MW01258191

a biography

This book is a special tribute to the great Houses of New York
and to those family dynasties that ruled New York high society
during the first third of the 20th century,
of which the **House of Kahn** stood tall.

for my grandmother
Clara Anne Williams
whose joy of art
I captured
and my mother Jane
who was born in Syracuse, New York,
at the start of the Roaring Twenties

THE
KAHNS
of Fifth Avenue

the
Crazy ***RHYTHM***
of
Otto Hermann **KAHN**
and the **KAHN** Family

First published in 2022 - 10 9 8 7 6 5 4 3 2 1
first edition
American version
ISBN-13 978-1916146587 (paperback)
a Williamson in America publication
iwp
i will publishing

Front cover image: The Pierre, the Metropolitan Club, and the more recent Park
Cinq, Fifth Avenue, New York City.

CONTENTS

Introduction

The KAHNS of Fifth Avenue is the biography of the financier Otto Hermann Kahn and the Kahn family. The family became one of America's most influential, wealthiest, and well-known of its generation. Within this account is the story of a boy, born into unimaginable riches, who went against his parent's wishes by forging a career in the entertainment industry. In doing so, he became one of the most documented musicians of the Jazz Age. That boy was Roger Wolfe Kahn.

In 2015 a chance discovery brought my attention to Roger through his brief association with Brooklyn-born jazz singer Adelaide Hall. The link was *Le Perroquet de Paris*, a chic nightclub Roger owned in New York City. Roger fashioned the club upon its Parisian namesake housed on the mezzanine of the famous *Casino de Paris* music hall. It was at *Le Perroquet de Paris* in New York in 1927 that Roger first met Adelaide Hall. What happened after their encounter was a turning point for both their careers.

The fact that Roger achieved immense fame at such a young age by leading one of the most popular dance bands of the 1920s is more often than not overshadowed by the addendum that he was the youngest son of the banking tycoon and philanthropist Otto Hermann Kahn. As such, his contribution to early jazz is often overlooked.

Through Roger's musical legacy, I discovered the Kahn family: Otto, his beautiful wife Addie, and Roger's three spirited siblings, Maud, Margaret, and Gilbert. Though all were individually fascinating, as a family, they were captivating. From that moment onwards, I was hooked.

To many Americans, the Kahns were akin to royalty; such was their lavish lifestyle. The family epitomized everything the 1920s represented; wealth, headiness, extravagance, liberalism, craziness, scandal, and jazz ... so much jazz. Then came the 1929 Wall Street Crash. Everything changed forever.

Lives can all too often be forgotten. What once was vibrant and relevant may become obscured by the passage of time. In *The KAHNS of Fifth Avenue*, I have attempted to bring back to life *the Crazy Rhythm of Otto Hermann Kahn and the Kahn Family*.

I. C. Williams, 2022

Ever Restlessly Forward
'Immer rastlos voran' – the Kahn family motto *

The KAHNS

PART I

LOOKING FOR THE BOY

1867–1924

The Kahn palazzo on the corner of Fifth Avenue &
East 91ˢᵗ Street

The KAHNS

1

THE RISE OF THE HOUSE OF KAHN

*If ever there was a child that could not have wanted
for more, then Roger Wolfe Kahn was that child.*

Installed in a suite of rooms on the top floor of Otto Kahn's magnificent Long Island country mansion was a miniature electric railway with fully operational tracks, locomotives, coaches, signals, station buildings, and all the workings to run such an extensive train set.[1] Yards of metal rail tracks, some laid out on tables, snaked from room to room. Only two door keys to gain entry to this suite existed; one key was with the housekeeper, the other belonged to Otto Kahn's youngest son Roger. It was behind this locked door that the young man, known to the world as Roger Wolfe Kahn, musician, composer, and aviator, would withdraw to and play with his model railroad, often for hours at a time, as he had done for years.[2]

This hideaway was Roger's sanctuary, where no one disturbed him. Here, he found balance and peace in a space where he could unwind and contemplate his future as he operated his trains. Gone were the demanding pressures and busy schedules that surrounded his everyday working life. Behind these walls, Roger's trains would arrive and depart from their stations without delays or disruption and travel as fast or as slow as he wished to drive them without anyone telling him what he could or could not do. It seemed ironic that his father, who built a vast fortune from helping to reorganize railroad systems, should have a son who was so fascinated by engineering and enthralled by model trains.

News of Roger's 'odd' hobby was leaked to the press in January 1930 when Roger was twenty-two. This random snippet of gossip was indicative of where his short life had led him. The media viewed any offspring of the wealthy financier Otto Kahn as 'public' property. Roger's eccentric behavior was rich fodder for reporters and columnists, who, at times, ridiculed him. The image of a solitary young man playing with his electric railroad inside his secret den revealed an aspect of Roger's life that the public was unaware of; his measured withdrawal from a world that had become fixated upon the sole mission of *looking for the boy*.

To understand how Roger reached this crucial point in his life at such a young age, and to appreciate exactly why he found it necessary to carve a new path for his future, we have to veer back, way back, to beyond his birth, and the birth of his parents, to identify the complexities and peculiarities that shaped his upbringing, and to examine the restrictions and advantages that came hand in hand with being a member of one of the most famous, influential and wealthy families of the day.

Otto and Addie Kahn's four children, Maud, Margaret, Gilbert, and Roger were born at Cedar Court, the Kahns' New Jersey country estate at Normandy Heights in Morris Township.

Roger Wolff Kahn was the fourth and last child to arrive. His childhood was not the typical upbringing that most children experience. As an heir to a financial dynasty, his doting and, at times, manipulative parents meticulously planned every detail of his future. No sooner had Roger gasped his first breath of New Jersey air than, like his elder brother Gilbert, his parents enrolled him on the register of a leading university. Having been born into an upper-class family, it was inevitable the brothers would attend one of the 'Big Three' American Ivy League institutions, Princeton, Harvard, or Yale. Princeton in New Jersey, recognized for its engineering, humanities, and science studies, was their choice for Gilbert. Their preference for Roger was Harvard in Cambridge, Massachusetts.

As the youngest sibling, Roger's brother and two sisters frequently spoiled him. His father affectionately nicknamed him 'Pip'; his mother showered him with maternal affection and was, at times, overly protective. Unusually, coming from Jewish lineage, the Kahn children were baptized into the Christian faith at the Episcopal Church in Morristown.

Ruffling Feathers

To piece together the Kahn family history and heritage, we must first travel back several generations to Europe. Otto Kahn's immediate descendants first settled in Germany along the Rhine Valley in the mid-18th century. The family spoke Yiddish. The locals regarded

Jewish immigrants as an underclass and gave them very few civil rights. Otto's paternal grandparents, Michael and Franziska Kahn, lived in the village of Stebbach in the Grand Duchy of Baden. The district was under the jurisdiction of Grand Duke Louis I. The Duke determined the laws under which foreigners could reside in his Duchy. Jews were permitted citizenship only if they worked in trade or money lending. Michael Kahn had intended to become a rabbi. However, his circumstances steered him along a different path. He spotted a yawning gap in the market for inexpensive soft mattresses and pillows, and in 1826 founded a family-run business in Stebbach manufacturing premium feather-bedding products. His foresight suddenly allowed the working classes the comforts of sleeping upon a soft bed, such as the upper classes did. After exhausting his supplies of goose feathers from the local area, Michael discovered he could import cheaper down of equally good quality from Hungary. Business boomed. With demand for his products exceeding his capacity to supply them, Michael took over the building adjoining the family home and converted it into a small factory.

Michael and Franziska (née Bär) had six sons: Bernhard (b. May 23, 1827), Marum (b. May 23, 1827 - d. June 4, 1827), Hermann (b. October 24, 1829), Emil (b. 1832), Leopold (b. 1841), and Sigismund. To assist their parents in growing the family business, each son worked at the Kahn factory at some point in their adolescence.

By 1848, the Duchy of Baden was under the authority of Leopold, Grand Duke of Baden. During the March Revolution of that year, the Duchy became a hotbed of revolutionary activities. Anti-Semitic riots swept the country, preceded by years of famine, disease, and mass immigration to America. For a brief period in 1849, during what would later be termed the Baden Revolution, Baden became the only German state to declare itself a Republic. In retaliation, the Prussian Army brutally suppressed the uprising and took control of the region. During this turbulent period of German democracy, Bernhard and Hermann (who was still only a teenager) became revolutionaries and participated in the riots. They delivered public speeches condemning the treatment of Jews and wrote rallying pamphlets calling for equality and unity. Then, armed with weapons and ready to lay down their lives for their beliefs, the brothers joined a band of insurgents and headed off to fight. As any mother might do, Franziska feared for her son's safety and kept a record of their activities in her diary.

Disappointingly, for the revolutionaries, the rebellion failed. The state took back control. The two brothers, along with thousands of militants, were branded traitors. The court issued warrants for their arrest. Both brothers resisted capture and escaped over the German border, Bernhard to France via Switzerland, Hermann to Antwerp.

Fearing for his life, in 1848, Bernhard immigrated to the United States to escape political persecution. Upon his arrival, he traveled to Albany, where his younger brother Emil had settled.

Bernhard readily took to the American way of life and found employment in a new profession, banking. Meanwhile, back in Germany, Bernhard and Hermann were convicted over their anti-monarchist activities. In their absence, they were indicted and sentenced to death.

In 1854, after carving a stable career for five years, Bernhard became a naturalized American citizen with the full intention of remaining in the U.S. to build a new life. 1854 was also significant for Michael and Franziska. Not only had they become the wealthiest Jews in Stebbach, but it was also the year they left Stebbach and relocated to the more prosperous city of Mannheim.

Over the next couple of years, the political climate in Germany became less volatile. With the appointment in 1856 of Frederick, Grand Duke of Baden - acting as Regent *ad interim* and considered a more tolerant and sympathetic governor - Michael and Franziska seized the occasion to call upon him to plead for their son's convictions to be nullified. The Kahns hoped he would take pity on their situation. At their audience, Franziska threw herself at the Duke's feet, begging for mercy for her two sons, insisting they were innocent and meant no harm. The Duke empathized with the Kahn family and assured them he would see what he could do but made no promises of a satisfactory outcome. He explained that it was not within his jurisdiction to overrule their son's sentences. True to his word, the Duke recommended the case go back to the courts, where each charge would be assessed individually for review.

After relentless petitioning, Franziska succeeded in having the indictment against Hermann retracted for lack of evidence. It was a massive victory for the Kahns. Upon receiving the news of his pardon, Hermann returned from Antwerp to the family home in Germany.

Bernard, having been a 'leader' in the insurgence, was not so fortunate. Michael and Franziska failed to secure any change in his conviction. Consequently, Bernhard remained exiled in America.

Increased pressure from Bernhard's parents finally persuaded him to return to his homeland to face the courts. When Bernhard arrived back in Germany in 1857, he discovered life had significantly changed during his absence. His parents now lived in some style in

Mannheim - a thriving industrial city pitched at the confluence of the Rhine and Neckar rivers - where life was considerably more convivial.

Franziska and Michael were thrilled to have their wayward son home and learn he was now a reformed man. His exile in America had undoubtedly had a decisive effect on him. He was confident, smartly suited, with handsome facial features, slicked-back hair, and a clipped beard, a son they could feel proud of.

Bernhard's return did not sit well with his brother Hermann. Almost ten years had passed since the two brothers parted company, and they were now no longer on speaking terms. A deep rift had developed between them that each brother was too stubborn to heal. Subsequently, Hermann uprooted his family and resettled in Frankfurt, where, with his brother Leopold, he established and managed the banking house Kahn & Co. The division between the two brothers continued throughout their lives, resulting in the two sides of the Kahn family rarely associating with one another.

Being practical-minded, Bernhard worked temporarily at his father's factory in Mannheim. He also did as his parents requested and appealed to the authorities for clemency, citing his forgiveness and reformed character. After careful consideration, the court dropped all charges against him.

Soon afterward, Bernhard met and fell in love with Emma Stephanie Eberstadt, a pretty young Jewish girl thirteen years his junior. On October 17, 1860, 19-year-old Emma married Bernhard contingent upon him remaining in Germany and not returning to live in the United States.

Although Emma was still on the cusp of her teenage years - she was born in Worms on October 29, 1840 - she was already displaying signs of her domineering character and driving ambition. Her father, Ferdinand Falk Eberstadt, had shown similar initiative and determination throughout his career as a businessman and politician; he was the mayor of Worms in 1849, a post he held until 1852. By 1857, the Eberstadt family had moved to Mannheim, where they freely embraced the city's many cultural and artistic activities. It was from this nonconformist background that Emma fostered her great appreciation and love of art and culture. The newlywed couple set up home in Mannheim, and on August 2, the following year, their first child Franz Michael was born. Seven more offspring followed: four boys, Robert August, Otto Hermann, Paul Friedrich, and Felix, and three girls, Clara Maria, Elisabeth 'Lili' Franziska, and Hedwig.

Following Michael Kahn's death in 1861, M. Kahn Söhne Bettfedern-

Fabrik (bedspring factory) continued for several years under the family's guidance before finally being sold. In 1867, Michael's sons, Bernhard, Emil (who had now returned to Germany), and Hermann, used part of their financial inheritance to establish the banking house M. Kahn Söhne. During the next few years, Bernhard became one of Mannheim's most prominent citizens and co-owner, along with his brother Emil, of two further banks, the Deutsche Unionbank and the Rheinische Hypothekenbank.[3]

Otto Hermann Kahn was Bernhard and Emma's fourth child and debuted in Mannheim on February 21, 1867. Otto and his siblings lived by all accounts an idyllic childhood surrounded by abundant affection from their parents, who greatly encouraged their children to express their artistic leanings. Their home was decorated with valuable works of art and regularly used as a locale for various cultural activities. Otto freely admitted throughout his life that he could not have been born into a more liberal and culturally aware family.

At the time of Otto's birth, Mannheim's Jewish population accounted for around 4 percent of the local community. Although Otto's parents were among this percentage, they were not observant Jews and did not raise their children in the Jewish faith.

The Mannheim, where Otto spent his childhood, although small in size, was experiencing significant expansion. 1867 marked a notable milestone for the city; it was the year when the newly built rail and road bridge opened, firmly connecting the municipality to the surrounding region. It provided a quick and easy method to cross the River Rhine. The structure directly linked Mannheim with the nearby city of Ludwigshafen on the opposite banks of the river. The railway also made the duchy's capital, Karlsruhe, easier to visit. The Rhine and Neckar waters were trade routes and vital for the city's economic growth. With industrial development came a cultural explosion. It was this dramatic artistic upsurge that filtered extensively into the home life of the Kahn family.

Although Emma was, at times, an overbearing and controlling mother, she did, in all faith, have her children's best interests at heart. She took it upon herself to determine the exact profession each one of her sons should follow and stressed this point to her husband, who, in all probability, was the one left to bear the news to his offspring. She also had a meddling hand in arranging her three daughter's marriages.

Otto developed a keen interest in music and literature at an early age. He played the cello and violin proficiently enough to consider furthering his musical education at college.[4] He was educated at the Classical High School at Mannheim and had written two five-act tragedies in blank verse by the age of seventeen, although they were never publicly performed.[5]

His elder brother Robert was a gifted pianist and left home to study music at the Hochschule für Musik Berlin. In Otto's quest to expand his academic interests, he also attended public university lectures on occasions. Otto had yearned to enter the music profession since his early adolescence. Alas, his hopes of following in his brother Robert's footsteps by enrolling at a conservatoire ceased when his father harshly announced he and his mother had decided his career must take a different route. That path would be in finance.[6]

Otto was desolate that he should have to forfeit his occupation of choice. To resolve the matter, he made a pact. He would fulfill his parent's wishes on the single proviso that if he sacrificed his musical ambitions to enter the banking profession, he be allowed to devote his free time to culture.[7] His parents agreed.

At seventeen, Otto moved to Karlsruhe to work at the local banking house of Veit L. Homburger. As a junior clerk, his menial duties included licking postage stamps and cleaning inkwells. Considering the branch sent out hundreds of circulars daily, this was no trivial task. In later years, Otto would jokingly declare that as a lad, he could lick his weight in postage stamps.[8] He also ran lunch errands to purchase 'sausages, beer, and other victuals' for his superiors. He remained at the bank for three years, steadfastly learning the rudiments of economics and diligently working his way up through the office hierarchy.

'It was a useful, salutary training, for it taught discipline and order,' Otto later confessed. 'One must learn to obey before he is fit to command. I suppose I must have wiped the inkwells fairly satisfactorily, for it was not long before I was promoted and had another novice to clean my inkwell and fetch my lunch.'[9]

Otto was a smart kid. He figured out early in life that if he labored hard and made sufficient money, he could have his cake and eat it.[10] This central motif of 'work hard, play hard' would remain constant throughout his life.

In 1888, Otto's banking career came to a temporary pause when his military service papers arrived. Conscription in Germany was mandatory for male citizens. Otto served as an Einjährig-Freiwilliger (one-year volunteer) in the Kaiser's Hussars 13th regiment stationed at Mainz.[11] In later years, he disclosed that his time in military service strengthened his resolve to succeed in life and taught him the principle of regulation and the importance of fulfilling and dispensing instructions.

After dutifully serving his required term, Otto was discharged and returned to work in the banking profession. For a brief spell, he was employed at his father's burgeoning bank M. Kahn Söhne, after which he secured a position at Deutsche Bank in Berlin. The company quickly spotted Otto's potential and offered him a post in their esteemed London branch. The proposal was too tempting for Otto to dismiss. He jumped at the opportunity, accepted the job, and packed his bags.[12]

In 1889, Otto journeyed to the UK and took up his new post at the London branch of Deutsche Bank, where he remained for almost five years. London was the world's money center, and Deutsche Bank was eager to expand its operation in the capital and increase credit for German trade. Otto arrived in the right place at the right time, and over the next five years, he helped build the branch into a highly successful agency.

In London, Otto lived in the Royal Borough of Kensington at 19 Sheffield Terrace, Holland Park, in a mid-Victorian, four-story, terraced house. He referred to it as his 'bachelor quarters.' The property stood opposite the Campden House estate and was a mere cuckoo's call from Kensington Palace and the fashionable shopping center of Kensington High Street. He shared the dwellings with two friends, Austrian-born Rudolf Schiff and Richard Rosenbacher, a stockbroker's clerk from Prague. They employed two live-in servants: a housekeeper Maria Scrutton, and her 21-year-old daughter Lizzie.[13] The banker Paul M. Warburg, who later became a business colleague and lifelong friend of Otto's, also lodged for a period at the address.[14]

Otto adored London and grew convinced he had found the country he would like to reside in for the rest of his life. The fact that hotelier César Ritz and the renowned master chef Georges Auguste Escoffier worked at London's Savoy Hotel confirmed to Otto just how pleasant life had become. In his opinion, the capital was most definitely 'a place worth living in.'[15] He even gave serious consideration to renouncing his German nationality and becoming a naturalized UK citizen.

London opened up an exciting world of culture that Otto could only have dreamed of back in Germany. His promotion at Deutsche Bank to deputy manager soon followed. With his salary increase, he signed the lease on a country property, Essex Villa, in the Buckinghamshire village of Datchet, not far from Eton College and Windsor Castle.[16]

In London, Otto became acquainted with Edgar Speyer, who ran Speyer Brothers, the London branch of Speyer's German banking house. In meeting Speyer, Otto came face to face with a kindred creative spirit and a cultural visionary. Speyer was hugely influential in London's music and artistic circles. Edgar and Otto mixed in similar bohemian enclaves. It was through this connection that the next chapter in Otto's life came about.

Just as everything was beginning to fall into place and Otto could not have felt happier, he clinched a dream job at Speyer & Co., a position that would lure him across the Atlantic to New York. The House of Speyer was one of the oldest and most influential international banking dynasties in Europe. The American posting was one Otto felt he could not ignore. Suddenly he was confronted with a dilemma, should he remain in London to further his career or explore his options in the United States? His irrepressible curiosity got the better of him. The opportunity was too tempting to reject. He accepted.

Nonetheless, in the back of his mind, he also understood that if the position and America were not to his liking, he could always return to the UK. Possibly with this understanding, on August 1, 1893, Otto submitted his UK Naturalization Certificates and Declarations form to the Home Office just before his departure to the States.[17] Later that month, the Secretary of State granted Kahn a Certificate of UK Naturalization. From his actions, some might think Otto had every intention of returning to the UK to live.

Kahn arrived in New York aboard SS *Havel* on August 9, 1893, aged 26, hauling a trunkload of aspirations and ambition.[18] Little could he have known exactly how large those dreams would turn out to be! Otto began working at Speyer & Co. on August 25 at their Manhattan headquarters in the Mills Building at 15 Broad Street.

It was Otto's first visit to the 'land of opportunity,' and he was hungry to experience everything New York had to offer. He rented lodgings at 26 West 34th Street in the Midtown South neighborhood. The thrill of walking along Manhattan's rectangular grid of avenues, bustling with New Yorkers shuffling this way and that, could only have caused his senses to heighten. The city was alive and buzzing with activity, and Otto longed to feel a part of it.

Otto had grown into a distinguished-looking young man with bright hazel eyes and an engaging smile. More interestingly, for the young ladies, he was a bachelor. Though he was relatively short in stature, just clearing five foot six, he commanded attention. Some thought him flamboyant, others European. Since his early twenties, he had sported a thick military-style mustache, which he waxed daily and kept immaculately trimmed. In later years it became his trademark.

Otto Hermann Kahn

In some respects, the timing of Otto's arrival in the U.S. could not have been worse. America was in the throes of a financial panic. Wheat prices had fallen, unemployment was rising, and stock market shares were on a downward spiral. Hundreds of banks had been unable to meet the public demand for cash withdrawals and subsequently ceased trading. Thousands of businesses had gone bankrupt. Under this gray economic cloud, Otto set to work in his most challenging role to date. In hindsight, this was the ideal testing ground for him to display his orderly work ethic, analytical mind, and deep understanding of finance. It would also test his resolve and prove to his employers how worthy he was for the job. The depression would last four taxing years, during which Otto toiled diligently at Speyer & Co. for two of them.[19]

Though his work was time-consuming, he did manage to return to the UK twice during this period. Once, in 1894,[20] and again in 1895,[21] when he traveled across Europe to study art and listen to music.

At one o'clock, on Wednesday, January 8, 1896, Otto's life took a significant change of direction. Six weeks before his 29th birthday, he married 20-year-old Addie Wolff,[22] the beautiful and somewhat sheltered daughter of New York banker Abraham O. Wolff. The ceremony took place beneath a bower of palms in the drawing-room of the Wolff Manhattan residence. The majority of their honeymoon was spent touring Europe[23] and lasted the entire year, at the end of which the happy couple returned to America. On New Year's Day, 1897, Otto took up his new post as a junior partner handling railroad business at the private investment banking house Kuhn, Loeb & Co., at which his father-in-law was a senior partner. Also joining the firm on the same day was Felix M. Warburg, brother of Paul M. Warburg.* Otto would remain working for Kuhn, Loeb for the rest of his life and eventually climb the ranks to become a controlling director.

The Wolff Heritage

Adelaide 'Addie' Wolff was born on June 10, 1875, in Manhattan, New York. Her mother Lydia (née Cohen) - a native New Yorker of German parentage, who married Abraham in 1874[24] - died in November 1885, aged thirty-two when Addie's birthday had just that year reached double figures. Consequently, the daily task of running and managing the family home and looking after her younger sister Clara had fallen upon Addie's capable shoulders.[25]

Abraham Wolff hailed from Edenkoben in Germany and grew up in an entirely different environment from the comfort and security his two daughters enjoyed. His Jewish parents were poor, barely scraping together enough money to survive. In 1850, when Abraham was twelve, his family immigrated to America to start afresh and settled in New York. Abraham's first job was as an office boy earning a weekly wage of $3. Within time, he'd saved enough capital to travel to San Francisco, where he established an importing business. However, he soon realized trade was more abundant in Ohio and relocated to Cincinnati. By 1873, Abraham had accrued enough wealth to retire from mercantile business. He returned to New York, where he changed his career and entered the banking profession as a clerk at Kuhn, Loeb & Co.

Few people, including his work colleagues at Kuhn, Loeb would ever have guessed Abraham was a multi-millionaire, so modest and unassuming was he in demeanor. To those who knew him, he came across as a very private man who appears never to have looked at another woman with a passionate eye after his wife Lydia's death and whose world revolved solely around the upbringing and welfare of his two pretty young daughters.

The family lived in a smart townhouse at 33 West 57th Street in the desirable Midtown region. Since the mid-19th century, the city's commercial yoke had begun to nudge further northwards along Fifth Avenue. Following this trend, affluent families began migrating towards Upper East Side, where they snapped up realty and built posh new family homes to suit their own design and wealthy lifestyles. The more private and residential locality between 34th and 59th Streets became highly sought after.

A neighboring family of the Wolffs was the Roosevelt, whose row house stood at 6 West 57th Street. Theodore Roosevelt Sr. and his wife Martha moved into the house in 1873 with their four children: Anna, Theodore Jr., Elliott, and Corinne.

Further along the road at 1 West 57th Street, luxuriously stretching half a block on the corner of Fifth Avenue, stood Cornelius Vanderbilt II's opulent French Renaissance-style townhouse. It was among this affluent neighborhood that Addie and her sister spent their formative years befriending some of the children of the good and great of New York.

Otto and Addie's attraction to one another was clear from the moment they first met. Addie's elegance and self-assurance, intensified by her graceful, upright posture, was hugely appealing to the eye. Her luxuriant hair, sculpted into a bun on the crown of her head, added height to her delicate five-foot frame. Otto must have known he was an extremely fortunate man to have taken her hand in marriage. For Addie, it was her husband's kind, wise eyes, charming smile, and impeccable, slightly old-school mannerisms that endeared him to her. What he lacked in height, he amply made up for in personality. Their eight-year age difference seemed irrelevant, especially as they shared common ground with their deep and passionate interest in art and culture. More important, for Addie's father, it was Kahn's business acumen that impressed him.

Addie's wedding was not the only celebration in January at the Wolff household; barely three weeks later, her sister Clara[26] wed Dutch émigré and New York banker[27] Henri Hendrik Pieter Wertheim.[28] They, too, went on a lengthy honeymoon and, upon their return, took up residency with Abraham at his New York home, a temporary arrangement until the couple acquired a house of their own.[29]

When the two sisters originally announced their engagements almost simultaneously, Abraham suddenly faced an unanticipated dilemma: what wedding gifts could he purchase for his two cherished daughters that would be equally thoughtful and appropriate? He solved this predicament rather unconventionally by building each daughter a country retreat.

During the Kahns' Grand Tour of the continent,[30] Addie developed her lifelong enthusiasm for Europe and its rich and varied culture. The couple returned to the States in excellent health just in time to celebrate the Christmas festivities bearing the good news that Abraham was to have his first grandchild.

When Otto took up his post at Kuhn, Loeb's offices at 27 Pine Street, he must have been very aware he was stepping into a company of high esteem, whose clients expected service of the utmost quality. The banking house was co-founded in 1867 (coincidentally, the same year Otto was born) by retired Cincinnati commission merchants Abraham Kuhn (a German Jew) and Solomon Loeb, a distant cousin of Kuhn's.[31] The company rose from modest beginnings, trading chiefly in government bonds and, more recently, in highly lucrative railroad securities. They primarily dealt with corporations. They did not deal with the general public. Kuhn, Loeb was now regarded as a powerhouse in American and international finance.[32] In 1849, to strengthen his family bond with Loeb, Abraham Kuhn married Solomon Loeb's sister Regina.

Abraham Wolff joined Kuhn, Loeb as a clerk in January 1875; the same year, fellow German, Jacob H. Schiff, entered the firm. As contemporaries, Schiff and Wolff became staunch friends. Schiff reinforced his position within the family-run organization four months later when he married Loeb's daughter Theresa. Their daughter Frieda (b. 1876) became Addie Wolff's best friend. In 1895, when Frieda married Felix M. Warburg, Addie was one of her bridesmaids.[33]

When Otto became Wolff's son-in-law, it continued the increasing trail of blood and marriage links within the company. Regardless of this connection, Otto's trajectory into Kuhn, Loeb was not guaranteed with certainty from the onset; Jacob Schiff, who had since become head of Kuhn, Loeb took an instant dislike to Kahn's manner and disposition. Otto liked to smile (unusual for a banker) and would smile often. He would also sing around the office. Yet, despite Otto's idiosyncrasies, Schiff approved Kahn's appointment as a partner out of respect and loyalty to Wolff.

Otto may have married into money, but how much of a fortune Abraham Wolff had accumulated over the years would not become apparent until his death. Notwithstanding, Wolff's son-in-law had every intention of forging a successful career of his own. As if to show his senior colleagues just how keen he was to make his mark, Otto would arrive at Kuhn, Loeb's offices punctually at 9:45 a.m. daily, a custom he adhered to from day one throughout his entire career.

Cedar Court, Morristown, New Jersey

Cedar Court stood amidst Morristown's exclusive Normandy Heights section and was not the usual New Jersey family residence. Constructed as two identical 40-room, Italianate, three-story villas, they were a cut above most of the other homes in the region. The twin properties stood at right angles to one another, connected by a covered loggia. With their red-tiled roofs and shuttered windows with folding sun canopies and decorative balustrade balconies, the villas captured the essence of Italian Renaissance architecture. At the front, they overlooked an entrance court inset with a sunken marble basin and ornamental water fountains. Their position atop a steep meandering hill afforded commanding views across meadows, countryside, and verdant woodland as far as Tuxedo and the Dover Mountains on the skyline. Sheep grazed on the sloping grass hillsides below, and in the near distance, a duck pond attracted wild birds. The estate took its name from the two proud cedar trees that stood at the entrance to the courtyard.

Abraham Wolff purchased this sizable tract in 1896 and had the matching redbrick villas built for his daughters as wedding gifts. Upon their completion in 1897, Addie and Clara moved into their respective homes with their respective husbands. However, what followed was not the fairy tale scenario imagined by the two sisters or their father.

Though the houses on The Heights (as the neighborhood was known locally) were not the most extravagant or largest in Morris Township, the properties were referred to as 'showplaces' and collectively acquired a unique identity. To live on The Heights was special, and the families that lived there knew it.

With its abundant green pastures and fresh country air, the suburbs of Morristown quickly became a favored rural escape for wealthy New Yorkers. Family's would scuttle down from the city's polluted landscape to spend weekends at their estates. The short distance from New York (a mere thirty miles or so) made the journey a doddle by rail.

Morristown had previously been an agricultural community and did not yet have the technological wonders New York City boasted; groceries were still delivered in a horse-drawn wagon, and horses pulled the local fire engine. Even the doctor visited his patients by horse and buggy. Locals viewed automobiles as a novelty, and when a vehicle clanked along Main Street, pedestrians would cough and splutter from the plumes of smoke and gasoline odor it left trailing behind. Regardless of the town's lack of modern facilities, the idyllic location and peacefulness encouraged well-to-do New Yorkers to snap up acreage and build fancy country retreats. Millionaire surnames such as Vanderbilt, Rockefeller, Dodge, McK. Twombly, McCurdy, Frelinghuysen, Claflin, and Kountze all owned substantial mansions in the surrounding district.[34] Local officials proudly boasted that more millionaires lived within a mile radius of Morristown Green than in any equal area in the world, a claim which was never verified.

The twin villas at Cedar Court were designed by the New York architects Carrère and Hastings. Addie and Otto's villa is the farthest in the picture.

In the spring of '97, life could not have been more agreeable for the Kahns, the Wertheims, and the aging Abraham Wolff as they settled into life at Cedar Court. A couple of months later, on July 23, Otto and Addie's first child, Maud Emily Wolff Kahn, arrived in the world. Maud soon acquired the playful pet name 'Momo.'

The Dawn of a New Century

At the dawn of the 20th century, there seemed little reason for the Kahns not to welcome the new era with optimism and open arms. Otto's career at Kuhn, Loeb was progressing steadily, and Addie was happily adapting to motherhood. As well as owning a country pile in New Jersey, the Kahns had moved into a comfortable New York townhouse at 8 East 68th Street, eleven blocks north from Abraham's abode. Addie had purchased the brownstone, five-story property in 1895 from Harriet and Sigmund Lehman of the Lehman Brothers investment banking family.[35] The house was built in 1882 and designed by Lamb & Wheeler. It stood on the south side of the quiet, residential street, and was adequately sized for a young, financially secure family and their servants. Conveniently for the Kahns, Central Park was close by, where Otto would go horse riding on one of his stallions. Most weekdays, Otto resided in Manhattan. But when his family was resident in Morristown, he would join them at weekends.

New centuries always take a while to gear up, and over the next few years, a series of tragic and unsettling events occurred that would drastically alter and shape the Kahns' lives forever.

Otto was by far the more gregarious and ambitious of all the partners at Kuhn, Loeb. His weekday evenings spent socializing in Manhattan amply catered for his taste for the high life and all things bohemian. His weekends, however, could not have been more different and were devoted to spending quality time with his young, ever-growing family. If Abraham and Otto stayed over at Cedar Court during the week, they would commute to New York together by train.

Monday, October 1, was just another routine day at the office for Abraham. Nothing particularly irregular or eventful took place during its course. He was purportedly in fine spirits when he left his desk that afternoon to board the early express back to Morristown. As he sank his body into the comfortably plump seat on the Pullman railcar, he must have felt an inner sense of satisfaction at the thought of spending a quiet evening at home in the company of his daughter Clara. That evening, supper and the conversation passed pleasantly. When Abraham stood from the dining table at around nine o'clock and left the room to visit the bathroom, there was no reason for anyone to suspect anything was amiss. A few minutes later, Abraham was found dead.[36] The doctor's report confirmed the 61-year-old had died instantly from heart failure. Friends and associates rallied around the Kahns and Wertheims to offer their sympathy and condolences. On October 2, the New York Stock Exchange formally announced his death from the rostrum.[37]

On Thursday morning, Abraham's funeral took place in Morristown, followed by the customary reading of the deceased's will. Abraham stipulated that: 'By the will, there are many charitable bequests, and several trusts established to provide annuities for various relatives and friends. The residuary estate is left to my daughters Addie W. Kahn and Clara W. Wertheim, who are to receive the income for life, and at their death, the principal is to go to their children.'

Gasps of astonishment came from those present at the reading when the extent of Abraham's fortune became known. That Wolff was a millionaire twenty times over was mind-boggling, especially as, for most of his life, he had lived such a modest and frugal lifestyle - the net worth of $20 million in 1900 is equivalent to over $610 million in 2020.[38] The largest part of his wealth was in trust. Addie and Clara were both now multi-millionaires. Their worlds were about to change dramatically.

Abraham's extraordinary life story must have struck a chord with Otto. The close similarities of their paths were evident; both were German American immigrants that had started their careers as office juniors, and both had taken up banking to advance their prospects. Whereas Wolff had secured his fortune, Otto was still mapping out his journey. Wolff believed his success at Kuhn, Loeb was down to his mercantile beginnings and his loyal friendship with Jacob Schiff. In later years, Otto would also cite Schiff as the person who taught him everything he knew about investment banking.

Addie's monetary inheritance directly altered the dynamics in the Kahn household, and for the immediate future, she wore the financial pants.

One month after Abraham's passing, the Kahns and Wertheims expressed their joy over the news that Addie was expecting her second child. Margaret Dorothy Wolff Kahn greeted her parents and sister, Maud, with a noisy welcome on July 4, 1901. From an early age, Margaret acquired the curious nickname 'Nin.'

The new century blew in a pervading air of optimism, where anything seemed possible. The modern world was growing faster with each passing year. As if to grab this air of confidence, the Kahns purchased a sizable tract in the Adirondacks to add to their ever-increasing property portfolio.[39] The house they built on the estate would be the first of many properties they would help design and create during the years ahead.

In 1901, architect William Coulter drew up plans for a luxury lumber chalet to sit on the gently sloping southeasterly facing bluff at Bull Point on the fringes of Upper Saranac Lake.[40] The Kahns christened the estate Bull Point Camp, and it became their official summer retreat. Their 'cabin in the woods' cost a mint to construct and resembled a cross between an English mock Tudor mansion and a classic Swiss chalet.[41] Its raised aspect gave a picture frame view of the tranquil setting across and beyond the lake. In winter, when the snow was deep, the camp became a place of wondrous beauty. Coulter incorporated all the latest amenities into the design, including electrically lit underground passageways connecting the main lodge to the surrounding buildings. There was even a boathouse from which to launch the Kahns' gas-powered boat.

Ironically, although Bull Point Camp was a joy to visit, the Kahns found their busy schedules afforded them little time to take advantage of it. Consequently, in 1905 they sold it to one of Otto's Wall Street associates, Henry Goldman of Goldman Sachs, banking a healthy profit from the transaction.

In 1902, five years after Clara and Henri tied the knot, they finally took possession of their own Manhattan home, an imposing newly built five-story Upper East Side townhouse at 4 East 67th Street. The limestone Beaux-Arts building crowned with a copper crested mansard was, without doubt, the most handsome townhouse they had seen and would make the perfect home for a young family. As if by creative planning, in the fall of that same year, the happy announcement of Clara's pregnancy came almost simultaneously with the news that Addie, too, was an expectant mother carrying her third baby. Clara's pregnancy was particularly significant as it was her third attempt to bear a child; the infants had died during her two previous births. The sisters were overjoyed at the prospect of their new arrivals. Addie's day of blessing arrived on July 18, 1903, a bouncing, healthy boy who was promptly named Gilbert Sherburne Wolff Kahn. During Clara's childbirth on Thursday, August 13, complications arose. The child was born sickly and lived only two hours. In the course of the delivery, Clara slipped into a coma from which she never regained consciousness and died two days later.[42]

Clara and her child's devastating and untimely death had a significant and immediate effect on the Trust Abraham had set up for his two daughters. As per the terms, the trust would be administered in Addie's favor. The financial provision for Addie and her progenies would now increase substantially.[43]

Just before Christmas 1904, the news from Germany that Otto's eldest brother Franz had passed away brought further sorrow to the Kahns' door.[44]

With Henri now spending less time in Morristown, the Wertheim residence remained uninhabited for lengthy periods. Although the Kahns continued to reside at their villa during the summer months, the ambiance and charm of Cedar Court had changed considerably since Abraham's and Clara's death. To cause further upset for the Kahns, there followed an unsettling incident at their property, one that held mysterious and worrying undertones for the family.

On the night of February 3, 1905, the Kahn family was staying at their Manhattan townhouse. Their Cedar Court property was unoccupied, aside from the live-in housekeeper who had retired to bed early. At around three o'clock the following morning, the housekeeper awoke to find her room malodorous with the pungent smell of smoke. She swiftly evacuated her bedroom only to discover thick smoke filling the corridor. By the time she reached the safety of the outdoor entrance court, the interior of the house was alight. James Fraser, the superintendent in charge of the grounds who lived in a lodge on the estate, was alerted. He contacted the local fire brigade. The nearest fire station was half a mile away in Morristown. When the horse-drawn wagon and crew finally arrived, the fire had ripped through the roof. Flames swallowed the upper and lower floors of the timber and brick building with such rapidity there was little time to save any of the expensive furniture and artworks housed inside, including a $100,000 Persian rug.[45]

Notwithstanding the combined efforts of the estate hands and firefighters, the Kahns' house collapsed. Paintings, furnishings, and objects of art valued at more than $400,000 were destroyed. Some newspaper reports put the figure as high as half a million dollars.[46] In praise of the firefighter's endeavors battling the blaze with limited resources and without necessary firefighting apparatus, they did succeed in preventing flames from spreading to the adjoining Wertheim property. That, in itself, was deemed a remarkable feat given the ferocity of the fire.

In New York, Otto and Addie were overcome with shock when news of the disaster reached them. In a matter of four years, Addie had tragically lost her beloved father and sister and her sister's child, and now the house her father had presented to her as a wedding gift had also been so harshly taken away from her.

The insurer assumed an electrical fault had caused the fire, although no tangible proof to support this theory was forthcoming. Another view, one more sinister, hinted that perhaps the incident had been an arson attack. This belief would become more compelling as the months unfolded.

The following day Otto arrived at the estate to inspect the damage and barely recognized what was once their beautiful home from the charred, smoldering shell. Chilling thoughts of what could have happened had the family been resident in the house scarred his memory for the rest of his life and resulted in him putting his family's safety at the forefront of any future building plans he might consider.

A few weeks later, Otto received more sad news, this time from Germany. His 77-year-old father Bernhard had died at the family home in Heidelberg.[47]

The Kahns now had no summerhouse at Morristown. Henri, on the other hand, had one he very rarely used. If the Kahn family wished to remain in Morris Township, the logical solution was to buy the Wertheim residence and take over the entire estate. They struck a deal, and the Kahns took possession of the property.

For the present, Otto and Addie concentrated on redesigning Cedar Court and commissioned the original architects Carrère and Hastings to oversee the project. By mid-April, any evidence of their former house had gone, and building work had commenced on the Wertheim villa adding a further wing in keeping with its overall Italian design. The annex would accommodate a ballroom. The grounds were re-landscaped by garden designers Brinley & Holbrook, and a squash court and two tennis courts were added. Just as the press had been keen to report the fire at Cedar Court, they were just as eager to chronicle the undergoing reconstruction work at the estate; 'At Cedar Court, work has begun on the new mansion for Otto H. Kahn. Considerable planting of rhododendrons has been done by Supt. James Fraser[48] and in the greenhouses, a promising lot of Ulrich Brunner roses are coming in for Easter.'[49]

It appeared to the world the Kahns had shrugged off their latest setbacks and were getting on with business as usual. Otto even treated himself to an 18-hole golf course designed by the noted architect Charles Blair MacDonald. The casual bystander might have questioned the extravagance of such an amenity, considering an excellent 18-hole golf course owned by the Morris County Golf Club adjoined the Kahn land.

There was, however, a simple explanation why Otto commissioned his bespoke golf course. For some time, there had been growing disquiet among a small but influential faction of the local Morris Township community who harbored vitriol towards the Kahn family. The Kahns viewed the hostilities as anti-Semitic, which was odd considering the family was openly aloof from almost everything to do with Judaism. Otto had been publicly humiliated when the Morris County Golf Club membership committee denied him membership. There was also a section of the local social set intent on excluding them from social gatherings. Regardless of such animosity, the Kahns stood their ground and refused to be shunted into the shadows.

Addie and Maud Kahn seated in raised box No. 11 at the Morristown Horse Show. Otto is standing in front of the box. It is one of the few photographs in the public domain of Otto and Addie together.[50]

In a show of unity, the family attended the prestigious annual Horse Show held by the Morristown Field Club, with Otto competing and, on several occasions, winning trophies. They also generously donated financially to local charities and sponsorships. But no matter what they did to benefit the community, a steadfast minority refused to accept their hospitality or offer of friendship. The aim of this clique seemed hell-bent on ridding the neighborhood of the Kahn family at any cost.

The fact that the membership committee at the Morris County Golf Club denied Otto's request to join caused ineffable embarrassment for the Kahns. Golf, whether played by men in plus fours or women in long skirts, tends to bring out the gamesmanship in a player. Otto's highly competitive streak was never too far from the surface. In a show of conciliation, Otto assigned the club a swath of land located alongside his estate and the club grounds. Their acceptance of the donation unwittingly shamed the club and its management over their hostile behavior towards him. In response to the gift, the club belatedly offered Otto membership, which he diplomatically never used,[51] while quietly professing he much preferred to play on his own private golf course.

Otto, competing in the horse-drawn carriage driving display at the Morristown Field Club. (Picture courtesy of The Library of Congress)

Not all of Morristown society showed the same hatred; Otto was a fully paid-up member of the Morristown Field Club on South Street and took part in many social and athletic events held by the club.[52]

Irrespective of local hostilities and tensions, Otto extended and developed the property over several years, making it entirely self-sufficient. He added additional acreage, bringing the total to 250.[53] The completed estate featured six workers' cottages, substantial stables for the family's thoroughbred horses, a carriage house, a fully operational farm and dairy, and well-stocked greenhouses. A covered sun terrace now occupied part of the area where the Kahns' former house had stood. The grounds contained: Japanese gardens, formal and sunken gardens, a rose garden, a pergola and sun terrace, a nature park inhabited with roaming deer, and a lake (designed by landscape architect and Morristown resident John Brinley) rippling with swans. A long, winding driveway fringed with maple trees led to the main house. In addition to golf, squash ball, and tennis, there was also a roller skating rink and a croquet lawn.

Many moneyed families of note owned estates in the neighborhood, one of the wealthiest being Mr. and Mrs. Hamilton McK. Twombly whose land adjoined the Kahns' boundary. With the cost of all the extra work undertaken at the property and considering the original price Abraham Wolff paid for the estate, Cedar Court was now estimated to be worth a cool million dollars.[54]

Otto's competitive spirit was never more evident than on the sports field.[55] He was an avid equestrian and liked nothing better than to exhibit his favorite black stallions, Starlight and Golight, in tandem or parade his two harness horses, Impetus and Icarus. In the 1904 annual Horse Show, Otto finished a respectable third in the carriage driving display, outridden by his neighbor Hamilton McK. Twombly, who came first.[56]

A view of the Kahn villa (center) from the rose garden at Cedar Court showing part of the pergola (left) and a corner of the squash ball court (right). (Picture collection of the North Jersey History Center, The Morristown and Morris Township Library)

The Kahns persisted in their efforts to integrate more within the local community. They opened the gates to their gardens at Cedar Court for horticultural displays and exhibitions, and in 1904 hosted a Chrysanthemum Show, which attracted flower enthusiasts and gardeners from across Morris County. Otto also became a director of the Morristown Trust Company, a State Member Bank with offices located in the center of Morristown.[57]

Much of the workforce employed on the estate came from local families. Otto always made a point of ensuring his workers were well looked after. Their annual staff party was renowned in the region.

Otto would hand over the keys to the house and allow his workers to party all day with only the finest refreshments and catering provided. Considering upwards of one hundred employees would attend, they were undoubtedly rowdy and memorable affairs.[58]

When the well-to-do families were in town, the local railroad station became a hub of activity. Each weekday the swanky 'Millionaire's Express' would carry the captains of industry and finance to and from their New York City offices. Some of the super-rich purchased personalized Pullmans, which they parked on sidings on their estates. To shelter his family from the embarrassment of being snubbed, Otto hired a private Pullman to transport his family when they traveled to the city for the day.

Perhaps, because of this continued unease, the Kahn family only resided at Cedar Court for short periods, usually during spring and fall, and made their primary home in New York City. With this in mind, in 1905, Otto purchased 10 East 68th Street, next door to the building they already owned at number eight. He planned to extend the property.

The Kahns' forty-acre deer park in the grounds of their estate contained thirty highly prized deer, which Otto was immensely proud of. Early in the morning of Tuesday, April 17, 1906, two ferocious dogs were deliberately set loose in the park, where they wreaked havoc.[59] That such a brutal and vindictive act of violence should see the innocent slaughter of eight deer and the wounding and maiming of several others came as another almighty blow to the Kahns. How dogs broke into the enclosure was baffling, as a high wire fence, impossible for animals to scale, encircled the pen. Later that morning, the caretaker discovered the dogs roaming the estate and shot them.

Who released the dogs into the enclosure remained a mystery. The attack only added to the growing catalog of unsolved crimes and violations that had plagued the Kahn family since they moved to Morristown. It seemed particularly telling that someone from the neighborhood should go out of their way to kill the deer to scare the Kahns. It was also a clear message that Jews were not welcome in the community. For Otto and Addie, this was one warning too many. Over the next few years, the Kahns spent less time at Cedar Court and put their efforts into purchasing or building new properties in different locations.

In another cruel twist, two months later, at Heidelberg in Germany, Otto's mother passed away.[60]

Throughout this cycle of loss and grieving, Otto and Addie took strength and solace in the joy of parenthood and the hope that a brighter future lay ahead.

The Harriman Connection

During the 19th century, the railroad became America's most important industry. With the mass production of steel in the 1880s, the expansion of the rail networks boomed. Its rapid growth encouraged investment in inner-city infrastructure, which provided a plentiful supply of employment opportunities. For the financiers who invested in the industry, such prosperity bestowed great wealth and influence upon them. Edward Henry Harriman was one of the most powerful railroad tycoons of the era. As Harriman's future business advisor, Otto's skill at brokering deals would become the stuff of legends.

American-born Harriman was a self-made multi-millionaire. He was chairman of the Illinois Central Railroad finance committee, admired for its deft management skills and foresight. Otto first met Harriman in 1894, when Otto had only been in New York for a few months and was still finding his feet at Speyer & Co.[61] Harriman's star was on the ascendancy; Otto's had yet to rise.

It was a time of change. The age of steam created the most significant transformation in America's history and shaped its future for many generations. Dubbed later as America's 'gilded age,' the prosperity that came from the expansion of railways coupled the nation and helped play a vital part in creating its future as a superpower. From this expansion, new millionaires emerged who made their fortunes in trade, steel, and railroads.

Harriman was one of Kuhn, Loeb's most important clients. Jacob Schiff personally handled all of Harriman's dealings. During the 1901 Northern Pacific railroad affair at which Harriman sought control of its stock and the subsequent panic on Wall Street that followed, Otto observed closely from the sidelines exactly how Schiff managed the operation, taking note of all the intricate details and transactions that occurred.

The corner of Wall and Broad streets was known as the financial crossroads of the world. It was on this corner that J.P. Morgan & Co. built their headquarters. In 1903, Kuhn, Loeb & Co. moved their headquarters into the newly constructed twenty-story office building at 52 William Street (anchored on the corner of William and Pine streets), two minutes' walk from the House of Morgan. Kuhn, Loeb occupied the first four floors of the building. The other sixteen floors they rented out. Kuhn, Loeb was second only to J.P. Morgan & Co. among private bankers and second to none in railway banking.

That same year, Jacob Schiff presented Otto with the Edward Harriman assignment. In doing so, Schiff must have been fully aware that Otto's reputation was now riding on the footplate of an American steam locomotive. For Otto, at last, he had a project he could sink his teeth into and establish his worth. Over the coming years, Otto's close affiliation with Harriman produced startling results. Harriman's shrewd dealings and dogged determination saw him succeed in every aspect of the railroad industry. In the process, his rail companies grew and prospered beyond any of his competitors.

It would be fair to say that Harriman became a mentor figure to Kahn; indeed, a close working bond developed. Harriman found Kahn's constructive mind and financial genius immeasurably valuable in expanding his vast enterprises.[62] Their working partnership was highly productive. In time, Otto became Kuhn, Loeb's chief liaison with Harriman.

Kahn's posting on the Harriman Syndicate saw him spending extensive periods absent from home and his growing family. He traveled from state to state, often alone in his own deluxe Pullman, crossing America's length and breadth, dealing with the complex financial transactions of reorganizing Harriman's railroad empire. Otto's analytical and practical mind focused on the matters at hand regardless of his yearnings to return to the bright lights of New York City. It was primarily through his alliance with Harriman that Otto began to build the Kahn fortune, which he would reinvest in property, bonds, culture, and art during the succeeding years.

2

THE NEW WIZARD OF WALL STREET

'The Kaiser's court was no more solidly founded on tradition than the Kahn household.'[1]

1907

Each year the Kahn family unfailingly retraced the familiar route across the North Atlantic and summered on the continent. 1907 would see no exception to that ritual.

On March 12, Otto sailed for Europe on the steamship *Kaiser Wilhelm* II.[2] One of his onboard traveling companions was Cornelius Vanderbilt III, en route to Paris with his family. Otto's trip was, for the present, primarily for business purposes. A few weeks later, his wife and children would join him for their annual summer vacation. Addie set sail at the beginning of May with her three children, two governesses, and two maids, plus a small mountain of deftly packed steamer trunks. The Austrian theater director Max Reinhardt was also booked on the same liner and had prearranged to meet Otto in Paris. The Kahns' extended trip would see them away from America for almost four months. Addie had recently learned she was expecting her fourth child and hoped the change of air and relaxation would greatly benefit her health.

1907 was a significant year for Otto. His diligence at Kuhn, Loeb was beginning to pay huge dividends. What's more, his business association with Edward Harriman had helped propel Harriman's and Kuhn, Loeb's profits into the stratosphere. Otto, too, was personally on course to becoming exceedingly wealthy, undoubtedly boosted by his directorships in several of Harriman's railroad, land, and other corporations.[3] Kahn's reputation in financial and cultural circles was leaping in brevity ten-fold. In April the press labeled him the new Wizard of Wall Street.[4] Otto had every intention of living up to the title.

In late February, during an investigation by New York's Interstate Commerce Commission into Edward Harriman's business affairs,[5] Otto had come to the attention of the American press and general public after being summoned as a witness.[6] Otto's ready and detailed answers to complex questions involving financial technicalities amazed members of the commission. For the lawyers and those hearing Kahn talk in public for the first time, he came across as an exceptionally skilled and knowledgeable speaker.

'Not only did he [Kahn] discuss hundreds of millions of dollars and hundreds of millions of shares of stock with absolute indifference, he showed that, although declaring himself to be merely a banker and in no sense a railroad man, he has a wonderful knowledge of railroad conditions and values.'[7] Testimony given at the inquiry revealed Harriman always consulted Kahn before buying control of any key railroad system and selling railroad stocks. A disclosure that confirmed just how close Kahn and Harriman's working relationship had developed.

The ascent in Otto's profile did not go unnoticed by his Kuhn, Loeb boss Jacob Schiff. Nor did the media's growing interest rush to Otto's head. If life's experiences had taught him anything, it was that the true value of wealth was not its magnitude but how hard you had worked to acquire it. In later years, when asked how he attained his fortune, he would openly reply, 'People are 'wealthy' because they leverage their money and take on risk and identify/seize market opportunities.' Such risks had become a daily practice for Otto.

At Kuhn, Loeb Otto was still working in a subordinate role, a position he found restrictive and at odds with his ambitions and leadership capabilities. As with all family-run concerns, the usual path to securing promotion came either with expansion, death, or retirement.

Addie's situation was somewhat different; she was born into a cushioned life amply provided for by her father's wealth. She knew little difference. Nevertheless, since her father and sister's death, no matter how well prepared she thought she might have been for life's big adventures, as the chief beneficiary to the Wolff fortune, she now found herself in totally unfamiliar waters. Her position as a woman of independent means would now require her to juggle her time wisely and effectively between her charitable associations and family duties.

For the moment, Otto knuckled down at Kuhn, Loeb knowing full well his time to excel would come. In the interim, his extracurricular philanthropic enterprises began to show significant results.

The Conried Metropolitan Opera Company

Otto's directorship of the Conried Metropolitan Opera Company came through his association with Kuhn, Loeb and not through his social contacts.[8] Jacob Schiff proposed Kahn for a seat on the board after being offered a directorship himself, which he declined. Before taking the position, Otto consulted his trusted friend Edward Harriman who advised him to accept. 'It ought to make a better businessman out of you,' Harriman purportedly replied. Otto became a director on February 16, 1903. The Conried Metropolitan Opera Company was a tenant of the Metropolitan Opera House. Theatrical impresario Heinrich Conried acquired the theater's lease and, as such, became the managing director.*

Kahn's appointment was a remarkable achievement bearing in mind the rampant anti-Semitic views held within various quarters of the organization. While Kahn was proud to be a Jew, perhaps the fact that he openly professed to be secular helped sway his fellow board members' decisions in toasting his selection. Nonetheless, now that Otto had one foot firmly wedged through the Opera House door, given time, he had every intention of scaling much higher within its ranks. That opportunity arose swiftly. In 1907 Otto was elected chairman of the executive committee of the Conried Metropolitan Opera Company.

The Met, as people affectionately referred to the opera house (and the company), had, since its opening in 1883, been the social domain of America's 'old' money, the personification of whom Caroline Astor (William B. Astor Jr.'s wife) was its doyenne. Consequently, her annual New York ball had long defined society and was the most sartorial social event of the New York season, if not the entire year. Her presence at the Met was felt like an earthquake tremor. Each Monday during winter, close to 9 p.m., she arrived shimmering in so many diamonds and emeralds she resembled a walking chandelier. Such was the grip of New York's established wealth; they influenced every facet of culture, right down to where you parked your backside in a theater.

The 'Met Set' was arguably the wealthiest and most influential social group in the world. When Otto was elected chairman of the board in 1908 (the year Mrs. Astor died), he dared to question their authority and single-mindedly set out on a mission to haul the company into the 20th century. Over the next two decades, he doggedly steered the Met to new, unscaled heights artistically and socially. He first reduced seat prices to a level affordable by ordinary folk. Next, he brought from Europe to New York some of the most astonishingly talented new wave artistes America had ever witnessed. Following Heinrich Conried's retirement from the Met at the end of April, Kahn invited Milan's Teatro alla Scala savior, Giulio Gatti-Casazza, to become a joint manager of the Met alongside impresario Andreas Dippel. Gatti-Casazza brought the eminent Italian conductor Arturo Toscanini with him as the Met's music director, who instantly raised the standard of performances. It was a brilliant coup for Otto to steer away from opera's spiritual home such a renowned maestro as Toscanini. 'A change from the old order to the new,' hailed New York's *Sun* upon hearing of the inventive appointments. Kahn was already the company's largest stockholder, owning 2,750 shares. With Conried gone, Kahn rebranded the company name to the Metropolitan Opera Company. The Gatti-Casazza/Dippel partnership lasted for two years (1908-10), after which Gatti assumed the role of general manager with a free reign on artistic innovation. Gatti-Casazza was a man of taste and culture. Under his management and Kahn's guidance, the Met quickly evolved and was soon attracting the world's foremost singers, musicians, conductors, and composers. Kahn now had the freedom to oversee every aspect of running the company and, as such, unapologetically steered it 'ever restlessly forward.'

The Met had an unwritten rule that no Jew could own one of the private boxes in the two-tiered 'Golden Horseshoe.' Both tiers held equal social prominence.[9] Even fellow Jew Jacob Schiff, who would visit the Met with his wife on Wednesday evenings, was only permitted to lease his parterre box No. 28.[10] Otto, who spent at least one evening a week at the Met during the opera season,[11] reconciled himself to having an arduous slog on his hands if he wished to change his associate board members' opinions regarding the constraint. For now, he resigned himself to watching performances from either the Director's Box or a public seat in the stalls.

Otto's creative vision was not just limited to the Met. His philanthropic ways began early on in his life. As a patron of the arts, he would fund diverse and experimental ventures, as well as conventional projects. His benevolence was already reaching out across the whole spectrum of American culture - in art, theater, music, writing, and dance. With his elevation within the Met, entire ballet companies and operatic and theatrical productions were now within his grasp.

Nonetheless, true to his hardened business sense, he did not suffer fools gladly. He could sniff out a con artist a hundred yards away.

Some saw his quest to expand and explore all forms of artistic expression as uncharted territory. If Otto liked a particular project, he instinctively believed, so too would the American public.

In Paris during late spring and for most of the summer of 1907, Otto rented a large apartment at 15 Rue Nitot,* a fashionable address in the 16th arrondissement close to Place des États-Unis (United States Square). It was here, Addie and the children joined Otto for their vacation. When in Paris, Otto would visit the art dealer and collector Henri Daguerre to purchase antiquities. From the French capital, Kahn wrote to a contact he had in Nauheim, Germany, expressing his anxieties regarding the current economic situation in the U.S: 'It looks rotten, very rotten in the financial world, but the darkest hour is just before dawn. It will become different again one day.' His fear that the monetary markets might take a nosedive did play out later that autumn.

On May 6, Otto attended a Gala dress rehearsal of Richard Strauss's *Salome* at the Théâtre du Châtelet.[12] In the audience were Baron Henri de Rothschild, William K. Vanderbilt, Sir Edgar Speyer,* and the promising young pianist Arthur Rubinstein. Otto had heard excellent reports of this German production and was keen to check it out. It was a radical opera that greatly appealed to Otto's avant-garde tastes, strewn with issues of morality and propriety ranging from sexual perversion, anti-Semitism, narcissism, and degeneration. It also featured the exotic, erotic, and much-discussed Dance of the Seven Veils.

A Conried production of the opera had premiered at the Met in January of that year and received unanimous disapproval by the directors and operagoers.[13]

'It remains to record that in the audience at this performance, as at the dress rehearsal on Sunday, the effect of horror was pronounced, many voices were hushed as the crowd passed out into the night, many faces were white almost as those at the rail of a ship, many women were silent, and men spoke as if a bad dream were on them. The preceding concert was forgotten; ordinary emotions following an opera were banished. The grip of a strange horror or disgust was on the majority. It was as significant that the usual applause was lacking. It was scattered and brief.'[14]

In a show of solidarity, although much to Otto's annoyance, Conried bowed to the moneyed patrons of the Met who demanded it was banned. As instructed, he canceled all future New York performances of the production. Perhaps Otto had been hoping the German presentation might fit more agreeably into the Met repertoire, especially now Conried was no longer an obstacle. Alas, it was not to be.

Otto returned to New York aboard the steamship *Kaiserin Auguste Victoria* in August.[15] Addie and their three children followed a few weeks later, arriving home in early September. No sooner had the Kahns set foot upon American soil than their whirl of social engagements resumed.

On September 26, Otto and his eldest daughter Maud participated in the opening day session of the annual Horse Show presented by the Morristown Field Club.[16] It was a three-day event, and the Kahn family had tickets for each day. On the first day, father and daughter had a healthy run of good luck, and both won ribbons. Otto scored highly in the Harness Horses over 15.1 hands category with his steed Coquet, and in the Saddle Horses not exceeding 18.2 hands category with his steed Supreme. Maud gained a respectable third in the Small Saddle category with her pony Tipsy. Although the spectator turnout was lower than anticipated because of the wet weather, the competition in the various classes was unusually keen.

On Saturday (the final day), the persistent rain submitted the course and the open-air wooden spectator's gallery to a heavy drenching. Regardless of the miserable weather, the event proceeded as scheduled.

The first competitor was Otto, exhibiting his new steeds, Director and Dictator.[17] Hundreds of ticket-holders braved the cold and rainy conditions to attend. Spectators filled every bench on the stand. Because the weather was so foul, the Kahn family sheltered beneath parasols in a private box on the tiered gallery. Just as the Ponies in Harness class got underway, a loud, distinct 'cracking' sound ricocheted in the air, as a crossbeam beneath one of the raised boxes snapped, and a section of the wooden stand collapsed. Spectators tumbled to the ground. Screams rang out as people nearby grasped the horror of what had happened. Panic ensued as those trapped on the upper level shouted frantically for assistance. Stewards ran forward to help the injured and carefully lifted them from the debris. Otto and his horses were signaled to a halt as the gravity of the incident became apparent. Luckily, Addie and her children escaped any injury and were safely escorted away to a waiting vehicle.

Just over three weeks later, on Saturday, October 19, Addie gave birth to a healthy baby boy and named him Roger. Rather unpromisingly, he arrived amid the 'Panic of 1907,' an economic crisis that saw stocks halve in value from the previous year.

The Kahn Clan

Roger's birth completed the Kahn clan of two boys and two girls. For Otto and Addie, the arrival of their latest child was akin to the icing on a very rich cake.

As was customary with wealthy families of the day, the children were assigned a governess, an English governess in the Kahns case. Addie was also a hands-on parent and would personally plan and monitor her children's daily activities with an exactness befitting a royal household. Yet, regardless of how strict and meticulous her actions may have appeared to a casual observer, they were applied with motherly fairness and instinct.

The children's schooling was as varied as their leisure activities were, combining traditional tuition with private tutoring alongside healthy outdoor pursuits for character building and relaxation. Addie's orderliness and attention to detail in scheduling their daily timetable was a necessity generated by her husband's lengthy absences; Otto's work commitments took him away from home for weeks at a time. One governess, who the family retained for many years, knowingly remarked, 'The Kaiser's court was no more solidly founded on tradition than the Kahn household.'

In some respects, Addie's perception of the world was a handover from the 19th century. She embraced change just as long as the proposed 'change' supported her viewpoint. She, too, was a strong woman. Her days were as diverse and as long as a 'diplomats' wife. She sat on numerous charitable committees' and board of governors and frequently attended recitals, social events, and society banquets. Hints of her strict matriarchal behavior are merely conjecture. Those that received a stern caution from her may well have exaggerated her firmness. With four children to watch over and countless staff on the payroll, and with as many residences to maintain as a royal family, she had every need to be thorough and orderly. It's fair to say, most people were in awe of her, especially in an era when many women were used to remaining unassumingly in the background.

The Kahn children's landscape was filled with privilege and adventure and determined by the seasons and the residences they occupied. A large entourage of staff accompanied them during annual summer trips abroad. In addition to a governess and maids, a tutor from New York was also on hand. In certain countries they visited, they would hire additional local tutors.

In some ways, the family displayed nomadic tendencies.

Otto's travels could see him spending at least a third of each year in Europe. Between his foreign excursions, he would tour America on business accompanied by his valet. The family also spent regular vacations at their holiday homes. Though Otto was indisposed most weekdays due to his demanding work commitments, he made a point of returning home at weekends to be with his family. He would unreservedly join in with all boisterous fun at home, taking great care to treat each child equally with as much love and attention as the other. Although he was not present for much of their early upbringing, his fatherly influence was never far away; he would regularly forward detailed guidelines regarding the children's meals, clothing, education, and so forth. His instructions would arrive by letter in the mail.

The Summers of 1908–1913

For the Kahn family, the six summers of 1908 to 1913 were idyllic, spent exploring the picturesque charms of the continent. With each visit, Addie fell more passionately in love with the European manner and way of life. So much so, she pleaded with her husband to arrange for the family to resettle in Europe. For Otto, it was not that simple. London and New York both had their attractions, but his roots in his adopted country had burrowed further than he could have imagined and would in time bury deeper. Nonetheless, for the moment, it was a proposal he gave serious consideration.

Roger's first visit to Europe came in 1908 when his family sailed first-class aboard the *Mauretania*, bound for Liverpool, England.[18] They departed from Cunard's Pier 54 on July 21, attended to by a small entourage of loyal servants, maids, and a governess.

Wealthy families did not holiday on the continent for a few weeks; they traveled for months, sometimes for a whole season. During these excursions, their staff had the unenviable task of hauling their employer's bulky luggage around with them. These same families would often return home considerably more laden than when they set off.

It was the age of the luxury liner, and the *Mauretania* was the pride of the Cunard Line. Dubbed an Atlantic Greyhound, such ships crisscrossed the ocean at record speeds in a bid to compete for the coveted Blue Riband. The *Mauretania* would go on to hold the award for nigh on twenty years. It was the first passage the Kahn family had taken aboard the *Mauretania*. Otto and Addie were hugely impressed with the level of service and the number of modern amenities on board. Over the next couple of years, the Kahns made a point of sailing on the *Mauretania* whenever they traveled as a family unit.

The London season ran from May through to the end of July. Hotels and societies organized many social activities and events during these three months to help keep tourists entertained.[19] This year, the UK's overcrowded capital was merely a stopover for the Kahns. Their next call was Paris, followed by a stay in Germany to visit Otto's relatives, where he and Addie were eager to show off their latest offspring.

On September 12, the Kahn family temporarily waved Europe goodbye as they boarded the luxurious *Mauretania* in Liverpool for their return voyage to New York.[20]

Back home in Morristown, the 13th annual chrysanthemum show was held on the last day of October by the Morris County Gardeners' and Florists' Society. A newly propagated chrysanthemum named after Addie scooped the top prize in its category. 'The Mrs. O. H. Kahn, a warm, bronzy red, has already received a certificate from the Chrysanthemum Society of America. In its class, we have seen nothing so attractive.'*

Ever since Otto had become chairman of the Met, his name had appeared frequently in newspaper society columns: 'On Monday night Otto Kahn of the Metropolitan Opera Company had a proscenium box where his guests included Mr. and Mrs. James W. Gerard,[21] Mrs. James B. Eustis [former Senator James B. Eustis' wife], and [composer and fellow Met board member] Rawlins L. Cottenet.'[22]

Aside from reorganizing the internal running of the Met, Otto now had more ambitious plans in the pipeline. His growing concerns over the lack of basic modern facilities at the current opera house encouraged him to draft plans to construct a new theater. It was a bold mission Otto would spend a considerable amount of time, money, and energy on during the years ahead.

In 1909, the Kahn family sailed to Europe a little earlier than usual, dropping anchor in Britain at the end of June. From the UK, they traveled to the continent, where they motored across France and beyond. In Paris, Otto and the Met's new general manager Giulio Gatti-Casazza had a meeting with the Neapolitan singing sensation

Enrico Caruso.[23] The tenor put his signature to a lucrative five-year contract with the Met that assured him three appearances a week for a yearly season of twenty-two weeks at $2,000 a performance. The total payment Caruso commanded from the agreement amounted to the colossal sum of $660,000.

Otto also made a special detour to Austria, where he visited his close friend Edward Harriman, who was convalescing after being diagnosed with exhaustion.[24] It was a poignant meeting for Kahn, as he observed firsthand the increasing decline of Harriman's health.

Harriman returned to the States shortly after Kahn's visit. A few weeks later, the great railroad baron passed away.[25] His doctor said he died from 'cancer in the abdominal region, or tuberculosis of the bowels.'[26] Upon his death, his transport empire controlled the Union Pacific, Southern Pacific, Central of Georgia, Illinois Central, and St. Joseph & Grand Island Railway, the Pacific Mail Steamship Company, and the Wells Fargo Express Company. He left a fortune estimated at over $200 million. His entire estate was left to his wife Mary, making her the richest woman in the country. On the night of Harriman's death, a reporter offered his sister Cornelia Simons (wife of the banker Charles D. Simons) his condolences. He then expressed how her brother was considered by many to have been the greatest man in America.

'Yes, he was the prince of them all,' replied a somber Mrs. Simons.

News of Harriman's death reached Otto while he and his family were still on vacation in Europe.[27] As such, Otto did not attend his friend's funeral, a constant regret that remained throughout his life

On each European trip, the Kahns added carefully selected pieces to their expanding art and antiquities collection. They were also investing wisely in quality works of art from Manhattan auction houses. On March 18, 1910, Otto caused the art world to gasp in astonishment when he purchased a magnificent tableau by Belgian master Frans Hals for an exorbitant price. After some lively bidding, *Family Group in a Landscape* finally achieved $500,000, with Otto out-bidding fellow art collector John Pierpont Morgan for the privilege.[28]

At the time, it was a record-breaking sum for such a painting. No sooner had Kahn taken possession of the canvas than he benevolently loaned it to the Metropolitan Museum of Art to display in their new Dutch Room.[29] The Otto and Addie Kahn Art Collection would grow considerably in size and value over the coming years, making it one of America's most important private collections.

Addie Kahn publicity photograph, ca. 1910.

Addie's profile, independently of Otto, was also on the ascendancy. Newspaper and magazine society columns noted her attendance at balls, dinners, recitals, and charity events. Requests for her to sit on the committees of charities arrived with regularity in her in-tray. Those she felt an affinity to, she offered her time and advice. In the spring of 1910, Gilliams Press Syndicate released a series of informal photographs of her. They came with the inscription, 'New picture of Mrs. Otto H. Kahn, well-known society woman. Mrs. Kahn is known as one of the best-gowned women in New York. She is a familiar figure at Newport, Ormond Beach, and other fashionable resorts.'

On occasions, Otto's addiction to hard graft would see him working an 18-hour day, seven days a week.[30] Such a taxing timetable would have been punishing on a 20-year-old, let alone a man in his mid-forties. He made it a rule not to bring work home from the office. Hence, the sporadic time he spent with his wife and children was extremely precious to him and his family.

It was in Kuhn, Loeb's boardroom, where Otto performed best. At meetings, he was quick, confident, impatient, and very, very smart. When a *New York Times* reporter quizzed Kahn on how he approached dealing with financial matters, the banker briskly replied, 'You have a suspicious disposition and are a little prone to distrust the motives of your fellow men.'[31]

Equally as important as his working day was the time Otto devoted to creativity. His attitude to artistic endeavors was far more fluid. Rather than questioning the whys and wherefores of each project he attached his name to, he would usually allow the spontaneity of the moment to take effect. He was also well known for being unflinchingly generous with his cash. Yet, despite his outward appearance of stiff restraint, his curiously, mischievous, and defiant side occasionally surfaced, especially during his extra-curricular activities.

In autumn, Otto journeyed in his private Pullman to the West Coast of America on business. On this round trip, he covered 10,000 miles.* Upon his return to New York in November, he accepted a position on the board of the Boston Opera House.[32] Many of the Met's productions already transferred to Boston. As such, it seemed logical to tie the two opera companies closer together using Kahn's influence as the thread.

When the Met secured the world premiere of Puccini's *La fanciulla del West*, it was a tremendous coup for Otto and the company. Tickets for the night were akin to gold dust. Even touts found it almost impossible to get their hands on any. The few they did secure had an asking price above $100. Otto despised ticket touts and purposely devised a new ticketing procedure. Anyone who bought a ticket had to sign for it upon payment and would only receive the paper ticket on the night of the performance after signing for it again. Ticket scalpers hated Otto for his actions. They could have cleared up in a single night if only they could have got their grubby hands on a ticket.

The media dubbed the occasion the 'greatest opera opening the city ever saw.'[33] Such publicity was priceless. With so many distinguished guests in attendance, security on the night was tight. 'Mrs. Otto H. Kahn was in pale gray and silver and wore diamonds,' observed New York society columnist Cholly Knickerbocker. One of the more amusing incidents of the evening occurred when a doorkeeper refused Otto admittance to the arena. When asked later about the episode, Kahn declined to be ruffled by the action of his subordinate.

'He did rightly,' said Otto. 'It was quite proper for him to refuse me admission if he did not know me. I think his salary should be raised.'[34]

In what could have been a public embarrassment for the Met, Otto cleverly diffused the situation by taking personal control of the outcome. However, despite his quick thinking, it did not prevent the press from gleefully reporting the incident in the papers.

Coronation–1911

The coronation of George V and his Queen consort Mary of Teck was taking place at Westminster Abbey on June 22, 1911. Many American families of note, including the Kahn family, arranged to travel to London to see the ceremonial displays and enjoy the celebrations.

The Kahns set sail from New York in March. Their departure created quite a gust of publicity, mainly because of the enormous price they paid for accommodations on the *Mauretania*.[35] The family and their accompanying staff occupied $11,000 worth of first-class staterooms and suites on the liner. In addition, they paid an extra $2,000 for cabin space and transportation charges on RMS *Caronia* to transport their three automobiles, chauffeurs, and additional servants. The *Mauretania* had been unable to accommodate the entire Kahn entourage, which amounted to over twenty passengers and considerable baggage.

'In the banker's immediate party are Mrs. Kahn and maid, Miss Maud E. Kahn and maid, Miss Margaret D. Kahn, maid and governess, Gilbert W. Kahn and nurse, and Roger W. Kahn and nurse. A valet attended Mr. Kahn. Mr. Kahn said he had leased Cassiobury House in Watford for the coronation. After the coronation, he and his family will tour Europe in their three automobiles. The banker said his vacation this year was purely a pleasure trip and that he expected to be home by August 1.'[36] The steamship company confirmed the

Kahns' booking for the voyage was the largest single reservation ever made for one family.

Before waving New York goodbye, Otto granted journalists a brief interview on the deck of the *Mauretania*: 'I see no cause for immediate financial worry in the U.S.,' he assured them. 'As far as I know, everything is satisfactory. That includes the finances of the Metropolitan Opera House as well. But the report that there is going to be a profit this year is wrong. We expect to come out even. At present, it looks as if we will be able to meet all expenses through the proper channels.'[37] Before heading below deck, Otto also confirmed Enrico Caruso was getting along just fine after a recent health scare that resulted in him canceling several appearances at the Met. Kahn added that he would not be surprised to hear that the singer's condition will have improved enough for him to appear next week. 'Caruso is more frightened than hurt,' Kahn explained, 'and to me, he seemed to be in perfect physical condition. He is like a small boy who is more scared than anything else. Although he has not been billed to sing at the opera next week, I think that there will probably be a pleasant surprise for the operagoers.'[38]

Though Otto claimed his four-month trip abroad was solely for pleasure, he did have some business to attend to regarding the Met. There was also the persistent rumor the press had latched on to about the possible relocation of the Kahn family to live permanently in the UK. Speculation had intensified over the past few years with each visit the Kahns made to Britain. Otto was reticent to disclose his plans just yet, so he remained tight-lipped on the matter. Meanwhile, behind the scenes, things were slightly different; Otto had already begun searching for a suitable property to purchase in the capital.

Over the coming months, the family's itinerary took them to Berlin, followed by a trip through Italy, with time spent in Paris, culminating in England for the coronation. Otto had leased Cassiobury House and its adjoining estate nestling in the heart of rural Hertfordshire as a base for the family. Servants that were not required to accompany the family across Europe stayed at the historic 56-room mansion. Otto also rented 95 Piccadilly, one of the smartest townhouses in central London. He chose the house specifically for its location; it directly overlooked the royal procession's route.

Cassiobury Park was the ancestral seat of the 7th Earl and Countess of Essex. The Earl, George Capell, was married to American heiress Adele Beach Grant of New York. She had sunk a considerable amount of her private wealth into the upkeep of the estate. Unfortunately, substantial inheritance costs had forced the Earl to mortgage the estate to the hilt. In a bid to raise funds, the Earl resorted to renting out the property.[39] This was not the first time Otto had leased Cassiobury to house his family during their visits to the UK; the short rail journey to London meant it was perfect for him to commute to and from the capital for business matters.[40] It also meant his family could enjoy the fresh air and long country walks the estate offered.

Cassiobury House

The Kahn family took up residence at their rented Piccadilly four-story townhouse the day before the coronation.

The property overlooked Green Park and Buckingham Palace beyond and had several balconied front windows to view the coronation parade as it passed by in the street below. 'Otto Kahn is said to have paid $2,500 for the front of a house on Piccadilly,' wrote an astounded tourist Martha Freeman Esmond to her friend in New York.[41] Otto's arrival in the capital sparked a flurry of interest among the press, with reporters following hot on his heels jostling for a scoop. The media were fishing for a story and convinced Otto had something hidden up his sleeve.

On coronation day, the Kahns threw a lavish party at the house catering for over a hundred guests at which many prominent Americans were present. Alfred Gwynne Vanderbilt and financier and attorney William Henry Moore threw similar parties nearby, with many guests moseying from one function to another. John

Pierpont Morgan rented a two-floor apartment on Piccadilly near Hyde Park Corner, where he entertained 150 friends.[42]

American writer Frederick Townsend Martin spent the night at the Kahns so he could watch the royal procession from the house. The celebrations left an indelible impression on him. 'I was awake all night,' he later recalled, 'and several times went out on my balcony overlooking Piccadilly to watch the masses of people who made a patient vigil to see their King pass by. They made such a noise that sleep was impossible.'[43]

Spectators and tourists jammed the streets in central London. Even the unseasonal rainfall could not dampen their spirits. Three processions snaked their way to Westminster Abbey: one comprising the royal guests, another for the Prince of Wales and members of the royal family, and a third for the King and Queen. Thousands of uniformed soldiers lined the route. Bunting decorated the streets. As the Gold State Coach bearing the royal couple passed by, banks of onlookers, some on raised platforms, leaned forward, waving white handkerchiefs, cheering their new monarch on his way. The Kahn brood joined in heartily, waving and jumping excitedly on the balcony as if their lives depended upon it. As each crowned head of state rode by on horseback, Kaiser Wilhelm II, among them, the children tried their damnedest to identify the ruler.

The Phantom Move to Britain

While Otto was in the UK, he turned to his friend Max Aitken for advice. Aitken had recently relocated from Canada to Britain and become an MP for Ashton-under-Lyne. Aitken found the UK so agreeable he strongly advised Kahn to move his family and business concerns, lock, stock, and barrel to England. Likewise, several eminent Conservative MPs were also actively encouraging Kahn to run for Parliament. Though the move would cause the Kahn family considerable disruption in their lives, Otto and Addie were carefully considering the matter.

Otto had grown to love New York and the American way of life, and a part of him wanted to remain loyal to the country that had bestowed so much good fortune and opportunity upon him. Yet, in a way, it was because of this bond he now felt trapped. There was also the small issue of a promise he made to Addie on their wedding day, vowing to establish a residence in the UK before he reached forty. He was now aged forty-four. Add to the equation his flirting desire to develop a political career, and the overall picture becomes more apparent. Otto had watched Aitken's meteoric rise in British politics with considerable interest. As a UK citizen, Otto would have a far better chance to achieve his political aspirations in Britain than if he were to stand for election in America. Taking all these factors into account, the Kahns quietly decided it would be more beneficial to be based in the UK than in the States.

In late summer, Otto hastened his return to America to break the news to his boss Jacob Schiff at Kuhn, Loeb, and to put his business affairs in order. When he disembarked at New York Harbor, he made no mention of his intended plans to the waiting newsmen, preferring to enlighten them on cultural topics.[44]

In his diary, he circled July 1, 1912, as the date for his family to permanently leave the U.S. Then, to start the ball rolling, he enrolled his two sons at Winchester College in Hampshire and instructed several London realty agents to find him a house suitable to accommodate a family of six, with servants quarters for fifteen.

In the ensuing months, not everything went according to plan. The power behind the throne at Kuhn, Loeb, was no longer thought to be Schiff. Instead, many considered Kahn to be the driving force. As such, Schiff was now taking a backseat role. Kuhn, Loeb's competitors J.P. Morgan & Co., were beginning to lose their dominance as America's senior private banking house. Kuhn, Loeb was on track to catch them up. If Otto left the States for the UK and handed the reins to someone else, he would be forfeiting the profits of all his hard labor over previous years. Kahn needed to consider the full implications of his proposal carefully. As if on cue, this came by way of his involvement with various cultural activities.

Over the next few weeks, Otto outlined his future intentions and goals for the Met.[45] When a *New York Times* journalist asked him if he believed Americans were a musical race, Otto's reply came as a jolt. 'Though we have not as yet been very creative in music, I think Americans are a distinctly musical people in that they are genuinely fond of music. It seems to be the art to which the soul of the American people responds most readily.' Otto then affirmed the American ear for music was far keener than that in Europe. 'We have set the mark, which must be reached in opera, for instance, higher than the Germans have.'

Mindful of Kahn's ancestry, his words must have come as some surprise to the reporter. Otto's reasoning as to why America's indigenous population had developed such an acute sense of hearing was he felt possibly due to the climate or some other powerful instrument of nature. As a nation of immigrants, he accepted their offspring would intuitively reject some of the things their parents embraced, thereby refining the younger generation's tastes and expectations to a point where their hearing was likely to be more acute than their parents. It's standard behavior that practically every parent experiences in a rebel adolescent and one that Otto and Addie would personally experience several years later with their children.

Kahn concedes that the American public is more exacting and discriminating in their judgment of operatic singing. It was a characteristic many European artists had discovered adversely after performing in New York. Without wishing to blow his own trumpet, Kahn then praises the Met for attaining a level of excellence akin to holding the 'championship ribbon' of the operatic world.

'The United States offers, I believe, a greater field and fuller opportunities for artistic endeavor than any other country at present, and this will be even more so in the future. I am convinced that in the 'renaissance period' of art, which is sure to come again sooner or later, this country will play a great, perhaps, the leading part.' Unknowingly, Otto's "renaissance period' of art' would de facto be closer in materializing than even he could have predicted.

When asked about his many accomplishments and subsequent wealth, Otto modestly acknowledged they were 'favored by circumstance and by the possession of those peculiar gifts which create success.'[46] Furthermore, he added a word of caution regarding the 'insidious tendency of wealth to chill and isolate' a person: remain 'approachable' and 'welcome contact with the workaday world to remain part and parcel of it. Never forget that the advantages, privileges, and powers' we enjoy, are ours 'on sufferance, so to speak, during good behavior.'

On December 2, Kahn cabled Max Aitken off the record to thank him for his advice and confirm he would follow his example.[47] His Canadian friend warmly welcomed the news.

Otto crossed the weathered Atlantic again in early January 1912 aboard the *Lusitania* and stayed in Britain for three weeks.[48] The fact that Oscar Hammerstein (owner of the London Opera House) was a passenger onboard the same vessel was significant. Kahn and Hammerstein had collaborated on a new agreement to combine forces with the Royal Opera House in Covent Garden. The alliance would see the two opera companies 'secure the best talent in the world at greatly reduced salaries by offering lengthy engagements and the interchange of the sensational stars.'[49] Hammerstein had made a brief visit to New York in early January to tie up any loose ends on the American side of the operation. Now the two impresarios were sailing to the UK together to finalize the deal in London.

The visit also allowed Otto time to catch up with various private matters, including his proposed relocation. Realty agents had scoured London's housing market and found a selection of properties for him to view. He regarded most of them as unsuitable, but one did capture his interest, 2 Carlton House Terrace. The magnificent mansion overlooked The Mall and St James's Park and was a short stroll to Trafalgar Square. Kahn's lawyer hastily opened negotiations with the vendor, Mrs. Maldwin Drummond. Included in the $500,000 purchase price was the property's valuable 17th-century French-style furniture.[50] Newspapers on both sides of the pond ran with the story: 'The house has twenty bedrooms, six or seven reception rooms, a very large dining room and a long ballroom. The marble staircase is famous, and the marble mantelpieces are among the best examples of their kind in London. Grinling Gibbons's carvings decorate the oak paneling in the library and dining room.'[51]

At 2 p.m. on Valentine's Day, RMS *Olympic* docked in New York Harbor at White Star Line's Pier 59. Crowds lined the quayside to greet the passengers. Onboard was Otto. As he stepped ashore, a pack of baying reporters pounced, jostling for a quote. Unbeknown to Otto, during his voyage, a London *Times* correspondent had wired an exclusive report to the *New York Times* announcing Kahn's decision to move 'within a year' to the UK to live. That such a report should appear in the papers was not in itself unusual. News and photographs of Otto's European activities often appeared in the newspapers. What annoyed Otto was how eagerly someone had leaked the content to the press. The correspondent, quoting one of Otto's 'friends,' inferred Kahn would also be entering politics. To Otto's surprise, he discovered he was front-page news on that day's *New York Times:* 'Members of the firm of Kuhn, Loeb & Co., who could be reached last night, refused to discuss Mr. Kahn's intended retirement or to say whether he would retain any interest in the New York banking house. Mrs. Kahn also declined to talk about her husband's plans.'[52] The press boys finally had their story; the Kahns were leaving America.

In August of that year, Addie and her children, accompanied by maids, governesses, and a nurse, returned to England on board RMS *Lusitania*.[53] Otto joined his family on September 16, having sailed with his valet on the *Mauretania*.[54] Their arrival signaled the start of the family's phantom residency in the UK.

The legal negotiations for 2 Carlton House Terrace had taken just over six months to finalize.[55] The purchase had been fraught with misunderstandings, not least the fact that Otto bought the house under duress after the owner misread a document he sent to her, which she believed to be a firm sale. Unhappy with his purchase, Otto promptly put the house back on the market for resale and instead took a year's lease (at the cost of $20,000) on the Earl of Londesborough's spacious townhouse, St Dunstan's Lodge, nestling in the lush surrounds of London's Regent's Park.[56] The Regency house, designed by Decimus Burton (a protégé of John Nash), was built in 1827 and incorporated a self-supporting quadrilateral 'Polygon Room' (or 'Tent Room'), giving the building a similar appearance to the Royal Pavilion in Brighton. The mansion stood among fourteen acres of well-kept lawns, trees, and shrubbery and was the largest private residence in the capital after Buckingham Palace. It acquired its name from the magnificent old clock with mechanical figures that stood at the entrance gates to the grounds. This remarkably well-preserved timepiece was designed in 1671 by the clockmaker Thomas Harrys for the façade of St Dunstan's Church in Fleet Street.

Pleased with the property, Otto extended the lease and called in a designer to redecorate the interior to match the beauty of an Aladdin's Palace, with features copied from those inside the St John's Wood house of Dutch-born artist, the late Sir Lawrence Alma-Tadema.[57] Once completed, Otto moved his family into their new abode in early 1913.[58]

To everyone's surprise, the Kahns and their fifteen servants lived in the house only briefly. Unexpectedly, in early February, Otto abandoned his English parliamentary adventure, upped sticks, and returned immediately to the States.[59] In April, Addie and their four children followed close behind, arriving back in New York aboard the *Mauretania*.[60]

Kahn offered no public explanation for his decision. Some hearsay suggested he was disgusted by internal struggles within the Tory party. Close friends believed he was too fond of America and could not bear the thought of being apart from it for too long. Others speculated whether he anticipated the possibility of war and, as such, sensed life in Europe would be too difficult for him and his family to endure. Otto never again spoke of any desire to hold public office. Nor did he express any thoughts of returning to the UK to live. When, in the future, journalists asked why he did not seek public office, Kahn delivered a stock reply, 'What little I may be able to contribute to the public weal, I can accomplish better in my present role than as a public official.'[61]

Contrary to this, an alternative account regarding Otto's phantom stay in London appeared in a newspaper report later that year. It suggested, Otto treated the purchasing of property and their subsequent renovation as a hobby and that while the alterations and decorations were in progress, he was in his element.[62] Upon completing the renovations, it became a different story; he tired of the house almost immediately and sought the quickest way to get shot of it. St Dunstan's Lodge was a classic example. Otto also claimed to be superstitious, and when Addie twisted her ankle from a fall on the outside terrace of the property, he took a great disliking to the place. Soon afterward, Otto put the house up for sale.

A few weeks after Otto's swift return to the U.S., the death of one of Wall Street's financial aristocrats occurred. On the last day of March, John Pierpont Morgan, head of J.P. Morgan & Co., passed away while on vacation in Italy, leaving his son John Pierpont Jr. (known to his friends as Jack), sole heir to his father's fortune estimated at $80 million. John Jr. directly took control of J.P. Morgan & Co. Was Otto forewarned about Morgan's ailing health, hence his speedy return to the U.S.?

There is nothing so redolent of the past as its vision of the future. Upon Otto's arrival back in America, he set out his grand design for the future.

Despite the Kahn family trying their hardest to assimilate within Morristown society, the local community continued to isolate them. Their predicament at Normandy Height's grew more intolerable with each passing year. In response to this unpleasantness, gradually, the family inwardly rejected their country estate in favor of their Manhattan abode and extended vacations in Europe. To address the situation, Otto drew up plans to construct a new country residence. It would be one of the largest private homes in America, second in size only to the magnificent Biltmore House built by George Vanderbilt.

In the latter part of 1913, Otto purchased 443 acres of land at Cold Spring Harbor on the northern region of Long Island, upon which he planned to build his dream country house. He then hired New York architect William Adams Delano of the firm Delano & Aldrich to design an impressive mansion modeled on a château in the Loire Valley region of France. The house would be perched atop a hill and overlook the district as a towering symbol of Kahn's stature and influence. The construction would take five years to complete.

No matter what country the Kahn family was visiting or what mansion they were residing in, their activities continued to fascinate the public. Reports of their comings and goings graced newspaper society columns weekly. Their lives appeared charmed and privileged way beyond the imagination of ordinary folks. During September at the annual Morristown Horse Show, Otto extravagantly forked out $106 for a box on the elevated stand so his family could watch the day's proceedings in comfort.[63]

Perhaps, it was the Kahns' willingness to openly display their wealth that irked the Morristown community and resulted in several residents behaving truculent towards them. Clearly, Otto's proposal to move his family to Cold Spring Harbor would be for the better. It would allow them greater freedom to express themselves without the need to check over their shoulder for their neighbor's approval. Moreover, Long Island would be an ideal place for them to spend summer breaks. Along its North Shore peninsula dubbed the Gold Coast, moneyed families lived happily away from scrutiny and the public's prying eyes. These families were A-Lister's long before the term became fashionable.

As if constructing one lavish mansion was not taxing enough, Otto simultaneously set about forming plans to build a substantial single-family townhouse in New York.

The Kahns' Manhattan Townhouse

As a statement of Otto's increasing affluence and position in New York society, the Kahns' five-story townhouse in Lenox Hill at 8 East 68th Street lacked grandeur. It also was not large enough for hosting elaborate banquets. By no stretch of the imagination did the property fit into the same bracket as the opulent mansions dotted along Fifth Avenue owned by the super-rich. With that in mind, Otto and Addie decided they needed a grander, more well-appointed townhouse with ample room for holding functions. The house would also require space to display their ever-expanding art collection and have room to accommodate their staff - a home fit for the Wizard of Wall Street. The property should also be a family home for their four growing offspring. Such a residence would not be easy to find and would more than likely need building.

In view of this, Otto purchased a freehold building on East 71st Street on the Lenox Library block. Before demolition began, Otto met up with his friend, steel tycoon Andrew Carnegie, who had built a luxurious palatial home on the Upper East Side of Fifth Avenue on the uppermost part of 'millionaire row.' On the northern side of East 91st Street, opposite Carnegie's red brick and stone mansion at number 2, was a vacant oblong lot that had already been leveled and was awaiting development. Substantial property lined two sides of the boundary. Otto had already had his eye on the land. During their meeting, Carnegie mentioned that many wealthy families were now gravitating towards the topmost part of the Upper East Side as he had done. As luck would have it, he happened to own the empty corner plot directly facing his own house and would, for the right price, be prepared to sell it. Its size was ideal for Otto's proposed new townhouse. Carnegie was a shrewd businessman. He spotted the area's potential, now known locally as Carnegie Hill, long before it became fashionable and scooped up several large tracts near his mansion. He intended to keep the neighborhood exclusive and sell land only to millionaires who had the same vision as he had and could afford to build a single-family mansion that would complement his abode. Otto was an ideal candidate for the vacant plot.

In 1913, Otto purchased the land from Carnegie on the northeast corner of Fifth Avenue and 91st Street for a reported $800,000.[64] One can only wonder if possibly Carnegie agreed to the sale after hearing of Otto's grand plan to build a spacious property modeled on the former papal chancellery *Palazzo della Cancelleria* in Rome?

On the northern corner of East 92nd Street at 1109 Fifth Avenue stood the French Gothic Revival pile belonging to Felix M. Warburg. Felix had commissioned young gun architect Charles P. H. Gilbert to design the house. Otto admired Gilbert's flare and contracted him and J. Armstrong Stenhouse to design his new mansion on the avenue.

Having purchased the Carnegie plot, Kahn no longer required his land on East 71st Street. In March 1913, Otto sold his East 71st Street plot to the wealthy heir, William Ziegler Jr. Construction of Ziegler's mansion took two years, going against the northward flow of Manhattan tycoons such as Carnegie. By the time Ziegler Jr. and his wife moved into their completed residence, the district had drastically changed. Most of their affluent neighbors had fled up Fifth Avenue along Central Park, and their former homes had either been converted for commercial purposes or razed. Luckily for Kahn, he sold the land to Ziegler at precisely the right time.

In February 1914, Otto hit the big screen with a cameo appearance in the fourth episode of *Our Mutual Girl* starring Norma Phillips.[65] He visited the Piping Rock Races to shoot his scene, where he appears alongside his friend August Belmont Jr. who owns the racetrack.[66] Mutual Film Corporation produced the 52-part serial. The one-reel episodes were shot weekly (much like present-day television soaps) and ran throughout the year at movie houses across America. The story follows the antics of a humble, young country girl named Margaret who visits New York City to stay with her wealthy aunt, Mrs. Knickerbocker (played by actress Mayme Kelso). It's the first time Margaret has been to the city of bright lights. A dizzy whirl of social engagements awaits her. Each episode documents the exciting places she visits and the interesting people she encounters along the way. *Our Mutual Girl* was a unique concept at the time and kept moviegoers interested enough to want to follow the young girl's escapades within bite-sized, ten-minute weekly installments.

In early June 1914, Otto signed a contract with the Manhattan building contractor Thompson-Starrett Co. to build his mansion on Fifth Avenue.[67] Construction of the four-story dwelling began almost immediately. By September, excavation of the basement had begun. With a proposed budget of $1 million, building works would take nearly four years to complete. When the house was finally ready for occupancy, 1100 Fifth Avenue would be the second-largest private residence in New York City.[68]

Later that month, the Kahn family departed from New York Harbor aboard Cunard's new RMS *Aquitania* 'the Ship Beautiful,' heading for Europe on an extended vacation that would last throughout summer. On the afternoon of June 16, shortly before three o'clock, *Aquitania* glided into the Mersey after completing her impressive maiden 'round trip.'[69] Onboard, she carried 2,649 passengers, the most ever recorded to have crossed the Atlantic from New York in a British vessel. So steady and smooth was the liner that the absence of vibration led many passengers to forget they were actually at sea. After she moored alongside Liverpool Riverside Station, the Kahn family was one of the first to disembark from D-deck.

A Pebble of Doubt

Mounting tensions between Germany and Russia were growing more hostile by the day. The crowned heads of Europe were at each other's throats. If one country declared war, it would affect everyone. That prospect grew ever closer on June 28, 1914, in Sarajevo, when an idiot kid got lucky and shot the Austrian Archduke Franz Ferdinand and his wife Sophie, Duchess of Hohenberg. The Archduke's assassination took Europe to the brink of war. That eventuality manifested one month later when Austria-Hungary declared war on Serbia.

The Kahns return to London was less frantic than had been in the past. Rather than staying in a hotel, they resided in Mayfair at the townhouse Otto had purchased the previous year. Over the next few weeks, Otto divided his time between business matters in the City and attending the ballet and opera at the Royal Opera House in Covent Garden. The family also spent an enjoyable day at the horse races in Berkshire among the fashionable crowd at Royal Ascot.

Otto was keen to negotiate a two-month lease of the Royal Opera House (provisionally penciled for February and March 1915) to present an opera directed by New York's Century Opera Company. Otto was chairman of the executive committee. Milton Aborn (managing director of the Century) had accompanied Otto to London to attend the meetings.

The Century Opera Company was founded in 1913 to present opera at low prices. City financiers subsidized it. That same year Otto had employed the brothers Milton and Sargent Aborn to run the company. Otto's only stipulation was that they develop and maintain it along the lines already stipulated.[70] The company had taken on the lease of the Century Theatre (known previously as the New Theatre) located at Central Park West between 62nd and 63rd and renamed it the Century Opera House.

Although the theater had only been operating since November 1909, it already had a checkered history. In 1906 a group of wealthy New Yorkers (Otto Kahn included) had combined financially to establish the New Theatre on the premise of building a theater for the masses: affordable, accessible, with low-priced tickets, showing quality productions. Two seasons in, and the plan disintegrated. The company folded. Poorly conceived with near-sighted goals were just some of the reasons cited for its failure. After a rebranding in 1912, the New Theatre became the Century Theatre, but that too went under, and in 1913 the Century Opera Company took over the lease.

Kahn and Milton Aborn appointed themselves as talent scouts on behalf of the Century Theatre as part of its policy to nurture outstanding young performers. However, one such brilliant tenor had eluded Kahn and Aborn's attempts to secure his services. As Otto explained to one local reporter, 'I am told there is a new tenor here who is a bricklayer by profession and a church choir soloist by avocation. I have not located him yet, but I have sleuths on his trail. If he is a better vocalist than a layer of bricks, I will engage him for the English season. I do not claim that he's a second Caruso, but in church circles, his voice is acclaimed the finest of the last decade.'[71] Aborn had already auditioned fifty singers in the past three days but had yet to find anyone that reached his exacting standards. That situation all changed when Aborn discovered the Welsh tenor and former coal miner, Hardy Williamson. The singer was dispatched instantly to New York to appear at the Century.[72]

As is often the case with well-laid plans, things can veer off course. Shortly after the Kahn family arrived in the UK, Otto received an urgent dispatch instructing him to return immediately to New York. Although Otto's visit was abruptly cut short, the rest of the family continued their holiday as arranged. Otto doubled back to America on July 9, on the German liner SS *Imperator*.[73] At Southampton dockside before departure, he relayed to reporters his hope that New York would soon see the Russian Ballet perform at the Met. When asked if he had secured the Royal Opera House on behalf of the Century Opera Company, he replied less confidently, affirming it was unlikely the season would go ahead.[74] The *Imperator* docked in New York on July 16. Meanwhile, over in Europe, political tensions were near breaking point.

In her husband's absence, Addie stepped forward to fulfill some of his engagements on behalf of the Met and attended several meetings in London with the Russian ballet impresario (and founder of the Ballets Russes) Sergei Diaghilev. On July 18, she wired her husband from London with details of the outcome of these meetings: 'Have had several interviews [with] Diaghileff [sic] about Ballet for New York. [Is] most insistent troupe should go [to] America this winter for urgent reason too complicated to cable upon which largely depend continuance of organization. Diaghileff [sic] willing to go even for 10 New York Brooklyn performances of which several matinees and some in Philadelphia, Boston, Chicago simply to keep company together.'[75]

Diaghilev never did get to America that winter. Due to the war, the ballet company got scattered across Europe. Diaghilev instead went to Italy. On October 10, he signed a contract with the Met's general manager Giulio Gatti-Casazza for a tour commencing in January 1916. In reality, Diaghilev was a man without a company, so he cajoled the Met into providing him with the means to create one. With an advance of $45,000, he suddenly had the luxury of experiencing a period of subsidized artistic freedom. Diaghilev spent the summer and autumn of 1915 in Switzerland, where he gradually and meticulously reassembled his ballet company. He promised the Met forty-seven dancers and his three biggest stars: Vaslav Nijinsky, Tamara Karsavina, and Michel Fokine. At the time he signed the contract, he had no idea if he could get them. Nijinsky was under house arrest in Budapest, and Diaghilev could not get his release.[76] When Otto got word of Nijinsky's predicament, he intervened and paid for the dancer's freedom.

Addie, along with her children, servants, and piles of luggage, journeyed from London in their three automobiles to Paris. From the French capital, the family planned to continue across Europe by car.

With political unrest on the continent increasing by the day, threatening to rip Europe apart, the Kahn family vacation understandably did not run to schedule. Three weeks into their trip, war broke out. An element of theatre all too often surrounds dramatic, life-changing events. In the Kahns circumstances, this quite literally became the case. With the outbreak of war on July 28, between 100,000 and 200,000 American tourists were stranded in Europe. All had to find a return passage home. Overnight, travelers' checks, letters of credit, and even some currencies were no longer accepted at banks or as payment at many hotels, shops, and restaurants. Exchange rates rose exorbitantly. Transportation became overwhelmed by the demand for tickets, causing some modes of travel to become unavailable, overbooked, or suspended indefinitely for fear of coming under enemy attack.

Forever the pragmatist, Otto summoned his family back to the States. But, due to unprecedented demand from American tourists and expats, the *Mauretania* (the Kahns' favorite ship) could not accommodate them. Thus, Addie and her children found themselves temporarily stranded in Europe without any passage home.

Panic set in.

London's hotels were packed to the rooftops. Some wealthy men who insisted upon staying at certain luxury hotels consented to accept servant's quarters rather than stay elsewhere.[77] The big hotels were turning away more customers than they could accommodate. Rumor had it that one western money king was so annoyed by his failure to secure rooms in one of London's West End hotels, he tried to buy the establishment.

When the British Prime Minister, Herbert Asquith, announced the declaration of war, Addie, along with her children, twelve servants, three vehicles, and a large number of steamer trunks, were holed up in central Paris in the luxurious surroundings of the Hôtel Ritz. After numerous cables and countless phone calls, arrangements to transport the entire family and their possessions to London were confirmed. From the UK, they hoped to book a safe passage to America. With some trepidation, the family set off from Place Vendôme and motored across France where, on August 4, they arrived under the veil of darkness at Dieppe on the Normandy shoreline. Here they caught a small ferry across the English Channel and landed safely at the port of Newhaven on the East Sussex coast. After further delays, the family arrived in London on the night of August 6, three days late, weary and exhausted, and checked directly into Claridge's Hotel.

Their journey was not without incident. Before boarding the vessel in Dieppe, French Customs impounded two of their automobiles. Onboard the ferry, anxious tourists and desperate refugees fleeing the conflict filled every corner of the boat. It was a harrowing ordeal for Addie and her children, who had never endured such an uncomfortable crossing before. To further hinder their discomfort, the party was traveling with sixty-five trunks of possessions. Some contained valuable jewelry, furs, and silver. Authorization for the luggage to make the crossing only arrived due to the exertions of a special agent at the American Express Company. When the Kahn family failed to reach London on the night of August 3, the following day's newspapers ran worrying reports implying the family had gone missing.[78]

Sheltered in the relative sanctuary of Claridge's, Addie paused for a few days rest to recover from the trauma she had just endured and to plan the remainder of her and her family's journey back to the States. The thought of a six-day Atlantic crossing confined on another overcrowded ship greatly distressed her. It was not an option she intended to take lightly and appealed for assistance from every contact she could muster. Her influence bore instant results. She was offered three alternative ships within the week but declined them all, fearing the accommodations would neither be spacious enough nor up to her exacting standards.

Such unreasonable and demanding behavior, especially during a time of political unrest, although objectionable to some, was not uncommon conduct for a woman of her standing and immense wealth. In her opinion, she was only doing what she thought was best for her family and those around her. For good or ill, not everybody viewed her actions sympathetically. Those, financially less fortunate, thought her priorities were back to front and deemed her behavior selfish and thoughtless and called for shipping lines to block the Kahns temporarily from traveling. In their eyes, the curtailing of certain luxuries seemed a meager price to pay in return for the assured safety of loved ones.

As the situation rapidly deteriorated in London, American businessmen and officials from the American Embassy thought it advisable to organize various committees to oversee the evacuations. A transportation committee conferred authoritatively with shipping companies; a financial committee held conferences with London bankers; a hotel committee arranged with hotels to accept American checks as payment. A diplomatic committee efficiently relayed all the goings-on to the American Ambassador in London, Walter Hines Page. At one point, it seemed as if no one could move a foot without forming a committee to approve it.

Emergency meetings were swiftly arranged, which the exiled tourists attended. Everyone wanted a quick solution to the present backlog of shipping travel requests. One group of refugees became so restive, cries of 'we demand that the United States send transports at once' were heard.[79] A New Jersey lawyer advocated an appeal be made to the belligerents to suspend hostilities to allow stranded Americans to be evacuated safely from the war zone. Those in attendance cackled like gulls over his lack of judgment. 'I'm afraid we count for little in the eyes of the belligerents,' advised the chairman.

A copious array of proposals were vigorously debated until, in desperation, one woman's voice rose above all the others and shouted, 'Stop this foolishness and let's get down to business and appoint committees!' The meeting ended abruptly. The great American exodus had begun.

Ironically, the fact that Addie found herself stranded in London, a city she adored, put her in a strange predicament. Perhaps she should stay put until things had quietened down a little. Over the next few days, Addie spent many vexatious hours correlating a satisfactory route home. Her efforts pushed her fondness for the city to the limit.

On August 4, Germany invaded neutral Belgium en route to its primary objective, France.

Finally, Addie succeeded in her task. After prevaricating in London for almost three weeks, she took some solace in the fact that she had managed to secure state apartments for her and her children on board the *Mauretania*, albeit entailed motoring up to Liverpool to board the vessel. The Kahns' luggage trunks - all sixty-five of them -

arrived at Liverpool docks ahead of the family. Addie and her brood were heading home. The ship departed from UK waters on August 29.[80]

By the time Addie, laden with children, arrived safely back in New York City, the war was about to take a more severe turn.

In the doubtful days of September 1914, Otto offered the assurance that unless Italy directly entered the war, the opera season at the Met would still go ahead.[81] Perhaps, to encourage ticket sales, he did not specify the alternative. His hesitance in doing so may well have been because he had yet to determine that option. Italy did not enter the war until the following year, and the Met opera season took place as intended.

Kahn also presented a series of brilliant premieres to aid the war effort and help lift people's spirits. The first was on September 14, at New York's Century Opera House. Performances of *Romeo and Juliet* and *Carmen* helped raise $5,000, which benefited the Red Cross war relief fund in Europe.[82] It must have given Otto great satisfaction to note many of his Wall Street associates attended performances, including his work colleagues from Kuhn, Loeb.

On October 22, Otto received the following cable:[83]

Naples Oct. 22

Sailing today aboard Canopic with Toscanini, Polacco, Setti, Romei, Farrar, Destinn, Bori, Hempel, Schumann, Caruso, Urius, Botta, Didur and minor artists. Within a few days will follow Weil, Goritz, Braun, Ober, Reiss and Rothier. Only missing artist, Gilly, prisoner of war, but hope for his release shortly. Canopic arrives Boston Nov. 2. Compliments from all
Gatti-Casazza

A copy of the wire arrived on the editor's desk at the *New York Clipper*. He decided to reproduce its contents in the newspaper to alleviate any fears friends and colleagues of the artists may have had regarding their safety. There had already been reports that French basso Léon Rothier was missing, presumed killed in action.*

Addie's abiding love of music, and her charitable endeavors to financially help worthy music students with their education, took on a more defined capacity in 1914. In November, news of a new arts organization she had founded to help young, gifted singers and musicians was announced in the papers.[84] The Music League of America began its first year by supporting twenty-five worthy candidates selected by an advisory committee from 115 applicants. A series of four concerts were scheduled at New York's Aeolian Hall to showcase the chosen artists, in the hope of securing future work and contracts. Among its sponsors were two of Addie's close friends, Mary Harriman (wealthy widow of the railroad magnate Edward Harriman) and Dorothy Whitney. The organization would grow in size and influence in the coming years, and its effect would spread throughout America.

At the beginning of the festive month, in an extraordinary move, various cast members of the Century Opera Company asked the management to reduce their salaries by 25 percent.[85] This unusual request came during the company's appearance for a limited season at the Auditorium Theatre in Chicago. Ticket sales had been miserable. The company's general manager Milton Aborn explained to the press why the cast had taken this measure. 'The people in the company realize that they ought to do something for the man who has done so much for them, and so they decided to help Mr. Kahn, who has stood the loss of the opening nights of our Chicago engagement. Mr. Kahn is able to stand any losses, which may come, but the fact that members of the company volunteer to help him by accepting a big reduction in salary demonstrates the harmony and cooperation which makes the Century Company unique.'

The spirit of the gesture, and the cast's willingness to take a cut in their salaries, made an indelible impression on Otto. What followed next made their act of generosity seem even more heartfelt.

In the last week of December, Otto made the difficult announcement that he had resigned from his post as chairman of the Century Opera Company's executive committee. The *New York Times* carried the story on its front page.[86] Kahn no longer wished to represent a company whose vision and direction appeared at odds with his. Yet, even though Kahn quit, he generously vowed to continue his financial support for the coming season. The Century's managers, brothers Milton and Sargent Aborn, issued a surprisingly bold statement soon after Kahn left. In it, they outlined a list of concerns they held for the company's future and squarely lay the blame for their current precarious financial predicament at the doors of its wealthy patrons.

'Society only judges opera by the price of the admission ticket. If we charge moderate prices, the millionaires won't come because they think they'll have to mingle with the so-called common herd.'[87]

The Aborns blamed this snobbish attitude as the cause for the recent suspension of the Century's forthcoming season at the Auditorium in Chicago. They then claimed that only 10 percent of the 'elite' actually liked opera and that the rest attended as a social function, some only to compare clothes. Finally, they maintained that many millionaires who agreed to back the Century financially 'got out from under and left Otto Kahn to foot the bills.' Such a damning public declaration must have come as a real kick in the teeth for Otto, especially as he had been its chief financial backer, having funded the organization to the extent of $75,000.[88] It was an expensive and particularly bruising lesson for Kahn to learn.

As the Aborn brothers were soon to find out, Otto's opinion carried considerable weight. After Kahn severed his ties, the company rapidly lost further patronage. Two seasons later, the enterprise went into receivership.[89]

3

A CHANGE OF DIRECTION

'Amongst the common meeting grounds available, one of the most appropriate is that of art. For art is democracy, art is equality of opportunity.'[1] Otto H. Kahn

1915

Otto helped the war effort in as many ways as he possibly could. Knowing he and his family would be unlikely to travel to Europe during the conflict and still unable to find a purchaser for St Dunstan's Lodge in Regent's Park, Otto offered the mansion and its grounds rent-free to the National Institute for the Blind. The institute jumped at the offer and duly set to work transforming the place into a retreat and training school for soldiers blinded in battle.[2] Through Otto's generosity, the British public noticeably began to warm to him.

The hostel opened on March 26 on the understanding their tenure would cease once the war ended. The main objective of the institute was to rehabilitate and retrain its residents in new skills. In the process, the blind learned how to cope with being blind.

'At the moment there are 30 men there,' reported *The British Journal of Nursing*, 'able-bodied except for the incapacity of the injury which has befallen them, but there are 25 more on the books, and more sleeping accommodation is to be added.'[3]

Blind teachers supervised the residents and taught them new trades and occupations to encourage them to be self-supporting in civilian life. The chairman and founder of the Care Committee, British newspaper magnate C. Arthur Pearson, who had recently become blind due to glaucoma, considered the lake in the grounds attached to St Dunstan's incredibly useful for the residents. Rowing was one of the best forms of exercise for the blind.

The Children's Early Years

As the I owned several properties, the children quickly grew accustomed to moving home. Winter at Palm Beach, spring in Morristown, summer on the continent, fall in New York, and so the cycle rotated year in year out. All four offspring received home education, and at the age of eleven, each child attended a private school.

In between the sporadic unhappy incidents at The Heights, the family's time at the estate did nurture some fond memories. Most afternoons, Maud, Margaret, Gilbert, and Roger were driven by their nanny to Morristown in a horse-drawn, fringe-topped surrey. They would spend time at King's Drug Store in the town center, where Eddie, the soda jerk, who presided over the soda fountain, would allow each child to mix their favorite ice cream soda or sundae.[4]

Addie maintained an extremely well-organized daily routine regardless of which country or property the family was in residence. When Otto's weekday work commitments drew him away from Morristown, he would devote his weekends entirely to his family. His Sundays usually started with a brisk morning walk with his exuberant brood in tow. Otto would stride along the tree-lined lanes attired in his tweed cape, looking every inch the country squire.

When Otto was absent from home for long spells, he kept a check on his children's schooling, more often by mail, as existing letters he wrote regarding their homework reveal.[5] Their language studies and reading material were of particular interest to him, as were details of the food they ate, which, together with Addie, he planned and approved in advance. One of the more fastidious batches of correspondence held in the Otto H. Kahn Papers at Princeton's Firestone Library reveal his dialog with hotel managers and rail companies when the family was abroad. He specifies in exact detail individual meals his children should eat. For example, roast chicken, mashed potatoes, snap beans, and 'freshly baked milk custard' for his children's main meal was his request in one dispatch written to the Great Western Railway.[6] The family would also carry supplies of tinned Walker-Gordon milk among their luggage during their travels.

Regardless of Otto's idiosyncratic behavior, he taught his children thrift and the value of money from an early age. To acquaint them with such matters, he opened bank accounts for each child before they turned twelve.

Roger's hazel eyes were every bit as soft as his mother's. So too was his luxuriant head of hair. As the youngest, Roger was doted upon by his parents and his siblings. Nonetheless, they also made a point of not wrapping him in cotton wool; all the Kahn offspring received equal measures of affection from their parents.

As the children grew older, the family spent more time at their Manhattan townhouse at 8 East 68th Street.

Having already reached their mid to late teens, Maud and Margaret Kahn began to draw attention from society columnists.[7]

Margaret had taken up dance classes. As a result, she was chosen to appear in a production at the Century Theatre for one matinee performance on March 4.[8] Under the banner, *The Children's Revolution*, more than two hundred youngsters were featured, presenting drama, dance, and pageant, in a historically accurate account of the life and times of the days when the American Republic was in its infancy. The show would benefit The Lafayette Fund – a charity devoted to aiding French soldiers in the trenches, assisting French hospitals, and helping the families of wounded soldiers and sailors. It was a big production with elaborate sets and expensive costumes. Though seats were costly, the show sold out. Also in the cast was a military band from the deaf and dumb institution and the dance troupe in which Margaret danced. The high point of the show was the Washington and Lafayette Inaugural Ball. In it, children, dressed in Colonial costumes, were announced by their real names and then the name of a distinguished ancestor who took a prominent part in the American Revolutionary War. The piece brought an outpouring of enthusiastic clapping from the audience.

Margaret Kahn, partnered with Gloria Gould (daughter of railroad executive George J. Gould), danced the minuet. Another group of children from the Michigan Indian Reservation presented a display of authentic Indian dances.

Otto and Addie encouraged their children to think out of the box. As such, they welcomed Margaret's stage appearance. Allowing their children to participate in such activities was a vital part of their education. The social restrictions imposed on women were still very much evident. More recently, Britain's suffrage movement had grabbed women's attention on both sides of the Atlantic. It seemed only a matter of time before Maud and Margaret took up the mantle and began showing their support.

Later that same month, Maud also appeared in public, although in a different setting. Her entrance was on the opposite side of the stage, in the auditorium.[9] The occasion was a charity Flower Show for the British War Relief Fund. The event took place in the Red Cross Tea Garden inside the cavernous Grand Central Palace exhibition hall. Maud, dressed in a crinoline dress and a sailor hat, sold flower seeds.

A couple of months later, 11-year-old Gilbert Kahn got in on the act when he trod the boards in a Lafayette Fund Fete. His performance was billed as part of a 'tableaux' of 'living pictures' and required him, along with many other children, to appear on stage in colonial costumes and uniforms. Gilbert represented an English lieutenant of the colonial period. The entertainment helped raise considerable funds to aid wounded soldiers in France.[10]

The war dramatically changed the travel patterns of many Americans. Families that devotedly crossed the Atlantic on their yearly pilgrimages to the continent now looked closer to home for their vacations.

On July 3, the I departed on their annual summer break. This year they traveled by rail to the northeastern state of Maine in New England.[11] Otto, fighting shy of a trip abroad, had rented George Washington Vanderbilt II's charming summer cottage Pointe d'Acadie in Bar Harbor for one month. The resort came highly recommended by his good friend Andrew Carnegie who had previously leased the property. Otto even had his prized stallions transported to the estate by private railroad car to compete in the local horse show during his stay.

As 1915 drew to a close, Maud Kahn's introduction into New York society drew ever closer. Her debut would be one of the highlights of the forthcoming winter season.[12] Understandably, the excitement and anticipation Maud felt became more intense as the big day approached. The ball would be a grand affair, and her mother took great pleasure in organizing the event. To ensure their eldest daughter received only the best, the I did as they had become accustomed to doing and threw a stack of money at it. The reception would take place on the first Friday in January.

1916

At the beginning of the year, Otto expressed his firm belief that the general business outlook for 1916 would be exceedingly bright and would fare much better than the previous year. Several other respected financiers, industrialists, and Wall Street bankers shared his optimism, including the National City Bank of New York president Frank A. Vanderlip.[13] It was with this mindset that Otto forged ahead with his major construction projects.

On January 7, Maud's big day finally arrived. Otto and Addie threw a spectacular ball to introduce their 18-year-old daughter into society. The staggeringly large guest list numbered 1,000 names. At the top of the list were the Vanderbilts, aspiring writer Mercedes de Acosta, and the young heiress Alice DeLamar.[14] Due to the sheer volume of guests and the elaborate catering requirements, the I hired Sherry's restaurant on the corner of Fifth Avenue and 44th. It seemed a fitting setting – Addie held her coming out party at Sherry's in 1894.[15] Sherry's advertised their restaurant as being the most magnificent and most expensive eating place in the world.

Before supper, guests enjoyed half an hour of entertainment. Enrico Caruso, the French actress Yvette Guilbert (who enacted one of her famous monologues), and the Russian prima ballerina Anna Pavlova featured on the program. Pavlova's performance came ten days ahead of the Ballets Russes American debut at the Century Theatre.[16] The dancer had briefly starred with the company in 1909.

The following day's *New York Press* applauded their performances: 'Few debutante entertainments given in the past five years have equaled the brilliance of last night's affair, and for two weeks society had looked forward to the ball with eager anticipation.'[17]

At Sherry's, guests took over three floors, including the large, ornately gilded and mirrored ballroom on the third, their smaller reception room on the second, and the first-floor Tapestry Suite. The party started promptly at ten and continued deep into the night, lasting until daybreak. Two large orchestras provided continuous music until the early hours when a light breakfast sobered up any remaining guests before they headed home. Press reports claimed Otto paid Caruso the astonishing sum of $10,000 for singing two songs.

The ball was a great success. Praise and thanks rained upon the I for hosting such a fabulous event. Though it was unreported whether any potential suitors for Maud's hand were in attendance, the party served its purpose, to introduce the eldest Kahn, daughter, into high society in style.

Just over a month later, Maud made another appearance in public, although this spectacle did not garner as much praise from the press as her debutante ball did. On February 18, she performed on stage alongside fellow suffragettes in a charity show to highlight the women's suffrage cause. *Melinda and her Sisters* was presented in the Waldorf-Astoria's ballroom and produced by the prominent socialite and suffragette activist Alva Belmont (née Vanderbilt). After six weeks of intense rehearsal, the operetta played only a single performance. The organizers hoped the concert would raise awareness and necessary funds for the Women's Party. With ticket prices topping $125 each, they quickly collected over $8,000.[18]

Though the production was termed 'amateur,' some of the cast were seasoned professionals. Elsa Maxwell (who would later establish herself as a journalist and premier society hostess) composed original music for the score, and actress Marie Dressler and Metropolitan Opera soprano Frances Alda took leading roles. In addition, a scattering of debutantes (Maud Kahn included) and fashionable society figures played supporting roles.

In reality, the operetta billed as 'a satire of smart society' came across as an airy trifle, noticeably lacking in any political speeches or propaganda to advance the suffrage movement. Even the Waldorf-Astoria's brilliant surroundings could not brighten the performance. British suffragette Emmeline Pankhurst's heartfelt battle cry, 'Be militant each in your own way … I incite this meeting to rebellion!' seemed to have fallen on deaf ears on this particular occasion.[19]

Otto's association with the Ballets Russes did not go as smoothly as hoped. Their New York dates and subsequent U.S. tour were neither the artistic nor financial success Otto and Sergei Diaghilev had banked on. Moreover, Diaghilev had shown his true colors as a meddling, temperamental megalomaniac.

When the company returned to New York in April for a four-week engagement at the Met, Diaghilev's foul temper caught him out. After cussing and striking a stagehand for annoying him, the technician's colleagues ganged up on the director. Only the intervention of a Met official prevented the director from sustaining a beating. That evening, as Diaghilev stood backstage in the wings watching the performance, a pig iron counterweight from above – used in the rigging system – came crashing to the floor, slicing a chunk out of Diaghilev's hat, narrowly missing the director's head.[20] No explanation for the accident ever materialized.

On April 12, Russia's leading *danseur* Vaslav Nijinsky – having now arrived in the States from his incarceration in Hungary – made his American and Met debut. The press and public instantly recognized his genius. When Diaghilev's company set sail on May 6 for Spain, Nijinsky stayed behind in New York. Otto had already decided Diaghilev must go for good, and any future tour by the Ballets Russes should have Nijinsky at the helm. Nijinsky agreed to Otto's proposal and signed a formal contract with the Metropolitan Opera Company on August 2, 1916.[21]

The second Ballets Russes tour commenced in New York on October 16, at the Manhattan Opera House, a week behind schedule due to an ankle injury Nijinsky sustained a week earlier. Their New York season did not live up to artistic or critical expectations and came to a sobering end on October 28. An arduous four-month stint across the States followed soon after. The tour turned out to be a fiasco, playing to half-empty houses, fracturing Nijinsky's confidence in the process. It was estimated the Met incurred a whopping $250,000 loss. Part of the problem was Nijinsky, who had no previous management skills and would dither clueless over the smallest of decisions. The other part of the blame fell at the Met's door for their exorbitant ticket prices and lack of PR skills in advertising in the relevant towns where the tour was visiting. The whole experience soured Otto's involvement with Diaghilev and put an abrupt end to his and the Met's sponsorship of the ballet company.

The Northaw Estate

When Otto purchased land and property, more often than not, it was on a grand scale. During one costly spree in 1914, he bought a substantial estate in Oyster Bay Cove on Long Island from Henry Herman Harjes, a former senior partner of the Paris-based investment bank, Morgan, Harjes & Co. The 170-acre Northaw Estate came complete with a 10-bedroom, colonial revival mansion, fronted with a white-pillared portico and semi-circular gravel driveway. Otto's original intention had been to increase the acreage and build a grander mansion.

Consequently, the Kahn family never stayed at the property. A few miles further along the island, Kahn had already snapped up a substantially larger tract on which he was now building his Cold Spring Harbor estate. As such, Northaw became surplus to his requirements. In February 1916, Kahn agreed to the sale of Northaw to a representative of the Cunard Steamship Company, Thomas Ashley Sparks.[22]

Fifth Avenue was the street of many automobiles and considered one of the most exclusive shopping districts in the world. The Kahns' 'his and hers' Rolls-Royce Landaulet limousines were often seen on the avenue threading their way among the traffic.[23] Along this vibrant thoroughfare, all walks of life mingled. It housed some of the city's most iconic buildings: The Metropolitan Museum of Art, New York

Public Library, St Patrick's Cathedral, the Waldorf-Astoria Hotel, and the Fuller (Flatiron) Building, not forgetting the Arnold Constable department store and the fashionable Dobbs hat shop at 244. Like an exotic bazaar, the colors, fashions, and continuous noise were an assault and pleasure on the eyes and ears. It was also home to luxury mansions and bordered Central Park, where the horse and carriage still reigned.

Steel signal towers positioned on inter-sections watched over traffic and pedestrians as they traveled this way and that on their daily business. Double-decker omnibuses clambered alongside noisy automobiles, hoisting in and spewing out passengers like a mechanical toy. Here the world came together in one almighty cacophony that represented the new spirit of America.

The Kahn family continued to reside at their East 68th Street townhouse throughout the building of their palazzo at 1100 Fifth Avenue, choosing to spend less time at their Morristown estate. To a casual bystander, it might have appeared Otto had gone into the construction trade; such was the extent of the family's building plans during this period. As well as overseeing complex designs for their magnificent country estate in Cold Spring Harbor, preliminary diagrams for a new summerhouse on the secluded island of Islesboro, Maine, were already on the drawing board. They were also searching for a seafront plot in Palm Beach, a resort the family had made brief seasonal visits to during the past couple of years.

122 North Ocean Boulevard

In early spring 1916, the Kahns returned to Palm Beach, Florida, for several weeks sojourn. They stayed at Lotus Cottage, nestling in the exotic grounds of the Hotel Royal Poinciana. With its varied leisure and sporting facilities, it was the ideal location for a family holiday. What's more, the visit fitted in neatly with their plan to build a retreat of their own in the fashionable resort.

Otto roped in his friend, the New York stockbroker and Palm Beach resident E. Clarence Jones, to advise him on various tracts available for development. After viewing several, Otto purchased an oceanfront plot in Floral Park at 122 North Ocean Boulevard for $11,500. The land extended from Sunset to Sunrise Avenue, along the palm-fringed and newly paved North Ocean Boulevard. Otto then hired Florida-based architect August Geiger to draw up plans for a new Mediterranean-style villa. Addie personally oversaw the interior decoration and furnishings with New York decorator A. A. Jones to reflect her sophisticated yet sympathetic and uncluttered style. Construction of the villa started in late summer the following year.

Throughout 1916, Otto continued to add more real estate to his property portfolio. In Manhattan, he purchased 6 East 68th Street, bringing the number of row houses he owned in the street to three.[24]

On May 16, the *New York Times* reported Kahn had slipped over to Paris, France, where he'd arranged in cooperation with the Marquis de Polignac (an aristocrat from one of France's oldest families) for the Symphony of Paris Orchestra to visit America later that year.[25] It was part of an arrangement he'd negotiated on behalf of the Franco-American Association for Musical Art, co-founded by Kahn with Clarence H. Mackay and William K. Vanderbilt. The objective of the association was to promote and encourage the appreciation of French music by facilitating trips to the U.S. by French singers and musicians.[26]

How long Kahn remained in Europe during this visit or where he traveled was classed strictly confidential due to the restrictions imposed on foreign nationals in Europe throughout the war. As such, personal travel details were not publicly accessible. However, by chance, in 2013, a morning coat with a matching waistcoat once belonging to Otto surfaced in an auction. Both garments, tailored from finely woven wool cloth incorporating a subtle diamond pattern, were handmade by London tailors C. F. Johns & Pegg. Inside the coat is a handwritten label inscribed 'Otto Kahn Esq. Nov. 1916.' Given this piece of evidence, it might indicate Kahn did visit the UK at some point in 1916.

Otto took great pride in his appearance and dressed every inch as society expected a wealthy Wall Street banker to dress. When in public, he was meticulous about the way he looked: whether in a wool suit with a neatly folded white handkerchief in his upper jacket pocket, complemented with English shoes and white spats, a jeweled tiepin and a fresh rose in his buttonhole; or attired in plus-fours, argyle socks, and brown brogues when playing golf; or wearing his trademark dark opera cape draped across his shoulders carrying his pearl-handled walking cane for an evening's performance at the Met. His image and how the public perceived him were paramount to him. Many of his expensive bespoke suits were handmade in Savile Row in London's Mayfair. One particular tailor he favored was Henry Poole & Co.; another was C. F. Johns & Pegg at 2 Clifford Street. His exquisite, handcrafted leather riding boots came from Peal & Co. at 487 Oxford

Street.

Eternally vain, in Kahn's eyes, a smart appearance showed the world stability, trust, and continuity, all vitally important attributes every reputable financier should display.

Somewhere in France

Although the Kahn sisters led exceedingly privileged lives compared with most young ladies of their age, they were not averse to rolling up their sleeves and getting their hands dirty. As members of America's upper class, Maud and Margaret were fully aware of the responsibilities expected of them and the challenges that lay ahead. Even so, the sisters were not ready to settle down to married domesticity just yet. Some of life's big adventures were still waiting to be discovered.

On July 29, 1916, Maud and her best friend Marianne 'Billy' Goodhue McKeever (daughter of the wealthy Wall Street investor Isaac Chauncey McKeever) set sail from New York aboard the French liner *Lafayette* bound for Le Havre in France.[27] Maud had only six days earlier celebrated her 19th birthday. With no set plan to adhere to, the girl's mission was simple: to volunteer their services to relief organizations in Paris to support the war effort.

The McKeever family lived at 120 East 65th Street, just around the corner from the Kahns. Both girls were raised and privately educated on Manhattan's Upper East Side. In a sense, this voyage would be Maud's rite of passage, her coming of age, for it was the first long-distance journey she had undertaken without being chaperoned by a parent or governess. Eleven days later, the two fresh-faced New Yorkers arrived in Paris, where they checked into the splendid Hôtel Plaza Athénée on Avenue Montaigne. Over the coming months, the hotel became their unofficial 'home from home.'[28]

Maud and Billy volunteered for war service without any formal orders and promptly joined the French Red Cross. Their first assignment was in the Paris Military Canteen at Gare Saint Lazare, where for long hours each day, they helped prepare and serve meals to soldiers and refugees.[29] Their duties were grueling and tedious and relieved only with brief spells of leisure when the girls would party like true Americans abroad. No doubt, a watchful eye was kept upon the two young heiresses by officials at the U.S. Embassy in Paris (where Ambassador to France, William G. Sharp, was based) lest the girls got into any bother.

On one occasion, Maud and Billy dined at the Café de Paris before catching a performance at the Théâtre Michel to see, 'the one and only real opera we went to.' Three potential male suitors joined them, including the U.S. banker William Henry Crocker's son William Crocker Jr. and his nephew Harry Crocker. As was expected, the girls were appropriately chaperoned by 'Mrs. Rogers.'

Leave was gratefully grabbed. Time spent wisely, reconnecting with emotions that had been folded away in a suitcase and forgotten. Then, in December, the girls arranged a trip to the French Riviera, traveling by train. They let their hair down in Cannes, played golf, and had a flutter at the beach casino.

During Maud's time in France, various reports filtered into the papers that several prominent Europeans, including a titled Frenchman, were wooing her. It was forecast she would return to the States either as the wife or fiancée of a Count or a Baron. As it turned out, such reports were mere conjecture.[30]

Otto's younger and closest brother Felix was now living in the U.S. In December, Felix acquired control of New York's Rialto Theatre after becoming its principal shareholder.[31] Felix was already a director of the Mutual Film Corporation,[32] who had signed movie actor Charlie Chaplin to a contract earlier that year allegedly worth $670,000.

With Otto Heinemann, Felix had also founded the independent record label OKeh that handled the U.S. distribution of Carl Lindström's two European record labels, Parlophon and Odeon.[33] Although Felix was a keen amateur cellist, his business interests and dealings in the entertainment industry were focused more on the financial side than the artistic.

Christmas came and passed, and Maud and Billy returned to their duties in Paris for a further short stretch before sailing home to America aboard SS *Kroonland* in February 1917.

Citizen Kahn–1917

1917 would be a hugely significant year for the Kahn family, not least for Otto. It was the year he finally received his U.S. citizenship papers.

Otto was incredibly proud of Maud's voluntary work.[34] Upon her return to New York, he and Addie threw a surprise welcome home party for her at Sherry's restaurant and invited a host of Maud's friends along.³⁵ Maud's thirst for adventure, however, did not stop there. A few weeks later, she crossed the Atlantic again, this time to England, where she offered her assistance to the British government. She arrived equipped with a brand new Ford Model T automobile paid for by her father and was put to work as a dispatch bearer for a London hospital, ferrying the wounded in her car.³⁶ It was challenging work, unsettling and long hours. Tending to the injured, witnessing brave men crippled by pain and fear was mentally draining. These were demanding times. Such experiences quickly molded young girls into strong women.

Through her volunteer work, Maud gained valuable life skills and forged many new friendships, which, post-war, led to her meeting her future husband, a fellow serviceman.

In mid-January, Jacques Copeau, the eminent and influential French theater director and founder of Théâtre du Vieux-Colombier, arrived in New York City at the start of a four-month goodwill lecture tour sponsored by the French Government. The underlining aim of the trip was to encourage American involvement in the war. Copeau also hoped to drum up interest in his own theater company. He'd disbanded the company in 1914 at the start of the war and hoped to reinstate it. His lecture tour went well, and, on a personal level, he rallied a measure of interest in his work with the Théâtre du Vieux-Colombier. Copeau accepted an invitation to dinner at the Kahns' East 68th Street home. During the evening, Otto and Addie impressed upon Copeau the importance of re-establishing his French theater company.³⁷ Otto offered to assist financially with the project and proposed an American tour. As a cultural ambassador, Copeau's visit achieved its goals.³⁸ The director accepted Otto's offer. At the end of his lecture tour, Copeau returned to Paris to reassemble his theater company with an $18,000 letter of credit in his pocket courtesy of Otto. Rehearsals ran throughout the summer. To further Copeau's objective, Otto leased the Shubert brothers Garrick Theatre at 67 West 35th Street in New York and promptly renamed it Théâtre du Vieux-Colombier. Kahn roped in the young Czech-born architect Antonin Raymond to redesign the theater's interior and appointed the interior designer and renowned socialite Mrs. Philip Lydig to oversee the decorative touches.³⁹

Tickets for the premiere went on sale and sold encouragingly well. Copeau returned to New York later that year on November 11, accompanied by his family, a troupe of twenty-nine actors, and large crates of scenery and costumes. The director proudly announced to reporters he'd managed to secure the release of six of his actors from war duties in the trenches. In an interview for *The Drama* magazine, he relayed his hope that 'for a time the Vieux-Colombier is going to find in America a second motherland.' Though renovations at the theater were still ongoing, the company opened on November 27 with an impressive production of Molière's comedy *Les Fourberies de Scapin*, coupled with a new piece, *L'Impromptu du Vieux-Colombier*. New York critics showered the actors with praise. The company settled happily into their new home, where they performed twenty-one different plays. The following year, at the close of their New York run in early April, Copeau and his troupe journeyed to Washington, D.C., and then to Philadelphia, where they presented a scaled-down selection of their repertoire in both cities'.

We're *'Camping Tonight'*

There was a side to Otto's character that was not readily apparent, a lighter, more playful trait that would keenly join in the fun and games. He was even known to mock himself if the occasion called for it. One such instance occurred in Washington, D.C., on Saturday, February 17, at the closing dinner of the season, hosted by the Gridiron Club (a journalistic organization). Three hundred guests attended. At President Woodrow Wilson's table were members of the cabinet, prominent government officials, and a sprinkling of business executives, including Otto.[40] For the after-dinner entertainment, there were various sketches and satirical musical skits; most were ad-hoc, unrehearsed observations, or off-the-cuff monologues. Otto joined in the fun by singing in a barbershop quartet alongside fellow guests, Thomas 'Tom' W. Lawson, financier Bernard 'Barney' M. Baruch, and president of the Guaranty Trust Company of New York, Charles 'Charley' H. Sabin. Reports of the evening's escapades leaked into the following day's newspapers.[41] The song lyric to *'Camping Tonight'* that Otto and his fellow barbershop cohorts sang surfaced in the dailies. The ditty - a homage to the Silent Sentinels - recounts the actions of the suffragettes currently picketing outside the White House gates in a bid to give women the right to vote. The women demonstrated silently, speaking only to reporters.[42] Otto was an advocate of the suffrage movement. His decision to perform *'Camping Tonight'* in front of President Wilson is a testament to his support. That aside, there was another underlining theme to the lyrical content:[43]

'We're camping tonight on the White House grounds,
give us a rousing cheer.
Our golden flag we hold aloft,
of cops, we have no fear.
Many of the pickets are weary tonight,
wishing for the war to cease.
Many are the chilblains and frostbites, too,
it is no life of ease.
They met Tom Lawson in the street,
Barney and Charles, and Ot.
He said: *'You boys appeared to know*
More than the public ought';
'Now won't you come to Washington and tell about the leak?'
They whispered: *'No, no, thank you, Tom,'*
and didn't give a squeak.
But Tom came, willing, eager, too,
and said they should be brought.
So Henry sent a Sergeant-at-arms for
Barney and Charles, and Ot.
'Now, boys,' said Bob,
'Come tell us all about this inside ring.'
They whispered: *No, no, thank you, Bob,'*
and didn't tell a thing.'

The 'leak'* referred to in the lyric, related to a charge brought against various individuals who, allegedly, profited in stock market transactions in December the previous year. Currently, there was an ongoing investigation into the matter in New York City and Washington, D.C. Prosecutors claimed they had prior knowledge of the president's peace note plans.[44] Those accused of improper dealings were financier Barney Baruch, attorney and private secretary of the president Joseph P. Tumulty, statesman and lawyer William G. McAdoo Jr., the president's brother-in-law Richard W. Bolling, and others close to the president.[45] When Baruch testified at the inquiry on January 9 in Washington, D.C., about his sales of stocks around the time of the peace note, he denied having any insider information. He also confirmed he had no business association with Otto Kahn, nor the man mysteriously referred to as 'Reich,' or anyone connected with the government.[46] When Otto took to the stand on the same day, he too confirmed he had no connection with any leak. Kahn was excused. Charley Sabin declined to reveal the source of his information. Thus, the panel dismissed Sabin from further questioning. The following week, financier Tom Lawson was hauled before the House Rules Committee in Washington, D.C., to divulge what he knew about the leak. Lawson calmly revealed that a congressman had told him about a stock gambling pool whose members included a Cabinet officer, a senator, and a banker. The congressman was Robert L. Henry, chairman of the Committee.[47] He then proceeded to name each defendant individually. He also charged that Paul M. Warburg, head of the Federal Reserve Board, knew about the leak. Lawson's sensational declarations, the most dramatic charges of scandal the capital had heard for many years, had the packed room in an uproar. More surprising, when Representative Henry later appeared on the witness stand, he denied any knowledge of the leak. The hearing was adjourned soon after.

Tom Lawson initially aired the subject of the leak to bring about a thorough investigation of the New York Stock Exchange. Lawson hoped the government would introduce incorporation and federal regulation as a result of its findings.

That Otto should have appeared in front of the president at a dinner attended by three hundred guests (including newspapermen) as a member of a barbershop quartet singing *'Camping Tonight'* is in itself odd. The fact that he sang alongside Lawson, Sabin, and Baruch, making light of the inquiry, seems even more bizarre unless they all held the unshakeable belief that the Committee would drop the investigation.

With much of the evidence already given, based on hearsay and assertions, and at the risk of the inquiry turning into a circus, the Committee on Rules favored abandoning the whole proceeding, believing reporters were to blame for the leak.[48] In the coming weeks, no further action was forthcoming, and the inquiry ended with the dismissal of all defendants.

On March 28, 1917,* after residing in America for 23 years and eight months, Otto relinquished his British nationality and became a naturalized U.S. citizen.[49] Nine days later, American Congress approved the joint resolution to fight alongside its allies Britain, France, and Russia on France's war-torn battlefields.

Shortly afterward, Kahn set out on a rallying tour across the Western States in a show of patriotism, delivering campaign speeches backing the U.S. Government's decision. He proposed several plans, including the immediate creation of a war finance board. He also declared Germany had deliberately planned the war and issued a stark warning to all militant Bolsheviks that American temper would not stand their trifling. Finally, in a call of unity, Kahn urged Americans of German origin not merely to do their duty for the

U.S. but to let their loyalty take active form. It was strong language for a man of German descent, but a stand Otto believed he had to make if he was to be respected by his fellow Americans.

Otto embraced change and made and spent a fortune cultivating it. In 1917 when he was elected president of the Metropolitan Opera Company - a role he assumed from the 1917-18 season onwards[50] - it came as the glaze on top of a very rich Opera cake. Kahn finally had the power to steer America's foremost opera company into the future. He already owned most of its stock. Taking overall control when the Met was still not operating to its full potential, living mainly on its reputation, appealed greatly to Kahn. He was confident he could turn its fortunes around for the long run.

Nevertheless, not everyone in the world of opera bowed in Kahn's presence. In contrast, some viewed him in a bad light, a meddling, pompous rich man who had no right sticking his nose into the bohemian world of music, art, and literature. To the general public, Otto appeared impervious to the brutal criticisms hurled at him, especially those from certain fractions of the media. Deep down, the slurs hurt. The scars would remain with Kahn throughout his life. His resolve, however, was deep-rooted, his determination committed.

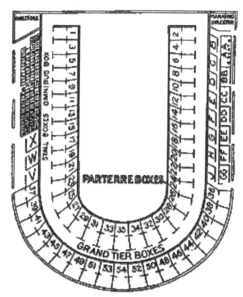

In 1917, Otto was finally permitted to own a parterre box [No. 14] at the Metropolitan Opera House.

In a surprise move later that year, Kahn was finally permitted to own a parterre box in the Met's hallowed 'Golden Horseshoe,' No. 14.[51] Whether as approval of Kahn's ascendancy in power or the simple detail that a box became available is unclear. What is certain is that no Jewish person before Kahn had ever owned a box at the New York Metropolitan Opera House. It was Kahn's choice to purchase it.

Throughout the 23 years Otto had lived in America, he had become known as a man of action, a man of his word. His name was recognized across the globe. A name synonymous with loyalty and trust. With increasing regularity, he was called upon to advise governments, leaders, and royalty. In the financial world, many regarded Kahn as the ablest reorganizer of railroads in the United States.[52] It was Kahn, who, in 1910, through prompt action, averted an imminent economic disaster by rescuing from collapse the famous Pearson-Farquhar syndicate that had overextended itself in a daring attempt to weld together a transcontinental system out of existing railroad lines. It was Kahn, too, who in 1906 played a principal role in the intricate negotiations leading to the listing of $50 million of Pennsylvania bonds in the first official listing of an American security in Paris. Kahn was also said to have taken an integral part in the tough negotiations that resulted in Kuhn, Loeb's recent issue of $50 million of City of Paris bonds, and $60 million of Bordeaux-Lyons and Marseilles bonds. Consultations also went ahead with Kahn during the recent formation of the $50 million American International Corporation (AIC) with its vast potential for furthering America's world position in trade and finance.*

'I don't know what we would have done without the counsel and practical assistance of Mr. Kahn,' remarked Charles Stone, president of AIC, when asked to comment on Kahn's help in establishing the organization. 'He is a wonder. His understanding of international affairs is amazing.'

When a journalist on the Pennsylvanian *Reading Times* asked Kahn what advice he had to offer to ambitious young men, 'Think,' he flashed back. 'The young man who applies himself seriously to thinking will, by and by, be amazed to find how much there is to think about. He should never be content simply to take things as they are. Nor should he be satisfied with accomplishing one task, no matter how worthy or important, but should continue thinking and thinking, and he will find many channels opening up for his activities.'[53] Kahn then advocated 'Acting' as his second word of advice. 'The young men and their elders in this country now have an opportunity such as has come to no other nation since the middle of the 17th century, when England rose to conspicuous greatness. Today every great nation except ours is under terrific strain and handicapped in the race for supremacy. We, being apart from it, and drawing immense materialistic benefits from it, have an unparalleled opportunity, not merely to make money, but to take a larger, broader, more influential, and a beneficent part in the world's affairs, in molding the destinies of mankind.'

Over the past seventeen years, Otto had worked tirelessly for Kuhn, Loeb, often sleeping only five hours a night, spending long spells away from his family, zigzagging back and forth across America reorganizing and remodeling rail companies into profitable concerns. The financial rewards he reaped for his arduous work were colossal. Money is for spending. It would be a crime not to spend it, he would later affirm. Hence, he earmarked a portion of his independent wealth for educating the public in the riches of art, theater, music, and literature. In this respect, Otto, the Maecenas, was like a child in a candy store. Europe was that confectionary store, brimming with artistic delicacies. The fun part for Otto was discovering and nurturing such talent.

For this reason, the Kahn family vacations abroad were the perfect escape, where Otto could release himself from the stresses of high finance. Furthermore, it was a ritual he and Addie would share yearly, sometimes twice within twelve months, health permitting. Such migrations could last anything from one to three months, depending on how expediently Otto could organize them into his working calendar at Kuhn, Loeb.

With the U.S. now engaged in combat, the carefree gaiety enjoyed by New York society took on a less spontaneous, more altruistic mood. Margaret Kahn, having just turned sixteen and feeling to some extent overshadowed by her big sister Maud - still stationed 'somewhere in England' - threw herself energetically into helping the war effort at home. It was an admirable decision for a teenage girl to make and one she did not take lightly.

Doubtless inspired by her elder sister's charitable work overseas, Margaret offered her time to various organizations connected to the U.S. national war effort. A picture of her perched halfway up a stepladder attaching a Government Liberty Loan poster to the façade of a building in Manhattan appeared in several newspapers.

'The time has come to conquer or submit,' warned President Wilson. 'For us, there is but one choice. We have made it.' The public took heed of Wilson's blunt rhetoric, and millions of ordinary American citizens invested their hard-earned cash into Liberty Bonds. 'Buy a war bond and help win the war,' proclaimed the message on the posters.

When Gatti-Casazza first took over the Met's daily management, most operagoers assumed he would favor Italian opera, as he was Italian, and ban German music. It did not take long to convince even the most skeptical that the new manager was a stauncher supporter of German opera than the former Met manager's Heinrich Conried or Maurice Grau had been, both of whom were native Germans.[54]

Prior to the Met's new season beginning later that year, the board of directors vetoed using the German language in the Met's repertoire. They deemed it unpatriotic. As a result, no performance of German opera took place at the Met during the 1917-18 season. When Otto publicly announced the temporary ban, not everyone agreed with the decision. President of the newly formed Commonwealth Opera Company (also based in New York), John Philip Sousa, adopted an alternative approach. He demeaned Kahn's action by announcing the Commonwealth Opera Company would produce German airs.[55]

'While I do not doubt that Otto Kahn has excellent reasons for his move, I do not think that patriotism demands any such expression. The German operas, which are popular with the people here, have been adopted by America, and are really American, just as American as an alien who takes out papers. America is not a geographical area, but an ideal, and because the writer of a piece of music happened to have been born in another geographical area does not make his music hostile.'

These were harsh words from a native-born American, especially one who denied any inclinations of pro-Germanism. Kahn firmly believed all opera should be sung in the language it was initially written and felt librettos suffered at the hands of the translators.[56] He certainly would not have entertained performing any German opera at the Met translated into English.

The press noted Sousa's dig at Kahn: 'Music is international, and I believe it is the force which will, in time, bind all the nations together. Music is the soul of the individual artist speaking to all nations. It is the one universal language. Great music is of all times and places.'

A few months earlier, 62-year-old Sousa had enlisted in the U.S. Navy to conduct the national band. 'I am for America first, last, and always. I am an American in a very strict sense, for all my ancestors have been in this country since the time of the Indians. So I cannot be accused of pro-Germanism. But I think music is beyond the boundaries of nations, and I cannot see any reason for excluding any opera by a composer who happened to be born in Germany.'

Kahn never publicly responded to Sousa's denunciations.

The following day, Kahn dropped by to see President Wilson at the White House to advise the president on the country's economy.[57]

The Cold Spring Harbor Estate Takes Shape

If a man's home is his castle, Otto certainly intended his new country house at Cold Spring Harbor to be just that. Otto may have been a futurist, welcoming and encouraging all things modern in art and culture, but it was to the past he looked for inspiration for his new mansion. Ideas for its design were adopted from the Château de Fontainebleau nestling in Seine-et-Marne in Île-de-France.

When Kahn sought planning permission from the local council to build atop Jayne's Hill - believed to be the highest point on Long Island - they rejected his request. Not to be discouraged, Kahn had his workmen build a hill of his own. The land was disturbed and elevated. It took two years to complete. Construction of the house began in 1917. The blueprint was Otto's vision, his new lover, and he raided his bank account weekly to keep her happy.

Residence for Otto H. Kahn On Jericho Turnpike, Woodbury, Now in Course of Construction

The Cold Spring Harbor house had a balance between the new and the familiar - the *Brooklyn Daily Eagle*, February 21, 1917.*

Over the next few months, the building's outline began to take shape, rising slowly, inescapably seen for miles around, scrutinized under the gaze of his affluent neighbors. Their wariness was ill-judged, for Kahn had commissioned one of New York's most highly regarded young architects to oversee the project, William Adams Delano. His reputation was impeccable.

By late August, the slate tile roof was in place, and the landscape architects Frederick L. Olmsted Jr. and John C. Olmsted of the firm Olmsted Brothers were hard at work planning the layout of the grounds.

The creative gardener Beatrix Farrand designed the more intricate formal gardens, which received the same high level of detail and attention. To add scale and grandeur, she created water features, rectangular parterres, and symmetrical vistas, complemented with stone statuary and boxed garden shrubbery.

Gossip continually encircled the Kahns, never more so than during the construction of their Long Island mansion during the war. Even their forward-thinking, free-spirited neighbors kept a watchful eye on the structure as it gradually dominated the horizon. Some of Otto's harshest critics openly disparaged him for his ostentation during a time of cutbacks and austerity. Yet, appearing unruffled by his detractors, Otto continued to flash his cash around.

Addie appeared more reserved in her manner and was genuinely concerned by such criticisms and how the public perceived her family. To help quell talk of excessive spending, she had certain design aspects on the estate modified. In a letter to the Olmsted Brothers, she wrote: *'we have made up our minds to continue the work very gradually not in a pretentious way.'* The Kahns scraped their plans for an Orangery. In its place, they ordered a 75-foot indoor lap pool.[58] Such an amenity appeared less frivolous and more practical. They abandoned diagrams for a terraced garden, and to appear thrifty, agreed to scale back the extent of the formal gardens. Thankfully for the Kahns, the building works were on schedule. If all went to plan, they hoped to take occupancy by the following summer.

The Sacred Flame of Art

On June 20, 1917, on a warm, temperate evening, three thousand people crowded into St. Nicholas Rink on West 66th Street, New York, to welcome the Civic Orchestra onto the stage.[59] The occasion was the opening night of a ten-week summer series of classical music concerts that included compositions by the German heavyweight's Beethoven and Bach, offset by lighter works by the French composer

Cesar Franck and the Russian composer Rimsky-Korsakov. Seats at 'popular prices' ranged from twenty-five to fifty cents. The rink looked spectacular, dressed in the banners of the United States, Britain, and France. Midway into the program, soprano Anna Case, with a large American flag draped around her body, sang a rousing rendition of 'The Star-Spangled Banner' with an orchestra of eighty players backing her conducted by Pierre Monteux. Case's interpretation brought the audience to their feet in a rousing display of emotion.

In his capacity as treasurer of the Civic Orchestral Society of New York City, Kahn delivered a speech from the podium. He thanked the audience for their enthusiasm and their belief in the neutrality of art.

'We are all Americans,' Kahn spoke assuredly, 'whatever blood flows in our veins, and we can say, as was once said long ago, that it is not for the honor, glory, or interest that we fight, but for the liberty alone, the most precious of those high and noble things that make life worth living. Another of those things is art, and in time of war, it is our duty to see that the sacred flame of art is not extinguished. The flag of art is neutral, and, please God, it always will remain so. [pause] I want to add a word of the appreciation with which all our hearts go out to sublime France [applause], and, to a distinguished son of France, Pierre Monteux, soldier and conductor.'

'The keynote of everything at this time is patriotism,' added Kahn, 'and we have arranged that at each one of these concerts a speaker on national issues will appear.' Kahn then stepped to one side and introduced Colonel Chatfield, who congratulated the society on its patriotic stand and splendid music. He then focused his address on recruitment.

Not all concertgoers that evening agreed with Otto and his fellow organizers. One such antagonist was the German-Jewish journalist and music critic Paul Rosenfeld who saw fit to decry the use of classical music as a magnet for drumming up recruits.[60] In his scathing write-up published in the August edition of The Seven Arts chronicle, Rosenfeld thought the concert shameful. He vigorously questioned the rationale behind the season of shows: 'One doubts whether irreverence, whether ignorance of values and disregard of them have, during the entire course of the war, assumed a form quite as contemptible as the one they are assuming at the concerts of the Civic Orchestral Society. For the sake of those who still attach some glamor to it, Mr. Kahn and his associates ought to remove the word 'patriotic' from the advertisements of their concerts.'

The Civic Orchestral Society was founded in 1916 by Kahn and other culturally minded guarantors. The society presented their first series of concerts that year at New York's Madison Square Garden, at which Chicago-born violinist Albert Spalding had been a soloist.[61] From a musical standpoint, the shows were a great success. The society was now keen to expand its range. It was hoped their current run throughout summer at St. Nicholas Rink would increase their reputation. Regrettably, critics were just as harsh in their reviews of the opening night performance as they were of their choice of repertoire. The *New York Times* asked for 'less shopworn works of early and modern France,'[62] while the *Musical Courier* complained, 'This is not the sort of music that one wants to listen to on a hot night in summer.'[63] The barn-like acoustics fared just as poorly as the seats did for their discomfort.

In response to low advance ticket sales, the society halved the run of twenty concerts. They blamed the cancellations on the unfortunate choice of venue. At the close of the season, Otto had the unenviable task of reporting to the guarantors that the sharp financial loss sustained would be greater than anticipated.

In this new age of celebrity, the press were already taking notice of the Kahn offspring. The two fresh-faced daughters in the main, but occasionally Gilbert would also get a mention. Presently, Roger was too young to be newsworthy; his time had yet to come.

That summer, Maud returned home to New York for another short break. Although many young American men had enlisted in the armed forces and departed for foreign shores, life in the city continued. Maud eased herself effortlessly back into the social whirl that was the debutante's privilege, attending receptions and parties. On August 16, she was a bridesmaid at her friend Margaret Clarkson Henderson's rushed wedding to Captain Otis Love Guernsey at the Church of the Heavenly Rest on the corner of Fifth Avenue and 90th. As a result of the hurried circumstances, Maud was Margaret's only bridal attendant and due to the groom's pressing army duties, there was no reception after the ceremony.[64] Soon after the wedding, Maud quietly headed back across the Atlantic to resume her role in the UK where she had volunteered to help the blind ex-Servicemen at St Dunstan's in London.[65]

On September 26, Otto delivered a patriotic address before the Chamber of Commerce in Harrisburg, Pennsylvania. His theme for the talk was *'Prussianized Germany: Americans of foreign descent and America's cause.'* He was also there to drum up support for the

Liberty Loan Campaign, of which he was a staunch supporter.[66] In his speech, Kahn urged Americans of German descent to give their full backing to the administration's war policies. He warned that Prussianism in Germany, 'with profound cunning, has instilled into the nation the demonical obsession of power-worship and world-domination.'[67] Kahn then articulated, 'For we Americans of foreign antecedents are here not by the accidental right of birth, but by our own free choice for better or for worse. Woe to the foreign-born American who betrays the splendid trust which you have reposed in him!'

After luncheon, Otto went on an hour-long tour of the city in an official limousine accompanied by Mayor J. William Bowman and David E. Tracy, president of Harrisburg Chamber of Commerce. Otto expressed how impressed he was with Harrisburg, which he termed Pennsylvania's most progressive city. The following day a telegram arrived from Hon. Frank A. Vanderlip of the Treasury Department in Washington, D.C., in which Tracy praised Kahn for his patriotic and unselfish assistance in connection with the Liberty Loan Campaign and vowed to pledge the Chambers hearty cooperation during Liberty Loan work.[68]

Much of Otto's spare time was occupied by writing, especially while traveling on long trips. His public talks were mostly self-written and were the ideal environment for him to judge public reaction to their content. Many of his essays would go on to form the genesis of his numerous published works.

A Singing Nation Behind a Singing Army

On September 27, the U.S. War Department appointed Otto as head of an advisory committee to provide entertainment for soldiers. In his role, Otto would oversee the organization and assembly of sixteen big frame marquee theaters, one for each of its national military cantonments. The advisory committee would collaborate with a theatrical committee, of which New York lawyer and theatrical producer Marc Klaw was the chairman.[69] By April 1917, the War Department Commission on Training Camp Activities was set up and began supplying entertainment and leisure-time activities to nearly a million and a half young men in training camps. They aimed to build morale and bring some resemblance of normality back into their lives.[70]

Each marquee could seat three thousand. Some of the best

theatrical talent in the States had volunteered their services. The entertainment calendar included motion pictures and live entertainment - the plan to screen movies required between eight to ten million feet of film a week. Books would also be available, courtesy of the American Library Association.[71] An organization to develop and encourage recruits to participate regularly in healthy athletic activity, preferably a competitive sport to help build their fighting instinct, was already in operation. Lectures on the harms of alcohol and prostitution were included, and any soldier disabled with a venereal disease was labeled a 'traitor.'

Some regarded the appointment of Marc Klaw as a controversial choice. As one-half of Klaw & Erlanger (entertainment management and booking agents), the company held a crippling monopoly on playhouses, theater circuits, and Broadway shows. As such, they determined the character of the plays to be presented, engaged the leading players and fixed their salaries, controlled ticket prices to the theaters, and took complete command of the booking arrangements, laying out the routes and dates in each city and town where the actors performed.[72] Klaw & Erlanger had created many enemies in the business. One bitter litigation suit brought against the company by the producer and impresario David Belasco had dragged on for six years, costing an estimated one million dollars in legal fees.[73]

Kahn's appointment to watch over the assignment sent a clear signal to Klaw to restrain his autocratic behavior. The committee's work was a huge success. It encouraged hundreds of entertainers from all rungs of the theatrical ladder to freely donate their time and energies, supplying the forces with many memorable hours of recreation.

Over and above the military instruction, the miracle of the training camps was how the imagination of America's youth suddenly became fused. In doing so, it depicted the real soul of America. The doughboys (a commonly used moniker in Europe for a U.S. infantryman during WWI) desire to express their inner feelings, transcended through the simplest medium, song. The impact of ten thousand singing soldiers, their hearts filled with passion, was not a sight, or sound, an officer in charge could easily forget. It stirred the spirit right to the core like no other emotion known to man.

America's late entry into the war saw 1.5 million troops stationed inside Europe by August 1918, of which over 300,000 were Black. The concept of organized mass singing in the training of an army was new. The idea originated at a meeting of the Commission on Training

Camp Activities on April 26, 1917.[74]

General John J. Pershing, commander of the American Expeditionary Force (AEF), and other far-sighted U.S. military officials were quick to notice the positive effect community singing had on the overall morale of their battalions. A singing army meant a happy, contented army, Pershing cabled to the U.S. War Department from France. Major General James Franklin Bell agreed. He, too, was convinced his troops' drive and confidence depended largely upon some means of self-expression. He viewed singing as the ideal medium; a vocal army would be a far greater force for victory than a silent one. 'A singing army is a fighting army,' insisted Bell at Plattsburg in April 1917, and with them, the spirit of America lived on.[75] The War Department, through the Commission on Training Camp Activities, took heed and placed trained song leaders in all Army training camps across America. Mass singing became an integral part of a soldier's daily routine.

Writer Carl Van Vechten said the only songs that influence a nation's music are those people sing. If recordings could capture for posterity the songs soldiers sing on the battlefields, then perhaps wars would never again be fought.

And so, American music went to war in the doughboy's lungs, heartfelt, democratic, adaptable to all his moods. For the soldier chose his songs well, sturdy old hymns for sacred moments, national anthems for ceremonial needs, old favorites for sentiment's sake, and jazz, so much …

'jazz.' [76]

Jazz from Columbus Circle to the World

Earlier that year, in January, five unknown musicians arrived in New York City from Chicago to perform at a restaurant on Columbus Circle.

The musicians were five clean-cut young guys from New Orleans. Fame initially enticed them to Chicago, where they came together as The Original Dixieland Jass Band. They then traveled to Manhattan, where in January 1917, they took up a residency in one of the city's top entertainment and restaurant establishments, Reisenweber's. On opening night, not all went to plan. Diners could not make heads or tails of the strange sound emanating from the band's instruments. By the end of their set, the room had emptied. Unsurprisingly, the band's gig got pulled. However, the management did not give up on the boys and booked them to appear at the opening of their smaller, second floor 400 Club Room on January 27.[77] In the interim, the band played a brief stint at the newly opened Coconut Grove on the rooftop of the Century Theatre, four blocks away on the corner of 62nd and Central Park West.

The Century Theatre was a cavernous place with lousy acoustics, stuck out on a limb a mile away from the theater district. The critics loathed visiting. The public echoed the same opinion. Since it first opened as the New Theatre in 1909, it had struggled to operate as a viable proposition. So when the Broadway producers Florenz Ziegfeld Jr. and Charles Dillingham signed a lease in Otto's office in May 1916, everyone involved hoped it would turn around the theatres' fortunes.[78] The pair produced a musical revue for the stage, and in mid-January 1917, opened a cabaret venue on its rooftop, the Cocoanut Grove.[79] Hey presto, the nightspot drew good business.[80] Customers were treated to a lavish midnight floorshow produced by Ziegfeld and feasted on a sumptuous meal. It was a costly evening out, aimed at the moneyed. The Century Amusement Corporation, which Otto part-owned, financed the venture.[81] The Cocoanut Grove was the ideal stopgap for the Original Dixieland Jass Band.

'Until You Visit Reisenweber's You Haven't Seen New York' claimed John Reisenweber in his advertisements.[82] The statement might well have been true. As its owner, he also bragged it was New York's *'Newest, Largest, and Best Equipped Restaurant.'* The four-story building certainly looked impressive from the outside, with its sidewalk to roof colonnades, tall windows, rooftop balcony, and a sidewalk cafe, grill, and bar. Inside was a ballroom and twelve dining rooms.

This was the beginning of cabaret nightlife culture in New York City. Reisenweber's was one of the first high-class establishments to offer the experience of a floorshow, live popular music, dancing, and dining all rolled into one, with twice nightly sittings.

Reisenweber's advertisement in the *New York Herald*, January 25, 1917, mentions The 'Jasz' Band, the Latest Western Rage.[83]

As a 'man about town,' it seems likely Otto could have caught a performance of the Original Dixieland Jass Band at the Cocoanut Grove or Reisenweber's if one considers he was abreast of most artistic movements in the city. Kahn was definitely in New York City during January.[84] Coupled with his role as chairman of the advisory committee for the Commission on Training Camp Activities and his involvement with the Century Theatre, it seems plausible his awareness of jazz music could well have stemmed from around this period.

The Original Dixieland Jass Band went down a storm at Reisenweber's 400 Club Room. By February 2, the restaurant was advertising them as The 'Jazz' Band, spelled with two z's.* By the end of February, new jazz bands had sprung up around the city like exotic truffles. Many were demanding exorbitant fees. The Original Dixieland Jazz Band now commanded a $1,000 price tag, unheard of for a five-piece band. Reisenweber knew he had struck the jackpot by giving the band their lucky break. To make sure everybody else in New York knew it, he had 'The Original Dixieland Band - Creators of Jazz' emblazoned in electric lights across the façade of Reisenweber's in Columbus Circle lest anyone should claim otherwise.[85]

November 1917

At a loyalty meeting of captains of industry, Otto announced he would be donating his income (after deducting his living expenses) for the duration of the war to the government and agencies engaged in the war effort.[86] He was the first American to do so. Jacob Schiff publicly commended Kahn's act of generosity. In response, Schiff contributed $200,000 towards a $5 million fund set up for Jewish war relief.[87]

1918

In early January, a cold front spread rapidly across the U.S. from the Rocky Mountains to the Atlantic coast and from the lakes to the gulf. The Weather Bureau branded it the coldest spell since 1893.[88] A severe blizzard crippled New York City's transport system. As snowdrifts grew higher, leaving many streets inaccessible, the Department of Highways used snowplows to keep some roads passable and traffic moving. With more snow forecast and a looming coal shortage, many of New York's rich folk packed their summer outfits and fled to the considerably warmer climes of Palm Beach.

Otto and Addie were due to make the winter trek to Florida. As luck would have it, they had delayed their visit until late February to allow their builders and decorators time to complete the fixtures and fittings and decorating at their new villa. Their rearranged schedule allowed Otto to fit several public engagements into his diary. One such function was a banquet in Chicago on Saturday, January 12, to deliver an address at the Chicago Bankers' Club. He also had several literary talks confirmed during the second and third weeks in January.

Kahn departed from New York's Grand Central Terminal at 6 p.m. on Friday, January 11, aboard the 20th Century Limited train accompanied by a party of financiers. By chance, his departure came just before the weather took a turn for the worse.

The overnight rail journey usually took twenty hours, arriving in

Chicago at noon on Saturday, providing ample time for Otto to check into his hotel and prepare for that evening's dinner. On Friday night, the blizzard worsened. The express progressed at a snail's pace, running hours late. On Saturday afternoon, external communications with the locomotive broke down; the fastest and most deluxe train in the world disappeared off the grid. Weather conditions deteriorated further. The train valiantly battled on through rising snowdrifts until finally it stalled and became stranded. The track ahead was impassable. Many of the passengers became deeply anxious as the snowstorm showed no signs of abating.

Late on Saturday evening, reports of the missing train filtered through to news desks. By Sunday morning, accounts of its disappearance appeared in the day's newspapers.

'Several of the Nation's leading financiers spent tonight [sic] in a snowdrift 'somewhere' east of Chicago aboard the 20th Century Limited, which departed from New York Friday afternoon. The party is headed by Otto Kahn of New York, who was to have delivered an address tonight at the banquet of the Chicago Bankers' club.'[89]

In Manhattan, the situation fared no better. Snow covered the cars and the sidewalks. Times Square remained blanketed in white. Further bad weather was forecast. Pathways had appeared on some of the highways cleared by plows. The occasional automobile drove slowly by, negotiating the mounds of snow on either side. In the Kahn household, Addie anxiously awaited news of her husband's safety and whereabouts.

New York Central Railroad Company approximated the train had halted somewhere east of Chicago, between South Bend and Elkhart. They hastily dispatched an emergency search party supplied with provisions and fuel to locate the stricken train. Onboard the carriages, there was little the passengers could do until the bad weather subsided. In the meantime, they had to sit it out, remain patient, and keep warmly wrapped. Otto must have been fully aware of the implications and dangers he and his fellow travelers faced. He was, after all, a serving director of Union Pacific rail.[90]

Rescuers shoveled through snowdrifts as tall as the train in a bid to find the marooned express. The longer it took, the colder those aboard became. Eventually, rescuers located the train, and frantic digging commenced. Some of the hardier male passengers clambered off the train to help. It took until late Sunday evening before the engine driver slowly maneuvered the 20th Century Limited into Chicago's LaSalle Street Station.[91]

Fellow guests at the dinner, traveling from different states, were stranded in drifts at unknown locations.[92] On account of the chaos, the banquet was canceled.

From Chicago, Otto did manage to travel on to Wisconsin. Here he gave a talk, *'The Poison Growth of Prussianism'* at the Milwaukee Auditorium. In it, he aired his views on the disarray of Germany's current political affairs. He urged Americans of German lineage to stand up for liberty and subsequently against Germany. His itinerary also included a visit to the University of Wisconsin the following day, where he presented an address titled: *'Frenzied Liberty; the myth of a rich man's war.'*

'As so often before, liberty has been wounded in the house of its friends. Liberty in the wild and freakish hands of fanatics has once more, as frequently in the past, proved the effective helpmate of autocracy and the twin brother of tyranny.'[93] When Kahn conveyed the line, 'We seek no place in the sun except the sun of Liberty,' one wonders if perhaps he spoke with a tinge of irony in his voice.[94]

Otto's current spate of public addresses coincided with the release of his forthcoming book *Right Above Race*. The contents of his talks were de facto 'chapters' lifted from the volume.[95]

The short promotional tour was a new departure for Otto. He had only recently hired the high-powered publicist Ivy Ledbetter Lee to handle his PR. Lee was a preacher's son from Georgia and a man of considerable flair and resource. He'd co-founded the public relations agency Lee, Harris & Lee, and was regarded by many of his clients, including John D. Rockefeller, as a PR genius. Kahn must have been a dream client for Lee, as the banker already knew most working members of New York's press corps by their first names, and when he met them, he greeted them as such. Lee also had extensive knowledge of financial matters from working for the brokerage firm Harris, Winthrop & Co., and as a Wall Street reporter.[96] Together, Lee and Kahn made a formidable team.

By mid-February, the Kahns' pink-tinted villa in Palm Beach was completed, furnished, and ready for occupancy. The newly christened Oheka Cottage (**Oheka** is an acronym for **O**tto **He**rmann **Ka**hn) gave the impression it had been transported brick by brick from southern Spain, so authentic was its Mediterranean character.

In late February, the Kahn family arrived in Miami aboard their private railroad car (that comfortably slept fourteen) to spend their first vacation in their new villa. Several houseguests accompanied them, including Otto's friend, banker Henry Rogers Winthrop.[97]

The pink-tinted oceanfront villa Oheka Cottage at Palm Beach.

The Palm Beach community was a close-knit colony, and social activities revolved around the beach clubs, casinos, hotels, and private estates of the wealthy. As if perhaps to express his gratitude for being welcomed warmly into the community, Otto invested financially in the local grocery store - Palm Beach Stores, purveyors of high-quality groceries. The store stood on the corner of Main Street and County Road, where, no doubt, the Kahns' housekeeper purchased most of the family's groceries during their stay.

The Kahn siblings readily embraced the more relaxed lifestyle, made new friends, and participated in healthy outdoor pursuits. Otto unwound from the rigors of his hectic Kuhn, Loeb duties by playing golf, swimming, spending afternoons at the horse races, and taking long leisurely walks along Ocean Boulevard with his dachshunds in tow. In the evenings, he bet thousand-dollar chips in Bradley's Beach Club casino.

The family fell so much in love with the resort that Otto acquired more plots over the coming years. Some were adjacent to Oheka Cottage, while others were along Ocean Boulevard, which he would speculate on as the coastline became more popular, making him a handsome profit. Otto also purchased 20,000 acres of ranch and timberland in Florida's Pasco County.* Oheka Cottage remained the Kahns' holiday retreat in Palm Beach for the next fifteen years.

The House on Carnegie Hill

1918 proved to be a period of significant upheavals, movement, and change for the Kahns. In early spring, the family moved into their magnificent Manhattan palazzo at 1100 Fifth Avenue.*

Otto and Addie's first function at their new home took place on the evening of April 9 to establish the French League in America and strengthen the two countries' already cordial relations.[98] Guests were treated to a light buffet and a musical recital by the French singer Robert Casa, who sang heartfelt songs of the trenches and the Latin Quarter in Paris. Visitors must have looked in awe at the exquisite decor and furnishings surrounding them, a testament to the refined taste and eye for detail of their wealthy hosts and their infinitely deep pockets.

A Mission to Europe

The call of Europe, irrespective of the war and the limitations and dangers it imposed, was too seductive for Otto to ignore. Hence, on May Day, he departed, accompanied by his valet, from New York Harbor aboard the Royal Mail steamer *Adriatic* bound for the UK.[99] The liner arrived seven days later in Liverpool from where Otto and his valet journeyed to London and checked into Claridge's Hotel.

What Otto did next and in what order is difficult to ascertain due to the restrictions prohibiting the publication of travel details relating to military personnel and civilians. What is known is that Otto was in London to prearrange his hazardous trip across Europe, to hold important meetings with various heads of state and government officials. Although the documents for these trips were 'top secret,' his itinerary verifies he did visit France and Spain.

Otto arrived in Paris at the tail end of May. Various dispatches published in newspapers confirm this. Considering Paris was under siege by the German army at the time of Kahn's visit, he most probably arrived by military escort to secure his safety. Otto later described this time in France as 'the most anxious and gloomy period, probably, of the entire war.'[100] German armed forces had begun their offensive on Paris between the Aisne and the Marne on May 27 and were fewer than fifty miles from the capital. The French armies were exhausted and wearied defending the road that led to Paris. It was no secret that morale was low in the Allied forces. The Germans were veterans and within sight of Paris and determined to bludgeon their way through. Otto could not have arrived at a more critical moment. On Tuesday, May 28, he held discussions in the French capital with government officials.[101]

Otto made two trips to the battlefront to see firsthand the challenges the Allied troops were up against.[102] The experience must have been unsettling for the former German Hussar, whose loyalties now lay firmly with the opposing nations. In Aisne, through a lull in the bombing, Kahn joined General Pershing for dinner in a château that had been hit by shellfire barely an hour earlier.

During this volatile time in Paris, Otto managed to finalize arrangements for the Orchestre de la Société des Concerts du Conservatoire to tour the U.S. He could barely contain his joy at accomplishing the coup and immediately cabled the good news to the States. Between fifty and sixty concerts were slotted into the itinerary, running from October 1 to January 1919. The National Bureau for the Advancement of Music hastily dispatched a bulletin: 'The purpose of the visit is to increase and advance an 'Entente Cordiale' between the two republics and was arranged between the French high commission and the United States Government as part of the extensive cooperation between them.'[103] The conductor André Messager, known for his work at the Théâtre National de L'Opéra in Paris, was contracted to head the tour.

From France, Kahn traveled overland to Spain. On June 19, he had an audience with King Alfonso XIII at the Royal Palace in Madrid.[104] Three months later, Sir William George Eden Wiseman (Head of British Intelligence Service in the U.S.) sent Lt.-Col. The Hon. Arthur C. Murray at London's Foreign Office two 'very secret documents' for his consideration. One of the documents was a ten-page translation of the discussion between King Alfonso and Kahn.[105] While in Madrid, Otto also had a meeting with Spain's Premier Antonio Maura Montaner, at which several Cabinet ministers were present.

Though Spain had remained neutral since day one of the war, it suffered crippling domestic economic difficulties. Severe poverty in the rural and southern regions, exasperated by high inflation, had forced internal migration into the big industrial cities creating overcrowding, tension, and uncertainty. King Alfonso and Premier Antonio Maura favored stronger ties with the allies such as America and the UK in a wish to strike up lucrative trade deals. As a result of his meetings, Kahn felt confident he had managed to secure closer ties economically between Spain and the U.S. and eagerly reported the outcome to officials back home.

At a diplomatic reception in Madrid, Kahn overheard a conversation between a pair of 'swarthy fellows' speaking Spanish.[106] They were unaware Kahn could understand their native tongue. One hinted of an imminent uprising of the Spartacus League in Brussels. What Kahn heard alarmed him enough to hurriedly leave the reception and head straight to see the British Ambassador in Madrid to inform him of his 'news.'

The Spartacus League (viewed as German Leninists) functioned as an underground faction during the war to stir up internal dissent to undermine German unity. The Ambassador forwarded Kahn's report that evening to London, where it went immediately to Prime Minister Llyod George, who, after investigation, found the information to be accurate. Kahn's prompt actions persuaded the Allied strategists to move ahead with their attack. A member of George's government later allegedly said the final armistice would have been delayed by as much as six months had it not been for the quick-thinking actions of 'secret agent' Otto Kahn.

On July 3, the University of Michigan awarded Otto an honorary Doctor of Laws (LL.D.) degree.[107] The following month, the French Government conferred upon him the *Chevalier de l'Ordre National de la Légion d'Honneur*[108] in recognition for his distinguished service to the allied cause.[109]

Before Otto left New York for the continent, he handed the keys to his Morristown house to the French director Jacques Copeau.[110] Otto had arranged to accommodate Copeau and his family, along with fifteen members of his Vieux-Colombier acting troupe for the duration of the summer. In mid-May, Copeau and his merry band of actors moved into the property. The remainder of the company returned to France. The rationale behind Kahn's generosity was to give the director and his fellow actors a base and the chance of a relaxing break in a conducive environment away from the stresses and strains of touring. Kahn hoped the change would imbue the company with fresh inspiration in preparation for their forthcoming second season in New York, opening in October. The run would feature twenty-nine plays, of which a dozen were new works. Their sponsor also hoped the troupe might present several open-air performances in the estate's grounds in appreciation for the fortunate circumstances they found themselves in.

Copeau, forever the taskmaster, swiftly instituted an arduous work ethic of rehearsals and healthy exercise that commenced early in the morning and ended in the evening before dinner. Complaints from the cast that he was pushing them too hard abounded, and rifts developed.[111] Sickness hindered progress yet further, particularly when Copeau became incapacitated with a bout of typhoid fever. Irrespective of the internal dramas, the second season opened in October on schedule at New York's Théâtre du Vieux-Colombier with 'Le Secret' written by Henri Bernstein. Copeau realized he would have to bow to public taste to make the company financially viable. Thus, his choice of productions reflected this. The second piece he presented was Pierre Beaumarchais's comedy in five acts, Le Mariage de Figaro. After garnering widespread acclaim from the critics, the company's future in New York seemed almost assured.

Otto's hospitality to the franc-pinching Copeau was not viewed so generously by the media. Soon after the theater company inhabited Cedar Court, the press disclosed the Kahn family would be spending part of their summer vacation at their sumptuous, new country estate on Long Island. It was estimated to have cost Otto over $11 million to construct. Although the château was still unfinished, the family did spend occasional weekends at the property during 1918.

At the close of the Vieux-Colombier U.S. season, the troupes' wicker costume baskets, marked with the company's distinctive two doves motif, were loaded onto the ship to accompany the cast on their voyage home to France. At the time, little did Copeau realize the last performance they'd presented in New York would be their unplanned American finale.

When Maud Kahn arrived back in New York on leave for the summer, she must have found herself slightly disoriented as she stood on Fifth Avenue, gazing up at her family's imposing new palazzo. It was the first time she had seen the completed building, let alone stepped over its front doorstep. Although her father was currently not in the U.S., her excitement at being welcomed home by her family must have been a tad diminished by her eagerness to explore the vast house. In particular, her private suite of rooms on the fourth floor.

Sagamore Lodge in the Adirondacks

During Otto's mission to Europe, his wife and children took an extended summer vacation, staying first at the Kahn estate on Long Island and then at Sagamore Lodge at Raquette Lake in the Adirondacks. Otto leased the camp from Margaret M. Emerson Vanderbilt, widow of Alfred Gwynne Vanderbilt Sr. He had drowned in 1915 as a passenger on the RMS *Lusitania* after a German U-boat torpedoed it. Thus, Margaret had inherited her husband's copious fortune. The Kahns were staying at the lodge for the entire month of August. Addie hoped her husband would join them later in the month upon his return from the continent.[112] Maud would also be joining them before returning to her war work in Europe.[113]

In previous years the Kahns had spent several enjoyable summers in the Adirondacks at their chalet at Bull Point. Since selling the property back in 1905, they had not returned to the area. The family was keen to escape the hustle and bustle of New York and its oppressive summer heat and reconnect with nature. The camp would be ideal. Trunks were packed, automobiles were loaded, and the Kahns set off to go 'roughing it.' The journey to Great Camp Sagamore took all of one day, by which time the youngsters were restless, full of anticipation at the prospect of what lay in store.

Sagamore Lodge faced the sweeping waters of Sagamore Lake and combined the design features of a Swiss chalet and a log cabin. To approach the lodge, visitors drove along a four-mile dirt track that crossed two bridges. At the second bridge, a horse-drawn carriage transported guests the last couple of miles to give them a taste of an authentic camp experience. The on-site amenities included an outdoor bowling alley, a playhouse, a boathouse with canoes, a full-sized tennis court, and numerous outdoor activities. There was even an original native aboriginal wigwam. After dinner, most of the action took place in the playhouse, which offered separate roulette, billiard, and ping-pong tables. The room's centerpiece was a genuine crocodile that Margaret shot on safari in Africa. It was used rather ingeniously as a tray to hold the ping-pong balls. The sprawling estate covered 1,526 acres, and outdoor sports ranged from kayak paddling to horse riding, garden croquet, and trekking.

After an exerting day of healthy recreation, the family spent most evenings relaxing in rocking chairs on the veranda. Refreshing nights of deep sleep restored everyone's energy for the following day. Otto returned to the U.S. in time to join his family at the lodge.[114] For all its quaintness and isolation, the vacation did what Otto and Addie had hoped it would do and recharged the whole family's batteries.

St. Bernard's School, New York City

Roger Kahn's first school was St. Bernard's Preparatory School on Upper East Side at 4 East 98th Street. He attended from the age of eleven. His parents chose to send him to an all-male private school in keeping with the family's social status. After completing his studies at St. Bernard's, Roger was expected to go to Groton and Harvard.

The choice of games at the annual Sports Day events gave an insight into the parents' social standing; their chauffeurs would compete in the chauffeur's running race. At one Sports Day, Addie Kahn presented a cup to the winner of the sack race.[115]

Attending school was challenging for Roger. He struggled with the regular curriculum and showed as little interest in athletics and sports as in studies or social activities.[116] Neither did he mix well with his fellow pupils. One subject he did show great aptitude in was music, especially harmony, theory, practical, and counterpoint. Since the age of six, Roger had studied music. The first instrument he learned to play was the violin, chosen by Addie because she was fond of its sound.[117] During the intervening period, Roger progressed to the piano, which he also played proficiently. From the keyboard, he advanced to the more rumbustious symphony drumming. On his 10th birthday, Roger received a professional drum kit and all the accompanying percussion as a special gift from his mother.[118]

Also, at the age of ten, Roger purchased a ukulele in the Ditson music store at 8-12 East 34th Street, just off Fifth Avenue.[119] When he handed his pocket money over to the sales assistant, he had the foresight to buy an instruction manual that explained how to play it. In later years, Roger would claim the ukulele was the instrument that lured him away from his school studies.

The Ditson music store was Roger's favorite store in Manhattan. Founded in Boston, Massachusetts, the Oliver Ditson Company was initially a music publishing house. After Oliver died in 1888, the company expanded into music instrument sales under his son Charles' direction. The Chas. H. Ditson & Co. music store in Midtown Manhattan occupied several floors of the Ditson Building and was one of many music-related businesses in the district. It was also a hub for musicians.

Roger and his brother Gilbert were firm buddies. Their four-year age gap did not restrict them from sharing the same hobbies and interests and meant they would happily compete in shared activities without the friction of one brother bullying the other. They also appear to have had an intuitive understanding of one another. In addition, they shared a deep-rooted passion for music, particularly modern, popular music, and it was through this common bond, the brothers became interested in jazz.

The Kahn brother's sudden infatuation with jazz music had not gone unnoticed by their parents. Presently, however, it showed no signs of disrupting their son's schooling, and as such, neither parent felt concerned enough to monitor their leisure activities. Gilbert had visions of becoming a banker like his father, and Roger showed a real flair for engineering. Otto harbored hopes that Roger might attend Massachusetts Institute of Technology and become an engineer.[120] Unless their current viewpoint altered, Otto and Addie were happy to allow their sons to tinker around playing jazz music in their free time.

In the meantime, Roger, having already mastered the violin, piano, drums, and ukulele, turned his attention towards the banjo, woodwind, and brass instruments.[121] His teachers at St. Bernard's continued to note Roger's lack of focus and engagement in the classroom and his reluctance to mix in social activities. They felt he was already displaying signs of an artistic temperament. Otto and Addie quietly observed his progress or lack thereof, although neither parent felt concerned enough by the boy's behavior to intervene.

Roger's visits to the Ditson music store were now becoming a regular occurrence. After school had turned out, he would head straight down to the Ditson Building and spend the remainder of the afternoon playing instruments in the store. Ditson's staff knew who the young lad was, on account of his surname, but never intruded or hassled him in any way, allowing him the freedom to practice on one instrument after another. The store's manager Harry L. Hunt always kept a watchful eye upon him. Roger soon became a competent guitarist in addition to mastering an array of reed instruments. Rather ingeniously, he asked his parents not to buy him Christmas and birthday gifts but to give him cash instead. With these funds, Roger purchased his collection of expensive musical instruments, which he kept neatly arranged on racks in his suite at home.[122]

Over the next couple of years, Roger mastered fifteen instruments, including various guitars, trombone, mandolin, viola, bassoon, tuba, French horn, harp, and cello, and all before he was out of short pants. Thus it's little wonder his private music tutor Jacques Kasner called him a bit of a musical prodigy.

On October 17, Otto made a passionate appeal to Americans of German descent. He urged them to 'strain every nerve to equal or outdo our fellow citizens of native birth,' by subscribing to the Fourth Liberty Loan. After bitterly assailing present-day Kaiserism for dishonoring all children of the Fatherland, Otto avowed, 'We men of German descent have a special reckoning to make with Kaiserism.

The whole world has been wronged and hurt by Prussianized Germany, as it was never wronged and hurt before. But the hurt done to us is the deepest of all. Our spiritual inheritance has been stolen from us by impious hands and flung into the gutter.'[123] Otto must have hearkened back to the younger days of his father and Uncle Hermann, who, like him, also stood up against autocratic rule and fought for liberty. Kahn declared that the war might be over before very long, and if that were to be the case, then the present issue of war bonds may be the last chance 'for some of us to obtain an adequate place in the pages of the book of honor of Liberty Loan subscribers. These pages will stand as a perpetual record, as eloquent as the casualty lists.'

Twenty-five days later, Otto's prophetic words came true.

On November 11, 1918, newspaper headlines announced in bold print:

PEACE - GERMANY SURRENDERS - SIGNS ARMISTICE TERMS.

The war was over.

Otto predicted great prosperity following peace, such as America had rarely experienced.[124]

The next day, Otto delivered a patriotic address at the United War Work Campaign Meeting of the Boston Athletic Association in Boston, Massachusetts. The talk was titled: 'When the Tide Turned - The American Attack at Château Thierry and Belleau Wood in the first week of June 1918.' Again, Otto spoke straight from the heart as he recalled the harrowing time he spent within sight of the battlefront during the week in question.

'America comes out of the war with her economic and moral potency and prestige vastly enhanced, with her outlook broadened, her field of activity expanded, her enterprise quickened, her imagination stirred, her every faculty stimulated.

The vista, which opens before us of America's future, is one of dazzling greatness, spiritually and materially. The realization of that vision cannot fail us if we but meet our problems in a spirit of true Americanism, of moderation and self-restraint and of justice and goodwill to all, rejecting alike privilege and demagogy, banishing all class rule, be it of capital or of labor.

In that spirit, let us grasp each other by the hand and thus resolved and united against enemies without or foes within, let us march on towards the high destiny that Providence has allotted to the country which in grateful pride and deep affection we call our own.'[125]

In New York City on December 21, Otto issued a typed statement to the press in light of the current investigation taking place by the Senate Committee in Washington, D.C., probing brewing and liquor interests and German propaganda. New York Attorney General Merton E. Lewis and Deputy Attorney General Alfred L. Becker had been summoned before the Committee to question their apparent abuse of their privileged position during the war.[126] Having been on the receiving end of anti-German sentiment, Otto wished to make his views on the matter clear:

'From the very beginning of the European war, I have demonstrated by my actions and spoken and written words, my abhorrence of Prussianized Germany, my utter hostility to her cause, and my active and whole-hearted sympathy with the cause of the allied nation. Within a few months of the outbreak of the war, I became and have continued to be ever since an object of abuse and attack in the German press.

I took my stand according to the dictates of my conscience and judgment. I have never wavered in the stand, either publicly or privately. I was known, widely, and to non-better than to German emissaries and the German Government. My record ever since 1914 of my support of the allied cause and in opposition to the German cause - not to speak of loyalty to the American cause - is clear, open, and unequivocal. If that record does not protect me against misrepresentation, misconception, or misinterpretation, nothing that I may say will.'

4

ELEVEN HUNDRED FIFTH AVENUE

THE KAHNS OF FIFTH AVENUE

'New wealth has been created at the expense of no one.'[1]
Otto H. Kahn

1919

Added to the Kahns' light-green, letterheaded stationery was now the address ELEVEN HUNDRED FIFTH AVENUE, although somewhat confusingly, the outdoor brass wall plaque read 1 EAST 91 STREET.

It was a grand building, built in the neo-Italian Renaissance style without any of the overly fussy ornamentations several of the neighborhood's mansions had succumbed to. The paneled inner front door was obscured to the passing public by a covered drive-through (*porte cochère*) accessed via two arched entrances on 91st Street. The porch allowed visitors privacy and the luxury of arriving in style, even in a downpour.

The house was the principal Manhattan residence of the Kahn family, and a small platoon of staff ran it, twenty-two of whom were live-in servants. Eighteen were British, and the remainder hailed from various countries on the continent.[2] Those listed on the payroll included 27-year-old Swiss Governess Helen Bourgere, 33-year-old English master chef Gottfried George, and Otto's 30-year-old English valet Vincent Boblick. Vincent had arrived in New York in 1911 and had traveled extensively ever since at his employer's beck and call.

The 80-room townhouse with its French limestone façade was also the Kahns' HQ and a museum to display their extensive art and artifacts collection. On the flat terraced roof was a small garden lodge, arched porch, and a fountain, with a backdrop of expansive views across Central Park Reservoir and the wooded parkland beyond. An inner courtyard with an adjoining terrace overlooked Fifth Avenue. On the second floor was an antique Louis XVI French salon used for entertaining.* Below stairs, a spacious, light, modern kitchen decorated in neutral colors, fitted with the latest 'French' top-of-the-range gas and coal metal stove awaited their cook, Gottfried George.

Otto and Addie's individual suites were housed on the third floor. All four Kahn offspring had private suites on the fourth floor reached either by the grand staircase or the electrically powered copper elevator.* Roger's suite overlooked 91st Street on the far eastern corner.*

Manhattan's 'millionaire row,' running along the northern length of Fifth Avenue on the Upper East Side, was home to many of New York's affluent families, including the Guggenheim residence at 833 Fifth Avenue, the Harry Payne Whitney abode a few blocks up, Mrs. Edward H. Harriman's mansion just east on 69th, the August Belmont place on 75th, and the famous Henry C. Frick mansion at 1 East 70th. On the northeast corner of Fifth and East 78th stood the James B. Duke palace, with banker John Henry Hammond's home at 9 East 91st Street.[3]

On New Year's Day evening, Addie hosted a small party at home for her daughter Margaret. Around a hundred guests attended, several of whom were Margaret's friends from high school. Also invited were some of the Kahns' new neighbor's. Guests danced in the magnificent Adam ballroom. The press keenly noted, 'Miss Kahn [who would be eighteen later in the year] will not make her formal debut for two years.'[4] The media's presupposition turned out to be incorrect. Margaret's debut was preponed to the 1919-20 season.

Maud and Margaret had blossomed into attractive, fashion-conscious young women who looked more like movie stars than the prim young ladies some may have expected them to be. Gone were the ringlets tied in ribbons from their childhood; short, coiffured bobs with loose-fitting dresses worn to the knee were now *de rigueur*, and they both smoked. The two sisters were immense fun to be around and enjoyed their enviable position in society.

Entertaining at home was no longer an obstacle for the Kahns; it was a pleasure, especially as they had a ballroom the size of a small concert hall that could cater for up to five hundred guests. In the years ahead, gold-embossed invitations to Kahn events became highly sought after. In the eyes of the older generation, 'new' money as opposed to 'old' was regarded as being slightly grubby in comparison. Against this backdrop, families of newly acquired wealth, such as the Kahn, McKay, and Carnegie, were allotted their position in high society.

At the beginning of February, King Victor Emmanuel III of Italy appointed Otto a Commander of the Third Class Order of the Crown to recognize his services on behalf of the allied cause, both before and after America's entry into the war.[5] Otto's jacket was suddenly becoming quite crowded with medals. It's fair to say Otto's wealth and business standing now rivaled that of the late John Pierpont Morgan. Through tenacity and diligence, Kahn had become a giant of American finance. For many American immigrants, Kahn's vast fortune became a symbol of what was achievable in the land of the brave. Moreover, his wealth allowed him to indulge in his many artistic passions. It also provided him with a stage from which to address the world on important issues and matters close to his heart. A platform he took exceptionally seriously, from which he would regularly address the public and governments on financial and political topics.

Addie was considerably more conservative in her approach to everyday matters than her husband was. Her calm manner could have been a result of her sheltered upbringing. Some viewed her as a stern matriarch. Such impressions may have arisen because of her demanding role running such a large household rather than being indicative of her personality. In truth, all she desired was what was best for her children.

The Kahn offspring, however, were of a different mold. They fully embraced the exciting new generation they were born into. Maud traveled the world unchaperoned, volunteered for military service, and broadened her mind through literature and the arts. Margaret, nearing eighteen, was bright, enlightened, a supporter of the suffrage movement, spoke her opinions openly and had an eclectic freethinking circle of friends. Unsurprisingly, of all the offspring, Margaret was closest to Otto and shared his deep love of art.

Of the two sons, Gilbert was the least like his father and exhibited none of Otto's grand mannerisms. He was quiet and unobtrusive. This year Gilbert would turn sixteen. He had already spent two years studying at Groton School, a private preparatory boarding college in Massachusetts, and would remain there for two more years.[6] Although he appeared more level-headed, even Gilbert had a bohemian side that encompassed most things modern. Like his younger brother, Roger, Gilbert was also a keen musician and played the banjo proficiently. In addition to the Kahn children being a product of their generation, they were also a product of their family's immense wealth. No matter how much they rebelled, they could not escape the fact that they were born with silver spoons in their mouths and, as such, were viewed as being supremely privileged. Some might even go as far as to say they were spoiled rotten.

The Kahn children must have been very aware of their father's standing in the world of finance, especially when accompanying him abroad. In some cities, he was received as if he was a visiting head of state or a minor royal. On occasions, crowds would form in streets and outside hotels where he was staying. The press and news cameras frequently documented his every move. Should a member of the public ask for a signed photograph, Otto would politely turn down the request. He made a point of only inscribing photos to personal friends. Newspapers listed his daily activities so often it must have been an unwritten practice within the Kahn household to consult them to check what he'd been up to the previous day.

Florida resorts were having their best season in history. The press now dubbed Palm Beach the American Riviera. Otto took advantage of the resort's increase in popularity by leasing out Oheka Cottage when it was unoccupied.[7] Business magnate John Durrant Larkin rented the villa for two weeks in late January, ahead of the Kahn family's arrival in mid-February.[8]

The Kahn sisters were thrilled to receive an invitation from Cornelius Vanderbilt III (known to his friends as Nelly) and his wife, Grace, to attend a reception and dance at their home at 640 Fifth Avenue. The event was the talk of the town and the first formal function the Vanderbilts had held since taking possession of their stately 85-room property after having extensive renovations undertaken. The lavish affair was in honor of officers of the 27th Division.

On Tuesday evening, March 25, Maud and Margaret arrived at the Vanderbilt mansion and were warmly received in the Great Hall by their hosts.[9] The French ballroom looked stunning, decorated with scented spring flowers, palms, and ferns. Five hundred guests danced to music provided by Conrad's Orchestra. At midnight a buffet supper was served in the French dining room, after which dancing continued into the early hours. The following day's society columns hailed it as the most brilliant party in New York since the war commenced. Not only did it honor the officers of the 27th Division, but it also affirmed Grace Vanderbilt's position as New York's prominent society hostess.

Shortly after, Maud returned to her relief work in the UK.

The Morning After

Otto's friendship with industrialist Andrew Carnegie had grown steadily over many years. It was a bond secured by mutual respect and common interests, businesswise, artistic, and philanthropic.[10] They also shared an avid passion for golf. Such was Carnegie's admiration for Kahn he offered him a seat on the board of trustees of the Carnegie Institute of Technology.[11] Kahn was now Carnegie's neighbor. Although the great man of steel was in his 83rd year, having retired in 1901, he still maintained a busy daily schedule dealing with his many charitable institutions.

On April 24, Otto visited Pittsburgh, Pennsylvania, as a special favor to Carnegie, to present an address before the Carnegie Institute. Titled *Capital and Labor - A Fair Deal*, it championed workers' rights. Pittsburgh was the home of the Carnegie Steel Company, which Carnegie founded in 1892. When Carnegie sold the company in 1901, the proceeds made him one of the richest men in history. To thank Pittsburgh, Carnegie funded and built several museums and learning institutions in the city operated by the Carnegie Institute. Today's event celebrated the Institute's 23rd birthday. Otto attended as the guest of honor and principal speaker. 'A man who is so many folded in his interests and sympathy is sure not only to be a distinguished man but also to be an interesting man,' assured the president of the institute's board of trustees, Colonel Samuel H. Church, in introducing Otto to the audience. His praise was genuine. He had personally known and admired Kahn for many years.

The subject Kahn chose for his talk was 'The Morning After,' by which he said he meant both the sound and problematic conditions arising from the war.[12] 'The principle on which we should deal with the labor question is very simple. It is the principle of the Golden Rule.'[13] Kahn laid out five points he concurred were necessary for every worker to perform to his full potential:[14]

1. The workman is neither a machine nor a commodity. He is a collaborator with capital.

2. The worker's living conditions must be made dignified and attractive to himself and his family.

3. The worker must be relieved of the dread of sickness, unemployment, and old age.

4. The worker must receive a wage, which not only permits him to keep body and soul together, but to lay something by, to take care of his wife and children, to have his share of the comforts, joys, and recreations of life, to be encouraged in the practice, and obtain the

rewards of thrift.

5. Labor, on the other hand, must realize that high wages can only be maintained if high production is maintained.

These five points were the doctrines behind Kahn's Golden Rule. Kahn was not alone in his thinking. Only a few weeks earlier in *The Wall Street Journal*, he had made public his personal view that the time was right for restarting constructive activities to encourage growth and help build the economy.[15] Simon Guggenheim, the new president of the American Smelting and Refining Company (ASARCO),* strongly agreed with Kahn, asserting the outlook was never brighter, an opinion shared by many other industry leaders.

Kahn's speech was full of drama and passion and exceptionally well received at the Institute. It was considerate, and good-hearted of Kahn to attend the celebrations and became even more meaningful in the months ahead.

When Maud Kahn returned to New York unexpectedly in early May, her parents must have been quietly relieved that their daughter was back home and in good health, given the influenza pandemic currently sweeping the world.[16]

Maud had worked abroad (with occasional breaks) for almost three years, right up and beyond the armistice. From the periodic news bulletins of her activities posted in the papers, she had become one of the best-known American society girls assisting on the continent in the hospitals and canteens during the war.[17] Her parents were now hoping she was back home to stay and would, given time, occupy her days with new interests and find herself a husband. Though Maud was pleased to be among her family and friends, she did not align her plans with her parents' wishes. Instead, Maud intended to return to Europe to resume her volunteer work, as and where it was required. Having left her motor vehicle parked 'somewhere in England,' she intended to reclaim it. Maud's confidence had grown immeasurably since her first overseas mission as a relatively naive 19-year-old back in 1916. Now aged twenty-one, she was a strong, independent woman of good moral character with a charming personality.

Maud made it clear to her parents she had only returned temporarily. After a short rest, she intended to head back to France and England.[18] This was not the news Otto and Addie had hoped to hear. Maud reassured them that her next assignment abroad would be her final one and last only a couple of months. After mulling the matter over, Otto and Addie conceded their daughter was far too strong-willed to have her mind altered. They supported her decision.

Presently, Maud longed to hang out with her friends, relaxing, partying, and catching up with all the society gossip she had missed.

On June 4, Congress passed the 19th Amendment that granted all American women the right to vote.

In July, Maud spent time with her best friend and traveling companion Billy McKeever at the McKeevers' grand house at Southampton on Long Island.[19] The arrangement fitted perfectly with her own parent's plans, who hoped to spend part of their summer vacation at their new country estate on the island. It also meant Maud would get to spend her 22nd birthday with her family around her before returning to Europe.

Cold Spring Harbor Estate

At last, Otto's country mansion was prepared, furnished, and ready for occupancy. That August, the Kahn family spent their summer break at the 127-room property. Otto had lavished an excessive amount of money building his dream country retreat; it was now time to enjoy it.* In one sense, the house would serve as a lasting legacy of Otto's overindulgence; in another, a gloriously extravagant folly of mammoth proportions. Upon completion, the property was the second-largest single-family home in America. Only the Vanderbilts Biltmore House in North Carolina pipped him to the post.[20]

Their Cedar Court estate could well have been the original blueprint for the new estate, only visualized on a grander scale; the entrance to the grounds was via a turnpike; a long driveway from the entrance gates led directly to the house. Only the architectural style and size of the property were adjusted. There was also a certain similarity in design and layout between Otto's new country seat and his great friend Clarence Mackay's Long Island pile Harbor Hill.

The estate was self-sufficient and housed a fully functioning farm supplied with livestock, orchards, fields stocked with crops, a dairy, stables, a sizable greenhouse complex, and an operational railroad station that served the estate's daily needs. A third of the land was wooded, and the remainder was farmland, chiefly pasture and hayfields.[21] Later additions to the grounds would include tennis courts, a racetrack, and an airstrip.

From a distance, the house resembled a French château but with none of the ostentatious gilding on the exterior. Instead, it came with a gray tiled roof, mansards, casement windows, and handcrafted wrought iron Juliet balconies. Inside, a maze of hallways, stairs, and corridors unfolded. Beyond lay a labyrinth of rooms and more passageways where servants and staff would scurry about their duties out of view from the family. Muted tones of creams and brown decorated the walls. A more comprehensive network of passages and tunnels lay beneath the house where there was idle talk of secret rooms. Otto employed a large company of workers to look after the estate, one hundred and twenty-six in total.

A palace fit for a king - Cold Spring Harbor Estate. (Aiglon Aerial Photos)

Rich walnut *faux bois* (fake wood) paneling lined the library walls, courtesy of a skilled *trompe-l'œil* artist. The effect was strikingly realistic. When greeting guests, Otto would stand at the top of a cascading horseshoe staircase in the entrance hall. The staircase was fashioned upon a similar one at the Château de Fontainebleau. As a reminder of his hometown in Germany, he had an emblem of a linden tree - a symbol of strength, healing, and community - engraved throughout the estate.

In the formal gardens, carefully framed views of vistas and hedged borders attracted the eye. With the onset of evening, outdoor lights lit up pathways and ornamental features in a coordinated display of 'showing off.' Such magnificence was indeed the perfect setting for the Wizard of Wall Street. As pictures of the house and grounds appeared in glossy magazines, Americans looked on in wonder.[22] How could one family live in such splendor when America was suffering the harsh consequences of austerity measures!

Some folks viewed the estate as the apotheosis of vulgarity and indulgence. Not surprisingly, Otto and Addie were fully aware of such opinions. But, in their eyes, they had made relevant and quite substantial cutbacks where necessary, so cared little for such gossip-mongering.

Each of the four Kahn offspring had a private suite comprising a bedroom, an adjoining sitting room, a dressing room, and a marbled bathroom. With so many rooms in the house, it became impossible to keep track of where everyone was at any given time.

When Otto was in residence, he would take a morning swim in the indoor lap pool and follow with a hearty breakfast in the dining room. Then, if he had work to attend to, his yacht would ferry him across East River to Manhattan.

The estate was a heroic attempt by Kahn to aggrandize and gentrify his family and his family's name. It may have looked as if it was from a bygone age, but it was inescapably connected with the modern world; it had underfloor heating, electricity, telephones, and all the latest household gadgets money could purchase. The decor reeked of Fifth Avenue interior design, although the furniture was authentic 18th and 19th-century selected from auction rooms. The house would never be a family home; it was Otto's show palace to live out his fantasies, a venue for inviting important guests for long, decadent weekend parties. It was also the perfect backdrop in which to house part of the Kahns' fabulous art collection. Their four Gainsborough portraits took pride of place on the walls in the reception hall.

When the weather was too lovely to be indoors, the gardens took on a life of their own. The glorious flowerbeds and boxed hedgerows shimmered in the sunlight bringing an essence of informality to the grounds. Work had already started on Otto's new 18-hole golf course. The golf architect Seth Raynor was designing it. Unfortunately for Otto, the assignment would take a couple of years to complete due to the scale and unevenness of the terrain.

The Death of Andrew Carnegie

On August 11, Andrew Carnegie died. His death came as a massive shock to his family and everyone that could personally call him a friend. Immediately following the announcement, it seemed as though the whole of New York momentarily came to a shuddering halt. The Lotos Club, where Carnegie was a lifetime member, lowered their flag to half mast over their building at 110 West 57th Street in a mark of respect to the great philanthropist.[23] America and Scotland went into mourning. Carnegie succumbed to bronchial pneumonia at his country estate Shadow Brook in Lenox, Massachusetts. His end came so suddenly that his daughter Margaret had been unable to arrive at his bedside to comfort him. Upon news of his death, messages of condolence poured into the Carnegie homes.

Carnegie's passing came as a particular blow to Otto, Addie, and the Kahn children, as well as the household staff at 1100 Fifth Avenue. The two families were exceptionally fond of one another. Carnegie's palatial mansion opposite the Kahns' home fell into darkness, with drapes in the lower rooms kept drawn throughout the coming days. Reporters remained vigilant outside the house in the hope of catching a relative or a friend of Carnegie's for a statement.

A simple funeral took place three days later, on the morning of Thursday, August 14. It was held without fuss at his Shadow Brook home and attended by his family and house staff and a handful of Carnegie's close work colleagues. Shortly after the service, his family accompanied the casket by train to New York for burial at Sleepy Hollow in Westchester County. Having started his career aged thirteen as a bobbin boy in a cotton mill in Allegheny City, Pennsylvania, no one, not even the world's most prophetic psychic, could ever have envisaged the illustrious career Carnegie was to follow.

Carnegie's famous expression 'dying disgraced' first appeared in an article about him in the *North American Review* in 1898 in which he said:

'The day is not far distant when the man who dies leaving behind him millions of available wealth, which were free for him to administer during life, will pass away unwept, unhonored, and unsung, no matter to what use he leaves the dross which he cannot take with him. Of such as these the public verdict will be, the man who dies thus rich dies disgraced.'

The once wealthiest man in the British Empire left an estimated fortune of around $30 million, having given to philanthropic causes during his lifetime through his Carnegie Corporation more than $350,695,653.40.[24] But, alas, he did not die to see his often-expressed wish that he might die poor.

The Belgian Royal Family

Albert, King of the Belgians, was the first ruling European sovereign to set foot on American soil. He and his consort Queen Elisabeth and their son, heir apparent Prince Leopold, stepped ashore at New York Harbor at 10:15 a.m. on Thursday, October 2, having arrived from Ostend the previous evening aboard the *George Washington* steamship.[25] It was also the day of the royal couples wedding anniversary. Their cross-country state visit would last a month and culminate in Washington, D.C., where Albert would address U.S. Congress on October 28.

The fair-haired, blue-eyed monarch was seen as a man of the people and doted upon by his subjects. He also had a curious history with America, for when he was heir apparent, he worked incognito in New York as a newspaper reporter under the guise of Al Raschid. At the time, he was in his mid-twenties and studying American industrial methods. At the time, his disguise remained a secret.

This official visit was the royal family's way of thanking Americans for their valued support in the war, during which Belgium had suffered decimation. Albert was also hoping to top up his homeland's coffers by encouraging investment in his beleaguered country. America went into overdrive, making the royals feel welcome.[26]

After stepping ashore, their majesties traveled by motorcade across the city, where cheering crowds lined the streets while ticker tape rained upon them. In Manhattan, the royal family stayed at the Waldorf-Astoria, occupying the third and fourth floors on the building's Fifth Avenue side.

On their first evening, the King and Queen attended an informal dinner hosted by Baron de Cartier de Marchienne in the East Room on the second floor of the Waldorf-Astoria. Prominent members of New York society attended, Otto and Addie Kahn included. Elisabeth wore a gold gown with a long sweeping train with diamonds glistening in her hair. Albert and the youthful prince wore Belgium army uniforms. Guests sat at a round table decorated with crimson dahlias and ferns, with the seating configured, so everyone knew everyone else to keep the atmosphere light and convivial. Dinner commenced at 8:30, and guests filed out at 10:45, with their majesties retiring directly to their suites. Onlookers waited patiently outside the hotel all evening to catch a glimpse of the royals and the invited VIPs.

It seemed appropriate that Addie had been invited to the dinner, for she was one of the patronesses of the Cardinal Mercier Fund set up in

1916 to help relieve the poor in Belgium throughout the war. Other prominent names on the committee included Addie's friends Mary Harriman and Mrs. John Pierpont Morgan.

The following day Albert visited the Woolworth Building and Wall Street. As his limousine entered the narrow streets of the financial district, what appeared to be the whole working population of Lower Manhattan was there to greet him. Wall Street and Broad Street were awash with brokers, bankers, clerks, stenographers, and messenger boys cheering the monarch. A squad of police officers had to push their way through the crowds to create a path for the King's automobile to pass. At the Stock Exchange, all dealings halted as soon as Albert entered the visitors' gallery. Escorting him was John Pierpont Morgan Jr., John D. Rockefeller Jr., and Otto Kahn. Luncheon followed in the mahogany-paneled dining room at the Bankers' Club.

On the West Coast, the royal party visited Culver City. Here they spent time at Ince Studios watching a movie being filmed. During the staging, Albert was noticeably taken aback by one of the more 'heated' scenes. He visibly blushed over the sight of a passionate lover's embrace sealed with a kiss upon his sweetheart's cheek.

At Niagara Falls, the monarch received a cooler reception - he got drenched by the rapids. After braving one particularly brisk trek along a cliffside walkway, Albert paused for a moment to appreciate the view. 'A walk like that is worth more than the cures in all our sanatoria,' he commented.

Upon their return to New York City, the royals attended more functions. On Saturday afternoon, October 25, Addie and her two daughters Maud and Margaret took afternoon tea in the company of Queen Elisabeth at the Vanderbilts home at 640 Fifth Avenue. Around 150 guests sipped Darjeeling and nibbled home-baked cakes and patisserie to the accompaniment of light music.[27] Elisabeth arrived shortly after 4:30, having been delayed by traffic. Earlier, she had visited her preferred jewelers, Cartier on Fifth Avenue, and followed on with a brisk stroll around an exhibition at the American Art Galleries viewing Belgian art.[28]

A large crowd amassed in the street outside the Vanderbilt mansion to catch sight of the Queen's arrival. Grace Vanderbilt welcomed Elisabeth into her home with all the aplomb of a seasoned hostess. The Vanderbilts went to great expense decorating the rooms with an abundance of fragrant flowers. Upon entering, guests would have been forgiven for thinking they'd stepped into the garden by mistake.

That evening, the royals attended the Metropolitan Opera House for a gala performance.[29] Otto took charge of the arrangements and laid on the finest entertainment he could assemble. The gala was the culminating event in the royal itinerary. All proceeds would benefit a fund set up to establish a medical institute in Brussels. Otto was the fund's treasurer and confirmed that $20,000 had already been subscribed in advance sales for boxes in the 'Golden Horseshoe.' Each box cost $1,000. In a generous gesture, many of the current box owners purchased their own, including the Kahns.

Ticket holders were requested to be seated by 8:30, for under no circumstances must the royal party be kept waiting for the performance to commence. As it turned out, the official party arrived almost thirty minutes behind schedule. During the delay, the seated audience struggled to remain composed. It was 8:55 when their limousine pulled up outside the Met's side entrance on West 39th Street, where Otto had waited patiently for nearly thirty minutes anticipating its arrival. As Albert stepped from the vehicle, Otto greeted him. Pinned on Otto's jacket were three decorations - the Italian Order of the Crown, the French *Légion d'Honneur*, and the Spanish Order of Charles II. Kahn immediately went into overdrive and whisked the King inside the building, trailed closely by Met board director Edmund L. Baylies who escorted the Queen and the prince. Three boxes in the Grand Tier awaited them. The boxes were donated for the occasion and decorated with a canopy of crimson velvet, fringed with gold brocade and gold tassels. Regular attendees to the Met said later that the show of jewels on display in the 'Golden Horseshoe' that evening surpassed anything they had ever seen before.[30] When the royals arrived in their box, the audience stood and applauded them for several minutes, delaying the performance further.[31] Artists on the bill included soprano Rosa Ponselle, operatic bass Léon Rothier and the pianist Sergei Rachmaninoff.

Otto and Addie watched the concert from their private box with their guests, writer and dramatist Lord Dunsany (Edward Plunkett, 18th Baron of Dunsany), and his wife, Lady Beatrice. Lord Dunsany was visiting the U.S. to undertake his first lecture tour. The papers described him as delicately handsome, standing six feet four tall, with a fair complexion, blue penetrating eyes, an abundance of light brown hair, and a military-style mustache. The 41-year-old attracted the attention of almost every woman that set eyes upon him.

Frustratingly for some, the gala did not proceed without glitches. During one intermission, Albert stepped out of his box into the rear corridor to speak to several committee members. He was still chatting when Met diva Mabel Garrison made her entrance on stage. As the orchestra struck up the accompaniment to her opening number, Miss Garrison noticed the King was not seated in his chair in the box. She immediately snapped her fingers to the conductor to halt playing. The music stopped. All eyes fell silently on the royal box. There was a nervous rustle of silk in the vicinity of the Queen's seat, and, while it cannot be said, she also snapped her fingers; she did something just as efficacious. Albert returned to his seat directly. Once the King was seated, Miss Garson resumed her center position on stage and signaled the conductor to commence.

The evening culminated with a stirring rendition of the Belgian national anthem *'La Brabançonne'* sung by Frenchman Léon Rothier, topped by an equally rousing chorus of *'The Star-Spangled Banner'* delivered by soprano Margaret Romaine with a vocal accompaniment by the Met chorus. Rothier gripped a Belgian flag during his number, and Romaine held the Stars and Stripes aloft throughout hers, bringing the concert to a frantic end, assuring curtain calls for all.

In November, King Albert decorated Otto with the Order of the Crown of Belgium.[32] 1919 was also the year when his daughter Maud was awarded the *Médaille de la Reconnaissance française* (Medal of French Gratitude) from the French Government for her voluntary wartime service aiding the sick and wounded.[33]

Edward, Prince of Wales

As if overseeing one royal occasion wasn't taxing enough for Otto, just over two weeks later, he had to go through the whole procedure again when Edward, Prince of Wales, arrived on American soil for an official visit. The prince had just completed a royal tour to Canada in an ambassadorial capacity representing his father, King George V. It was the first visit to the U.S. of a Prince of Wales since his grandfather Albert Edward visited in the same role in 1860.

New York's winter season customarily coincided with the Metropolitan Opera House's premiere and the National Horse Show's first night. The 1919-20 opera season opened on November 17. The year also saw the return of the debutante 'coming out' parties.

On November 18, the Met played host to Edward, Prince of Wales, at a special evening gala held in his honor. Earlier in the day, Otto had made specific arrangements with staff at the Met on how to greet the prince should they come into contact with him during his attendance. Upon his arrival, Otto would escort him to a parterre box.

Just as the Belgian royals had been late when they arrived at the opera, so too was Edward, almost half an hour, to be accurate. The prince was due at the Met at 10 p.m. But when the clock struck ten, Edward did not appear. He was still at a previous dinner engagement at the Waldorf-Astoria. When he realized the setback, he left the hotel and made a rush for the theater. At his disposal to escort him was a motorcade of the Mayor's Army Guard and twenty traffic cops on motorcycles.

Outside the Waldorf-Astoria, crowds of curious onlookers had gathered to see the prince off. At the Met, an even larger mass of spectators had formed to witness his arrival. All along the route, from Sixth Avenue through 39th Street, people lined the streets. It seemed wherever Edward went, the crowds followed. Mass adulation was a new experience for the young prince and one he was still coming to terms with.

By the time Edward arrived at the Met's private side entrance, Otto and Clarence Mackay were flagging from boredom. After exchanging quick pleasantries, they promptly escorted his highness up the stairwell (imaginatively transformed into a leafy bower to mark the occasion) and along the rear corridor to John Pierpont Morgan Jr.'s parterre box No. 35 in the center of the 'Golden Horseshoe.' Sharing the box with the prince was 1st Viscount Grey of Fallodon, Assistant Secretary of State William Philips, and Admiral Halsey. General Pershing, Mrs. Grover Whalen, and Mrs. Rodman Wanamaker would join the party later in the evening. After delivering Edward to his box, Otto made his way to his private box where Addie and their two daughters Maud and Margaret, were seated with their guest Mrs. Edward M. Houseman.

The audience were already settled in their seats, having listened to soprano Florence Easton and contralto Kathleen Howard enact the third scene of the first act of Carl Maria von Weber's *Oberon*. They had also watched the second scene of the third act of the ballet *Samson and Delilah*. After that, the stage curtain fell. The audience was now twitching restlessly in anticipation of Edward's arrival.

Upon seeing the prince enter his box, four thousand operagoers rose to their feet and welcomed him with spontaneous applause and hearty cheering. 'Three cheers for the Prince of Wales,' called out a voice from the stalls and were given freely in response. As the orchestra struck up the first few bars of the British National Anthem, Edward stood awkwardly to attention, like a bashful schoolboy, visibly overwhelmed by the reception he was receiving.[34]

In the royal box, Edward made light of the seating arrangements and waved Admiral Halsey into the front seat reserved for the guest of honor. Halsey was having none of that and insisted the prince be seated in it. Still, Edward fooled around further, much to the audience's enjoyment, they, having now cottoned on to the prince's tomfoolery.

'He's the sweetest thing you ever saw,' uttered a smitten young girl standing tiptoe in the dense crowd crammed into the rear corridor beneath the 'Golden Horseshoe.' Some had been waiting over an hour and a half to catch a glimpse of the dashing prince. Edward did not disappoint his fans. He looked immaculate, attired in a dress suit, with his brown hair slicked back with pomade. Although he was no longer a youth, he was still a tad self-conscious and at times behaved like an irrepressible teenager, filled with fun and spirit, a trait he craved to let out in some manner or other. His inquisitive smile and boundless energy were electric.

Glimpses of his mischievousness surfaced in various ways during the evening. First, in the flying leap with which he took the three steps leading up from the leaf-lined stairway into the upper entrance lobby, followed by the playful manner in which he entered his box in the 'Golden Horseshoe.' These were all light-hearted gestures from the prince, undoubtedly intended to put those around him at ease.

When the auditorium lights dimmed, the stage curtain rose on the opening scene to Ruggero Leoncavallo's *Pagliacci*. The young prince, leaning his elbow on the rail, settled down to enjoy the golden voice of Enrico Caruso acting the lead role of Canio, the head of a Commedia troupe. A short fragment of Verdi's *La Forza del Destino* brought the evening's program to a climax. Then, just as the prince was about to depart, the orchestra sprang into a rousing rendition of *'The Star-Spangled Banner.'* Finally, a colorful display of American and British flags unfurled from the rigging above the stage, bringing the gala to an explosive finale. The evening eventually wound up within sight of midnight at 11:40.

When the prince left his box, he got caught up in another jumble of guests; this time squeezed into a narrow rear corridor. Further ahead lay the stairwell to the street, which, likewise, was lined with onlookers. All had gathered to give the prince a memorable send-off. Treating the hindrance like an athlete might at a sports event, Edward shook as many of the hands that stretched out to grab his, along the corridor, down the winding stairs, to the outside sidewalk. From here, he was escorted into a limousine and driven back to his temporary lodgings on the battlecruiser HMS *Renown* anchored on the Hudson River.

In response to the hundreds of letters of support he received from the public during his visit, which the prince physically was unable to reply to individually, he wrote an open letter to the city of New York. Copies were dispensed to newspapers on November 22, one day before the prince set sail for home. The message appeared word for word in many publications:

November 22, 1919

HMS *Renown*

I wish to leave a message for the city of New York before I sail today, and I hope that you gentleman of the New York press will publish it for me. The people of New York have welcomed me with such kindness that I cannot leave without saying a few words of farewell.

I refuse entirely to say good-bye [sic], whether you like it or not, I am going to pay the United States another visit as soon as I can, because I like it so much, and I wish to see much more of the country and its people, including the Great West.

There is one thing I should particularly like you to say for me in the press. I have had hundreds of charming letters since I came to the United States, and not a single disagreeable one. I wish that all these letters could have been answered. They have been too many to make this possible, but I hope their writers will let me thank them in this way for the many nice things which they have said.

New York has been so kind to me that I can never forget this first visit. As I have said before, I am proud to be a New Yorker in my own right, and I am determined to see more of the great city as soon as I can. One can never have enough of such hospitality as yours, and I hope all the people of the city will realize how grateful and appreciative I am.[35]

Edward P

Prince Edward's American visit came to an end on November 23. In the morning, he attended an investiture ceremony on HMS *Renown*, where he awarded military medals to American and British officers and civilians in recognition of their bravery in the war. An informal lunch followed to thank all the dignitaries who had acted as hosts during his stay. Among the guests were Reginald Vanderbilt, Clarence Mackay, and Otto and Addie Kahn.[36] After the reception, guests lined the pier to bid the prince farewell. As the battle cruiser slowly moved away from the harborside, well-wishers cheered and waved him goodbye. Shortly after, the battleship USS *Delaware* fired a 21-gun salute. The *Renown* replied after the last shot had died away, then picked up speed and cruised into Upper New York Bay. As the ship faded into the horizon, back on the quayside, patrolman Phillip

Leffert released five trained carrier pigeons headed for the *Renown*. When they arrived on board, they were immediately caged. Five hundred miles out at sea, the pigeons were released to carry back to New York messages of thanks from the prince.

The Carry On Tea Room

Addie was a patroness of countless committees, councils, charities, and organizations, both in America and abroad, which would take up an immense amount of her time.

Recitals, functions, charity sales, and fundraising events were held regularly in New York to help boost monies for the war effort, many of which were organized and sponsored by prominent women in society. One of the more novel associations Addie gave her time to was the Carry On Tea Room. To raise funds, they rented a tearoom at 587 Fifth Avenue, renamed it the Carry On Tea Room, and opened it daily for three hours in the afternoon from three until six. All the profits from the sale of beverages and cakes aided the Federal Board for Vocational Education, which helped house and re-educate men disabled in the war.[37] It was a unique idea and one that caught on with great enthusiasm among women of riper years that took afternoon tea. By sharing the responsibilities, all the ladies involved with the association were assigned shifts on the rota to wait on tables in the tea parlor, Addie included.

As part of this year's Christmas festivities, the Kahn family attended the Met on Saturday, December 27, for the premiere of the new opera *L'oiseau bleu (The Blue Bird)*.[38]

The four-act fairy story, masquerading as a children's opera, is based on Belgian playwright Maurice Maeterlinck's 1908 play of the same name, with a music score composed by Albert Wolff. Otto championed the work, and the Met financed the production. Maeterlinck was present for the opening performance at which Wolff conducted the Met orchestra. The opera was traditional family entertainment and ideal for the festive season.

Ticket sales from the premiere aided The Blue Bird Campaign for Happiness, an initiative set up rather optimistically by Mrs. William K. Vanderbilt Jr. to promote more joy in the world.*

Representatives from some of New York's most notable families attended. In the foyer and during intermissions, *L'oiseau bleu* souvenir booklets were sold by the booklet committee (program vendors) to boost donations. Maud Kahn and her friend Billy McKeever were employed as sellers. As a special dispensation, Otto also allowed his son Roger to sell programs, but only during the Christmas performances, to earn himself some extra pocket money.

A young Roger W. Kahn (left) captured through the stage door window at the Metropolitan Opera House as composer Albert Wolff (center) and set designer Boris Anisfeld (right) pose for a photographer during rehearsals of *L'oiseau bleu*, December 1919.*

The public flung its arms around the new work, and most of the performances sold out. The Met hoped they had finally discovered a worthy alternative to their usual Christmas production of Engelbert Humperdinck's *Hansel and Gretel*.

1920

'Ahead lay a decade of chromatic craziness.'

With the Great War's turbulent years now firmly behind, post-war America took on an elevated air of sanguinity. To future historians, the 1920s would represent a decade of optimism and adventure. But, to those that lived through it, life would never be the same again.

The Roaring Twenties symbolized the times and shifts in standards; tradition became flexible, society challenged rules, inventors and scientists explored brave new ideas. Liberalism thrived. Bold artistic creativity excelled. The restrictions and shackles instituted by previous generations no longer held sway. Women had secured the vote and now had a voice.* Society felt driven to live for the moment. Freedom was precious, never more so than on the tailwind of a war.

Throughout the '20s, women's fashion reflected this newfound confidence and became more daring. Paris fashion houses embraced the gamine look; shorter hemlines and slimmer silhouettes freed the body and the mind. Silks and satins, combined with richly detailed beading, thousands of handsewn sequins, or fur-trimmed cloaks, coordinated with Egyptian motifs or Chinese embroidery, were just some of the influences plundered from all four corners of the globe. This fluidity of movement soaked into every cul-de-sac of the female wardrobe.

Across Europe and America, energetic new dance crazes swept the dance floors. Music simmered to a soundtrack of jazz. As happened in most homes, the Kahn household embraced every facet of this exciting collision of creativity. The family could not get enough of what the Twenties had on offer. And taste they did.

The 1919-20 debutante season was deemed the most notable on record in number and size of gatherings, due mainly to their suspension during the past four years of war.[39] During the coming three months, over four hundred parties took place at which more than a hundred daughters of prominent New Yorkers received their formal recognition as debutantes.

Margaret Kahn was one such debutante, and Otto and Addie threw one of the most lavish parties of the season to introduce their teenage daughter into New York society. On New Year's Day night, the Kahns' Fifth Avenue palazzo was ablaze with light and color as they flung open their ballroom doors to welcome over three hundred guests to Margaret's debut.[40] The room looked magical, decorated with festive greens, reds, gold baubles, and palms.[41] A sit-down dinner followed the introductions, after which, at the stroke of midnight, the real party started. An orchestra played the latest foxtrots and dance tunes while the two young Kahn brothers keenly joined in, playing their banjos. Even Maud, who had now officially retired from her war duties, was home for the occasion.[42]

For the Kahn family, 1920 was to be a year of joy and happiness. Eight days in, on the afternoon of Thursday, January 8, at four o'clock in the Kahns' splendid Adam ballroom, Addie hosted the third (in a series of six) *lecture-musicales* presented under the auspices of the

Advisory Council of the Schola Cantorum of New York. The German-born composer Kurt Schindler conducted the performance,[43] and several hundred music lovers turned up to hear the recital.

Eight days later, on January 16, something quite unprecedented happened, Prohibition. The Eighteenth Amendment of the U.S. Constitution came into immediate effect in every state throughout America. How this would affect people's social habits, no one had the vaguest idea. Not that an alcohol ban would impact the Kahns or any other wealthy American family's behavior. Prohibition for them just made it a bit more fun to get intoxicated.

What Next!

An off-Broadway revue seemed like a highly daring enterprise for young, teenage, society girls to become involved in, but that is precisely what happened at the end of January when *What Next!* - an original musical comedy with a score composed by Deems Taylor - opened at the Princess Theatre for a two-week run. 'Music tuneful and lyrics clever, while specialties and dances feature,' claimed *The Sun* newspaper's sharp opening night critique.[44]

All profits from the show were earmarked for the Girls Protective League and the New York Probation and Protective Association. As such, the majority of the cast donated their time freely. However, the first-night reviews were far from riveting. Many were peppered with telltale adjectives politely pre-warning any prospective ticket purchaser not to expect a too highly polished show, as this was principally an amateur production, albeit was conceived and produced by theatrical professionals. That said, the revue was by all accounts immense fun to be in.

Rehearsals progressed at a slow pace throughout January. By opening night, some cast members were still unsure what their role entailed. The company included a dance troupe of sprightly, teenage debutantes called the All Night Rollics Girls, most of whom had never trodden the boards before. Margaret Kahn was in the corps, as were her friends Billy McKeever and sisters Beatrice and Sheila Byrne and Dolly and Kitty Kimball. Maud Kahn was also in the cast. Beatrice had a named part, 'the Spirit of Dreams,' and was assigned the role of *première danseuse*.[45] Luckily, there was a thread of plot running through the three acts, but how much of a story depended on the audience's imagination. A diamond necklace is stolen at a country house party by a bogus Duke and is recovered in the finale by an

amateur detective. The third act, titled *The All Night Rollics* - a tribute
to a *Ziegfeld Midnight Frolics* number, danced by a high-kicking,
feather-wearing chorus line of young girls - gave the audience a good
indication of what to expect from the production. It later transpired
Florenz Ziegfeld Jr. helped stage the piece. One cheery reviewer
declared the specialties were 'well worth seeing,' claiming the young
debutantes 'would make almost any Broadway showman envious.'
Several *tableaux vivants* [living pictures] - girls positioned in artistic
poses - intermittently decorated the stage. Maud and Margaret Kahn
had their names listed in the program, and newspaper reviews
singled out their performances.

With first-night seats priced at $50 and boxes at $150 apiece, the
audience was made up primarily of proud parents and wealthy
friends of the cast. Interestingly, the newspapers did not mention
whether Otto or Addie Kahn were among the first-nighter's
attending. Perhaps, the two elder Kahns intended to catch the show
after it had ironed out any teething problems, or were they
forewarned to stay away?

What Next! summed up precisely what the society columnist in the
Sunday edition of the *World* thought of the production.[46] His notion
of who should or should not appear on a public stage did not sit
kindly with the producers or performers. 'What Next! Blanketty-
blank-blank-dot-blasted [sic] if I know!' He then proceeded to
lambast the cast for taking part. 'With young ladies of high society
turning handsprings on the public stage and kicking their toes into
the flies for the delectation of the sinister eyes of any sort of mixed
audience that pays the price of admission, neither I nor anybody else
can tell what will happen next.'

Following a brief pause to dot an 'i,' the columnist then explains
why he felt so offended by what he had seen. 'With the exception of a
few of the midnight revues and cabaret performances, there is hardly
a girl and music show on Broadway more frankly unclothed. ... It was
something that should never have been seen outside of a private
house before an invited audience.' He then, finally, insisted, 'Had I
witnessed such a performance in a private house, of course, my lips
would be sealed, but a public exhibition is another matter.'

The *Sun and New York Herald* were far kinder in their half-page
write-up and thought the society girls danced like professionals.[47]
Even the girls dance trainer Miss May Leslie jumped to their defense,
'Let me tell you that the society amateur is a better chorus girl than
the professional and is worth the same salary if she needs the
money.'

As might be expected, the show played to capacity houses.

A Surprise Announcement

Maud Emily Wolff Kahn photographed at
the races.

Roger Kahn was twelve when his eldest sister Maud got engaged to
the British soldier and war hero Major John Charles Oakes Marriott,
D.S.C.M.C.[48]

Otto made the surprise announcement on Sunday, February 15. The
news hit the papers the following day.[49] Maud was aged twenty-two,
her fiancé was three years older. John was the youngest officer in the
British Army of his rank to be awarded the Distinguished Service
Order and Military Cross. He also received the French *Croix de Guerre*
for his outstanding bravery during the war.

When news of the engagement broke, Maud was holidaying at her
parent's villa in Palm Beach. Her sister Margaret was with her, as was
her future husband and several close friends. The marriage came as a
total surprise to everyone; even Maud's pals were unaware. It was a
match made in heaven for the two romantics who were smitten with
one another.

The media ran the story, and pictures of the happy couple appeared
in glossy magazines and the dailies. Some reports even hit the front

pages.[50] The majority claimed wrongly that the romance blossomed three and a half thousand miles away in England during the war, where Maud met her future husband while carrying out volunteer duties for the British forces. However, the savvy journalist Maury Paul, writing under the pseudonym Cholly Knickerbocker, discovered otherwise.[51] Knickerbocker's exclusive surfaced in the *Palm Beach Post* on February 19.

It was a post-war romance. The couple met at an informal dinner party at the Kahns' Fifth Avenue mansion six months prior. Friends said it was 'love at first sight.' There followed an ardent courtship. John was Maud's ideal beau, grounded, handsome with dark blonde hair and the obligatory military mustache worn by men of the era, well-educated, hugely protective, and great fun to be around. He had a reassuring sense of understanding about him that comes to a person after experiencing life to the full. He was the only son of Charles and Gertrude Marriott of Stowmarket in Suffolk, England. Both his parents were deceased. He was now ready to settle down and raise a family of his own.

In his article, Knickerbocker states, Maud holds 'the coveted position of being the most beautiful woman in Palm Beach this season or any previous one' and praises her outstanding qualities and achievements. 'Maud Kahn is one of the most popular and talented young women in metropolitan society. She is more than a mere society girl and, like her daddy, possesses an executive ability, which is nothing short of amazing. Despite the fact that she will inherit a vast fortune at some future day, Maud is a young miss of very simple tastes and devotes the greater part of her time to charitable enterprises.' Knickerbocker ends his piece by congratulating Major Marriott on capturing one of the prettiest and cleverest young women in Gotham society.[52]

The day before news of her engagement broke, Maud drove south to Florida to spend a short break at her parent's villa. Accompanying her was her sister Margaret and a couple of friends, including Billy McKeever. Maud left New York in her father's car and planned to unwind with her friends around her, away from the media's glare and intrusion. Intentionally, Maud did not reveal to Cholly Knickerbocker that John was also staying with them in Palm Beach. Neither did she divulged any of her future wedding plans. Those details were well and truly under wraps.

John was presently serving as a General Staff Officer to the British Military Attaché at the British Embassy in Washington, D.C. He was currently on leave and had arranged to spend time with his future bride driving across America. Furthermore, he'd recently applied for a transfer back to the UK to join the Scots Guards. His application had gone through, and his return to Britain was imminent.

On February 20, *The Sun and the New York Herald* reported that the Kahn party, without John, had departed by car from Palm Beach the previous day and were heading for Kingsville, Texas, to spend time at a ranch before heading to California to visit the main Pacific coastal resorts. They planned to return to the Empire State in April.[53] How much of the report was fabricated by the Kahns to keep the press off their backs is unclear. What is certain is that John did accompany Maud during part of the trip.

Otto and Addie arrived in Palm Beach for a short stay at their villa the day after Maud departed. The elder Kahns returned to New York two weeks later, where Otto set sail for the continent. Addie remained in Manhattan to organize preparations for her daughter's marriage. In May, Addie and the rest of the Kahn clan intended to travel to the UK to join Otto. Plans for Maud's wedding had to be in place before their voyage.

By March, Maud and John's coast-to-coast tour of the States had taken them as far as California. In Pasadena, they checked into the exotic Mediterranean-style Hotel Green. The lavish complex was one of Pasadena's leading tourist destinations. The grounds had three extensive annexes, lush gardens, and its own Santa Fe Railroad station right on its doorstep. It was a winter resort for wealthy easterners, and Maud and her party had no problem fitting in. What did come as a surprise was what followed. No sooner had the Kahn party checked in than, suddenly, the *Los Angeles Herald* plastered a picture of Maud and John on their front page under the heading, 'New War Romance Bared in Pasadena.'[54] Did the leak come from an over-talkative hotel lobby staff member, or did a roving journalist just get lucky?

A few weeks later, having kept the journalists artfully at bay, Maud and Margaret set off on their return journey home. They arrived back in New York in mid-April. On April 14, the two sisters accompanied their mother to the spectacular 2nd Annual Aviator's Ball at New York's Ritz-Carlton Hotel.[55] Once again, the media were out in force. The American Flying Club had organized the event. Many members of the army, navy, and air force were present. Addie helped arrange the evening's entertainment that included a feisty performance by a troupe of Russian dancers. The ballroom looked spectacular, decked out with the most impressive aeronautical display outside an aircraft hangar; hot air balloons floating in cotton clouds, with airplanes suspended from the ceiling directly above dancers on the dance floor.

Photographers were hoping for that elusive romantic image of Maud and John, arm in arm on the dance floor. The Kahns, however, were far too adept at dancing one step ahead of the press. No such picture materialized.

In May, the Kahn family joined Otto in London for their first European vacation since 1914. From the UK, their itinerary took them to France and Italy.[56] In London, they stayed at Claridge's and in Paris at the Hôtel Ritz. Otto also planned to spend three weeks in the French colonies in Africa dealing with matters arising from the war.[57] Addie and her daughters had a long shopping list of items to purchase for Maud's forthcoming wedding, and what better cities to shop in than London and Paris!

The Europe of 1920 was not the Europe that welcomed the Kahn family back in 1914. Otto discovered the key European economies were not as buoyant as he had expected. They had suffered more during the last year from the effects of peace than the impact of war.[58] In part, he blamed this paradox on the controlling influence of the Peace Treaty makers at the Versailles Peace Conference. On the other hand, he did find the UK was prospering. In his opinion, London was still the financial center of the world. 'England's position is the result of geographical, economic and psychological factors, racial qualities, and the experience and practice of centuries.'[59] The talks Kahn held with Russians in Paris revealed their hopes that the ruling Bolshevist oligarchy would soon collapse. Rather tellingly, Otto never made it to Germany this trip. However, he did have a meeting in Paris with the head of the German economic mission, sent to France to confer with delegates appointed by the French Government. Otto also met several captains of industry who had recently arrived in the country. The overriding feedback from the meetings was that the West had nothing to fear from the Junker, Militarist, or Hohenzollern party.

During May, Otto visited Tunis and Algiers, traveling two thousand miles by road. He was immensely impressed by the country's diversity of natural resources and the historical sites he saw.[60] Otto had hoped to visit Belgium and several other countries. However, his trip was curtailed due to his eldest daughter's impending marriage. As a result, he only managed to journey to the French Colonies in Africa. Addie also shortened hers and her children's visit and returned to New York ahead of her husband to organize the final preparations for Maud's big day.

The provisional date for Maud and John's wedding was June 9. The couple later revised the date to June 12.[61]

In the meantime, Otto telegraphed his wife in New York to inform her his return to the States would be delayed, and the wedding date would need rescheduling.[62] Otto was having difficulty securing a passage from England. As the wedding day fast approached, another announcement appeared in the newspapers with the amended date of June 15.[63] Owing to the church's small seating capacity, only relatives and a few close friends were invited to the ceremony. Luckily, Otto secured a reservation on the SS *Imperator*, scheduled to arrive in New York a few days before the wedding.[64]

The media went to town reporting what they were now labeling 'the society wedding of the year.'[65] From the many detailed accounts written up in the newspapers, the reception was going to be huge, catering for a thousand guests, and would take place at the Kahns' Long Island estate.

In the run-up to the happy event, Maud and Margaret spent several relaxing weekends at the estate, throwing small informal house parties for their friends. The East River's watery expanse did not keep the press at bay in their efforts to cover every aspect of the two sisters' comings and goings. Gossip and updates were fed regularly to the public. 'Another hospitable house in Long Island is that of the Otto H. Kahn's,' the *Gazette-Times* informed its readers.[66] 'Maud and Margaret Kahn have given delightful parties over each Sunday at the Kahn estate, which, by the way, beggars description. Until I saw the Kahns' country place at Woodbury, I imagined I had gazed upon the last word in country houses. But, well, there is nothing finer in all America, and to attempt to tell of the wonders of the place would be to attempt the impossible.'

On June 5, the press keenly reported that Otto had departed from Southampton aboard the SS *Imperator* and was on his way across the Atlantic. Then, confusingly, further bulletins appeared, confirming he was on board RMS *Celtic*.[67] The mix-up arose after Otto initially booked the *Imperator*. The ship's owner, Cunard, had pulled the liner from service to undergo an urgent overhaul, which was still not completed. Photographs of Otto smiling, looking casual and relaxed on the deck of an 'ocean liner' before his UK departure appeared in the newspapers. On the same day, Major John Marriott arrived in New York from England aboard the SS *Lapland*. John had already taken up his new London posting with the Scots Guard. He'd been granted three weeks' leave to attend his wedding.

Otto finally made it back to New York aboard the *Celtic* on Friday, June 11,[68] four days before his daughter's marriage.

The Wedding of the Year

Maud's wedding day finally arrived. The Kahn household awoke early. There was still plenty to organize and set in motion. Like a military maneuver, the servants and staff adhered to a strict schedule, arranging everything according to plan. Chefs from Sherry's restaurant assisted with the catering. Much of the food had been prepared in advance in Sherry's large kitchens on Fifth Avenue and delivered to the Kahns' Long Island estate, where a small battalion of waiters would serve every whim and need of the 1,000 guests. Otto and Addie had every intention of giving their daughter a reception the likes of which New York had not seen for many a year.

The simple ceremony took place on a beautifully sunny afternoon at 4:30 in the quaint little church of St John's nestling on the North Shore of Long Island.[69] 'Picturesque and brilliant,' wrote the *Washington Herald* in their account of the joyous occasion.[70] Rev. Harry A. Barrett performed the service. Scarcely more than a hundred guests fitted inside. A Scots Guard welcomed guests at the church entrance dressed in a vivid red coat and fur busby. The bridegroom, and the best man Major General H. K. Bethell, together with the ushers (members of the British Embassy in Washington, D.C.), also came attired in military uniform.[71] The church interior was decorated with a blizzard of blooms and looked enchanting. Every flower was homegrown on the Kahn estate. Clusters of white roses tied with white ribbons trimmed the pews, arrangements of peonies colored the chandeliers, roses adorned the chancel. The scent of blossom lingered in the air.

All eyes fell upon the bride as Otto proudly led his daughter down the aisle to the sound of music played by a string trio and a harpist. Maud had never looked lovelier, dressed in a gown of ivory satin embroidered with a thousand seed pearls.[72] A simple string of pearls adorned her neck, a wedding gift from her mother. In her hands, she cupped a bouquet of flowing white orchids. Shadowing the bride, assisting with her train, walked her maid of honor Margaret and four bridesmaids, of which her best friend Billy McKeever was one.[73] Maud's two unruly brothers Gilbert and Roger looked equally dapper, rigged out in pageboy suits with knickerbockers adjusted below the knee.

After the ceremony, the bridal party and congregation were ferried in vehicles to the Kahn estate for the reception. A special 'wedding' train was on hand to transport additional guests non-stop from New York to Cold Spring Harbor railroad station, from where they were ushered by a fleet of coaches directly to the function.[74]

Maud was the first of the Kahn siblings to be betrothed. Her wedding was also the first to be held at the Kahns' Long Island estate, which *The Sun and New York Herald* columnist perceptively noted had yet to be christened.[75] 'It [the house] looks as if it has been transplanted from France, and with its grounds is one of the finest estates on Long Island.'

The names on the guest list read like a *Who's Who* of New York high society. They included: the Vanderbilts, Rockefellers, Winthrops, Morgans, August Belmonts, Warburgs, Princess Cantacuzène of Romania, Mrs. Bainbridge Colby (wife of the Secretary of State), Harry Gloster Armstrong (the British Consul General in New York), Gaston Liébert (the French Consul General in New York), Comte Roger de Périgny, and William Adams Delano. Many were personal friends. Members of the diplomatic corps from the British Consulate in New York, politicians from Washington, D.C., and people connected with Otto and Addie's many charities also attended.

Maud and John and the hosts received guests in the library. An extensive buffet was served in the dining room and outside at tables on the terrace. After everyone had eaten ample, the bride cut the cake with her husband's sword, and the best man proposed a hearty toast to the newlyweds and the bride's generous parents. Then, late into the small hours, guests danced in the ballroom to the accompaniment of Markel's Orchestra before departing or bedding down for the night in one of the many guestrooms.

The public's interest in the wedding was considerable. Newsreel footage of the reception appeared in movie houses, including New York's Rialto Theatre. The following day's papers and magazines printed a rush of photographs of the happy couple with descriptive accounts of the bridal gown.[76]

The newlyweds spent the first night of their honeymoon in a guest suite at the Kahn country mansion. On Thursday, they set sail for the UK. John had instructions to report for duty with his regiment in London.[77] Among the broad array of gifts the couple received, Otto presented them with the keys to a house in London and a summer place in Ascot near Windsor.[78]

In the days immediately after the wedding, life at the Kahn household quietened considerably. Otto and Addie returned to their customary routine of attending concerts, plays, and charity events. On Tuesday, June 22, they went to the first night of Florenz Ziegfeld Jr.'s *Follies of 1920* at the New Amsterdam Theatre. New York society turned out in force for the opening. Ancient Egyptian architecture and motifs heavily influenced the set designs and costumes. In their write-up, *The Sun and New York Herald* shouted, 'Ziegfeld *Follies of 1920* is a blaze of color and beauty. Truly aesthetic and humorous appeal is the keynote of the new production.'[79] Irving Berlin had contributed a dozen songs, and his catchy melodies greatly added to the show's success. The comedy antics of Fanny Brice and her husband W. C. Fields had the audience in stitches and almost ripped the building's seams open. It was rare for Otto and Addie to be out together without family or friends accompanying them. Visit's to the theater were one of the few public activities they enjoyed as a couple.

In July, Otto issued a press statement summarizing his recent impressions of Europe.[80] First, he denounced The Treaty of Versailles for sowing seeds of dissension among its member nations and channeling discord throughout the world. He argued that 'instead of peace and settlement, they have wrought dispeace and unsettlement.'

Regarding the American 'War Credits,' he was of the firm opinion the U.S. was carrying this immense burden of expenditure without any compensating material return. He firmly believed America should take the initiative in straightening out this matter to mutual satisfaction without awaiting further approaches on the subject from their Allied companions, thus preventing it from becoming a continuing source of embarrassment, uncertainty, and vexation. He based his opinion on certain abnormal factors, including the initial conditions attached to the loans and the economic problems that presently confronted the Allies.[81] He did not expect normal conditions in France and Italy to return in the immediate future and urged American investment in these two countries so they could purchase coal and other raw materials.

The news that Otto had sold his country estate in Morristown hit the front page of the *New York Times* in July.[82] To be accurate, the Kahn family had abandoned the property almost two years earlier after their Cold Spring Harbor house became habitable. The sale drew a line through all the unhappiness and anti-Semitism they had experienced at the hands of their unfriendly neighbors in New Jersey. Cedar Court changed hands for a cool $1 million,[83] a tidy sum that came in handy for the Kahns after the total expenditure of their daughter's wedding had finally been totted up.

September brought the sad but not wholly unexpected news of Jacob H. Schiff's death. His leadership at Kuhn, Loeb had taken the company to the fore of America's investment banking world, challenging J.P. Morgan's grasp. With his passing, the balance of power shifted within the company. Otto became a senior partner. Kuhn, Loeb was now directed by a quartet of senior partners, Mortimer L. Schiff (Jacob's son), Felix M. Warburg, his brother Paul M. Warburg, and Otto.[84]

With the added responsibility and workload that came with Otto's promotion, those closest to him assumed he might reduce some of his extracurricular interests. How wrong could they have been! Otto continued just as he had done over the previous two decades, discovering, guiding, and nurturing new artistic talent and advising charities, companies, and committees on which he sat. His exhausting lifestyle seemed frantic to most people, and few could keep up with him.

On September 22, Kahn addressed the Chamber of Commerce in Dayton. 'Our Taxation System' was the theme of his talk, during which he explained his belief that America's taxation system was far too complicated for its own good.[85] One month later, Kahn spoke in Pittsburgh, Pennsylvania, at the second National Industrial Tax Conference, where he delivered a similar speech. His swipe at the government was duly noted by local politicians, financiers, and the newspapers. 'It is not necessary to say much about the excess profits tax,' Kahn assured his audience, 'as its harm is recognized and all desire its repeal. In theory, it is a just tax. I do not think it has always added to cost, although everyone tries to pass it on. My main objection is against its application. It is so hard to administer that it is practically unworkable without civil service experts. Also, I think excessive surtaxes should be abolished.'[86]

Signs that Otto's health was beginning to cause concern to those closest to him began to surface in the fall. Such worries proved well-founded.

Otto suffered a stroke.

All the warnings had been there; Otto just failed to take note. His medical condition came as a huge shock and a stark warning to him, his family, and his friends. Otto had repeatedly pushed his body to the limit for years. Now his body had rebelled. He was fifty-three and no longer as robust as he imagined.

Addie cleared Otto's diary, and for the next two months, he was confined to bed, recuperating at 1100 Fifth Avenue. His physician instructed him not to unsettle himself with any troublesome work-related matters. When Otto felt stronger and able, he journeyed to White Sulphur Springs in West Virginia to further his recovery. The health resort was renowned for the rejuvenating properties of its mineral springs. Should Otto crave any relaxing diversions, it also had an 'adequate' golf course and a small casino. After a restful stay at the resort, he traveled to his villa in Palm Beach, where he remained periodically until March the following year.

Otto's enforced convalescence was a trying experience for him. He had little time for confinement and longed to be back amid the action, whether in business or a cultural sphere. As such, Addie had to ban friends and work colleagues from visiting him. Even without Otto at his office desk, the wheels of finance still rotated, and life continued its jagged course. A fact Otto found difficult to accept.

In early November, when things could not have gotten much worse for Otto, something quite extraordinary blew in from nowhere. To add to Kahn's stress levels, an individual unknown to him accused him of being an illegal immigrant. National newspapers hungrily splashed the accusation across their front pages. The Kahns were baffled by it all, as was everyone else who knew them.

Mrs. Clara L. de Poy, in a letter delivered by a messenger to U.S. District Attorney Leroy W. Ross in Brooklyn, charged that Otto's citizenship papers were illegal.[87] It was unclear who Mrs. de Poy of Great Neck, Long Island was or why she should suddenly bring about such an allegation. Nonetheless, what ensued was like something out of a Keystone Cops movie.

On Tuesday, November 2, the United States presidential election took place. Otto and Addie were registered to vote in their Long Island constituency. Early that morning, two mysterious strangers arrived outside the local polling station in Cold Spring Harbor, where the Kahns were due to cast their vote. They remained throughout the day until the premises shut in the evening.[88] The watchers, a female, and a male, asked every person entering the building the same question; did they know Otto Kahn, and if so, did they know if he had cast his vote in the election. They explained the reason for their actions was to prevent 'foreigners from voting.' Word of their presence reached the Kahn house at Cold Spring Harbor, where Addie was in residence. Later that day, Addie arrived at the polling station in a chauffeur-driven automobile. She was escorted into the building by her driver, whose intent was to shield her from reporters or imposters. Addie cast her vote and left without being apprehended by the two 'plain-clothes detectives.' Due to his convalescence, Otto did not visit the polling station.

Three days later, the district attorney released details of the charge brought against Otto by Mrs. Clara L. de Poy to the press:

'I hereby call upon you to commence action against Otto H. Kahn of Woodbury, Long Island, to rescind and declare void the so-called naturalization papers issued to him on the ground that said papers I believe to be illegal.'[89]

Mrs. de Poy clarified in her letter that she had no personal vendetta against Mr. Kahn or his family and that she merely wanted justice carried out. Her demand to have Kahn's citizenship papers revoked came about because she wished to make sure 'no foreigner' voted that was not legally registered to do so. The New York Times implied Mrs. de Poy had connections with a pure ballot organization.[90]

In his written reply to the claimant, the District Attorney asked her to visit his office on Monday, November 8, with her attorney, William Eastman of Mineola, to reveal the nature of her information, which he assured her he would investigate without delay.

That same day, Otto's counsel Paul D. Cravath, issued a statement denying any wrongdoing.[91]

Cravath specified that Mr. Kahn did not vote at the recent election due to illness and instead convalesced at his home at 1100 Fifth Avenue. He also explained that although Kahn became a naturalized British subject in 1893, he received his first American naturalization papers in 1907 and his final documents in 1917. Even though Kahn's papers were out of date, the Court of Common Pleas in Morristown, New Jersey, had granted his U.S. citizenship because he was entitled to it under a decision of the U.S. courts that covered New Jersey. Furthermore, Cravath claimed Kahn was issued his final documents using an act of Congress validating all naturalization certificates filed before January 1918 upon declarations of intentions filed before September 27, 1906.

According to Mrs. de Poy, Kahn made his first application for citizenship in New Jersey in 1906 but took no further action until 1916, when he applied for his certificate.[92] Mrs. de Poy asserted the request was outlawed because Kahn failed to apply for the certificate within the permitted seven-year period. Irrespective of this fact, she alleged Kahn received his papers in 1917. Having had the records searched, she felt confident Kahn was not a U.S. citizen despite his naturalization papers.[93] Mrs. de Poy also informed the district attorney that staff treated her discourteously when she visited the

Cold Spring Harbor polling station on Election Day.

Deputy Sheriff Amza Biggs of Suffolk County, New York, was notified on November 2 of two strangers acting suspiciously outside the polling station, detaining voters as they went about their business. The deputy sheriff confirmed that no one inside the building knew the identities of the couple.

On Monday, November 8, Mrs. de Poy presented her evidence to Leroy W. Ross. After conducting a thorough investigation into the matter, Ross released a statement on November 23.[94] Kahn's citizenship papers were legal, Ross stated. 'Mr. Kahn's declaration of intention became valid, and there can be no question that he is now, and has been since May 9, 1918, a citizen of the United States.'[95] He also clarified that the two 'plain-clothes detectives' outside the polling station at Cold Spring Harbor on Election Day were, in fact, Mrs de Poy and Fred Burlingame of 266 Madison Avenue, Manhattan.[96] Although Ross believed more than seven years had elapsed between the time Kahn filed his declaration of intention to become a U.S. citizen and his final petition, Congress did pass an enabling act on May 18, 1918, under which Kahn's declaration of intent became valid.

Ross thought Mrs. de Poy had been duped into believing Kahn was an illegal immigrant,[97] although he did not mention who it was that had deceived her.

The elder Kahns put Christmas week aside to entertain at home. Gilbert returned from Groton School, where he was boarding, and Margaret, who was still living under the family roof, invited some of her New York pals over to join in the festivities. Roger perked up, too, now that his brother was home for several weeks' break. When Gilbert was away, it changed the whole dynamics of the household, especially for Roger. With Gilbert around, life took on a kaleidoscope of possibilities. The brother's antics usually involved fast automobiles, motorcycles, and lots of music-making.

Addie opened the house to welcome a specially invited audience to a festive afternoon *lecture-musicale* presented by the chorus of The Schola Cantorum. It was their second show at the Kahn abode that year.[98] During the concert, the Australian pianist Percy Grainger gave a talk on 'The Arts of Cyril Scott,' accompanied by illustrations on the piano played by Grainger and readings of Scott's poems.[99] The Kahn brood were keenly encouraged to attend such events.

Just because Otto was presently convalescing, it did not imply he was inactive; his secretary could still type him the odd letter or two or even a full public address. One such speech, in which he presented an argument in favor of a sales tax, was delivered at the House Ways and Means Committee in Washington, D.C., on December 21.[100]

He also informed C. Arthur Pearson in London that now the war was over, he wished to have St Dunstan's Lodge in Regent's Park returned to him. Otto had alternative plans for the property.

Pearson kicked up a monumental fuss and petitioned Kahn to extend his goodwill and, in turn, lengthen the Blind Institute's tenancy at the property. The institute was still very much in operation and would be difficult and costly to evacuate and rehouse. Pearson roped in some hefty names to back him; Dowager Queen Alexandra and Winston Churchill included. As would generally happen when Otto's benevolent nature came into effect, he rescinded and allowed the institute to remain in situ for a few more years. Tragically, early in the negotiations, Pearson drowned after knocking himself unconscious in his bathtub.

The estate was finally returned to Otto in 1927 when the institute moved to new premises.

5

GILBERT TAKES A HIT

'Young Kahn Hit by Auto - He and Girl Near Death'[1]

1921

During January, the Kahns spent a three-week family vacation at their winter home in Palm Beach, traveling from New York aboard their private rail car. Margaret stayed only briefly as she had booked a passage to the UK to spend time with Maud. On the coast, Otto's convalescence was less restrictive and more physical. Some mornings under the warm Florida sun, he would swing by the golf club for a leisurely round. Occasionally, after lunch, he might head out sailing for the afternoon, always being careful not to overexert himself. After a pleasant break, Addie and Roger returned to New York, where, on Thursday, February 3, they sailed for the continent aboard RMS *Aquitania*.[2] The ship docked in Southampton six days later.[3]

Addie, and Roger's European trip, would last almost seven months and take in France, Italy, Switzerland, and Holland. They, too, intended to visit Maud in the UK, staying first at Claridge's in London, followed by a short get-together at Maud's new country retreat near Windsor. Roger would receive private tuition throughout the trip and attend the Conservatoire de Paris for lessons in music composition. When Otto was fit enough, he hoped to join them for brief periods between his visits to various European health spas if his physician permitted him to travel abroad.

In the meantime, Otto remained in Palm Beach to continue his recovery, where he welcomed several houseguests to join him. Gilbert returned to Groton School to resume his studies. On the second Sunday in February, Otto and his guests motored to Miami to attend a swimming gala showcasing local girls and boys.[4] It was a welcome change to Otto's daily routine.

Otto had already been quietly planning to build a new smaller villa on land he had purchased neighboring Oheka Cottage on the northern side. Now seemed the ideal time to push forward with the idea. It would make a perfect holiday home for his two daughters. Kahn selected the Florida-based architect Bruce Paxton Kitchell to design the villa. In May, he signed a $40,000 contract with Brown and Wilcox Company, the same firm he employed to build Oheka Cottage four years earlier. Construction of the new property got underway later in the year.

Otto rented Oheka Cottage out to the newspaper proprietor Ogden Mills Reid and his wife, Helen, during the second week of March. Cutting his stay short, Otto returned to New York.[5]

Margaret was due back in the States in early March. She sailed from Southampton aboard the SS *Imperator* on February 26, bearing heaps of news and gossip she was itching to share with her father. The *Imperator* approached Lower New York Bay as scheduled on March 5.[6] Annoyingly for all aboard, before reaching Upper Bay and New York Harbor beyond, the vessel dropped anchor and was held in quarantine due to a health scare onboard. Physicians from the Public Health Service boarded to check passengers for a suspected typhus outbreak in steerage class.[7] Owing to the length of time required to conduct such examinations, the ship remained moored offshore for longer than anticipated. It took until 4 p.m. two days later before the *Imperator* could dock in New York Harbor, and passengers were finally allowed to disembark. The following day's papers reported a hundred steerage passengers were escorted off the ship at Hoffman Island in Lower New York Bay and taken to a quarantine station for further examination.

Reassuringly for Margaret, she was given the all-clear.

Gilbert's Motorcycle Accident

Sunday, March 13, should have been just like every other Sunday for 17-year-old Gilbert Kahn. The fact that he was home from Groton School for the weekend, spending time with his father and sister Margaret at the family estate on Long Island made the day that little bit special. Life at the house was quieter than usual, as his father was still on the mend and under strict orders from his physician to take things easy. His mother and brother Roger were across the pond visiting the UK. Not that Gilbert was too concerned by their absence, as there were plenty of activities and distractions on the estate to occupy him. Gilbert, like Roger, had a fixation with motorcycles and cars and racing them. Cold Spring Harbor had some ideal paths and tracks for competing along, something Gilbert and his brother participated in regularly, much to their parent's disapproval. Some of the quieter, country roads that crisscrossed Long Island were also good for racing along. As the weather was agreeable, Gilbert headed off for the afternoon on his motorcycle to visit several of his favorite outposts on the island.

At around five o'clock on his return home, Gilbert drove through leafy Huntington Village and then headed south along New York Avenue (a partly residential road) towards West Jericho Turnpike. The journey from Huntington to Woodbury usually took him around ten minutes. As the road was empty, Gilbert was traveling at some speed. A little way ahead of him, an automobile came into view driving steadily in the same direction as him towards the turnpike. Gilbert soon caught up with the vehicle. As he prepared to overtake the car, it reduced its speed and turned left to enter a private driveway. Gilbert miscalculated the speed he was driving. Instead of swerving to avoid a collision, his motorcycle careered straight into the side of the vehicle. He hit the automobile squarely, and with such a terrific force, it hurled the car into a shallow ditch beside the road. The vehicle partly rolled over in the process. It then temporarily righted itself onto its wheels before losing balance again and tumbling onto the ground, crushing Gilbert and his motorcycle beneath it.[8]

Four occupants were inside the car: 21-year-old driver Olive Crowe and three passengers - Miss Crowe's mother and their friends Mrs. Mildred Fitch and Edward Staudenmaier. Upon impact, the driver was thrown forcefully against the dashboard; she fractured her skull on one side near the base. She also suffered internal injuries and lay unconscious slumped in a heap beneath the steering wheel. The other passengers escaped relatively unhurt aside from bruises and shock and managed to crawl unaided from the overturned vehicle.

Fortuitously, an automobile drove towards them on the opposite side of the road moments after the collision. Its driver Morris Kassel immediately braked and jumped out of the car to help. After righting the overturned vehicle, he was able to reach Gilbert. Kassel carried Gilbert's unconscious body over to his car and placed him inside. He then did the same with Miss Crowe. Afterward, he drove at speed to nearby Huntington Hospital. The surgeon in charge, Dr. Willoughby Pendill, and his assistant Dr. Warren Kortwright attended to the two injured patients and took X-rays of their skulls. From the initial diagnosis, Miss Crowe's chances of recovery were small. As far as Dr. Pendill could determine, Gilbert's skull was not fractured though he confirmed he had suffered a severe concussion of the brain. He had also broken his right ankle in several places and sustained multiple bruises. Both patients remained unconscious.

After determining Gilbert's identity, a police officer contacted the Kahn estate on Long Island to speak to the head of the family. Otto was not home. He had returned to Manhattan by boat. By chance, Margaret was in residence. After receiving the news of the accident, she drove immediately to the hospital. Word reached Otto a little later, at 1100 Fifth Avenue. As any doting father in his privileged position might do, he summoned his best driver to bring his fastest automobile, to drive him to collect two of New York's finest physicians. Those physicians were Dr. Charles G. Taylor of 10 East 61st and Dr. John J. Moorhead of 115 East 64th. Together they traveled at speed to Huntington Hospital. When they arrived later that evening, Gilbert and Miss Crowe remained unconscious with no noticeable improvement. Otto wired his wife in the UK with news of the accident and to prepare her for the worse. The two New York physicians conferred with Dr. Pendill and Dr. Kortwright. All agreed Gilbert would require an operation if he did not regain consciousness during the night.

Otto and Margaret and the two physicians maintained a constant vigil at Gilbert and Miss Crowe's bedsides. All they could do was pray that the two patients would pull through. It would be a long, tiring night for everyone concerned.

The family's prayers were answered.

On Monday morning, Gilbert showed slight signs of regaining consciousness. A hospital bulletin described his condition as 'propitious.' Sadly, Miss Crowe displayed no noticeable signs of improvement. The doctors still feared she had little chance of recovery. A further bulletin issued later that day stated little change. Both patients required a thorough examination before the hospital could release any further details.

Overnight, reports of the accident ricocheted across America like a pistol bullet firing over the starting line at a greyhound race. Which paper could get the story out the quickest? Monday's newspapers from New York to San Francisco and almost every other city in-between ran with it. 'Banker Kahn's Son and Girl Critically Hurt in Collision' led the Brooklyn Daily Eagle on its front page.[9] 'Young Kahn Hit by Auto - He and Girl Near Death' hollered the Chicago Daily Tribune across its front page.[10] 'Groton Schoolboy Hurt' stated the local Groton, Massachusetts daily.[11] 'New York Bankers Son is Hurt' affirmed the San Francisco Chronicle.[12]

Over the coming days, Gilbert's condition slowly improved.[13] He regained consciousness and gave an account to the police of the lead-up to the accident. Throughout this critical period, Otto and Margaret remained at the hospital. Addie and other family members received updated bulletins as they were issued. The principal of Groton School, Rev. Endicott Peabody, was contacted and notified of the situation. At present, there was no indication when Gilbert would be well enough to return to his studies. Miss Crowe also regained consciousness, although her injuries were considerably more severe than Gilbert's. She provided the police with her version of the accident, as did the passengers traveling in her car, but their perspective differed slightly from Gilbert's. It transpired the accident happened in front of Olive Crowe's home at New York Avenue, Huntington.

Passenger Edward Staudenmaier's version of events ran accordingly: 'Both vehicles were traveling south on New York Avenue at five o'clock, Miss Crowe's car being in the lead. When Miss Crowe arrived opposite the roadway leading to her home, she glanced at the rear and gave a signal for turning to the left. No one was in sight. The car turned slowly, left the concrete roadbed, and was crossing the trolley tracks, which run parallel to New York Avenue when the motorcycle crashed into the car. Mr. Kahn, rider of the bike, dropped almost instantly across the rear wheel of the cycle and then slid slowly to the ground. He lay there unconscious. The shock of the collision had thrown Miss Crowe's head violently against the upright holding the top, and she slid down under the wheel.'[14]

Undoubtedly, the initial quick actions of Morris Kassel helped save Gilbert and Olive Crowe's life.

Gilbert remained hospitalized for the following week, after which an ambulance transported him to the family's Woodbury home to commence his long road to recovery. His parents felt the large estate would be the ideal place to convalesce. Otto hired a nurse to visit twice weekly. Upon his arrival, Gilbert found the house was not the fun-filled home he was used to, on account that his brother and mother were abroad, and all his friends were at school. Otto was still on the mend and had social commitments in Manhattan to attend, and Margaret had college to keep her occupied. Gilbert soon began to feel isolated. After several days of being cooped up at the large, unwelcoming mansion, Gilbert asked his father if he could convalesce at Fifth Avenue to be closer to him and Margaret. He could also occasionally have his friends round to help cheer him up. After enduring almost five months of recovery himself, Otto sympathized

with his son and agreed to the arrangement. On March 24, an
ambulance from Huntington Hospital transferred Gilbert from
Woodbury to Manhattan.[15]

Overall, Gilbert's injuries would lay him off school for one year.[16]

Sweet Baby John

Sweet baby John was born in London on Saturday, April 2, the first
child to Maud and John Marriott and Otto and Addie's first
grandchild.[17] After all the heartache and unpleasantness the Kahn
family had endured over the previous six months, news of John's
birth brought a welcome gasp of joy to the Kahn household. Addie
and Roger were in London, staying at Claridge's Hotel when Maud
went into labor. Addie rushed over to the Marriotts home to be at the
childbirth.[18] Both the baby and Maud were doing fine. Over in
America, Otto, Margaret, and Gilbert were thrilled at the news and
could hardly wait to see the new arrival. If everything went to plan,
all three hoped to make it to the UK in a month or two.

Given Otto's recent health scare and the fact he was now aged 54,
Otto and Addie decided it was time to reassess their finances and rearrange the management of their property portfolio. Their three
houses in East 68th Street - numbers 6, 8, and 10 - had already
received internal and external renovations by the Beaux-Arts
architect Harry Allan Jacobs, whose flair for decorative façades Otto
greatly admired.[19] In April, the Kahns sold their five-story 'English
basement residence' at 8 East 68th Street.[20] Between 1921 and 1922,
they offloaded properties 6 and 10. They also formed a company to
administer their property holdings.[21] Such action would secure the
family homes should anything unforeseen happen to Otto.

Spring in New York promised an assortment of social events,
mostly weddings, but perhaps as a mark of the changing times, some
alternative gatherings also appeared in the calendar. One date that
drew media attention involved Margaret, who had for some time
been attending ballet class. Ever since her appearance the previous
year in the stage musical *What Next!*, Margaret had taken her ballet
tuition exceptionally seriously.

'Dancing is the newest exclusive fad, and so many of the
distinguished daughters of multi-millionaires are learning to
pirouette while advocating the introduction of a National American
Ballet,' disclosed journalist Helen Hoffman in the *South Bend News-*

Times.[22] Miss Hoffman certainly thought Margaret and her dancing friends matched her description perfectly. Hoffman alleged this sudden influx of feet tapping and arm waving was derived from a wide-spreading movement to establish an American National Ballet. She claimed the longed-for concept was about to be realized. Seemingly, America was to have its own National Ballet under the guidance of self-styled ballet mistress Mlle. Desiree Lubovska, an established interpretive dancer and prominent figure in early 20th century American dance.

Lubovska was, in fact, a creature of her own creation. She was no more Russian than any of the other girls born in the Minnesota street where she grew up. What Lubovska had done was reinvent herself and adopted a mysterious Russian heritage as a way of capitalizing on the glamor and allure of real Russian prima ballerina Anna Pavlova, the reigning queen of ballet. Princeton University was hosting a summer ballet school where the educated toe was heading. In arrangement with the newly-formed board of the National American Ballet, fifty of New York's most promising dancers enrolled at the school.

Margaret was considered for a placing at the summer ballet school at Princeton but did not make it. So instead, she joined her father and brother Gilbert on a trip to Europe.

The month of May always saw a marked exodus of society from New York City, with most wealthy families heading to the continent or their country estates. On May 3, Otto, Margaret, and Gilbert accompanied by a valet, maid, and a nurse set sail on the RMS *Aquitania* for Europe.[23] The restful voyage, fine cuisine, and fresh air would greatly benefit them all. Just sailing first-class across the Atlantic on such a splendid liner was an event in itself. Passenger lists would regularly contain many prominent American and foreign travelers, notable names that still stand out today. The *Aquitania* docked at Southampton on May 10, from where the Kahn family caught the boat train directly to London. Here they joined Addie and Roger at Claridge's Hotel. After the dramatic events of the previous few months, it was an emotional reunion for everyone. The following evening, Otto and Addie were entertained at dinner by King Albert and Queen Elisabeth of the Belgians.

During this visit, Otto would not be spending long periods away from his family to attend to business matters. On this trip, his well-being was his main priority. Days spent at various spas would aid his health immensely. One such stay in southeastern France was at the Hôtel Royal in Évian-les-Bains on Lake Geneva's shores, where the mineral water springs were renowned for their rejuvenating benefits.

In June, Otto was appointed *Commandeur de l'Ordre National de la Légion d'Honneur* of France. The French Prime Minister, Aristide Briand, personally presented Kahn with the distinction at a special award ceremony in Paris.[24] During the occasion, Otto received a decorative fifty-five-page autograph album. Inside were original sketches and watercolors by French artists, along with quotations and inscriptions from composers and other prominent cultural figures. The album came bound in dark maroon Moroccan leather embossed with a striking green and yellow floral motif designed by the French bookbinder René Kieffer.[25]

Otto was still in Europe when his friend Enrico Caruso passed away. The unexpected news came as a profound shock to him and everyone else. The tenor died on August 2 in his native city of Naples at the Hotel Vesuvio, where he was recuperating after recently undergoing six operations and a blood transfusion. America took the news of his loss as deeply as Italy and the rest of the world did.[26] Reporters clambered outside the New York Met hoping for a statement, but none was forthcoming. Otto, Gatti-Casazza, and everyone connected with the opera company was on vacation.

Reports of Otto's outings to Europe often appeared in local newspapers and magazines of the countries he was visiting and in the national press in America. It was a convenient way for Addie to keep track of him. On occasions, photographs of Otto would emerge that must have made her think and look twice. One such picture taken on August 10 in France on the beach in Deauville captured her husband dressed in a bathing costume relaxing in the close company of an attractive, bathing-suited, young female. The lady in question was reclining on a beach towel with Otto kneeling awkwardly beside her. There's a look of surprise etched upon Otto's face as he notices the camera pointing at him. When the photograph appeared in the papers, the identity of the young lady remained a mystery. *The New York Tribune* reported on the same day that Otto had delayed his expected return to the States (booked to depart from Southampton on August 15) under orders from his European physician, who feared the strenuous journey might cause his patient to have a relapse.[27] Although Otto's health had improved, his doctor felt he still required further rest.

At Deauville, the Irish painter Sir William Orpen took his sketchpad along to the Kahns rented villa and captured drawings of Otto and one of the Kahn daughters.[28] In the evenings, for relaxation, Otto would visit the Casino with his long-standing friend Lord Beaverbrook to socialize rather than play at the gaming tables.[29]

From Deauville, the Kahns returned to London. Two weeks later, after biding Maud farewell, the family, accompanied by their maids and Otto's private secretary James S. Dartt and valet Alan Carthurst, departed from Southampton docks aboard RMS *Olympic*.[30] Though taken under extraordinary circumstances, the trip had brought the whole family together for the first time in several years.[31]

When Otto arrived back in New York, he issued a statement mourning his dear friend Caruso's passing and praised the singer's outstanding talent and charisma. He also announced a special memorial concert at the Met scheduled for Sunday, February 19, the following year. The celebration would feature many of the leading artists and conductors who had performed alongside Caruso on stage.[32] Proceeds from the event would benefit the Caruso American Memorial Foundation, of which Otto was an active officer. The foundation hoped to raise an endowment of $1,000,000 to assist talented and deserving American music students.

On September 29, Otto received lawyer's papers informing him of two lawsuits for damages filed against him. An automobile he owned, driven by his chauffeur George Cheshire Jr., had collided with a horse-drawn carriage in which two passengers were traveling. The occupants were thrown clear from the wagon and sustained severe injuries.[33] The accident happened on Long Island on December 13 the previous year. It was a private summons brought by the claimant's John W. Cromwell, aged 70, and his daughter Leonora, both Huntington residents. Mr. Cromwell suffered two broken ribs and internal injuries, and his daughter sustained a broken arm and collarbone, along with various cuts and bruises. The case went ahead on November 1.[34] In his defense, Kahn's driver Cheshire Jr. claimed the glare from the lights of an approaching automobile temporarily blinded him, and he did not see Cromwell's wagon in time to avoid the collision. The Jury ruled in favor of the plaintiffs, with the verdict against Kahn. The judge awarded Cromwell and his daughter damages totaling $2,000 and court costs.[35] Kahn did not instruct his attorney to register an appeal against the court decision.

Otto slowly eased himself into a less rigorous work schedule under the guiding watch of Addie and his physician. At the beginning of October, he journeyed to Washington, D.C., where, on October 3, he took luncheon with President Warren G. Harding at the White

House.[36] After lunch, the pair had a private meeting. Otto had already publicly declared his support of tax reform to facilitate the healthy growth of American businesses.[37] A few weeks later, the president signed the Revenue Act of 1921 that introduced sharp tax cuts across the board.

Maud and John, with their infant son, crossed the pond at the beginning of November. Their trip to the U.S. coincided with the family reunion over Thanksgiving. It was John junior's first trip away. On November 14, Otto, Addie, Margaret, Maud, and her husband John had a family evening at the opening night of the Met's current season.[38] The house was packed to the gods, graced by royalty, the diplomatic corps, and the *crème de la crème* of fashionable high society. It was so well attended it prompted a *New York Tribune* columnist to express memories of pre-war openings when the event rivaled some of the most prestigious gala affairs of the Old World. As usual, box holders arrived fashionably late, with many guests coming on from dinners. It was after 9 p.m. when the curtain rose on Verdi's *La traviata* with Italian coloratura soprano Amelita Galli-Curci performing Violetta in her Met debut with Beniamino Gigli at her side in the role of Alfredo. Although the splendor of the occasion was undoubtedly compelling, operagoers found it difficult during the intermissions to refrain from dwelling on memories of that most incomparable tenor Enrico Caruso.[39]

Roger and Gilbert did not join their family at the Met. They remained at home where, as the house was empty, they could play the kind of music they liked, jazz. At last, Roger was happy; he had his brother at home. Just being in his brother's company gave Roger a boost of confidence. Gilbert stayed at home until he was fixed up, which took until the following summer. He never did return to Groton School. In the meantime, Gilbert was taught at home by private tutors to ready him for Princeton, which he would enter in the fall of 1922.[40]

Roger, who had just turned fourteen, was set to enter Groton School that fall.[41] But, due to his continuing health and emotional well-being issues, all that changed after Gilbert's motorcycle accident. Otto and Addie deemed it would be more beneficial for him if he studied at home for the time being with private tutors so that they could keep an eye on him. Rather than going to Harvard University, Otto and Addie now hoped Roger might attend Princeton.

Roger was going through that awkward phase that many teenagers go through, preferring to repeatedly wear the same old clothes, tinkering with oily machinery, and being generally unsociable. However, when Gilbert was around, there was a noticeable transformation. Roger came out of his shell, and his humor and engaging manner returned. Although Gilbert's musical skill was not as distinct as Roger's, he liked nothing better than to strum along on his banjo, accompanying his brother, playing jazz and the classics, sometimes for hours at a time. The house would regularly resonate with the sound of the two brothers playing music, which was one pastime their parents encouraged.

It was to his mother that Roger turned to for emotional support. They remained close throughout their lives. Addie may have come across to those not acquainted with her as a formidable woman, uncompromising, and at times intimidating, but underneath her refined exterior nestled a heart imbued with compassion and kindness. She was the perfect companion for Otto. She was also a devoted mother and a tireless charity campaigner championing causes from emancipation for women to caring for stray dogs and animals. It was to his mother that Roger also turned to for understanding, and Addie unfailingly fought Roger's corner throughout most of the battles he encountered with his father.

In 1921 Otto was elected vice president of New York's esteemed Philharmonic Symphony Orchestra Society.

Otto was also the treasurer of the School Art League. It was a non-profit enterprise initiated to support art students with their education and development and, as such, still exists today. In December, he accepted an invitation to their eleventh annual luncheon at the Hotel McAlpin in Herald Square, Manhattan. In his address, Otto apologized for not donating more of his free time to the League's cause and, for that reason, felt impersonal in praising it.[42] In an attempt to lessen his guilty feelings, he relayed an incident that happened to him when he was a young banker learning his trade.

'I was taken to the opera by my boss, who was a rich man among the rich men of the place, but instead of listening to the beautiful music, he immediately fell asleep.'

It was the first time Otto had visited an opera house, and it left an indelible impression upon him. He claimed the experience made him feel like a plutocrat from his sense of cultural superiority over his companion, for he immensely enjoyed the music and spectacle of the performance. In contrast, his wealthy companion slept through it, barren to the pleasure. Kahn ended his speech with the hopeful message, 'The country is young, and it is full of talent lying around waiting to be guided.'

At the time, little could Otto have imagined just how prophetic, personal, and close to home those last words would turn out to be.

1922

As the months passed and Otto's health grew more robust, his work commitments progressively increased. Soon he had returned to his former hectic routine of cramming as many meetings into a day as his secretary could fit onto the pages of his business diary. Otto would famously conduct meetings one after another, with some lasting only minutes. He may have been a financial wizard, but he was also an astute businessman, and his most expensive commodity was time or the lack of it. For Otto, time indeed was priceless. When he was appraising an artistic venture, it was far cheaper for him to authorize the funds than to spend precious hours discussing a long, drawn-out proposal. If the aspirant had a viable proposition, Otto would sanction the funds, repayable with interest if the project was a success. His philosophy was to encourage and advise without being heavy-handed: 'I am trying, in various ways, to prove a reasonably satisfactory investment.'[43]

Flapperitis

America had pulled through the deadly influenza pandemic of 1918. Now it had a new scourge to concern itself with, flapperitis.

It was official; New York City had an epidemic of flapperitis, so said Miss Janet Richards (a Washington social worker) during a lively meeting of the Girls' Protective League at 1100 Fifth Avenue. Addie had invited the League to hold their meeting at her home to discuss and raise awareness of the dangers to women's morality lurking on every parquet dance floor around the city.

Was jazz sinful? It was a pertinent question, and something, no doubt, Roger and Gilbert were aching to know the answer to.

The feisty, all-female debate took place on February 16. Apparently, or so Miss Richards would have everyone believe, well-bred and educated girls, instead of being the personification of purity, refinement, and innocence, were taking the initiative in cheek-to-cheek dancing, midnight automobile frolics, and other heated 'carryings-on.'

'Why,' Miss Richards declared, as she thumped her notebook on the table, 'things have come to such a pass that every mother has reason to fear for her sons' safety.' She then implanted yet further alarm in everyone by forewarning that conditions had lately become 'deplorable.'[44] Had Roger and Gilbert been listening through the door keyhole, one wonders whether their hair might have stood on end.

Meanwhile, the newspapers picked up the story and had a blast. 'Flapperitis has mother's fearing for their sons,' read the header in Utah's *Ogden Standard-Examiner*.[45]

'Do Flappers, vamp boys?' asked the presiding Chair.

'It's 50-50,' said Mrs. Jessica Payne, who boohooed Miss Richards' assumption.[46] Mrs. Payne, who had a grown son, declared boys were just as responsible as the girls for the relaxed modern-day freedom of manners seen between the two sexes. 'Boys refuse to dance nowadays with a girl who wears corsets. Are the girls responsible for the fact that they remain wallflowers if they wear corsets to a dance? Certainly not!' Mrs. Payne had a point. Was fashion to blame for the relaxed standards in etiquette, or was it just mirroring the era?

'Standards, concerning what constitutes good manners, have undergone a great change. Girls, and boys, are much freer in manners than was formerly the case,' explained Mrs. Payne. 'However, there is no corresponding increase in immorality. Girls realize nowadays that their virtue is their most priceless possession. And their increased freedom of manner toward the opposite sex is not accompanied by an increase in immorality. If we must rebuke our young people, let them equally share the criticism.'

Reassuringly, the majority of the ladies attending felt flapperitis had not yet reached seismic proportions. Nonetheless, a few definitely thought the storm was heading their way from the concerned expressions on their face.

Alternately, Rev. Phillip Yarrow, superintendent of the Illinois Vigilance Association, felt modern-day music was definitely having an impact on the moral standards of today's youngsters. He referred to jazz as, 'a pathological, nerve-irritating, sex-exciting music,'[47] which kind of summed up the whole ethos of jazz.

Whether Addie took any of the points raised at the gathering seriously is not recorded, but one can safely assume she had as much fun debating them as the press had writing them up.

Not every female association held the same concerns expressed by the Girls' Protective League. In October of that year, the New York State Federation of Women's Clubs held a convention at New York's Hotel Commodore at which their progressive-minded president, Mrs.

Thomas G. Winter, spoke in praise of the flapper. 'I'm all for the flapper,' confessed Mrs. Winter.[48] 'If the truth be known, we were all flighty when we were young. I know I was mighty silly, but we tried to conceal it from our parents. The young people of today don't try to conceal anything. They are enjoying that freedom toward which ages of history have been working, and having this freedom almost frightens them. This heritage of freedom has to be paid for by responsibility and self-control. Everything worth having must be paid for; the more worth the having, the higher the price.'

At the age of fourteen, Roger graduated from knickerbockers into trousers.[49] It was also the age Roger learned to play the saxophone. It was this instrument that, in later years, he confessed defined his career path.

Life in the Kahn household was never dull or quiet, and Roger had every intention of raising the volume. In the Adam ballroom, he installed his drum kit. He played them almost daily. Roger's jazz apprenticeship was pretty much self-taught, practicing alone, playing various instruments to the accompaniment of his pianola.[50] Now that Gilbert was home, he had a willing accomplice to join him.

Roger's frequent visits to the Ditson music store were beginning to pay big dividends. He could now play practically every instrument in the store, all self-instructed. His favorites were the piano and the saxophone. Any customer who happened upon the youngster rummaging through the instrument racks, or perfecting a new tune on a clarinet, or thumping out a run of toe-tapping rhythms on the tom-toms, would feel quite satisfied that 'if necessary, he could play 'Yankee Doodle' on a monkey wrench.'[51]

At the beginning of March, after the Jewish Relief Drive calculated they would have a $40,000 shortfall in that year's theatrical quota, they hastily arranged a midnight charity performance at the Palace Theatre for Saturday, March 25. Tickets for the event went on sale to the public the following Monday morning, When Otto heard about the Drive's predicament, on Monday morning, he generously purchased the entire first loge for $1,000.[52]

By the end of Tuesday, the house had sold out.

An exhibition in New York of works by British-born artist Albert Sterner opened on April 3 at the Fifth Avenue gallery of Jacques Seligmann & Co. The display lasted for two weeks. Among the twenty exhibits was a portrait of Margaret Kahn.[53] Margaret's growing interest in photography and art, and the city's vibrant art scene, would, in the years ahead, see portraitures of her captured by several proficient artists.

'I Would Rather Put in a Piano'

'Do you believe that music might deter people from committing crime?' asked New York City Mayor John Hylan to Otto Kahn during a meeting at the City Hall on April 4.[54]

Otto attended the public hearing in support of a bill passed by the previous legislature to authorize the city to construct a college to study music, drama, and performing arts.

Secretary Joseph Haag of the Board of Estimate (an administrative body responsible for making decisions and policies regarding various civic matters) pointed out there were many schools in the city to study music, but no conservatoire for higher education. The proposed development would fill that gap.

Otto took to the stage and spoke to the packed assembly in favor of the project, citing his firm belief that art was good for the human psyche. 'The objects of democracy mean not only getting larger wages for the people but also getting them what they want in an artistic way, for there is a strong desire in their soul to get an outlet for their emotions. I believe some of the causes of crime today come from a desire to get away from the dullness of everyday life.'

It was a philosophy Dr. Eugene Noble (director of the Juilliard Foundation), who was at the gathering, wholeheartedly supported. When Mayor Hylan asked Otto whether he thought music could help reduce the crime rate, Otto replied affirmatively. Hylan may have picked up on this point because the press had recently ridiculed him for his failure to decrease law breaking in the city. One newspaper went as far as suggesting he ought to 'put a cop in everybody's house.'

Otto had a better solution. 'I would rather put in a piano. Wealth is only a matter of dollars and cents, but the man who can hear good music is better off than the man and woman who sit chattering in a box at the Metropolitan Opera House. Art is not highbrow stuff; art is democracy and education and social influence and enables people to give their souls an airing, and they need airing now and then. Bring art to the people, and you'll bring the people to art.'

It was an inspiring speech concerning a subject that was dear to Otto's heart. Predictably, not everyone agreed with him. One columnist in *The Leader* in Guthrie, Oklahoma, believed the ability to appreciate music and art was born in an individual and could not be 'planted like sweet peas or cabbages.'[55]

Towards the end of the meeting, attendees agreed the new building should be a permanent memorial to honor the city's fallen soldiers in the war. With no opposition to the measure, at the close of the hearing, Mayor Hylan announced he would approve the bill.

In late April, the Kahn family minus Otto sailed for Europe. Due to Otto's work commitments, his departure was delayed until the following month. In the UK, Addie and her family moved into Taplow Court for the summer, a mid-19th century Victorian mansion rented from Lord Desborough, set high above the River Thames near Maidenhead.

Before Otto left the States, he arranged for the Metropolitan Museum of Art to loan his Italian old master *Young Knight in a Landscape* by Vittore Carpaccio, which he acquired in England two years earlier.[56] The painting went on public display in Gallery 30, where it remained for several months. It was a gesture Otto welcomed; he much preferred the thought of the public having the pleasure of viewing artworks from his collection than keeping them shuttered away while he was absent.

Otto departed from New York aboard RMS *Olympic* on Saturday, May 13, bound for the UK. Also traveling on board was his friend and fellow financier John Pierpont Morgan Jr.[57]

While in London, Otto met up with John Pierpont Morgan Jr. again. This time for business talks.[58] Morgan Jr. was en route to Paris to confer with other bankers about a proposed international loan to the German government of $200 million to encourage economic stabilization. The loan went ahead, and when Morgan Jr. floated it on the U.S. market, it rapidly became oversubscribed.

Otto was reunited with his family at Taplow Court, from where they journeyed to France. In Paris, the Kahns took up residence at the Hôtel Ritz. While Addie and Margaret shopped and toured the galleries, Roger studied music composition at the Conservatoire. Otto combined work with pleasure and met up with the Met's general manager Gatti-Casazza who was busy auditioning aspiring new talent to export to New York.

On June 3, Otto attended Sergei Diaghilev's premiere of *Mavra*, a one-act comic opera composed by Igor Stravinsky with a libretto by the Russian poet Boris Kochno. Diaghilev was anxious to impress Otto in the hope he would offer a New York transfer. Diaghilev even loaned Otto his private box at the Théâtre National de L'Opéra to view the performance. The twenty-five-minute piece received scant praise from the audience and the press. Otto feared it too short, 'I liked it all, then- poop- it ends too quickly.'[59]

Soon afterward, Otto accompanied Gatti-Casazza to Austria. In Vienna, they auditioned several promising singers. They also met up with Czech soprano Maria Jeritza, whose debut at the Met the previous year in Puccini's *Tosca* had created quite a sensation. The press reported that Kahn and Gatti-Casazza were keen to secure Jeritza for the Met's forthcoming season.[60] In an unprecedented move by an established composer, Munich-born Richard Strauss agreed to conduct his controversial opera, *Salome*, in a one-off performance given exclusively for Otto and Gatti-Casazza. He hoped they might reconsider the Met's ban of the work.[61] Strauss was made Music Director of the Vienna State Opera in 1919. Presently, he was away from the city, so he journeyed back specifically to conduct the piece. The concert took place on Sunday, June 11.[62] With its heavy erotic themes and images of necrophilia, several opera companies firmly refused to include *Salome* in their repertoire. After its infamous 1907 U.S. premiere in New York, the Met was now one such company. Although Kahn favored restaging the work, *Salome* would not return to the Met stage until January 1934.

On Monday, June 12, Otto attended a luncheon at the British Embassy in Vienna, hosted by Sir William Athelstane Meredith Goode,[63] - a representative of the British government in Austria.[64] As Otto left the Embassy, he freely voiced his opinions to the waiting press regarding Austria's current economic crisis. 'The present desperate situation of Austria is a logical consequence of the Treaty of Saint-Germain-en-Laye, which was a piece of political and economic lunacy.' The Allies and the Republic of German-Austria signed the agreement on September 10, 1919. Otto insisted it was 'one of the great political blunders of our time.'

Nonetheless, he remained optimistic about Austria's future. 'Austria and Vienna are indispensable integral parts of the life of Europe.' His short outburst ended with words of hope: 'The desire is growing everywhere to repair the damage wrought by that pact.'

On July 11, Otto arrived in The Hague accompanied by the German Jewish financier Max Warburg (Felix M. and Paul M. Warburg's brother). They attended the Hague Conference together.[65] When news of their attendance reached the press, it prompted worrying rumors to circulate in the media concerning private deals with the Soviet Delegation.[66]

To scupper further harmful press, Otto issued a statement that stressed the danger in central Europe was more pressing than the Russian problem. He assured reporters, 'The conference with the Russians will bring useful results and will lead to a closer approach to unity of views and policies on the part of England, France, and the U.S., in respect to the Russian situation.'[67]

Whether Otto slipped into Germany during this trip to Europe is unclear. However, the likelihood that he met up with some of his relatives (possibly liaising in a neighboring country) is probable, especially as his eldest sister Clara Maria Jonas (née Kahn), passed away in Berlin at the beginning of the year. Such a reunion would have been appropriate if only to pay his respects to his sister's two daughters (his nieces), Margarethe and Eva.

Otto returned to London from The Hague on July 16.[68]

Otto set sail for the U.S. in the second week of August aboard RMS *Mauretania*, a few weeks ahead of his wife and children. Traveling with him was his valet Frederick W. Cooper and private secretary James Dartt.[69]

Six days later, on August 15, as the luxurious ocean liner glided gracefully into New York Harbor, the familiar outline of Manhattan's towering skyscrapers must have been a welcome sight for Otto. For America was now his home, and New York embraced its favorite financier in style.

As usual, photographers and reporters were there to greet Kahn and jostled for a front position on the quayside, eager to seize a story for their papers. As Otto stepped briskly down the gangway, one journalist called out, 'Welcome home, Mr. Kahn!'

'How was your trip abroad, Sir?' called out another.

'Very satisfactory,' replied Otto.

At the foot of the walkway, Otto paused to allow photographers to seize a picture, after which his secretary escorted him directly towards Customs. On this particular day, no exclusive was forthcoming. Otto had other things on his mind.

Addie, Margaret, Gilbert, and Roger, accompanied by their maid Miss Lydia Cooper and Roger and Gilbert's tutor Lorraine Doty, arrived back in New York exactly one month later during the second week of September.[70]

The result of a poll announced in September conducted by *The Jewish Tribune* named the 'twelve outstanding Jews in America,' as chosen by its readers.[71] Topping the list was 62-year-old Louis Dembitz Brandeis, an associate justice of the Supreme Court of the United

States. Otto made the longlist of candidates totaling 174, joining fellow Kuhn, Loeb partner Felix M. Warburg. Not unexpectedly, Otto did not make the shortlist of twelve, unlike his colleague Warburg who did. For someone who openly denied practicing the Jewish faith, Kahn must have found it surprising to see his name on the list in the first place.

Builders had completed the Kahns' new two-story, Italian-style villa in Palm Beach for their daughters, and it was now ready for occupancy. Otto christened it Sunrise Villa, after Sunrise Avenue. During its construction, Maud's commitments and plans had altered quite dramatically. She had married, relocated to the UK, and given birth to her first child. Margaret, however, was still undecided where her future lay. In the interim, Otto temporarily leased out the villa. Pennsylvania steel magnate Jacob Leonard Replogle and his wife Blanche immediately rented the property for an annual rent of $7,500. The couple became so enamored with the place and the laidback Florida lifestyle, they put in an offer to purchase it. In the fall of 1922, Otto sold Sunrise Villa to the Replogles for the modest sum of $135,000.

Peter of Forkland

Two hundred and five dogs made it into the ring on the first day of the eighth annual Shepherd Dog Show on October 17 at the 104th Field Artillery Armory in New York City, including Roger Kahn's German Shepherd, Peter of Forkland. It was the biggest specialty dog show ever presented by the club. The armory, at 1988 Broadway, was usually home to the New York National Guard unit. Today, a platoon of four-legged friends took over the place, barking and yapping, and mischievously bringing havoc among the regulated formality of its usual activities.

Shepherd dogs were now one of the most popular breeds in America.[72] Categories ranged from a 'puppy' class (for dogs aged six to nine months old), a 2nd 'puppy' class (for dogs from nine to twelve months old), a 'novice' class, an 'American bred' class, and many more categories besides. Dr. Kurt Roesebeck (president of the German Kennel Club) arrived from Hanover in Germany to participate as the head of the judging panel; so prestigious was the event. Judging was fierce. The competition was equally intense. Every dog shown in the ring received a rating; grades were excellent, very good, good, satisfactory, or zero.[73] Few of the participating dogs received a rating higher than good.

Roger brought his faithful companion along to enter it in the 'American bred' class. He held high hopes it would win a prize. When the moment arrived, Roger proudly exhibited the dog's handsome profile in the ring, taking the course without fault. In response, he garnered rousing applause from the audience for his and his dog's efforts.

Each dog owner was willing his canine to win. Things were looking good for Roger. Even the head judge was German. When the moment came to announce the winners, a wave of silence guillotined the air:

'In the American bred class, the fourth place goes to ... (a lungful of breath hugged the moment) ... Peter of Forkland.'

Roger was not ecstatic with the result, but neither was he saddened by it. At least his dog had been placed and came away with a rosette. In their coverage of the event, the *New York Tribune* published a particularly unfavorable review of the 'American bred' class winner. 'Ewi Rex, owned by Mr. J. C. Quirk ... was far from being the best-typed dog, more of the truck horse style, but he undoubtedly won on not being so shy as the others.'[74] The reviewer in his appraisal of the other dogs in the same category concluded: 'What seemed the best, but placed fourth, was Peter of Forkland, a beautiful, outlined dog, wonderful feet and a beautiful mover, owned by Roger W. Kahn, son of Otto Kahn.'

Roger was a determined lad and eager to make his mark on the world. How he would achieve that, he had yet to fathom out. He had already decided he wanted to be either a musician or an engineer. His only obstacle to date was convincing his parent's such occupations were noble enough for him to pursue. Both subjects fascinated him and occupied his time obsessively. He was an inveterate tinkerer with mechanical gadgets and was self-tutored in electronics. He liked nothing better than figuring out how machinery was configured and operated. His list of achievements included numerous radio receivers built from kits, and a complete car engine, for which he remodeled the vehicle's chassis.

Fortunately for Roger, his brother Gilbert shared his interest in music and, to some extent, mechanics.

Copies of *Radio World* and *Popular Mechanics Magazine* lay scattered upon Roger's desk in his fourth-floor suite at 1100 Fifth Avenue. Here he spent hours surrounded by his electric tools and instruction manuals constructing the latest device that had grabbed his imagination.

It was no secret in the Kahn household that Roger was obsessed with jazz music. Every servant from the scullery maid upwards knew about it. He played jazz on his instruments, on the record player, and on his radios. He made a determined effort to learn everything he could about jazz. Even Gilbert had become hooked. It was also one of the prime reasons his father had taken such an interest in its development.

Though Roger had seen *Madame Butterfly*, *L'oiseau bleu*, and *Tosca* performed at the Met, this was as far as his operatic education had progressed. He much preferred modern-day music.

Roger was still only at the shallow end of fifteen; a full ten months had yet to pass before his 16th birthday. If staid, rigid conformity had framed his upbringing, then once Roger reached sixteen, he had every intention of raising a rebellion. Jazz music was the perfect medium for him to express his insurrection.

In mid-November, Georges Clemenceau, former French premier, aged 81, visited America to encourage Americans not to be ambivalent about European politics.[75] During his brief stay, he delivered thirty rousing speeches reminding audiences that if they forgot a war had ever taken place, another one would occur. Otto offered his hand of hospitality to the elder statesman by placing his country mansion at his disposal. Clemenceau did indeed visit Kahn's Long Island estate to take a rest from his busy schedule.[76] Clemenceau also delivered an evening address at a packed Metropolitan Opera House on Tuesday, November 21, which he called the most important speech of his career.[77] During it, he exposed his fear that another civil war was on the horizon, more horrible than the previous one.

6

BALLROOM SYNCOPATION

'It's wonderful! ... An old lady visitor was astonished and thought that radio came down the chimney.'[1] Roger W. Kahn, May 1923

1923

It was apparent to both Gilbert and Roger they were never going to be part of the 'cool' gang, either in college or any other educational institution. If they wanted to get ahead in life and gain the respect of their elders and peers, they would have to carve a niche of their own making rather than relying on their parent's connections. As such, the brother's ethos of 'work hard, play hard' was probably a result of their lifestyle and determination to stand on their own two feet. Although being the sons of one of the most eminent investment bankers on the planet had its advantages, it also came at a hefty price and numerous disadvantages. Roger would openly punctuate this fact in umpteen interviews throughout his life.

Gilbert had a more practical outlook on life. Although he was musically minded, he was more of a musical tourist than a regular inhabitant and held no desire to enter the music industry as a profession. Banking was his career of choice. His musical interpolations were purely for fun, as a way of him releasing some of his excess energies. The social aspect of music was also very appealing, which, for a young man soon to reach twenty, was seriously important. It is unclear whether Gilbert acquired his shortened name 'Gil' from his family, but what is certain is his friends, particularly those throughout his education at Princeton, referred to him as such. Indeed, in later years, his wide circle of friends, including the brother and sister stage stars Fred and Adele Astaire, endearingly called him by his pet name.[2]

Shortly after Gilbert entered Princeton as an undergraduate, the art historian Charles Rufus Morey of the Department of Art and Archaeology invited Otto to sponsor various lectures at the university by European scholars. After some consideration, Otto agreed to fund the scheme for two years to the tune of $1,500 a year. He later extended the offer for a third year.[3] Some cynics among the faculty may well have viewed Otto's generous gesture as a sweetener in the hope that Gilbert might receive preferential treatment at the university. However, from the few accounts where Gilbert mentions his schooling, there is certainly no reason to suggest he was treated any differently from other students of his year.

Roger, for the present, had less conventional ideas forming in his mind. Though his initial intention to study engineering at university was still very much on the cards, the thought of it would become less appealing the closer his 16th birthday approached.

When WJZ Radio invited Roger to fill a thirty-minute slot playing popular songs on his saxophone, Roger must have thought all his birthdays had come at once. With his parent's consent - for they had little reason to dissuade him otherwise - Roger jumped at the chance and accepted the invitation. The program was aired in early spring and gave the public a clear indication of Roger's ability as a musician. Furthermore, it brought his talent to the attention of some very influential New York musicians. One of those musicians who took note of the young kid swinging a mean saxophone was the bandleader Paul Whiteman, who was regularly scouting for talented new musicians.

The broadcasting boom of 1922 had seen a profusion of independent commercial radio stations springing up across America. Since its inception on November 2, 1920, radio had become the best and quickest method to deliver a message to the public.[4] WJZ, owned by Westinghouse, was launched on October 1, 1921, and transmitted programs from Newark, New Jersey. In May 1923, Radio Corporation of America (RCA) bought the station and relocated the whole set up to Radio Broadcast Central in New York City. Their new studio was on the 6th floor of Aeolian Hall at 29 West 42nd Street.

Before they moved, Roger recorded his radio debut from WJZ's single-room studio in Newark. The announcer began the program with a short introduction: 'We take great pleasure in introducing Roger Kahn, son of Mr. Otto H. Kahn, the famous financier. Mr. Roger Kahn, though only 16 years old, is an expert player of the saxophone, and he will now entertain you with a number of selections.'

A slip-up by the announcer increased Roger's age by an additional year. He was still only fifteen when the program aired. Whether Roger fibbed intentionally about his age to appear on the show or whether the announcer made an error is undocumented.

Roger played as many of the latest hits from stage musicals and dance halls that he could squeeze into the allotted half-hour, one after the other, uninterrupted, in quick succession, with little or no conversation between numbers. He played his saxophone with 'zip and vim,' hardly pausing for breath, reported *The Wireless Age*.[5] It was an impressive debut for a teenager, delivered confidently, and displayed few nerves. The more astute listener might have presumed the young guy playing must indeed have been a professional musician; he sounded so relaxed with his instrument. The praise Roger received when the program aired made a deep impression on him and encouraged him to consider taking his music a step further, although in what capacity he was still unsure.

Interestingly, the blunder over Roger's age cropped up again a few weeks later in a magazine article published after his radio debut. This time, the culprit was Sam Loomis, a journalist, who likewise documents Roger's age as sixteen.

Loomis heard the boy's performance on WJZ and was fascinated by the fact that the son of a wealthy banker of international fame, known for his patronage of the arts, should be more interested in jazz than classical music. His curiosity prompted Loomis to interview Roger for a magazine article he was writing for *The Wireless Age*.

When Loomis arrived at the Kahn mansion on a Saturday morning to conduct the interview, the butler directly led him upstairs to the music room where Roger was practicing his saxophone. Also in the room accompanying Roger was a drummer who turned out to be Roger's brother, Gilbert. The brothers were happily jamming along to a mechanical piano. Gilbert was tapping out rhythms on various instruments such as tom-toms, rattles, bells, and gongs. The pair continued playing for a while, leaving the journalist in two minds whether or not he'd just stepped into a Broadway cabaret.

Gilbert was home from Princeton for the weekend, and Roger had completed his studies until Monday. The rehearsal was part of the boy's recreation hour when they had the freedom to do as they pleased. The room contained an assortment of musical instruments, all neatly arranged on racks. Loomis noticed a selection of saxophones of differing sizes, a banjo, a violin, and a clarinet, but failed miserably to identify by name all the drum paraphernalia lying haphazardly around the floor. Then, there was the spooky self-playing piano, whose keys were slapping ten to the dozen as if played by a pair of ghostly hands.

After the music ended, the duo introduced themselves to their visitor. Loomis was instantly taken by their ease and friendly nature. Neither displayed any airs and graces and came across as just regular, down-to-earth lads, 'such as you will find in thousands of homes,' revealed Loomis in his article. He takes note of Roger's wide eyes and small, grubby hands that hardly seem large enough to play the saxophone. Roger openly admits he's mad about jazz and that he's a huge radio fan. He also talks about his collection of cars and his keen interest in mechanics and engineering. Roger confesses to already owning a Rolls-Royce, a Bugatti, a Mercedes, and a redesigned Ford Model T. That's some collection for a 15-year-old!* It was his Ford, with an upgraded engine for added speed, which he installed, that gave him the most pleasure, especially when he got the chance to take it for a spin along the many pathways on his father's Long Island estate.

Delving further, Loomis asked what career path Roger was thinking of following, and had he considered becoming a banker like his father? Roger categorically dismisses the notion. 'Oh, no! I'll leave that for my brother. I want to be an engineer.'[6]

As if to emphasize this fact, Roger points to a radio set he's in the process of assembling from a kit. Diagrams and various internal parts belonging to the device lay on a tabletop in the room. He admits to already owning five other radios, including a six-tube radiofrequency rigged up in his bedroom with a loop and loudspeaker. A tradesman had recently installed a mast on the roof to give better reception. Roger claims it's his inquisitive mind that steers his desire to become an engineer.

On his way to the interview, Loomis had wondered what attributes it would take to become as successful as Roger's father. Was it Otto's vitality and strength or some hereditary gene? After meeting the Kahn brothers, he professed to notice qualities in them they could only have inherited that drive a person to accomplish their goals surpassingly well. The effects he felt created a greater understanding of things and concluded such intellect had to have been genetic.

Loomis then pressed Roger for his thoughts about radio and its growing significance in the world. 'It's wonderful!' enthused Roger, who kept repeating his answer while switching on a radio set in the room, allowing the apparatus to speak for itself.

After listening to the radio for a few moments, Roger recounted an amusing incident that happened in his apartment upstairs when an old lady came around to visit him. She overheard the radio playing and was astonished by it, and wondered where the sound was emanating from. She had never heard a radio before. 'She looked around and saw all the windows closed, and then said, 'Do you mean to say that it comes right through the walls? Doesn't it come down the chimney?' She then looked up the chimney to see for herself.'

In relaying this light-hearted anecdote, Roger felt the old lady's reaction was typical of radio's alarming effect on a person when hearing it for the first time.

The apparatus she referred to was the radio Roger had installed in his bedroom that operated using an indoor loop to pick up reception. Since her visit, he had added a stylish Radiola Grand to his collection that used the outdoor antenna erected on the roof. Loomis informs his readers that with the addition of the rooftop aerial, the notion of radio seems somehow not to be as startling to the uninitiated, for it seems pretty reasonable to hang up a wire in the air and catch something with it.

The Wireless Age was the nation's foremost radio magazine. Roger's inclusion in it was immensely significant in bringing him to the attention of American radio listeners. The full-page article was printed in the May edition and came with an accompanying picture of Roger posing with his saxophone. After reading the article and learning about the Kahn brother's lifestyle, one wonders whether Loomis left the Kahn residence with an additional list of questions to the ones he arrived with that he had yet to find answers for.

As a direct result of Roger's radio broadcast, he struck up a friendship with the bandleader Paul Whiteman.[7] In some respects, Whiteman became his unofficial mentor. Whiteman and his orchestra were the house band at New York City's Palais Royal, a restaurant cum dance hall on the corner of Broadway and West 48th Street. Although Roger was technically underage, it did not stop him from visiting the Palais Royal night after night to listen to Whiteman's orchestra playing live on stage. Roger's attendance became so regular that Whiteman, in an unprecedented move, made a place for the youngster at the back of the orchestra so he could sit and study at close range the band's methods. On occasions, Roger was also encouraged to join in and play any instrument he may have brought along.

Radio Roger

Roger was smitten with radio and everything to do with it. Nowadays, he might easily have been labeled a bit of a nerd. At home, he maintained a workshop in which he studied all the latest technology. Here, he built new receivers from radio kits. In his bedroom, he had six home-built radios positioned around his bed. In the evening, he would tune in to a different frequency on each receiver and listen to the broadcasts through his clunky metal earphones. He particularly liked Western orchestras.[8]

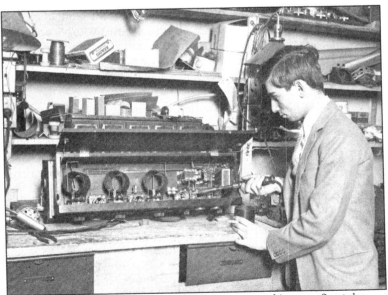

Roger in his workshop at 1100 Fifth Avenue, working on a five-tube Neutrodyne radio receiver, which he has constructed.[9]

Even though radio was still in its infancy, broadcasting companies were eager to exploit its increasing popularity. New York already had four major broadcasting stations: WEAF, WJZ, WJY, and WHN. All listed regular live broadcasts in their schedules featuring jazz orchestras from hotel ballrooms and dancehalls across the metropolis. At the time, music comprised more than two-thirds of radio programming. Roger's fixation with dial twisting meant he could listen to many of these transmissions at home.

Radio had one significant advantage that bars and restaurants could not compete with; there was no off-season on the airwaves. Consequently, radio always had an audience. Theater owners became increasingly anxious over the popularity of etherized entertainment. So much so, they began looking for ways to overcome this obstacle and hopefully to attract larger audiences in the process.

The first network broadcast in radio history simultaneously aired by more than one station took place in January 1923 and was carried, linked by telephone wires, by two stations, WEAF, New York, and WNAC, Boston. The content of the presentation consisted of a saxophone solo that lasted five minutes.[10]

The name of the musician playing the instrument has since disappeared into the fog of time. Yet, ironically, a couple of months later, the American public first became aware of Roger's musical talent through the same mediums of radio and saxophone. It seemed inevitable that the radio would play an even larger part in the youngster's future. How integral a part had yet to be determined.

In early 1923 Otto's prized 18-hole golf course on his Long Island estate was completed. It was a beautifully groomed course, difficult and exacting to construct, but a challenge architect Seth Raynor undertook with great enthusiasm. Otto was responsible for helping to dig many of the bunkers. Some of the greens were replicas of ones Otto had played on in various countries during his travels. Raynor drew on his experiences as an engineer to design the fairway: breathtaking vistas, two bridges spanning the gulches on the fourth hole, upright fountains dancing in the lakes, and sinuous curves on the cart paths, which all blended pleasingly with the landscape. With the link now operational, Kahn spent as much time at the estate in the pursuit of perfecting his swing as his busy schedule would allow.

Roger was never one to miss out on any opportunity that arose in his pursuit of new distractions. Rather imaginatively, he devised an alternative use for the cart path as a speed track and accordingly found great enjoyment racing his customized Ford Model T along its route. He did this in full view of his father, who kept a sobering watch in between practicing his tee shots on the fairways.

Otto hated losing at golf, and when he did, he was sore. To lessen the eventuality of such events, he took a mental note of where his golfing partner's balls landed most frequently. He then secretly had traps installed in those positions hoping his actions would scupper his opponent's chances of winning. In Otto's eyes, all was fair in love and golf.

Like her parents, Margaret Kahn also inherited a love of the arts and developed a keen interest and an uncanny eye for recognizing gifted, aspiring artists. On March 20, she found her way to Arnold Genthe's photographic studio in Lower Manhattan at 100 Fifth Avenue, where she sat for him. German émigré Genthe worked in the soft-focus pictorialist medium and specialized in portraitures and dance photography.

Genthe's style of creating artistic images by manipulating the surroundings rather than producing conventional shots appealed greatly to Margaret's interest in contemporary art. It was a form that suited Margaret's natural features. One of the striking portraits Genthe captured of Margaret shows her gazing inquisitively into the lens, her large brown eyes, still with a flash of youthful innocence in them, seemingly searching for answers.[11] The photograph appeared in an early retrospective exhibition of Genthe's work.*

Otto's Plan to Buy the Hippodrome

In May, the papers announced Otto had begun negotiations with United States Realty Corporation to purchase the New York Hippodrome for a price above $3 million.[12] Otto's reason for buying it was so his friend, theatrical producer Morris Gest, would have a venue to stage Max Reinhardt's mammoth spectacle, *The Miracle*. Reinhardt's European production, which boasted music by Engelbert Humperdinck, had been a runaway success and garnered praise from critics and theatergoers alike as it made its way across Europe. Kahn had seen the play numerous times and was mightily impressed. He was now keen for American audiences to savor the experience.

The Hippodrome stood on Sixth Avenue between West 43rd and 44th and was the largest vaudeville theater in the world, with a seating capacity of 5,200. Its owners had recently earmarked the building for demolition to construct a 'controversial' office block in its place. Kahn's offer to purchase the site halted the intended redevelopment. In the interim, not everything went to plan. Gest invited Max Reinhardt over from Europe to view the Hippodrome and to cost up an American production of *The Miracle*. Annoyingly, the estimate came in way over budget at around $500,000, and that was before the curtain had risen.[13] Kahn rejected the quote and asked Reinhardt to submit a more reasonable estimate. Reinhardt refused, so Otto pulled the plug and sent the producer packing. He also withdrew his offer to the United States Realty Corporation to purchase the theater.

However, this would not be the last time the mighty Hippodrome would feature in the lives of the Kahn family. The following year Otto would be back at the theater for an entirely different reason.

Meanwhile, Otto's initial interest in the colossal venue encouraged the Keith-Albee Corporation (a popular movie and vaudeville theater chain) to acquire a lease on it, thus halting its demolition. Overnight, the company turned the house into a variety theater with an entertainment policy similar to that of New York's famous Palace Theatre.

Spring and Summer in Europe

Otto revisited Europe in the spring of 1923. The trip combined business and pleasure, but primarily business, to study the working operations of major continental operatic companies. In April, he returned to Berlin and attended an important meeting at the Staatsoper Unter den Linden at which several officials from the Berliner Staatsoper were present. Otto went as the Met's official representative. His family did not accompany him on this particular journey to Germany, although they had arranged to join him later in Europe.

On May 16, Roger submitted an application form to the New York City passport office for his first individual passport.[14] He had previously traveled abroad on his mother's documents on which his name appeared. Roger's passport was issued on May 21.

As summer banished spring, Addie and Roger and a small entourage of staff crossed the Atlantic to join Otto on the continent. It's fair to say the Kahn family zigzagged across the ocean as casually as some folk might catch a local streetcar and probably thought as little about the procedure as most people would do when riding a trolley car. For the Kahn family, this was just a normal part of everyday life, nothing special, only a mode of transport to get them from A to B and back again. What was important was what was waiting for them at the end of the voyage.

In France, Roger resumed his tuition at the Conservatoire de Paris. This year his New York music tutor Jacques Kasner accompanied him to Europe. Kasner was busily preparing Roger for entering university. French-born Kasner had an interesting background, having arrived in America as an economic migrant. He quickly established a career on the concert stage as an exceptionally gifted violinist, performing solo recitals at the Aeolian Hall and other important venues. He also gave private violin and music tuition and was recommended to Addie as a possible tutor for Roger. After interviewing Kasner, Addie immediately employed him. Kasner was now aged 48. Any thoughts of furthering his stage career had faded. Jacques and Roger had become firm friends and traveling companions, and it was through their teacher-pupil relationship, Roger's musical talent flourished. Kasner would, in later years, express to journalists his belief that Roger was a musical prodigy.

From France, the family traveled to Belgium, Holland, Germany, Austria, Hungary, Italy, and Switzerland before returning to France and then driving to Spain. In September, in Vienna, large crowds of Austrians gathered outside the hotel where the Kahn family were staying. All were hoping to catch a glimpse of Otto. Since his assistance during the Great War, Kahn's reputation and fame had increased throughout Europe. Every time he stepped out into the street, members of the public would besiege him, which greatly hindered his movements in the capital. He was a guest of honor at a banquet, which many prominent Austrian financiers and industrial leaders attended.[15] At the dinner, Otto gave a speech in which he praised the new head of state Monsignor Ignaz Seipel: 'The whole atmosphere of this country has been changed. On every hand, one meets with evidences of the thorough transformation that has been affected. How is this? I believe it is because you are so happy as to have a man at the head of the state who really belongs among the few great statesmen of our time.'

In Budapest, Otto met the financier Baron Leopold Popper de Podraghy at a government meeting.[16] Kahn told the Hungarian authorities that Kuhn, Loeb & Co. would not contribute to any loan to the Hungarian government unless its ministers took steps to stop the discrimination in their country against Jews.[17] By coincidence, the Baron, one of the wealthiest industrialists of the former Austro-Hungarian Empire, was married to the opera singer Maria Jeritza.

Otto also managed to finalize negotiations with Mme. Jeritza for her to sing during the next season at the Met.

By the time Roger reached his 16th birthday, he had grown into a handsome young man. Though still boyish in looks, an attribute enhanced by his thick, dark brown tousled hair, there was a noticeable air of maturity about his demeanor that far outstretched his youthful years. He was short in stature - his passport describes him as five foot four - with brown puppy dog eyes and weighed 125 lbs. He disguised his skinny physique by wearing three-piece wool suits, even indoors. His greatest passion was cinnamon buns

Like his father, Roger was hyperactive. It was this trait that helped fuel his restless spirit. Impatience appears to have been an underlying trait in both Gilbert's and Roger's DNA. The downside to Roger's lack of patience resulted in him abandoning projects just as rapidly as he had attained interest in them. Nowadays, a physician might identify such behavior as obsessive, compulsive tendencies. However, in the 1920s, the medical profession viewed such conduct differently, and more often than not, brushed it off as overactive leanings and thought nothing more of it.

Unusually, for a boy that had been surrounded from birth by an out-going, loving family, Roger was an intrinsically shy, reserved young man and, at times, a bit of a loner. This trait was possibly a throwback to his early days living as the youngest child in an impossibly busy household. Yet, irrespective of his self-effacing character, his restrained manners made him instantly likable by everyone that met him.

In Europe, Roger celebrated his birthday in style, welcoming his future with an air of expectancy.

The Kahns Return to New York

The Kahns' European jaunt lasted almost four months until the tail end of October. Putting holidays aside, the family departed from Southampton docks on October 31 aboard RMS *Olympic.*[18] Included in their party were Otto's valet Frederick Cooper, his private secretary James Dartt, and Roger's music tutor Jacques Kasner.

When Roger arrived back in New York, there was a visible change in him. The boy appeared more grown-up and more self-assured.

By the time Roger reached his 16th birthday, he had grown into a
handsome young man.

Theoretically, Roger was still a student, as he had not yet completed
his college preparatory studies. As far as his parents were concerned,
his next step in life would be to attend university. Considering
Roger's love of music and his deep interest in jazz, it should therefore
not have come as a surprise to his parents when he announced he

would like to hire a jazz band and rehearse with them at 1100 Fifth Avenue. However, this was not the case. The news came as a jolt to his mother and father, who initially strongly objected to the proposal. Once they had allowed the idea to circulate a little and breathe and given themselves time to mull it over, they came to a compromise. They would pander to their son's hobby and allow him to hire a band to rehearse with, on the understanding that this was as far as it went. They may also have consulted Roger's music tutor Jacques Kasner, who, most likely, would have approved of the arrangement. The matter was settled. To help advance Roger's musical development, Otto agreed to pay for a band of musicians to visit the Kahn house once a week over the next few months.

Roger must have been over the moon when his father announced the good news. He knew just the band he wanted to employ, the Arthur Lange Band. One assumes Roger chose the Lange aggregation because they were local (New York City-based), consisted mainly of jobbing musicians, and were reasonably priced. That said, there is possibly a more important reason why Roger went for the Lange unit - Arthur Lange's arranging skills. Lange worked as Paul Whiteman's arranger. Through Roger's attendance at the Palais Royal performing with the Whiteman orchestra, he grasped just how integral Lange's arrangements were to the Whiteman sound.

Roger led his first jazz band in the fall of 1923. The rehearsals were unusual, to say the least, for they were conducted, under strict secrecy, behind closed doors. The doors in question were the splendid double doors belonging to the magnificent Adam ballroom in the Kahns' Fifth Avenue mansion. Neither was there an audience to witness the musicians in action. Only the inner sanctum of the Kahn household and the musicians in the band were privy to the goings-on.

Why all the secrecy, you may well be thinking?

The emergence of post-war big-band jazz catered to the publics increasing vogue for dancing. White orchestras monopolized Manhattan's midtown café and hotel music scene, fronted by baton-waving maestros such as Vincent Lopez, Paul Specht, Abe Lyman, and Paul Whiteman. Their leaders were regarded as celebrities and could command substantial fees. Other units, like The California Ramblers and Arthur Lange Band, were mainly made up of session musicians, whose members would change often.

Most big hotels in New York City with a ballroom or tearoom employed an orchestra, as did every Broadway musical. The scope for jobbing musicians was immense. Some players comfortably performed three or more engagements a day before bedding in for their evening stints at Manhattan's diverse nighteries. The musicians in Arthur Lange's band were the same; professional musicians paid for playing their instruments in various locations. The Kahn gig was just another assignment. They had no reason to believe otherwise. Neither did anyone else.

It seemed only natural the musically gifted young Roger Kahn would want to be a part of this fascinating new music scene that was taking place right on his doorstep. So it wasn't that it was all done in secrecy; it was just a paid rehearsal in the musician's eyes.

Arthur Lange's twelve-piece orchestra had a residency at Cinderella Dancing, a large dance hall on Broadway and 48th that catered for up to 1,700 gyrating hips on its parquet dance floor. Lange wrote the arrangements and orchestrations for the band. Many bandleaders in New York regarded him as the city's foremost music arranger, hence his involvement with Paul Whiteman. As such, his unit was self-contained and attracted some of the best jobbing musicians available.[19] Lange played no instrument on stage, preferring only to conduct.

Lange and his musicians rehearsed with Roger one afternoon a week. The session took place after Roger had completed his studies for the day and usually lasted a couple of hours.

As such, Roger's weekday timetable ran accordingly: Breakfast at 7:30, after which he had just enough time for a brisk walk before his tutors arrived at the mansion and lessons commenced for the morning. He toiled over French, German, English, Latin, physics, history, politics, and business studies from nine until one o'clock, much like any other young student might. After lunch, Roger was free to resume his music tuition with his tutor Jacques. The arrangement suited all parties concerned.[20]

Rehearsals with the Arthur Lange Band progressed at an encouraging pace. Soon, the usually serene Kahn mansion was reverberating to the sound of hot syncopated cross-rhythms. Even the intricately plastered ceiling and mirror-paneled walls could not dampen the sound seeping from the first-floor ballroom where Caruso had previously sung and violinist Friedrich Kreisler had performed. India rubber earplugs were distributed to the house staff, lest the 'noise' should distract them from their chores. Addie also wore a pair when she was in residence if the rowdiness became too intolerable for her to endure.

The assignment was a classy gig for the Lange musicians, a little unusual but in some respects quite cushy. How could any cash-strapped musician upon entering the Kahn home have not marveled at the fine 18th century antiques, old master oil paintings, and Persian carpets that adorned the rooms! The building was, after all, in parts, a museum. What made the visits more compelling for the musicians was that the kid who organized them could play like a pro.

Roger spent weeks rehearsing with the band, developing the sound, and helping arrange the orchestral parts. He played a combination of the many instruments he was proficient in and even took the baton on occasions.

Some musicians quit due to other commitments, and new members replaced them, more competent players with a deeper understanding of jazz. Slowly, Roger built a cohesive unit of skillful musicians around him, all striving for the same goal: success.

How many months the rehearsals continued is vague; one report suggests they lasted around half a year. Any plans Roger was forming for the band, he kept close to his chest, presumably because of the opposition he knew he would encounter from his parents. Roger was also taking private lessons in harmony from the esteemed American composer and pianist Rubin Goldmark, who counted the aspiring composer George Gershwin as a pupil.[21] It could also have been around this time that Roger took composition lessons from George Gershwin.[22]

Jazz music had progressed in leaps and bounds since Paul Whiteman first became hooked on it. The term 'jazz' had now become connected to almost everything: 'magazines, movies, melodramas, comic strips in Sunday newspapers, and even politics, because they are noisy and full of vigorous rhythm,' concluded Paul Whiteman in a magazine interview.[23] 'They express our national humor. This is jazz. Why shouldn't a dance orchestra do the same thing?'

Whiteman first experimented with jazz arrangements when he formed his first dance band in San Francisco late in 1918, just after the war ended. His New York City debut took place two years later when his orchestra landed a residency at the Palais Royal. 1920 was also the year he signed an exclusive recording contract with Victor Talking Machine Company. Soon after, he scored his first million-selling hit.

The jazz arrangements the Whiteman band played were not open for improvisation. They were fixed, noted, orchestrations for capable soloists. The lack of freestyle expression in his music would, in later years, prompt some purist music critics to renounce Whiteman's influence on 'real' jazz. He was called a jazz catalyst early on in his career, which in some respects, he was. He certainly popularized jazz and made it more accessible to the masses. The symphonic arrangements he introduced to jazz resulted in the term 'symphonic jazz,' which Whiteman's orchestra was the first to develop.[24]

In December, Whiteman announced that his orchestra would perform a jazz recital, the first of its kind, in February the following year at the Aeolian Hall.[25] His reason for staging the concert was to give music lovers a real insight into present-day jazz music.

'My recital is to be purely educational. I intend to point out, with the assistance of my orchestra, the tremendous strides which have been made in our popular music from the day of the discordant jazz, which sprang into existence about ten years ago, from nowhere in particular, to the melodious music of today, which - for no good reason - is still called jazz.'[26]

It was a bold move for the music maestro.

'I am convinced that most people who ridicule the present so-called 'jazz' and refuse to condone it or listen to it seriously are quarreling with the name 'jazz' and not with what it represents. Neither my protest nor the combined protests of all musicians will change the name. Jazz it is, and jazz it will remain. If I am successful in breaking down only a small portion of the antagonism toward jazz, which is so prevalent among lovers of music, oratorio, and symphony,' asserted Whiteman, 'I will feel amply repaid for my efforts, and so will my associates.'

Whiteman revealed he had commissioned the composer Victor Herbert to write an American suite for the recital and that Irving Berlin and George Gershwin were contributing original works.

It turned out, Whiteman had approached Otto Kahn to help stage the concert. The two held an informal meeting earlier that summer in Europe, most probably in Paris, to discuss it. Kahn had been supportive and offered his assistance and suggested they go ahead with the proposal this coming winter.[27] February 12 was the agreed date. Whiteman also disclosed that Kahn's son Roger, whom he called 'an ardent saxophone enthusiast,' may also be featured on the program. The bandleader failed to mention that Otto would be one of the principal financial backers of the concert.* That news would be announced later in a few weeks.[28]

~

December in Manhattan

Roger had already been actively searching for talented musicians in Manhattan to rehearse with long before he announced to his father that he wanted to hire a band. In the evenings, when his parents were attending social functions, he would slip out of the house and visit bars and hotel ballrooms where he snuck in, usually unobserved, to listen to the house bands that were playing. It was during these excursions that he hatched the idea of forming a band.

'I don't know when I started in music,' Roger would later confess to journalists.[29] 'Ever since I can remember, I loved it. There was something in me that made music.'

After studying to master the symphonic drums for two years, Roger discovered the joys of the saxophone when he came across the instrument in Ditson music store. In learning to play it, he began to realize its possibilities. Since taking up the sax, Roger had become proficient in playing the clarinet, flute, piccolo, and trumpet. 'For a long time, I was an outsider, an amateur. I happened to be the son of a rich man, which is a good thing or not, according to the way one uses or abuses it. The real musical fellows probably thought my music was just the fad of a rich man's kid. I didn't know how to get acquainted with them. I used to slip away, so no one would know who I was, and try to get acquainted.' Finally, his tenacity paid off; musicians began to take him seriously. 'Probably it was the saxophone that gave me the entrée to the best jazz circles.' Those same musicians imbued confidence in him and encouraged him to put his next plan into action, to form a jazz orchestra.

Over the coming festive season, the Arthur Lange Band continued to play their lucrative bookings, which this year included a two-week stint at the Mark Strand Theatre as a pit band, in addition to their residency at Cinderella Dancing.

The Mark Strand was New York's first house specifically designed to show movies. It seated almost 3,000 people and had the most luxuriously decorated interior many of its customers had ever seen. The press likened it to a palace when it opened, hence the phrase 'picture palace.'

Lange and his band were surprised by the reception and the big salary they earned at the Strand. So much so that Lange seriously considered going on an American road tour playing only picture houses, a move he had previously shied away from because his musicians were not under contract.[30] Lange even went as far as to hand in his notice at Cinderella Dancing.*

Lange's sudden change in direction came as a shock to Roger and unsettled him. It also made his arrangement with Lange and his band untenable. If Roger wanted to continue hiring Lange and his musicians' services, he would need to act speedily.

Roger came up with a plan. Quietly, without telling his parents, he began hiring musicians for his orchestra and, rather shrewdly, put them under contract. Using his savings, he paid the musicians well, and in return, the musicians continued to turn up punctually for rehearsals at the mansion. Roger then waited for the storm to break, as break, it surely would.

In the meantime, December brought many welcome distractions to the Kahn home. As customary, the house became a hub of activity over the festive season, with numerous parties committed to the calendar.

Gilbert returned home from Princeton and was just as keen as his brother to forget all about schooling. Gilbert had endured the endless cycle of traditions and pranks bestowed upon first-year students and had now settled into a routine of intensive study. But even he was experiencing a niggling sense of uncertainty about his future.

Otto's brother Felix was in town. On December 21, the pair attended the gala world premiere of Cecil B. DeMille's epic new silent movie, *The Ten Commandments*.[31] Felix was a director of Paramount Pictures Corporation that was distributing the picture and Otto was a stockholder. The George M. Cohan Theatre in Times Square was hosting the event. It was one helluva night; roped barriers, newsreel cameras, and thousands of movie fans blocking the street hoping to catch a glimpse of their favorite celebrities. Spectators were not disappointed: Gloria Swanson, William Randolph Hearst, Ricardo Cortez, and many more VIPs received rousing cheers as they made their entrance on the red carpet. Inside the theater, the audience was spellbound for three hours, howling and applauding wildly as one dramatic scene segued into another. At the finish, viewers clapped incessantly for over five minutes.

While the elder Kahns were out on the town partying, so too were their offspring, although, for Roger and Gilbert, their excursions involved catching the hottest jazz band in the hippest bar they could blag an entrance to.

7

A SONG WITH NO KEY SIGNATURE

'Jazz is America's contribution to music. It is the artistic expression of American exuberance.'[1] Otto H. Kahn, March 27, 1924 *

1924

'What's the matter with Jazz?' asked *Étude* magazine in their January 1924 edition.[2] 'First, jazz, at its worst, is an unforgivable orgy of noise, a riot of discord, usually perpetrated by players of scant musical training who believe that their random whoops, blasts, crashes and aboriginal tom-toming is something akin to genius,' exploded the attention-grabbing first paragraph. The description could well have been how a certain fraction of society viewed jazz. That said, in the third paragraph, the writer softens his approach to readdress the equilibrium by airing some of the finer qualities of jazz: 'in the music itself there is often much that is charming and genuinely fascinating when written and played effectively.' Though hardly revelatory, this statement could easily be said of any music genre, whether hillbilly, ragtime, classical, or blues.

Indeed, what the writer aimed to put across was just how divided public opinion was towards jazz. The publicity jazz generated in newspaper column inches was phenomenal. Everybody appeared to hold a viewpoint, whether good, bad, or indifferent, and that factor, to some extent, helped push jazz into a different musical stratosphere. Jazz was now a dominant musical force to be reckoned with, and its development would continue to evolve just as erratically as it had advanced over the past few years.

Paul Whiteman was, by some margin, the most successful jazz bandleader of the day. He could command $10,000 a performance and was a tremendously influential figure in helping the growth of jazz and aiding its exposure. He never claimed to play Chicago's Black improvisational jazz; his style was a refined, polished crossover and blended elements of jazz and classical music within scored dance arrangements. Whiteman's forthcoming concert, *An Experiment in Modern Music,* was timed perfectly to tap into the public's riven opinion towards jazz. It would celebrate jazz's 'progress' from its backstreet bar origins to the now mighty concert hall.

No sooner had jazz arrived than it rapidly began to evolve into countless breakaway genres. Symphonic jazz was one such variant. As the name implies, it was jazz music arranged specifically for a symphonic orchestra. The sound was bold, exciting, and wholly modern. It questioned the public's perception of jazz. Some critics called it the white man's interpretation of Black jazz. The French labeled it *musique légère* (light music). It was Paul Whiteman that brought symphonic jazz to the forefront.

Whiteman and his orchestra had already successfully taken symphonic jazz into dance halls and theaters throughout the United States and across the Atlantic to the UK. More recently, he had brought it into millions of ordinary American homes via wireless. His recordings were also hugely popular. Like many other musicians and composers of the era, Whiteman was now keen to experiment further with jazz to see where it would lead.

It was symphonic jazz that greatly interested Roger more than any other interpretation, and it was to Paul Whiteman that Roger looked for inspiration. In Roger's mind, Whiteman embodied everything he aspired to accomplish.

American Symphonic Syncopation

Though Black jazz and white commercial jazz had sprung from the same origins, their paths had organically divided and were rapidly growing further apart. Symphonic jazz was one of the more apparent strains of that evolution. French modernist composer Darius Milhaud became aware of this juxtaposition after visiting America in 1922. He observed firsthand the jazz music played in Harlem and its counterpart played downtown in Mid-Manhattan. Milhaud heard Paul Whiteman's orchestra perform at the Palais Royal and commented on how slick and well managed the band was and how they played directly into the mass production market catering to the record-buying American public. He positively believed the music he heard in Harlem was what he termed 'authentic' jazz. He felt Paul Whiteman's music was arranged symphonic jazz with a high level of musicality, where nothing was spontaneous, and everything was measured. Milhaud believed Black jazz had evolved separately, alongside its white equivalent, because of the different cultural influences and forces it picked up along the way. He argued that this vein of jazz was less constrained and still in touch with its primitive African roots.

The drama critic Paul Nivoix in an article he wrote back in October 1923 for the French journal *Comœdia*, explained his belief that symphonic jazz was neither classical nor jazz and that it was Americanized music composed and performed purely for commercial gain. He praised Otto Kahn's efforts in helping bring forth the 'renewal' of jazz music:[3]

'The jazz band is king. Be it at dances, the cabarets, and even in the houses of the good bourgeoisie - to speak truthfully, we are starting to tire of it. Reassure yourself; the jazz band is going to renew itself. Here, on this subject, is the latest news that comes to us from America: The jazz band is in full reform. Otto [H.] Kahn's millions - or at least a part of them - are going to push the movement. If everything goes well, the ordinary jazz band will be replaced by American symphonic syncopation.'

'Roger Wolfe Kahn, the youngest son of the famous banker ... has invented this new name. He has promised to devote his life to the glory of the saxophone and all its ersatz substitutes.'[4]

What Roger had done was to take the basic concept of symphonic jazz and developed the idea further. He did this by writing syncopated arrangements of popular classical pieces and would test them out during his rehearsals with Lange and his band. One such work, which he adapted into a rhythmic dance tune, was the cavalry charge theme from Rossini's *William Tell Overture*. He also arranged *Méditation* from the opera *Thaïs* into a foxtrot.

'The theme of the *Méditation* is played on the violin by a young laureate of the Vienna Conservatoire, while the banjos and saxophones rage on. The result is unique,' exclaimed Nivoix, sounding more alarmed than pleased by the effect. Undoubtedly, Nivoix was no fan of symphonic jazz. It attacked his sensibilities, and in his opinion, spelled doom for authentic jazz.

The Miracle

Almost ten years after Otto had initially attempted to present Karl Vollmöller's religious play *The Miracle* to New York audiences, it finally opened at the Century Theatre on January 16, 1924.*

With a cast of 700, it was a miracle it opened, considering the dramas, financial costs, and setbacks the production and its team endured in staging it. Morris Gest's spectacular presentation received a multitude of praise and denouncement in equal measures. *Brooklyn Life* magazine called it 'the most notable spectacle the theater has ever known in the history of the world,' a powerful statement for a powerful production.[5] Most critics hailed it as a delight for the eye and the mind, but many religious organizations and sects thought it scandalous. Anti-Catholics denounced the play as 'Catholic propaganda' and circulated leaflets saying as much and threatened legal redress. In one such pamphlet, distributed outside the Century Theatre, the producer Morris Gest, financier Otto Kahn, director Max Reinhardt, and even the composer Engelbert Humperdinck (a Lutheran) - who wrote the music for the production but had since died - came in for a bashing:[6]

'Max Reinhardt, the Austrian Jew, Morris Gest, the Russian Jew, Otto Kahn, the German Jew, these three alien Judas Iscariot tools for Jesuitical propaganda will never be permitted to build their theater in New York City in which to continue their subtle work of luring Protestant American manhood into their alien Roman Catholic activities - a work evident throughout the recent stage production of *The Miracle* at the Century Theatre.'

In a prodigal move to keep the show 'exclusive' and 'sold right out,' Gest reduced the theater's seating capacity, making it even more difficult for the public to purchase a ticket.

The Miracle ran until November, playing 298 performances, more than any other production staged in seventeen European capitals. The original financial investment Kahn and Clarence Mackay forked out to stage the production was $600,000.[7] Within ten months, it had taken $2 million at the box office. The interest payments Kahn and Mackay received by the end of its run reached over $600,000 each.[8]

Otto took great pleasure in inviting talented new performers into his home. On January 20, the tenor Roland Hayes performed a special recital in the ballroom at the Kahns Fifth Avenue mansion.[9] It was the first private concert Hayes had given in New York City. The singer had only recently completed his first headlining American concert tour, during which he performed at the prestigious Carnegie Hall. Hayes received an impressive $1,000 check from Otto for his performance.

February blew in an unprecedented wind of change in the Kahn household. During the next few weeks, the whole dynamic within the Kahn family shifted from the old guard to the new.

Victor Recording Studios–February 4

Word of Roger's musical goings-on came to the attention of the bosses at Victor Talking Machine Company. Eager to hear what this youngster had to offer, they invited him into Victor's recording studio to lay down a couple of tracks. On Monday, February 4, after his studies, Roger and ten hired musicians headed across town to New Jersey. Victor studios made test recordings of '*What Do You Do Sunday, Mary?*' and '*You.*'* They recorded one take of each number. It's interesting to note, the artist's name written on Victor's ledger alongside the two tracks is Roger Wolfe and Orchestra, without a hint of the Kahn name. The band's line-up contained two saxophones, two cornets, a trombone, banjo, violin, drums (traps), piano, and a tuba. For the present, Victor did not offer the teenager a recording contract. However, they now had a clearer indication of the young prodigy's capabilities and commercial potential.

Roger's Stage Debut Announced–February 7

Three days later, in a front-page scoop in *Variety*, Mina Schall (a former burlesque performer turned budding journalist) in her report, *Rich Catch*, gleefully announced to the world in bold headlines: 'OTTO KAHN'S SON, ROGER, IN VAUDEVILLE WITH JAZZ BAND.'[10] The revelation that an adolescent son of one of the richest men in America was to launch himself on the unsuspecting public as a jazz musician, thereby turning his back on the groves of academe, came as a complete surprise to most everyone, including Roger's parents. When the news broke, New York society was rife with gossip about the Kahn kid.

In an instance, the article annihilated the years of careful PR management the elder Kahns had manipulated to keep any whiff of scandal regarding the family or its name out of the newspapers.

Following on, Schall purrs: 'Defaulting as conductor of orchestra - Rehearsing in Kahn's Fifth Avenue home - Band will be billed as Roger Wolfe's Orchestra' - altering the spelling of Wolff to Wolfe. Schall did not divulge how she came about this maelstrom of furtive information. No doubt, her source was close to the Kahn camp. As one might imagine, its immediate impact rose more than a few eyebrows over at the Met, as well as inside the Kahn household.

In the main body of her article Schall then discloses at a furious pace all the meaty gossip:

'Roger Wolfe Kahn, the son of Otto H. Kahn, financier and patron of the arts, will shortly debut in vaudeville as conductor of a jazz orchestra that will have as its guiding spirit the services of Arthur Lange, one of the leading arrangers in the country. The band will be known as Roger Wolfe's Orchestra, with his surname omitted for professional reasons. It has been rehearsing at the Kahns' Fifth Avenue mansion... The band has booked a flurry of ultra-social dates it being in the nature of a lark for the scion of the Kahn house.'

After her initial bombshell, Schall continues by discharging some hard-hitting shrapnel:

'The youngster has been an ardent addict of the saxophone. It was Paul Whiteman's original intention to introduce the lad at his forthcoming concert [on] February 12 to illustrate what effect jazz music has had on the younger American element. Otto Kahn incidentally is one of the patrons of the Whiteman concert. Tommy Gott, the 'hot' trumpeter of the band, will be the business manager of the new orchestra, which will have the same personnel as that of the original Arthur Lange band.'

The cat was out of the bag. Roger's reaction to the exposé is unstated, but judging from his subsequent actions, he remained focused and resolute, irrespective of the grief his parents dealt him. On the positive side, as any PR agent would have a client believe, any publicity is good publicity, especially if it's free. The monetary value of a scoop on the front page of *Variety* was incalculable. The following day, three major dailies featured the story on their front pages, and

countless others printed it inside. Overnight, Roger became the talk
of the city without ever having stepped a foot on stage.

Back at 1100 Fifth Avenue, Otto and Addie hit the roof. After reading
the article, they ordered Roger into the library where, behind closed
doors, they subjected him to an interrogation of the 'nth degree. To
begin with, he had not consulted them over his intentions. Secondly,
he was jeopardizing his future career as an engineer. Thirdly, he was
not in a financial position to fund such a venture, and, lastly, the
reputation of the family's good name was at stake. What happened
next resulted in several conflicting reports. One journalist [in later
years] attempted to recount the dialog that might have occurred
during the heated ticking-off, though how faithful the account is, is
questionable.[11]

'Otto Kahn was fingering a newspaper. 'Kahn's Son Jazz Leader,'
said the headline over the piece.

'You'll have to give this up,' announced Otto Kahn.

'No,' said Roger.

'How are you going to pay your men?'

'I've been wondering,' conceded Roger.

'All right,' said Otto Kahn, evidently confident of the outcome of his
son's venture. *'I'll give you the money to cover two weeks' salaries.
After that, you're on your own.'*

If only the altercation had been that civil. In reality, it turned out to
be otherwise. Roger may have been his mother's favorite child, but
even she was 100 percent behind her husband on this one. In no
uncertain words, they banned Roger from performing on a public
stage with his band. They also forbade him from using the family
surname in connection with any of the band's activities.[12] As far as
Otto and Addie were concerned, the matter was settled there and
then and wished to hear no more about it.

Roger returned to his fourth-floor suite, where he remained nursing
his wounded pride for most of the day. The wrath of his parents came
as a massive blow to him, considering how much time and effort he
had spent over the past few months rehearsing with Lange's band,
preparing for his public debut.

Roger's quiet withdrawal from Paul Whiteman's upcoming concert
at the Aeolian Hall also became a topic for speculation, bearing in
mind Otto was one of the show's main financial backers and one of
George Gershwin's principal patrons. Was this Roger's punishment
for disobeying his parents? In all probability, Roger's parents had the
final say on the matter.

In The Nature of a Lark–February 8

Otto and Addie were still dealing with the fallout from the public unveiling of their youngest son's unruly activities when another bone-shattering spoiler appeared in print the following day. This new disclosure published in the *New York Clipper* came under the tantalizing heading: 'Otto H. Kahn's Two Sons Broadway Jazz Musicians.'[13] The header then revealed, 'Roger Wolfe Kahn Preparing Vaudeville Act - Gilbert Kahn, Princeton Student Also Playing Intermittently with California Ramblers as Lark,' before finally adding, 'Kahn Sr., Vexed?'

Though the scoop had an element of truth to it, the reporter shaded the facts to fit the paper's angle, that being of two renegade sons of a wealthy banking family turning their backs on their parents.

The reporting also slipped up in places; it referred to Roger as the elder son and Gilbert as the younger. With some of the facts cherry-picked verbatim from Mina Schall's scoop in *Variety*, curiously, the *New York Clipper* also appeared to have had their own informant.

'Roger Kahn is an accomplished saxophonist,' expressed the *Clipper*, laying no doubt as to the fact that this admission had come from someone who had heard the boy play. Regarding Gilbert's musical aspirations, the reporter specifies, 'Gilbert Kahn is not known to have any professional hankerings at present, but he also is an accomplished jazz musician. As a Princeton student, he finds time on every trip to New York to rehearse and play with the California Ramblers. Arthur Hand, the leader, is a friend of his, and young Kahn may be seen almost every weekend at the Broadway cabaret. In addition to playing the saxophone, he can strum a banjo with the best of them.' The Broadway cabaret mentioned was the Monte Carlo Restaurant beneath the Roseland Ballroom on 51st.

The article concludes by noting their father's purported views on the topic. 'What the older Kahn thinks of these jazz leanings on the part of his offspring is not known, but it is rumored he does not regard them so highly, particularly when the commercial angle enters.'

All was not rosy in the Kahn camp. Otto was not happy, neither was Addie, and Roger most definitely was not pleased. Gilbert was at Princeton and had yet to show his allegiance to his brother. In an unexpected twist, another side to the story would soon come to light.

~

Otto and Addie Attend an Art Dinner–February 10

In the meantime, to help quell the gossip and show a united front, Otto and Addie did as they always did in trying situations; they put on their glad rags and a brave face and had a night out on the town. On Thursday evening, two days before Whiteman's mammoth concert at the Aeolian Hall, Otto and Addie attended a dinner marking the fifth annual exhibition of The New Society of Artists.[14] The function was held in the main exhibition room of the Anderson Galleries, on Park Avenue and 59th Street. Many notables in the art world attended, including interior designer Elsie de Wolfe, art collector Mrs. Vincent Astor, photographer Arnold Genthe, gallery owner Frederick G. Keppel and attorney Paul D. Cravath. During the evening, there was much talk about Paul Whiteman's upcoming concert, at which many of the dinner guests would be attending.

To say there was a buzz in the air about the Whiteman concert would be an understatement. Tickets sold out as soon as they were released. Besides the antics of the Kahn brothers, newspapers had talked about little else during the past week. Understandably, the pressure on everyone involved in the project was immense, especially for one composer who had more riding on this concert than anyone. That person was George Gershwin.

An Experiment in Modern Music–February 12

Whiteman commissioned George Gershwin to write a piece for piano and orchestra. Gershwin wrote *Rhapsody in Blue* in a matter of weeks. During the afternoon of February 12, chosen to mark Abraham Lincoln's birthday, Gershwin premiered the work at the Aeolian Hall.

The hall was shaped like an elongated barn, adorned with a narrow mezzanine balcony. It was an odd building, dark and airless (it had no ventilation system). Organ pipes lined the back wall of the stage. Even the hard, wooden, foldup seats were uncomfortable to sit on. By no stretch of the imagination was it the ideal venue for a long, drawn-out performance. Nonetheless, most critics greeted the concert with enthusiasm.

Whiteman had the stage decorated with oriental embroidered silk screens and exotic-looking potted palms to brighten the place up. His orchestra was spread across the stage on three tiers, with Gershwin's black concert grand singled out on the left. Also included in the program were new pieces by Irving Berlin and Victor Herbert.

Many esteemed classical musicians, including Leopold Stokowski, Sergei Rachmaninoff, Fritz Kreisler, Jascha Heifetz, and John Philip Sousa, were in the audience.* Broadway stars fraternized with classicists, the converted rubbed shoulders with skeptics, for there appeared to be no division in their curiosity.

Otto cleared his diary for the afternoon to attend, as most probably did his impressionable younger son Roger, who would have cornered himself a ticket at all costs.

Backstage before the concert began, Gershwin was said to have felt extremely nervous. On stage, his performance was electrifying and emotionally charged. By the fifth and final theme of *Rhapsody in Blue*, Gershwin was euphoric. Whiteman later said he was surprised to realize tears were trickling down his cheeks during the central theme.

Rhapsody in Blue was the most impressive individual highlight of the presentation. 'It was a lengthy number, but its intricate arrangement of the clever rhythm made a deep impression. To the learned musical critics, it was the outstanding subject of discussion, and in the line of symphonic jazz music, it presents a toothsome morsel for thought.'[15]

After his performance, Gershwin was presented with a silver cigarette case as a special memento from Otto Kahn, Irving Caesar, Paul Whiteman, Irving Berlin, and various other friends (totaling thirty) to commemorate the occasion.[16] Whiteman claimed the concert was purely an educational experiment; after the event, no one could deny a jazz milestone had taken place.[17]

Nonetheless, the concert drew divided opinions.

One critic described it as 'a highly ingenious work of sweeping brilliance.' Another felt it was full of unexpected tonal contortions and musical somersaults that kept the listener on the edge of their seat.

Otto Not Displeased With His Son–February 15

Three days after Whiteman's historic Aeolian Hall concert, an extraordinary report appeared in the *New York Clipper*, stating Otto was not in the least bit displeased with his son Roger or his son's hankering for a career as a jazz musician.[18] Neither was he vexed about his son's activities, as had been widely reported in the media over the past few days. On the contrary, Otto was helping to steer and advise his talented teenage son by putting at his son's disposal a thesaurus of professional connections and business expertise. Otto was also keen for his son to include several classically trained musicians in his band's line-up selected from the finest symphony orchestras in the country. The monetary value of which he professes no vaudeville circuit or cabaret club could contemplate paying. Otto also wished the media to know that his son's band would be known as Roger Wolfe's Orchestra, with the Kahn dropped from the title for professional purposes. The orchestra was rehearsing regularly at the Kahns' Fifth Avenue townhouse under Otto's guidance and with his full knowledge and approval. Otto was also eager to announce that negotiations were already underway for the orchestra to perform a limited run on Broadway at Keith's Palace Theatre.

What brought about Otto's sudden change of attitude is not made clear in the article, but one only has to read between the lines to realize something did not add up. Was this swift turnaround a direct result of Whiteman's hugely successful concert, or was it the machinations of Otto's inventive PR guru Ivy Lee at work? For whatever reason Otto issued this statement, it was more likely an exercise in unifying the Kahn brand for the sake of their public image. In truth, the original leak to the press disclosing Roger's musical activities had put the elder Kahns in an embarrassing position. Their disapproval of Roger's craving to be a professional jazz musician appeared totally at odds with their philanthropic work and artistic patronage.

As if to clear the air, Otto journeyed south to Palm Beach to grab a change of surroundings.*

The 'flurry of ultrasocial dates' Mina Schall referred to in her *Variety* exclusive that Roger and his band would shortly be undertaking had yet to be announced. In the meantime, had Mina delved a little deeper, she might have discovered that Roger was about to make his live debut performing at a private social function. Mrs. Horatio Nelson Slater, a wealthy Fifth Avenue neighbor of the Kahns, known to her friends by her first name Mabel, was the host. The dinner for sixty guests took place on February 18. Addie was a guest. For the occasion, Roger played the violin.[19] Guests of honor at the soirée were Prince and Princess Alfred of Hohenlohe.[20]

Mabel inherited a textile manufacturing fortune (estimated to be worth more than $20 million). The estate came from her husband, Horatio Nelson Slater, who passed away in 1899 - leaving her with four young children to raise. She was a great friend of Addie Kahn.

Mabel and Addie sat on the lecture committee of the advisory council of the Schola Cantorum. They occasionally hosted charity recitals on behalf of the singing school at their respective homes. Mabel lived primarily at her country estate in Bar Harbor, Maine. During the winter season, she occupied her luxurious Manhattan apartment at 907 Fifth Avenue overlooking Central Park.[21]

Mabel had an unusual pastime; she was a prolific amateur inventor and had amassed a personal fortune from the royalties she received from some of her creations. In 1904 she patented a refrigerator (ice cooler) and held patents relating to various other gadgets, including movable eyes in dolls, atomizers, and a military blanket.[22] Through Roger's fascination with engineering, he forged a friendship with Mabel. It is possible the 'old lady' Roger referrers to in the article published in the May 1923 edition of *The Wireless Age* was, in fact, Mabel.*

Here's the rub: Journalist Mildred Hardenbergh came up with a theory explaining why she believed Otto and Addie had arrived at the predicament they now found themselves in regarding Roger's musical aspirations. She offered her version in an article titled: 'And The Daddy of Opera Raised a Jazz Baby Boy - Surprising Situation of Rich Mr. Kahn.'[23] 'Everybody said that Papa Kahn did not wish his son to play in public. But when his orchestra was to play at the Fifth Avenue home of Mrs. H. N. Slater at a dinner she was giving in honor of the Prince and Princess Alfred Hohenlohe where Roger would play the violin solo, Mama Kahn stated she could see no objections to her son accepting an invitation to play at a friend's home!'

Whatever messages Otto and Addie were sending out to their son and everybody else around them, their bulletins were becoming increasingly more muddled by the day. The day following the dinner, Addie traveled to Palm Beach to join her husband at their villa.

In a surprise development, immediately after playing at Mabel's party, Roger and his band was offered their first public gig. The venue was the Knickerbocker Grill. The gig was still a secret. Roger had not announced it to the press, and neither did his parents know. As they were currently in Palm Beach, Roger decided not to tell them.

The Knickerbocker Grill–February 26

The Arthur Lange Band had now left their residency at Cinderella Dancing. In its place, they had taken a temporary slot at the Lomax

Club in the Romax Building at 47th Street West, off-Broadway.[24] Lange was receiving $1,800 weekly for the gig.

To secure Lange and his musicians, Roger arranged with Lange to take over his band starting February 26. The deal guaranteed Lange the full $1,800 weekly fee the band presently commanded at the Lomax Club. Roger did this behind his parent's back. Roger had certain addendums inserted in the contract. The most specific was that the band would go under the name of the Roger Wolfe Orchestra. Lange would remain as musical director. In addition, Roger would play an assortment of instruments as and when he chose.[25] To keep things above board, Roger formed a corporation through which legal matters involving his musical activities would be carried out and documents signed.

Roger had already secured the band's first paid engagement through his corporation at the Knickerbocker Grill for one week from Tuesday, February 26. Meanwhile, the Lange band continued playing at the Lomax up until the week ending Sunday, February 24.[26]

On Tuesday, February 26, an advertisement appeared in the *Sun and the Globe* newspaper announcing the Roger Wolfe Orchestra premiere that evening at the Knickerbocker Grill.[27]

When Otto was told about the advert in the paper, he called Roger for an explanation. That Roger dared to defy his parents was one thing, but to do it so publicly was too much for Otto and Addie to stomach. In their view, Roger had overstepped the mark. It was time for them to curb his wayward behavior.

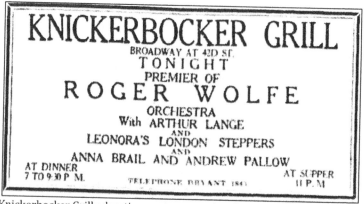

Knickerbocker Grill advertisement announcing the Roger Wolfe Orchestra premiere, *The Sun and the Globe*, Tuesday, February 26, 1924.

The Knickerbocker Grill hugged the southeast corner of Broadway and West 42nd Street, just a few steps away from Times Square and the theater district. The restaurant was formerly part of John Jacob Astor IV's elegant Hotel Knickerbocker. The hotel initially catered for the 'rich and smart set' during a time of prosperity. It quickly became a place to see and be seen in.[28] Astor's son Vincent inherited the hotel in 1912 after John Jacob and his wife died on the *Titanic*. Following Prohibition and the downturn in the economy, the business went into a steady decline. In 1920, the hotel closed its doors for good, but the Grill remained open as a going concern, serving Chinese and American cuisine, and was still a regular haunt for the bright young set. It was the perfect venue for Roger to launch his band.

In preparation for that evening, the management had positioned tables and chairs around the dance floor in a horseshoe arrangement. The stage was a raised wooden platform facing the dancers. The setting afforded everyone a comfortable view and ample room for dancing. The famous 'Knick' bar - where an early version of the dry martini cocktail was concocted in 1912 - ran the entire width of one wall and always attracted a busy pre-theater crowd.

The Knickerbocker Grill, Chinese and American restaurant.

Late that afternoon, as the band was setting up their instruments on the stage in readiness for a soundcheck, some unexpected visitors arrived in the lobby: Otto, accompanied by a Musicians Union official and a representative from the American Federation of Labor. Roger's father had traveled up from Palm Beach, especially to confront his son.

Otto's explosive arrival in the restaurant brought the soundcheck to an abrupt halt. Kahn Sr. was in no mood for compromise or teenage shenanigans and immediately challenged his son. A robust exchange of words followed, the gist of which saw Otto ban Roger from appearing on stage with his band. Next, the American Federation of Labor representative stepped forward. He informed Roger that as he was not a member of the American Federation of Musicians, he would not be permitted to perform in public without first obtaining a Musician's Union membership card. As for the present, he advised Roger to sit this one out and watch from the sidelines as his band performed.

Roger was livid. So too was Otto.

Kahn Sr. promptly left the building with his two officials in tow, leaving Roger behind to pick up the pieces. Not only did the youngster feel humiliated and belittled in front of his twelve musicians, but it also left him in a difficult predicament. The management had contracted the band on the understanding that Roger would appear on stage with them.

Roger was well aware of his parent's apprehensions over his musical aspirations. He also realized he would require their full support if he were to make a go of it. What he had not anticipated was just how far they would go to prevent him from achieving his aims.

Otto's demands were not unreasonable; only in Roger's eyes, he deemed them unfair. Oddly, it was the Kahn family history repeating itself. Like Otto, Roger was the fourth child, and like his father, Roger was also a gifted musician. The pattern could not have escaped Otto's thoughts. Roger was now practically the same age Otto had been back in Mannheim when his father denied him the opportunity to follow a music career. If Otto were to deny his son the chance to express his artistic leanings, he'd be casting a dye for deep resentment further down the line.

Although Roger disagreed with his father, he did respect his father's decision.[29] For the moment, Roger was grounded; his debut was unceremoniously put on hold.

The Roger Wolfe Orchestra went ahead as planned and performed that evening at the Knickerbocker Grill. Upsettingly, for Roger, he was not among their ranks. The restaurant sold out, with standing room only at the bar; requests for reservations far outstretched their capacity. The band tore through their setlist, one number after another, until diners could no longer remain seated. The dance floor soon filled with gyrating couples, all intent on having a good time. What was so striking about the band was their professionalism. Somewhat unjustly, relegated to the sidelines, was the youngster that brought it all together. From his table, Roger pounded out the rhythms with his cutlery, played solos on his imaginary saxophone, and kicked his heels hard on the floor as his band played a killer set. The bandsmen received rapturous applause at the end of each number, the resonance overflowing into the following day's rave newspaper reviews. By a curious twist of fate, the imposing of a ban on Roger had a countereffect; it brought the press sniffing for a story and served only to strengthen Roger's resolve to pursue his dream.

The 'Knick' did such profitable business that week the management extended the band's engagement.[30] Each night the band performed, Roger listened attentively, egging his musicians on, dishing out encouragement, howling enthusiastic 'yelps,' releasing his teenage inhibitions. After the show, he'd return home elated and head straight to his fourth-floor suite where he'd work late into the night writing new song arrangements.

Of course, Otto and Addie read the newspaper reviews saying how terrific the Roger Wolfe Orchestra was, and of course, they heard fantastic feedback from their daughter Margaret and her circle of friends who had been to see the band. They would also have heard how disheartened their son was, and how could they be so disapproving of him when all the young lad wanted was to be a musician? Of course, it broke their hearts as much as it broke Roger's, but, for the present, neither side would step down.

Otto and Addie would also have been aware of the tension in the house. No doubt, the servants kept them in the picture with accounts of Roger's behavior and his comings and goings. But, regardless of all these factors and all the chiastic patterns of custom and tradition, for the time being, no matter whose side you were on, it seemed as if everyone was looking for the boy.

Relief for Roger came at the weekends when Gilbert returned home from Princeton. The two brothers went everywhere together. Roger would follow Gilbert to the Monte Carlo Restaurant, where Gilbert played his saxophone and banjo with the California Ramblers. Gilbert accompanied Roger to the 'Knick' to watch his brother's orchestra perform. Each held the other in high esteem, and their mutual respect bound the brothers together.

To help further his music career, Roger applied to the local branch

(802) of the American Federation of Musicians for membership. He sat an entrance exam in front of a board of five examiners. He chose to play the saxophone and drums for his practical appraisal to demonstrate his musicianship.[31] Roger passed the exam with a commendation and paid his $50 admission fee. He now had permission to play live anyplace in New York.[32] With his Musicians Union card taking pride of place in his wallet Roger took to his next task, to convince his parents to lift their ban on him playing in public.

The news that Roger had joined the union appeared in the papers. When a journalist asked Otto for his views on his son's music activities, Otto's response was somewhat dismissive.

He later issued a statement, insisting, 'I do not turn up my nose at that form of music, notwithstanding crudities and imperfections. On the contrary, I see in it the inauguration of a genuinely and distinctively American way of musical expression, which even in its present initial stage has produced some interesting and noteworthy results and which gives every promise of leading to serious and essentially American artistic achievement in due course of time.'[33] Otto ended with the advice that every young man should develop his natural talents.

Publicity and Public Display's–February 29

Wherever the Kahn brothers went, the press were not far behind. Dodging reporters had now become a pastime and led to yet further complications. In a joke publicity stunt, a photographer captured Gilbert on stage alongside music cohort Arthur Hand - violinist and leader of the California Ramblers. The picture appeared in several newspapers, creating more ripples of disapproval from the Kahn elders. More surprising was the revelation in *The New York Clipper* on February 29, purportedly based on inside gossip, claiming Roger was contemplating severing connections with Arthur Lange's unit.[34]

Whether Roger or Lange was keen to initiate the parting, the report did not stipulate. Nevertheless, regarding the band, it did infer that Lange would 'doubtlessly secure its return from the Kahn name.'

Following the picture in the newspapers of Gilbert on stage with the California Ramblers, Otto and Addie hit the panic button and pulled the drawbridge up. Gilbert had gone too far. Back at the Kahn mansion, Otto ordered the immediate family into the library for crisis talks. Otto and Addie were more than willing to foster their son's musical ambitions, just as long as those artistic desires revolved around classical music and symphony orchestras. Why jazz, they decried, and why did everybody make so much fuss about it? And, why did the New York sheets have to run a column every time their two sons tuned an instrument? These were all matters neither Otto nor Addie could fathom out.

Gilbert was fast approaching his 21st birthday and had matured into a strong-minded, determined young man. When Otto questioned Gilbert over his leisure time activities, Gilbert fought his corner, unrepentant, and saw no reason to apologize for partaking in an activity his father proudly endorsed through his philanthropy. Sharp exchanges followed. Otto reiterated by stipulating every person residing under his roof abided by his rules.

Gilbert was unapologetic for his behavior and stormed out of the house. He went missing for an entire week, causing considerable anxiety in the Kahn household. This time Otto's strict demands had gone too far. Gilbert returned home in his own time when things had calmed down a little. When all was said and done, he was only sticking up for himself and his younger brother. Things changed after this episode, slowly but noticeably. The boys were, in time, given more freedom than they had experienced before and the liberty to make their own mistakes.

Roger's Plan

Roger hated being at loggerheads with his parents. To help diffuse the situation, he calmly approached them with a working plan. Firstly, he questioned why being a rich man's son should jeopardize his choice of career. Then, he asked his father for a financial loan to help pay the musicians in his band. He vowed he would pay back every dollar he borrowed once he had achieved commercial success. He then announced he would be putting his college studies on hold.

Roger had not yet completed his college preparatory classes and currently spent four hours studying with private tutors each morning. Jacques Kasner was also still employed as his music teacher. Roger confided in Jacques many of his current difficulties and concerns, especially as his brother Gilbert was away during the week boarding at Princeton. Jacques was nearing fifty; an age gap of over thirty years existed between pupil and teacher. On account of this, Roger probably viewed Jacques as an uncle figure rather than a buddy. Indeed, at times their relationship appeared much closer than the bond between Roger and his father.

Initially, Otto and Addie were vehemently opposed to Roger's business proposition, believing it was a passing boyish fancy.[35]

With time, after giving it more consideration and being satisfied by their son's sincerity, they agreed it would be far wiser to allow Roger to play out his whim than to deny him the opportunity to make a go of it. Nonetheless, they still stood firmly by their 'three rule' directive: no directing in public, no playing in public, and no use of the family surname. It is unclear whether they also put a timescale on his activities, but they certainly put a cap on the loan he requested.

To pay his musicians' wages and keep the band functioning, Roger asked for a $25,000 loan from his father, a substantial amount for any 16-year-old to borrow.[36] His father never blinked twice at the request, preferring to write a check there and then. However, upon handing it over, Otto made it explicitly clear that this would be the full extent of any loan he would grant and that it was not a gift and would require repaying.

Certain sections of the press implied Otto had encouraged Roger in his musical ambitions from the beginning and, as such, had 'angled' Roger's first jazz band. Patronage was, after all, Otto's modus operandi. Allegedly, Otto's original idea was to form a supergroup of highly skilled musicians that would have included his son. After Roger's intentions appeared in *Variety*, he shelved the plan. A report in the *New York Clipper* on February 29 stated the *Variety* exposé had 'crabbed' a lot of things for Otto's venture.[37] Again, was this the hand of Otto's publicist Ivy Lee?

Roger had tumbled into the spotlight haphazardly and for all the wrong reasons. It was his tenacity that saw him through his present difficulties. His father may have provided the money, but Roger invested his time, talent, and effort into the project. As Otto knew only too well, following a music career would be fraught with complexities and obstacles for his son that would intensify due to the Kahn connection. During an interview Roger gave in later years to the journalist Louis Fribourg, he explained how he dealt with the situation he unexpectedly found himself in and how he literally had to persuade his parents that nothing was 'degrading nor obnoxious in associating the family name with jazz.'[38]

'My father, you know,' Roger stressed, 'is a devotee of classical music. To him, jazz was a medley of tin pan syncopation, and he would not think of permitting me to devote my life to it. I respected his opinion, but I could not agree with him. I believe jazz reflects the spirit of our age and that it is as genuine and artistic as classical music. It requires just as subtle rhythm, just as much design, technique, and originality, and since I have talents in that direction, I intend to see whether I cannot hasten its universal acceptance as art.'

Roger was determined to build around him the finest jazz ensemble In New York. Over the coming weeks, he devoted long hours to band rehearsals and arranging music scores. Using the Lange orchestra as a nucleus, he drafted in new musicians, namely, concert-pianist Ray Romano from Mal Hallett's Roseland combination[39] and several Boston Philharmonic Orchestra members.[40] Already in the band were the hot trumpeters, Tommy Gott and Earl Oliver. Gott had previously worked in Whiteman's orchestra, and Oliver had played for General Pershing's military band overseas.

He paid his musicians generously, from $150 a week upwards, with the accent usually on the up, knowing full well other bandleaders would not be able to afford to poach them.

'I had to pay the regular rates of the musicians' union; in some cases much more where I had to have a certain man, and he was hard to get,' Roger later explained to journalist Zoe Beckley, in an article published in the *Brooklyn Daily Eagle*.[41]

'I bargained and haggled. I visited an attorney, not father's, to help with contracts and advise me about borrowing from banks in case father shut down entirely on the source of supply. I figured that with his name and my persistence, I could borrow.'

Paying such large salaries meant he was losing $600 a week at the Knickerbocker engagement, bearing in mind the fee he received from the management was $1,000.

Surprisingly, news of Roger's penchant for jazz gradually began to seep into all manner of publications before he had even set foot on a stage. One journalist in the society magazine *Brooklyn Life* wrote how the young musician had become captivated with the saxophone, a 'queer-looking instrument that wails so beautifully.'[42]

To make extra income at the 'Knick,' Roger assembled an in-house presentation titled *London Night*, a floorshow representing London's nightlife with guest appearances from several cast members of the Broadway production *Charlot's Revue of 1924*.[43] Perhaps Roger took his inspiration directly from the UK, where news of a dance craze was sweeping London. 'Craze fills all halls in [the] city each night,' claimed New York's *Sun and The Globe* newspaper.[44] This sudden flood of exertion was mainly due to the American musicians who made up most of the 'hotter' jazz orchestras performing at the venues. Their European counterparts had, seemingly, 'never learned to play jazz music well enough to satisfy the discriminating.'

Unbeknown to his parents, Roger did break one of their conditions; in the excitement of the moment, he would pick up an instrument and play along with his band. During this 'cooling down' period, daily life at the Kahn residence resumed a semblance of normality, with Roger and Otto both climbing down from their respective mantles.

During late evening, on March 10, a worrying incident occurred. Otto's chauffeur-driven limousine was targeted by another driver whose car persistently tried to block and run Otto's automobile off the road.[45] As the two vehicles sped ahead, the wild driver was unremitting with his assault. Fortunately, patrolling police officers witnessed the clash and promptly intercepted, pulling over the offending car and arresting its driver. Only the skill and level-headedness of Otto's driver Thomas Hill prevented their vehicle from crashing. The following day in the Traffic Court at Magistrate House, Francis McFarland, an electrician, was fined $30 for reckless driving. McFarland never gave any explanation for his behavior.

On Tuesday evening, March 11, the Knickerbocker management permitted WJY Radio to transmit a live performance of Roger's orchestra direct from the venue. The broadcast went out on *The Clipper* - a weekly two-hour radio show sponsored by the *New York Clipper* newspaper.[46] For that particular evening, the program was extended to four hours to accommodate the Kahn orchestra's radio debut and relay their whole performance. The two largest wireless outlets in New York were WEAF and WJY. For an unknown band to secure a live link with such a prestigious station was a significant achievement.

The radio presenter announced the band as Roger Wolfe Kahn's orchestra under Arthur Lange's direction. To everyone's surprise, Roger made intermittent appearances playing in the line-up.

'The band is a corker,' raved the *New York Clipper*, 'and would prove a sensation in vaudeville. It's a question where it best qualifies for a café, just like Lange was criticized for bringing too fine an organization into a dance hall when he opened the new Cinderella.'[47]

The broadcast was so favorably received that WJY transmitted a second live performance from the 'Knick' by the Kahn band the following week.[48]

One evening, after attending a performance at the Met, Otto and Addie arrived unannounced at the 'Knick' to hear their son's orchestra play. Roger was on stage. When he saw his parents in the audience, he remained where he was and continued playing. At the end of the set, Roger left the stage and sat at his parent's table. That evening, Otto and Addie realized just how genuine their son's passion for jazz was. It also became apparent to them he had assembled a fine orchestra of gifted musicians. Soon after, slowly and without any noticeable fuss, they conceded their disapproval and, without saying as such, overlooked his occasional unannounced stage appearances. Yet, despite their backing down, Roger still did not get their approval to use the Kahn surname.

At the Met, Gatti-Casazza signed a new five-year contract to stay on as the company's general manager, bringing his reign as New York's 'King' of opera to sixteen years. During his administration, he had produced over 100 operas for the company.[49] In a press statement, Mr. Gatti, as he was familiarly known, thanked his boss for his vote of confidence. 'I am very grateful to the president of the board of directors of the Metropolitan, Mr. Otto H. Kahn, for the new proof of confidence he has given me and for the praise he has so graciously bestowed upon me publicly.'[50] It was a significant milestone for Gatti-Casazza and a feather in Otto's cap, having masterminded the deal.

Roger had no previous experience with the commercial and financial side of the entertainment industry. As such, he had to learn the business fast, from the bottom up. However, at no point did he appear daunted by the magnitude of the task ahead of him. To keep his players fired up, Roger knew he had to ensure work came in regularly. He was also aware that at some point, he would need to arrange publicity and advertising, set up a vaudeville route, and make disk recordings to achieve wider recognition. Many orchestras were looked after by a management company and often employed a publicist. Roger had every intention of running his band along the same lines.

Even the press noticed how well organized some of today's jazz bands had become. The *New York Clipper* claimed this was one of the reasons why there were so many prominent aggregations and why jazz musicians were in a healthier position than ever before. 'This is illustrated by the importance attached to the concerts of Whiteman and [Vincent] Lopez and the entrance of such wealthy boys as Roger Wolfe Kahn into the jazz field.'[51]

Competition in New York City was keen, and many new bandleaders were only too willing to undercut other bands to bag a prestigious residency. Given his current setup, Roger was already better placed than most up-and-coming bandleaders. However, if nationwide success beckoned, Roger knew things would change. Being tied to the job 24 hours a day would take its toll. That's when he would employ a business manager to take care of his personal affairs. Roger had yet to determine his overall role within the band, whether as a musician or leader. For the present, Arthur Lange led the band, but for how much longer was debatable.

When it became apparent to the Knickerbocker manager that young Kahn would not be gracing the stage nightly with his presence, he sacked the unit.[52] Roger was already $3,000 in the red. Unfazed by the turn of events, Roger set out to find an alternative residency. A lucky break followed when he secured the band another live radio broadcast, which aired on March 20 on station BO.[53]

Away from all the hullabaloo of their son's activities, Otto and Addie resumed their rounds of carefully chosen social functions. On the evening of March 21, Addie attended a literary costume ball to aid the Independent Artists Association held on the roof garden of the Waldorf-Astoria Hotel. Guests were encouraged to dress in costumes representing their favorite character from a book.[54] Addie's character remained a mystery. The ball was knee-deep in debutantes on the hunt for a swashbuckling husband. The following afternoon, Addie co-hosted a Tea Dance at the Hotel Majestic to help raise awareness of civic affairs.[55] The entertainment included a community sing-along led by the Peoples Chorus of New York, followed by tea and dancing.

Early Sunday morning, on March 23, a mysterious fire broke out at the Kahns' Cold Spring Harbor estate and destroyed the chicken houses on their farm, roasting over 2,300 poultry.*

Two days later, a front-page report in *The Jewish Transcript* claimed Otto's net worth had increased to a hundred million dollars, and he was now the wealthiest Jew in America.[56] As if to celebrate the fact, the Kahns were added to America's elite '60 families' list.[57] Their tax figures (issued in the 1924 Federal Tax Register) listed them at number thirty, with an aggregate net income for the year of $1.4 million.[58] The Rockefellers were the richest on the list, with an estimated worth exceeding $2.5 billion. The Ford, Mellon, and Du Pont fortunes topped $1 billion, with the Vanderbilt, Whitney, and Harkness family wealth individually valued at $800 million.

~

Strange Diversion–March 30

'The strange diversion of Otto Kahn's son, who spends his weekends from Princeton blowing a saxophone in a Manhattan 'white light' restaurant,' reported the *Brooklyn Daily Eagle* header.[59] The journalist failed to mention why playing the saxophone was perceived as being odd. He did, however, go into great detail about Gilbert's hedonistic lifestyle away from the classroom.

Otto Kahn's son, Gilbert, runs counter to his father while blowing his saxophone.

Gilbert was a part-time member of the California Ramblers. The band had built a strong following on the local college circuit. They also played regularly at the Ramblers Inn on Shore Road in Pelham Bay Park and the Post Lodge in Westchester. More noteworthy were their appearances at the prestigious Palais Royal and Hippodrome in New York City. Presently they were contracted at the Monte Carlo

Restaurant in Manhattan, where Gilbert would sit in with them and blow his saxophone at the weekends. Their violinist Arthur Hand ('Art' to his friends) was the bandleader and cut a dashing figure with his clean-cut looks, slicked-back hair, and willowy physique.

Art and Gilbert were good mates, of equal age, and shared remarkably similar tastes, from music to motorcars, down to the sporting hobbies neither pursued. Gilbert's inclusion in the Ramblers line-up was as an occasional guest musician and not permanent.

When the *Eagle* reporter asked Art about his friendship with Gilbert, Art readily replied, 'we like to have him with us. He's a prince of a boy and a good musician besides. He's what you might call a 'typical American collegian." Art hesitated for a moment and then laughed before correcting himself, 'no, better than the typical if you know what I mean.'[60]

The newspapers got a big kick out of the story of Otto's two sons being jazz buffs, mainly because of his standing as a patron of the arts and for being chairman of the Met's board of directors.[61] It gave their readers something to chat about, and that's what their readers liked, a bit of gossip. Frustratingly for Roger, the label would cling to him for the rest of his life; he would forever be referred to as the son of banker Otto Kahn. Although Roger's parents had presently barred him from using the Kahn surname in association with his musical endeavors, it did not deter journalists from craftily inserting the Kahn tag when reporting about him.

No one could have foretold the rapidity with which Roger's career took off. After leaving the 'Knick,' Roger signed a contract for his band to perform in the musical slot at the Rivoli picture theater at 1620 Broadway. The three-week engagement began on Monday, March 24. The band was billed as the Roger Wolfe Symphony Jazz Orchestra and played six numbers before the feature movie.

'Roger Wolfe's Symphony Jazz Orchestra rendered half a dozen popular song hits and almost stopped the show,' hollered the *Brooklyn Daily Eagle*.[62] The Rivoli was an independently owned movie house and the sister theater of the Rialto. Felix Kahn - Otto's brother and Roger's uncle - was the Rialto Theatre Corporation's dominant shareholder and controlled both theaters.

On the evening of March 26, Otto visited the Rivoli to hear his son's band play. Otto and Roger entered the theater by the stage entrance. Instead of Roger taking a position on stage with his orchestra, father and son sat together in the stalls in row A. After the band had played their set and Otto was leaving, reporters pounced, asking him what he thought of the performance:[63]

'Splendid,' he replied assuredly. 'I'm all for it. One thing is certain, no European orchestra could play that kind of music like that. Jazz is America's contribution to music. It is the artistic expression of American exuberance.'

Otto may have left the theater with a spring in his step, but he was still adamant he would not allow his son to lead his orchestra in public. I have no objection to say any boy developing his talents, especially my own son,' he acknowledged. 'Anything is better than loafing. My son seems to be able to play any instrument in the orchestra, but I don't want him to play in public, at least not now. When he gets older - but we'll cross that bridge when we come to it.'

Annoyingly for Roger, it seemed his father's mandate, forbidding him from playing music in public, remained.

The band changed their repertoire at the Rivoli weekly. On the evening the *New York Clipper* reviewer was present, they opened with an up-tempo version of '*California, Here I Come*' followed by a syncopated arrangement of Anton Rubinstein's *Kamennoi Ostrow*. A jazzier number titled '*Maybe*' preceded the band's encore of '*Saint Louis Blues*.'[64] The critic dubbed it a 'corking orchestra' and picked out Earl Oliver and Tommy Gott's trumpeting as 'standing out smartly.' He also praised the banjoist. Encouragingly, the *Clipper* believed the outfit could easily be a smash in vaudeville or a stage production if it chose that route.

No sooner did the band finish their residency at the Rivoli than they took over as the resident pit orchestra for the Broadway revue *Vogues*. The excitement and immediacy of a live stage musical would leave an indelible impression upon Roger.

Vogues - a musical revue in two acts with original music composed by Herbert P. Stothart - had opened at the Shubert Theatre on March 27.* It was produced by Lee and Jacob Shubert and was the brother's first attempt at staging a musical revue. The Shuberts hoped to emulate the producer Florenz Ziegfeld Jr.'s trusted *Follies* and *Frolics* format comprising comedy skits and dancing girls, wrapped up in a satin bow of catchy tunes. Most critics gave the thumbs up, but the show found little favor with the public due to the lack of top draw names in the cast. In mid-April, to stimulate ticket sales, the Shuberts enlisted the Roger Wolfe Symphony Jazz Orchestra to take over pit duties. Their selection generated wide publicity for the revue.

Finally, Roger got to play with his orchestra in public. Ironically, his appearance was not on stage. 'Because the regular banjo player is ill,

Roger Wolfe Kahn is playing the banjo nightly in his *Vogues* orchestra,' reported the *New York Sun*.[65]

American novelist Theodore Dreiser saw *Vogues* at the Shubert Theatre and wrote about the experience in a letter to his cousin, aspiring actress Helen Patges Richardson, who later became his wife. 'Last night, I went to one of those crazy musical shows all by my lone - *Vogues*. It's just like all the others, *Greenwich Village Follies* and so on, and I knew that, but the comedians - Fred Allen and Jimmy Savo I have seen in vaudeville before - years ago. I had a good laugh at them or, rather, at Fred Allen, who reminds me of some old-time, quirky character I have seen somewhere. This is the show in which Otto Kahn's son plays the banjo in a jazz orchestra. There was much talk of it here in the papers at the time. The leading woman Odette Myrtil, French and with an accent, didn't interest me, and the chorus wasn't much.'[66]

On April 2, at New York Harbor, Otto and Addie waved goodbye to their beloved grandson John Marriott. John Jr. was sailing back to the UK with his nurse on RMS *Berengaria* to be reunited with his parents.[67] His temporary stay with his doting grandparents had brought an element of impish playfulness into the household that they would sorely miss.

Perhaps to celebrate his lucky break in *Vogues*, on April 3, Roger ordered a new custom-built (to his design) Bugatti from the coachbuilders *Lavocat et Marsaud*. The 3/4 seater, with an open touring body, was assembled at their factory in Boulogne-sur-Seine, France, and shipped to New York later that year in September.

Last summer, Margaret's interest in New York's art world had brought her in contact with Basque painter Ignacio Zuloaga y Zabaleta. Zuloaga's society portraits were highly sought after in wealthy New York drawing-rooms and were often painted-to-order, an easy trick many artists applied when they were short of money. Zuloaga painted a portrait of Margaret, probably commissioned by her parents. The composition shows Margaret masquerading as a Spanish princess; a black tassel shawl draped loosely upon her open shoulders is gathered tightly around her folded arms, beneath which a ruched satin flamenco-style dress exemplifies her body.[68] She stands erect, almost forthright, against a typically Spanish scenic background gazing directly at the viewer. Somber notes of black and green dominate the coloring. The picture commands attention. On April 24, the canvas went on public display at the 23rd Annual International Exhibition of Paintings at The Carnegie Institute in

Pittsburgh, Pennsylvania. The exposition ran throughout the summer of 1924.[69] It was Zuloaga's first showing at the Pittsburgh Salon. Matisse, Picasso, Derain, Friez, and Vlaminck were all represented, as was the controversial Spanish painter Anglada whose luminous and stylistic female figures were the sensation of the exhibition.

In early spring, Roger commissioned lyricist Joseph O. Donovan to write lyrics for a foxtrot he'd composed.[70] In April, Roger submitted the composition titled 'Why!' to Jack Mills Inc. publishing house. Mills accepted the dance tune for their catalog. Roger was now officially a published composer. Even the New York Times seemed impressed enough to report the news.[71] The Music Trade Review went one better and asserted the publisher was onto a winner, 'Musical critics unanimously declare the song has 'hit' possibilities. The vast amount of daily paper linage, which young Kahn has received, will do much toward rapidly establishing his songs.'[72] It was the first composition Roger had tendered to a publisher.

During a candid interview Roger gave with the journalist Nunnally Johnson published in the Brooklyn Daily Eagle, he recounts the problems he faces with his parents over their refusal to accept the profession he's chosen to follow.[73] In the process, rather tellingly, Roger depersonalizes his father when mentioning him, preferring to call him 'he,' clearly signaling that the rift between father and son had not yet healed.

The reader can almost sense from the outset young Kahn is in for a grilling. To set the scene, Johnson first reveals there may be a faint glimmer of hope on the horizon, as Kahn Sr. has yet to interpose any objection to Roger playing the banjo in the orchestra pit for the musical revue Vogues.

'The banjo player got sick.' Roger explains. 'He,' [that's Mr. Kahn, clarifies Johnson] 'hasn't said anything.' Roger contemplates for a moment the possibilities of something developing before the day is over. 'He's even been down to hear me. But I don't know how long it will last.' Roger pauses for a moment before continuing. 'Well, he didn't say anything at first when I said I was going to get an orchestra together. He didn't think anything would ever come of it. He never said a word against it.'

Choosing his words carefully, Roger follows on, 'The first thing I knew about his not liking it was when I told him that we'd signed a contract to play in the Knickerbocker Grill. Then he was much against it. But he's always fair.'

Johnson then asks how his mother feels about it all.

'She was much against it.'

'But how could you sign a contract at your age?' queries Johnson.

'We had incorporated. The corporation signed it.'

An effective strategy: Roger had taken legal advice beforehand, something no doubt he learned from his father.

'They [his parents] told me that I could do whatever I wanted to. No, they didn't say anything about my being a banker. That's my brother at Princeton that's going to be a banker. Well, you can see I thought that music was my line.'

Roger's music tutor Jacques Kasner is sitting in on the interview, which takes place in Roger's suite at 1100 Fifth Avenue. Kasner reveals to Johnson how Roger would have taken up aviation, except his mother was dead against it, and that Roger was going to look into it as soon as he reaches eighteen. Roger's fascination with flight stemmed from his many European trips abroad with his parents.

In the room where the interview is taking place are several model sailing ships encased in glass cabinets. Roger confesses to having started his model-building hobby when he was eleven.

Returning to Roger's music ambitions, he confides, 'I've got to get a restaurant. An orchestra has to have a restaurant and a show. The show by itself won't be enough. I can't even break even as it is now. I've got to see somebody today about that. If we can play a restaurant and a show, everything will be fine.'

Roger insists he's pretty conservative regarding jazz music and offers no allegiance to Paul Whiteman's recent movement to elevate the genre classically. To do so, he thinks, would be like upgrading a cabbage to be a rose.

'I think Whiteman's wrong,' insists Roger. 'He's getting ahead of the game. He's taking too much of the jazz out and getting too classic. I think you ought to leave that jazz touch in it. Whiteman is just spoiling good jazz to get cheap classical music. None of that for me.'

When Johnson asks how long Roger intends to stick it out as a struggling musician, especially as his parents are so opposed to the idea, Roger answers hopefully: 'Just as long as it holds out. They said I could be anything I wanted, and I want to have this orchestra. He [his father] is much against it, but he hasn't said anything this week. I think he's going to let me go ahead for a while now.'

One can sense how intensely angry Roger is about the predicament he now finds himself in.

'There's one thing I shall insist on,' stipulated Roger, 'everything about my orchestra must be entirely American. The players will be American, and every bit of music played will be American.'

Ironically, the National Bureau for the Advancement of Music, for which Otto was chairman of their National Music Week Committee, had arranged to hold their first synchronized music event across America from May 4-10.[74] The festival would celebrate music in various forms with concerts and performances from musicians at all stages of their education. 452 cities and towns were participating fully in the event, with an additional 328 to a lesser extent.[75]

The underlying philosophy of the organization was simple: 'Music Week is, to some extent, different from all the other special 'weeks.' It is a 'drive' for music by the friends of music, but it is also the occasion for participation in and receiving of pleasure, thus making it independent of any propelling force from behind. Its strength comes from the universal, yet sometimes unconscious, human need for music. Participation ranges from the elaborate concert and pageant to the simple home *musicale*, with a place sometimes even for the five-finger exercise beginner.'[76]

In the foreword of the National Music Week program, Otto provides the following quotation: 'Art is not the plaything of opulence. It is a robust, red-blooded thing. It is true equality of opportunity. In a world too much given to accentuate the things which divide us, it is one of those fundamental elements which unite us and make us kin in common understanding, common feelings, common reactions. It is true democracy, knowing nothing of caste, class, or rank.'[77]

In the light of recent events, it must have seemed odd to the public that Otto's philosophy did not extend to his own flesh and blood.

Dr. Lee DeForest was hailed as a radio genius, having invented the audion tube to transmit sound waves over distances. He was now occupying his time as a talking motion picture producer. DeForest's Phonofilms were classed as shorts, usually lasting around five minutes, and featured vaudeville and music stars, prominent political figures, and current news items. The reels used synchronized soundtracks. DeForest produced them as appetizers, viewed before the main feature film. It cost around $1,500 to convert a movie theater so it could screen Phonofilms.

Under Felix Kahn's watch, the Rivoli Theatre on Broadway was one of thirty-four theaters on the East Coast that had installed the DeForest sound system.

On Sunday, May 4, a leader in the *Brooklyn Daily Eagle* announced, 'Roger Kahn and his Band in Phonofilms.' The report sensationally went on to reveal, 'Roger Wolfe Kahn, millionaire bandmaster, whose jazz orchestra is the latest sensation on the Great White Way, has extended his endeavors into the motion picture field. Mr. Kahn and his jazz mates will be seen in a new DeForest Phonofilm, which in plain language means talking movies, at the Rivoli Theatre in another week or two. This will mark his first public appearances as [hitherto] he has confined his musical activities to non-participant managing of the orchestra. In the new film, young Kahn will play the banjo.'[78]

Roger had already been strumming his banjo with his band in the orchestra pit at the Shubert Theatre, covering for his regular banjoist who was sick. He had also snuck in an occasional appearance at the 'Knick' without announcing it. However, he had not as yet officially performed live on a stage with his orchestra. That eventuality would arrive sooner than the press predicted.

Upon reading the story, one wonders whether someone behind the scenes was beginning to pull a few strings for Roger, be it his Uncle Felix, a friend, an associate, or possibly even his father! It's also noteworthy that Roger's stage name appears in print for the first time as Roger Wolfe Kahn. Had Otto and Addie now revoked their 'three rule' policy of no directing in public, no playing in public, and no using the family surname? What is also intriguing is why the reporter chose to label Roger a 'millionaire bandmaster,' considering his present finances were in such a precarious state.

The *Eagle* also confirmed Roger and his orchestra would be 'doubling' (along with their assignment in *Vogues*) at Loew's State Theatre in Times Square, where they would appear for one week beginning Monday, May 12. The Loew's gig would mark Roger's first vaudeville appearance and bring him into contact with thousands of school kids during the matinee and early evening performances. Roger's potential and youthful appeal had suddenly become blatantly apparent to everyone around him. From this point forward, the crazy rhythm of Roger Wolfe Kahn commenced.

Predicting *Vogues* would only have a limited Broadway run, Roger set about securing a café residency.

Word soon circulated that Roger's band would be following on the heels of the mighty Whiteman Orchestra at the Palais Royal. The youngster would also be leading the outfit and playing his saxophone.[79] The rumor was correct.

Not content to sit around, Roger had negotiated a residency at the hip dance hall taking over the baton from his mentor and friend Paul Whiteman. That he secured the gig in favor of all the other heavyweights in town immediately ranked his band among the top five in the country. It was a massive boost for Roger and his musician's morale and reputation. Suddenly, the Roger Wolfe Orchestra was a contender. They were doubling nightly from a Broadway theater into a Broadway nightspot.

However, the press could smell a rat.

Inspired Propaganda

The Palais Royal was a classy establishment; it had an oval dance floor, served expensive food, and all its patrons wore evening dress. At the far end of the room was a mechanically operated sliding stage. The Palais Royal was the forerunner of what later became termed a 'nightclub.' A line of gleaming, black cabs was always in attendance outside, waiting to grab a fare to take happy customers home, or if they were really happy, on to their next venue. Playing the Palais Royal was a big deal. The events surrounding Roger's engagement there are significant, not least for the outrage it caused among fractions of New York's music fraternity and the press.

'Kahn gets the Rapp,' ran the New York Clipper leader on May 8.[80] 'Kahn's Band Replaces Rapp - Inspired Propaganda thought behind it - Sympathy for Rapp.'

The Rapp in question was bandleader Barney Rapp. The Palais Royal management had unceremoniously sacked Rapp's orchestra after appearing there for only one week to make way for the Kahn aggregation. Inspired propaganda was said to be behind Kahn's installation, with Paul Whiteman himself airing his dissatisfaction over the move. The bandleader had personally selected the Rapp organization to supersede him. Whiteman had played a long run at the Palais since 1920, and any band that replaced him would need to have pulling power. After playing only one week at the venue, the management decided Rapp did not have enough drawing power to attract punters. The music fraternity had been satisfied with Rapp's choice, as had the press, but the public thought differently.

Both communities suspected someone pulled wires to get young Kahn the gig. The Clipper even went as far as to dissect Kahn's current streak of good luck. They noted how Vogues originally opened on Broadway with Duke Yellman and his Irene Castle Orchestra as the in-house band. When the Paul Van Loan Orchestra replaced Yellman, Van Loan lasted less than a week before the Kahn outfit took over.

'It is not unknown that the [Kahn] orchestra played three weeks at the Rivoli on a booking arrangement in which Felix Kahn - a financial power in the Famous Players-Lasky Corporation - had no little say. It is also not unknown that the *Vogues* salary for the Wolfe band is nothing to brag about, and it is rumored the young scion of the Kahn house is personally making up the difference.' Indeed, Roger was making up the difference with money from the loan his father had granted him. The *Clipper* ended their stinging report by expressing, 'Musical Broadway's sympathy is entirely with Rapp.'

Roger and Whiteman may well have been friends, but they were also professional rivals. In definition, the standard of musicianship and draw of both units was high. As far as the management of the Palais Royal was concerned, it was clear cut; Roger had more pulling power than Rapp.

The Kahn band made their Palais Royal debut on Monday evening, May 5. When they appeared under the delicately tinted lights on the raised stage, young Kahn was not among their ranks. However, in a surprise move the following evening, Roger made his live stage debut alongside his musicians. He got to play his Paramount banjo and conducted one number during each set.[81] His unit also featured his recently published song *'Why!'*[82] Roger was ecstatic, in fact, so happy, he remained on stage with his band all evening, playing right up until the venue closed in the early hours of Wednesday morning.[83]

What is more extraordinary is who was there to witness Roger's debut. Attending the Palais Royal on Tuesday evening to publicly support their son was Otto and Addie. Accompanying them were several prominent guests; Reginald Claypoole Vanderbilt (the youngest son of Cornelius Vanderbilt II), Samuel Guggenheim, Mrs. William Randolph Hearst (Millicent), and Rhode Island socialite and occasional silent movie actress Mrs. Morgan Belmont (Margaret).* Did Roger hold back on his debut to accommodate his parent's visit or was it another cleverly orchestrated publicity stunt!

Possibly, to capitalize on Roger's youthful draw and the enormous press exposure he was currently receiving, the supervisor of recreation at New York's Park Department, James V. Mulholland, booked Roger and his orchestra to headline the annual 'May Day on the Green.' The concert took place on May 24 on the sheep meadow in Central Park.[84] The huge event attracted 10,000 school children as well as their accompanying adults. The youngsters were transported from schools to the park in city busses and given free ice cream and cakes while being treated to a concert of music, song, and dance.

Otto had his fingers in many pies, and assorted pies they were too.

From the moment he woke up in the morning until the minute he laid his head upon his pillow at night, he occupied his mind with some project or another. *Brooklyn Life* reported on May 31 that Kahn was now a stockholder - along with Condé Nast, Mrs. Frederick W. Vanderbilt, and around forty others - of the exclusive, recently opened *Lido Venice* restaurant at 35 East 53rd Street. The eatery was decorated in a pseudo-Italian style, with original, hand-painted murals by Pieretto Bianco; one represented San Marco's Basin in Venice. The cost of the interior decoration alone exceeded $90,000. The Italian theme even extended to the exterior, where Juliette balconies wrapped their rails around each window. With its private dining areas, ideal for intimate occasions, the restaurant attracted an elitist crowd. In charge of the kitchen was a Basque cook, who, by all accounts, produced superb authentic Italian cuisine. *Lido Venice* was dubbed society's own, and high society flocked to it.[85]

Roger and his orchestra remained at the Palais Royal for precisely one month, during which they continued doubling down the road at the Shubert Theatre in *Vogues*. Kahn's Palais Royal engagement ended when police raided the place and closed it under the padlocking order for alcohol consumption.[86] Was this the outcome of a vendetta orchestrated by a rival bandleader or club owner?

Hoping his current setback was a fluke, Roger set his sights on an even bigger prize; a residency at one of New York's elite hotels.

In early June, midway through the *Vogues* engagement, Roger was informed by Milton Shubert (theater owner Lee Shubert's nephew and assistant) that the band's salary would be reduced, owing to the axing of the weekly matinee.[87] Roger refused to accept the pay cut. Milton was furious and told young Kahn sharply, 'You're through.' Roger immediately marched his band over to the Hippodrome, where they were promptly hired as a 'special attraction' to run over the Convention period. Milton got wind of the booking and did not fancy his chances running *Vogues* against the Kahn orchestra at the Hippodrome. Milton contacted his boss, Uncle Lee. Lee immediately notified Roger that Milton had no authority to hire or fire anybody connected with *Vogues* and insisted Roger and his orchestra return to the show forthwith. Lee then sweetened his tone a little as he told Roger, besides, he was anxious to renew an option clause in the band's contract.

Roger stuck to his guns. He did not intend to take any cut in salary. Besides, the band's contract only had three days left before it expired.

The Shuberts demanded they see the original agreement. Roger held back in supplying the papers. His representative had them, and at this precise moment, he was in Chicago. As such, Roger could not produce the document in the time requested by the Shuberts. With threats of legal action, crushingly, Roger and his musicians returned to the production.

Saxophone sales were up, so too were sales of banjos, especially the tenor banjo.[88] Some of the credit for this demand in sales came down to bands such as Whiteman's and Kahn's, affirmed the *Brooklyn Daily Eagle*: 'Jazz is melodic, it has a swing that gets into the blood, and it's here to stay. Such men as Paul Whiteman, Roger Wolfe Kahn, Paul Specht, and Ted Lewis have shown what jazz can be - very different from the beating of tom-toms, [and] the noisy racket that the unskilled jazz players give us.' *Variety* agreed: 'In this day of so-called modern music it doesn't seem possible to create music without at least one or two saxophones, the saxophone seemingly personifying the age and its music.'[89]

Paul Whiteman		Vincent Lopez	
Isham Jones		**Abe Lyman**	
HARRY RESER	*The Endorsement of Famous Orchestra Leaders Helps Music Dealers Sell* **Paramount Banjos**		ACE BRIGODE
BILL BOWEN			KEITH PITTMAN
BEN BERNIE			ARNOLD JOHNSON
SLEEPY HALL			MANY OTHERS
S.S. Leviathan		**Barney Rapp**	
Roger Wolfe Kahn		**Ben Selvin**	

Paramount Banjos advertisement, July 5, 1924.

The Hotel Biltmore at 43rd and Madison

The Hotel Biltmore was renowned for staying one step ahead of the game. News of Roger's engagement at the hotel sent ripples of astonishment throughout New York's entertainment industry. 'The kid's a genius!'

A Biltmore residency was the plum job every bandleader coveted. How Roger secured the Biltmore gig was in itself an astonishing feat. On Wednesday, June 4, Kahn marched his orchestra over to the Biltmore to audition for John McEntee Bowman, president of the Biltmore hotel chain. Bowman offered Roger the gig on the spot.[90] The band officially commenced their Biltmore residency the next day at the Cascades' seasonal opening in the hotel's rooftop ballroom.

The Biltmore was a prestigious gig. Many of New York's top orchestras had tendered for it. Bowman was so impressed with the Kahn outfit he tied them to a year's contract. The terms stipulated they play at the afternoon tea dance from five to seven and during supper atop the hotel in their spacious ballroom, the Cascades. When the Cascades shut for the winter, the band would entertain diners in the elegant Bowman Room, named after the hotel's owner. Roger's weekly pay was $2,500, plus an additional 50 percent from the tea dance covers (approx. $300), totaling $2,800: the highest salary ever for a steady hotel orchestra attraction.[91] Most of New York's top hotels employed an orchestra and many financial benefits followed from such a residency. Roger's perseverance had paid off.

Bowman added a clause in Kahn's contract that stipulated Roger must personally lead his orchestra on a mutually arranged quantity of evenings each week. Being the shrewd businessman he was, the hotel magnate instantly recognized the pulling power Roger and the Kahn brand held, especially among the wealthy guests the Biltmore attracted.

More unusual was another term Bowman agreed to in his haste to secure the Kahn unit; the notification that Roger would be traveling abroad with his parents later in June. Several musicians from his band would also be accompanying him to perform a series of concerts in Europe.[92] During their two-month absence, Roger pledged to employ equally proficient replacements. Under Otto's patronage, the band aimed to give concerts on the boat and at Deauville, Monte Carlo, and other summer resorts.[93]

New York was considered the world's hotel capital for its number, size, and quality. Moreover, the hotels were far more modern, incorporating the latest fittings and luxuries to meet the increasing demand for high-class accommodations. The esteemed Biltmore was one of the most comfortable. It was also one of the largest, housing 1,000 rooms, of which 950 had en suite bathrooms. The colossal building, located conveniently in the heart of the shopping and theater district, occupied an entire block directly facing Grand Central Terminal. It also featured a connecting tunnel with the railway station, which offered guests the convenience of never having to step outside into the street.

The Biltmore Hotel, New York

The imposing façade and twin towers of the Biltmore overlooking Vanderbilt Avenue.

Its rooftop ballroom doubled as the Cascades, an imposing, cavernous space that functioned primarily in summer. An ornamental balcony overlooked the hardwood dance floor, and three enormous drop chandeliers presented the illusory effect of light cascading down from the heavens. Wide, lofty, floor-to-ceiling windows dressed in heavy drapes lined the walls on three sides.

Beneath the arched windows at the eastern end of the room was a three-tiered, curved stage where the orchestra performed. Another striking feature of the room was its sliding roof that would be hand-cranked open on warm, clear nights to allow guests to dine and dance beneath the stars.

The palatial Biltmore ballroom atop the south tower where guests would dine and dance beneath the stars.

The nightspot was one of the most glittering and spectacular in the city. To be hired as its resident orchestra was deemed in music circles to be a significant fillip for any band's career.

The Cascades summer season officially opened on Thursday, June 5, and was exceptionally well attended.[94] The following day's *New York Evening Post* reported that among the many exciting features presented that evening was 'the famous Roger Wolfe Kahn Orchestra, under Roger Wolfe Kahn's direction.'[95] The paper also noted the redecoration of the ballroom. 'The color scheme is refreshingly cool in its green tones,' with the coolness heightened by the splashing water in the fountain.

The following afternoon the Kahn orchestra performed their first tea dance where, due to Prohibition, a selection of teas replaced cocktails. During the muggy summer weather, afternoon tea in the

Biltmore's outdoor Italian Gardens was a must for any well-heeled shopper. The 12th-floor gardens were high enough to wash away the noise and bustle of Vanderbilt Avenue below yet protected from the sun and wind by the overlooking walls of the building's twin towers. Advertisements declared it 'the most popular and coolest room in New York,' which, it probably was on a hot summer's day. It was also one of the choicest settings for meeting friends after a long day shopping before heading home by train.

The Tea Room loggia and a section of the outdoor Italian Gardens (right) on the mezzanine floor of the Biltmore.

In winter, the band remained indoors in the warm, covered logia. Outside, in a miraculous transformation, the roof became a magical ice skating rink, planted with real conifers and imitation snow.

It was the ideal gig for Roger, inasmuch that he only lived up the road. Conveniently, he could drive himself down to the hotel, arrive outside the front entrance, hand over his car keys to an attendant to park the vehicle in the garage, and appear on stage leading his band all in a matter of minutes. In truth, Roger enjoyed working at the Biltmore so much he played there practically every afternoon and evening.[96] After milking the tea dance, the band would hot-foot over to the Shubert Theatre for the evening performance of *Vogues*, after which they'd return to the Biltmore to entertain diners at the Cascades.

Roger was correct in his assumption that *Vogues* would not see out the summer. The show's ticket sales did pick up, but not enough for the Shubert brothers to consider extending its run. Nevertheless, the discipline of a nightly performance was a valuable experience for Roger, one he had eagerly sought. The Kahn orchestra remained with the show until the final curtain fell on July 12.

The Tyranny of Parents

Gilbert may have been studying economics at Princeton in the hope of becoming a banker, but even he had a rebellious side to his nature. While his father was currently away in Europe on business, news of Gilbert's extracurricular exploits hit the front pages again, and all for the wrong reasons.[97] The eccentric German poet, dancer, and nobleman Baron Willy Sebastian Knobloch Droste, who liked performing near-naked on stage, was in New York City promoting his ideology, the 'Tyranny of Parents.' On June 21, he held a public crusade and fundraiser at the Waldorf-Astoria to launch an international association based on his beliefs. His gripe was with titled and wealthy parents that refused to allow their artistically gifted offspring to pursue a career in the arts and, if they did, to suffer the indignation of ostracism or, worse, disinheritance. Whether Gilbert related wholly to the exotic Baron's notion or thought it sounded like a bit of a laugh is not made clear, but he did attend the rally to show his support. The press pounced on Gilbert and plastered his face across the dailies. It was a story made in heaven and fell right into Baron Willy and the media's lap.

'To have a title and be the son of a rich man is more terrible than to be a poor boy who can make his own way,' wailed Baron Willy in one of the quotes the papers chose to print.

Although the newspapers labeled Gilbert a 'prospective member,' he never did sign up for membership.

Addie and Roger, accompanied by several trunks packed with musical instruments, arrived in the UK port of Southampton aboard RMS *Berengaria* on July 2.[98] Traveling with them was Roger's music tutor Jacques Kasner.[99] After disembarkation, all three journeyed to London by train, where they joined Otto at Claridge's Hotel.[100]

George Gershwin was in London for the summer, working on orchestrations for his new stage musical *Primrose*. He was lodging with Alex Aarons and his wife Ella at their apartment at 10 Berkeley Street, a ten-minute walk from Claridge's.[101] Gershwin's musical was scheduled to premiere in September at the Winter Garden Theatre in Covent Garden. While in London, the Kahns met up with Gershwin socially. Roger even wangled himself the chance to play in Gershwin's thirty-piece orchestra - whether at rehearsals or a performance of *Primrose* in the theatre's orchestra pit, is unclear.[102] When the Kahns' stay in the capital ended, the family journeyed to France and then to Italy.

During Roger's absence from New York, Arthur Lange resumed his role fronting Kahn's twelve-piece orchestra.[103] Lange's sterling dance arrangements still dominated the band's repertoire and were a testimony to his talent and guiding influence. Exactly how long Lange intended to continue playing underdog would be put to the test during Roger's time away.

Music journalist Abel Green witnessed the band performing at the Cascades just after Roger had departed from American shores. In his review, he noted: 'Despite the hugeness of the Cascades Room, the spacious and one of the most beautiful roof gardens in New York, none of the effects are lost. The personnel are high grade and considerably high priced, and only such as a wealthy man's son could afford to engage. It is not unknown that the band's engagement in *Vogues* or at the hotel alone could not make it pay for the musicians, although both combined certainly does. Yet, with all that, young Kahn is said to have run behind $15,000 so far in his venture, having each man under personal contract and guaranteeing a regular weekly salary, regardless.'

Those salaries all had to be paid promptly during Roger's absence.

Green also noted that Lange was still not satisfied with the ballroom's acoustics, feeling the band's sound might benefit from being closer to the dancers. He suggested positioning the group on the dance floor instead of on the raised platform. Green also confirmed that trade at the Cascades was sensational, which the management wholly accredited to the Kahn unit's draw.

Roger's hope of taking some musicians to Europe with him to play selected dates had not gone as planned. His musicians were unable to obtain the labor permits necessary for them to work abroad.[104]

Trailing around Europe was probably the last thing Roger wanted to do at this moment in his life, especially as his band was receiving such favorable reviews at the Biltmore. However, travel had its attractions: he could check out the local music scene, catch up with the latest aeronautical developments, and hook up with any fellow musicians visiting the continent. Roger's parents also expected him to undertake some 'serious study' during the trip, which is presumably why his tutor was accompanying him.

Although Roger was abroad, he still had to keep an eye on his business matters back home. His band was running up a weekly loss of $600, which he subsidized using his father's loan.[105] With his paycheck from the Shuberts about to end, Roger now had to fathom out a way to guarantee additional bookings to keep his band afloat. He had already begun to repay some of his creditors and put himself on a budget of disbursements. The last thing he wanted was to run out of capital. It, therefore, came as a surprise when *Variety* revealed, 'Son of Otto Kahn Reported to Have Made Business Connection with Father.'[106] Finally, Otto had reached out to his son with an offer to help.

Roger planned to co-produce a stage musical earmarked for a fall premiere and had already developed a working agreement with a prominent Broadway producer. *Variety* anticipated Roger would most probably use the Kahn orchestra in the production. Otto showed keen interest in the venture and announced he would financially back it to the limit. 'If the boy wants a theater of his own, he can have it.' Otto was finally on board.

To earn extra cash for his band, Roger came up with the novel idea to trial Sunday dances at the Cascades. The first session attracted a fair-sized crowd.[107] Dancing on Sundays was regarded as undignified by most of the luxury hotels. That aside, the encouraging turnout paved the way for regular Sunday dances at the Biltmore.

The band also took to the airwaves direct from the Cascades in a live hook-up with WJZ.[108] Through the wizardry of wireless, the band's music entered the living rooms of thousands of new listeners who, Roger hoped, would become fans. Their first evening broadcast on July 8 was so well received, WJZ committed to a regular weekly slot from the Cascades.

The newspapers already referred to the teenager as a millionaire bandsman. The *Brooklyn Daily Eagle* went one step further: 'If one wishes to end the evening riotously, tune in on WJZ, where is Roger Wolfe Kahn with his multi-millionaire jazz.'[109] Within a matter of weeks, Roger's earning potential had multiplied. The media were now feting the Kahn band as the next big thing on the East Coast and ideal for exploitation.[110] On July 26, WJZ aired a live afternoon transmission of 'Roger Wolfe's Biltmore Tearoom Orchestra,' which became a regular weekly feature throughout summer.

~

In Italy, Otto held meetings with Morris Gest, Sergei Diaghilev, and Max Reinhardt at the ever-fashionable Lido in Venice. Here, over outdoor lunch, they discussed a new, yet to be disclosed, venture.[111]

A couple of weeks later, the Kahns returned to the UK, where they traveled to Scotland. Otto had rented Whittingehame House, a large country manor near Haddington in East Lothian. The neoclassical mansion was home to former British Prime Minister Arthur James Balfour, Earl of Balfour.[112] Balfour referred to the surrounding region as a 'paradise for golfers,' which was why Otto was attracted to the area. While in Scotland, Roger and Jacques learned to play the bagpipes,* no doubt breaking the calm and serenity Otto had paid the Earl so extravagantly for in the process.

After a short stay, Otto felt the draw of the big city too hard to resist and returned to the U.S., leaving his wife and son to continue their vacation in the Lowlands. Otto arrived back in New York with his valet on August 12 aboard the *Majestic*.[113]

No sooner had Otto departed from UK shores than Gilbert arrived in Southampton on August 8, having sailed alone from New York aboard RMS *Olympic*. Gilbert traveled by train directly to Scotland to join his family at Whittingehame House.[114] Roger was thrilled to have his brother with him, especially as Scotland had many curious customs and traditions to discover.

As well as walking the rugged foothills and swimming in the local river, the brothers also found time to play music. The change in surroundings inspired Roger to compose eighteen jazz melodies. One composition titled *'Cal, Cal, Cal, Cal Coolidge'* exalted the merits of Calvin Coolidge.

Coolidge was running for re-election as President of the United States.[115] Roger wired the ditty to the president's Washington campaign office for their approval, on the understanding that if the president liked it, he could use it on his campaign trail.[116]

Coolidge did indeed like the song. The following day Roger received a message of thanks from the president's secretary, Mr. C. Bascom Slemp, confirming they would incorporate the piece into Coolidge's campaign.[117] Roger promptly wired a copy of the manuscript to his orchestra at the Biltmore, instructing them to plug it at every performance they played leading up to Election Day. In a new departure for Roger, he wrote the lyrics as well as the music:

Cal, Cal, Cal, Cal Coolidge
You're quiet and honest and plain
But your actions indicate
That you've been picked by fate

To guide our ship of state again
Cal, Cal, Cal, Cal Coolidge
You're true as the Red, White, and Blue
Say, the USA can hardly wait
Until next fall election date
Just watch us while we demonstrate -
America wants you.

Treading the Boards

'Roger Wolfe Kahn readying his jazz band for vaudeville.'[118]

Variety had already intimated Kahn's unit would go down a storm on the vaudeville circuit and that any savvy controller who coaxed him over to tread the boards could make rich pickings. That exact scenario unfolded almost word for word.

When impresario E. F. Albee (of the Keith-Albee Theater chain) phoned Otto to discuss whether Roger would appear in vaudeville, the response Albee received was not what he had anticipated. Mindful of his son's lack of business acumen, Otto took the liberty to negotiate there and then a lucrative fee and a firm engagement for Roger and his band to perform at New York's Hippodrome. Since Otto's recent return from Europe, the papers had made much of his softening approach over his son's musical interests.[119] Otto never divulged the fee he negotiated. Meanwhile, the band was placed on a guaranteed retainer for one year under contract to Keith-Albee.

Variety was quick to pick up on Otto's business dealings for his son. Their columnist Abel Green reported in his weekly editorial that contemporary musicians thought Otto, 'a pretty good agent to affect a booking with E. F. Albee personally,' and wondered if he was available to 'worry about their bookings on the usual commission!'[120]

Roger Wolfe Kahn's Hotel Biltmore Orchestra, 'by kind permission of John McEntee Bowman, Hotel Biltmore,' opened at the mammoth Hippodrome on Monday, August 25, for an indefinite run. The band closed the first half of the show.[121] At the end of their debut performance, they received rapturous applause from the audience. Sitting in the stalls was Otto, beaming, the proudest father in the house. Unfortunately for Roger, he was not present; Roger, Gilbert, and his mother were still in the UK and would not be returning home until late September.

'In all, the entire show was a masterly show, conceived and executed on a level beyond anything heretofore known in any bill on vaudeville. Two or three weeks of this pace will make the Keith's Hippodrome a bonanza.'[122] By attending the show, Otto gave out a clear message to his critics that everyone, no matter how stubbornly inclined, should welcome change and offer a guiding hand to new talent, even if that talent happens to be their offspring. It was a monumental change of heart for Otto.

The Prince of Wales Revisits America

On August 29, Edward, Prince of Wales, arrived in New York aboard RMS *Berengaria* on an informal visit. As anticipated, there was great excitement surrounding his arrival. The city rose to the occasion.

Many grand private parties took place in his honor; a couple, in particular, on Long Island. As was customary at such affairs, a top orchestra entertained the guests. Edward made no secret he was an avid jazz enthusiast, unlike his mother Queen Mary, who, 'among other things, hated it.'[123] Fierce rivalry from New York's biggest bands created a headache for the hosts of these events, with each under-cutting the other to secure a booking to play in front of the prince.

Paul Whiteman agreed to perform at Clarence Mackay's reception on September 6 at his palatial Long Island residence, Harbor Hill, set in 648 acres in Roslyn. The newspapers wrongly reported Vincent Lopez and his Orchestra were the agreed band at the event. It was with some annoyance that the managers of Lopez and Whiteman respectively issued blunt warnings to the press demanding an instant retraction and apologies over the mistake; such were the hostilities between Lopez and Whiteman.[124]

Otto attended Clarence Mackay's party, and while there, he invited Edward over to Cold Spring Harbor for an informal round of golf. The prince keenly accepted the offer. Edward was the houseguest of industrialist James Abercrombie Burden Jr. and his wife Florence at their vast Long Island estate Woodlands, set in a landscaped park in Syosset.[125] The Burdens were neighbors of the Kahns. When reports of Edward's reckless partying on Long Island reached his parents back in the UK, the prince later implied his father, King George V, banned him from ever returning to the States again.

Addie, Gilbert, Roger, and Roger's music tutor Jacques Kasner departed from the UK aboard RMS *Aquitania* on September 27, bound for the U.S.[126]

Just before Roger's return, Arthur Lange quit the Kahn orchestra. Although Lange's leaving was not unexpected, it was a setback. Lange stated musical differences and his wish to devote more time to arranging had influenced his decision.[127] He also moaned that the grind of rehearsals and doubling from the Biltmore into the Hippodrome had worn him down. Whatever his reasons, he did form a new band directly after parting company from Kahn, leaving his motives for resigning questionable.[128] Lange did, however, confirm he'd continue arranging music for Kahn's band with the assistance of Hugo Frey and Domenico Savino.* Tommy Gott and a new boy, violinist Joe Raymond, took turns conducting the unit in Roger's absence, and Gott, with Otto's occasional guidance, continued to manage the band.

When Roger initially set sail for the continent with his mother, he promised her he would not pose for any press photographers or give interviews while he was away. He did this to appease Addie's dislike of the media. Before he returned to America, to get around this, he wired a press release to a pal in New York for him to hand out to reporters at the dock upon Roger's arrival.

When the *Aquitania* dropped anchor at New York Harbor, Otto was at the quayside to welcome his wife and two sons home. Roger's friend was standing beside him, clutching copies of Roger's press release to distribute to the reporters. Otto asked to see it. After reading it, he chuckled his approval, 'Not so bad.'

As soon as Roger was back home, everything changed. Roger now took on a more visible presence and stepped into the bandleader's role. As their director, Roger put his hand to stage design, lighting, and styling the band's image, besides writing arrangements and composing new material. The band was Roger's vision, and he surrounded himself with a strong team to assist him. Due to his lack of business experience, he hired a personal manager Bert Cooper (husband of the dancer Bessie Clayton), who had previously managed vaudeville acts.[129] He also engaged George B. Evans to handle the press and day-to-day admin.

The band's gig at the Hippodrome lasted three weeks and was a big success. Discussions of further vaudeville dates were ongoing but had yet to be confirmed. For the present, Roger concentrated on steadying the ship, getting attuned with being in charge, and bringing about changes gradually when necessary. To keep the money coming in, the band continued their weekly radio hook-up with WJZ and Sunday evening dances at the Cascades while fulfilling their regular contractual obligations at the Biltmore.

~

Gilbert and Anne

When Gilbert announced his engagement to tobacco heiress Anne Elizabeth Whelan on October 9, it came as no surprise to his or Anne's family or anyone else that knew the young couple. Anne was the daughter of Charles Augustus Whelan, president of the United Cigar Stores of America. Gilbert and Anne were both aged 21 and had been dating for some months.

News of their engagement hit the front pages,[130] as did their hastily planned marriage arrangements released the following day.[131] Their sudden rush to tie the knot raised a few eyebrows among society, with any notion of impropriety hurriedly expunged, citing the couple's unbridled love for one another as the reason behind their hurry to exchange vows. The marriage would unite two families of social prominence and wealth and be deemed an ideal match by both sets of parents.

The following day, Anne accompanied Gilbert to the Marriage License Bureau in the Municipal Building, where they obtained a permit to wed. The couple earmarked November 19 as the date for the wedding and booked New York's Ambassador Hotel as the venue. The pressure to get everything organized in five weeks grew more challenging as the big day approached.

In late October, the *New York Times* disclosed that Otto had been invited to be Mayor of New York on a reform Republican ticket.[132] Though flattered at the proposition, he declined, stating he could best serve the public as a private citizen doing what he was already doing.

Gilbert and Anne's Marriage–November 19

The Italian Garden at the Hotel Ambassador had never looked lovelier or more colorful. Even the sun appeared to bless the union as it broke through the clouds when the couple stepped arm in arm as husband and wife into the garden. One thousand guests were there to greet them.[133] The ceremony followed the rites of the Roman Catholic Church. The *New York World* was quick to point out that the Catholic Church only gave consent for the service after the bridegroom (a Protestant) had reached an agreement, specifying the newlyweds would raise any children from their marriage in the Catholic faith.[134] The report also mentioned Gilbert might, at a later date, take up the same religion as his bride.

The Vanderbilts, Astors, and Mackays turned up in their finery to witness the uniting of two family fortunes. The media dubbed it the most outstanding reception of the social season.

The bride carried a bouquet of white orchids. Her sister was a matron of honor, and Gilbert's sister Margaret took on bridesmaid duties. Gilbert's buddy and Princeton scholar, Leonard Jarvis Cushing, took the role of best man, while Gilbert's brother Roger assumed usher's duties. The wedding cake stood seven feet tall.

After the reception, guests were treated to an evening dance in the Louis XV ballroom at the Ambassador.

Early next day, the happy couple departed for Hot Springs, Virginia, where they planned to spend several weeks honeymoon, relaxing, playing golf, and horse riding. Upon their return, a spacious Manhattan apartment at 55 East 72nd Street awaited them, a gift from the bride's parents.

That Gilbert should wed while still being a Princeton under-graduate created a headache for him. He now felt more inclined to earn an independent living than continue his studies for the next two years. That dilemma, however, would be temporarily put to one side and determined in due course after the newlyweds returned from their honeymoon.

Plans For a New Opera House

The Met's 40th opera season began on Monday, November 3, with *Aida*. The old opera house was starting to show its age.

Otto had recently announced his intention to submit plans to the Met's board of directors for a modern new opera house in Manhattan. The building would have up-to-date backstage facilities, a more spacious proscenium, and seats at affordable prices for people of modest means.[135] He believed the present theater was archaic, inutile for real music lovers, and hindered the promotion of music drama. Regrettably, not all operagoers or, indeed, Met directors shared his views or vision.

Over the next seven years, Otto and Addie worked tirelessly to promote their plans and objectives for building a new opera house for the city. Their perseverance, no matter how commendable or visionary, would be tested to the limit and ultimately have a detrimental effect on Otto's health. For now, it was the start of the project, and Otto and Addie were imbued with a spirit of anticipation.

The Little Theatre, Brooklyn

When Otto attended a meeting on November 11 at the Brooklyn Chamber of Commerce to support the Little Theatre campaign in Brooklyn, he did so as a sponsor and enthusiast. Almost two hundred Brooklyn residents turned up, including leaders in art, and business, all offering their backing for the project. The cost to construct and equip the new theater was $200,000, with almost half already subscribed. A drive to secure the balance was agreed upon and scheduled to launch on November 18.

Otto was the principal speaker at the meeting. His talk left an indelible impression on all those present.

Kahn began his address by explaining the importance of art in daily life and how it pays much higher dividends than we realize: 'the lives of most people are cast on gray backgrounds. Even lawlessness may only be a reaction to the conditions imposed by everyday drudgery.'[136] The rich returns Otto had personally received from his interest in art he claimed were 'tax-exempt dividends that no Congress can touch. Art is true democracy and knows neither class or caste; Wall Street and Socialists can meet here on common ground.'

The shared interests Otto spoke of brought him effectively on to the subject of music, a topic close to his heart, and, more precisely, jazz and its current influence on the younger generation. 'It is easy enough to deride or disparage, but any movement which in its rhythm, and other respects, bears so obviously the American imprint, which has divulged new instrumental colors and values, which has taken so firm a footing in our own country, aroused so much attention abroad and is an object of such great interest to foreign musicians visiting here - any such movement has a just claim to be taken seriously.'

It was a direct jab at skeptics of jazz.

'True, in respect of music, jazz demonstrates itself as yet rather in appreciation and cultivation than in creative ability, but it is reasonable to expect that out of the ever more widely cast seed of comprehension and proficiency, there will spring the final fruitage of creation. Moreover, it does not seem to me, beside the point to allude to the fact that America did create [within the recent past] a musical expression - imperfect as yet and spotted with crudities, but vigorously alive, characteristically novel, and distinctively its own.'

Otto then offered a comparison to support his stance.

'Just as gypsy, and similar bands, in the southeastern countries of Europe, are an expression of the art of their respective peoples, so a first-rate jazz band, or particularly a first-rate Broadway revue or musical comedy, with its swiftly rushing pace, spontaneous grace, zest and swing of its dancing, the tang of its humor, the kaleidoscope of its color, the hustling, palpitating rhythm of its orchestra, have more claim to be ranked as an approximation to American art than a savorless grand opera composer with painstaking erudition and technical impeccability after the model of Wagner, Debussy or Strauss.'

Otto believed jazz was intrinsically American, and he had every intention of establishing such a claim there and then on behalf of his adopted country. 'It is said that jazz cannot be looked upon as characteristically American because it is traced back to African origin. It remains nevertheless true that America has seized it and made it its own. You might just as well say that Theodore Roosevelt was not wholly American because his origins can be traced back to Holland. Or, in a more frivolous vein, you might say that a cocktail is, or rather was, not a peculiarly American product because ingredients composing it are of foreign origin.' Otto was well aware of the power of the media and that every word he communicated would be in print the following day.

'There is a vast amount of talent among players and composers of jazz. It will have to purge itself of crudities; it will have to frown upon vulgarity; it will have to aim, as some of its leaders do, at evolution from its present stage. We should try to help and hasten that process.

Instead of turning up our noses at jazz, in superior musical virtue and fastidiousness of taste, we ought to take the attitude of spurring it on with friendly interest, of setting it the task of progress toward further and higher achievement, and of giving actively sympathetic encouragement to every sincere attempt to develop this peculiarly American product into a fruitful contribution to musical art.'

Whereby Otto rested his case in the full knowledge, he had done what he set out to do, to get as many column inches in the next day's newspapers as possible to help further the causes of Brooklyn's Little Theatre movement and jazz.

Jazzin' the Met

When the bandleader Vincent Lopez casually announced earlier in the year that he would like to hold a jazz concert at either New York's Aeolian Hall or the Metropolitan Opera House, at which he would focus on the subtleties between a symphony orchestra and a modern dance orchestra, he probably had no idea his wish might come true.[137]

Otto gave consent for Lopez and his fifty-piece jazz orchestra to perform an afternoon concert at the Met. The show went ahead on Sunday, November 23. It was the first jazz concert ever presented at the opera house. For the occasion, Lopez augmented his orchestra with a twenty-piece saxophone section. In popularity stakes, Lopez was forever tailing Paul Whiteman, and that grieved him. With this show, Lopez hoped to catch up with his rival and narrow the gap. The recital was an undeniable success and combined all-American classical music with a selection of modern pieces.

Lopez was a natural showman. His secret for presenting a good jazz program was variety: 'I get back from my audience just as much rhythm as I give out, provided I am playing the right kind of music.'[138] That music was jazz.

The notion of a jazz concert at the Met brought outrage in operatic circles, not least from those who performed there. 'Impresario Giulio Gatti-Casazza surrenders the baton to Vincent Lopez,' wrote the *Springfield Missouri Republican*.[139]

To help counter any ill-feeling by opera buffs, Lopez released a sympathetic statement to the press before his concert: 'Mr. Lopez is conscious of the distinction, and the responsibilities thrust upon him, and he intends making his debut there the first real exposition of the possibilities of jazz in its best and highest sense.'

The irony in Otto's actions cannot have escaped Roger's attention.

The backlash to Otto's sudden defense of jazz, and there was a backlash, a major one, hit newspapers globally.

'Kahn on Jazz!' read the leader in the *Music Courier*.[140] 'His words have been reported all over the world, a fact that is far more interesting than the words themselves,' whined the *Courier*.

'If Tom, Dick, or Harry had made the same or similar statements, not a single newspaper would ever have quoted them to say nothing of the editorial mention, which has also been accorded the remarks of Mr. Kahn. Even if Tom, Dick, or Harry were musical experts far more qualified to speak of jazz than is Mr. Kahn, their words would have been received with (perhaps) respectful silence. But Mr. Kahn has millions; he is a sponsor of the arts, has a son who directs a jazz band; therefore, what he says is of importance to the news-seeking press.'

The Times headed its editorial with the comment: 'His Opinion Will Not Be Accepted.' They then openly contradicted Kahn.

The World was less antagonistic, agreeing, 'his thesis is sound' and 'jazz, whether we like it or not, is American.'

The *Courier* ranted, it was 'pleasant' of Kahn to have defended jazz, but how much better if someone of 'real musical' merit had stepped forward in its defense. Alas! The *Courier* sighed; no such musician or composer volunteered. The *Times* dug the knife in further, voicing, if jazz expresses the American spirit, then the American spirit was, 'in a very bad way.' Such views would no doubt rage on for many years to come.

Not long after, Otto announced he wished to produce an authentic American jazz opera on the Met stage. Predictably, the press threw their arms up in horror.[141] Otto approached George Gershwin, Irving Berlin, and Jerome Kern with the honor. All three replied they had empathy with the concept but were ill-equipped to write such a production. Many thought Kahn had again jumped in when he had no right to. Some papers suggested his son Roger's musical adventures were the stimulus behind the idea.

The *Music Trade News* joined in the discussion. 'Everybody's talking about it! Everybody has an opinion - so, let's have a symposium,' and requested its readers to join the debate by submitting their views for publication.

Composer and philanthropist Eleanor Everest Freer hastily penned a reply: 'Art is based upon nothing but talent and technique, it needs no clap-trap or jazz basis, as Otto Kahn advocates, and when Americans take the operatic destinies of the country into his own hands, then only, will the country produce art and opera.'

Journalist and foreign correspondent Charles Henry Meltzer aimed straight for Otto's jugular: 'Mr. Kahn again rushes to the defense of the noblest national art - well, he is able to treat the Metropolitan as a toy.'

The most astounding part of it all, stressed the *Springfield Missouri Republican*, was that no less a person than Otto Kahn had stepped forward with the offer in the first place.[142] Their denouncement was based upon Otto's initial refusal to allow his son Roger to follow a career as a jazz musician. The journal even went as far as to assert, 'his son, Roger Wolfe Kahn, was really the pioneer of the family.'

Irrespective of the furor in the newspapers, jazz showed no signs of wilting away into a darkened corner. Indeed, quite the opposite scenario was happening in America and on the continent. On Wednesday, December 10, diners in capitals across Europe embraced a live dual transcontinental jazz broadcast from Philadelphia (via Wanamaker radio station WOO) and the Wanamaker Auditorium in

New York (via network WNYC). The cities across Europe that tuned in for the transmission included London, Paris, Vienna, and many others.[143]

In December, Gilbert and Anne returned to New York from their honeymoon, wildly happy, and immediately set up home in their new apartment on East 72nd Street. Gilbert had made the momentous decision to cut his college studies short and to leave Princeton as a sophomore, having studied only two of his four-year degree. He planned to forge a career in banking. He secured a job as a clerk at the Equitable Trust Company's head office at 37 Wall Street, deciding it was wiser for him to gain a firm grounding away from his father's influence.[144] Nonetheless, it was common knowledge Otto was a director and trustee of the Equitable Trust. Otto was also a great friend of James Irving Bush, vice president of the company.

Perhaps Gilbert might have stayed on at Princeton and graduated had he not found all the benefits and trappings from being a son of one of the wealthiest men in the world so distracting.

At midday on December 23, WSB Atlanta Radio broadcast a performance of the Roger Wolfe Kahn Orchestra.[145] Two days later, on Christmas day evening, the Kahn family gathered around the wireless to hear Roger and his orchestra featured on *Christmas Frolic* aired from 8 to 9 p.m.[146]

In the embers of December, Roger could reflect upon the goals he had achieved throughout the year with a sense of pride. That said, he was not one to rest upon his laurels. Roger may have gained his father's approval, but he had yet to win favor with certain sections of the media. The new year would bring countless challenges for the young musician and yet more obstacles to overcome.

PART II

SITTING ON TOP OF THE WORLD

1925–1929

Roger Wolfe Kahn

The Twenties were a charming, carefree decade. The Kahns epitomized all that glittered and all that was golden.

8

HOWLING WOLFE

'It's just that the music is in me, and I have to get it out.'[1]
Roger W. Kahn

1925

Otto was working from his Kuhn, Loeb office at 52 William Street on January 2 when he dictated a brief note to his secretary addressed to James B. Pond. He invited Pond to attend a luncheon on January 7 to welcome the British politician and writer Edward Hilton Young to New York.[2] Young was the British Liberal Member of Parliament for Norwich. He had previously worked as the Financial Secretary to the Treasury under Prime Minister Lloyd George. He was now a Privy Counselor and was in the U.S. on a brief visit to give talks.

James B. Pond was the son of impresario James Burton Pond who owned and ran the Lyceum Theatre Lecture Bureau that organized lucrative tours for writers and speakers. Mark Twain, Arthur Conan

Doyle, Booker T. Washington, and Winston Churchill were all represented by Pond. Pond Sr.'s death in 1903 resulted in his son taking over the family business. Pond was handling Young's speaking engagements during his visit to the States.

Forty-three leading bankers and other prominent men had so far accepted Otto's invitation to the gathering.

In Otto's letter to Pond, typed on Kuhn, Loeb's distinctive light-green letterheaded stationery, he asks, 'Please let me know when Young will arrive. I ought to see him for a few minutes some day before the luncheon.'

The note perfectly illustrates how Otto would skillfully arrange meetings that sometimes lasted only 'a few minutes' to allow him to fit all his appointments into his busy schedule.

Like his father, Roger also effectively adopted this work ethic to run his music business alongside his role as a creative artist.

Gilbert and Maud had now flown the nest, leaving only Roger and his sister Margaret at home living with their parents. Though each offspring had a private suite of rooms, they still had to abide by their parents' rules and respect their wishes when residing under the same roof. Roger still conducted rehearsals with his band at home, where he also dealt with the intricacies involved in running a successful musical unit. With the band's increased workload, the arrangement was not always convenient for his musicians. Roger was also devoting more time to his arranging and composing. Bearing this in mind, it became glaringly apparent to Roger and his parents that he would have to rent an office to run his business more efficiently.

The office Roger rented at 1607 Broadway was a mere hop away from Manhattan's busiest intersection Times Square, where the illuminated advertising boards of later years had yet to mask every square foot of every building's façade. Presently, they were still recognizable for the purposes they were originally built. Only theaters had the brash, eye-catching billboards to entice passersby to rush into the box office and purchase a ticket. Times Square was as much a symbol of the city as was the Statue of Liberty, and it was around this midtown region that the cultural heart of the city beat.

Roger's office was not the tiny breadbox one might imagine, like the ones squashed into Tin Pan Alley, with blank walls housing an upright piano. It was a plush, streamlined suite. He even engaged a secretary. Emblazoned on the front windows in black lettering larger than those on his father's bank (and just as big as those of songwriter Irving Berlin whose office was directly above) was the name, Roger

Wolfe Kahn.[3] From now on, this would be Roger's music headquarters and business office. Conveniently, the building also housed Ringle's Rehearsal Studio.

Paul Whiteman had a booking agency, as did Vincent Lopez. It seemed only a matter of time before Roger had one. He employed a booker to handle his engagements and those of any orchestras he might wish to represent. One of the first units Kahn's organization signed was the Kentucky Serenaders, securing them a residency at the Hotel Belleview in Belleair, Florida.[4]

The marketing of Roger Wolfe Kahn was just as important to Roger as the music he played. What the public perceived him to be would influence how they related to him as a serious artist or not. To the general public, Roger's life had been predetermined by a series of markers - his surname, his family's wealth, the houses he lived in, etc. They were all components he had no control over. To achieve his career goals, Roger felt he had to change people's perceptions of him.

Given this, Roger hired George D. Lottman as his full-time publicist. Their working relationship was an immediate success, so much so, the whole office took on a different dynamic, more fun and less pressured. Both were creative souls and eager to make a mark in their chosen professions. Lottman remained with Roger for many years. They also became firm, lifelong friends and would, on occasions, go on vacations and business trips together.

George was 24 when he began working for Roger and was married to Betty Court (a vaudeville singer with the Court Sisters). Before setting up as a freelance radio press agent, he worked as a feature writer on the *New York American* broadsheet and at *Women's Wear* magazine.

Under Lottman's guidance, Roger's career took on an entirely new dimension. George's job was to promote Roger in a positive light and keep the public interested in him. As Roger's flack, George came into his own and soon built up a sound reputation as a man that got things done. Overnight, Roger's public image changed for the better. To keep the media interested, George regularly fed news agencies bulletins and updates on Roger's activities.

Roger's next move was to arrange a vaudeville tour. To test the waters, the Kahn Orchestra, with Roger blowing sax, participated in an Actor's Fund Benefit at Jolson's 59th Street Theatre. The show took place on Friday afternoon, January 23, and sold out, grossing $25,000 for the fund. Kahn's orchestra was the first act on stage and played four numbers to 'plenty of applause.'[5] Also appearing on the bill was George Gershwin.

The band's performance was enough of a success for Roger to push ahead with preparations for a tour of New York and Brooklyn vaudeville houses spanning several months. The dates were timed to fit seamlessly with the band's residency at the Biltmore and were a way of introducing Roger to a broader audience, an audience that he hoped would fall head over heels for him.

Popular Bill at the Hippodrome

The following week the 'Million Dollar' bandleader appeared at New York's Hippodrome on a million-dollar bill with a 'Million Dollar Baby.' It was Roger's first appearance there but his bands second. The family-oriented eleven-act presentation catered primarily for youngsters on their half-term break. A heterogeneous mixture of acts appeared on the bill, ranging from the drag artiste Karyl Norman to the Hippodrome Girls (dance troupe) dressed as wooden soldiers and a balancing dog named Teddy, whose intelligence was almost human. Topping the bill was the 6-year-old superstar Baby Peggy (Peggy-Jean Montgomery) in her vaudeville debut. She was better known for her screen appearances. On stage, she romped around in a little net frock accessorized with white socks and patent leather pumps, telling comedy sketches and singing with all the poise of a grownup. She was labeled the 'Million Dollar Baby' due to her $1.5 million Universal movie contract.

Roger Wolfe Kahn and his Inaugural Orchestra were the third act in the running order and shone for all the right reasons. Roger added 'Inaugural' to the band's name to highlight the news his band was to perform at the Inaugural Ball in Washington, D.C., following Calvin Coolidge's presidential inauguration ceremony. The stage set at the Hippodrome was minimal, dressed with a backdrop of purple velvet upon which hung an enormous American flag offset by a gold-painted staircase on which the Kahn band stood.[6] Violinist Joe Raymond handled directing duties. This arrangement allowed Roger to focus on playing his saxophone, during which he 'manipulated torrid notes' and took a bow at the conclusion. Various staged effects colored their performance, including an unbilled female dancer performing jazzy steps to a scorching rendition of 'Stars and Stripes Forever.'

The presentation proved so popular it ran for several weeks through to the end of February, with all three daily shows selling out. *Variety* reckoned that three-quarters of the audience were juveniles to see Baby Peggy; such was her phenomenal drawing power. They also noted the genuine enthusiasm and noise the younger members of the audience generated exceeded any hand clapping by the elder element present. It was a smart move by the Shubert brothers to include Roger on the bill; his appeal to the youngsters was instant and, in their eyes, elevated him from 'curiosity' act to star status and teenage music sensation. It, therefore, came as no surprise when Victor Talking Machine Company (known informally as Victor Records) signed Roger to an exclusive recording contract during his engagement at the Hippodrome.

On Valentine's Day, Otto departed from New York on the SS *Duilio* for an extended business trip through Europe. He planned to visit Italy, France, Spain, and England.[7] The tour would see him away from the U.S. and his family until early June. At the quayside, when a reporter asked him about the possibility of him arranging loans with foreign Governments, Otto declined to make any comment.

The 35th presidential election had taken place the previous year on November 4, at which the incumbent president and Republican, Calvin Coolidge, was elected to a full term. Coolidge had served as president since President Warren G. Harding's death on August 2, 1923. The idea of a Charity Inaugural Ball had flourished since its inception in 1921. It was the vision of Mrs. John Allan Dougherty, treasurer of the Child Welfare Society. The ball was conceived as a charity event to benefit children.

News of Roger's invitation to perform at the ball surfaced in the papers as early as mid-February. United News Pictures was the first agency to grab the story and released a pleasing photograph of Roger clutching a Conn saxophone with their report: 'Millionaire's son to lead orchestra at Inaugural Ball. Roger Wolfe Kahn, son of Otto H. Kahn, youngest orchestra leader of standing in the country, has been chosen to lead his orchestra, one of two, which will furnish music at the Inaugural Ball on March 4 in Washington. Roger organized his orchestra a year ago and, by being selected to supply jazz at the most important national function of the year, becomes at seventeen, the leader of the first jazz band in the land.'*

Coolidge would have preferred not to have had a ball, finding the expense wasteful. He was also still in private mourning over the tragic death of his 16-year-old son Calvin Jr., who had died from a blood infection the previous summer.

Otto's departure to foreign shores meant he missed the president's inauguration ceremony. He also missed his son's performance at the

The Charity Inaugural Ball souvenir program, March 4, 1925.*

PROGRAM FOR THE INAUGURAL BALL AT THE MAYFLOWER HOTEL
EVENING OF MARCH 4TH, 1925

UNITED STATES NAVY BAND ORCHESTRA

CHARLES BENTER, *Director.*

9 to 10 P. M.

* * *

1. Grand March, "CORONATION".....................*Meyerbeer*
   From The Prophet

2. Overture, "FINGAL'S CAVE"......................*Mendelssohn*

3. Finale from the "SYMPHONY IN F MINOR"....*Tschaikowsky*
   No. 4, Opus 36
   Fourth Movement, Allegro Con Fuco Andante

4. Grand Scenes from the Opera, "LOHENGRIN".........*Wagner*

5. Suite of two numbers:
   (a) "WOODLAND WHISPERS" (Characteristic).....*Czibulka*
   (b) "WHISPERING FLOWERS" (Characteristic)....*Von Blon*

6. Valse de Concert, "ROSES FROM THE SOUTH".......*Strauss*

7. Ballet Music from "FAUST" (Suite Number One)........*Gounod*
   (a) Tempo di Valse, (b) Adagio, (c) Allegretto, (d) Moderato
   Maestoso.

8. Excerpts from the Musical Comedy, "WILDFLOWER"..*Youmans*
   Finale, "STAR SPANGLED BANNER"

* * *

DANCE ORDER OF ROGER WOLFE KAHN ORCHESTRA

Beginning at 10 P. M.

1. The Only Only One
2. I Want You
3. Tokio Blues
4. I'll See You in My Dreams
5. Pleasure Mad
6. Rose Marie
7. Waters of Minnetonka
8. Oh, Mabel
9. All Alone
10. Me and My Boy Friend
11. Tea for Two
12. My Best Girl
13. Peter Pan
14. You and I.

Intermission

15. Lulaby
16. Why
17. Good-bye Sunshine
18. Tango
19. June Brought the Roses
20. Indian Love Call
21. Roses of Picardi
22. Fascinating Rhythm
23. Lady Be Good
24. So Am I
25. Call of the South
26. Tell Her in the Springtime
27. Florida
28. Shine

* * *

DANCE ORDER OF VINCENT LOPEZ' ORCHESTRAS

Beginning at 10 P. M.

1. Fox-trot, "Oh Joseph"
2. Fox-trot, "Rose Marie"
3. Fox-trot, "Me and My Boy Friend"
4. Fox-trot, "Follow the Swallows"
5. Waltz, "Shadowland"
6. Fox-trot, "Cold, Cold Mamma"
7. Fox-trot, "Tea for Two"
8. Fox-trot, "Driftwood"
9. Fox-trot, "Lady Be Good"
10. Waltz, "Memory Lane"
11. Fox-trot, "Charley My Boy"
12. Fox-trot, "Fascinating Rhythm"

Intermission

1. Fox-trot, "Indian Love Call"
2. Fox-trot, "I Can't Get the One I want"
3. Fox-trot, "Adoring You"
4. Fox-trot, "Eliza"
5. Waltz, "What'll I Do?"
6. Fox-trot, "Too Tired"
7. Fox-trot, "Spain" (Tango)
8. Fox-trot, "Limehouse Blues"
9. Fox-trot, "Charleston"
10. Waltz, "All Alone"
11. Fox-trot, "Prince of Wales"
12. Fox-trot, "Good Night Ladies"

The dance order of the Roger Wolfe Kahn Orchestra and Vincent Lopez Orchestra - Charity Inaugural Ball souvenir program, March 4, 1925.

inaugural ball held at the Mayflower Hotel. However, Otto did purchase a box for the occasion, which he gave to Mrs. Lawrence Townsend (of Washington's fashionable Du Pont social circle) to entertain her guests in.[8] Nearly 5,000 people turned up for the dance, filling the ballroom, the great dining room (cleared for dancing), the long corridor (which ran between the two), and the adjoining garden. In truth, so many people attended, they appeared to take possession of the whole building, packing into every available space and walkway.

Five orchestras played during the evening, of which the United States Navy Band, Vincent Lopez, and Roger Wolfe Kahn were the most notable. The *New York Evening Post* rated the Kahn ensemble as the jolliest and pointed out that several of their twenty-eight numbers received bursts of applause from the dancers.[9] Although President Coolidge chose not to be present at the ball, preferring to retire to bed early at 10 p.m., Vice President Charles Dawes and his wife Caro did show up.

An interesting stage view of dancers in the Mayflower Hotel's ballroom during the Inaugural Ball, March 4, 1925.

Neither did Addie, Margaret, or Gilbert catch Roger's performance that evening. Addie and Margaret were enjoying a relaxing break at Oheka Cottage in Palm Beach. Gilbert and his wife Anne were also holidaying in Florida as guests of Anne's parents and were staying at the Whelan's villa Belleaire in The Oranges.[10]

Upon Addie's return to New York in March, her busy calendar of social functions resumed almost immediately. One of the more noteworthy events she attended was the world premiere of the one-act opera, *The Garden of Mystery*, composed by Charles Wakefield

Cadman.

In late spring, Addie employed a new personal chauffeur, Robert McCulloch, who hailed from the coastal town of Dornoch in the Highlands of Scotland.[11] Robert remained loyally in Addie's service for many years.

The U.S. was experiencing a period of rapid economic growth and social change that would become synonymous with jazz, the 1920s, and Calvin Coolidge's presidency. Later dubbed by the media as the Roaring Twenties, the roar would increase in volume right up until the end of the decade. For the present, life was good, and consumerism continued to rise to even greater heights never before seen in the American economy. One such commodity that Americans bought by the truckload was phonograph records.

On Tuesday, March 10, Roger led his Biltmore orchestra into Victor Studios in New Jersey to record his debut single.

'Hot-Hot-Hottentot,' composed by Fred Fisher, was the first track Roger and his orchestra laid down. They captured four takes. Historically, they were one of the last batches of acoustic recordings Victor ever made; almost every session afterward was recorded electrically. Arthur Lange arranged the song, proving he did remain true to his word.[12]

Between the four takes recorded, takes 1 and 4 ended up trashed. The 2nd take was released, with the 4th held as a backup should it be required.

Although there is no vocal on the recording, at 0:44 seconds into the track, a voice calls out 'Hottentot.' The simplest explanation of Hottentot implies an indigenous South African warrior or tribesman from the Khoikhoi tribe. The German-born songwriter Fred Fisher may have used the term to appeal to the current trend for Black music.

At the same session, Roger also recorded 'Yearning (Just For You),' a composition by Benny Davis and Joe Burke, which delivers a bright vocal refrain by Elliott Shaw.

Victor released 'Hot-Hot-Hottentot' backed with 'Yearning (Just For You)' the following month, on April 24.[13] As with the launch of any new recording artist, the label had high hopes for their latest prodigy. The two tracks showcased Roger's and his talented band of musicians, versatility. Colored promotional posters depicting a woman wearing a pompadour wig accompanied the record's release and appeared in music stores and on billboards across the States.[14]

An advertising poster for *'Hot-Hot-Hottentot'* and *'Yearning.'*
These were Roger's first recordings released on Victor Records.

Roger was now a Victor recording artist.

(Prints and Photographs Division Washington, D.C., George
Grantham Bain Collection, Library of Congress)

Disappointingly, the tracks did not sell as well as Victor and Roger had hoped. Consequently, the record company held back Roger's second offerings until later in the year, much later, late November, to be exact.

Fire on Long Island

On March 24, a grass fire took hold on arable land in Huntington, Long Island, and spread to adjoining estates.[15] Huntington Manor Fire Department attended the initial outbreak but could not contain or stop the fire from spreading. As flames leaped from hedgerows to forests across acres of land, the blaze drew ever closer to the Kahn estate. One hundred firefighters and many local volunteers valiantly fought to dampen the flames and prevent the fire from spreading and damaging more property. Although the Kahn mansion was not yet in immediate danger, cottages and farm buildings bordering the estate were. The fire raged for hours. Eventually, it was brought under control and extinguished, averting any risk of the Kahn residence from being engulfed by flames.

Roger's orchestra business was at last beginning to pay dividends. His deal with Victor paid him $1,000 for every recording date he attended.[16] His orchestra currently commanded $2,200 a week in vaudeville. Vincent Lopez had put a $3,000 price tag on his vaudeville engagements. Within time, Roger's rate would surpass that amount. He also received requests to play on the college circuit, where he could increase his fee by $500 to $1,000 for a personal appearance. On top of this amount was his steady weekly salary from the Biltmore of around $2,800. His booking agency also commanded a cut from every gig or residency they secured for the bands they represented.

Understandably, some of the more established members of New York's music fraternity were a bit sore about this new kid's financial pulling power. On the downside for Roger, all the additional work he was attracting added extra hours to his already lengthy workday.

To help reduce his band's weekly expenditure, Roger reshuffled the personnel, bringing in less costly yet equally talented musicians.[17] Pianist Al Mitchell came on board to complement Ray Romano, the ace pianist already in the band. Mitchell had previously headed a combination signed to Paul Whiteman's agency.[18] Under Roger's leadership, Mitchell also took over as the band's chief arranger, relinquishing the necessity for any future involvement with Arthur Lange. Other members that were released, whose salaries had risen considerably due to Roger's munificence, were told by their new employers to 'come down to earth' regarding their future earnings.[19] After doing his sums, Roger calculated his band was now self-supporting.

Roger premiered his newly streamlined band on Sunday, April 13, at a National Vaudeville Association benefit at the Hippodrome, during which Roger played his saxophone.[20] The confidence and alacrity of the musicians showed. The press deemed the new roster 'hot.'

The summer season was fast approaching, and the Cascades atop the Biltmore was scheduled to reopen its doors in June. Roger was determined to have the slickest band in New York in preparation for its reopening. Kahn's agency was already negotiating a summer vaudeville tour for him, expected to play in New York's Keith-Albee houses that would run simultaneously with his residency at the Cascades. Roger knew he had to get his band blisteringly hot if he was to impress his peers as well as the discerning public. As part of the present reshuffle, one of the last new members Roger contracted was violinist Joe Venuti.[21]

Majesty Limited

In Paris, Otto dined with the recently elected French Prime Minister Paul Painlevé and his Minister of Finance, Joseph Caillaux.[22] They discussed, among other things, the French War debts. Otto made it a custom never to disclose the intricacies and minutiae of such meetings publicly. When a leak appeared in the newspapers professedly from Otto, outlining various points considered during the dinner, Kahn blew his top and denied ever having delivered them.[23]

In a correction Otto cabled to the press, he insisted: 'I have been scrupulously careful not to say one word in public during my stay in Europe on the question of the foreign debts to America except in one speech, before an American club in Paris. On that occasion, I said it would be unbecoming to speak on the question of the French debt, a question which I hoped would be settled before long in a manner satisfactory and honorable to both nations. At a private dinner later, at which no reporters were present, I cautioned the gathering against placing too much dependability on words from America that wound susceptibilities, declaring even journalists and politicians were not cloaked in infallibility.' His words were a stinging rebuke to the peddlers of untruths.

In London, on the final leg of his tour, a reporter for the *London Evening News* grilled Kahn on his opinions of jazz and whether he still believed it to be the future of music.[24] Otto hated it when reporters assumed they knew his mind better than he did.

'Of course, I hold no such belief,' Kahn replied curtly. 'What I do think is that, notwithstanding the imperfections of present-day jazz, there will develop out of it in the future, a genuine and significant American contribution to the art of music. ... True, it is traced back to African origin, but America has taken it, modified it, and made it, its own.'

It must have appeared to Otto that in some obscure way, he'd now become an unofficial spokesman for the cause for furthering jazz, so interested were the media in his views of it. Admittedly, he had traveled farther than most people and, therefore, seen the effect jazz had on diverse cultures across several continents. 'I have just completed a journey, which took me through a good part of Europe and some of Africa,' Kahn explained. 'Jazz was to be met with, everywhere, even among the Arabs.'

To many critics, jazz's organic growth into a legitimate art form proved challenging to understand or define. Otto conveyed his theory as to why this should be:

'Jazz is majesty limited,' he declared, 'and affected with crudities in its present stage; its failings 'jump at the eye' as the French say, or rather, 'at the ear'; but it does characteristically mirror some of the conditions of our modern life. It has rhythm and dynamics and seeks - what is too often neglected by the more 'high-toned' of modern composers - melody. It is sincere and spontaneous and stands robustly on its feet, boldly disregardful of rules and precedent.'

Kahn spoke as fluidly as any accomplished musician might when emphasizing a particular phrase in a musical piece. At the end of his explanation, Kahn affirmed, 'I look upon jazz as a phase, as a transition, not as a completed process.'

The 'completed process' Kahn references presently appeared to be a long way off, judging by his response. When the reporter inquired, 'Will there ever be jazz opera, Mr. Kahn?' Otto must have bitten his lip in frustration at being repeatedly asked the same question. Being clairvoyant was not one of Otto's métiers; neither was he inclined to favor supposition. Otto was clear and decisive in his reply:

'Jazz opera strikes me as a contradiction in terms. In its literal meaning, it is utterly unthinkable. But I do hope that some of the young American composers who, at present, are devoting their talents to producing jazz dance music and jazz songs will tackle more important and more exacting tasks. I hope some of them will try their hand at opera and endeavor to express themselves in their own way Similarly, with the book and story - let it too be drawn from the fullness of present-day life.'

Otto backed up his belief with a simple statement: 'True art is eternal, but it is not stationary.' The progression of any art form is imperative for its development. Jazz was still in its preliminary stages. Its evolution would depend purely upon the public's interest in exploiting and nurturing it.

When the reporter craftily inquired whether Kahn was encouraging his son Roger to follow a jazz career, one can sense Otto deemed the whippersnapper had overstepped the mark. 'My son's development is, of course, no matter of public interest, least of all outside his own country. If I speak of his activities in music, I do so merely to illustrate a phenomenon of which, from my own observation, I see him as a typical example. His inherited taste and gift for music manifest themselves, thus far, mainly in what are among the essential American traits, namely, rhythm and dynamics. Hence, he is drawn now to what, for want of a better term, is comprehensively called 'jazz,' and expresses himself in that musical idiom.' Otto then revealed plans were in the pipeline for Roger to further his music studies at a European conservatoire. He was keen to observe what effect such an education would have upon his son in the future.

The 'Boy Wonder' of Jazz!

In early June, Otto's return to New York coincided with the Cascades' reopening at the Biltmore,[25] where Roger and his orchestra would be playing nightly throughout summer.[26]

During Otto's absence, Roger had composed a musical comedy score in collaboration with lyricist Louis Brea tentatively titled *I'm For You*.[27] William Cary Duncan had written the book, and Edgar Macgregor was tipped as a likely producer. Rehearsals were already penciled for late summer with talk of a fall premiere. Roger had expressed his wish to abstain from using his father's influence or patronage, fearing reports of nepotism might jinx the production.[28] As such, Edward Royce had been lassoed as the show's chief sponsor and director, with any financial input from Otto, placed on a back-burner in reserve, should it be required at a later date.[29]

Roger, the Society Sleuth

In June, speculation was rife in Manhattan's smart drawing rooms that Otto Kahn's errant teenage son Roger was now thinking about becoming a full-time detective.[30] The story even crept into society gossip columns. Not wishing to put a hot rumor to bed or indeed miss the opportunity of scooping an exclusive, the press got to work sniffing out the facts behind this amusing tale. It soon came to light that the conjecture had an element of truth to it; Roger was indeed acting as a part-time sleuth, albeit on a case-by-case basis as and when the New York Detective Force called upon his services. The boy detective had even been elected an honorary member of the elite '400' force and earned his detective star by helping to catch a thief.*

In a full-page report, the *Springfield Leader* revealed the details and how it had all come about.[31]

Over the past couple of years, a well-documented spate of unsolved society crimes had taken place around New York City and its wealthy suburbs: robberies, burglaries, and even a suspected murder. The offenses usually involved vast sums of money or expensive jewelry. Most of the felonies had baffled the victims and the authorities.

The previous year during Edward, Prince of Wales's visit to the U.S., one such high-profile burglary occurred at a party the prince was attending. The million-dollar country home of Joshua A. Cosden at Sands Point on Long Island was the crime scene. The costly pearls of Mrs. Cosden worth $150,000 and gems belonging to houseguest Lady Mountbatten valued at $42,000 were the items stolen.[32] The break-in happened in the early hours of Tuesday morning on September 9 while the party was in full swing. The Cosdens had even hired extra security stewards to keep reporters and photographers at bay. That the prince was a guest appears not to have dissuaded the crook or 'crooks' in the slightest. Indeed, the prince's presence seems to have been a blessing in disguise.

Joshua A. Cosden had made his multi-million dollar fortune in the oil fields of Oklahoma. At the time of the party, the Prince of Wales was a houseguest at the Burden estate a few miles along the Gold Coast.

Whether any member of the Kahn family attended the Cosden party is unknown, as no guest list was made available to the media. However, Otto did attend the Mackays Long Island party for Prince Edward on September 6. So, theoretically, Otto may have been a guest at the Cosdens bash on September 9.

From Roger's perspective, the thief had to have known the hosts. It had all the hallmarks of an inside job, as did most of the other similar burglaries.

Intruders in darkened bedrooms were made even more mysterious and fascinating in the public's imagination when robbery after robbery happened without the cops bringing the perpetrator to justice or locating the booty.

Roger's cover was blown during a dinner at the Hotel Biltmore, at which he was presented with a gold badge and made an Honorary Member of the New York Detective Force.[33] At seventeen, he was the youngest member of the association. Special guests at the event included Detective Dennis Mahoney (president of the New York Detectives' Association) and around a dozen members of the New York police force. Roger's father was also present. The *Brooklyn Daily Eagle* wondered whether, from now on, hostesses would be inviting the teenager to their soirees to watch over their silver spoons and wedding presents?[34]

During Roger's induction speech, he expressed how it was not the fault of his 'full-time' colleagues [detectives] that they were born to the 'blue' rather than the 'purple.' By definition, beaten before they started when it came to solving society crimes. Roger pointed out that the malefactor who preyed on the rich would have to be someone who understood their psychology. Roger felt, with his upbringing, he was in the perfect position to outsmart the villain. He also made clear he had no desire to take any credit away from the police force but would merely be there to assist them.

Detective Dennis Mahoney clarified that Roger was appointed because he showed a genuine willingness to help the police solve 'society crime' mysteries. He did not reveal how many felonies Roger had given his hand to or helped bring about a satisfactory outcome. Otto declined to make any public statement to the press about his son's latest activity.

Later that evening at the Kahn home came leaked reports of merry laughter among family members as Otto recounted the evening's events. From then on, it became a family in-joke that whenever the police came knocking at their heavily bolted front door, they need not worry, for, in all probability, the cops would be seeking the assistance of young Roger to help solve a crime.

When a daylight robbery occurred later in the year at New York's Plaza Hotel, the whole city gasped in astonishment. In one fell swoop, $750,000 worth of jewelry disappeared from the 6-room suite of F. W. Woolworth heiress Mrs. James P. Donahue. New York cops called it the boldest jewel theft in history. Among the items spirited away under the perfumed nose of Mrs. Donahue as she lay soaking in her en suite bathtub was a $50,000 10-carat diamond ring and a heavy rope of pearls valued at the eye-watering figure of $450,000. This was serious bling. The thief astutely disregarded four imitation ropes of pearls good enough to fool an oyster; such was his expert eye.[35] Reports stated Mrs. Donahue felt physically sick when she discovered the robbery. Mrs. Donahue need not have feared, for help was close at hand, closer than she could ever have imagined.

Roger racked his brains over this one. The fact that a maid and her dresser were waiting in an adjoining sitting room made the robbery even more audacious.

Maud and Margaret viewed their younger brother's sleuth work with great amusement and ribbed him at every opportunity that arose when a 'young detective' might be called upon for assistance.

Trips Away

It was off-season in the city. The Met was shut. New Yorkers were readying themselves for their summer vacations. Several members of the Kahn family were heading to Europe. This year Roger was planning a change and would instead remain at home throughout the coming months.

In mid-July, Addie crossed the Atlantic aboard RMS *Olympic* accompanied by her brother-in-law Felix Kahn and her maid Madelein Garcin.[36] In London, they stayed at Claridge's Hotel. A week later, Addie journeyed to Ascot to spend time with her daughter Maud and grandson John. Before leaving the U.S., Addie had opened up the grounds at Cold Spring Harbor to allow the public to view the many colorful flowers and shrubs in bloom.[37] Gardening was an interest Addie had grown a great fondness for and one she hoped to engage in while pottering around her daughter's garden in Ascot.

Gilbert and his wife Anne had sailed to the UK on RMS *Berengaria* a week ahead of Addie with their private lady's maid Marie Metzner. They were also staying at Claridge's in London, where they met up with Addie.[38]

Gilbert had now been working over six months as a junior clerk at the Equitable Trust Company.[39] When he first took up the post, some detractors forecast he might not fit into the rigid pattern of full-time employment such as banking proffers. Initially, the sheer size and intricacies of the organization had baffled him. Yet, despite his earlier concerns, Gilbert had now settled comfortably into his role.

'The whole bank performs like a highly organized and perfected piece of machinery,' expressed Gilbert in the company's in-house newspaper, *The Equitable Envoy*. 'Each employee seems to have such a full and detailed understanding of his duties, and all show the same eagerness, the same precision, and the same fidelity to the company.'

The dependability that impressed Gilbert in his colleagues was now evident in his behavior. His work associates found him likable and pleasantly sociable without 'swank' or 'side.' Encouragingly, those close to him also felt he'd inherited some of his father's ability for understanding the complexities of financial matters.

Otto had always encouraged young scholars to experience aspects of life they had not encountered before. He would regularly donate his box at the Met to music students so they could enjoy top-class performances. He was also known to pay bursaries for gifted pupils to study at University. One memorable act of benevolence Otto financed was an extended weekend cruise for five hundred affiliates of the American-Hungarian Chamber of Commerce and their families. He hired the SS *Presidente Wilson* for a return voyage from New York to Nova Scotia. The liner left New York Harbor on Thursday, August 13, and arrived two days later on a bright, warm morning in Halifax. Otto paid for the entire cruise, so members of the Chamber could enjoy an outing in the 'old-fashioned' manner still operating in Europe.[40]

During the same weekend, Otto invited Roger and his orchestra to Long Island to spend Sunday relaxing at the Kahn estate.[41] Otto's 61-foot yacht *Oheka* transported the musicians (with their bulky instruments) along the East River to Oyster Bay. The band even struck up a tune or two while on board. One of the musicians who spent time exploring the grounds was the impressionable young violinist, Joe Venuti. He even managed to fit in a round of golf. Joe was astonished at the affluent lifestyle the Kahn family led. Upon returning to the Big Apple, he recounted his experience to his friends: 'It's nice, but it's not for me.'[42] Venuti believed in spending his money as and when he earned it enjoying life to the full. The orchestra gave a performance for the staff and, in return, were treated to a delicious homemade clambake.[43] The musicians slept overnight at the house and returned to Manhattan the following day, arriving back in time for their advertised performance at the Biltmore.

When Otto stayed at his Long Island estate in summer, he would commute to Manhattan on his yacht *Oheka*. The 35-mile trip could take up to one and a half hours, time enough to unwind from his hectic work schedule. Ninety tranquil minutes on the water soaking in the view, eating fresh lobster sandwiches, catching up with the broadsheets was Otto's reward at the day's end. The crew had grown used to the many children who'd swim out to greet the vessel upon its return to Oyster Bay and would generously dispense leftovers to them from Otto's afternoon tea; treats such as home-baked peach shortcake.

In August, news reports confirmed Roger was to establish a School of Jazz Music.[44] The academy was housed in the handsome Dakota building on Central Park West at 72nd Street, and the first term began in the fall.[45] The school bore Roger's name and was governed by him. Roger contracted many of the musicians in his band as faculty members to tutor in their respective fields: Tommy Gott on cornet and brass; Vic Berton - deemed by some to be the world's best drummer - supervised the drumming division; Arthur Schutt and Ray Romano taught piano; Joe Raymond tutored the violin, and Arnold Brilhart, Harold Sturr, and Dick Johnson taught saxophone and reeds. Although Roger was a multi-instrumentalist, he chose only to instruct in the art of arranging and orchestration. The curriculum targeted 'advanced' music students, and the first semester was limited to musicians from New York orchestras.[46]

The academy officially opened on Wednesday, November 18. Many celebrities from the world of popular music attended the launch. Vincent Lopez, Ray Miller, and Ben Bernie all offered welcoming speeches to the students.[47] One of the first classes was a special concert by Roger's Biltmore Orchestra to illustrate the fusion of jazz and classical music.

Also, in August, Roger announced he would be lending his name to other orchestras after his father had now permitted him to use the Kahn surname as a business proposition.[48] Upon hearing the news, the editor of *Variety*, Sime Silverman, contacted Roger to suggest his fledgling booking agency might increase its business if he advertised in his publication.[49]

Roger took heed of Silverman's advice. Regular adverts in *Variety* followed. Such marketing affirmed Roger Wolfe Kahn meant business.

Gilbert and Anne returned to New York in mid-September following their two-month trip to Europe.[50] Addie arrived back shortly after, rested, and ready to resume her social and charity engagements. The new cook Jessie Macrea from Scotland had settled in at 1100 Fifth Avenue and become an integral member of housekeeper Mary

Hogsett's efficient team of fourteen servants.[51] Addie's personal chauffeur Robert McCulloch, whom she employed earlier in the year, had also proved to be an exceptionally trustworthy and able employee. Gilbert resumed his duties at Equitable Trust with a noticeable spring in his step following his promotion within the company. Being home also allowed Gilbert to continue his saxophone lessons, which Roger had been giving him.[52]

"The Personnel Is High Grade and Considerably Worthy."—*Variety*.

ROGER WOLFE KAHN
AND HIS
Hotel Biltmore Orchestra

EXCLUSIVE VICTOR RECORDING ARTISTS

THE MOST IMPOSING ARRAY OF INDIVIDUAL INSTRUMENTALISTS IN
ANY SINGLE DANCE COMBINATION IN AMERICA

JOE RAYMOND, Violin			ARNOLD BRILLHART } Reeds
TOM GOTT } Trumpets		ROGER WOLFE KAHN	DICK JOHNSON
LEO McCONVILLE		Director	HAROLD STURR
			"CHUCK" CAMPBELL, Trombone
ARTHUR SCHUTT } Pianos			ARTHUR CAMPBELL, Bass
RAY ROMANO			DOMENICK ROMEO, Banjo
			VICTOR BURTON, Drums

UNTIL DECEMBER 31st, 1926, AT THE HOTEL BILTMORE, NEW YORK

"The Second Best Dance Combination in America."—*Billboard*.

Roger Wolfe Kahn and His Hotel Biltmore Orchestra, *Variety*, Sept. 9, 1925.[53]

Roger and his Hotel Biltmore Orchestra commenced a three-week, end-of-summer tour on September 21.[54] Their first gig was at the prestigious Palace Theatre in the heart of Times Square. The bill contained a hotchpot of variety acts.[55]

Young Kahn had already built a wide following among New York's café society.[56] His manager hoped this snap tour would broaden his appeal. In an astute move, John McEntee Bowman allowed Roger to link the Biltmore name with the Kahn brand, deeming the publicity it generated would be mutually beneficial.

On opening night, the house sold out. When the curtain rose, revealing Kahn's twelve-piece orchestra immaculately attired, with each musician posing perfectly still with their respective instrument, there was a noticeable stirring in the audience. Standing in front with his back to the auditorium was Roger. As soon as he raised his baton, the band leaped into action. Their first number was a foxtrot. When the youngster turned and glanced briefly towards the myriads of faces gazing back at him, he bowed his head slightly to acknowledge them before returning his attention towards his band. Roger was a born leader and a natural stage performer rolled into one. Slicing the air with his baton, pacing the rhythm in clockwork precision, all eyes in the theater were on him. The band played with pace and skill throughout their twenty-minute set, slick professionals to the core, sleeker than a jar of pomade. The 'boy wonder' of jazz had tailored his routine specifically for the masses, and the audience loved it.

ROGER WOLFE KAHN
ORCHESTRA
HOTEL BILTMORE, NEW YORK

Playing a Limited Vaudeville Tour of the
Greater Keith-Albee Theatres in New York
and Brooklyn

Roger Wolfe Kahn Orchestra, *Variety*, Sept. 30, 1925.

The following week the Kahn orchestra breezed into the Riverside Theatre for a seven-day engagement, followed by a week at the E. F. Albee Theatre in Brooklyn. They shared the bill with vocalist Nora Bayes and hoofer Bill 'Bojangles' Robinson. The notices were spectacular.[57]

As well as directing his orchestra, Roger also played the drums, cornet, saxophone, trumpet, banjo, violin, and piccolo on stage,[58] concertinaing from one instrument to another without pausing to catch his breath. It was a novel idea and meant Roger remained the focal point of the performance.

'Young Kahn and his associates were given a rousing reception when the names went out on the enunciators,' reported *Variety*.[59] The band performed 'eight numbers with three as encores' and took full advantage of the generous amount of time allotted them 'in the No. 3 spot.'[60]

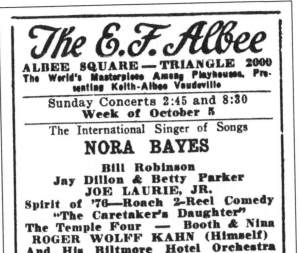

Roger and His Biltmore Hotel Orchestra at the E. F. Albee Theatre.

Top of the bill at the Palace meant you had made it. Broadway was laid at your feet. After Roger's storming debut at the venue, Keith-Albee's booking office, in an unprecedented move, announced the immediate return of Kahn and his orchestra for a solid three-week run opening on October 5. Reports claimed it was probably the quickest return date to the Palace in any artiste's career.[61] What was so astonishing was that it happened so early in Roger's career. Some entertainers could wait for twenty years before securing a slot on the bill at the Palace. Even more bizarre was that Roger declined the three-week booking, preferring to play only one week due to the heavy work commitments already confirmed in his diary.[62] He did, however, negotiate an additional engagement to run over Christmas and New Year's Eve.

On Monday, October 12, Roger's return to the Palace did not disappoint his fans or the critics. When the curtain rose, Roger took command of his band with the flair of a seasoned professional.

'Young Kahn leads with a quickness and earnestness that may have been combined with some nervousness on Monday night. But he knows what he is doing and controlled the men all of the time.'[63]

As the adrenaline rush kicked in, a mighty wall of sound confronted the audience, beckoning them to tap their feet, wave their arms, sway their bodies or, do anything, just as long as they did it in time to the wildly infectious rhythm the band was delivering.

'One flash at this Kahn boy ... and you will wonder how his father ever happened to traverse the world looking for high art talent when he had it right at his own dining table. It's funny, too, when it's so well known that every member of high or low art the world over knows, or knows of Otto Kahn - and are expectant of or from him. And his own kid most likely can make 60 percent of those from the high or low staked by his father look foolish for natural talent. The Kahn turn well earned its several encores. It's quite an orchestra for a youngster to have organized.'64

Was this the same, diffident, insecure boy of only a year ago? It appeared not. Roger had blossomed into a first-rate performer.

'While bands nowadays are no novelties and it must be an exceptional one to distinguish from the other, the Kahn orchestra has a name and music with both distinctive. That makes this orchestra of extra value for vaudeville, as it must for the Hotel Biltmore.'65

The following week Roger celebrated his 18th birthday.* The day brought an unexpected gift - a hallmarked silver conductor's baton presented to him by his band members.66 It was a touching gesture, appreciated more so by the birthday boy because his musicians knew firsthand the struggles and challenges he had overcome to reach this point in his life. The silver baton became Roger's lucky mascot, and from that day forward, he used it at every stage performance he gave.

Kahn's band now ranked among the top orchestras in America for showmanship and musical brilliance, a fact clearly stated by one reviewer after catching the band's performance at the Cascades given directly after a show at the Palace. 'That the organization musically rates as one of the best hotel bands in the United States, not alone New York, is the natural thing, considering the personnel.'67

That line-up included: Roger Wolfe Kahn, various instruments and conductor; Joe Raymond, violin and stand-in conductor; Tommy Gott and Leo McConville, trumpet; Arthur Schutt and Ray Romano, baby grand piano; Harold Sturr, Arnold Brilhart, Dick Johnson, saxophone section; 'Chuck' Campbell, trombone; Vic Burton (aka Berton), drums and percussion; Arthur Campbell, tuba, and Domenic Romeo, banjo.

The grudging premise that Otto, through some imagined connection with the Hotel Biltmore management, had made Roger's residency at the hotel possible was 'mere supposition,' stated journalist Abel Green in *Variety*.68 Roger's critics may have barked over Otto's initial financial input in helping his son establish his band, but the tide had turned. The Kahn organization was now self-supporting. Roger had personally lost a considerable amount of money in keeping the band afloat over the past year, but his determination had paid off. His bank account was in the red, and he was making a healthy profit, enough to start clearing his financial debt to his father. After deducting his weekly outgoings, Roger was now making over $500 a week profit.[69]

Now that his son's band was commercially viable, Otto became a regular visitor to the Hotel Biltmore, where he would often invite friends and business associates for dinner. He already subscribed to at least half a dozen press clipping agencies to keep informed of his family's increased media coverage. In moments of fatherly pride, he would confide how much he cherished some of his son's most flattering press notices to the extent of carrying them about in his coat pocket so he could show them to people.

At the end of Roger's short vaudeville tour, he returned to work on a new stage musical he'd intermittently been scoring. It went by the tentative title of *Miss Moonbeam*.[70] He hoped to complete it within the next couple of months. Two notable librettists were collaborating with him on the project. Roger also placed a new composition, 'Nobody Loves Me,' containing a Lew Brown lyric, with Shapiro-Bernstein publishers.[71] Later in the fall, Roger contracted the talented acoustic guitarist Eddie Lang to join his Hotel Biltmore outfit. Lang arrived via a recommendation from a fellow band member, violinist Joe Venuti. Band members were also quick to take advantage of the band's current popularity. Drummer Vic Berton authored the book *Tips on Tap* published by Robbins-Engel Inc. It was the first 'how to play drums competently' instruction manual of its kind.[72] Trumpeter Tommy Gott also got the writing bug and completed his debut, an instruction manual for budding trumpet players.

Roger's tight work schedule meant his appearances at the Biltmore were limited. So when Lee DeForest released a new Roger Wolfe Kahn movie short in the fall, it helped keep Roger's name in the public's mind. The film hit the screens at theaters fitted with the new DeForest sound system, which conveniently included the ones owned by Roger's Uncle Felix.

In a sponsorship deal with the musical instrument manufacturer C. G. Conn Ltd., Roger endorsed their latest range of brass instruments, 'not because of the similarity of their names, but for their musical qualities.'[73] As part of the deal, each musician in Kahn's brass section received a complimentary instrument.

George and Ira Gershwin's musical, *Lady, Be Good!*, had completed a successful run on Broadway and was now destined for a premiere in London. Happily for Otto - who initially invested $10,000 in the show on the strength of one song, '*The Girl I Love*,' which was later dropped - the production had made a profit.* The transfer to England would feature Fred and Adele Astaire, who had starred in the Broadway show. In an unexpected move, Roger, and his orchestra, were invited to join the London production. Regrettably, for Roger, he could not accept the offer due to his contractual obligations at the Biltmore.

In the wake of the recent critical acclaim bestowed upon Roger, Victor decided now was the ideal time to put the Kahn unit back in the recording studio. The absurdly titled '*Bam Bam Bamy Shore*' coupled with the novelty rag '*Look Who's Here*' were the two new tracks the band cut.[74] Victor used the session to test their newly installed electrical recording process.[75] As such, Roger's masters were the first to be released in the world using this new technology.

The recordings hit the stores in November. Victor hoped the Christmas market would increase demand and bolster Roger's chances of sailing into the charts. One could easily have imagined flappers dancing to the tracks at home around their gramophones. This was commercial music for the masses. With records now selling in their millions, young Kahn had every intention of grabbing a slice of the action. Furthermore, Victor saw fit to book Roger and his band into their Camden studio for one day a week for practically every remaining week in the year.

Even though Roger had signed to Victor as an exclusive artist, he also recorded under a nom de disk for Cameo, Pathé, and Perfect, going by the names of The Cascadiacs and The Deauville Dozen.[76] The bands were formed as studio units with session musicians hired solely for the project. In October, Roger recorded two instrumentals: an energetic foxtrot created by Arthur Schutt titled '*Pep*,' and '*Dreaming of Tomorrow*' composed by Joe Sanders. Pathé released both tracks under the Deauville Dozen moniker.*

No matter how much Roger accomplished, the media still held the widespread belief he would soon tire of his 'hobby' and find a proper job, perhaps something along the lines of what his brother Gilbert was doing.[77] How wrong could they have been! On the contrary, Roger intended to prove all his cynics wrong by making music his life's work and openly admitted he aspired to gain honors akin to Paul Whiteman. Roger's music empire already incorporated a booking agency, music school, and a publishing house. Furthermore, he was a recording artist, stage performer, and composer. *Variety* also confirmed Kahn's contract at the Biltmore, which was due to expire this coming December after an 18-month residency, had been renewed.[78] The extension was for a further six months.* No matter what the media assumed, Roger had no intention of laying his baton down anytime soon.

When the Board of Taxes and Assessments announced the largest single jump in New York City property valuations since 1897, the news must have brought a double-edged smile to Otto's face.[79] Incredible leaps in hotel and theater valuations were recorded, along with significant increases in personal assessments. The Metropolitan Opera Company's revenue for the year was $4,350,000, showing steady growth over the previous year of $300,000. Otto's tax bill for the year had increased by $50,000.

In October, Otto treated himself to a large tract of around 500 acres in Sachem's Neck on Shelter Island, on the eastern end of Long Island.[80] The purchase reestablished the integrity of the plot to operate as a real estate investment. Presently the terrain was arable farmland and a nature reserve; what Otto proposed to do with the land he never publicly revealed. For the time being, the landscape remained unaltered.

Otto was very open about his views on publicity and the role of today's media: 'This is the age of publicity, whether we like it or not. Democracy is inquisitive and won't take things for granted. It will not be satisfied with dignified silence; still less with resentful silence.'[81] His publicist Ivy Lee was renowned for being a skillful manipulator of the press. On November 2, Otto graced the cover of *TIME* magazine. No one could underestimate the impact and importance of a heavyweight news magazine such as *TIME* committing a front cover to Kahn. It reaffirmed his position as the Wizard of Wall Street.

When a journalist questioned Otto about his diet and where he got his colossal amounts of energy from, Kahn replied flippantly, 'one of the essentials is a supply of the milk of human kindness.'[82]

Mr. Kahn & Mr. Gatti

'At four o'clock on a dull afternoon last month, a Lincoln motorcar waited outside the office door of the Metropolitan Opera House in Manhattan. Some nondescript fellows who were arriving in twos and threes at the same door glanced at their watches and then, nervously, at the big car where it crouched beside the curb, glittering in the gray air as if its glass and brass and nickel work were lit with a secret sunlight. For whom was it waiting?'[83]

The Met was the leading opera company in America. In its present ill-equipped theater, it was a challenge for the management to maintain the high standards of its productions expected by the public. In December, Otto announced his ambitious plan to build a modern state-of-the-art opera house in Columbus Circle. The new theater would extend an entire block, along West 56th and 57th, between Eighth and Ninth Avenues, on land Otto had purchased specifically for the project.[84]

Otto fully expected opposition. His judgment was correct.

The notion of such a bold plan brought a maelstrom of objections from all walks of society, not least those voiced by numerous directors of the Metropolitan Opera Company. Regardless of such disapproval, Otto quietly pressed ahead with the project of his own accord. Over the next few months, the black Lincoln limousine with glittering glass, brass, and nickel work parked outside the Met's stage door became a frequent sight during late afternoons. For the moment, no further statement from Otto was forthcoming. When the Met's general manager Gatti-Casazza, who some likened to 'an iceberg with a beard,' was pressed for his opinion on the topic, he offered his standard reply, 'No comment.'

On November 27, Otto delivered an address at the Carnegie Institute of Technology in Pittsburgh, illustrating the importance of drama in American Universities and independent theaters.[85]

It was a compelling talk aimed at rallying new support and additional finance into the industry. Kahn cited from experience his successes and defeats as an impresario and spoke about his costly yet failed attempt to create the New Theatre Company. He culminated by urging thoughtful guidance and providing more opportunity to young talent, a lesson Otto had learned personally closer to home.

Fame

Orchestras were big business. Every theater, hotel, bar, and ballroom had at least one resident band playing most evenings. The idea of DJs and piped music had not yet been conceived. The only form of musical entertainment came from a live orchestra. Paul Whiteman's income had steadily risen year upon year. His earnings for 1925 were his highest to date, paying $800,000. Similarly, Roger's booking agency was doing terrific business.

During the past few months, Roger had focused on strengthening the line-up of his Biltmore Orchestra by contracting some of the most sought-after musicians in New York. After the latest shake-up, only three players from Arthur Lange's original unit remained: trumpeter Tommy Gott, clarinetist Owen Bartlett, and tuba maven Arthur Campbell. His most recent recruit was the hot and technically brilliant trombonist 'Miff' Mole.

Lucky Boy

It was handy for Roger having the songwriter Irving Berlin working directly above his own office at 1607 Broadway. The two composers' would often pop into each other's workplace to check out one another's latest compositions. It also meant Roger could get permission personally to record any new Berlin songs he liked.[86] On November 19, Roger and his Biltmore Orchestra recorded an instrumental rendition of Berlin's 'A Little Bungalow.' On November 27, they laid down a version of Berlin's 'Lucky Boy.' Both songs came from the upcoming Broadway musical comedy *Cocoanuts* featuring the Marx Brothers.* Victor earmarked the tracks for an early January release in the New Year.

Roger had already completed the scores for two musicals. In December, he embarked upon the ambitious task of writing a jazz symphony, which he provisionally named *Americana.*[87] The basis of the work explored themes from several popular African American spirituals. The *Music Trade Review* reported a major record label had already made arrangements to record the piece upon its completion.

Roger worked long hours on his scores and orchestrations, sometimes laboring well into the night.[88] He would lock himself away in the music room he'd created on the top floor of the Kahns Fifth Avenue mansion. Some evenings, between shows, he would scour cabarets and cafés looking for new talent to sign to his booking agency, such was his commitment to his work.

As the end of the year beckoned, Roger herded his finely augmented twelve-piece Biltmore band into Victor's Camden studio to record 'Rhythm of the Day.'[89] The song, composed by Donald Lindley with lyrics by Owen Murphy, was featured in Earl Carroll's Broadway revue *Vanities* and singled out as the show's novelty hit.

The band laid down four instrumental takes of the number, but Victor chose not to release any of them. Why remains a mystery to this day. Was the band's adaptation considered too modernistic for current tastes?

Did Victor get cold feet?

At the same December recording session, Roger laid down another instrumental, *'A Cup of Coffee, a Sandwich and You,'* a catchy tune with an even catchier title. Victor did finally release this track three months later.

Roger was undeterred by Victor's apparent nervousness at releasing *'Rhythm of the Day.'* If anything, it spurred him to compose more original tunes, no doubt in the hope of securing his record company's favor. One such piece was the lively foxtrot *'Following You Around.'* Surprisingly, it took two years before Roger got around to recording the song. In the meantime, Remick Publishing signed another of Roger's new compositions, *'Let Me Be The One For You,'* with lyrics by his publicist George D. Lottman.[90]

Many critics still viewed Roger warily as 'the new kid on the block,' who was financially reliant upon his father's wealth. It was a misconception the press fed to the public for sensationalism and one Roger would struggle to eradicate for most of his life. If nothing else, his superb band was a testament to his talent and tenacity. What the critics failed to recognize was just how determined the kid was.

The public's fascination with Roger was growing considerably. He began to get recognized in the street. New Yorkers would stop him on the sidewalk and request his autograph. Store assistants would greet him by his surname. Similarly, his local Manhattan deli Gertner's began to take more notice of this energetic young lad that would rush in for lunch every other day; having a celebrity frequent your eatery was always good for business.

Such is fame!

Roger became aware of this 'shift' in people's reaction towards him and began to act accordingly. His image received a makeover; out went the high-street three-piece suits, in came an entire closet of bespoke replacements.

Even his local deli Gertner's in Times Square saw fit to name a sandwich after him, the RWK, the meat ingredient of which Roger later confessed to a journalist, was not particularly to his liking. Still, nevertheless, he felt obliged to order one whenever he dropped by for lunch.[91] It so happened the 18-year-old had a particular aversion to pastrami (one of the main ingredients of the RWK) dating back to his childhood.[92]

Another aspect of his increased fame resulted in a steady stream of business proposals; most were inappropriate, money lending, or blatant begging letters. Even some of his trusted musicians were prone to trying their luck at squeezing a further pay rise out of him. In response, Roger toughened up. For every musician he employed, he knew there were a dozen others equally capable and talented who were eager to take their place. In doing so, he quickly learned that handshakes might not be so honorable where money was concerned.

On the morning of Christmas Eve, Otto attended the funeral of his great friend and newspaper proprietor Frank A. Munsey. The ceremony was held at the St John the Divine Cathedral in Manhattan.[93] The one-time newspaper magnate, and owner of eighteen journals at different times throughout his career, died owning only two, the *New York Sun* and *Evening Telegram*, having merged or sold the rest. Munsey possessed the rare power of undivided concentration. He kept a cool head when all around him chaos prevailed.[94] He made and invested millions and, in his will, bequeathed a large chunk of his fortune to the Metropolitan Museum of Art. Kahn and Munsey held tremendous regard for one another, together with a mutual love of opera. In a final act of deference for his friend, Kahn was an honorary pallbearer at his funeral.

Work in the Kahn household did not stop for Christmas. Roger and his orchestra played every evening at the Hotel Biltmore throughout the festivities.[95] The band also doubled with a short New York City vaudeville tour. On Monday, December 28, Roger presented his week-long Christmas special at the Palace Theatre with an augmented orchestra of twenty-five men. The following week they began a fortnight stint at the colossal Hippodrome.[96]

On Tuesday evening, December 29, jazz missionary Paul Whiteman and His Greater Concert Orchestra staged a one-off concert at the Metropolitan Opera House. The show was Whiteman's *Second Experiment in Modern Music*. It featured George Gershwin's one-act jazz opera *135th Street* (previously titled *Blue Monday*). The program also aired, *A Little Bit of Jazz* by John Alden Carpenter, *Mississippi Suite* by Ferde Grofé, and *Circus Days - Eight Pictures from Memory* by Deems Taylor. Whiteman commissioned Taylor's piece, especially for the event.[97] Otto was present at the performance. Roger was unable to attend due to his vaudeville commitments. Although the recital was well-received, it did not have the same impact as Whiteman's earlier concert at the Aeolian Hall in February the previous year.

Nonetheless, Otto was adamant a homegrown American jazz opera was a viable concept that would inevitably occur. Composer Deems

Taylor disagreed. When journalist and budding author Harriette Ashbrook interviewed the composer about his thoughts on jazz and the idea of an American jazz opera, Deems was quite specific in his views: 'I think it's grand. I like it. I wrote a jazz composition for Paul Whiteman. I get a lot of fun out of it, but I don't agree with those who think a jazz opera can be written successfully. I think the chances of it being done are slim. Opera, you see, is emotion. Jazz is stimulation, not emotion. It makes your feet go, but it doesn't affect your tear ducts. It's all right for expressing the mood of your hero when he's all 'jazzed up,' stimulated, excited. But what are you going to do when he dies. You'll have to fall back on music.'[98]

At the age of sixteen, Roger had plunged himself into debt with a loan of $25,000 from his father. By the end of 1925, aged eighteen, Roger had worked himself out of debt, repaying his father the total amount advanced. 'That was one of the happiest days of my life,' Roger would later recount. Roger Wolfe Kahn Inc. was a profitable commercial enterprise.[99]

Some critics accused Roger of treading on Paul Whiteman's toes. In truth, nothing could have been further from the mark. Roger was of his own making and had his own direction to follow.

At the end of the year, Roger could look back with a sense of pride at the mammoth obstacles he had overcome to pursue his ambitions and reach this point in his career. He had his own business and employed a personal manager and a publicist. He had also secured an exclusive record deal with Victor and private sponsorship deals. But, more important, he had won over the respect and support of his parents. Roger now hoped what lay ahead was everything he had been striving so hard to achieve, financial and artistic success.

9

THE DREAM PALACE

There was a young belle at the Biltmore
who fell for the current jazz score
when she danced without veils
to the saxophone's wails
security had to be called for

1926

New York City was a whole different ball game for jazz. The thought of going elsewhere to perform was not an option for Roger. It seemed a ludicrous misuse of time and energy to him. He much preferred to stay around his home patch, for it was in New York City that Roger felt most comfortable and at ease. The question wasn't whether or not he enjoyed traveling or visiting different cities; the inconvenience of long tiresome journeys irritated him. He favored the notion of speed, to arrive at a destination without the drawn-out hassle of getting there. In this respect, flying was his perfect ally, and in aviation, Roger found an instant companion.

The 1920s are often referred to as the 'golden age of jazz,' where ermine touched velvet, and diamonds barked at paste. Hairstyles, like skirt lengths, became shorter, the missionary position became passé. Prohibition nurtured more alcoholics than ever before. Drug-ladled parties became the new bohemian rage. Roger had not yet acquired a taste for alcohol. He smoked, as did every member of the Kahn family. Abreast of his clean-living habits was his desire to become a pilot. You couldn't be as high as a kite and still expect to fly a plane in a straight line. His reactions had to be fast, faster than most. Flying lessons began almost as soon as Roger's bank balance tipped over into the red. He signed up for a tuition course at Roosevelt Field on Long Island and got his initial thrill of sitting in front of a cockpit control panel in a Sikorsky Winged Standard two-seat trainer aircraft. It was in this single-engine plane he received all his primary flight training. His instructor was A. Tunstall. The first plane Roger bought was a Sikorsky monoplane.[1] His preferred airfield was Roosevelt, ideally situated not far from his father's Cold Spring Harbor estate.

The Orchestra Business

Variety decided January was as good a time as any to announce that Roger had altered his band's name to the Roger Wolfe Kahn Orchestra, even though Roger and most newspapers had been calling it as such for many months prior.[2] Roger was now officially the poster boy of jazz and the bandleader the public wanted most to see. Hence, his reluctance to travel out of New York to tour with his orchestra had put a price tag on his head. He could now command $500 to $1,000 extra just for making an appearance. This additional currency meant the Kahn orchestra could demand as much as $3,800 a week in vaudeville. For colleges or private functions, they commanded a similar fee.

At the beginning of the year, *Variety* also revealed Roger's recording sessions with Victor had significantly increased over the past few weeks. Six new recordings from the Kahn stable were due to drop on Friday, January 8: *'You Told Me To Go,' 'Lucky Boy,' 'I'm Sitting on Top of the World,' 'I Never Knew,' 'Down and Out Blues,'* and *'A Little Bungalow.'* The label was determined to harvest a big hit from their young prodigy.* According to *Variety*, Victor Records were keen to exploit the Kahn name and the Hotel Biltmore tie-up. The company had already booked a succession of studio dates for the band throughout the coming months.

Roger's slick instrumental take of *'Down and Out Blues'* got the thumbs up from Abel Green in *Variety*, who hailed it 'a corking low-down indigo wail.'[3] Green was also impressed with Kahn's arranging skills and the versatility of the orchestra. Like many young musicians, Roger was eager to carve his own musical niche. In an attempt to set himself apart from his contemporaries, he took to describing his music as 'futuristic.'

Throughout January, Victor's Camden studio reverberated with the toing and froing of Roger and his musicians. The studio captured four more excellent tracks: *'Song of the Flame,'* *'Lantern of Love,'* *'Baby'* and *'Looking For A Boy,'* the latter having danced in from the Gershwin brother's latest stage musical *Tip-Toes*. These were the band's first recordings with their new guitarist Eddie Lang.[4]

Victor's January promotional blitz in record stores across the States, along with a national newspaper advertising campaign, soon paid dividends; Roger's recordings began to make an impression on the sales charts. Their perseverance paid off; Roger had a minor hit on his hands with *'Lucky Boy.'* By early February, *'I'm Sitting on Top of the World'* peaked at No. 9, giving the teenager his first notable top 10 success. In its wake, Roger's popularity rose yet a further notch.

The orchestra business.

The daily schedule of a successful bandleader made ordinary nine to five jobs seem a doddle. A typical day in their diary lasted from around 9 a.m. through to two o'clock the following morning, seven days a week, and could read as such: awake early - a two-hour band rehearsal followed by two hours attending to office business, all dealt with before lunch. In addition to a theater matinee performance, the afternoon could include working on future projects, interviews, studio sessions, and radio recordings. In the evening, the bandleader would head his orchestra playing dinner music at a hotel, tailed by an evening pit performance at a Broadway theater. Following this, a return visit to the hotel to play late-night dance music, ending with a possible appearance at a nocturnal club or two.[5]

Roger's engagement diary was equally as plump. The exercise of composing music seemed almost an inconvenience and extravagance as far as putting time aside to undertake the task.

During the evening of Friday, January 22, at the Academy of Music on the corner of East 14th and Irving Place, Roger and his Hotel Biltmore Orchestra headed a charity concert for the Brooklyn Newspapermen Club Fund.[6] All 4,000 seats for the event sold out in advance. It was terrific news for the fund and splendid PR for Roger, especially as New York's newly elected Mayor Jimmy Walker and every journalist and newspaper of note across the city would be in attendance.

One of the first cultural assignments Mayor Walker coordinated in his initial term of office was to hold more open-air concerts in Central Park throughout the summer months, especially jazz concerts.[7] Already penciled in were performances by Paul Whiteman, Roger Wolfe Kahn, and Vincent Lopez, along with a possible recital by the American composer and conductor Edwin Franko Goldman.

The day after Roger's performance at the Academy of Music, Otto delivered a controversial address at the Hotel Astor in New York before the Foreign Policy Association. During his speech, he spoke of fascism in glowing terms.[8] Otto's opinions on current Italian political matters appear to have been formed by his impressions from spending short spells in the country during his travels to Europe and his friendships with several native Italian's now resident in America. It was common knowledge no other organization was in a better position than the Foreign Policy Association to bear on the ears of foreign governments in a bid to help shape foreign policies. They achieved this by coordinating the results of independent unbiased research and polls. In accepting the invitation to deliver an address, one assumes Otto knew of the association's influence on foreign governments. Otto was said to have come across as being 'quite an objective speaker.'[9]

'In formulating judgment on *fascismo*, two things should be kept in mind,' expressed Kahn. 'First, it so happens that Italy is inhabited by Italians and not by Americans or British, and what applies and appeals to us need not necessarily apply and appeal to them. Secondly, in the case of every people, more essential even than liberty, and therefore taking precedence over it, is order and national self-preservation, actual and spiritual. Indeed, true liberty is impossible unless there is order and an adequately functioning government.' Kahn later concluded: 'To anyone who knew Italy then, the change, which came over the country with the advent of Mussolini, is little short of miraculous.'*

If Kahn Wants a New House, Let Kahn Pay For It!

'If Kahn wants a new house, let Kahn pay for it!' were the words of financier Robert Fulton Cutting (president of the Metropolitan Opera and Real Estate Company) upon receiving a confidential twelve-page dossier from Kahn. In the document, Otto outlined the inadequacies of the Met's current theater and why the Metropolitan Opera Company should build a new one to replace it. No wonder Cutting and fellow directors of the real estate company were up in arms over Kahn's proposal; they were, after all, the owners of the building, which the Met leased. How dare Kahn suggest replacing it with a brand new state-of-the-art theater![10]

A couple of weeks later, when Otto publicly announced his intentions to build such an opera house, a multitude of supplicants (many with their personal interests at heart) rushed forward, professionals, tradespeople, and general operagoers, all vying to be involved in the project and offering their services, some for free.

The Metropolitan Opera House was, without question, the home of the country's best operatic productions. It was also the bastion of New York's high society. The present opera house at 1411 Broadway between West 39th and 40th opened in October 1883. The building was now considered by many to be antiquated and unfit for purpose. Otto was adamant the city needed a modern, more democratic theater to stage contemporary, cutting-edge productions. Not everyone shared his vision, most notably a considerable portion of the board of directors who deemed the proposals too radical. The opera house realty was valued at around $10 million and jointly owned by relatives of the benefactors that originally invested their cash in building the theater back in the '80s. All thirty-five held a parterre box in the 'Golden Horseshoe.'

As a result, each box holder owned an equal thirty-fifth share in the building. A condition of ownership stipulated the boxes must remain in the same family of the original shareholder from generation to generation. Disposal of the boxes was not permitted. Regardless of this clause, Otto somehow purchased box No. 14. Kahn now proposed to uproot the opera company and rehouse it in a new theater that he assured would be 'bigger, better and more democratic than the Metropolitan.'[11] He suggested building the theater on land he had acquired on the corner of West 56th and 57th Streets for $3 million the previous October. He also intended to reduce the number of parterre boxes to thirty and have them leased rather than owned.

At a meeting on January 22, the directors of the Metropolitan Opera Company reluctantly admitted Otto's plan was not such a bad idea after all and agreed in principle to move forward with the building of a new opera house. To help fund the project, Vincent Astor, William K. Vanderbilt Jr., Edward S. Harkness, E. Roland Harriman, and Frederic Potts Moore accepted directorships on the Metropolitan Opera Company board.[12] Otto also suggested the new building should be self-sufficient and contain a theater and offices, so the rental from the offices would help subsidize the opera house. For practical reasons, the board approved the structure should be perpendicular - a skyscraper.

The saga of the Met's new theater and the indecision and objectionable behavior pitched by Robert Fulton Cutting and several Met board members in obstructing Otto from progressing with the project would continue for several seasons to come. Their bickering sent Kahn into a deeper and deeper depression over the matter. It was never going to be a smooth ride, but no matter how persuasively and determined Otto promoted the venture, the project would never get beyond the starting block.

On Monday, January 25, the Jean Goldkette Band from Detroit made their New York debut with a two-week engagement at the Roseland Ballroom. In Detroit, pianist Goldkette was dubbed the 'Paul Whiteman of the West.' Many of New York's notable bandleaders and musicians attended the opening show to check out this hot new contender. Jostling for tickets were Whiteman, Sam Lanin, and Roger Wolfe Kahn.[13] Goldkette's reputation in his home city (where he held a residency at the Graystone Ballroom) was enviable. Goldkette also ran his own School of Music in Detroit. The Goldkette outfit was highly disciplined and celebrated for its unique instrumental harmonies and orchestral arrangements. Goldkette and Roger were also stablemates at Victor Records. As a kind of peace offering to Goldkette, Roger and Sam Lanin conducted one number each with the Goldkette band during the concert.[14]

Roger had recently hired John S. Martin to manage the increasingly busy Kahn booking office.[15] The agency now had a chain of orchestras on its books, and business was booming. Some of the bands they presently represented included the New Porters, the Dopey Dozen, the Society Serenaders, the Mayfair Melodians, and an all-female orchestra named the Debutantes.[16] All of the bands played exclusive sets chosen and arranged by Roger. The more successful Kahn became, the more lucrative were the offers that arrived on his office desk. Requests for him and his musicians to endorse merchandise steadily flowed in. To have the Kahn name attached to a product was perceived as a distinct sign of quality. Roger was just as happy for his fellow bandmates to grab a slice of the action as he was for himself, and in 1926 various advertisements began to appear in music trade papers with members of his band promoting an array of products. Vegaphone ran an ad campaign featuring a smartly attired Tony Colucci (banjo player in Kahn's orchestra) that had a picture of Tony posing with a Vegaphone banjo strapped across his shoulder.

Alongside Colucci's image ran the snappy caption: *'Tony Colucci, Roger Wolfe Kahn's Orchestra - A prominent artist in the banjo circle, is Tony Colucci, now with the famous Roger Wolfe Kahn's Recording Orchestra. The artist of his caliber desires the finest banjo possible, and the Vegaphone has been Mr. Colucci's choice.'*[17]

Such endorsements were beneficial money earners for musicians and a helpful way to promote their careers.

Roger's unerring knack of hiring talented musicians meant other bandleaders often tried to poach them. In retaliation, Roger also applied the same strategy. In the latest reshuffle, saxophonist Alfred Evans jumped Ross Gorman's outfit to join the Kahn stable.[18] Despite Keith's booking office crying out for the Kahn aggregation to headline at their New York vaudeville houses,[19] in February, Roger opted to 'double' his band on the highly lucrative college prom circuit.[20]

On January 30, the *Literary Digest* published an article titled 'King Jazz and the Jazz King.' In it, they announced: 'There is a boy who will not reach his nineteenth birthday until after this is printed, who is making more money in a year than the President of the United States receives. This boy is Roger Wolfe Kahn, son of Otto H. Kahn.'[21] In truth, Roger was now earning so much money he was unsure how much he was exactly making. No sooner did the checks arrive in his in-tray than he spent the money paying salaries and all the other expenses that went hand-in-hand with running a successful orchestra and booking agency. The journalist pointed out how in eighteen months, Kahn junior had startled the music world by building a musical empire rivaling those of Paul Whiteman and Vincent Lopez that now threatened to surpass them.

'In addition to organizing and directing the world's highest-priced (and some musicians declare the best) jazz orchestra, directing and controlling twelve others, writing songs, and composing musical comedies, this boy is organizing and laying plans for a great semi-symphonic orchestra to develop the foxtrot theme and to place jazz on a higher standard as a distinctive type of American music.' The symphony the journalist referred to, which Roger was still working on, was *Americana*.

'We are not fully up to the possibilities of this new type of musical expression. There are glaring faults, musically, in most of the jazz, and these faults must be eradicated. Someone will do it, and I want to contribute something toward its development.'

Furthermore, Roger was negotiating the lease on a club in upper Manhattan to establish the city's first high-class $5 cover charge nightspot. He was hoping to target the fashionable and wealthy. Currently, the project was momentarily in abeyance, awaiting his father's consent.

The boy's energy and talent appeared limitless.

The above interview took place at Roger's Broadway office, throughout which Roger appeared in a playful mood, having convinced the journalist he was the office secretary and not the famous musician he had come to interview. Roger's manager Bert Cooper arranged the meeting for 11 a.m. Cooper had yet to turn up, hence the confusion over Roger's identity. Roger happily went along with the charade, clearly loving the temporary anonymity during which he could either bad-mouth himself or big himself up. He chose to do the former. Thirty minutes later, Kahn's publicist George Lottman entered the office. Roger introduced George to the journalist but failed to indicate he was engaged in a prank. The journalist proceeded to ask George various questions about his boss, which he dutifully answered. Only when Kahn burst out laughing did the journalist and George twig that he'd been playing them both along.

A few days later, Roger packed up his orchestra and transported his musicians to the warmer climes of Florida, where they checked into the plush Miami Hotel Biltmore.[22] It was Roger's way of giving his boy's a break, albeit a working holiday. The orchestra performed at the hotel daily during their stay. In their absence, Roger installed his sub-unit, the Deauville Dozen, at New York's Hotel Biltmore. The Deauville Dozen was one of Roger's recording outfits consisting of exceptionally hot session musicians. As the pay was good and the gig prestigious, the musicians made themselves available to deputize. The Biltmore boss John McEntee Bowman didn't mind which musicians played at his hotel, just as long as the stand-in band came with the Kahn seal of approval and name tag.

Before Roger and his musicians traveled to Florida, they had one important gig to attend on Friday, February 5, in the ballroom at the Hotel Biltmore - the twenty-sixth Fordham Junior Prom, at which Roger and his orchestra would be officiating.[23] All six hundred tickets sold out in advance. The hotel received a transformation for the evening, decorated with Fordham banners and colorful bunting. Over 1,200 students turned up for the event, 600 more than expected.[24] Despite the Biltmore ballroom's reputation as being 'the most spacious dancing room in town,' the management must still have been mightily impressed by the turnout. In a pre-arranged hook-up, WOR broadcast Kahn's performance live over the radio.[25] In the coming months, further Prom dates for the Kahn band included Yale, Georgetown, and Mount St Vincent.

The Florida break came as a welcome respite, allowing Roger to catch up with his parents, brother, and sisters, who were holidaying (some with their respective partners) at Oheka Cottage further up the coast in Palm Beach. The Palm Beach coastline had rapidly gained a reputation as a playground for the rich. During the season, a typical day on the beach would attract more celebrities and members of the smart set than a journalist could squeeze into a society column: Otto Kahn chatting to T. Coleman du Pont (politician and owner of New York's Waldorf-Astoria Hotel), with Florenz Ziegfeld Jr. nearby shaded under a straw parasol; Lady Dimity stretched across a beach towel attracting much attention in her figure-hugging bathing suit; Chicago broker Phil Charters scanning the financial pages of the New York Times checking his investments. The beach was just as good a place to socialize and conduct business as were the adjoining restaurants and clubhouses. Due to its stunning location, Oheka Cottage attracted many transient visitors. In January, the Austrian writer, and Max Reinhardt's aide-de-camp, Rudolf Käthchen Kommer, whose friendship with Otto had grown over the past few years, called by and spent several days enjoying the Kahns' hospitality.[26]

In mid-February, the Kahn party left Florida earlier than usual and returned to New York City, leaving their villa in the capable hands of their resident housekeeper and staff.[27] The family's early departure was to accommodate the arrival of Mrs. William K. Vanderbilt Jr., who had rented the property from Otto.

The trouble with the press scrutinizing the Kahns' every move meant the public could keep a detailed track of their whereabouts. Such media exposure had its drawbacks.

In the early hours of the morning on February 18, two men shaded by nightfall arrived on the grounds of Oheka Cottage.[28] One of the intruders was carrying a large hold-all bag. The two men peered through a front window to check for any movement indoors before proceeding to the rear of the premises, where they found a shaded window to force open. Satisfied that no one was awake, the man with the hold-all removed a metal crowbar from his bag. Asleep upstairs, unaware of any potential danger, was the multi-millionaire socialite Mrs. Vanderbilt.

The man with the metal crowbar jimmied the window open. The latch broke with little resistance. He then slid the window up as far as it would go and began to wriggle in through the gap.

Unbeknown to the would-be burglars, the villa had all-night security surveillance. On duty was the night watchman William Keely.[29]

A shot rang out.[30] Whence it came, the intruders were unsure. The gunshot did the trick. The two burglars bolted and fled the scene, leaving their crowbar behind.

The nightwatchman appeared outside on the rear terrace wielding a pistol. A second shot rang out into the cool night air - another warning shot.

In their flight, the two intruders leaped over a hedge and then fell out of view.

The sound of an automobile engine being revved up could be heard nearby. Car lights lit up the road. Two more gunshots followed the car as it sped away into the unforgiving darkness.

The police put all passages from Palm Beach to the mainland under guard, but the would-be burglars escaped.

'Attempted Robbery at the Kahns Home,' read the slug line in the following day's papers. It was a close call for all concerned.

Looking For A Boy

There was a sense of glamor about Roger: his good looks and boyish floppy hair, along with his dark, inquisitive brown eyes, appealed to the youngsters as well as to the slightly older, more sophisticated brigade. There was also an element of the untouchable about him. He was one of those rare beings in show business that had talent, was pleasing to the eye, and was extremely marketable. As a brand, the Kahn label stood head and shoulders above most of their contemporaries. They didn't have to court the press; journalists courted them and keenly documented their every move. It's also fair to say the Kahn family was savvy at using such marketing to further their own goals.

Roger Wolfe Kahn – poster boy of jazz.

With Roger's recording of *'I'm Sitting on Top of the World'* bringing in a whole new level of interest in the teenager, Victor Records were keen to capitalize on its success. Newspapers were clamoring to interview the young protégé. Some reporters were luckier than others. Hughie Fullerton, under his nom-de-plume Paul Kinkead, was one of the luckier ones.[31] Fullerton interviewed Roger for *Liberty* journal in what transpired to be the writer's first article on jazz, which he simply titled *Jazz!* Throughout their meeting, Roger remained true to his character and placed Paul Whiteman at the top of the list in the jazz hierarchy.[32] Fullerton states the whole world had gone jazz mad from east to west. Roger insisted he was not in the slightest bit fazed by the interest or attention he was receiving. In New York City alone, the Musicians Union reckoned approximately twenty-five thousand men and a couple of thousand women were playing instruments in more than three thousand orchestras, most of which specialized in playing jazz. In the U.S., the jazz business accounted for $100 million in salaries for the musicians alone.

Over the coming months, Roger put on his writer's cloak. He wrote a series of articles for various publications, including *Liberty* journal and the *Saturday Evening Post*, about his career as a bandleader and jazz music in general.[33] 'Memoirs at 18' was one of the articles he penned.

In February, Victor Records put out four new tracks by Roger and his Hotel Biltmore Orchestra: *'Looking For A Boy,' 'Lantern of Love,' 'Baby,'* and *'Song of the Flame.'* 'For a youngster, Kahn's rise to prominence has been extraordinary,' exclaimed *Variety*, who thumbnailed his phenomenal ascendency down to Kahn and Victor's 'painstaking building up with choice material' and as ever 'tip-top' instrumentation.[34]

Touring was a highly lucrative pastime for some jazz bands. Roger, however, was still hesitant about leaving the comforts of his home turf. Paul Whiteman and his orchestra had just performed out West at San Francisco's Automobile Show. For the privilege, he pocketed $25,000 for a week's work on a 75-cent gate.[35] Whiteman attracted such immense crowds to his daily performances that punters became too distracted by the music to purchase automobiles. Although it was deemed a mighty success for Whiteman, the car manufacturers were of two minds.

If Roger was to reap the substantial financial rewards his name and music were now attracting, he had to get his band and American symphonic syncopation out on the road playing to the masses.

After their two-week assignment in Florida, the Kahn band returned to New York City, where on February 19, Roger took his musicians back into the recording studio. This time the group laid down an instrumental dance version of *'Bluin' the Black Keys,'* a new composition by the band's pianist Arthur Schutt. Unfortunately for Schutt, who would have been hoping for some hefty royalties, Victor Records rejected the track and shelved the recording. Victor's actions indicate they had the final say over the material Roger released commercially, thereby exercising their right to overrule the artist's judgment.

5th Avenue Club

It was no secret Roger was hankering to open his own club. His only drawback was the financial expenditure of such a venture. When the songwriter and impresario Billy Rose, owner of the 5th Avenue Club, approached Roger to take over the nightly entertainment slot at the premises, Roger accepted.[36] Although the club was not the ideal venue, the experience would give Roger a valuable insight into the machinations of running a private club. Kahn installed one of his 'substitute' dance orchestra's into the club under the direction of maestro Don Lindley. They opened on March 6 with a $5 cover charge under the proviso that the 'millionaire bandsman' would make 'periodic personal appearances between 12 - 1:15 a.m.' Given all of Roger's other daily commitments, the gig was pushing it a little even for a youngster with boundless energy.

Back in the Kahn booking office, unburdened from any emotion, the enterprise seemed doomed from the start. After only two nights, Roger stormed out of the venue, finding the whole experience a grind, distasteful, and not to his liking.[37] Although his aggregation led by Lindley temporarily remained in situ, they too were pulled once Billy Rose found a replacement.

'Friday Nights Radio Program Should Make Theaters Worry' ran the header in *Variety*.[38] The broadcast in question was aired on WJZ New York on March 19 under the banner *WJZ Ninety Minutes*: an hour and a half of live music exclusively given by Victor recording artists. The quality of music performed was deemed so excellent, two of the entertainment weekly's, *Variety* and *Music Trade Review*, wrote full-page critiques of the transmission.[39]

Victor Records pulled out all the stops to promote their younger artists, particularly bandleaders Roger Wolfe Kahn, Jack Shilkret, George Olsen, and the vocalists Franklyn Baur, Helen Clark, and Ed Smalle. The show featured twelve acts and was relayed to over half a dozen radio stations, pulling in a large audience. Roger and his orchestra played five numbers, including his latest Victor release, '*Song of the Flame*.'[40] A couple of months earlier, Franklyn Baur had recorded a vocal refrain on Roger's track '*You Told Me To Go*' that Victor issued back in January. The previous year, singer Elliott Shaw had delivered a vocal on Kahn's '*Yearning (Just For You)*.' However, Roger had never played live on the radio with a vocalist, nor had his orchestra performed on stage with one. Presumably, this situation existed because he had yet to discover a vocalist that reflected his overall sound. Roger recorded with several other vocalists over the following months - Johnny Marvin, Henry Burr, Frank Bessinger, and Billy Jones - although none became a regular member of the outfit.

A revealing insight into the cutthroat inner politics operating within the Metropolitan Opera Company came from the French-born mezzo-soprano Raymonde Delaunois during an interview she gave in which she expressed her great sorrow for Otto Kahn. As might be expected, the newspapers were quick to pick up on it:

'If Otto Kahn were the manager and not the chairman of the board of directors of the Met, this very rich house would be a very artistic house. But he has other occupations, and the young singer just whistles gently. It must be a terrible thing for an artist like Mr. Kahn to be simply a banker.'[41]

Mademoiselle Delaunois was so troubled by the prevailing situation at the Met that she quit performing there to star in a new operetta written especially for her by Anita Loos of *Gentlemen Prefer Blondes* fame.

Beautiful Thought

Roger's reluctance to travel far afield with his band led one Canadian newspaper columnist to declare that should Roger ever decide to go as far as Montreal or Toronto to play, his visit would allow some keen, young journalist the opportunity to write a topical poem to mark the occasion commencing: *'In Canada did Roger Kahn unstately pleasure tunes decree.'*[42]

One sure way of getting Roger out on the road with his band was to play the College proms. On Friday, April 16, in another 'surprise,' Roger traveled from New York to Philadelphia by train with his specially augmented thirty-one-piece orchestra to perform at the University of Pennsylvania's annual Ivy Ball. It was the social event of the season. The organizers had already sold several thousand tickets.[43] Perhaps, Roger's keenness to appear at the prom was because Jean Goldkette and His Orchestra were also on the bill. They were traveling from Detroit.[44] The College promoted it as a friendly 'battle of the two bands,' with an 'all-night party' atmosphere.

The ball concluded seven days of social activities to celebrate Ivy Week. This year the event was held off-campus in the spacious ballroom belonging to the Penn Athletic Club. Those attending got the use of lounge rooms, an adjoining promenade, and a garden balcony. Dancing got underway at 11 p.m. sharp and continued non-stop until 5:00 a.m. For those chancers hoping to gatecrash, the steering committee issued a stern warning stating a strict door policy would operate only permitting ticket holder's entrance.[45]

Roger meant business and enlarged his outfit to thirty-one musicians, just for the occasion. Both bands arrived at the venue armed with their instruments, ready for battle.

A review in the following day's *Pennsylvanian* painted a riveting account of the evening praising all concerned, especially the steering committee, the bands, and the guests who attended.

'Under brilliant lights and midst elaborate decorations, with lilting music as an accompaniment, whirling couples brought Ivy Week to a successful culmination last night,' declared the *Pennsylvanian* reporter. 'Roger Wolfe Kahn and his Hotel Biltmore Orchestra and Jean Goldkette and his Orchestra vied with each other throughout the entire program and that their efforts were successful was attested by the appreciation and applause of the dancers.'[46]

Such was the last-minute rush for tickets by hundreds of students, the *Pennsylvania* noted, the most overused phrase heard on the night was, 'I lost my ticket.' The same reporter hissed, 'The Ivy Ball was crash-proof.'

From all accounts, the Kahn and Goldkette bands hit on all sixes, with each band playing just as deftly as the other, leaving no doubt the only winners that evening were the students who attended.

On the following evening back in New York, three saxophonists from the Kahn band - Arnold Brilhart, Alfred Evans, and Harold Sturr - joined Rudy Wiedoeft in a special one-off recital at the Aeolian Hall, promoted by the Associated Music Dealers of New York.[47] Wiedoeft was regarded by many to be the premier reed virtuoso in the world. The recording artists, soprano Virginia Rae and tenor Franklyn Baur joined the saxophone section on stage.[48]

The secretary of the Associated Musical Instrument Dealers of New York was none other than Harry L. Hunt, manager of the Ditson music store. The same store where Roger had spent many an afternoon before becoming the success he was today. Allowing his saxophone section to appear at the concert could well have been Roger's way of showing gratitude to Harry and the Ditson company for the encouragement they proffered upon him in his younger days.

In response to the added workload the Kahn office was handling, Roger promoted his publicist George Lottman to general manager. George, however, still retained his position as Roger's PR.[49] George had hitherto allotted his work activities to various clients. Roger now signed him to an exclusive two-year contract. The deal gave Roger the freedom to devote more time to composing music. He began working on ideas for a new jazz rhapsody titled *Birth of the Blues* and embarked on a project christened *Spiritualana* based on old-time camp meeting songs.[50]

Now Roger was no longer cuffed to the office, he could pursue a few more social activities. He gave saxophone lessons to his friend Paul

Berlenbach - an avid jazz enthusiast and current light heavyweight boxing champion. He also spent weekends racing his custom-built Bugatti at 95 mph across his father's country estate.

During the evening on Sunday, May 2, the National Vaudeville Artists' association held a massive fundraiser in New York to celebrate their tenth anniversary and raise money for their Benefit Fund. The organization billed it as the largest such event to date in the theatrical world. The N.V.A was a considerable concern that boasted nearly 20,000 members, all working in vaudeville. They had recently acquired a large estate near Saranac Lake, 40 acres of timbered land in the idyllic Adirondacks, and built a 200-bed hospital and sanatorium named Spion Kop. The purpose behind this year's drive was to help finance the completion of the facility. They also hoped to put money towards up-to-date equipment for treating tubercular patients.

Performers drawn from all walks of the theatrical world jumped at the chance to offer their assistance, bringing opera, drama, burlesque, circus, vaudeville, acrobatics, music, ballet, film, and comedy together under a quintet of theatrical roofs.

The five monster 'super shows' would start simultaneously at 8:15 p.m. at five of the biggest theaters in New York City: the Metropolitan Opera House, the Manhattan Opera House, the Hippodrome, the Century Theatre, and the New Amsterdam Theatre. Twenty-two thousand seats went on sale to accommodate demand. Over three hundred acts volunteered their services. With so many distinguished stars confirmed, no one artist could be billed as a headliner at any of the five theaters. As such, artists were listed alphabetically.[51]

The event was a mammoth undertaking that guaranteed every artist would perform at all five theaters during the evening. Each theater had a different running order to adhere to. To ensure there were no delays, a fleet of 100 automobiles transported the 800 performers from theater to theater. Squadrons of police were involved in the maneuver, maintaining a right of way in all the streets the N.V.A. vehicles traveled. Thus, from the north to the south, central Manhattan came to a virtual standstill for several hours.

Fred Stone, president of the N.V.A., personally guaranteed that the time slots allotted to each entertainer had been allocated precisely to the minute, so there would be no delays or waits for audiences or performers. The endless line of automobiles at the artistes' disposal would be a feat in coordination never before attempted anywhere and, probably, impossible except in Manhattan because of its simple grid of straight avenues and adjoining streets. Among the huge list of entertainers who volunteered their services was Al Jolson, George Jessel, Houdini, and the Roger Wolfe Kahn Orchestra. Roger finally got to perform at the Metropolitan Opera House.

George Lottman's managerial direction In the Kahn office soon began to show significant results. The Hotel Ritz-Carlton in Atlantic City had recently engaged a nine-piece Kahn band headed by Abe Effig. Several other large hotels at the resort - the Hollywood Inn, the West End, the New Jersey, the Winston Inn, the Sea Gate, and the Coney Island - had all hired a Kahn band as a seasonal attraction.[52]
  Roger also appointed a new booker for his agency, Nat Chaiken.[53] In the Adirondacks, the exclusive Paul Smith's hotel - where President Coolidge and his family were due to spend their summer vacation - booked Roger Wolfe Kahn's Collegians for the season. In New York, the Roseland Ballroom employed another Kahn unit, Mattlin's Melodians, as their house band. In May, the Society Buds, an eleven-piece female orchestra handled by the Kahn office, commenced a picture house tour.[54] Business was so brisk; Roger opened a branch of his booking agency in the Woods Theatre Building in Chicago.[55]

The Kahns excursions to the continent had unearthed some remarkably talented artists. In the process, the family helped give many of them a beneficial leg up the career ladder and a fast track to appear on the American stage. The Kahns' backing and contacts were highly sought after in every country they visited. One performer that Addie personally sponsored was the Spanish-born diseuse, singer, and actress Raquel Meller. The Spanish diva created quite a fuss when she arrived stateside to begin a season at New York's Empire Theatre. Billed as the *Spanish Girl*, Meller was guaranteed a paycheck of $6,000 a week.[56]
  Her arrival kicked up a storm of publicity because of her crushing desire to be so unsociable. Addie greatly admired Señorita Meller's talent and strength. It was through Addie's connections that the singer was making her American debut. So enamored was Addie by her, she bought every seat in the Empire Theatre on the only preview night of Meller's run at the extravagant cost of $17,500. Moreover, Addie used her private funds to pay for the tickets. Otto's acquiescence of his wife's indulgence on this occasion was admirable. Why anybody should buy the entire seating allocation of a theater is questionable. That said, the takings were donated to charity. Yet more baffling was that Addie missed the performance, as she and her daughter Margaret nipped over to Europe for a short visit before

Spanish Girl opened on April 14.[57]

Meller's reclusive behavior during her trip was said to reflect her unease at being unable to communicate with her host country in their native language; she spoke only her mother tongue, Spanish, and was in the process of learning French. When Meller arrived in New York aboard the SS *Leviathan*, news leaked out that, to supplement her first-class suite, she had attempted to book an additional deluxe suite to accommodate her two Pekinese dogs. Meller's meteoric rise to fame in Spain and other European countries had made her a fortune that she'd astutely invested in diamonds and real estate. The singer was also fond of cheap theatrical jewelry. When her jewels got impounded at customs for appraisal, she found herself with nothing sparkling to wear on her evening visit to the Metropolitan Opera House as guests of the Kahns. In exasperation, she ordered her manager to hurry up the customs officials, hoping they would release her jewelry.

'I'll try to get the valuable pieces by tonight,' explained her frantic manager.

'Oh, don't bother about them,' replied Raquel. 'It's the cheap gypsy jewelry I want.'

In France, Meller lived in splendor in Versailles and Nice. In New York, she and her Pekinese resided at the Hotel Ambassador in a 5-room suite, which she found cramped and wholly unsuitable. During the day, she stayed indoors, knitting shawls, her feet rarely touching Manhattan's sidewalks. Renault automobile agency placed a car at her disposal, which she had little use for. After a tour of the West and a brief stopover in Hollywood, she had only one further plan ... to return to Paris.

Although it appeared to the outside world that life within the Kahn household was spontaneous and privileged beyond comparison, the family did operate by a rigid set of rules and routines. When the *New York Herald Tribune* editor phoned the Kahn residence late one evening to talk to Otto, a most abrupt footman greeted him on the other end of the line. The editor discovered to his inconvenience just how strict the Kahn house rules were.

'Mr. Kahn has retired, sir,' replied the footman.

'Well, wake him up; it's an important message,' the editor insisted.

'No, only the butler is allowed to wake Mr. Kahn.'

'Let me talk to the butler, then.'

'But he's asleep also,' said the footman.

'Wake him up. I've got to talk to Mr. Kahn.'

'But I wouldn't dare to do that, sir. Nobody is allowed to wake the butler.'[58]

For the past year, Gilbert Kahn had worked at the Equitable Trust Company learning the banking trade. The time had arrived for him to travel to Europe to study the methods and conditions of various foreign banking houses.[59] His training would keep him away from America for around eighteen months. Upon his return, plans were already in place for Gilbert to join Kuhn, Loeb & Co. Gilbert's first stop would be Paris, followed by London, where, in both capitals, placements awaited him at J. Henry Schroder & Co. There was also talk of him journeying to Amsterdam and Germany, where, in the latter country, he might take a short temporary position at the family-owned Kahn bank. Arrangements had been made for Gilbert's wife Anne to accompany him during his time abroad. The couple departed on the SS *Leviathan* from New York Harbor on May 22.

Twin Peaks Bohemia

The bohemian vibe of Greenwich Village was not the carefree, laidback, nonconformist ambiance of Montmartre in Paris. That aside, it did have a certain charm that attracted artistic types to inhabit and frequent the neighborhood. Otto was drawn to the area, as was his daughter Margaret. On occasions, they would visit together to check out what was happening. The idea of 'slumming it' appealed to their risqué sense of aesthetic. In one instance, Otto arranged an afternoon meeting at a local Village café with an enterprising young architect, who had a business proposition he wanted to put to Otto. The entrepreneur was Clifford Reed Daily.

At 102 Bedford Street in West Village stood a dilapidated five-story house that Daily had grand ideas of renovating and transforming into an artists' quarter. Otto liked the idea and warmed to Daily's entrepreneurial spirit. He agreed to financially back the venture. Two years on, and the renovations were completed. Twin Peaks, so named because of the buildings fanciful appearance - not too dissimilar to a Swiss cuckoo clock with two individual pitched roofs - was now ready for tenancy.[60]

The twelve individual studios, aimed at artists, photographers, and writers, could be rented for an affordable $68.50 a month. Daily hoped his 'island growing in a desert of mediocrity' would inspire a new collective artistic movement.

The house officially opened to paying residents on the afternoon of May 21. At the opening ceremony were Otto and Daily, Mayor Jimmy Walker, Princess Amélie Troubetzkoy (an American writer married to the Russian artist Prince Pierre Troubetzkoy), representatives of the Churches, and several hundred local villagers. Photographers were there to capture the moment. Otto stood on the sidewalk outside the house, politely shaking hands, to the point where he began to feel a little self-conscious about his meager involvement in the project, apart from opening his checkbook.

'I don't understand,' Kahn faltered during the short speech he gave at the cutting of the ribbon. 'I have done many things for my city and its people, but I have never before been thanked so greatly out of proportion to the aid I may have rendered. Yet, I am glad the Village feels I have helped it. I am more than delighted to have discovered the Village and to have been discovered by the villagers.'[61]

At 2:30, Princess Troubetzkoy set a flame to a brazier of acorns, as an offering to the mythological Greek god Pan in a pagan ritual that newspapers were quick to note, was probably the first such offering ever proffered upon Pan in New York. The incense of acorns - chosen because they are the seeds of the great oak tree - represented wisdom, longevity, rebirth, and a promise of future strength.

Potential residents of Twin Peaks went through a strict vetting process regarding their suitability, and a housekeeper, Helen Todd, was duly installed to oversee the running of the premises.[62]

The idea of living within an artists' enclave of bookstores, cafés, bars, and late-night clubs, greatly appealed to Margaret and her whimsical notion of what it must be like to be an afflicted artist. Without hesitation, upon her return to New York from Europe, she rented a studio of her own at Twin Peaks and moved in. Her presence went totally against the whole ethos of the venture - 'An inspiring home for creative artists.' Margaret was hardly homeless, nor was she a struggling artist. Whispers of nepotism crept in.

Margaret soon discovered that living as a bohemian in a commune of artists, actors, and writers, was not all it was made out to be. She quickly tired of the experience and before long returned home to the gracious splendor of Fifth Avenue.

The Castillian Royal

In June, the Kahn orchestra came to the end of their two-year residency at the Hotel Biltmore.[63] Initial reports claimed Roger was seriously considering signing with the Arthur Spizzi Syndicate with the thought of gliding his band into a lucrative picture house tour.[64] The booking agency dealt with circuits rather than single theaters. It turned out the lure of touring and being away from the comforts and familiarity of his daily routine did not, in the end, appeal to the 18-year-old. Not unexpectedly, Kahn's band still had to be paid, irrespective of whether they were performing or not. To tide the group over, George Lottman promptly secured a weekly summer residency at a New York roadhouse, The Castillian Royal, on the Pelham Parkway.[65] Here, unbeknown to Roger, he got billed as the 'Millionaire Maestro,' a label that displeased him. A further hindrance was that Roger would have to appear with his band twice a week as part of the deal.

Castillian Royal advertisement, Roger Wolfe Kahn for the 'Entire Summer Season', *Variety*, June 16, 1926.

The Castillian Royal, The Woodmansten Inn, and Pelham Heath Inn were located on Pelham Road, a busy highway running east and west from New York City to Pelham Bay. All the venues had a slightly dubious reputation for underhand politics, customer grabbing, and rumors of selling illicit gin. Why Roger agreed to such an engagement is anyone's guess. The venue was certainly a few rungs down the ladder from the refined luxury his band had become accustomed to at the Hotel Biltmore. Inevitably, the residency was doomed from the start. Roger hated it, his musicians rebelled, and several quit the band, namely, violinist Joe Venuti, pianist Arthur Schutt, and Kahn's stalwart drummer Vic Berton.[66] F. Stanley King, the drummer from Barney Rapp's orchestra, was recruited to take Berton's place.[67] Lottman tried dressing up the gig by arranging a tie-up with WEAF

Radio to broadcast live from the venue when Roger was performing. The Kahn band opened at the start of the third week in June. How long they would stick it out was anyone's guess.

Songwriter Irving Berlin was making $300,000 a year on royalties from his compositions.[68] Roger was keen to concentrate on his songwriting and scoring abilities rather than leading his band in a roadhouse.

At the beginning of June, Victor dropped two new Kahn recordings: his rendition of Irving Berlin's *'At Peace With The World'* (with a vocal refrain by Henry Burr), coupled with the foxtrot *'I'd Climb the Highest Mountain (If I Knew I'd Find You).'*[69] Once again, Roger was the first artist to record the new Irving Berlin composition. Towards the latter part of June, Victor released another Kahn disc, *'Somebody's Lonely,'* with a vocal by Henry Burr.[70] Since leaving the Hotel Biltmore, Roger had simplified his band's name to Roger Wolfe Kahn and His Orchestra, dropping the Hotel Biltmore reference from the title.

The summer heat was unrelenting. New Yorkers in their thousands flocked to the coast at weekends to liberate their lungs from the cities fumes. On Sunday, June 19, the number of day-trippers visiting Coney Island reached 400,000.[71] As a result, roadhouses were drawing in a brisk trade. The most reliable barometer of business for any inn came via its washroom concessionaire; this year at the Castillian, it was the best in its history.

Even with the increase of customers at the Castillian, Roger was still not happy. At $2,000 a week, the band was only breaking even. At the Hotel Biltmore, they had cleared more than $2,800.[72] Berton, Schutt and Venuti may have left the group, but as a unit, they still had a galaxy of stars within its ranks with the likes of Tommy Gott, Joe Raymond, Harold Sturr, Alfred Evans, 'Miff' Mole and Arnold Brilhart. Those stars did not come cheap. A *Variety* journalist summed up the current situation the Kahn unit found themselves in with a single sentence: 'Probably not the choicest 'spot' for this aggregation; the roadhouse is chiefly a means to keep the organization intact until fall.' Roger wanted out. The establishment's co-owner, Al Goldman, informed the press that Kahn had signed the contract to play until September 15, so he was stuck there. The band's reviews were fantastic, which shows just how hot they were.

'The boys are generous in their dance sessions and their delivery seems to inspire an insatiable appetite for more of the Kahn brand. The leader himself, tooting a mean clarinet among some 18 other instruments he is capable of handling, is an attraction because of his style. As a conductor alone, the boy is a natural baton-wielder, maintaining a strict tempo that leaves nothing wanting. Further analysis of the band is extraneous. Its progress to the front on its merits, sans the aura of the 'name,' is accounted for by the proficiency of this entity.'[73] Irrespective of their excellent reviews, Lottman had to turn things around swiftly to keep the unit functioning. That break came sooner than anyone had anticipated.

Brand Kahn

Away from his band's predicament, Roger Wolfe Kahn Orchestras Inc. was growing from strength to strength. The Kahn name was now a brand. 'Each unit offered is sold with the Kahn 'label' - thus virtually compelling us to guarantee merit. Nationally publicized units - peerless in personal - now available for those who discriminate.'[74]

One of Kahn's units was confirmed for a ten-week stint at the beachfront Hotel Ritz-Carlton in Atlantic City, commencing early July, followed by a picture house tour in the fall.[75] The lads over at the Castillian Royal would have willingly handed over their bonuses for a chance at the gig. A steady stream of talented musicians queued daily outside Kahn's Broadway office, all hoping to be represented by the company.

When the opportunity to appear at the 'Biggest Carnival of the 20th Century' arrived on Roger's desk, he jumped at the chance. Anything to get his musicians out of the Castillian was a godsend. The theatrical and sporting event was scheduled for Sunday afternoon on June 27 at New York's colossal Polo Grounds in Upper Manhattan.[76] There were three stadiums at the grounds; the largest was the home of professional baseball and American football. The idea of an orchestra performing such a large open-air concert was acoustically mind-boggling. Playing in what could loosely be termed a bathtub would cause the sound to dissipate into thin air.

The carnival would benefit the United Jewish Campaign, with grandstand seats selling at $2 and box seats at $25. Over one hundred entertainment stars plus a handful of prize-winning pugilists had signed up to appear. It would also host the World's Amateur Champion Charleston Contest, with prizes of $1,500 in gold up for grabs. Also planned was a comedy baseball game between the Friars' and the Lambs' actor's clubs.

Singer Al Jolson and the world's lightweight champion boxer Benny Leonard had agreed to thrash out a three-round comedy-boxing exhibition at which producer George M. Cohan would referee. Jack Delaney (light-heavyweight boxing champion of the world) and the American lightweight boxer Sid Terris would be on hand to offer encouragement. Another feature was a tug of war between the choruses of every Broadway musical in New York. Sixteen orchestras were listed to furnish music for the event from top bandleaders such as Vincent Lopez, Ben Bernie, and Roger Wolfe Kahn. Theatrical stars already confirmed included the Marx Brothers, Ann Pennington, Sophie Tucker, Fanny Brice, Marilyn Miller, Houdini, Mae West, and 'Bugs' Baer. Mayor Jimmy Walker would be on hand to lend his support to the proceedings.[77]

On the day, everyone who agreed to appear did, and the event was a monumental financial success raising $75,000.[78]

Over 1,000 dancers competed in the Charleston contest. The judges found it hard to decide on one winner as so many of the entrants were excellent. Roger and his orchestra played in front of an audience estimated at over 35,000, their largest to date. All the entertainers and athletes joined in the costumed grand finale parade.

There was, given time, one performance that would become more memorable than any other on the day; Houdini's thrilling stunt, suspended from a steel cable, stretched across the length of the Polo Ground. From it, he managed to free himself from a straitjacket in record time. Incendiary blonde Mae West, currently starring on Broadway in her outrageous self-penned comedy-drama *Sex*, accompanied Houdini with his act. Sadly, Houdini's performance would turn out to be the last benefit show he ever gave. Three months later, he was dead.

In mid-July, Otto and Addie invited a few select friends to join them for a summer break in New Hampshire. One of the guests was Otto's private secretary Elizabeth 'Beth' Mutke. They lodged first at the fashionable Fabyan House in Crawford Notch, just beyond Bretton Woods.[79] A few days later, the party traveled to the Balsams at Dixville Notch. Here the mountainous and wooded landscape attracted many trekkers' intent on tackling the ascent to Mount Washington's summit. The trip gave Otto a welcome respite from the everyday stresses of city life.[80] With little to distract him, it also gave him time to prepare himself for his upcoming business trip to the West Coast of America.

News of Roger's impending debut as a stage musical composer appeared in *Variety* in late July.[81] There was something of the devil in the report implying that perhaps the youngster would not live up to expectations, or maybe he had taken on more than he was capable of doing. Roger wrote the score in collaboration with two Broadway heavyweights, lyricists Lew Brown and Buddy DeSylva, both known for their input in George White's hugely popular *Scandals* revues. As with any new musical venture, it's the sum of all the components that creates either a sure-fire hit or a miserable miss. The press would have to wait a while longer before they could cast their verdict.

In the meantime, Roger opened a new branch of his booking agency in the fashionable resort of Newport, Rhode Island. He put Henry Lodge in charge of the operation.[82] Lodge was foremost a musician and composer who, through his family connections, had a wide acquaintance with the social set in Palm Beach and Newport. With Lodge in charge, Roger and Lottman felt they could trust his musical expertise and judgment.

Roger's plans to expand his booking agency abroad were underway, with Paris earmarked as the first major European city for a new branch. The Paris office would operate in association with the American bandsman Billy Arnold. Billy already had a firm footing in the French capital, having lived there since the Great War. Roger also planned to open similar branches in Deauville, Cannes, Biarritz, and other popular resorts. Lottman had arranged to travel to France in

September to oversee the opening of the Paris office.

After carefully considering the proposal, Roger agreed to undertake a short vaudeville tour around New York City, primarily to get his orchestra out of the Castillian and back on stage in front of a more appreciative audience. In doing so, he would have to revoke his contract with Al Goldman, which had him tied until September 15. Thankfully, Goldman was wise enough to realize that getting on the wrong side of the Kahn family was not a brave thing to do, especially with the influence and clout their name carried. Goldman agreed to adjust Kahn's contract, thereby releasing his orchestra early from their contractual commitments.[83] The band was hugely thankful to young Kahn and prepared themselves for a Loew's theater vaudeville tour.[84] Yet further good news arrived when New York's Palace Theatre confirmed a two-week headlining engagement in August, with other major metropolitan houses to follow. At last, it felt as though the old band was back in business, back in the footlights where they belonged.

Even though the Kahn organization was knocking out bulletins with unremitting regularity, behind the scenes, something else was in preparation, something bigger and bolder than any other orchestra leader had done to date. That news was not yet ready for release.

A Curious Incident and Even Stranger Coincidence

Roger did not just confine his love of speed to the roads and the air; it also extended across the water. Like his father, Roger had also purchased a yacht, albeit not a grand vessel like Otto's. Roger used his 30-foot boat mainly for commuting from Manhattan to Long Island, where he moored it at his private dock in Cold Spring Harbor. As his father had done, Roger also christened his yacht using an acronym of his name, **Roweka**. The boat could achieve 32 knots an hour and operated on a 12-cylinder Liberty airplane motor, which, more than likely, Roger had installed.

On Monday, August 2, a report arrived at Hunter's Point Police precinct that Roger's $10,000 boat had gone missing from its private mooring, presumed stolen.[85] The police sent out notification of the theft to all river precincts across the city. Roger had only purchased the boat five days prior.

The following morning Hunter's Point Police precinct received several calls from boatmen, all with similar sightings of a 'fancy-looking boat' having washed up high and dry on the mudflats along

Newton Creek near Penny Bridge at Laurel Hill. Detectives Thomas Layton and Thomas Devery headed upriver in a speedboat to investigate the sightings. They soon located the mudflats where they did indeed find a 'fancy-looking boat' that had run aground.

The officers sent out a call for backup. Within the hour, an entire Marine Division of river police arrived to extricate the yacht from the grip of the slushy mudbank. They managed to refloat the vessel successfully. From its registry number, detectives ascertained Roger owned it. Furthermore, the yacht was in relatively good order, except for a slightly bent crankshaft.

When detectives questioned boatmen working nearby at Newton Creek, the plot thickened. A middle-aged man had initially arrived on the yacht early the previous afternoon. A short time later, the boat sailed up the creek as far as Mussel Island, after which it returned and dropped anchor near Penny Bridge. It then ran aground. The said yachtsman pottered on deck for a short while before disembarking. He then set off along the riverside. At Newton Creek, he approached the boatmen and asked them to keep an eye on his vessel, as he had to visit Albany to get cash to purchase parts needed for repairs. The man in question never returned.

The police notified Roger they had reclaimed the yacht. They also told him they believed it was probably stolen to sell on to bootleggers in the rum-running trade. As such, money could have already exchanged hands, although, on that point, the detectives were not sure. They advised Roger to retrieve his yacht directly to prevent its theft a second time. Bootlegger's operated frequently across the busy waterways around Manhattan, mainly under the cloak of darkness, shipping illicit liquor across to the mainland in whatever vessels they could get their hands on.

In a strange coincidence, a Pierce-Arrow car crashed outside the metal gates of the front entrance to the Kahns' Cold Spring Harbor estate. When the abandoned automobile came to the attention of a passerby, he called the police. What the cops unveiled was even more bizarre. The smashed-up overturned vehicle was laden with liquor. Was this a flunked booze delivery to the Kahn estate? After the accident, the driver had escaped from the wreck and flagged down a passing motorist who drove him to Smithtown, where doubtless he intended to muster help. Not so! Once in Smithtown, the fugitive stopped another vehicle and hitched a ride in a different direction, presumably to confound the authorities who were now on his tail.

Rumors of illicit alcohol concealed on the Kahn country estate thrived but were never proved. Likewise, Otto's wine cellar was hidden securely under lock and key away from public view. Were the two incidents connected, or was it just a sequence of random events?

During an extraordinary interview Roger gave to the *St. Petersburg Times* published on August 5, he revealed he had become tired of jazz and yearned to do something more fulfilling. 'It gets tiresome having an orchestra. I used to think it was wonderful but not anymore. I want to do something real. I want to compose music. I have already published three songs, and that's where the fun is.'[86]

What brought about this sudden craving for a change in direction probably stemmed from several factors: the responsibility of having to pay weekly paychecks to the musicians in the ten orchestras that bore his name, coupled with paying the salaries of his agency staff; his increasing passion for aviation; and his genuine desire to spend more time composing music. Roger was still a teenager, a couple of months away from his 19th birthday, and was undoubtedly just as keen to enjoy himself as any other teenager might.

Was Roger having a bad day at the office? The journalist does not disclose. Roger's drive to build his music empire into the most successful in America was never going to be a smooth ride. There would be off days. Or was this to be a long-term discontentment? Time alone would be the judge. Roger did reveal he was already making plans to travel to Europe in two years to study music composition. Putting his future aspirations aside, Roger had a more pressing announcement he wished to deliver; the scoop he and Lottman had held back for release. Finally, the venture had secured his father's approval. Roger was to open a New York nightclub in October.

If Roger thought he led a pressured life before he made the announcement, it would be ten times more demanding after airing the news. From that moment onwards, his days would become a relentless blizzard of activity, time schedules, and near nervous breakdowns.

Kahn Back At The Palace–August 9, 1926

Commencing Monday the following week, Roger and his orchestra headlined at the Palace Theatre in Times Square.[87] They closed at the Castillian on Sunday night and glided effortlessly onto the Broadway stage with all the aplomb of seasoned professionals as if they'd never been away. The boys felt good to be there, back amidst all the action and bright lights. There was a real buzz in the air. The musicians were itching to show the public just what they'd been up to since the last time they graced the boards.

'Kahn back at the Palace,' screamed the headlines. New Yorkers came out in force to welcome back young Kahn and his orchestra.

The Club Bug

*'Then I got the club bug and started Le Perroquet de Paris
on 57th Street. And, oh gosh, what it cost me to run it!'*[88]

From late summer 1926 through to the following spring, everything in Roger's life revolved around his nightclub.

Le Perroquet de Paris was the distinctive name Roger chose for his highly anticipated new club on West 57th Street in Manhattan's nifty fifties. Another club, *Le Perroquet*, run by French entrepreneur Rene Racover already existed in Paris. The Parisian counterpart was housed above the entrance lobby of the *Casino de Paris* and was hugely popular. With Racover on board as a partner, Roger hoped their New York operation would be equally profitable. Roger's place occupied Ciro's former restaurant. Even before the nightspot had opened, the press were hailing it the 'Club of Dreams.'

It would be the most impressive nightclub in New York City to date. Roger had taken out a ten-year lease on the premises at 146 West 57th Street for an annual rental of $23,000.[89] Racover would receive a 49 percent interest with Roger holding control. With all the money Roger was earning, he was anxious to invest his profits into something legitimate and credible. A nightclub seemed an ideal venture in which to make that investment.

When Roger first suggested having a nightclub to his father, Otto phoned singer and Ciro's restaurant owner Harry Richman. He offered to purchase Ciro's, lock, stock, and barrel.[90] Otto was good at precipitating actions rather than talking about them. It was what he was used to doing. Initially, Chapman thought the call was a practical joke. However, after being assured the offer was genuine, Chapman finally agreed to Kahn's proposal. Otto would also help finance the venture.

In taking over Ciro's lease, the Kahn-Racover combination acquired all the assets and liabilities of the former establishment. The assets included the best-equipped kitchen in a New York nightspot. The debts on the room entailed a sum of $40,000 'in the red.'

The idea behind the club was simple: to open the most luxurious nightclub in New York and station Roger's original Victor recording orchestra there with Roger conducting the band nightly in person. It would be a classy proposition, formal and exclusive, featuring a cabaret, a set meal menu, and a high cover charge, all of which would appeal to the wealthy socialites that wore good taste on their lapels and splashed money around like cologne. With the Kahn brand, Roger's top-class orchestra, and Racover's French connection, the arrangement looked set to make a mint.

The press went to town heaping praise upon the venture with all the enthusiasm of a young kid embracing a new toy, so much so that things quickly got out of hand. Everyone wanted to get in on the action: tradesmen, investors, entertainers, chefs, etc. The list grew daily.

Roger summoned a meeting with his band. The club was currently undergoing renovations and would open in around six weeks. In the meantime, Roger halted all future live appearances, which meant trimming the current Palace Theatre run, and placing any future Keith-Albee vaudeville bookings temporarily on hold.

Understandably, the musicians were not happy with the arrangement. They had bills to pay and mouths to feed. Roger put them at ease: they would still receive their full weekly salaries up until the club opened, after which things would revert to normal. The impromptu hiatus would allow his musicians to take a well-earned break, visit family and friends, or chill out and take things easy. It also provided time for Roger to take temporary leave away from all the madness in New York.

The band could not believe their luck. Not only were the musicians being paid to do nothing, but they could also take on recording or session work as and when it came about, just as long as it did not interfere with any of Roger's plans for his orchestra or club. What Roger failed to tell his musicians was who would be paying their salaries.

Otto and Addie were due to take their summer vacations but had decided not to spend them together this year. Instead, Otto had chosen to travel by train across America to visit the West Coast for business reasons. As customary, Addie opted to sail to Europe and invited her daughter Margaret to accompany her. Aware of the tremendous strain Roger was under with all his work obligations, Addie insisted her son join her, if not for the entire six-week duration, then at least for a part of it. Although Roger could see the benefits of such a break, he had to remind his mother that he was solely responsible for paying his musicians' weekly salaries. If he didn't work, he would not be able to fulfill that commitment.

Addie refused to listen, and by way of making it easier for her son to say 'yes,' selflessly offered to pay his musicians their full salaries while he was absent. Roger accepted his mother's offer.

Over the next few weeks, Addie forked out $11,000 in musician's salaries so her son could take a vacation.[91] It was an unusual arrangement, but then most things the Kahn family did, defied the norm.

Setting aside his mother's generosity, Roger deemed it would be far more beneficial and fun for him if his valued buddy and agency manager George Lottman accompanied him on vacation. George, too, was under mountains of pressure and in dire need of a break. Although it was not the family holiday Addie had envisaged, she agreed to her son's proposal. Instead of sailing to Europe, Roger and George would take to the open road and cross America in a Marmon touring caravan that Roger had recently purchased from the wife of the theatrical producer Albert Herman Woods.[92] The vehicle had been specially adapted and came equipped with a kitchenette (complete with a refrigerator) and separate shower facilities, which Mrs. Woods paid over $9,000 to have installed. Roger would catch up with his father on the West Coast.

Addie would have Margaret to keep her company, and they could meet up with Maud and her family (who were holidaying in Europe) and Gilbert and his wife, who were still living on the continent.

On the morning of Saturday, August 14, the rubber hit the road; Roger and George headed off in the Marmon on their motoring adventure across the vast American landscape with Los Angeles as their destination.[93]

With the Kahn family away, their Long Island home was closed for the season. In the family's absence, the noted artist Austin Montgomery Purves decorated Otto's lap pool with elaborate underwater frescoes. The murals, painted on panels, were attached to the sidewalls of the pool.[94]

In New York City, renovations at Roger's nightclub progressed at a steady rate in a bid to get the room ready and prepared for its official opening. Overseeing the project while Roger was absent was Rene Racover. Racover was also a director of the French Line shipping company and had managed to secure contracts for Kahn dance bands on all of its fourteen vessels.[95] It was a prestigious assignment, worth a tidy sum.

Before August bowed out, Victor handed the public a parcel of new Kahn recordings, most notably his medley of Raquel Meller's American hits: '*My Toreador*,' '*Poor Scentless Flower*,' '*Your Wonderful Lips*' and '*Who'll Buy My Violets*.'[96]

One wonders if, perhaps, Roger recorded these as a memento for his mother, knowing of her great admiration for Señorita Meller. Victor also released Roger's version of '*Cross Your Heart*' from Philadelphia's hit musical *Queen High*, and his take on the Richard Rodgers and Lorenz Hart song '*Mountain Greenery*,' written for the *Garrick Gaieties 1926* stage revue. Everyone at Victor had a good feeling about '*Mountain Greenery*.' When Abel Green reviewed the latter two tracks in *Variety*, he assured the record-buying public they were 'brilliantly scored and distinctively rendered.' Victor hoped to bag a late summer hit by capitalizing on all the free publicity Roger and his nightclub venture were generating in the press.*

The announced opening of *Le Perroquet de Paris* was October 1, with a proposed $3 cover charge.[97] By late August, this had changed - the projected entry price had risen to $5, and the launch date put back to 'on or about' November 1.[98]

When Otto traveled, he traveled in style. During his lightning trip to the West Coast, he journeyed in the luxury of his own private railroad carriages attended to by several servants. He invited a small, select group of guests to join him; some were business associates, others were personal friends. Among the party was the vice president of the Equitable Trust Company of New York James Irving Bush, influential publisher Condé Nast, author David Gray, journalist and editor of *Vanity Fair* Frank Crowninshield, Leonard Jarvis Cushing of Famous Players-Lasky Corporation, Vice-Admiral Ernest Augustus Taylor of the British Royal Navy, and Lt. Colonel Norman Thwaites of the British Army. It was an eclectic assemblage of traveling companions. Otto had arranged the trip for three reasons: 1. Business - to seek out investment opportunities; 2. Bonds - to get acquainted with people and forge new friendships; 3. Pleasure.[99] The 'hurried' tour would take in around twenty-five cities.[100]

During the outward journey, Otto made a fleeting visit to Canada, where on September 2 in Toronto, the Kahn party attended the Canadian National Exhibition. The day had been set aside as 'Music Day.'[101] The directors of the exhibition threw a special luncheon in Otto's honor. In return, Otto gave a suitably prepared address encouraging the many benefits derived from music and the arts.

When the train reached the West Coast, it swept south, visiting various towns along the coastline. In Monterey, the Kahn party spent several days relaxing and playing golf at Del Monte Lodge at Pebble Beach.[102]

In Santa Barbara, Otto learned to his amusement the local press were keener to hear news of his son's proposed nightclub than details of his own activities.[103] It was a strange turnaround, the father being brushed aside for updates of his son. Nonetheless, Kahn assured the journalists he was entirely behind his younger son's planned nightclub. The aim of the club, he emphasized, was not merely to add to New York's exotic nightlife, but also 'to introduce musical compositions and development of merit to the public and bring to public attention new talent, especially among young people who under present conditions have very little chance to get an audience.'

Rumors had already leaked to the media that the club would have a mirror dance floor and that the glass-topped tables would contain bowls with live goldfish swimming inside. Otto was eager to play down the expense and extravagance of the renovation, preferring to focus on the aesthetic appeal of the 'picturesque' club.

In Los Angeles, Kahn put aside time to play more of his favorite sport, golf, and swam regularly in the ocean. He also met up with his son Roger and Roger's buddy George, who had managed to arrive in one piece considering the immense scale of their endeavor, driving across the entire length of the continent.

Wall Street investment had, to present, poured over $2 billion into the American film industry, the bulk of which paid for the building of new picture houses. Otto engaged actively in encouraging financiers to invest in the industry. Through his efforts, he had been elected a member of the board of Paramount Pictures. It seemed appropriate that Otto should stop by in Hollywood to catch up on his investments.

The movie-making business greatly interested the Kahn family. Otto, Addie, Gilbert, and Roger were all keen to explore its financial and creative possibilities. This fascination even extended to Otto's brother Felix, who owned several theaters. Otto firmly believed that cinema was a form of art. When Otto arrived in Tinsel Town, the townsfolk treated him like visiting royalty.

Hollywood, which now had more stars than the heavens, had experienced an unexpected transition, a kind of self-inflicted identity crisis. The movie studios were still coming to terms with the talkies and all the implications and problems this technological advance brought.

Vice-Admiral Ernest Augustus Taylor (far left), unidentified (2nd left), Douglas
Fairbanks (3rd left), Frank Crowninshield (4th left), Otto Kahn (center), Leonard
Jarvis Cushing (4th right), Charlie Chaplin (3rd right), David Gray (2nd right), Lt.
Colonel Norman Thwaites (far right), late-summer 1926. (Copyright © Roy Export
Company Limited)

Universal Studios' prolific output of factory system low-budget
westerns, short comedies, and melodramas were showing their age
and had now become clichéd. New blood and a new creative vision
were needed to bring the studios and their movies up to date.

When Otto and his party called in on Charlie Chaplin Studios, they
met its famous owner. Also present was the actor Douglas Fairbanks.
Chaplin was in the middle of filming his latest movie *The Circus*. He
was dressed in character wearing his trademark bowler hat, clasping
his bent walking cane.* Otto and the comedy actor struck up an
immediate rapport.

A few days later, the Kahn party resumed their itinerary at
breakneck speed traveling southwest to El Paso in Texas. Roger bade
his father farewell and, with George, went eastwards by train, leaving
his motor vehicle in L.A. to be transported later by rail. Roger and
George had an important date lined up on October 3 in Chicago,
which they could not afford to miss.

In El Paso, Otto and his traveling companions met local commerce executives over breakfast. Later in the day, they visited Fort Bliss army post to pay their respects to General Edwin B. Winans.[104] *

In Dallas, the start of the SMU Aggie football game was delayed fifteen minutes as a courtesy to Otto and his guests to allow them to arrive in time to see the kick-off.[105] Kahn even managed to stop by Houston to weigh up business possibilities, before the group finally departed on their long journey home to New York.

Chicago Bound–October 3

Roger Wolfe Kahn was in Chicago!

It was an important day for young Kahn and his eponymous orchestra. It was also a hugely significant day for the Orpheum Circuit as they revealed to the public their sparkling new vaudeville house, the New Palace Theatre. It cost $12 million to construct. It certainly looked expensive: designed in the opulent French Baroque style, inspired by the Château de Versailles. Headlining the bill as its opening attraction for the entire week was Roger and his band.

Roger's visit to Chicago was the first out-of-town run for the Kahn orchestra. For the privilege, they were pocketing the handsome fee of $4,200, a record figure.[106] He'd accepted the engagement because of the delay in opening his nightclub in New York. He wanted to keep his musicians fired up. Orpheum's publicity machine went into overdrive; Roger appeared on the front page of practically every paper in northern Illinois.

The theater opened in a blaze of glory.[107] Stars of stage and screen and many society folks made an appearance, with some traveling in from New York City. Dignitaries representing Chicago included Mayor William Emmett Dever.

Curiously, the building resembled a luxurious hotel, with much space devoted to the grand lobby, foyer, promenades, and lounges, with additional rooms for smoking and writing. Upon entering the auditorium, theatergoers stopped in awe to admire the magnificent gold and ivory color scheme. Orpheum had provided every convenience possible, from fresh, clean air pumped into the ventilation system to spacious double-upholstered seats. There was even a maid and page service on hand. The auditorium seated 2,500, all with a clear, uninterrupted view of the enormous stage. Every modern electrical and mechanical device known to stagecraft was housed backstage. Even the large, airy dressing rooms came equipped with shower baths and many other up-to-date amenities. The Met in New York City must have been seething with envy.

The inaugural performance took place on Sunday afternoon, on October 3, with a full supporting bill compered by Will Mahoney. There was no doubt who the public in their thousands had flocked to see - Roger Wolfe Kahn and his Society Orchestra.[108]

As the curtain lifted, Kahn's musicians remained perfectly still on stage, holding their respective instruments. In front stood Roger with his back towards the audience. As the band jumped into their first number, Roger turned briefly and peered out into the vast auditorium. A visible shiver of anticipation stirred among the audience, followed by a spontaneous round of applause. Roger acknowledged the welcome with a slight bow of his head and a cheeky grin. Roger had grown a mustache![109]

The 'boy wonder' of jazz looked totally at ease as he steered his band faultlessly through a well-rehearsed routine. The orchestra played with competence and drive. There was no room for mediocrity; each musician was a seasoned professional. It was a tried and tested formula aimed at the masses. As each number folded neatly into the next, the audience lapped it up. Roger was on a winning streak. The reviews were sensational.

At one performance later in the week, something quite unexpected happened on the stage. The incident would make trombonist 'Miff' Mole quiver with nervous recollection for many years to come.[110] It took place during the number 'Tiger Rag.' As 'Miff' stood from his chair to grab a hot solo, he let rip in his inimitable style. Trained upon him was an enormous arc light that captured his gleaming brass trombone and Derby hat mute. As the number furiously gathered pace, building to a mighty crescendo, 'Miff' raised his trombone high into the air at the exact moment it peaked. At which point, the front end of his horn exploded outwards and flew over his shoulder, falling with a distinct clank onto the stage, sending the audience crazed with excitement. 'Miff' kept his cool as if it was all part of the show, then calmly walked over to the offending mute, picked it up, fitted it back into place, and kicked straight back into the number. He proceeded with another hot phrase before finishing the chorus with a climax, bringing the audience to their feet with a standing ovation. 'Miff,' in thinking he had messed up, had created one of the highlights of that evening's performance.

'Roger seriously considered keeping it in as part of the act!' recalled 'Miff' during an interview many years later.

Kahn and his orchestra completed the engagement at the New

Palace Theatre triumphant, after which they returned to Manhattan fully charged and ready to take on a week's booking at the E. F. Albee Theatre, Brooklyn, commencing on October 11.[111] After this, there followed a further week at New York's Palace Theatre, at which Roger introduced his latest composition, 'You Should Know.'[112] At the end of the Palace run, Roger and his orchestra went straight into rehearsals for the opening of Le Perroquet de Paris, which was presently on schedule to open at the beginning of November.

Addie and her daughter Margaret returned to New York from their European vacation on October 21 aboard the Aquitania.[113] They arrived in preparation for the launch of Roger's club. Regrettably, they returned too late to help celebrate Roger's 19th birthday on October 19. Neither was his brother around for the occasion; Gilbert was still working in Europe.

New York's nightlife had a ritual all of its own, where folk moved in and out of circles depending upon their mood and financial constraints. The Village flapper chose supper at the Biltmore for its low cover charge, dancing, and jazz accompaniment, whereas the aristocrat much preferred dining at Sherry's. The livelier establishments, such as Casa Lopez and Club Richman, attracted the Broadway beauty, followed by an appearance at Reuben's or Club Caravan.

Lowlife devotees took supper at the Colony or swung by Harlem's Cotton Club, which stayed open late until breakfast. For those romantically entwined, Small's, with its low lights and soft music, usually sufficed. The choice was limitless for the rapacious visitor in town for the night: Texas Guinan's rowdy 300 Club, The Owl for Black entertainment, or the Colony to rub shoulders with regulars such as Gloria Swanson, Elsie de Wolfe, and a few of the Vanderbilts. If your motor was still running by closing time, it was on to Reuben's for that out-all-night feeling.

The advent of Le Perroquet de Paris brought a new kid on the block, and anyone worth their weight in gold, be it actual or metaphysical, expected an invitation to its unveiling. The timing of Roger's club could not have come at a better moment, for on the same night Le Perroquet de Paris was set to open, New York's latest opera season launched at the Met.

Reams of newspaper articles prophesized the club's apparent extravagance and luxury. To help fuel such coverage, George Lottman drip-fed regular updates to the media. As the opening date grew ever closer, the demand for tickets to its premiere grew even greater. Rather astutely, the nearby Club Mirador, expecting a massive overspill of customers unable to get into Kahn's joint, announced a $10 entry charge for the same night. Roger immediately increased his cover to match it.[114] New York high society was chomping at the bit, poised on their toes, crazed with anticipation.

The press claimed Otto was financially underwriting the club and had already forked out a colossal $250,000.[115] A large proportion of the money had gone on fixtures and fittings. These included: a silver and beaten copper stage proscenium cleverly positioned to give an uninterrupted view of the orchestra from all corners of the room; glass-topped tables fitted with individual aquariums containing live goldfish; six live parakeets in domed metal cages. However, the real star attraction was the translucent floor, using underfloor and overhead lighting, giving customers the illusion of dancing on light. The revealing nature of how such an effect might inadvertently illuminate women's legs and their undergarments enlivened gossip columns.[116] It was not the first club to have a glass floor; that distinction went to the producer Morris Gest who ordered a similar one in 1918 (designed by Norman Bel Geddes) for his cabaret theater (the former Cocoanut Grove) atop the Century Theatre. Roger's club was, however, the first in New York to have a mirror floor.[117]

In keeping with the French theme, chic hand-painted invitations for the opening night, costing 50 cents apiece to create, were mailed in advance from Paris to distinguished guests and celebrities.[118] Roger even had a new entrance with an overhead canopy constructed on 57th Street. As the opening got closer, the press night arranged for Sunday, October 31 (the day illusionist Houdini died) got canceled as contractors were still working on-site.

Frustratingly, at the last moment, just before the roped barriers went up across the sidewalk and the red carpet was rolled out, the premiere was postponed again. The custom-made tables with glass tops, destined to display the acrobatic goldfish, had arrived but not to the specifications as ordered. They required immediate alterations before being installed. A further delay arose when a fuse blew, blanketing the establishment in darkness. These were crazy days, and the tabloids were lapping it up.

'Everything was ready but the electricity,' said the man in charge of the lighting Henry G. Bulitta. Consequently, the electrical effects, of which there were seventeen (including forest fires and moonlight), did not operate as expected. 'If we flick the switch to make the effect of a thunderstorm, a rainbow would come instead. When we turned the switch that would have shown up the goldfish, it lit up the parrot cages. We expect to open Friday.'[119]

Irrespective of the delay in opening, Roger raised the first-night cover charge yet again, this time to $25! The news sent New Yorkers into hyperbolic overdrive. The press worked themselves into a frenzy.

Kahn fever swept the city.

Roger Wo[lfe Kahn]

Enterprises for the [...]

Le Perroq[uet...]

America's [...]
After-[...]
Rende[...]
at 146 West 57th. St[...]

in assoc[...]

Rene R[...]

ROGER WOLFE KAHN ORCHESTRAS, Inc.

R-W-K *units insure*
PERFECTION IN PERSONNEL
PRESTIGE OF NAME

Inferior organizations have no place here. There is a name to be protected—a standard that must be adhered to. Each unit offered is sold with the KAHN Label—thus virtually compelling us to guarantee merit — Nationally publicized units now available for those who discriminate. — Each unit personally assembled and rehearsed by ROGER WOLFE KAHN.

Roger Wo[lfe...]

Executive Offices
Phones—Ch[...]
George D. Lottman—Gene[...]

Le Perroquet de Paris

Opens

Le Perroquet de Paris Finally Opens

Friday, November 5 - the big day arrived. *Le Perroquet de Paris* flung open its doors to the public.

'Dream Palace Opened in New York by Young Kahn,' blazed *The Evening Independent* headline.[120]

And so it was! Never in the history of New York's nightlife had there been such a brilliant opening for a nightclub.[121] West 57th Street echoed with the sound of cabs, limousines, onlookers, and partygoers arriving, all with their sight aimed clearly in the same direction, upon the immaculate red-carpet runner laid across the sidewalk outside *Le Perroquet de Paris*.

The jostling, yelling, screaming, and pushing, the arrivals and commotion, the squeals of joy and gasps of excitement vividly set the tone as stars and celebrities lined the red carpet to pose for photographers. Like an exotic bazaar, the chilled air became infused with the trail of expensive fragrances. New York's elite and fashionable converged in a mighty show of support for Roger and his Dream Palace as Manhattan looked on in wonderment.

A steady flow of vehicles pulled up to the curb throughout the evening and spewed their guts out onto the sidewalk. Autograph hunters stood their ground, pouncing on ticket holders as they stepped from limousines, scattering innocent bystanders with their impetuous assaults.

Photographers held their cameras aloft in the hope of capturing that one exclusive image that might grace the following day's papers. The glare of their exploding flashlights lit up the street. When tousle-haired actress Fannie Ward appeared, the crowd lurched dangerously forward as cries of 'Fannie' punctured the air. The ensuing chaos resembled a scene at a movie premiere. Such was the noise and fire-cracking delight emanating from spectators as they shoved restlessly ahead to steal a closer look.

The Little Parrot

Le Perroquet de Paris was the jewel in New York's nightclub coterie. On opening night, it sparkled like a De Beers South West African diamond. From wall to wall, the club shimmered with wealth. The air buzzed with excitement. No facet of detail had been overlooked, from the waiter's black tie and tails to the cigarette girls revealing outfits, down to the ultramodern decor - the last gasp in glamor, simply designed, yet with an eye for grandeur in its furnishings, art, and mural decorations.¹²² The room was a homage to sophisticated elegance, an artist's canvas upon which to feast one's eyes.

Otto's checkbook had worked wonders. The centerpiece of attention was a $12,000 exquisitely designed French bandstand that assured the ultimate in acoustics, lit by an elaborate lighting system that would bring credit to a Broadway production.

The copper and silver bandstand at *Le Perroquet de Paris*. Note its reflection in the mirror dance floor. On the right of the picture is Roger's instrument rack holding the eighteen instruments he played nightly at the club, ca. 1926.

The widely discussed mirror dance floor did, with the flick of a switch, cleverly lose its power of reflection when used for dancing, saving ladies the awkwardness of any embarrassing blushes. It worked as such: when switching the lights off, the dance floor became a mirror, reflecting the ceiling, where the moon and heavenly stars appeared. When turning the lights on beneath the floor, the mirror effect disappeared, and the lights changed color in fascinating succession: from purple to green, from blue to violet, and so on, changing the mood of the room to reflect the music.

Harry Richman officiated as the emcee; Jimmy Durante had

declined an offer to host due to an alternative engagement he'd accepted at a rival venue.[123] Rene Racover was assigned the roles of general manager and front of house greeter, overseeing the smooth running of the operation during opening hours, leaving Roger time to concentrate on musical matters. Entertainment ran nightly from 11 p.m. to 2:30 a.m. to catch the theatrical profession as well as the general public. Roger insisted on the voluntary 2:30 a.m. curfew, taking into account Mayor Walker's designated club closing hour of 3 a.m.

The theme of the cabaret show was one of shifting variety, seamless like sand upon a beach: a dance, a comedy act, a dance, another specialty, etc., with Roger's orchestra providing accompaniment and leading the dancing throughout the evening.

Such a sophisticated spectacle was unusual for a nightclub. The format, conceived by Roger, was quite groundbreaking for the time. The diner traveled on a journey through jazz rhythms, from Paris to Cairo, then overland to the Zulu Kingdom, before sailing the ocean to India. The music moved along the Hindustan path and then to Japan in South Asia, but not necessarily on the same route each evening. Sound effects and mood lighting added to the ambiance. 'Perhaps the music carries to the brain the picture of a sunset. Immediately a full-fledged red sun sinking in the sea appears on the stage, and red light is shot up through the transparent floor. A scantily clad dancer representing the sun motif appears suddenly from nowhere, and twirls and twists to the beams of four spotlights, which illuminate her entire person.'[124] The show was a revelation and demonstrated what inspired choreography could achieve within a club environment by utilizing the concept of reinterpretation.

The room comfortably seated 550, although the architect never designed it for mass patronage. Instead, Roger and Racover aimed to attract the ultra-cool, strictly formal society babes with enough cash to corrupt.

Expensive gifts - termed 'special favors' - were presented to each woman as she entered the club: either a bottle of Jean de Parys exquisite perfume *Sous le Gui*,* or a pretty French porcelain doll.

Premiere souvenirs costing $60 each were on sale from an attractive cigarette girl, should a gentleman feel the urge to impress his accompanying wife or girlfriend.[125]

Rubbing shoulders at the host's table were Irving Berlin and his wife (heiress) Ellin Mackay, Condé Nast, Mr. and Mrs. Harry C. Cushing III (Mrs. Cushing was Reginald Claypoole Vanderbilt's daughter, Cathleen), and Roger's incredibly proud parents accompanied by his sister, Margaret. The latter brought along her fashionable coterie of friends with her.

Roger presents a bottle of the coveted French perfume *Sous le Gui* to Mrs. George D. Lottman (Betty) at *Le Perroquet de Paris*.[126]

Though Roger was a 'reluctant' performer, he was undoubtedly a star with a distinctive style, and guests to his club expected to see him in person on stage conducting his orchestra. In theory, it was the perfect gig for the youngster, a mere five-minute drive from home. It also allowed him time during the day to concentrate on other matters such as composing and arranging and any further musical projects he had in the pipeline.

The reviews over the following days were fabulous. 'The last gasp in smart nightclubs,' shouted *Variety* breathlessly. 'Ultra-artistic with an ultra 'In' following [with] the millionaire maestro's own crack dance band. Be sure to make it!'[127] Reservations flowed in with a measure of urgency attached to them: people wanted to see the place for themselves. In his lengthy appraisal in *Variety*, Abel Green acknowledged the club was as spectacular as all the pre-launch hype had intimated.

'The new *Le Perroquet* looks like a handsomely plumed bird, not grubby (grungy) or raucous in its prattle, as is the wont of some parrots, but a dignified, beautiful object that will fetch plenty of attention from the truly 'nice' people. Of course, Jimmy Durante and his conspirators have not been prospering for naught, but there is an equally large field that will like Roger Wolfe Kahn and his café just like the undersigned likes Kahn, his café, and also Durante.'[128]

A swish Manhattan nightclub was every bandleader's dream. Roger was now the owner of the most beautiful nightclub in New York, if not the Western Hemisphere, and he was still only a teenager.[129]

The Way Forward

This winter, Manhattan nightclubs took on an unusually lavish appearance, with each club vying for custom from their closest counterpart, using as many hackneyed tricks to increase attendance figures as they could muster. Mid-Manhattan was a playground for the rich. Many clubs tried mimicking *Le Perroquet* and adopted a Gallic theme, hiring French managers and entertainers. The Russian influence of the previous year created by immigrant Slavic nobility was now deemed passé.[130] The glittering enterprise that was *Le Perroquet de Paris* stood far and away ahead of its competitors.

Along with overseeing the running of his club, Roger still had recording commitments and stage projects to undertake. On November 4, Kahn and his orchestra swung by Victor studios to lay down two new tracks, George and Ira Gershwin's '*Clap Yo' Hands*' and Harbach, Hammerstein, and Friml's '*We'll Have a Kingdom,*' the latter featured a vocal by Johnny Marvin. On November 24, Kahn recorded '*Tonight You Belong To Me,*' showcasing celeste player Nathaniel Shilkret. He also captured the upbeat '*Wouldn't You!*' with a rhythm guitar solo by Eddie Lang. Franklyn Baur handled the vocals on both numbers. Another visit to the studio on December 14 delivered '*Tenderly Think of Me*' with a vocal injection by Frank Bessinger and '*Tell Me Tonight,*' again featuring Shilkret on celeste.

Requests to play at society engagements and College dances arrived regularly. The quantity increased ten-fold over the festive season, adding tea dances and balls to the list. Most of them, Roger declined. Instead, many were undertaken by one of his dozen or so orchestras that either carried his name or that his agency represented. The Collegiate Ramblers was one such band that benefited greatly from Roger's opposition to playing out of town.[131]

Irrespective of Prohibition, or perhaps because of it, New York clubs were doing a roaring trade. However, as business partners, Roger and Racover were never destined to become the nightclub barons of New York City. Their jellylike partnership never settled into a cohesive working relationship. Both directors had different visions of how the business should grow. For Roger, his aim was clear; he wanted to run the entire operation himself. With this in mind, Roger offered to buy out Racover's cut.[132] Racover accepted, banked the money, and fled back to Paris, where he felt considerably more at home.

Roger referred to *Le Perroquet* as being more like an art studio café. It was a huge financial undertaking, and Roger had a large weekly payroll to fork out. At weekends the premises attracted capacity attendance figures, seating as many as 575 covers. With suppers taken into account, business was brisk, in fact, so good, the doorman was turning customers away on Friday, Saturday, and Monday.

The Scandal of the Northern State Parkway

The scandal of the Northern State Parkway was, at the time, less of a scandal and more of an outrage. The scandal came to light much later.

New York City Parks Commissioner Robert Moses, whose authority stretched across five boroughs, proposed a new highway to generate a smoother traffic flow across Long Island. On paper, the route went straight through Otto's country estate, kissing goodbye to his expensively designed 18-hole golf course in the process. The highway also encroached upon estates owned by several other moneyed families: the Vanderbilt, Phipps, Grace, Ryan, Hennessy, Whitney, and Morgan. When Otto received notification of the plan, he was livid and immediately summoned his attorney Grenville Clark.

In theory, the project was sound; in practice, the route was badly mapped. The impact it would have on farming communities was catastrophic. In late 1926, Moses (who, through his marriage, was related to Otto)* instructed surveyors to reroute the highway three miles south, thereby sidestepping Kahn's estate along with the majority of the other wealthy landowner's tracts. Irrespective of the change, the new route would still cause havoc for the local farming communities. Moses disregarded their pleas. Construction of the road went ahead.

In the 1960s, correspondence was unearthed between Grenville

Clark and Robert Moses that revealed Otto had secretly donated $10,000 to Moses to assure the Parkway bypassed the Kahn estate.[133] The money allegedly paid for surveyors fees. Robert Moses remained in power for 44 years and would later be labeled as the man, more than any other, that defined the shape of modern New York, but at a cost; a grievance, New Yorkers are still coming to terms with.

Last Will and Wishes

The Swedish-born opera singer Lydia Lindgren arrived in the U.S. in 1913, aged 19. Her fresh-faced Nordic features, flaxen hair, and gentle smile brought her to the attention of the Metropolitan Opera Company in 1914, more especially Otto, who personally took her under his wing. Lindgren soon became a featured singer at the Chicago Opera House and the Met, where she had built an excellent reputation for her strong, clear diction and powerful voice. However, beneath her calm, measured stage appearance laid a troubled cauldron. The press dubbed her the 'Swedish nightingale.' Otto's early friendship with Lindgren took on various roles: mentor, father figure, with talk of a romantic attachment. Lindgren had since married operatic tenor Raoul Quirze and the couple resided in Flushing, New York. However, her bond with Otto was more binding than either let on and had become a matter of continued fixation for Lindgren on various levels, especially financially.

On December 6, the singer visited Boston, Massachusetts, and checked into a suite at the Copley Plaza hotel. After writing three letters - with one marked 'My Last Will and Wishes' - she ordered a taxicab and went to a local drugstore where she purchased a small bottle of liquid. She returned to the cab and asked the driver to take her back to the Copley Plaza.

As the driver glanced in his rear-view mirror during the journey, he saw Lindgren slump forward onto the cab's floor, where she remained reeling in agony.[134] The cab driver immediately drove to Boston City Hospital, where doctors ascertained she had swallowed the contents of the bottle she had purchased from the drugstore marked iodine. Whether her bid to kill herself was a serious attempt or a marker to attract attention can only be guessed. Physicians were hopeful the 42-year-old singer would recover.

The cops found the three letters Lindgren had written before she attempted suicide in her handbag: one addressed to 'the Public Administrator,' one to her husband, and the third inscribed to Otto H.

Kahn, New York.[135] When the singer was well enough, she held a press conference in which she clarified her reason for writing a letter to Otto. 'I wrote Mr. Kahn because he has befriended me, as he so often befriended other singers, and has befriended the profession itself.' The reporters did not believe her explanation and suspected it was an appeal for Kahn to use his influence to help her husband's career. The actual contents of her letter to Kahn remained secret. In a thoughtfully considered statement, released after she had fully recovered, Lindgren cited insomnia, nervousness, and despair as the reasons that compelled her to down the iodine draught.[136]

Parrots Landing

Once *Le Perroquet de Paris* was up and running, the regular cover charge remained at $5. In paying the entrance fee, guests expected top entertainment, which Roger and his orchestra and cabaret revue delivered nightly. Viennese-trained exotic dancer Maria Ley was one of the more avant-garde specialty performers featured in the floorshow.[137] In an interesting side note, in April 1928, Maria became Roger's cousin-in-law after she secretly married his German cousin, Frank Gerhart Deutsch* - the millionaire son of his aunt 'Lili' (Otto's sister Elisabeth).

In a surprise development, the parrots were proving exceptionally good for business. The strikingly colorful birds had acquired a reputation for being excellent mimics. The sound of their squawking provided in equal measures great delight and extreme annoyance to the clientele.

So coveted were the expensive *Le Perroquet* souvenirs that Roger opened a small *Le Perroquet* gift shop beside the entrance to the club, where the general public could purchase similar items.[138]

On Friday, December 17, at 7:30 p.m. Roger and his orchestra broadcast live from the plush new studios of radio WABC. Handily, they were housed on the 17th floor of Steinway Hall at 109-113 West 57th Street, just along from *Le Perroquet de Paris*.[139] The program coincided with WABC's inaugural transmission and gave Roger ample opportunity to promote his nightclub and introduce his latest composition, '*El Tango del Perroquet*.'

The festive season came all too soon, and New Year's Eve fell upon the club. As 1926 dragged its worn-down heels towards the finishing line, Roger had every intention of saluting the New Year in spectacular style and slapped on a $40 cover at *Le Perroquet de Paris*.

For those souls wishing to welcome midnight in the comfort of their own home, Radio WEAF broadcast live from Independence Hall in Philadelphia via various packed nightclubs along the route. One of those clubs was *Le Perroquet de Paris*.[140] Through the wizardry of radio, each club relayed fifteen-minute music segments, alternating from venue to venue.

The program aired at 10:30. It was a mammoth undertaking for the station, whose producer was hoping the links would be seamless. They were. When the time hit 11:44, the hook-up went live to Philadelphia. Inside Independence Hall, Mayor W. Freeland Kendrick welcomed listeners with his greeting for a splendid and beneficial 1927. On the stroke of midnight, his wife rapped the Liberty Bell twelve times, after which the music of Roger Wolfe Kahn and His Orchestra hit the airwaves direct from *Le Perroquet de Paris*. The sound was as crystal clear as the ringing of the Liberty Bell. The linkup was everything Roger loved about technology and music combined. The Kahn Orchestra had a blast and played the longest set of the presentation. They began with a jazzy rendition of '*Stars and Stripes Forever*,' arranged by musical director Harold Stern. Then came '*You Should Know*,' '*Sunday*,' '*Desert*,' '*The Birth of The Blues*,' and '*El Tango del Perroquet*,' with Roger handling the microphone in person for a Happy New Year salutation upon parting.

The parrot had well and truly landed.

10

THE YEAR NEW YORK WENT CRAZY

*'What an eyeful he would have had at Roger Wolfe Kahn's jazz palace,
where goldfish swam in the very tables and one danced over mirrors.'*[1]

1927

Throughout Manhattan's atlas of nightclubs, top orchestras played every night of the week, pumping jazz music into the very soul of New York. Every successful bandleader had a nightclub. Roger had now joined that elite list. *Le Perroquet de Paris* shimmered with class. Even the doorman who welcomed guests as they arrived was expensively kitted out in the smartest uniform, hat, and gloves money could buy.

Jazz shook the city into action night after night. It seeped from its every pore. 'There is no curfew' was the catchphrase at the Salon Royal, an all-night café in the Hotel Acropolis on West 58th Street. Radio WMCA regularly broadcast from the premises. Over the airwaves their emcee would craftily exploit the free publicity by repeatedly announcing their catchphrase, much to the annoyance of other Manhattan club owners. The café reveled in the fact that it could sidestep the three o'clock closing regulation through the technicality that it was inside a hotel. Under the said law, hotels of fifty rooms and over were exempt from any restrictions and, as such, could stay open all night if they so wished. This argument coaxed a lot of business away from the nearby clubs.

As within any big city, nightclub politics was challenging for the owners and the customers alike. Some unscrupulous proprietors were known to play wayward tricks on their patrons to encourage them to spend more or prevent them from moving on to another establishment.[2]

It was this 'competitive' spirit that kept Roger continually on his toes, finding novel but legitimate ways of keeping his clientele happy and keen to return to his establishment time and again. Good publicity is a significant factor in any club or restaurant's longevity and success. Roger was luckier than most entrepreneurs'; he already employed one of the best publicists in the entertainment business, George D. Lottman. George made it his business to ensure *Le Perroquet de Paris* received regular mentions in every good daily and entertainment column in the state.

Even though Roger was still in his teens, many viewed him as being top of his game. Some less fortunate bandleaders who had yet to make a name for themselves tried every trick in the book to get a few column inches in the papers. One such musician Henry Santrey, an Australian bandleader who had yet to set foot in the U.S., inserted a sizable placement in *Variety* craftily advertising Kahn's name alongside his own while assuring readers there was only 'one Roger Wolfe Kahn' and there was only 'one Henry Santrey.'[3] It was a cunning tactic to snatch the public's attention. Otto's concerns that the Kahn family name might somehow get tainted or misused commercially due to his son's career had not been an overprotective parent's whimsical exaggeration.

A radio plug was always a good way of attracting extra business. Roger did one better and signed with WEAF to broadcast live from his club every Friday evening from ten past ten for an hour.[4] Roger hoped the added exposure would bring in the hungry after-theater crowd and help promote his recordings.

Victor dropped two new recordings from Roger and his orchestra in January: the up-tempo '*Wouldn't You!*' presently featured in the *Greenwich Village Follies*, and the enchanting, melodic '*Tonight You Belong To Me*,' both furnished with a vocal by Franklyn Baur.[5]

Keeping in line with Roger's aim to push his own compositions, in January, he signed an exclusive year-long contract with Jack Mills Inc., authorizing Mills to publish all his standard, commercial, and instrumental numbers.[6] The first works to get the Mills treatment were six of Kahn's rhapsodic compositions plus his characteristic tango, '*El Tango del Perroquet.*' The number was already going down a storm at *Le Perroquet* and was used as the opening and closing tune on Kahn's WEAF radio show each Friday evening.[7] The Mills contract excluded Kahn's show numbers. Roger was presently writing the entire score for a new musical comedy titled *Hearts and Flowers*, for which he had already composed roughly thirty songs.

Some of Kahn's musicians at *Le Perroquet* proved to be only temporary and moved on to other gigs as and when work materialized. In January, trombonist 'Miff' Mole rejoined Kahn's orchestra after taking several months' hiatus playing with Ross Gorman and His Earl Carroll Orchestra.[8]

Around this time, the young clarinetist Benny Goodman, accompanied by fellow aspiring musicians Glen Miller and Harry Greenberg, visited *Le Perroquet de Paris* to check out the Kahn orchestra. In Goodman's autobiography, published twelve years later, he recounted the experience as if it had happened only a few days prior. '... before we opened, we went around to the *Perroquet*, where Roger Wolfe Kahn had his band at the time, with Lang, Venuti, 'Miff,' Tommy Gott, Leo McConville, and several other good men. I liked this band a lot because the kind of guitar Eddie Lang played was absolutely new at the time, and his use of the instrument was pretty much responsible for it taking the place of the old banjo. ... Though musicians never cared much for fiddle in a dance orchestra, Venuti was the first fiddle player to make sense in a jazz band.'[9]

Just as Roger would overhaul the musicians in his orchestra at the club, he would also revamp the floorshow. One of his featured acts Ramon and Rosita, a male and female dancing partnership, unexpectedly resigned after securing a nine-month engagement on the continent.[10] In their slot, Roger contracted Moiret and Fredi, a little-known dance duo comprising Fredi Washington and Al Moiret.

In the autumn of 1926, a young, Black, inexperienced actress named Fredi Washington - the girl with a boy's forename - auditioned to act opposite Paul Robeson in a new play. Much to Fredi's surprise, she got the role. The play was *Black Boy*. Robeson was a protégé of Otto's. Otto had helped finance Robeson's career in various projects over the past couple of years. During Otto's involvement with this particular play, he became acquainted with Fredi Washington. B*lack Boy* opened at Broadway's Comedy Theatre on October 6, 1926, and received a unanimous panning from the critics. Regrettably, for those involved, it closed in November after playing only 37 performances. Due to the risqué element of the play - a Black love story, something unheard of on a Broadway stage at that time - Fredi thought it advisable to take on the alias of Edith Warren and was billed as such in the theater program. When the show closed, Otto introduced Fredi to his son Roger, possibly at *Le Perroquet de Paris*, for it was at the club Roger hired Fredi and her dance partner Al Moiret to appear in his floorshow.[11] Moiret and Fredi - at a pinch, the name almost had a French ring to it - performed exotic dance routines. Fredi would, in later years, find fame as a film actress.

Birdsong

To the public, it seemed an epidemic of bird fever had descended upon Tin Pan Alley. Every songwriter of worth appeared to get their foot on the perch. Over the next twelve months, a volary of bluebird, blackbird, red robin, and birds-eye view numbers swept the airwaves and dance floors.

The sudden appeal of birds originated from the previous summer when Gene Austin's version of *'Bye, Bye Blackbird'* became one of the biggest selling hits of 1926, nestling on the top spot for twelve weeks. Henry Hall and His Gleneagles Hotel Band followed on the bird theme with their tender *'Bird Song At Eventide,'* which also fared well.

To cash in on all the free publicity birds were suddenly attracting, Roger penned his own bird ditty, *'El Tango del Perroquet.'* In January, sticking with the feathered wings, Roger laid down another bird song for Victor, *'A Little Bird Told Me So.'* This, too, became a foot-tapping favorite with dancers at *Le Perroquet.*

Throughout 1927 a flock of bird-related songs flew off the lyricist's nib. There trailed, *'The Dicky Bird Hop,'* *'Hello Bluebird,'* *'A Little Birdie Told Me So,'* *'Two Little Love Birds,'* *'When The Love Bird Leaves The Nest,'* *'Lucky Bird'* (from the Broadway musical *Hit The Deck*), *'You Remind Me of a Naughty Springtime Cuckoo,'* *'Just a Bird's Eye View of My Old Kentucky Home'* and *'I'm Tellin' the Birds, I'm Tellin' the Bees.'*

Several became big sellers, including Vincent Lopez's rendition of *'Hello, Bluebird,'* which peaked at No. 3 in the sales charts, and *'Two Black Crows, Parts 1 & 2 (The Early Bird Catches the Worm)'* by Moran & Mack that glided smoothly to the No. 1 spot. To top them all, Irving Berlin composed the vastly popular *'Blue Skies'* that gave the whole menagerie a colorful palette upon which to fly.

Popular music was not the only musical genre the dawn chorus rustled the feathers of. The acclaimed Italian conductor Arturo Toscanini had live birds singing during an afternoon performance of

La Primavera (Spring), from Vivaldi's orchestral concerto No. 1, *Le Quattro Stagioni* (*The Four Seasons*).[12] *

At Manhattan's Hotel Commodore, the resident dance orchestra had a live bird chorus accompany them. The hotel management housed the aviary in their garden restaurant to entertain guests during afternoon tea. The orchestra's leader Bernard Levitow would tell customers the birds 'practice their parts.'

The biggest bird of the whole menagerie was yet to land, and when it taxied in at the beginning of 1928, it came as such a surprise, it rattled the cage of every impresario on the Great White Way. That bird would be a blackbird.

In the meantime, the errant parrots at *Le Perroquet de Paris* continued to cause much concern for the staff with their mimicry and much hilarity for the clientele. The birds became so popular with customers and good for business that Roger increased their number and added some canaries for good measure.

At noon on Thursday, February 3, a fire broke out in the basement beneath the Kuhn, Loeb & Co. offices in the Kuhn, Loeb building at 52 William Street.* Employees speedily evacuated their offices. Though thick black smoke filled the building, its fireproof construction prevented flames from spreading to the upper floors. The fire temporarily cut off telephone communications in the area, bringing chaos to the financial district. An estimated 15,000 office workers from nearby buildings blocked surrounding streets as they watched the drama unfold. Otto was holidaying in Palm Beach when the incident happened. Firefighters could not determine what caused the blaze. Curiously, 22 years to the day, the Kahns villa in Morristown burned to the ground under similarly mysterious circumstances.

With Otto and Addie in Palm Beach for several weeks' stay, Roger decided to travel further south and booked a trip to Havana, Cuba. He invited several friends along - his agency manager George Lottman, bandleader Ben Bernie, and the music publisher Irving Mills. The party were due to depart from New York on February 6.[13]

Roger already had a Kahn orchestra contracted at the Seville-Biltmore Hotel in Havana.[14] Other luxury hotels on the island were crying out for an in-house jazz band. Roger figured it would be a handy way to give him and George a short break while securing some profitable contracts.

Before Roger's departure, in a surprise announcement, New York's Hotel Pennsylvania confirmed that Roger and his orchestra would be taking over from the George Olsen Orchestra as the hotel's new resident band. They would premiere in late March.[15] Doubling his group between *Le Perroquet* and the Pennsylvania would make for a tight schedule. Vitaphone Film Company also verified Roger was to shoot two film shorts in Manhattan on February 14.[16] Annoyingly, for young Kahn, he had to forfeit his trip to Cuba. Within 24 hours, Roger had booked and canceled a vacation, secured one of the most prestigious hotel residencies in the country, and bagged two films.

A further report inferred Roger had motored to Atlantic City in New Jersey to grab some relaxation and checked into the fashionable Ritz-Carlton hotel.[17] The resort was a firm favorite with New Yorkers. The press hooked onto the story revealing another side to the tale. According to a report in *Variety*, Roger had been explicitly instructed by his father to take a break. Allegedly, he was now staying at a health resort in Lakewood, New Jersey.[18] Otto had prescribed the rest after observing his sons' daily ritual of working non-stop into the early hours of the morning. As a result of the unsociable hours, Roger's health had deteriorated to a point where his parents now felt the need to step in and assert an upper hand.

The breather could not have come at a worse time for the youngster, especially with all the additional business he was attracting. Nevertheless, Otto had personal experience of what can happen through burning the candle at both ends, having suffered a stroke six years earlier. It was easy to postulate how Roger had become a victim of his own success; in truth, it was more down to the fact he hated delegating and much preferred doing things himself.

Every musician in town had heard of *Le Perroquet de Paris*, but few got the chance to step inside, due mainly to the hefty prices the club charged. A 'classy' rich man's joint was the consensus most jobbing musicians had of the venue. Such talk did not deter some musicians at the top of their game from frequenting the club, such as Paul Whiteman and Vincent Lopez. Roger and Whiteman were often pitted against one another in the press, though in reality, there was no denying Whiteman was the crowned king of jazz.

On Monday, February 7, upon Whiteman's return to the East Coast from an extensive American tour, another tribute for the maestro awaited. When the bandleader stepped off the train at New York's Grand Central Terminal, the baton brigade was there to greet him.[19] A motorcade of thirty vehicles transporting the orchestras of Vincent Lopez, Ben Bernie, George Olsen, Fred Rich, Benjamin A. Rolfe, Ernie Golden, and Roger Wolfe Kahn escorted Whiteman to Times Square.

From there, they drove to the City Hall for an official ceremony to honor Whiteman for his services to music.[20]

In February, Roger's recording of 'Tonight You Belong To Me,' composed by Lee David with lyrics by Billy Rose, peaked encouragingly at No. 11 in the sales chart. Kahn fared even better with his instrumental of the Gershwin brothers 'Clap Yo' Hands,' which charted at No. 9 in the same month. Yet still, that elusive No. 1 hit had yet to fall into Roger's hands. To keep up the momentum and cash in on Valentine's Day, Victor rush-released Kahn's adaptation of 'Tenderly Think of Me.' The number was already a dance floor filler.

On Valentine's Day at the Manhattan Opera House, Vitaphone produced two film shorts, Nos. 468 and 469 titled *Night Club*.* Both films featured Roger and his thirteen-piece orchestra and gave viewers a flavor of New York nightlife. The choice of venue instantly raises the question, why weren't the films shot inside *Le Perroquet de Paris*? Perhaps filming would have interfered too much with the day-to-day running of the club. Film No. 469 has a guest appearance from the teenage singing/dancing duo, the Williams Sisters, who perform 'Thinking of You,' snatched from the Broadway musical *The Five O'Clock Girl*. The two sisters, Dorothy and Hannah, aged eighteen and sixteen respectively, hailed from Taylor in Pennsylvania and had only recently settled in New York to pursue that much-coveted dream of making it big in show business.

The two film shorts were part of the Vitaphone Varieties series and were released in picture houses a few weeks later in March. In the main, reviews of Roger's performance were highly favorable, with one Texas journalist in the *San Antonio Express* noting: 'Roger Wolfe Kahn's specialty on the Vitaphone is undoubtedly the best subject offered since the installation of the device. His instrumental harmony is wonderful and original ... and the Williams Sisters act brings the act above par for any circuit.'[21]

In film No. 468, Roger and his band perform 'El Tango del Perroquet,' 'Following You Around,' and 'I'm Telling the Birds' - the latter number has an added accompaniment by the novelty jazz ensemble the Mound City Blue Blowers. Kahn brings the sequence to an end with a rendition of Irving Berlin's classic 'Blue Skies.' Yet, again, Roger was visibly plugging the bird theme.

The soundtrack on film 469 contained 'Indian Butterfly,' 'My Heart is Calling You' with a vocal by Henri Garden, 'Thinking of You' featuring the Williams Sisters, and for the finale 'Yankee Rose.'*

The Mound City Blue Blowers (in the foreground) on set at the Manhattan Opera House.* Roger is standing to the left with his orchestra seated in the background. *Night Club*, No. 468. (Picture © Duncan P. Schiedt Photograph Collection, Archives Center, National Museum of American History, Smithsonian Institution, Washington, D.C.)

Vitaphone's 'sound-on-disk' musical shorts were immensely popular with audiences and theater managers alike, who found attendance figures increased when they incorporated a Vitaphone film on their variety bill. *Le Perroquet de Paris* currently featured all of the performers on the two Kahn shorts in its floorshow.

The Williams Sisters

Roger became aware of the singing and dancing Williams Sisters in Chicago back in 1925 when he visited the city on business.

The sisters started in show business as juvenile performers on the vaudeville stage in Pennsylvania. As a variety act, they soon gained featured billing and garnered favorable reviews. Hannah Annette (b. July 16, 1910)* and Dorothy (Dorothea, b. August 19, 1908) came from Taylor, Lackawanna County, PA, and were first-generation daughters of Welsh immigrant parents Thomas C. Williams (b. February 8, 1888) and Mattie (Martha, b. 1887). Also living with the family was Mattie's eldest daughter Leona Evans (b. 1906). Thomas worked down the pit in the local coal mine in Taylor.[22] The family counted their money carefully.

Hannah (left) and Dorothy (right) of the Williams Sisters with Roger (center) looking dapper, captured in a movie still from *Night Club*.

When the girl's parents separated, it was left to Mattie to bring up her children.[23] As a single-parent family, they moved to Scranton, where Mattie worked as an usher in a local theater, probably accounting for how and why her two daughters Dorothy and Hannah entered the theatrical profession at a young age. From newspaper reviews dated as early as 1918, the sisters, aged 8 and 10, were already treading the boards as a duo with modest success.[24]

AFTER THE THEATRE AT
LE PERROQUET DE PARIS
*
ROGER WOLFE KAHN'S
two latest
"Discoveries in Divertissement"
*
THE WILLIAM SISTERS
decidedly different and
HENRI GARDEN
extraordinary operatic tenor in a remarkable
repertoire of songs—old and new
*
Other innovations in entertainment and
Roger Wolfe Kahn and his Orchestra
*
145 West 57th Street
Reservations — Circle 4400
Le Perroquet de Paris
Couvert $5

A tasteful advertisement for the stylish *Le Perroquet de Paris*.[25]
Note the incorrect spelling of the Williams Sisters.

When the girls hit their teens, they were encouraged to travel to New York City to try their luck on Broadway. They arrived in Manhattan during the excitement and vibrancy of the early Jazz Age. The first Broadway show they appeared in was George White's *Scandals of 1924* at the Apollo Theatre. The revue had a musical score composed by George Gershwin, ran for a lengthy 196 performances, and stood the girls in good stead. It introduced them to Broadway audiences and brought them to the attention of producers and bandleaders. One of those bandleaders was Charley Straight, who, in 1925, invited the duo to Chicago to perform with his orchestra at the Rendezvous Café. Straight had one of the largest café followings in the city.

Roger became aware of the sisters in Chicago when he saw them appearing with Charley Straight and his Rendezvous Orchestra. The gifted cornetist Leon Bismark 'Bix' Beiderbecke was a member of the band. At the time, Roger admired the sister's professionalism enough to remember their names. In April 1926, the Williams Sisters made their first recordings with Straight and his orchestra; '*What a Man*' and '*Hi-Diddle-Diddle.*'[26] They also made occasional radio broadcasts with the Straight combo. That same month the sisters secured an engagement at Chicago's newly renovated Merry Garden Ballroom backed by Billy Tucker's Orchestra.[27]

From the 'Windy City,' the duo journeyed to Kansas City for a summer booking with Charley Straight and his Orchestra at The Muehlebach Hotel.[28] At this point in their career, Charley appears to have become the girl's unofficial mentor. From Kansas City, the sisters returned to Chicago to perform in Roy Mack's latest *Frolics* revue, aptly titled *Frivolous Frolics*. A mention in *Variety* gave high praise to the youngsters: 'Williams Sisters, exceptional team of usual harmony, get off to a flying start and stop the show completely. They are not over 18 and a treat to behold.'[29] The duo were so popular with Chicago audiences they were held over for the second edition of *Frivolous Frolics* that opened in late August. 'The Williams Sisters ... are a big surprise. Their unique and cute manner of singing is stopping the shows. As a café attraction, these kids are a bet.'[30] Amazingly, the sisters featured in the third edition of *Frolics* that premiered in October.[31] It was from the strength of these performances that the sisters secured a Victor recording contract.

Their growing popularity did not go unnoticed with other bookers and bandleaders: in particular, the Chicago-based theatrical company, Balaban and Katz (B&K), who operated several theaters in the 'Windy City.' In early January 1927, B&K offered the Williams

Sisters a three-week contract, which the girls declined. As a result, the corporation blacklisted the act. Regardless of the ban, the duo appeared at the palatial Granada Theatre on Chicago's north side in opposition to B&K's Uptown Theatre on North Broadway. B&K was a subsidiary of Publix Theatres Corporation, founded in 1925 as an affiliate of Paramount Studios. In 1926, the Famous Players-Lasky Corporation bought a controlling interest in Balaban and Katz. Roger's father was a member of the Paramount board. Roger's Uncle Felix was on the Famous Players-Lasky Corporation executive committee. Felix was also a member of the Paramount board.[32]

News of the sister's blacklisting hit the national papers.[33] At this point, Roger stepped in and invited the pair to New York City to appear at *Le Perroquet de Paris*.[34] Roger featured the duo at his club and personally okayed their 10-week contract for $400 a week.[35] Hannah was sixteen when she started working at *Le Perroquet de Paris*. Their performance impressed Roger enough to offer them a single number in one of his forthcoming Vitaphone shorts.

Le Perroquet was not the first New York nightclub to hear the eccentric stamping and crooning harmonies of the Williams Sisters. September 1926 saw the twosome performing at Texas Guinan's raucous 300 Club.[36] How long they remained there is anyone's guess, as Guinan's club was notorious for being padlocked by the cops. After paying the levy, Guinan would reopen in a different venue a few days later. The young sisters also graced the stage at the cozier Avalon Club in November of the same year.* Yet, more surprising, a few weeks into the girls' tenure at *Le Perroquet* came the news that Broadway impresario and producer George White (of *George White's Scandals* fame) had placed the sisters under a two-year contract for a reported sum of $650 a week.[37] This took place right under Roger's nose.

Before the siblings left Chicago, they had canned four recordings for Victor - their first for the label - highlighting their distinctive harmonizing. *'I've Grown So Lonesome Thinkin' of You'* and *'Sunday,'* were captured on December 15, 1926. Three days later, they recorded *'Sam, The Old Accordion Man'* and *'Nothing Else Matters Anymore.'* The latter two tracks got the thumbs up for an early spring release.[38] Slotted between their own Victor sessions, the sisters vocalized on another Victor track, *'He's The Last Word,'* with Ben Pollack's Californians. No matter how one viewed the duo's chances of making it big, things for the Williams Sisters were undoubtedly on the up.

Happy Birthday Mr. Kahn

Otto's 60th birthday on February 21 took much the same course as every other working day in his business diary by putting in a full day's shift at his Kuhn, Loeb office. The milestone was fittingly noted and remarked upon by news agencies worldwide, more in context with his celebrity status than as a groundbreaking achievement. When a reporter from ACME News approached Otto and cheekily asked if he could proffer any advice to the younger generation on this, his special day, Otto paused thoughtfully for a moment before handing over several words of guidance: 'Work hard, avoid getting into a mental rut, cling to your ideals, because, such stuff as dreams are made on, is valuable stuff.'[39]

In a rare move, perhaps to celebrate the occasion, Otto permitted one journalist an exclusive interview with him, which took place in Kahn's mahogany-paneled private office at Kuhn, Loeb. The Mexican caricaturist and occasional writer Mauro Gonzàlez conducted the interview. It had been an unalterable rule of Otto's throughout his career never to give newspaper interviews. Today, Otto broke that practice. Gonzàlez had been commissioned by a journal to sketch an official caricature to celebrate the renowned banker's 60th birthday.

When Gonzàlez arrived at Kuhn, Loeb, he was surprised to find the place had 'something of the movie palace about it,' Otto being very much the star of the show. Before meeting 'the great, little guy' inside his inner sanctum, Gonzàlez was passed from one 'flunkey' to another, much like an item of clothing tossed around in a washing machine. When finally the pair met, Gonzàlez immediately noted Otto had aged; his black eyebrows were shaggier, and his thick military mustache was now quite gray. Otto's second-floor private office overlooked the Caledonian Insurance building in Pine Street; Otto could see the firm's 'Caledonian' signage through the window from his desk. During the brief time Gonzàlez was permitted to sketch, Otto remained seated at his desk. He spoke openly and with ease about various topics, 'relevant or irrelevant on satire, drama, philosophy, the opera, and everything else.' The interview gave a rare insight into a man who few ordinary folks got to meet. In the published article 'Judging the Stars' (accompanied by the Gonzàlez caricature of Otto), the reader can detect how much of an indelible impression Kahn left on the artist.[40]

The prime reason why Otto was treating his birthday much like any other day was due to his impending departure from American shores on the forthcoming Saturday aboard the SS *Leviathan*.[41] His three-month trip to the continent would see him visiting Yugoslavia to purchase artworks and Italy to find new musical talent.[42]

On Saturday, when Otto turned up at New York Harbor with his valet Frederick Cooper, reporters were taken off-guard. Kahn's name was not on the passenger list, and, as such, none of the attending press had expected to see him. When a journalist inquired why the banker's name was not on the list, Otto revealed, 'If my name is given out as a passenger several days before sailing, I am pestered with scores of trivial propositions, which people try to urge upon my attention. Merely by remaining off the list, I am able to live my normal life the same as any other person. When it is known that I have sailed, I can't be bothered.' That said, Otto thanked the reporters for their belated birthday wishes, then took his leave and boarded the liner. Also traveling in first-class was Otto's friend Max Reinhardt.

While passing through London, Kahn called into the office of the European Merchant Banking Company, of which he was a partner.[43] The newly created company represented Kuhn, Loeb's interests in Europe. Kuhn, Loeb partner Gordon Leith managed the office.

Addie arranged to join her husband on the continent in late spring. In his absence, she kept herself busy attending a string of social engagements. On the first day of spring, she visited the Grand Central Palace for the opening of the 14th International Flower Show. New York's Horticultural Society presented the event. A torrential downpour kept attendance figures lower than anticipated. Inside was a profusion of exotic blooms. Although Addie did not win the coveted Holland Cup crafted from solid gold, her primula malacoides picked from her Cold Spring Harbor greenhouse did scoop a second prize.[44]

On the afternoon of Friday, March 11, Addie welcomed the public to her Fifth Avenue home for a charity performance by the Pius X Choir of the College of the Sacred Heart.[45] Addie and her daughter Maud were patrons of the school. The all-female choir was made up entirely of students currently attending the college. Liturgical and polyphonic music and ancient chants filled much of the program, although the girls did complement it with some lighter original compositions and contemporary pieces. Addie felt a close affinity with the college; the recital directly benefited them financially.

Settling In

Where once alcohol was king, now cordials reigned. Sodas on West

57th Street ruled.

The attraction of *Le Perroquet de Paris* was undeniable. Even the wholesome American tennis ace Helen Wills - dubbed 'Little Miss Poker Face' by sportswriter Grantland Rice - was spotted bopping on the mirror dance floor. The club garnered glowing reviews for its ambiance, decor, and entertainment. Kahn's orchestra had never sounded better: 'the Kahn syncopators are a never-ceasing wonder with their musical prowess. They attract a certain musically wise following just because of their advanced musical style.'[46] Yet, regardless of how much praise the club received, the place was hemorrhaging money. Higher than anticipated outgoings and unjustifiable expenses meant the weekly profit margin failed to meet expectations. With each weekly loss, Otto's cash injection looked more and more likely to run dry. In a bid to help stem the seepage, Roger made a series of sweeping cutbacks. He abandoned the Parisian example of giving expensive complimentary souvenirs to ladies upon arrival - namely, a bottle of premier French perfume. This overhead alone saved him $2,000 a week.[47] He scaled back on the number of cabaret performers and welcomed guest artistes who paid him for the privilege of appearing there.[48] He also cut down on advertising; George Lottman was already doing a splendid job wangling free press coverage in all the best society columns and diaries. The $5 cover charge remained.

Roger continued his weekly hook-up with WEAF radio, which was also broadcast live on Saturday evenings, feeling the additional exposure benefited the door takings.[49] In a bid to cut down on the time he spent traveling back and forth between 1100 Fifth Avenue and the club, he rented an apartment on 57th Street above the club where, on occasions, he would sleep over.[50] On Sunday, April 7, the Actors Fund of America, in association with the British Artists Fund, held a special dinner at *Le Perroquet de Paris* to benefit their $1.5 million endowment campaign.[51] Tickets cost $25 ringside and $15 elsewhere, with all proceeds being handed to the British committee to aid their work on behalf of the Actors Fund of America.[52] The event received a lot of press exposure due mainly to the attendance of Charlie Chaplin and Gertrude Lawrence.[53] Otto was the chairman of the Actors Fund drive but, on this occasion, was unable to be present as he was away in Europe.

Roger's most recent song to be published by Jack Mills Inc., '*Following You Around*,' had received encouraging feedback from radio stations, nightclubs, and the public. As a result, many bandleaders were chasing Mills for the rights to record it.[54] There was also talk that Roger might appear in a new Irving Berlin musical slated for a Broadway summer premiere.[55] Things were presently in the planning stage.

To keep the money flowing in and his musicians happy, Roger took the entire *Le Perroquet* floorshow, including the Williams Sisters, into the Strand Theatre for a weeklong headlining vaudeville engagement opening on Sunday, March 6.[56] The presentation attracted many customers who would not have been able to afford the entrance fee to see the show at *Le Perroquet*. The Kahn unit played a straight up-tempo set of pop numbers spliced by three specialties, two composed by his band, with the Williams Sisters bowing in with three songs to ease the tempo.[57] The orchestra burned up twenty-four minutes playing five numbers and pleasured the viewers with one encore, keeping things slick and punchy. The only time Roger spoke to the audience was to introduce the Williams Sisters. The theater took $38,700 at the box office, proving Roger could still pack a punch on Broadway.[58] The big news on the horizon was confirmation of Roger and his band's forthcoming opening at the Hotel Pennsylvania on March 30.

Just Kidding Around

With *Le Perroquet de Paris*, young Kahn had achieved the exotic. Next came the fun and frolics.

Hannah Williams was pretty, slim, and lithe, with thick auburn hair. Her dark eyes danced along with her act and fell teasingly upon the laps of young men in the front row of the audience at *Le Perroquet*. Her naive sense of humor endeared her to her friends and admirers, not least her new boss, Roger. He, too, became captivated by her flirtatious charms and fresh, seemingly unaffected nature. He took her to the theater and to fancy restaurants. He talked to her about the many things he wished to achieve in life and how he hoped to get married one day, settle down, and have children. From all accounts, Roger was drawn to Hannah the moment he first saw her. Only her young age had been a stumbling factor in preventing any romantic dalliance. However, during a newspaper interview Hannah gave in May 1932, she revealed that she and Roger had secretly gotten engaged at the time. The veracity of this disclosure is further backed up by the reporter's account of how it came about:

'When she [Hannah] was only 15, working for a Chicago nightclub with her sister, Roger saw her and [later] signed her up for his New

York nightclub. The second night she worked for him he took her out, and three weeks later they were engaged.'[59]

Hannah was young, impetuous, and inexperienced in the ways of the world, especially those concerning wealth and fame. Her 17th birthday was not until July 16. An adolescent crush was hardly a solid foundation to base one's future, let alone build a successful career. Hannah adored the attention, but quite what she had cooking in the back of her mind had yet to come to the fore. For the time being, the pair were an item, albeit a heavily guarded secret one, and would often spend time together, away from the flash and glare of Roger's nightclub, chilling out in each other's company.

No matter how rewarding and glamorous it might have appeared at the time, being a club attraction did not equate to being featured as a top-of-the-bill Broadway or vaudeville star. The Williams Sisters were well aware of this dichotomy and had, for the future, set their sights on treading the boards of legitimate theaters. Nightclubs had paid the rent for the past two years and allowed them to develop their act. However, their starring role had yet to materialize. Their next step was to make that dream happen.

Although Roger had hired the sisters to appear at *Le Perroquet* as a double act, he also handed Hannah a featured solo spot singing '*Hard Hearted Hannah (The Vamp of Savannah)*' while gyrating seductively on the mirror dance floor.

Irrespective of Roger's guidance and the attention he lavished upon the sisters, the pair had signed a two-year contract with the Broadway impresario George White. Their actions must have put Roger's nose sorely out of joint. In all probability, this issue, more than any other, contributed to the loved-up couple arguing and calling off their engagement.

The Place of the Rising Sun

Otto had already arrived in Paris by mid-March[60] and was now on his way across Europe in his quest to study 'art, science, business and politics,' as well as taking in some less taxing pleasurable pursuits en route. He arrived in Berlin around March 18 with his son Gilbert and daughter-in-law Anne. Gilbert was still living on the continent, furthering his studies in the banking profession. Otto's presence brought a welcome break to the couple's daily routine. During their ten-day visit to the capital, Gilbert and Anne stayed with Otto's sister Elisabeth 'Lili,' wife of the CEO of the German General Electric

Company, Felix Deutsch.

On March 19, Otto revealed to a reporter how he was seriously contemplating purchasing two German jazz operas, *Royal Palace*, composed by Kurt Weill, and *Jonny spielt auf*, written by Ernst Krenek. He wanted to produce them at the Met in New York.[61] While in Berlin, Otto arranged meetings with the German head of state President Hindenburg, Wilhelm Marx (Chancellor of Germany), and the Foreign Minister Gustav Stresemann. When Otto spoke as guest of honor at the American Club of Berlin, he talked favorably about Germany's many attributes. Nonetheless, he was noticeably hesitant to play the role of the protagonist lest it should make him the target of some well-aimed missiles in the press.[62]

Otto traveled to Italy from Germany, where his trek to Asia Minor progressed via the warm Adriatic, Ionian, Mediterranean, and Aegean Seas aboard the Duke of Westminster's yacht *Flying Cloud*. The April cruise took in Sicily, Athens, the Greek islands, and parts of Turkey. Kahn had chartered the 282-foot schooner and its 40-member crew for a month and invited several interesting and like-minded guests along for the all-male cruise. On the passenger list were the novelists Arnold Bennett and David Gray, sculptor Jo Davidson, *Vanity Fair* editor Frank Crowninshield, and the marine artist Paul Dougherty.[63] The theatrical producer Morris Gest joined the party in Venice.[64] Kahn hoped the indulgence of such a cruise would facilitate privacy and some well-earned rest.

Le Perroquet de Paris to Close

'The most beautiful nightclub in America is not the triumph that it might have been,' reported the *Chicago Tribune*, forlornly.[65]

The shock announcement that *Le Perroquet de Paris* was to close its doors for the spring and summer season came just as Roger and his orchestra were preparing to open at the Hotel Pennsylvania.

New York society planned everything around the four yearly seasons. In summer, the wealthy vacationed on the continent or at their country estates. Most of Broadway's chic nightclubs would close for the duration. The financial implications of keeping a club running during 'dry' season were too crippling.

Although Roger had managed to cut some of the deficit, the club's expenditure was mounting daily. His hard work, late nights, and the enormity of the endeavor he had taken on were beginning to take their toll on his health. After consulting his father, Roger decided the only action to take was to shut the club. Coupled with the stress from his break-up with Hannah, Roger was in urgent need of a change.

Whether to save face or with good intentions, Roger announced the club would reopen in the fall, probably in October, to coincide with the opera season opening.

As if to reinforce Roger's press release, Argentinian dance duo Ramon and Rosita, who had scored such a success at *Le Perroquet de Paris*, also issued a statement. They would be returning to Roger's club after their summer residency in France, where, coincidently, they featured at Rene Racover's *Le Perroquet* in the French capital.

For the present, Roger knuckled down to the business at hand. *Le Perroquet* would close on April 1. In the interim, Roger and his orchestra calmly, without any publicity, commenced their warm-up gigs at Manhattan's plush Hotel Pennsylvania.[66]

The Hotel Pennsylvania was located directly opposite Pennsylvania Terminal at Seventh Avenue, between 32nd and 33rd. It was advertised as the world's largest hotel. Each one of its 2,200 rooms boasted an en suite bathroom. The hotel's owner Ellsworth M. Statler personally managed it, and it was with Statler that the buck stopped.

For Roger, his residency at the hotel was a blessing. It could not have come at a more opportune time.

Statler gave the band two weeks' grace to rehearse and prepare for their official opening. This arrangement granted Roger, and his musicians, the freedom to tailor their act specifically for the hotel's two venues - the Pennsylvania Grill and their more select roof garden. It also gave Roger time to figure out what his long-term vision was for his future.

Opening at The Hotel Pennsylvania

The rivalry between top bandleaders was fierce. The Pennsylvania gig had not been cut and dry. There were several tenders submitted for the berth, with some leaders prepared to undercut to secure it.[67]

Outgoing bandleader George Olsen recommended Vincent Lopez to fill the vacancy, Ellsworth M. Statler favored Kahn. After considerable debate by the hotel management, the Kahn unit bagged the job. Once installed, Roger had every intention of showing everyone just how worthy he was of the position.

The coveted residency was this season's plum job. Not only would it help promote Kahn's record sales, but George Lottman had also negotiated a guaranteed fee of $2,050 with an additional 50 percent

from covers after reaching a certain quota. This arrangement would
see Roger's weekly salary top the $3,000 mark. Kahn's contract was
said to be exceptional, considering the conservativeness of the Statler
organization and their reserved reaction to dance music. Kahn's
guarantee, alone, topped everything paid to bandleaders at the hotel
before him. That aside, the hotel management was not keen on
'doubling' and openly discouraged it, something Roger had always
defended as a musician's right. The deal saw the band playing six
dinners and six suppers weekly, twelve in total, with no Sunday
performances.

In addition, Statler stipulated that Roger must undertake eight
personal appearances a week. Statler had made this dispensation in
deference to Roger's parents, who were concerned about their son's
well-being due to his unhealthy practice of working late until all
hours of the morning.

On the evening of March 30, Roger Wolfe Kahn and His Orchestra
premiered at the Pennsylvania Grill.[68] The room was heaving, as was
the sidewalk outside. It seemed as though the whole of New York
high society had turned out for the occasion; such was the rush for
table reservations.[69]

Roger and his band were a dab hand at delivering highly polished
performances at fashionable venues and held nothing back. The
band's presentation was stylish, slick, and nothing short of
sensational. The following day's reviews were a testament to their
professionalism and competence and a joy for Statler, Roger, and his
musicians to behold.

Mr. Statler was so impressed with young Kahn that he dislodged
George Olsen as general music director of the Statler chain of hotels
(after only recently choosing him) and appointed Roger in his place.
He also permitted Kahn's musicians their practice of 'doubling.'
Roger's manager also arranged for the Kahn orchestra to broadcast
weekly from the Pennsylvania Grill via a live tie-up with radio WJZ.

On Friday, April 1, Roger and his orchestra gave their final show at *Le
Perroquet de Paris* before temporarily dimming the lights in the
club.[70] At the time, there was no denying it broke Roger's heart to see
his beautiful nightclub idly sitting vacant. Over the next few months,
Roger tried everything humanly possible to pay the financial debts he
owed on the establishment so he could reopen in the fall with a clean
slate.

Roger Wolfe Kahn, Himself and His Orchestra, opened
at New York's Hotel Pennsylvania on March 30, 1927.[71]

Also on April Fool's Day, Victor resumed their relentless assault on
the public's consciousness by releasing a new Kahn record, *'Yankee
Rose,'* a peppy, dance-inspired instrumental that had already proved
popular in Kahn's repertoire. The song was currently featured in
Roger's Vitaphone movie *Night Club*, now playing the picture house
circuit.[72] Victor was hoping this would be the big hit the Kahn
organization merited.

It was not to be.

In the interim, at 1607 Broadway, Irving Berlin popped downstairs from his office to Roger's office on the floor beneath to tell the youngster about a new song he had just written, that everybody who heard it was in raptures over. The song was 'Russian Lullaby.'

Two weeks later, on April 14, Roger and his orchestra, along with Henri Garden's golden larynx, recorded Berlin's 'Russian Lullaby.' Berlin had composed a gem.

A Chain of Orchestras

No sooner had Roger led his orchestra through the doors of the Hotel Pennsylvania than he set about putting together a proposal to install a Kahn dance orchestra in all the Statler hotels. It was a mammoth proposition that young Kahn hoped would net him a $1 million profit. Roger had already consulted his father over the initial idea, and Otto had given him the thumbs up.

Preliminary negotiations between Roger and J. Duggan (Statler's senior assistant), and Milton Statler, the 19-year-old adopted son of Statler Sr., moved briskly forward. The deal would see $2,340,000 being paid to the youthful bandleader over 12 months, with Roger providing thirty personally trained orchestras in return, one for each of Statler's hotels. After initial talks, Roger submitted the bid to Statler Sr. He was currently considering the proposition and had expressed a wish to consult Otto Kahn about the matter before making his final decision.[73] If Roger could bag the deal, he could instantly pay off his debts at his nightclub and reopen it in the fall. The dailies pounced on the story, with several leading with it.[74]

Roger's business plan stood as follows: The average weekly salary of a jazz orchestra was $1,500. Thirty such bands equated to $45,000 a week. That figure multiplied by 52 (weeks) gave the grand yearly total of $2,340,000. Of that sum, Roger would reap a profit just short of $1,000,000 (around $640 commission a week per band). No wonder Roger's father was impressed with the figures.

'Even father will have to admit there's more money in jazz than in bonds,' grinned Roger to a plucky reporter from the Brooklyn Daily Eagle. The journalist had craftily tracked the bandleader down to Statler's office at the Hotel Pennsylvania to grab an exclusive statement.[75] That Ellsworth M. Statler even bothered to consider a million-dollar business proposition from a teenager indicates just how seriously he took young Kahn. 'Maybe I'm a musical nut!' pondered Roger aloud, as the reporter listened intently, pencil at the ready, 'but this is one time where I think I've done credit to the Kahn banking name. I bet father didn't have dreams of that much money when he was my age. I'll have to ask him when he comes back.'

Otto was still away in Europe.

During the snatched interview, Roger handed the reporter an encyclopedic-sized, leather-bound scrapbook to glance over. It contained press clippings of himself that his father had proudly collected, neatly pasted in by office staff at Kuhn, Loeb. The journalist looked suitably impressed. 'And now I'm becoming a businessman, my father will have to kill the fatted calf, I guess,' joked Roger, tongue in cheek. 'I'm sure if this thing goes through, I'll make a go of it. Jazz is no longer a fad; it's a reality.'

Over the next few months, Roger and Milton Statler developed a firm friendship. Not only were they of a similar age - Milton was one year older than Roger - they both had influential fathers that were self-made millionaires. Similarly, both teenagers shared a great love for motor racing and the addictive allure of speed and fast automobiles. Roger even had Milton 'rattling the drums' on occasions at the hotel.

Suddenly, as if overnight, Roger Wolfe Kahn was everywhere: on the radio, on the big screen in picture houses, plastered across billboards, appearing at College Proms,[76] playing at benefit concerts, littering newspapers and magazines, revolving on record players, and heating up the dance floor at the Pennsylvania. You could not get away from the lad. It was as if he had the Midas touch. Naturally, his mother and father were well aware of what was going on around them, but what they had yet to comprehend was just how famous their son had become. His fame was spreading globally and quickly. The Kahn name had now truly evolved into a brand.

Roger's latest new tune to hit the dance floor was '*Gentlemen Prefer Blues*,' his response to novelist Anita Loos' witty satire *Gentleman Prefer Blondes*.[77] Also in the pipeline was his stage presentation *Hearts and Flowers* (a parody on musical comedy). This was the show Roger had collaborated on with the writer and enfant terrible Ben Hecht,[78] which had recently taken on board the producer Horace Liveright.[79] Rehearsals were earmarked to start in summer.[80]

The National Association of Orchestra Directors'

Eight bandleaders - Paul Whiteman, Vincent Lopez, George Olsen,

Roger Wolfe Kahn, Ben Bernie, Fred Rich, Benjamin A. Rolfe, and Ernie Golden - founded the National Association of Orchestra Directors' (NAOD) in January 1927. They appointed a jazz arbiter, lawyer Julian T. Abeles, to run the organization on a salary of $25,000 a year.[81] They aimed to bring in force a set of rules within the music industry that musicians, bandleaders, record companies, and their associates could endorse. They also sought to make reasonable rules to avoid aggressive competition in making recordings and other forms of reproduced music. They hoped every bandleader in America would become a member of the association. A spokesman for NAOD stressed, 'American jazz today is a big business, and like all other big businesses, it must have its arbiter.'[82]

A committee was appointed to visit hotels, nightclubs, and dance halls to observe and instruct other orchestra leaders on playing the correct renditions of songs. Members 'were determined to get at the root of the so-called bad jazz which, they deemed, brought all jazz into disrepute.'[83]

Indecent dancing was another issue the committee was keen to get to the bottom of. If flappers were the instigators of vulgar cavorting, then Broadway certainly encouraged it. Concerns over young ladies' morality were still raging in polite salons throughout New York high society. To help get a clearer perspective of the fad, the committee agreed they would visit nightclubs to investigate at close hand what exactly brought about this exotic behavior in females.[84]

They determined jazz music was undoubtedly a dominant factor in their behavior, however, as was whatever beverage the young lady might have guzzled beforehand.

On Easter Sunday, April 18, NAOD hosted a concert at the Hotel Astor to aid its benevolent fund.[85] The show was like no other show given by dance orchestras before, for it featured every musician from fourteen top bands. The units advertised as taking part were Ben Bernie, Roger Wolfe Kahn, Vincent Lopez, George Olsen, Fred Waring, Benjamin A. Rolfe, Sam Lanin, Ernie Golden, Jacques Green, Mal Hallett, Johnny Hamp, Ben Selvin, Fred Rich, and Irving Aaronson. Paul Whiteman and his orchestra were also hoping to appear. In total, 250 musicians participated, with the various directors taking turns to conduct. It was a mammoth undertaking. With tickets priced at $3.50, the event raised $10,000. The show struck up at 8:30 p.m. sharp and crossed the finishing line after midnight. Ben Bernie wired the Astor to inform NAOD he was stuck in Chicago on a contract and could not appear. Roger also wired to apologize; he was held up in Chicago on business and would not be attending the event personally, although his musicians would participate.[86]

Three days later, Paul Whiteman resigned from NAOD citing, 'his displeasure with the organization's move from strictly fraternal activities to combined business ventures.'[87] Similar discontent among other bandleaders saw NAOD wind up its operations at the end of the year.

Those Williams Sisters

After *Le Perroquet de Paris* shut its doors, the Williams Sisters hot-footed it back to Illinois, where they appeared on the Orpheum circuit. They first played the mighty New Palace in Chicago,[88] then graced Minneapolis for a week.[89] There followed a week in St. Louis and a return engagement at the Palace Theatre, Chicago. However, after completing the first two weeks, the duo canceled all their remaining Orpheum bookings.[90] They alleged the Orpheum dates overlapped with their forthcoming picture house appearances in Chicago. The sisters then opened at Chicago's Capitol Theatre on April 18. Other Marks Bros. and Cooney dates followed, after which the duo played a two-week engagement at the Green Mill Café. In late summer, they were scheduled to start rehearsals on George White's upcoming musical comedy *Manhattan Mary*, with a cast that included Ed Wynn, Lou Holtz, and Elizabeth Hines.[91]

During the sisters' appearance at Chicago's Capitol Theatre, Roger arrived in the city for 'business' matters.[92] The day was April 18, when he was due to appear at the NAOD concert at the Hotel Astor in New York. During his stopover, he met Hannah. They argued severely and parted on bad terms. Their quarrel was most likely work-related or regarding their former personal relationship, or both. Under this cloud of disharmony, Roger returned to New York to resume fronting his orchestra at the Hotel Pennsylvania.

In late April, Roger and his orchestra visited a new recording studio to master a batch of recordings for Victor. The music complex on East 58th Street was inside Liederkranz Hall, a brownstone building built in the German Renaissance style. 'It was spacious, and the walls and ceilings were all of ornately gilded carved wood,' recalled one musician that recorded there.[93] It claimed to have the most effective acoustics of any building in the city. Victor was keen to try and capture this 'quality' - timbre - on record. During the previous fortnight, the engineers had made several experimental demos. As the technicians grew more confident with the equipment and acoustics, they were keen to start recording live orchestras. The first band Victor called in was their house orchestra, The Troubadours. Roger's unit was invited next. Their line-up was ideal to trial: three violins, three saxophones, two cornets, a trombone, tuba, banjo, and piano and drums.

The orchestra laid down four takes of '*South Wind*' and three versions of '*One Summer Night.*'[94] Both numbers had a vocal by Henri Garden. Nathaniel Shilkret produced the tracks. Victor considered none of the '*South Wind*' takes suitable for release and destroyed all copies. Hence, Roger and his musicians were called back into Liederkranz Hall a couple of weeks later and canned two fresh instrumental renditions of '*South Wind*' without Shilkret at the helm.[95] These two masters were deemed far superior to the last takes and were held by Victor for future release. While the band was in the studio, they delivered two additional tracks: three instrumental variations of '*Where the Wild, Wild Flowers Grow,*' of which two versions survive, and four takes of '*Calling,*' with a vocal by Franklyn Baur. Victor approved two versions of '*Calling*' for release. As a rule, Roger produced all his recordings and had previously worked with only one other producer, Edward T. King. From Kahn's recording history to date, it was evident his involvement with a producer was always a bit hit and miss and usually took longer to complete. Notably, Kahn's 1926 recording of '*Cross Your Heart*' took eight attempts before the producer Edward T. King called it a wrap.

Encouragingly for Roger, his recording of '*Following You Around,*' with a sentiment that could easily have mirrored his relationship with Hannah, was gaining considerable radio exposure and high sheet music sales. It was a brilliant confidence boost for the youngster and clearly showed his ability to pen a memorable tune.

Given Roger's challenging work schedule and his unease at taking time off, Addie stepped in; using her motherly persuasion, she insisted her son accompany her on an all-expenses-paid trip to Europe where they would meet up with Otto. As a carrot, she also invited his agency manager George Lottman to join them. By coincidence, Roger and George had some business to conduct in Paris, connected with the Kahn booking agency operating there. Roger accepted his mother's offer. Reservations for the pair were booked on the SS *Leviathan*. The ship was due to depart in just over a week on May 21.

Had Addie sensed something else was amiss with her son, possibly something to do with that 'showgirl' in Chicago?

Princeton House Party

The 1927 Princeton University House Party took place on the weekend of May 13 and 14, precisely one week before Roger left for Europe.

For Kahn junior, the gig was extremely significant; Roger and his orchestra were one of the headlining acts. The event had been the talk of the campus for months. Admission tickets had sold out way in advance, and no wonder, the line-up of bands listed alongside the Kahn unit was jaw-dropping: the Jean Goldkette Orchestra (with cornetist 'Bix' Beiderbecke), the California Ramblers, Fletcher Henderson's Orchestra, and George Olsen and His Music. All of the artists taking part were at the peak of their popularity.[96]

Performing at Princeton was noteworthy for Roger because it had been one of the chosen universities he and his parents had considered for him to attend. Although it was later agreed, Harvard would probably have been more suitable, considering his interest in engineering. Princeton was also the University his brother Gilbert had studied at, and in that regard, many of Gilbert's jazz-mad former classmates would probably be present. Indeed, the band Gilbert had been a guest player in, the California Ramblers, had a sizable following among the undergraduates on the campus.

The House Party was memorable for all the right reasons. Two of the weekend's many highlights belonged to Beiderbecke, whose dazzling performances with the Goldkette Orchestra, one given on Friday evening and a smaller, abbreviated set on Saturday, astounded everyone that witnessed them.

The 'Kid' of 25

On the day before Roger departed from New York, an event of great historical importance took place on Long Island that had Roger and every other flight enthusiast in the USA gripped. At 7:52 a.m. on Friday, May 20, Charles A. Lindbergh set off from Roosevelt Field in his *Spirit of St. Louis* monoplane in an attempt to fly the Atlantic non-stop to Paris. On that gray, dull, drizzly morning, as the single-engine plane began its unsteady takeoff rumbling along the muddy runway, it only just managed to clear the telegraph wires at the end of the airfield. Newsreel cameras were there to capture the occasion, some no doubt wondering if they would ever see the fearless pilot again.

Sightings of Lindbergh's aluminum-colored plane were spotted above Newfoundland and excitedly reported over the radio airwaves as Americans tuned in by their thousands to follow his progress.

Roger and his band were performing that afternoon in Schenectady at the Union College Junior Prom.[97] Throughout the day, young Kahn kept a close ear on the regularly updated bulletins on the radio.

Overnight, something extraordinary happened as Lindbergh's spirit of adventure began to grip the imagination of humanity around the globe.

The following day Addie, Roger, and George Lottman left New York Harbor on their journey to Europe aboard the luxuriously fitted SS *Leviathan*.[98] The majestic liner departed promptly at two o'clock, crowded with Americans making the spring dash across the Atlantic to the continent via Southampton and Cherbourg. Every first-class suite and cabin was reserved. Accompanying the Kahns were two maids and a valet. Many reporters and journalists were traveling in second class, making the crossing in the hope of documenting Lindbergh's flight to France.

The *Leviathan* was the flagship of the United States Line fleet, and George was in for a real treat. Any thoughts Roger retained of Hannah Williams were temporarily packed away as he began to unwind, relax, and enjoy the leisure time on hand. During his four-and-a-half-week trip away, Roger planned to visit London, Paris, and Berlin.

A few weeks before Roger's departure to Europe, Paul Whiteman commissioned him to write a piece of music, possibly a rhapsody, for a movie Whiteman was to appear in and suggested it be along the lines, though not imitative, of Gershwin's *Rhapsody in Blue*.[99] It was too good an opportunity for Roger to pass up. Moreover, Roger already had a piece he'd been quietly working on that would fit the directive perfectly, *Birth of the Blues*. Accordingly, Roger intended to set aside time during his trip to complete work on the assignment.[100] Whiteman also proposed to perform the composition with his orchestra during six concerts he was giving later that year in the fall.

That Saturday evening, after flying thirty-three and a half hours non-stop through foul weather, nightfall, and little or no sleep, Charles Lindbergh finally caught sight of the glittering lights of Paris. At 10:24 p.m. local time, just north of the capital at *Le Bourget*

Aérodrome, Lindbergh's plane glided out of the darkness and into the history books as it made a near-perfect landing. Lindbergh had achieved his dream and, in doing so, changed the world. It was that immediate. From obscurity, the 25-year-old former airmail pilot became one of the most famous people on the planet.

News of Lindbergh's colossal achievement was wired globally, including onto the SS *Leviathan* while at sea, where celebrations lasted well into the night.[101] Back in New York, newsreels of Lindbergh flashed across the screens in picture houses; some were even playing on the same bill as Roger's Vitaphone movies.

Overnight, Roger changed his plans. Unsurprisingly he was now in a rush to reach Paris as soon as was humanly possible.[102]

Films showing at the Wintergarden in Jamestown
during the weekend Roger departed from
New York aboard the SS *Leviathan*.

Back in Chicago, even though B&K were still boycotting the Williams Sisters, the duo had managed to keep themselves busy performing in variety shows at the Granada and Capitol picture houses. On May 23, the girls were due to appear at the grand opening of the newly built Marbro Theatre owned by the Marks Bros. Annoyingly for all concerned, due to the installations running behind schedule, the Marbro unveiling was postponed.[103]

After a five-day delay, the Marbro finally swung open its doors to the paying public on Saturday, May 28.[104] Upon arriving at the theater, customers could have been excused for thinking they were entering a Spanish Baroque palace; such was its ornate grandeur. Crystal chandeliers, magnificent marble, mirror, and gilt fittings, a yawning lobby, sweeping corridors, and a rising double-horseshoe staircase stunned theatergoers as they flowed in. The 5,200-seat auditorium drew a big audience to see its variety show *In A Magic Garden* and the feature film *The Love of Sunya*, starring Gloria Swanson. The Williams Sisters' act, accompanied by Benny Meroff and his twenty-piece band, was a feature of the stage production and praised for its delivery:

'Williams Sisters cleaned up, as usual. Did two numbers and an encore and turned down offers for a second. The girls gave the show its second strongest point; though whether they drew their weight is a question.'[105]

Though there was very little sibling rivalry between the sisters, Hannah, being the edgier, more talented, one of the pair, was always singled out for more attention by the press. Hannah was hot-headed; it took a lot to coax her down when she got on her plinth. After her heated argument with Roger, she saw red and did a foolish, immature reprisal, no doubt, to get her own back at Roger. She immediately attached herself romantically to another bandleader, Charles Kaley, who was the conductor of the house orchestra at the Granada picture theater, where the Williams Sisters had recently featured in the cast. Within two weeks of the couple meeting, they got engaged.[106]

Charles Kaley was a vocalist and bandleader. He was signed to Columbia Records and had dreams of becoming a film actor. The self-styled 'singing bandleader' had moved to Chicago from the East in the spring of that year. He was now working with his twenty-piece band alternating between the Marbro and the Granada picture houses. Born in the quiet backwater town of Red Cloud in Nebraska on June 16, 1902, Kaley, aged 25, was just over eight years older than Hannah. Handsome, in a fatherly manner, clean-cut Kaley put up no resistance to Hannah's advances.

Hannah lied to Kaley about her age and told him she was eighteen when she was still only sixteen. Because Kaley was so intent on marrying the bobbed-haired dancing dynamo, he suspected nothing was amiss and proposed to her. Unbeknown to anybody else at the time, Hannah accepted.

For the first two weeks in June, the Williams Sisters remained in Chicago performing at the Marbro in the variety show, *In A Magic Garden*. Yet, again, the girls were playing in opposition to the B&K

theaters and, although the company was still shunning the sisters, the ban appears to have had little effect on other circuits booking the act. If anything, it seems to have had the opposite outcome.

With rehearsals for George White's upcoming musical *Manhattan Mary* on the horizon, Hannah's work in Chicago was drawing to a close. In the interim, Hannah and Kaley took the liberty to head off together on a week's vacation without informing anyone. While they were away, they got hitched.

When the pair returned to Chicago, all hell broke loose.

In London, Addie, Roger, and George checked into Claridge's Hotel. It was the first time George had visited the UK, let alone seen the plush interior of Claridge's. No doubt, he was mightily impressed with his digs. After staying only a couple of days, Roger and George sailed across to France, where in Cherbourg, they caught the maiden Cherbourg to Paris airline flight, and in the process, made history as the first passengers to do so.[107]

Back in the U.S., at the beginning of June, Victor rush-released Roger's rendition of 'Russian Lullaby' in a bid to corner the American market before any competitors ran the course with it.[108]

It was an excellent decision; the sentimental ballad captured the hearts of millions and rocketed Kahn's disk to the top of the U.S. sales charts, where it happily revolved for fifteen consecutive weeks.* Yes, over three months!

Roger finally had his No. 1 hit.

For the remainder of the year, life for the teenager went crazy.

It was while Roger was in Paris that reports of Hannah's marriage filtered through to him. Not surprisingly, Roger was livid when he heard the news, as was Hannah's sister Dorothy, as too was their mother, Mattie.

In her rush to get hitched to Kaley, Hannah appeared to have overlooked the fact that she was underage. Her 17th birthday was not until July 16. Her marriage was illegal in the eyes of the law.*

Hearsay in the past had circulated along Broadway that Hannah and Roger, before their split, had secretly become engaged. Had Roger's parents discovered this small 'detail' and, unbeknown to Roger, deviously arranged for the Williams Sisters to be blacklisted in Chicago, hoping they might quietly disappear from the scene?

Perhaps Roger had discovered what his parents had done and subsequently gone to Chicago behind their backs to try and persuade

Hannah to return to New York. Instead, the couple argued, and Hannah rejected him. These imponderables were just some of the questions certain show folks were now beginning to ask.

Lindbergh mania eclipsed everything else in the world at that moment in time. There was no getting away from the euphoria that surrounded the man, his spirit, and the extraordinary progress of aviation. Roger reveled in it all and got equally wrapped up in the whole ballyhoo and excitement that embodied Lindbergh's remarkable achievement. Roger even drove out to *Le Bourget Aérodrome* and charted a plane, which he flew from Paris to London, and then back. Whether Roger was in a particular rush that day or whether in the act of defiance, one of his flights took place in particularly severe weather conditions. So dangerous that Lindbergh was warned against making a similar flight on the same day from the same *aérodrome* in his *Spirit of St. Louis*.[109] Lindbergh departed from Europe on June 3, not by wings, but from the port of Cherbourg aboard the specially chartered ship USS *Memphis* courtesy of the U.S. Government. Back in America, the public excitedly awaited the pilot's return to bestow a hero's welcome upon him.

Oheka II

There must have been considerable interest in New York when the 73-foot German-built cruiser *Oheka II* arrived on the Hudson River, having sailed from Canada. *Oheka II* was the brand new yacht Otto commissioned master shipbuilder Otto Lürssen to build at his shipyard in Vegesack, Germany. The *New York Times* and many other newspapers noted its arrival on the Hudson. *Oheka II* was, after all, the fastest privately owned vessel in America, and the event was something of a curiosity for New Yorkers to witness. The yacht, fitted with three Maybach VL2 V-12 airship motors, had already been put through its paces with a test in Germany on the River Weser, where the yachts American Captain, William T. Young, was present to witness its handling. Young had been particularly impressed with its beauty and elegance and its excellent position in the water. He referred to it as 'the best yacht he ever saw.'[110] Otto paid in the region of $90,000 to have it built, and it cost over $100 daily to operate.

Delivery of the boat to its new home on Long Island had taken several weeks, traveling from Lürssen's shipyard via the River Weser to the River Elbe up to Hamburg. From Hamburg, it traveled by steamer to Montreal, Canada. From Montreal, Captain Young navigated the cruiser down the Saint Lawrence River to Lake Champlain and through the Champlain Canal to Albany, New York. Young now planned to conduct a series of speed trials to check the boat's endurance and capabilities. He hoped she might break the speed record from Albany to New York City of 4 hours, 21 minutes, 57 seconds.*

Oheka II speed trial on the Hudson River.

The first-speed trial took place on June 8. Although Otto was not in the U.S. to witness it, the test still went ahead. The weather that day was ideal, a little overcast, but with no harsh winds, perfect for the matter at hand. The route started at the Albany Yacht Club and traveled downriver to finish at the Columbia Yacht Club. *Oheka* II departed at precisely 1:18 p.m. At 2:10, she passed C. H. Evans Brewing Company at the Albany Pump Station cruising at 29 knots. Encouragingly, she'd covered the first thirty miles of the course in 50 minutes. By 2:55, the yacht headed by the old lighthouse at Rhinecliff, averaging 30 knots. At 3:22, she passed under the Poughkeepsie Bridge at a rate of 32 knots.

Just as the ship was making good time, the Captain misjudged her angle just south of West Point Academy, and the boat ran aground on an unbuoyed mudbank damaging two propellers.[111] The trial came to an abrupt halt. Thankfully, the cruiser sustained only limited damage and managed to limp a further seventy-five miles under one engine operating at 15 knots, reaching the Columbia Yacht Club at 8:08 p.m. This was not the finish Captain Young had predicted to the newspapers. Frustratingly, *Oheka II* did not break the speed record that day as intended. Nor would it be repaired in time to pick up the Kahn family when they returned from the continent later that month. On a happier note, newspapers reported the following day that the vessel had set a record for the first half of the course from Albany to Poughkeepsie, lowering the time by over 9 minutes set three years previously by L. Gordon Hamersley in *Cigarette IV*.[112]

When *Oheka II* was eventually delivered to Otto fully repaired later in the year, it cut the sailing time from Long Island to Manhattan down to 55 minutes.

The Kahns summer jaunt in Europe took an indefinable shape. Roger hurled himself into writing his new composition for Paul Whiteman and advanced his flying pursuits during free time. In between, he met up with a New York friend, 19-year-old Virginia Franck, who he first met a couple of years earlier when they appeared on the same vaudeville bill at the Riverside Theatre in Manhattan. Virginia was a 'specialty' dancer and had just finished a Broadway run in the musical comedy *Criss Cross*. She had traveled to the continent to try her luck in Paris and was presently featured at the *Café des Ambassadeurs* under the curious stage name Viva Regor.

Roger took Virginia for a flight one afternoon in a plane he had chartered at *Le Bourget Aérodrome*. A reporter got wind of their liaison and was there to greet them upon their return. He snapped pictures of the couple, which they happily posed for holding hands standing beside the plane.

Roger also put time aside to travel to Berlin, where he met up with his father, his brother Gilbert and Gilbert's wife, Anne. He also met up with his sister Margaret and his aunt 'Lili.' Although the visit was only brief, it gave Roger time to reconnect with his family in a way he'd been unable to do during the last six months.

At times, it was easy to forget Otto was of German Jewish origin, with his distinctive clipped English accent and gentile appearance. His conversation was 'rapid, precise, lucid,' and when something captured his imagination, he had a habit of twisting a corner of his waxed mustache. 'Otto could not walk in public without attracting attention.'[113] His name was also a prompt to get projects moving; if Otto was interested in an artistic proposal, it was deemed worthy of public attention.[114]

Roger had now reached that point in his career where he was sufficiently successful enough in being recognized for his talents and abilities, other than being just the youngest son of Otto Kahn. After meeting Roger a couple of months earlier, the songwriter cum part-time columnist William Jerome noted in his column how modest the youngster was, with not a grain of pretense about him. He found this surprising, being mindful of Roger's lineage and fame. 'He has everything that goes to make up a 100 percent, real man. If the big American jazz opera is ever written and this young American doesn't write it, take it from me, it won't be written.'[115]

Unlike his father's suave, pristine appearance, Roger's dress sense was less groomed. With his short stature and tanned complexion, Roger did not look dissimilar to a young Irving Berlin. He was skinny. His weight came in at around 57 kilos. His sincerity and enthusiasm made him instantly likable.

Nevertheless, Roger had about as much fashion style as a button. With his 20th birthday approaching, Roger took a more sobering interest in his appearance. He smartened himself up, cut his floppy dark brown hair, slicked it back with pomade, and introduced a defined side parting on the left. In London, he bought an entire rack of suits from Savile Row, fifty in total, and shipped them to New York with boxes of silk ties and crisp new cotton shirts. He now, in all seriousness, began to look the part of a successful bandleader.

When Lindbergh arrived back in America on June 11, the National Broadcasting Company (NBC), in association with most of the other radio stations throughout the American broadcasting network, officially named the day 'Lindbergh Radio Day.' In addition to the official ceremonies in Washington, D.C., Lindbergh programs were transmitted on stations WEAF, WJZ, WRC, and the Pacific Division. Plans were made with the Washington reception committee, headed by inventor John Hays Hammond Jr., to link the nation from coast to coast to broadcast the Lindbergh ceremonies in Washington. An estimated 30 million people tuned in for the event.[116] Although Roger was not in the country to personally honor the aviator, his orchestra was. The band dedicated two numbers to the aviator via their weekly WJZ radio link from the Hotel Pennsylvania. First, '*Lindbergh, the Eagle of the USA*,' followed by '*The Road to Mandalay*,' which, the announcer told listeners, could be the road 'Lindy' may follow someday if his luck keeps on shining.

The Kahns Return From Europe

The RMS *Majestic* set sail from Southampton on June 15, with the Kahn family occupying several first-class suites.[117] Over the next few days, Otto was especially keen to spend time completing an address he'd been preparing. The six-day voyage would also give Roger time to contemplate his future and rearrange his engagement diary for the remainder of the year. The way he saw it, the world was changing fast, faster than even he had imagined. It was the beginning of the aviation industry, and Roger intended to be a part of it. He'd not felt this charged up for a while and instinctively knew his career path was about to change radically.

Otto's three-month trip to Europe was the longest he'd undertaken for several years. He'd visited Britain, France, Germany, Belgium, and Italy and made brief stops in the Baltic States, Greece, Turkey, Yugoslavia, and Dalmatia. The trip had been eventful in more ways than Otto had anticipated. He missed an important appointment with Mustafa Kemal Pasha in Constantinople due to the Turkish leader's sudden departure to Angera. That mix-up aside, he undertook conversations with Mussolini in Italy, Prime Minister Raymond Poincaré in France, and the Foreign Minister Gustav Stresemann in Germany. In Belgium, he had an audience with His Majesty King Albert.

On the weekend before Otto departed from Paris, he satisfied his passion for golf and teed off at Ormesson golf club on the city's outskirts. For the privilege, he paid $111 a hole. Otto was so impressed with the course and how the staff looked after him, he generously tipped 50,000 francs to the club as he left.[118]

On June 21, the *Majestic* anchored in New York Harbor at Pier 54.[119] As the Kahn entourage prepared to go ashore, Otto appeared on A Deck promenade looking relaxed in a flannel suit and a fedora hat. He gazed at the crowds waiting along the quayside, more out of curiosity than in an attempt to recognize anyone. It appeared particularly busy. After one last cigarette, he returned inside.

A short while later, the Kahn family disembarked. As Otto stepped ashore, a magnesium lamp exploded. Feet scuffled, rushing, pushing. Otto was ambushed.

'Welcome home, Mr. Kahn,' called out one whippersnapper.

A small cluster of journalists gathered around the banker, all baying for a story. Unusually for Otto, he had little to recount. Europe's economic situation had generally improved, and things were far better today than they had been a year ago, but that was hardly a newsworthy headline.

When pushed by one insistent newshound to comment on the economy, Otto shut down the reporter instantly: 'The subject is too big to be condensed down to a few minutes of conversation.' That said, Otto bade farewell and returned to his family as they made their way to the arrivals terminal.

Otto was not the only member of the Kahn family reporters pounced upon that afternoon. When they caught sight of Roger, they made a beeline for the youngster. He was, after all, at number one in the sales charts with 'Russian Lullaby.' One particularly clued-up correspondent inquired how he found the music scene in Europe. Roger readily answered. 'The production of jazz music abroad is better than ever before, though the European cannot completely grasp the rhythm which characterizes American jazz.'

He also denied recent reports claiming he was about to organize a 'jazz syndicate,' and then, to the surprise of all, announced he was to devote most of his time in the future to composing rather than actively performing with his orchestra.[120]

The press boys had their story.

Over in Illinois, reporters were hot on the heels of Mattie Williams, Hannah's mother. Mattie frog-marched her teenage daughter to Circuit Courthouse in Cook County to have her offspring's marriage to Charles Kaley annulled. At the same time, Mattie decided it would be a blessing to have her own dysfunctional marriage to her absent husband Thomas terminated, citing cruelty, and the small matter of a seven-year separation, as the grounds for her divorce. The judge granted mother and daughter their annulments on the same day, June 30.

Later, when a journalist asked Roger for his thoughts on Hannah and Kaley's legal separation, he denied holding a torch for the girl and claimed he bore no malice and wished her well. 'I'll say this much,' he elaborated, 'I was very sorry to learn that another fellow got her. But that doesn't mean I could have had her if he hadn't.'[121] The media appeared unconvinced by Roger's dismissive stance.

After the annulment, Kaley continued much like before by picking up his baton and fronting his jazz band in Chicago. Interestingly, he did add a new number to his repertoire, 'Hard Hearted Hannah (The Vamp of Savannah).'[122] Meanwhile, upon Roger's return to the Hotel Pennsylvania, he made a point of playing Irving Berlin's more upbeat 'Blue Skies' during his performances.

The Circus at Hotel Pennsylvania

New York City was experiencing a heatwave upwards of 80 degrees. Coney Island recorded a million visitors on July 3, the highest number ever logged at the beach resort.[123] The following day, two million extra people arrived in Manhattan for Independence Day celebrations. To add to the occasion, the management at the Hotel Pennsylvania redesigned their rooftop restaurant. Erected over the stage was a huge candy-striped circus tent beneath which the Kahn band now performed, with balloons and other circus paraphernalia strewn about the room.[124] The novelty theme was in response to the public's desire for more spectacular productions. Roger took on his role of ringmaster with great glee, cracking his whip whenever his musicians stepped out of line. The tent proved so popular with customers it remained in situ until the end of August.[125]

Victor Records dished out new Kahn recordings with steady regularity throughout the year to capitalize on the youngster's continuing success and the constant media attention he attracted. The four tracks Roger mastered in spring at Liederkranz Hall finally hit the record stores over the summer months.[126]

When Otto made an impromptu call at his son's booking agency at 1607 Broadway, the office was so busy no one recognized him.[127] After waiting a few minutes, a young office girl approached and offered her assistance. Otto could see from her lack of experience that she was new at her job and had no idea who he was. He asked if he could see her boss. 'Who should I say is calling?' inquired the young girl. Otto humorously took on the alias of a jobbing musician seeking employment. His chosen instrument was the saxophone. When Roger finally appeared to meet the musician, Otto's disguise was lifted.

Roger now had ten orchestras in New York working under the Kahn name. His agency also handled many other bands. Musicians would regularly drop by the agency looking for work. To keep his Hotel Pennsylvania unit exclusive, he named it the Roger Wolfe Kahn Original Orchestra. Roger also renegotiated his contract with the Statler organization to cut back on his live appearances. The new arrangement meant he could now appear with his band as and when he chose.[128] This gave him greater flexibility and more time to compose music and work on other musical projects.

Throughout summer and into the fall, the popularity of Roger's recording of 'Russian Lullaby' continued unabated. The Brooklyn Daily Eagle noted after listening to one of his live radio broadcasts, 'Berlin's 'Russian Lullaby' was superbly played.' Their admiration for the bandleader and his musicians did not stop there: 'We listened for quite a while to Roger Wolfe Kahn's orchestra, and we enjoyed it hugely. Mr. Kahn's players move along as smoothly as a superclass motorcar on a new concrete road, and there wasn't a single jarring sound.'[129]

Unexpected and sad news arrived at the Kahn household, informing Otto his cousin, Sir George James Graham Lewis, 2nd Baronet, head of the London law firm Lewis & Lewis, had been tragically killed in Montreux in Switzerland.[130] On August 8, 58-year-old George, having just left the Grand Hotel, entered the railway station opposite, where he stumbled and fell into the path of an oncoming train. Sir George was Otto's aunt Elizabeth Lewis' (née Eberstadt) son.

4 a.m. Summons

In the early hours of the morning on Wednesday, August 10, Roger was driving his sleek, black sedan through Brooklyn along Eastern Parkway on his way to Long Island. Through his rear-view mirror, he noticed a patrol officer on a motorcycle in pursuit. The cop first spotted Kahn's car when it sped past him along Eastern Parkway. He immediately gave chase, driving up to 55 mph to catch up with the vehicle. Several blocks ahead at Albany Avenue, the cop overtook Roger and signaled him to pull over to the curb. Roger pulled over on the corner of Eastern Parkway and Rogers Avenue, at which point the officer, Patrick O'Connor, drove up alongside and apprehended him.[131] When the officer informed Roger he'd been racing over 45 mph along Eastern Parkway, Roger reached into his glove compartment and removed a special deputy police commissioner Gold Badge, which he promptly showed to the officer.[132] The badge was presented to Roger by the City of New York Police Department a couple of years ago when he was involved in undercover detective work.* It afforded the holder dispensation if caught speeding. The cop was unimpressed with the badge and told Roger that it no longer held any weight as the current administration had withdrawn it from circulation.[133]

'I'll have to give you a ticket charging you with driving at over 45 mph,' insisted the officer, bluntly.

'I didn't think this machine was capable of it,' replied Roger, flippantly, sounding more surprised by the car's agility than the fact that the cop was issuing him a summons.

The officer asked to see Roger's driver's license and then asked his occupation and address. Roger answered 'musician' and gave his address as 1100 Fifth Avenue, Manhattan. The cop served Roger with a summons to appear in court on Monday, August 15, charged with a speeding violation. He also assured Roger he had at times been driving at up to 53 mph. The incident occurred at 4 a.m. At no point did the cop appear to recognize the identity of the famous motorist.

News of the offense swiftly appeared on the front pages of many of that day's newspapers and, not unexpectedly, caused an almighty rumpus in the Kahn household.

On Monday morning, Roger arrived early at Brooklyn Courthouse only to be met by a pack of reporters lurking outside the front entrance. Roger pushed his way past them into the lobby of the building without making any statement. Inside he met up with his attorney. They proceeded into a smaller hall adjoining the courtroom, where they waited for their case number. When it was called, Roger and his lawyer entered the court. Also present was the traffic officer Patrick O'Connor who had issued the summons.

After hearing the charge, the magistrate asked the defendant, 'How do you plead?' Roger's attorney replied, 'guilty.'

It was Roger's first offense, and, as such, he received only a stern warning from the magistrate and a $25 fine.[134] Pleased with the outcome, Roger left the courtroom 'grinning.' Outside, Roger gave a brief statement to the reporters, 'hereafter I'm going to confine my speeding to airplanes because I can go as fast as I like.'[135] It later transpired that although the officer had every right to confiscate the Gold Badge, he allowed Roger to keep it.

The presiding magistrate, Harry Howard Dale, who imposed the fine on Roger, had no idea the defendant was the son of Otto Kahn until reporters told him later that day. When asked had he known this information beforehand, would it have altered his decision, the magistrate expressed his indifference. 'That fine would have been imposed on anyone, poor or rich, after a plea of guilty.'

The news that Roger would be cutting down his appearances at the Hotel Pennsylvania brought some restlessness among his band. Their worries that the gig might get pulled manifested in their offstage antics. In intermissions, saxophonist Arnold Brilhart and several other band members had adopted the pastime of making paper airplanes and flying them around the hotel. Violinist Joe Venuti went one step further and constructed a cardboard plane measuring 10-foot-long.[136] He decided to see if it would fly in the street and roped in three waiters and a busboy to help carry the craft out of a backroom, across the dance floor, onto an outside upper balcony directly overlooking Seventh Avenue. From there, Brilhart and several fellow musicians hurled the plane into the air with great gusto, where it flew briefly before nosediving like a lead weight hitting a traffic cop in the street below. The officer stormed into the hotel and promptly arrested everyone in the band.

Le Perroquet to Close For Good

It was the age of speed, and Roger was in a desperate rush to reach the finishing line. The whole point of him flying his expensive airplanes and driving his costly cars was simple - speed! As with most rally drivers and flight enthusiasts, Roger had become what the media now termed a 'speed demon.' That aside, the label did little to describe how he presently spent most of his waking hours, for his impossible workload was beginning to weigh him down.

The time had come for Roger to pull in the reins, recover any outstanding payments, and streamline his business operations. He filed a suit against Billy Rose for an unpaid salary totaling $917 arising from his band's short tenure at the 5th Avenue Club the previous winter.[137] *Le Perroquet* had been hemorrhaging money. No matter how much cash Roger and his father poured into it, they still could not get the place to pay dividends. The 'parrot' had become a dead duck perched upon Roger's shoulder. To ordinary folk, the nightclub appeared pretentious and out of touch. It never had the earthy appeal of Harlem's nightspots that catered for a broader spectrum of clientele. Neither was a drop of alcohol drunk on the premises, ginger ale being a favorite. That aspect alone was a drawback. Its exclusivity could well have been its downfall. Harlem clubs were synonymous with having an element of 'risqué' attached to them. Risk and entertainment went hand in hand.

Roger's establishment was not the only New York operation that experienced financial difficulties; Paul Whiteman's folly in the former Cinderella's lasted only a few weeks. Bandleader Irving Aaronson's endeavor at 159 West 49th opened and closed in exactly nine days.[138] Club Mirador and the Lido had both shut for the season. It may well have been the Roaring Twenties, but if Roger wanted to rise above the din, he knew he had to roar louder.

Father and son came up with a plan. The original lease for the club still had nine years more to run. They had to find a new tenant to sublet the premises. *Le Perroquet de Paris* would not be reopening in the fall.

Otto had an air of authority about him, not in a forthright manner, more from the confidence and wisdom he exerted that came with experience. Roger was now displaying signs of his father's fortitude. If Roger had to close Le Perroquet for good, he was determined not to allow this setback to overshadow his career. He would mark its cessation down to experience, albeit an expensive lesson, and transmute his energies into his many other creative projects.

The fallout from Le Perroquet's closure personally hurt Roger's pocket and his pride, $200,000s worth.[139] The press had a field day reporting the club's demise. It would become the fodder of gossip columns for years to come.[140] Some thought Roger had been unwisely generous. 'Generosity withers on Broadway like a potted flower in a furnace room.' Others put his financial loss down to naivety. No doubt, the idiom 'you can't run before you can walk' sprang to many people's minds. That said, it was fun for the Kahns and everyone involved in the venture while it lasted. Columnist Herbert Corey wrote a fitting epitaph: 'the only regret I can feel is for the goldfish.'

Roger now had more time to concentrate on his composing. He channeled his energy into completing the new stage show he was working on with lyricist Al Dubin.[141] Roger's agency manager George Lottman and Abel Green (Variety journalist) had collaborated on the book. With Roger's appearances at the Hotel Pennsylvania reduced to two or three nights a week, his violinist Joe Raymond took over as the leader in his absence.

In early August, Roger announced he would compete in the New York to Spokane transcontinental air race in September.[142] For the victor, there was a $10,000 prize up for grabs. It wasn't just the money that encouraged Roger to sign up; it was the acclaim and acknowledgment that came with winning. He intended to fly in his new custom-built Bellanca monoplane equipped with a Wright Whirlwind motor, which the manufacturer was still assembling. The craft had already cost him $40,000. He would also fly solo. The Spokane Chamber of Commerce sponsored the race, and more than 100 pilots registered to participate in the various competitions over the five-day event. Possibly as an early 20th birthday gift for Roger, Otto purchased a German-made Dornier Wal seaplane to add to his son's growing collection of aircraft.

A few weeks later came an even bigger surprise when Lottman issued another press statement from the Kahn office confirming Roger would be retiring from performing for good.[143]

Speculation that Roger would turn his attention more to aviation in the future had been rife in the media for some months, but no one had expected his retirement from the stage. *Variety* revealed on their front page the real reasons behind Roger's decision to quit. He was fed up with the temperamental attitude, bickering, in-house fighting, and general pettiness of some of the musicians he conducted business with. Hence, he had decided to disband his orchestra and to step away from having any direct involvement with his booking agency.[144] By severing contact with his musicians, it gave him an open field upon which to graze. In the future, Roger would concentrate solely on composing music. The stage musical he had written with a Ben Hecht libretto was now ready for development. His new futuristic 'blues' rhapsody, which Paul Whiteman had commissioned, was presently being scored by Ferde Grofé in preparation for Whiteman and his orchestra to premiere in the fall.

In August, Roger's publishing contract with Jack Mills expired.[145] Although Kahn and Mills parted on good terms, Roger decided to freelance as a composer and would, in the future, place his music scores with different publishers. From now on, George Lottman would handle all aspects of Roger's career.[146]

As his publicist, personal manager, and confidant, George intended to make sure Roger and his orchestra bowed out in style.

On September 1, Roger flew to Hartford, Connecticut, to appear at the Bond Ballroom atop the smart Hotel Bond for a special one-off appearance fronting the Julie Wintz Orchestra. Kahn's agency had secured a residency for the band at the hotel.[147] Roger only agreed to appear after the hotel's owner Harry S. Bond assured Kahn there was a suitable airfield nearby for him to fly into.

The Unsubtle Art of Subterfuge

On September 2, the news broke that Roger was to wed the dancer, Virginia Franck.[148] The report came totally out of the blue. The following day further details, accompanied by a picture of the couple holding hands, emerged on the front pages of several national papers.[149] The editorials claimed the couple first met in September 1925 when they appeared on the same vaudeville bill at the Riverside Theatre in Manhattan. They struck up a friendship that, over time, developed into a romance. Last winter, Roger and Virginia secretly became engaged. A few months later, the couple quarreled, separated, and went their own way.[150] In spring, Virginia headed to Paris alone to take up a dancing engagement at the *Café des Ambassadeurs*. She adopted the stage name Viva Regor (her surname being suspiciously similar to her ex-boyfriend's name - Roger spelled in reverse). In late spring, Roger arrived in the French capital, where the couple reconciled during a flight in a plane Roger was piloting. When the plane landed at *Le Bourget Aérodrome*, the couple smiled and posed for pictures in front of the aircraft and announced they had made up.

The account sounded feasible except for one aspect; no one at the Kahn residence would confirm or deny the story.[151] A big question mark hung in the air. Where had Virginia Franck suddenly materialized from, and how come word of the engagement had only just surfaced? Something did not add up. Several news editors could smell a rat.

The exclusive had emanated directly from 19-year-old Virginia Franck, who hailed from the village of Lynbrook in Nassau County. She was a bona fide friend of Roger's; in fact, the couple had, as the story mentions, reconnected in Paris during Roger's recent visit there. Virginia had also posed with Roger for a reporter at *Le Bourget Aérodrome* after taking a flight piloted by young Kahn. The picture circulating on the front pages of numerous dailies was one of the snapshots taken that day at Le Bourget. The first piece of the puzzle any editor worth their salary had to solve was who sold the picture to the press?

The report also alleged Roger would, at times, fly his plane over Virginia's family home on Long Island when she was staying there to impress her. The Francks' house was around twenty-five miles southwest of the Kahns' Cold Spring Harbor estate.

On Sunday, September 4, the storyline diversified when conflicting newspaper reports claimed Otto and Roger had individually denied the claims. Miss Franck was less forthcoming.[152] Some newspapers were still undecided whether to believe the Kahns dual rebuttal. Correspondent Corinne Rich claimed in the *Milwaukee Sentinel*, 'Both Parties Silent but Broadway Prepares for Wedding.'[153] The media also noted that Virginia had taken to wearing Roger's gold monogram signet ring, the one he usually wore on his little finger.

When Virginia's father was questioned on Saturday, September 4, at the Franck family home regarding the Kahn denials, he claimed Virginia had spent the previous day with Roger at the Kahn estate on Long Island. 'My daughter is 19 and is capable of making up her own mind. Roger is a fine boy, and I like him.'

When a reporter tracked down Virginia for a comment, she insisted, 'I've known Roger for three years, and we're good friends. Why, he wants a little bit of a home, not like the big, fine one he lives in now.

He often comes here to my home to visit.' She then teased, 'well, I may have some wonderful news before long. Roger told me not to say a word about anything, and I'm not, as you see.'[154]

Two days later, on September 6, further reports about the couple's proposed marriage appeared in the papers. This time Roger adopted a firmer stance. 'It is utterly absurd,' he insisted. 'I have never been engaged to Miss Franck, and I am never going to be engaged to her. I met Miss Franck nearly two years ago. Then I saw her once or twice in Paris, and we had our picture taken standing beside a plane, which I had been flying. But there has never been any understanding of marriage between us, or anything approaching it.'[155]

Regarding the gold signet ring Virginia had taken to wearing, Roger confirmed he had given Miss Franck such a ring a while ago and that it had no significant meaning attached to it other than it was a gift.

When finally a journalist contacted Otto by phone to clarify the situation, Otto reaffirmed the whole shenanigan was ridiculous. 'Roger is only a boy of nineteen,' he said. 'He has never been engaged to her, and he is not going to be.'[156] No doubt, with that off his chest Otto slammed the receiver down.

In truth, what happened in Paris between Roger and Virginia was as follows: Roger and Virginia had their pictures taken while standing by an airplane after the couple had taken a flight together. Shrewdly, the Parisian photographer mailed Virginia and Roger 25 prints each, with a bill enclosed. Even shrewder, Virginia sold one of the photographs to the *Daily News* together with a vague suggestion that she and Roger were an item. For this juicy yarn, she received many thousands of dollars' worth of free publicity.[157] The story was a hoax. She and Roger were never engaged and had no intention of swopping gold wedding rings. The trouble was, the scoop went viral.

Had Roger, Virginia, and George Lottman cooked up the tale together as a publicity stunt, or did Virginia go it alone? Frustratingly, that detail never came to light.

Amusing, endearing, charming - the account of two youngsters in love had a simplicity that captured the public's imagination. Albeit did have a grain of truth to it, the female character was, in fact, an imposter. The press already knew about the Pennsylvania youngster Hannah Williams who ran off with an older bandleader and got hitched underage to spite her ex-boyfriend, who, in reality, was Roger. The real couple in love in this mix was Roger and Hannah. But, for the present, the newsmen had their hands tied with threats of legal writs if they pursued such lines of reportage and dared only assimilate whispers or hint at such speculation.[158] While all the individual elements of the truth appeared in print, they were not stitched together with the same typewriter thread.

A stern ticking off was the probable comeback Roger drew from his father for dragging the family name into murky waters. As for Hannah, the producer George White unexpectedly terminated the Williams Sisters contract in the Broadway-bound production *Manhattan Mary*. Instead, the sisters were encouraged back to Chicago to appear in White's latest touring production of his aptly titled *Scandals* revue.[159] Hannah's girlish charms may have blinded her ex-husband Charles Kaley, but not everyone fell for them.

As for Virginia Franck, the actress danced effortlessly into the chorus line of the Broadway production, *Padlocks of 1927*.* In the coming months, Roger turned his attention to other concerns, primarily his re-invention.

Roger's Farewell

Initially, Roger had signed a twelve-month contract at the Hotel Pennsylvania; his imminent 'retirement' opened a floodgate of interest from bandleaders itching to bag the sought-after residency.

For the foreseeable future, Kahn's booking agency at 1607 Broadway would carry on operating. The part-time bandleader Peter Van Steeden Jr. was brought on board to run it.[160] Roger would continue to honor his recording commitments with Victor. George Lottman would continue managing Roger's business affairs.

The 'blow-off' George arranged to make sure his boss bowed out in style took place at the Hotel Pennsylvania on Saturday evening, September 24.[161] The grillroom was packed wall-to-wall with friends and fellow musicians to witness the disbanding of one of the country's hottest bands. Some viewed it sorrowfully as the end of an era. The following week the Kahn band remained at the Pennsylvania until Thursday without Roger at the helm, after which Johnny Johnson and His Orchestras took over the spot. As to the immediate plans of the crack musicians in Kahn's band, some, like trumpeter Tommy Gott, formed their own units, while bandleaders such as Don Voorhees immediately snapped up some of the others.[162]

Roger's music career began in earnest three and a half years ago; those closest to him viewed his sudden 'retirement' more as a temporary anchor, a dry-docking. Dismantling. Refitting. It certainly gave the press something to dwell on. But, for Roger, it would be a blessing and a significant moment in his career. He had a thicket of ideas floating around his head and was raring to get to work on them.

September bestowed several early birthday gifts upon Roger, most notably the one he purchased himself, a brand new Salmson aircraft. It was his third airplane. In early September, he traveled to Rockford in Michigan to collect it.[163] The machine was custom-built for competitions and aerobatics rather than for comfort. He planned to fly it in the upcoming transcontinental air race from Roosevelt Field to Spokane. Roger would proudly boast he had never suffered from airsickness and could weather any extreme flight conditions or turbulence he encountered. However, his next flight would test him to the limit. Roger was so keen to get the craft back to Long Island that he flew it using no compass or navigation other than a conventional railroad map. Whenever he lost his way, he descended into the nearest open field and asked the local farmer for directions to Buffalo or Albany or wherever he had to be. He made the trip home in five and a half hours. Roger's new customized Bellanca, a replica of the 'Miss Columbia' monoplane, which by all accounts would be the last word in aerial luxury, was still at the manufacturers. The plane was currently having a bathroom, complete with a shower, installed, and it would not be ready in time for him to fly in the National Air Races, hence his purchase of the Salmson.* As it turned out, Roger withdrew from entering the air race.

Another advance birthday present came from *TIME* magazine when they featured Roger on the front cover of their September 19 edition, earning Roger and Otto the accolade of becoming the first father and son to be figured individually on the jacket.[164] Yet more noteworthy, Roger was the first jazz musician to adorn the frontispiece of *TIME*. He was also the second teenager granted the privilege; opera singer Marion Nevada Talley (also aged 19) had the initial honor in March 1926.*

Gilbert's intention of carrying on the Kahn family banking tradition grew a giant step closer to realization when, in mid-September, he arrived back in New York with his wife Anne aboard the *Majestic* to take up his new post at Kuhn, Loeb & Co.[165] It also meant Gilbert would be home to celebrate his brother's birthday on October 19.

The call of adulthood beckoned. Roger's teenage years were fast approaching their finale. His 20th birthday arrived with a tinge of poetic license. Roger marked the occasion with undignified abandon away from prying eyes. A necessary deterrent, for Roger, continued to attract media attention almost as frequently as his eminent and industrious father.[166] One only had to leaf through the dailies to find a mention of Roger somewhere among the tittle-tattle gossip columns.

Otto's philanthropic and building enterprises continued unceasingly. He'd recently financed the renovation of a five-story building on West 10th Street at number 244.[167] The smart, modern studio apartments were now ready to accommodate budding writers, artists, singers, and actors. The rental was $60 a studio per month. The lodging-house complemented the one Otto already owned in Greenwich Village named Twin Peaks.

Reports that Kahn was to personally underwrite any deficit occurred by the director Max Reinhardt and his theatrical company of thirty during their forthcoming eight-week tour of the States caused a few raised eyebrows at the Met.[168] The curtain rose on November 1, with the troupe's weekly expenses anticipated to reach $30,000. Otto was also understood to be behind the importation of the Irish Players who were destined for New York's Hudson Theatre in late fall.[169]

During the year, various construction works and repairs took place on properties owned by the Kahns, including the completion of a new automobile house designed by Charles P. H. Gilbert at 422 East 89th Street.[170] The purpose-built garage could house ten vehicles and had upper quarters for twelve tenants. It was here their four Scottish-born chauffeurs resided. The Kahns practice of hiring Scot's chauffeurs came about after a recommendation from Andrew Carnegie, whose own drivers had all been born in that apparent cradle of drivers, Scotland.

October also delivered Otto the pleasing news that the Japanese government had conferred upon him the Order of the Rising Sun.[171]

The day Roger got his pilot's license, he took his plane up for a solo flight to celebrate.* He now had his eyes set on a transport pilot's license just as soon as he'd put in the required number of flying hours.

In a candid interview published in the *Brooklyn Daily Eagle* on November 8, Roger spoke about the many struggles he had faced since becoming a bandleader.[172] In some respects, it was probably one of the most revealing interviews he had given to date. 'Kahn Abandons Jazz Band to Become Composer,' announced the eye-catching caption. 'Father didn't mind the noise around the house but balked when son wanted to conduct in hotel dining rooms.'

Roger explained with little restraint exactly why his father had withdrawn his encouragement and financial support for his sons 'fad.' When Roger first took up playing jazz, it was his passion. It quickly grew into an obsession, so much so that he would spend several evenings a week crawling sidewalk bars, clubs, and hotel restaurants looking for jazz musicians to rehearse with. When he launched his professional music career, he initially drew irreverence from many newspapers, attracting such headlines as 'Money King's Boy Goes Jazz' and 'Bankers Son Bosses Band.' Several years later, Roger was now turning to those same editors asking for acceptance on his terms. The young musician was well aware of the risk he was taking.

Presently, Roger had quit playing on stage and changed his musical direction to concentrate on composition. He had sacked his band and installed himself in his Broadway office, where he was now doing what Irving Berlin did so successfully in his office, one floor above - writing songs all day.

'I can play any instrument, and I know the theory of music and harmony and how to write scores - I ought to, I've been at it ever since mother made me study violin at the age of six - but running tea dances and nightclubs is something else again. There are times when I think I started too young. I was only fifteen when I got the band together.'

Now at the age of twenty, Roger claimed he had grown weary of fighting his parents with one hand while conducting his orchestra with the other. His childhood quest for noise had now merged into an adult's taste for peace on all fronts.

To some extent, Roger's frustration at continually being treated like a kid by the media helped him decide to quit performing live. Upon reflection, he conceded his club venture was wrong by design and was destined never to work. Nightclubs were renowned for being fickle, nurtured upon a fashion, a whim, or a trend. When the scene buckled, the hard facts of finance kicked in, and, like his father's checkbook, the club closed.

Roger liked familiarity and structure in his personal life and his career. The circus that surrounded him had become stifling and difficult for him to maneuver around. It was inevitable a break-up of some sort was on the horizon. He was, after all, first and foremost a Kahn and, as such, would always attract attention and gossip, an intrusion he found increasingly more challenging to handle or accept.

Due to his exceptional success, the hours in his day had become preoccupied with a dozen things at once. To make those significant changes in his life, he realized he had to prioritize and concentrate on what he wanted.

That, he had decided, was composing and flying airplanes.

Once Roger had left the constraints of the Hotel Pennsylvania behind and wiped his hands clean of running orchestras, his daily routine took on a calmer, less maddening ritual. During the day, if the weather were fine, he could usually be found at an airfield. Although Otto refused to accompany his son on any flights, he commissioned a landing strip on the grounds of his Long Island estate to enable Roger to fly in and out.[173]

Roger in the open cockpit of a Curtiss JN-4 biplane preparing for a solo flight at Curtiss Field.

Roger's attraction to aviation was much like his attraction to auto-racing, purely that of sport. 'I'm interested in it as I am in golf or polo. But music will always be the real interest of my life, particularly composition,' he told correspondent Hortense Saunders who tracked him down at Curtiss Field.[174] Metropolitan New York had four airfields, three on Long Island and one on Staten Island.[175] All were privately owned or run by the military. Curtiss and Roosevelt on Long Island were close to one another and ideally located for the Kahn estate.

It was at Curtiss Field that Roger kept his Sikorsky monoplane. The second time Roger flew solo was over his father's Long Island estate, so his parents could share his buzz. He then dipped over Broadway to get a new viewpoint of his office. Though his family declined his invitations to fly with him, his buddies Johnny Schiff (Mortimer's son) and William 'Billy' Bateman Leeds Jr. keenly took up his offers. 'It's a great life,' Roger assured Hortense Saunders. 'It beats nightlife and nightclubs.' Pictures of Roger sitting in the cockpit of the Curtiss biplane he used for training purposes began to appear in the dailies. The more hours he spent in the air, the closer he came to acquiring his transport pilot's license.

Roger was known to arrive at airfields casually on his motorcycle and would drive right up alongside his plane before climbing on board.

Autograph hunters would spend all day hanging around airports waiting to spot a celebrity and then pounce. The lack of security was glaringly apparent, prompting one newspaper reporter visiting Curtiss Field to express how 'casually' the airplane business was operated.[176] 'There is no section formally roped off for landing purposes, and since a plane may taxi an unconscionable length before coming to rest, great danger really menaces the crowd of avid sightseers.'

This onslaught of day-trippers and fanatics became a regular occurrence at the airfields and an irritation for Roger, who would dodge them whenever possible. As might be expected, some were keener than others.

One evening in Manhattan, after Roger had parked his car on 46th Street close to Broadway and gone off to attend a function, he returned to discover a thief (or thieves) had broken into his vehicle. Stolen was his 'flying jacket, two pairs of riding breeches - like those [Charles] Lindbergh wears - and a pair of riding boots, such as Lindy never owned.'[177] Roger appealed to the police for help tracking down the culprit(s) and the missing items. The cops informed him that the chances of retrieving them were slim.

In November, Roger moved into a Manhattan apartment at 100 Central Park South.[178] It was a temporary arrangement, where, on occasions, he would stay if and when he needed his own space.

The *Blackbird's* Nest

A fortuitous set of coincidences followed. The juxtaposition of Harlem brash and Manhattan chic came together.

In December, upon a recommendation from the songwriter Jimmy McHugh, who had enjoyed several memorable evenings at *Le Perroquet de Paris*, the impresario Lew Leslie offered to rent *Le Perroquet* on a six-month lease.[179] Rather than having the place sit idly dark, Otto accepted Leslie's proposal. Roger reluctantly handed over the keys. The deal cost Leslie twenty thousand smackers and a split of the profits.[180] Leslie christened the club *Les Ambassadeur's* after one of his favorite Parisian haunts. He intended to launch the latest edition of his popular *Blackbirds* revue at the venue in January.

Although Leslie had thought it prudent to change the club's name, he planned to keep a French theme running throughout the interior decoration and commissioned French mural artist Adrien Drian to repaint the lobby.[181]

In addition to being a successful Broadway producer, Leslie was also an experienced club promoter and fully understood the cachet, attraction, and strength the Kahn name carried. In a crafty move, he exploited the connection on initial publicity, informing the public, 'Les Ambassadeur's, formerly Roger Wolfe Kahn's *Le Perroquet de Paris*.' It was a smart marketing strategy if he could get away with it - and, for the time being, he did.

New Year's Eve Madness

Where once 'birds' had been the lyricist's lucky charm, suddenly everything went 'crazy' ... '*Crazy Words, Crazy Tune* (*Vo-do-de-o*).'

To wish the madness of the year farewell, George Lottman sent Easter cards in lieu of Christmas greetings to confuse everyone. George was possibly inspired by the Anti-Christmas Card League of America, which prohibited its members from sending Xmas cards.[182] On December 30, Victor Records rounded out the old year by releasing a double-sided disk from Roger and his orchestra of 'The Hours I Spent With You' and 'An Old Guitar and an Old Refrain.'[183] Radio Broadcast journal thought 'the first was a fair waltz' but decided 'An Old Guitar' (a foxtrot) cried out to be tangoed to.'[184]

Newspapers on New Year's Eve predicted the absurdity of Prohibition would probably see the wettest celebrations on record. Some New York nightclubs ran advertising campaigns blatantly guaranteeing that despite the 3 a.m. curfew and the threat of law enforcement, they would continue the revelry until at least eight the following morning. Irrespective of the law, there were plenty of clubs, bars, restaurants, and hotel ballrooms to choose from, each vying for the customer's cash.

Lew Leslie took full advantage of the lucrative trade over the holiday season and opened Les Ambassadeur's to the public with songstress Adelaide Hall accompanied by the Kahn Orchestra. Roger reassembled his musicians, especially to play the gig.[185] It was a calculated publicity stunt by Leslie to welcome in the New Year and advertise his lavish new nightclub and the launch of his forthcoming edition of Blackbirds, which would premiere at the venue in January.

11

AMERICA'S NEW SON

'An engagement announced in New York society circles is that of Miss Margaret Dorothy Kahn to John Barry Ryan Jr., son of Mr. and Mrs. John Barry Ryan of 18 West 10th Street, New York, and grandson of Thomas Fortune Ryan. The marriage will unite families long identified with New York and prominent in the social and business worlds. It is to be a short engagement, and the marriage will be celebrated in New York next month.'[1]

1928

The formal announcement of Margaret and John's engagement and their proposed marriage brought an unscheduled burst of activity in the Kahn household. Even the cold chill of the January air could not dampen the excitement that ran through the servant's quarters when news of their betrothal broke. Naturally, Margaret's sister Maud would have to return from England. There would be scores of visiting guests to house, not to mention the dinner, reception, and menus to arrange and all the other preparations that go into hosting a marriage of this caliber. After all, this was the union of Otto and Addie's youngest daughter, so understandably, the expense was no issue. The wedding was to take place on February 9.

Margaret was 26. Her fiancé 27.[2] The fact that John Barry Ryan Jr. was the grandson of financier Thomas Fortune Ryan, known to be one of the richest men in America, brought an undeniable air of anticipation about the union. The press implied John Jr. was a prospective heir to part of his grandfather's fortune. It was a dynastic alliance made in financial heaven. Otto and Addie, who were currently occupying their villa in Palm Beach with their houseguest Mrs. William Batemen Leeds Jr. (formally known as Princess Xenia Georgievna of Russia), could not have been happier with the news.[3]

Kahn's Daughter to Wed John Ryan Jr., Reporter And Heir to Fortune

Margaret Kahn.

However, as later became apparent, the reception would not be the lavish occasion as assumed by the press, but a low-key affair, as requested by the bride, with only a select group of family and guests attending. As her sister Maud could not make the journey over from the UK, Margaret dispensed of bridesmaids. Neither was the term 'wedding links two fortunes' literal, as a feud had long existed between the house of John Barry Ryan and that of his wealthy father.

Unlike Thomas Fortune Ryan, who made his millions in tobacco, insurance, and transportation, his grandson John Jr. had taken a career outside of business and finance to work in journalism. He presently worked for the *Newark Ledger* in Philadelphia and was previously hired by the *Inquirer*, the *Morning* and *Evening Ledger*, and *The News*, all in the same city. When confronted by a journalist on a rival paper and asked if he specialized in any particular department at the *Newark Ledger*, John's reply summed up his down-to-earth approach and hard-working ethic, 'No, I'm just a plain reporter - that is good enough for me.'[4]

When the columnist Charles H. Joseph announced the marriage in the *American Jewish Press*, claiming the Kahn family worshipped at St Bartholomew's Episcopal Church of New York, Otto was livid and had his secretary issue a damning response to the ill-informed journalist. 'You say that I joined in later life, the Episcopal Church. Permit me to say that you are mistaken. I have not joined the Episcopal or any other church. A year ago, I made the following statement for publication, 'Religious observance is instilled in one's youth. My parents were not practicing Jews and did not bring me up to be a practicing Jew. But I never left Judaism and have no idea of doing so.' That statement continues to hold good.'[5]

The start of the New Year propelled Roger's career forward with a gust of renewed optimism. On January 6, Victor released his euphonious rendition of '*Among My Souvenirs*,' a song composed by Horatio Nicholls, which Kahn delivered with a first-rate vocal by Harold 'Scrappy' Lambert.* The score for his latest stage venture, the musical comedy *Here's Howe!*, was almost completed.[6] In a surprise move, Roger received an invitation to conduct the Cass Hagan Orchestra. They temporarily had no leader and had a string of performances looming at various theaters in and around New York.[7] The fee was substantial. When Roger went to hear the band rehearse, he was impressed enough to take on the assignment. The dates ran throughout the second half of January. Although the job was intended to be low-key, the press got wind of it. The news left George Lottman with the awkward task of announcing that even though Kahn had retired from stage work, speculation that he would be conducting the Cass Hagan Orchestra for a limited engagement was correct.

At the end of January, another press release issued by the Kahn agency confirmed Roger and his Recording Orchestra would perform a snap tour around New York throughout February on the Fox theater circuit. The shows were billed as Kahn's farewell headlining vaudeville appearances.[8] It all sounded a little messy, but no doubt, Roger's sizable fee made the outing worthwhile.[9] The first dates saw the maestro playing four nights at the 3,000-seat Academy movie palace on East 14th Street, from February 9. The date could not have been more conflicting in the Kahns' social calendar for February 9 was the day Roger's sister Margaret was to wed John Barry Ryan Jr.

Roger and His Recording Orchestra
at The Savoy.[10]

The day of Margaret and John's wedding took on the appearance of a snowstorm; such was the chilliness of the weather outdoors and the profuseness of white blooms adorning the interior of the Kahns Fifth Avenue ballroom. A blizzard of white welcomed the 160-plus guests that gathered for the occasion. Even the three-tier wedding cake ordered from the master baker Madame Blanche Le Ralec came decorated with white bells, white blossom, and white putti, making merriment among the white sugar frosting.*

Throughout the reception, Margaret endearingly called her husband 'Johnny,' and during Otto's toast to the happy couple, he professed of his youngest daughter, 'It is my deliberate conviction that you are the nicest girl in this here republic.'[11]

Over the next few days, pictures of the itinerant reporter and his pretty bride graced the pages of newspapers and magazines, many taken on the deck of the SS *Leviathan* as they set sail on their honeymoon to Europe. From the UK, they planned to travel to the South of France and then to North Africa before returning to set up home on Long Island.*

The Luxurious Art of Flying

Roger's new custom-built, six-passenger Bellanca monoplane was finally delivered. The body of the ship was black, trimmed with gold paint. The interior cabin came fitted with seats upholstered in genuine leather, modern lighting, curtains, and surfaces lined with black and silver cloth. In preparation for sitting his transport pilot's license exam, Roger arranged for the head of the Syracuse District for Flying Safety, Mr. L. M. Boggs, to test fly the plane on February 14 to check it was in full working order.[12] The machine passed with flying colors. To keep it secure, Otto leased a private hangar at Roosevelt Field to house the plane.[13]

Roger Wolfe Kahn Becomes Flier Just to Idle Around in Air Sedan

Above—Roger Wolfe Kahn's new Bellanca plane. Lower left shows luxurious interior of ship. At right is the composer-flier.

Inside view of the cockpit control panel of Roger's new Bellanca.[14]

Roger took his flying interests extremely seriously. He was a member of the newly formed Manhattan Aero Club, which already boasted over 125 active members, and sat on their Advisory Board.[15] The popularity of airplanes for private use was steadily rising, especially among the wealthy. Enthusiast's such as Henry Francis du

Pont, Harold S. Vanderbilt, Vincent Astor, and Earl D. Osborne all owned private planes and flew them regularly.[16] When a journalist asked Roger if he was thinking of aviation as a paid profession, he categorically denied any career change. 'I haven't any intention of taking up commercial aviation,' he confessed, shaking his head.[17] 'That's a lot of nonsense. I've got my own plane, and I have a pilot's license, and I like to fly, but I'm not trying to make any money out of it.' The reporter approached Roger at Curtiss Field, just as he was about to take up his Salmson for a spin.

The weather conditions that day were particularly windy and not ideal for flying. Despite this, Roger still flew his plane. For fifteen minutes, he circled the field, making sure to keep out of the path of any regular commercial planes. He then glided in over the hangars, balancing the wings like a spirit level, before landing as smoothly as he had taken off. As he climbed out of the cockpit, he slid his aviator goggles up onto his forehead and acknowledged the reporter that had stayed to watch his aerial display.

'There's a strong wind up there,' Roger remarked to the press boy. 'It's not much fun today. You have to work all the time. You have to tend to business or goodbye.' Roger threw his hands up in the air and managed a mischievous smile before heading off towards the hot dog shed on the corner of the field.

Otto celebrated his 61st birthday in Florida with Addie and several friends.[18] He even made a brief trip to Havana.[19] There was talk he might follow this break with a whistle-stop rail trip to the West Coast, returning to New York City sometime in April. Perhaps the time away would help him recover from the enormous personal disappointment he bore after realizing his dream of building a new Metropolitan Opera House had finally fallen through.[20]

Over the past two years, Robert Fulton Cutting had become the thorn in Otto's side throughout Kahn's drive to bestow New York with a new opera house. American-born Cutting was also a prominent, moneyed philanthropist with a keen interest in music and the arts. Through Cutting's efforts to help reform the city government and encourage the building of low-cost housing, he was dubbed 'the first citizen of New York.' Cutting's unceasing objections to Otto's proposal had ultimately worn Kahn down to the point where, in early 1928, Otto abandoned his dream altogether.[21] Otto's admission of defeat was a sore burden he would find difficult to recover from fully.

Otto immediately put the site on West 56th and 57th Streets, which he'd bought for the project, back on the market.[22] He then transferred his attention to the development of large tracts of woodland he'd scooped up in the Peconic Bay section of Suffolk, Long Island, on which he hoped to encourage the construction of home colonies.[23]

The *Blackbirds* Effect

From mimicking parrots, Roger's former nightclub had now become home to a flock of singing blackbirds.[24] *The Blackbird Revue* opened as a floorshow at *Les Ambassadeur's* in January, showcasing Adelaide Hall. By March, it had morphed into an extended two-act revue renamed *Blackbirds of 1928*, with a company of forty. 'The greatest aggregation of colored artists ever assembled in an after-theater rendezvous,' declared advertisements in the newspapers. 'Lew Leslie's *Ambassadeur's*, formerly Roger Wolfe Kahn's *Le Perroquet de Paris* - open nightly and Sundays from 10 p.m. to closing.' Leslie was determined to use the Kahn name alongside his own for as long as he could get away with it.

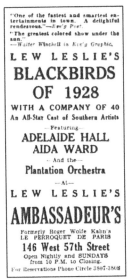

Blackbirds at the *Ambassadeur's*.

Blackbirds had evolved into something far bigger than any of the artists appearing in it could ever have imagined possible at the time. Whether it was down to the astounding songwriting talents of Dorothy Fields and Jimmy McHugh, or Lew Leslie's irrepressible determination, or Adelaide Hall's dynamic stage presence and vocal calisthenics, or just the unique conglomeration of the troupe as a whole, was difficult to determine. When something magical happens on stage, it is best not to dissect it and theorize; otherwise, the magic dissipates. Nevertheless, the show stirred the public's imagination like no floorshow before it and had them slipping their hands into their wallets, purchasing tickets to see it not just once but twice, thrice, and so on.

There was no getting away from the fact that Leslie was a canny entrepreneur. In rounding up supporting artists for the show, he enticed some star performers away from Harlem's mob-owned Cotton Club. But, in doing so, his temerity backfired. As a result, he received a stern warning from the Mafia that his club would be firebombed if he continued the practice. The reprisal never happened, but the danger and intimidation were real.

The public adored the show and flocked nightly in their hundreds to see it. The influential showbiz columnist Walter Winchell called it 'the greatest colored show under the sun.' And Winchell had clout! Winchell's thumbs up encouraged Leslie to commission Fields and McHugh to write a second half to the show. Such brilliant reviews were good news for Roger, as it now meant Leslie might extend his six-month lease on the venue.

Here's Howe!

'Here's to the flapper, good and kind;
let's drink her health in toddy.
She's nothing much upon her mind
and less upon her body.'[25]

Blackbirds of 1928 may have been kicking up a sweat on the mirror dance floor over at Kahn's old nightclub, but Roger now had a show of his own to focus on. Rehearsals for the new Aarons and Freedley musical comedy *Here's Howe!* for which Roger had co-written the score got underway on March 6. The title had a history and was not wholly original; it had appeared in several literary mediums, most recently a *Here's How* cocktail mixology book.[26] The Mask and Wig Club of the University of Pennsylvania had adopted the name for one of their stage productions.[27]

At rehearsals, the show came together surprisingly quickly. However, some orchestral arrangements on certain numbers were thought unnecessarily complicated. To iron the problem out, on the following Saturday, Roger flew his plane down to the Jersey resort of Atlantic City to confer with Alex Aarons over the score's orchestrations.[28] Such work is always best carried out away from the hustle and bustle of the theater. It also gave the pair time to catch a well-earned breather before returning to New York on Monday morning to resume rehearsals.

The production team of Alex Aarons and Vinton Freedley customarily loaned their talents to only one show a year. They had recently produced the Broadway hit *Funny Face* (starring Fred and Adele Astaire) berthed at the Alvin Theatre. The Gershwin brothers had written the score, and authors Fred Thompson and Paul Gerard Smith had devised the book. Breaking from tradition, Aarons and Freedley agreed to produce *Here's Howe!* and brought Thompson and Gerard Smith on board to write the book. Irving Caesar provided the lyrics. It was a massive stroke of luck for Roger to have such a talented and proven team around him.[29] The musical was destined for a spring premiere and booked into the Broadhurst Theatre at 235 West 44th Street. Allen Kearns (who had been pulled from *Funny Face* to appear in this production), Irene Delroy, and orchestra leader Ben Bernie and his band were among the cast's principals, with choreographer Sammy Lee committed to staging the dance routines.[30] Rehearsals were scheduled to continue throughout March, with a short out-of-town tryout tour commencing in April.

Actress Irene Delroy, who played the role, Joyce, was such a cutie she could easily have been the artistic inspiration for the cartoon caricature Betty Boop - the similarity of their facial features was striking. Despite her likeness, this was not the case. The character had not yet been created, and when it was, two years later, the likely source for that distinction went to the singer Helen Kane.

Although Roger no longer had an orchestra, he was still under contract with Victor Talking Machine Co. As such, he had to hire session players to make any future recordings. On March 14, he took thirteen jobbing musicians into New York's Victor Studios to lay down the Harry Woods composition *'She's a Great, Great Girl.'* Victor saved two of the three takes captured. He also recorded the James P. Johnson ditty *'Give Me The Sunshine'* with golden-voiced Franklyn Baur during the same session. Roger was fortunate to bag Baur; the singer was currently hot property, having enjoyed considerable success in Ziegfeld's recent Broadway edition of *Follies*.[31] Baur was also the highest-paid vocalist singing on the radio.

Trombonist 'Miff' Mole never showed up for the first tune, and at the last minute, a replacement took his place. That musician was 23-

year-old Jack Teagarden, who blew a 32-bar solo on the track literally off the cuff, 'wearing the largest hangover on Manhattan Island,' Kahn later recalled. When Victor released *'She's a Great, Great Girl'* a few weeks later, Teagarden's improvised solo made a big impression. It was one of Teagarden's first recordings.

In mid-March, Otto headed west from Palm Beach to Hollywood by train to escape the stresses of big city life. Accompanying him in his Pullman party was John L. Lancaster, president of the Texas and Pacific Railway, the 'aristocrat' Prince Francesco Ruspoli (8th Prince of Cerveteri) from Rome, English author Beverley Nichols, Otto's trusted companion Rudolf Kommer, playwright and novelist David Gray, vice president of the Equitable Trust James Irving Bush (regarded as the 'handsomest man in America'), and his loyal friend, publicist Ivy Lee. The break genuinely was for relaxation purposes but became a widely documented publicity exercise thanks to Ivy's intervention - Otto the Magnificent takes on Hollywood![32]

The train pulled in at various stations en route to Los Angeles, taking in New Orleans, El Paso, and New Mexico. On March 15, Kahn and his party alighted at Lake Worth. The newspaper magnate Amon G. Carter had invited them to lunch at his sprawling country estate Shady Oak Farm.

The following day the train made an early morning stop at Union Station in El Paso. Kahn had an 8 a.m. breakfast meeting with local businessman Warren Pilcher and various executives at the El Paso Club on the roof of the Hotel Hussmann. Pilcher hoped to secure a $1.5 million investment for a proposed new sportsman's hotel in the city. During a cooked breakfast of chops and scrambled eggs, Otto chatted to reporters. When asked his impressions of the city, Kahn responded enthusiastically, 'El Paso is among my favorite spots. That is no bull.'[33] As if to reiterate the fact, he then added, 'I like the west. I get more pleasure out of it than I do out of Europe.'

The journalists were taken aback by Kahn's frankness.[34]

'I believe in answering all questions,' Kahn reassured everyone. 'I was told when I started as a banker to keep dignified in silence. That simply means building a wall around yourself. Dignity, which needs the protection of silence, is not worth having.'

The rushed stop in El Paso lasted a mere two hours, after which the tour deluxe resumed its journey.

During early evenings the group stopped off in the nearest town to dine at the best hotel, where it had been prearranged for eight blonde-haired sirens (usually young actresses from a local show) to keep the guy's company. Otto aimed to add a little innocuous *amusement* to the proceedings. Doubtless, some folks misconstrued his intentions. For their trouble, each temptress received a $100 bill hidden discreetly under her dinner plate. Author Beverley Nichols in his memoir *All I Could Never Be*, denied any sexual activity took place.[35] He also noted Otto always remained the faithful husband. That said, Nichols further let slip Otto much preferred the company of sedate, middle-aged, firmly brunette females and that he would retire earlier than his traveling companions at the end of the evening, back to his sleeping compartment on the train. As photographs suggest, it's noticeable that not all the actresses were blonde.

On the rear of the train: James Irving Bush (far left), Beverley Nichols (2nd left), Otto Kahn (center), David Gray (far right), and six of the eight 'sirens' hired to keep the party amusing, March 1928. (Courtesy, Fort Worth Star-Telegram Collection, Special Collections, The University of Texas at Arlington Libraries)*

By the time the train shunted into LA's Central Station, the 'blonde' enchantresses had silently vanished.

In sunny California, Otto took a stroll in the newly opened Botanic Garden in Mandeville Canyon, Brentwood. Here he planted a New Zealand laurel tree in the Forest of Fame, a stretch of land reserved for growing and nurturing trees planted by notable visitors.[36] Charles

B. Hopper, a director of the Garden Foundation, escorted Otto to the planting. A photographer from ACME News captured the occasion. Otto put on a cheery face; business as usual. It was good PR. A man who plants a tree could never be called a pessimist!

Otto plants a laurel tree at the Botanic Garden, Brentwood.

The film capital was heavy with celebrity gossip. Writer, Carl Van Vechten, found Hollywood people dull and rich. The place did stretch his imagination, though, and gave him a fertile source of material from which to draw inspiration. One story he had great pleasure in regaling was how Otto Kahn was entertained at dinner one evening in Hollywood, at which sixty blondes were present. 'Another evening, he was entertained at a dinner at which sixty brunettes were present. That is the way you can order things in Hollywood.'[37] Little wonder Otto found the city so alluring.

A few days later, in Salt Lake City, Otto gave a speech outlining business conditions in America and the effect the forthcoming presidential election would have on the nation. During his talk, he leaked news about his youngest son Roger, confirming the rumor his son was shifting away from directing orchestras to work in aviation.[38] How soon the transition would take place, Otto did not specify. The report came totally out of the blue.

Meanwhile, Addie sailed in the opposite direction, heading for the UK's cooler climes to spend a short break with her daughter Maud and to be at her grandson John's 7th birthday party on April 2.[39]

By coincidence, April 2 was also the date *Here's Howe!* held its first tryout performance, which took place at the Chestnut Street Opera House in Philadelphia.[40] For some inexplicable reason, the show appeared in local newspaper advertisements as *And Howe!*[41] Roger flew out to be there. The launch did not go as well as the producers or Roger had hoped. Over the coming days, the producers made significant alterations to the running order and the script. More favorably, *Variety*, in their review, thought it 'a good, lively summer show.'[42] The reporter also mentioned a 'luscious' young lady named Virginia Franks playing the third female lead. Was this Roger's former belle from Long Island, the dancer Virginia Franck?

Upon Otto's return to New York, a reporter from a William Randolph Hearst-owned newspaper contacted Kahn to verify a scoop he was about to publish claiming the banker had given five 'actresses' $5,000 each to study in Europe. With his lawyer's help, Otto killed the story there, and then, although, allegedly, it did have some veracity attached to it. While in Hollywood, Kahn had offered to pay for an actress to visit Salzburg in Austria to study drama with the director Max Reinhardt. He also gave money to another actress towards a scholarship in New York.[43] The last thing Otto wanted was to be associated with another scandal. Such an exposé would have been devastating for his reputation, his career, and his family. The reveal was further proof, if Otto needed it, that the press were on his tail waiting for him to slip up.

After hearing of Otto's tricky predicament, a Paramount executive with a sympathetic ear cabled Kahn with some wise words: 'You probably know motion picture girls will say and do anything that will get them a trip or publicity.'

After two weeks in Philadelphia chafing at the bit, the cast of *Here's Howe!* headed for Boston, where the show anchored for a two-week berth at the Shubert Theatre.[44] Here, the producers planned to iron out any final anomalies in preparation for its Broadway entrance. Roger flew out to Boston in his new Bellanca six-seat monoplane to check on the shows progress, giving the plane its maiden short-haul flight in the process.[45]

Irrespective of its name change, the show fared well at the box office in Philadelphia, taking $42,000 during its two-week tenure. In Boston, the show grossed $21,000 in its first week.[46] By the time the unit reached Broadway, the billboards were back advertising it as *Here's Howe!* Also added to the company was the English comic actor Eric Blore. Interestingly, Virginia Franks was no longer in the cast.

Broadway had 23 theaters dark (a considerable amount) as it approached the testing summer season.[47] Any new musical faced stiff competition from established hits such as *Funny Face, Rosalie, The Three Musketeers, Greenwich Village Follies,* and *Show Boat.* If *Here's Howe!* was to stand out, it had to offer hit songs, a strong plot, and engaging performances.

Here's Howe! premiered at the Broadhurst Theatre on May 1. The first night reviews were mixed, with most middling or fairing above average.[48] Sammy Lee's choreography received high praise.[49] The actor William Frawley in his role as 'Sweeney' Toplis, literally stopped the show nightly. He could do no wrong in his comedy portrayal. However, the problem most reviewers had with the show was its weak storyline. Broadway heavyweight Walter Winchell attended the premiere as a personal guest of the show's producers Aarons and Freedley.[50]

In his first-night appraisal, the *Variety* critic Abel Green made it known, '*Here's Howe!* is no world-beater as a musical and, as such, not intended, but it is a satisfying enough spring entry that will get some coin for a nice stay and turn a profit for all concerned.'[51]

Other individual highlights Green thought worthy of mention included the 'winsomely captivating Irene Delroy'; the bandleader turned actor Ben Bernie, who handled 'dialog and business like a legit'; Allen Kearns as the juvenile 'labored rather well'; and Ben Bernie's orchestra, 'a revelation' playing the score from the stage and pit 'like vets.'[52] He also expressed how the real outstanding numbers in the show were chiefly Kahn-composed.

The dance number 'Crazy Rhythm,' handled superbly by Dan (Ben Bernie), Cora (Peggy Chamberlain), and Mary (June O'Dea), stopped proceedings nightly. The song had HIT plastered all over it. It was so irrepressibly catchy that the audience left the theater humming it on the way out.

Otto's name invariably cropped up whenever discussions about the financial backing for the show arose. Otto categorically insisted he had no monetary involvement in the production. Indeed, the journalist Abel Green affirmed Roger would deem it shallow glory if the show proved a success under those circumstances.

The packed premiere attracted a mixture of first-nighters: society folk, the Broadway mob, Tin Pan Alley artisans, and nightclub habitués. Many were associated with the creators or sponsors of the production. Here's Howe! was Roger's musical theater debut and, as such, always was going to attract enormous interest from the public and press alike. Such publicity would play either in his favor or, depending upon its content, against him. Roger was no fool; he knew there would be an element of risk attached to anything he put his hand or signature to; that was the nature of the beast.

After the reviews had gone to press, all anyone involved with the production could do was sit it out and await the public's reaction. Quite unexpectedly, over the coming weeks, something quite magical happened ... 'Crazy Rhythm' became a big, fat hit.

Crazy rhythm
Here's the doorway*

Worldwide recognition of Roger's songwriting abilities arrived soon after Victor released his rendition of 'Crazy Rhythm,' along with the other memorable song from the score 'Imagination.'[53] Both songs were individual hits. 'The titillating contagion of 'Imagination' and 'Crazy Rhythm' will do much to ballyhoo Here's Howe! on the dance floors and the radio.'[54]

You go your way
I'll go my way
Here's goodbye to you

Crazy Rhythm sheet music went on to sell over a million copies.[55]

'*Crazy Rhythm*' epitomized the madness of the Twenties and all the fun and carefree abandon the era represented. The composition lifted your spirits higher than a weather vane. It was the kind of song that made you feel like a millionaire walking on air. Caesar's lyrics were witty and smart in equal measure and, more important, easy to remember. Kahn, Joseph Meyer, and Caesar were determined to write an out-and-out hit for the show. With '*Crazy Rhythm*,' they accomplished it. The song was inescapable. It was one of those simple tunes that the brain cells would not let go of no matter how hard you resisted. *Ritmo Loco, Verrückten Rhythmus, Ritmo Folle, Rythme Fou*; in whatever language you heard it sung, '*Crazy Rhythm*' did exactly what Caesar's lyric, and Kahn and Meyer's 32-bar rhythmic melody set out to do - ignite the dance floors. *'Crazy Rhythm'* was a self-assured instant classic.

An opening night on Broadway is like no other. A kind of magic fills the air. It's the night that can mark a show's success or failure, a hit or flop, although this is not always the case. The hope that *Blackbirds of 1928* would sit it out at Roger's nightclub throughout summer was not to be. Lew Leslie had grander ideas for his baby chicks. He pulled the show out of *Les Ambassadeur's*, revised it further, added more acts to the cast, including the sensational hoofer Bill 'Bojangles' Robinson, packed it off on a brief out of town trial run, after which he installed it on Broadway at the Liberty Theatre two streets away from the Broadhurst where *Here's Howe!* was playing. Was this a coincidence or another clever marketing ploy? *Blackbirds of 1928* opened on Broadway eight days after the premiere of *Here's Howe!* but not all initially went according to plan for Mr. Leslie.*

In early May, the Williams Sisters arrived back in New York City to perform at the Little Club. Their re-emergence was low-key. *Variety* got wind and noted that although Roger and Hannah had a 'mad' on for over a year, they had since patched things up and were now on speaking terms.[56] A few weeks later, the Williams Sisters eased themselves into the more exclusive Club Richman at 137 West 56th Street, where they opened for George Olsen and his Orchestra. The sisters remained there throughout the summer.[57]

On May 14, at the monthly meeting of the directors of Paramount Famous Lasky Corporation, Gilbert Kahn was elected to the board.[58] Alongside his father and Uncle Felix, Gilbert would be the third member of the Kahn clan to sit on the board.

The Dutch Treat Club

When an invitation arrived on Roger's desk from the exclusive Dutch Treat Club, Roger must have thought it a good omen.

The Dutch Treat Club was conceived in 1905 and rose from the ashes of the former Cloister Club; a luncheon and dinner club that, according to George Barr Mallon (one of its founder members),[59] 'sprang to life in the late 1880s, when the men sported very tight trousers in glaring checks, and the women protected their rear approaches with jutting bustles; when the telephone was an exotic luxury, and the unmarried lived in boarding houses.'[60] Membership was select and aimed towards aspiring writers, musicians, and stage performers of merit and worthy illustrators who worked for periodicals or the broadsheets. The club's name came from the principle that everyone paid 'Dutch.' Meetings took place on Tuesday lunchtimes (copy date day for the then publishing world) in a top-class Manhattan hotel or restaurant.

The midtown Hotel Martinique was a favorite hangout for New York's 'artistic' set and a regular meeting place of the Dutch Treat Club. Its motto, 'the best without extravagance,' summed up the hotel perfectly. It was situated on 49 West 32nd Street opposite the Hudson tube and close to the theater district. Vaudeville and Broadway entertainers, artists, writers, and Greenwich Village bohemians would congregate at the café and barroom for informal luncheons and early evening cocktails.*

On Tuesday, June 5, the Dutch Treat Club threw a private luncheon at the Martinique to honor the *Here's Howe!* cast and production. Roger, Joseph Meyer, and Irving Caesar represented the writers, and Irene Delroy and 'Fuzzy' Knight attended from the cast. Columnist Karl Kingsley Kitchen officiated as the emcee.[61] Such an invitation from what was perceived as an 'influential' private members club was seen by those involved in *Here's Howe!* to portend a positive sign for the show's future. Spirits among the cast that day were high, and, though much liquid refreshment was drunk during the meal, all cast members present did make that evening's performance.

The Summer of '28

Since its transfer into a theater, the reviews for *Blackbirds of 1928* had been mixed, and, like *Here's Howe!* performances were not selling out. Leslie's production had a big cast totaling over a hundred performers. It was a huge financial undertaking to keep the show ticking over, especially as he was still running and paying the rental on *Les Ambassadeur's* and handing over a cut of the profits from the club to the Kahns. Opportunely for Leslie, the lease on the club lasted only until the end of June.

When the warmer summer weather arrived, things started to pick up.* More customers were around. However, with the sweltering heat came a different issue, air conditioning, or the lack of it. Most New York City theaters did not yet have air conditioning. Many theaters along Broadway left their exterior exit doors ajar to create a current of air running through the building to help keep audiences cool. In doing so, music from the orchestras would waft out onto the sidewalks. Outside the Liberty Theatre where *Blackbirds* was playing, passersby would catch strains of '*I Can't Give You Anything but Love, Baby*,' '*Diga Diga Doo*' and '*I Must Have That Man*,' belted out by the joyously talented Adelaide Hall. Some pedestrians would instinctively stop to listen; some just caught a cadenza floating in the air; others would linger a while longer to hear whole songs. The same procedure happened outside the Broadhurst with *Here's Howe!*, but for most people, the music emanating from *Blackbirds* somehow sounded more exotic, more Harlem, more risqué. It was the element of risk, Leslie's clever marketing, the astoundingly brilliant songs from Dorothy Fields and Jimmy McHugh, along with the multifarious talents of the *Blackbirds* cast that proved to be the hidden ingredients that created the jewel that *Blackbirds of 1928* became.

Here is where we have a showdown
I'm too high, and you're too low down
Crazy rhythm, here's goodbye to you

If ever a show should have been a success, it was *Here's Howe!* It had all the right ingredients for being a smash. So what went wrong? The book was the root of the problem. The plot could easily have been written on the back of a tram ticket: 'a summer musical comedy about the Cinderella of a motor car factory.' This specific twelve-word phrase was plastered across advertising billboards, unwisely, as it turned out. Yet, for all its simplicity, the storyline was not strong enough to carry a whole Broadway production. The verdict would be a bitter pill to swallow.

Although *Blackbirds of 1928* and *Here's Howe!* contained different content, they were, figuratively, running against each other, given they were both musicals featured on Broadway. Each show also had a big summer hit; '*I Can't Give You Anything but Love, Baby*' from *Blackbirds* and '*Crazy Rhythm*' in *Here's Howe!*

Alas, public interest in *Here's Howe!* was not enough to fill the 1,100-seat theater. At the end of June, the show quietly bowed out of the Broadhurst. *Here's Howe!* closed.* Though it delivered what would become one of the most enduring jazz numbers of the era, *Here's Howe!* was no match against its competitors. Fortunately for the songwriters Kahn, Meyer, and Caesar, '*Crazy Rhythm*' attained greater success. The sheet music alone sold over a million copies. As for *Blackbirds of 1928*, the show defied the box office slump and became the biggest hit of its kind on Broadway.

The *Rhythm* of the Waves

The long, hot summer of 1928 brought New Yorkers out of the tenements and into the streets. Temperatures soared. The heat eradicated any semblance of normality. The days melted into a wash of burst hydrants and flavored ice carts. Not even the weather forecaster had predicted days like these. All decency and manners were abandoned on the sidewalk, replaced by shades, straw hats, and flimsy garments. No one had the energy to move, let alone work.

Theaters continued to keep their doors and windows wide open to keep the air circulating and the customers inside. Wafts of Adelaide Hall opining '*Diga Diga Doo*' drifted along Broadway, keeping the traffic tides flowing and the pedestrians entertained. The city was jazzing on its axle.

Oheka II with passengers and crew cruising en route to Long Island.

Finding the summer heat insufferable, Addie Kahn slipped over to the UK in mid-July, her second visit within months.[62]

Plying the waters of Long Island Sound, aboard his sleek princess *Oheka II* became Otto's new pastime. Shuttling to and from his country estate to his Lower Manhattan office was now a doddle and a pleasant way to unwind after a hectic day of high-powered business meetings.

Otto could enjoy a leisurely breakfast and catch up with the news in the morning papers on the outward journey. On his return, he could savor a light tea and relax with the evening papers without fear of being bothered by any irritating interruptions. With his wife away, the summer heat gave Otto a worthy reason to spend more time at his beloved Long Island estate. It was also the perfect weather for throwing his infamous rumbustious weekend parties.

The end of the long, hot spell came when the rains arrived. A torrential downpouring that wet everyone outdoors through to their skin.

Poor Roger!

Dear Sir
In one of your recent issues, you state that my son Roger, on attaining his majority next October, will come into the possession of a large fortune.
Ordinarily, I would not discuss in print my personal affairs or those of my children. If I depart from that principle in the present instance, it is because I believe the public impression that Roger, at the age of 21 years, will become the recipient of a fortune is apt to be unfortunate for him and detrimental to his career.
I deem it my duty, therefore, as Roger's father, to state that the report, above referred to, is wholly without foundation and that no fortune, large or small, awaits my son on the occasion of his 21st birthday. I shall greatly appreciate it if you will have the kindness to publish this letter in the columns of your paper and thanking you in advance. I remain, faithfully yours,
Otto H. Kahn [63]

Poor Roger!

Speculation of the impending handout Roger would receive on his 21st birthday in October was already appearing in gossip columns as early as July,[64] hence his father's handwritten denial to the press.[65] The young man still had two and a half months to wait until he received even a birthday card, let alone 'come into the possession of a large fortune.'

Also, in July, a story leaked to the press that Otto had sunk $80,000 into *Here's Howe!* without Roger's knowledge.[66] When Roger found out, he was livid and stated he would not have entertained the production had he known about his father's financial involvement.[67]

Otto retorted that he invested in all of Aarons and Freedley's stage shows and was not brought in especially for *Here's Howe*!

After Lew Leslie vacated *Les Ambassadeur's*, the niggling problem of the club's lease reared its head again. Hence, the nightclub went back on the rental market. When picture house owner Mike Mindlin proposed transforming the venue into an independent movie theater, Otto and Roger jumped at the idea. Mindlin already owned one picture house, so he had a good knowledge of running such an enterprise. They struck a deal. Mindlin would pay an annual rental of $21,000 for the site plus an additional 25 percent of the net profit.[68] Mindlin also agreed to cover from his pocket the expense of remodeling the establishment.

Otto already owned Twin Peaks and another studio rental property in Greenwich Village. He now added a further building to his rental portfolio, The Tiniest Little House, a restaurant that had been in business for seven years. It was referred to as the neighborhood's smallest and most novel café but had never turned over a healthy profit. Otto intended to convert the space into living quarters.[69]

At the beginning of August, Otto departed from New York on board RMS *Aquitania* to join his wife in the UK.[70] He also intended to visit Europe in search of cultural pursuits. It was a trip he was particularly looking forward to.

Roger had not performed live on stage for around six months. His retirement was about to come to an inadvertent end. In Times Square, a new ballroom named *Star* was due to open on September 1, with the Roger Wolfe Kahn Serenaders billed as the house attraction.[71] Kahn signed a contract to appear on a week-by-week basis on certain prearranged nights. Needs must when necessity calls. The fee was way too tempting for him to decline.

Beautiful Vienna

'I drowsed in beautiful Vienna.
Beethoven called me, 'anywhere, anywhere, out of this mess.'
Yet, I should love what is light to Otto Kahn and Morris Gest.
Who plays the devil in Everyman?'[72]

Otto's trip to Europe was just as productive and eventful as he hoped. In Salzburg, Max Reinhardt agreed for his new production of Tolstoy's *Redemption*, produced by Morris Gest, to play a two-week engagement on Broadway in mid-November, with actor Alexander

Moissi filling the lead role. Otto arranged to financially back the visit.

At the Hotel Adlon in Berlin, Otto held a private meeting with Dr. Hugo Eckener, the mighty *Graf Zeppelin* dirigible designer.[73] They discussed a loan for $14 million to set up the Ocean Air Transport Company to establish a regular passenger and cargo airship service between the United States and Germany, the first of its kind. Eckener was about to depart on his maiden transoceanic flight to America from Germany, commanding the *Graf Zeppelin*.

Before Kahn returned to America, he made a brief unexplained visit alone to Ramsgate on the southeast coast of England, where he spent a night at the Granville Hotel. A feature of the Granville was its spa facilities - it had twenty-five different types of baths, including Turkish. Staying at the hotel were Sir Robert and Lady Fox Symons, Sir William Crawford, Lady Ashfield, The Hon. Grace Lowrey Stanley, The Hon. Ada Cunliffe-Lister, and The Hon. Mrs. H. Huntsman.[74] Did Otto visit this relatively small seaside resort for business, pleasure, or health, or did he spend the evening with a lady friend? He journeyed southwest to Southampton the following day, where he boarded RMS *Olympic* to return to New York. Accompanying Otto on the crossing was his trusted valet, Frederick Cooper.

The day after the *Olympic* set sail, the British press reported that twelve of the passengers collectively were purported to be worth one thousand million dollars.[75] Most of the dozen mentioned, headed by Otto Kahn, were members of New York's elite 'Four Hundred' (not to be confused with the Gilded Age 'Four Hundred'). They represented many of the new world's vast money-making enterprises: steel magnates, publishers, builders, as well as bankers, and lawyers.

When Otto stepped ashore at New York Harbor, he was told of the disastrous impact the September 17 hurricane had left on the Florida coastline and inland at Lake Okeechobee, causing catastrophic damage to property and land and claiming considerable loss of life. The Kahns' oceanfront villa withstood the storm and sustained only superficial damage. However, their neighbors, the Replogles, were not so lucky; their house and grounds took a terrific battering, causing the uprooting of many trees and shrubbery.

Americana

One of the most inspiring things about living in such a cosmopolitan city as New York was the ability to absorb artistic influences from an array of diverse cultures. It was from this melting pot Roger pulled inspiration for *Americana*.

Roger had been working on his *Americana* concept for several years: arranging melodies from old American gospel songs and reworking them within the framework of a symphony. When the writer and producer Joseph Patrick McEvoy offered Roger the commission to compose the entire score for a new edition of a musical revue he had produced on Broadway two years earlier titled *Americana*, Roger was hesitant at first to accept the job.

His assignment for *Americana* came on the heels of *Here's Howe!* closing. Perhaps he felt it was too early for him to jump straight into another Broadway show. Or, given the circumstances, maybe it was the best thing for him. The fact that McEvoy had named his revue *Americana* was too much of a coincidence for Roger to ignore. He signed the contract. Work on the score commenced immediately.

With a book written by McEvoy, *Americana* had previously been staged at the Belmont Theatre in 1926, where it ran for a healthy couple of seasons, playing 224 performances. The score nurtured the Gershwin brothers song *'That Lost Barber Shop Chord.'* When the show folded in February 1927, McEvoy was particularly saddened by its fate, especially as it had been his big stab at producing a hit show. Undeterred, the author believed the concept still had gas in its tank; hence, one of the reasons why he roped in Roger.

A year and a half later, a new adaptation, totally overhauled, with a fresh score, updated choreography, and additional dialog, was the vision McEvoy was now selling to the public and press. McEvoy was known to be a bag of wind at the best of times. On this occasion, the media gave him the benefit of their doubt. Broadway serenely awaited the outcome.

For his second edition of *Americana*, McEvoy gathered around him a talented crew; Dutch set designer and art director Hermann Rosse, costume designer John Held Jr., and the popular cartoonist Rube Goldberg.[76] Roger had watched the growing success of *Blackbirds* with great interest. The cast in *Americana* was to have a Black and a white chorus. The singer and composer J. Rosamond Johnson would lead the Black ensemble. It was this concept that contributed to Roger accepting the commission.

Rehearsals were fraught with tension due mainly to the fact that McEvoy had total control over the whole production. The buck stopped with him. A newsreel shot during rehearsals and shown in New York picture houses ahead of *Americana*'s Broadway premiere gave a rose-tinted glimpse of what the public could expect.[77] The reality was somewhat different.

Joseph Patrick McEvoy wrote plays, revues, books, and other literary material for a living - most fetchingly, the sentiments inside greetings cards. Uncharacteristically, he resembled a prizefighter, or perhaps a wrestler. He was quite an imposing figure in Broadway circles. You either liked him or loathed him; there was no middle ground. When he spoke, his hectic mop of unruly hair flew in all directions, and his tremendous mustache wobbled. Wearing his trademark trilby, with a Havana cigar perched permanently between his lips, he could just as easily have passed for a gangster. Yet, beneath the brim of his hat, he possessed the kindest eyes many people had ever gazed into. He first made a name for himself writing *The Potters* newspaper serial published in several hundred dailies across America.[78] The series ran successfully for seven years. His stage productions had been relatively profitable, but he was still hoping to strike gold with a whopping, big hit. His latest literary offering *Show Girl* had received pretty good reviews, and some critics believed he was on a 'roll.' Even Florenz Ziegfeld Jr. hired him to write comedy skits for his *Follies* revues. Ziegfeld stated McEvoy loved his own jokes so much he would steal a bow to audience hisses.

McEvoy's comedy was very much the humor of the day, satirizing the many ridiculous customs of everyday Americans. He exploited this vein heavily in his previous *Americana* production, enticing the public to pay for the privilege to laugh at themselves. Reports claimed the theater management once evicted him from the auditorium during one of his shows for laughing so loudly at his own jokes.

The 1928 edition of *Americana* had a three-week tryout in Boston at the Colonial Theatre, where the comments were favorable.[79] Takings at the box office hit $18,000 in its first week.[80] The general agreement was that it had a good chance of going over big. *Variety* thought 'the show has the makings of a good revue with some minor recasting and the addition of more talent, but there is a lot to go out.'[81]

While the show was playing out of town, Roger killed time by offering to help Nassau County Police Force with their air search for a fugitive gunman. The man they were after was Howard Abrams, who, the police believed, had attempted to murder his wife, Helen, with a bullet.[82] The incident took place on October 15. Abrams was the proprietor of the Twentieth Century Lodge roadhouse near Huntington on Long Island. Since the shooting, the culprit had been on the run. Roger flew his biplane low over the wooded terrain on Long Island to help flush the gunman out. After almost two weeks of the cops scouring Long Island, Abrams finally surrendered at Flatbush Avenue railroad station.[83]

Roger's 21st birthday came and went without the hullaballoo many of the tabloids had anticipated. No million-dollar endowment was presented to him by his father or mother. Nor was there any extravagant party for the media to pick over the carcass of like vultures the following day. Instead, Roger had more important things to occupy his mind and time, primarily taking care of any last-minute orchestral arrangements for the score of his latest Broadway offering.

Americana opened on Broadway on Tuesday, October 30, at Lew Fields' Mansfield Theatre. Although the press termed it a 'revival,' it was an entirely original production, with new comedy skits and a specially written score. Celebrities turned out in force to witness its launch; *Variety* reviewer Arthur Pollock noted Fanny Brice off to the left and Otto Kahn to the right.[84] During the show, Texas Guinan, who was also in the audience, saw herself satirized by a 'talking' dummy and appeared to enjoy it.

Roger delivered some cracking tunes: '*Life as a Twosome,*' '*Young Black Joe,*' '*He's Mine,*' and the oddly titled novelty '*The Ameri-Can-Can,*' a take on the French Can-Can. Once again, Irving Caesar collaborated with Kahn and supplied lyrics for many of the songs. '*Life as a Twosome*' was cherry-picked from *Here's Howe!* It was one of the songs from the production that everyone agreed had been rashly overlooked during its initial airing.

In an attempt to cut costs, McEvoy produced and directed the entire show and cast no big draw names in any roles. The most noteworthy cast members were Frances Gershwin (George and Ira's sister) in her Broadway debut, the Black vocalist J. Rosamond Johnson, dancer Joe Donahue, and the Roger Wolfe Kahn Orchestra playing in the pit. A surprising late addition to the cast was the Williams Sisters, who had recently featured with Paul Ash and His Orchestra in the stage revue *Parisian Nights* at New York's Paramount Theatre.[85]

Sketches parodying Prohibition were common practice in revues, and *Americana* delivered several. First-night reviewers labeled them 'mediocre.' Though various cast members came in for criticism, 'there were some fine moments' from J. Rosamond Johnson, Joe Donahue, and the Kahn Orchestra. The novel touch of having two large choruses, one African American and the other Caucasian, was also praised. However, the novelty of having actors on roller skates during a satire based on Eugene O'Neill's *Strange Interlude* said more about the low-cost production value than the added value to the show.

Fate, and predominantly the lousy reviews, took its toll almost instantly. Although numerous critics implied the cast was just not up to scratch, perhaps upon reflection, McEvoy had to admit the show's failure fell upon his broad shoulders and had been all too hurriedly put together.

Events came to a head backstage the following Monday afternoon. Bearing in mind McEvoy's heavy build and Roger's scrawniness, the confrontation took on the manner of a heated exchange of words rather than an all-out bout of fisticuffs.[86] The outcome was decisive; McEvoy quit *Americana* there and then without any financial compensation and gave Roger consent to do as he saw fit with the show. Roger had a memo pinned to the backstage noticeboard informing the cast that due to a dispute among the producers, from immediate effect, the show would close. *Americana* shut on Monday 5 November after playing only five days and seven performances on Broadway.[87]

When Mike Mindlin's Little Carnegie Playhouse opened its doors on November 2 at Roger's former nightclub, newspapers praised it for being one of the most delightful little theaters in the country.[88] Featured on the screen that day was the Soviet silent movie *Ten Days That Shook the World*, directed by Sergei Eisenstein. 'It is clever, but a bore,' claimed critic Mordaunt Hall in his *New York Times* review. The film celebrated the tenth anniversary of the 1917 October Revolution that overthrew the Kerensky Government. Although the art-house movie theater was named the Little Carnegie Playhouse, Mindlin had enlarged the interior. It now incorporated a splendid Art Deco auditorium and foyer, courtesy of the renowned Viennese designers and exponents of modernistic decoration, Wolfgang Hoffmann and his wife, Pola. Gone were the glass tables, mirror dance floor, parrot cages, goldfish bowls, and palm trees; in their place were row upon row of plush silver and black velvet seating, 409 seats in all. Opposite the Playhouse at 145 West 57th Street, as if to complement it, opened a new café, the Russian Art Chocolate and Russian Tea Room owned by Vienna-born ballet dancer Albertina Rasch.*

Otto was a dependable Republican voter and had contributed financially to the party for many years.[89] His allegiance to its leader and candidate for the 36th quadrennial presidential election, Herbert

Hoover, was assured. That said, Kahn was not a blind Republican loyalist, and during the 1928 campaign, openly aired his preference for the repeal of Prohibition.

In a letter Kahn wrote in response to an irate critic, in which Kahn defends his personal beliefs, the banker puts across some convincing reasons for his enduring support of Herbert Hoover.

'My sympathies are, and have long been, with the liberal and progressive element in politics. I would not knowingly vote for a reactionary. In 1920, Mr. Hoover was hailed by leading spokesmen for the progressive cause as the man best fitted for the presidency. While cautious of speech, reticent in promise, averse to resounding professions, he is the same wisely constructive liberal and humanitarian now that he was then, additionally qualified by eight years of governmental experience. If there be any who will vote for him in the expectation of a stand pat administration, they greatly mistake the man.'

'As I view the elements of the situation, including particularly the platform declarations of the two parties, I fail to see any valid reason why you should expect me, or any other Republican, though fully appreciating the merits and the vigorous, colorful, attractive, personality of Governor [Al] Smith, and though opposed to Volsteadism, to depart from usual party affiliations in the forthcoming presidential election.'[90]

In late October, Otto made a brief visit to Washington, D.C., where on the 25th, he breakfasted with Herbert Hoover at Hoover's home. After the meeting, Kahn declared to the waiting press corps his support of the Republican nominee as the man who can bring about prosperity 'benefitting all the people.'[91]

Voting took place on November 6.

Hoover won overwhelmingly, securing forty of the forty-eight states.

In some respects, *Americana* had been Roger's dream as much as McEvoy's. Because Roger received genuinely favorable reviews for his score, he felt encouraged enough to salvage the production. In doing this, he turned to the show's musical director Don Voorhees for assistance on the proviso that Roger could secure financial backing to restage it.[92] *Variety* claimed McEvoy had sold the show to young Kahn. Roger and Otto denied it and maintained that a new revue with a new producer was underway. McEvoy stated he had spent $30,000 cash on *Americana* before it appeared on stage and assured everyone the production had no outstanding debts. What Roger was unaware of, that would later come to light, was that his father had loaned McEvoy the initial $30,000 to stage the show.[93] *

Roger did not intend to sink his capital into the venture. To this intent, he consulted his brother Gilbert, who put out feelers to try and dig up interest downtown in Wall Street where the money was. Gilbert came up trumps. The finance was guaranteed.

In remodeling the show, Roger drew some of his inspiration from Lew Leslie. The new edition would have Black and white performers, although not in a strict 50/50 ratio. The whole caboodle was conceived, rehearsed, and put through its paces in two weeks. Roger roped in comedian Julius Tannen to emcee on a percentage and salary basis and hired comic writer 'Bugs' Baer to pen new sketches. Kahn's orchestra remained on the payroll. Several recruits joined the cast: actresses Ula Sharon, Frances Shelley, and Virginia Watson, dancer Carl Randall, and the comedian 'Bozo' Snyder. Tellingly, the Williams Sisters remained. After a rushed rehearsal, the show played three nights in Springfield before its Broadway induction.

On November 23, the news that Thomas Fortune Ryan, aged 77, had died hit the headlines. His grandson John and granddaughter-in-law Margaret were at the Ryan mansion at 858 Fifth Avenue when the great man passed away.[94] The Virginia-born traction and tobacco tycoon was reckoned to be America's 10th richest man and left an estate valued at $141 million.[95] *

New Americana

New Americana flew in on the tailwind of Blackbirds of 1928 and opened on November 29 at the Liberty Theatre. Blackbirds had only recently vacated the Liberty and transferred to the Eltinge Theatre next door. New Americana and Blackbirds were, literally, playing head-to-head.

Sadly for the cast of New Americana, the Blackbirds' magic did not rub off on them; the following day's notices were abysmal. A scathing review in the Brooklyn Daily Eagle penned by Arthur Pollock left no doubt in the reader's mind exactly which side of the starting block New Americana sat. He kicked off by likening the shows 'virtue of being unconventional, informal, sympathetic' to being 'rather like something thrown together hurriedly to give someone a good time.'

He then advised, 'informal revues are best when original, and the original sections of this one are not numerous enough (nor original enough) to stand out against the banalities with which the thing is splashed.'[96] As for the cast: Tannen chatted and had wit. Randall danced, well. Sharon danced too. The Williams Sisters took inspiration from the actress Zelma O'Neal in her role as Flo in the musical comedy *Good News*. 'Bozo' Snyder clowned gracefully, though it was difficult for Pollock to judge why he wasn't funnier, and the Roger Wolfe Kahn Orchestra wrapped the whole package up with tunes that were 'good enough.' He also noted that Roger was not out front leading his men; Don Voorhees was. In the Graphic, the acting Mayor of Broadway, Walter Winchell, ranted, 'not a good show,' and the *Telegram* matched his sentiment, 'misses the mark six times out of seven.'[97]

New Americana had stiff competition from *Blackbirds*, *Hello*, *Show Boat*, and *The Three Musketeers*.

Variety, in their summary, praised Kahn's score as being the most notable feature of the whole production,[98] as did the reviewer from *Brooklyn Life*: 'Roger Wolfe Kahn's orchestration was the best part of the show, and the entr'acte, where each player had a little solo of his own, was very effective.'[99]

Did *New Americana* suffer the same outcome as its ill-fated sister?

Yes. Even the famous ticket 'King' Joe Leblang at his Times Square discount ticket agency could not shift tickets for the show. Roger must have watched in awe at the crowds flocking nightly next door into the Eltinge Theatre where *Blackbirds of 1928* was selling out. Where was he going wrong? He could not fathom it out.

New Americana was, if nothing else, magnificent in its brevity and bit the dust on December 5 after only seven performances, giving barely enough time for the public to decry it. It was a huge, personal blow for Roger, a defeat he took deeply to heart.[100] If anything, *Blackbirds'* success was an index to where he was going wrong, only at this moment in time Roger was not in the right frame of mind to see it.

Being judged so harshly by the media cannot have been easy for Roger to stomach, especially at such a young age. Roger's escape was to fly his plane and disappear for hours. If not in his plane, he would drive across Long Island in one of his fast automobiles. Such irrational behavior was as worrying for his parents as it was for his friends. Roger had yet to come to terms with the fact that life was a succession of human failures, and it's the knocks and how he took them that would turn the boy into a man.

Whether in a stab of frustration at the old dinosaur the Met had become, or purely to ruffle a few dusty feathers among the short-sighted bureaucrats that now controlled it, Otto claimed the regular operatic repertoire had grown terribly rusty.[101] His one operatic exception was Giuseppe Verdi's *Ernani*, due to a particular melodic attractiveness and some brilliancies of orchestration. Perhaps his loyalty to the grand dame of Broadway was beginning to wear thin. His commitment to it had unquestionably taken a plunge.

'Broadway Legits in Panic' ran the front-page headline in *Variety* on their December 12 issue. 'Business Shot, But Few Hold Up.'

It had been the worst season in years for musicals and dramas along the Great White Way, with presentations tumbling like dominos. Twenty-five theaters were already dark, despite the tricky Christmas spell looming ahead when more shows would likely follow suit.

Business dropped so noticeably after Thanksgiving that theater managers went into a blind panic and jointly decided radical action was needed. The Shubert Organization led the flow by announcing their houses would temporarily remain dark and reopen for the more lucrative Christmas week, prompting several other theaters to adopt the same principle. Another ten productions shut voluntarily to cut costs and vouched they would reopen over the yuletide holiday. According to Equity rules, attractions may lay off the week before Christmas without salary liability.

It seemed ironic that of all the times Roger should launch a new show, he chose one of the worst seasons Broadway had ever suffered. In hindsight, it could well have been viewed economically as a litmus paper of what lay ahead; only that melodrama had yet to unfold.

Some might have claimed Roger was cocooned in a privileged world of wealth that gave him a clouded vision of reality. On the contrary, he knew the value of a buck as well as anyone. Roger ended the year in the red, slightly up on the previous year, to the sum of $210,000.[102] *New Americana* had not proved to be the lifeline he had banked upon either artistically or financially. Yes, it transpired his father had underwritten the show, but Roger had every intention of paying back his father every dollar.

To help reduce some of his debt, Roger set out on a brief vaudeville tour. Being a Kahn, he had certain provisos added to his contract. He turned down the offer of an out-of-town engagement guaranteeing $3,500 a week from Keith's, stating he preferred to stay around New York.[103] To that avail, Kahn and his eponymous orchestra set off on a manic sprint around the metropolis, performing two shows a night, alternating in different theaters. The tour took wing on December 30 when he played the first half of the program in Flushing[104] and then, after a mad dash across town, performed on the second half of the bill at the Coliseum. It was a calculated move to double his fee. Roger also arranged for the Williams Sisters to appear on the bill as a featured act.

Over the past few months, Hannah Williams had slowly, without fuss, worked her way back into Roger's good books. Whether Addie and Otto were quite as accepting and forgiving of the impulsive young girl was still very much a matter open for debate.

12

HOT DEPRESSION JAZZ

'Roger Wolfe Kahn and His Orchestra have just returned to vaudeville and will be heard in a rousing program of modern music with special arrangements and novel effects. Featured with his band are the Williams Sisters, personable and talented singers and steppers.'[1]

1929

*V*ariety asked, 'Was it worth the experience?'[2] The entertainment weekly referred to the $500,000 loss Roger and Otto had collectively incurred during the past five years since Roger had been active in show business. 'That 500 grand is well-nigh a pittance alongside of the Kahn family fortune,' was, the paper assured its readers, a reasonable amount to pay for such an experience. Whether Otto and Roger agreed, *Variety* failed to mention.

The article did reveal that Roger and his orchestra would be making an appearance at New York's prestigious Palace Theatre, where the

bandleader planned to present a self-contained show complete with
a supporting cast that would include the affable Williams Sisters.

Victor dropped two new recordings from Roger in January, *'A Room
With A View'* and *'Dance, Little Lady.'* 'Some intricate brass work
punctuates the orchestrations,'[3] noted *Variety*, and were an excellent
testament of Roger's arranging skills. Once again, Franklyn Baur took
command of the microphone. On *'A Room With A View'* violinist Joe
Venuti elegantly stole the number from under everyone's nose
during his meandering 8-bar solo. Both tunes arrived from Noël
Coward's joyful West End revue, *This Year of Grace*, which had
recently transferred over the pond to Broadway. These would be
Roger's penultimate recordings on the Victor label. Roger ranked as
one of Victor's top-selling artists.[4] His record deal had favored Victor,
not Roger. Now that his three-year contract was coming to an end,
Roger had decided not to renew it when it expired in April. Roger
was determined to get a larger slice of the profits from any future
record contract he signed.

Due to the strong public interest in Roger, his manager George
Lottman segued more dates into Roger's current tour; appearances at
the E. F. Albee in Brooklyn, the Fordham, the Flushing, and a return
to the Coliseum were all confirmed for January.

Playing such a tight schedule was a career move Roger had
stubbornly fought against over the past year after the last tour had
left him physically exhausted. The band's outing at the E. F. Albee
debuted on Sunday, January 6. They shared the bill with the feature

movie *Captain Swagger*.[5] On opening night, things did not go to plan. Roger came down with a high temperature and a fever. He'd contracted a nasty bout of influenza. His physician immediately ordered him to remain in bed.[6] On Monday, the Albee Theatre announced the Kahn unit had canceled due to illness.[7] The rest of the tour was postponed and hastily rearranged for the coming weeks.

Influenza hit Roger hard. He spent the next two weeks cooped up in his apartment existing on a diet of home-cooked soup prepared by his mother's cook, with only his German Shepherd dog Peter of Forkland to keep him company. His illness could not have come at a worse time.

Neither were his parents around to offer hands-on support or to help cheer him up. They were vacationing in sunny Palm Beach at Oheka Cottage with their daughter Margaret and son-in-law John Ryan Jr. The Kahns had invited Lady Diana Duff Cooper (who was en route to Nassau) and Prince Dmitri of Russia as houseguests. The supreme Russian monarchist's council had recently chosen Prince Dmitri's brother Prince Nikita as emperor and successor of the late Czar Nicholas II.[8]

During the visit, Otto went deep-sea fishing for the first time after being encouraged to give it a try by his son-in-law John Ryan Jr. Whether it was beginners' luck or indicative of Otto's skills as a fisherman, he caught the largest kingfish ever plucked from Palm Beach waters, weighing in at a whopping forty pounds and eight ounces.[9] The fish gave Otto a mammoth struggle lasting one hour and nineteen minutes before he finally landed it unaided on the boat's deck using a five-ounce tip and nine-thread line.

Otto's remarkable catch instantly made him into something of a celebrity among local fishing clubs and fishing enthusiasts. As news of his sizable catch spread further afield via newsprint, offers of fishing club memberships speedily arrived through his letterbox in their dozens.

'We are picking our members. We want the cream of Who's Who in America,' wrote the Palm Beach Sailfish Club president in his letter inviting Otto to apply for membership. The club advertised itself as 'the most exclusive sports club in the world.' Otto must have been thrilled with the invitation, for not only did he immediately join, but he also used his influence to help provide mortgage financing for the club's subsequent expansions. Otto also donated a silver trophy cup, which he attached his name to, for the winner of the annual Sailfish Derby Division Competition.

As the following week dragged on, Roger could bear lying in bed no longer and rallied his musicians to recommence their tour. On Monday, January 14, the unit appeared at the Flushing Keith Theatre in a program containing a mixed bag of variety acts. Irene Ricardo (a singing comedienne) appeared in the first half, trailed by Maharan and Big Rosie (a novelty turn featuring the only trained wild elephant on the American stage.) Roger and his orchestra appeared in the show's second half after Maharan had safely returned the elephant to its enclosure.[10] The Kahn unit then moved on to the E. F. Albee Theater in Brooklyn for a week's engagement from Sunday the 20th.[11] By the time the band hit the stage, they were firing on all cylinders. They proved so popular that the booker extended their contract for a further week.

Roger also received the encouraging news that his song 'Imagination' (co-written with Meyer and Caesar) had been slotted into the current London production of the musical comedy *Funny Face*, starring Fred and Adele Astaire.[12]

The winter season in Palm Beach lasted around six weeks, after which the resort would hibernate. The lockdown occurred straight after George Washington's birthday on February 22, whereafter only the caretakers of the large estates would remain. This year Otto returned to New York earlier than usual. His family and houseguests - *New York Herald Tribune* proprietor Ogden Reid and his wife Helen

- remained in Palm Beach. Kahn had several Broadway premieres to attend and various business matters to arrange. His decision was ill-timed. No sooner did he arrive back at his cavernous, draughty Fifth Avenue mansion than he too came down with a bout of influenza and a high fever.[13] His physician ordered him to remain housebound for the coming week. Although Kahn's condition was thought not to be too serious, his physician still arranged for two nurses working 12-hour shifts to be on 24-hour duty at the Kahn abode.[14]

In a letter Otto wrote from New York to his daughter Margaret in Palm Beach, mailed just after her first wedding anniversary, he pines: 'I should love to be with you in the pink palazzo by the southern sea, but there is really no sense your being in this relentless city because during the day the evil spell of the office claims me.'[15]

On the evening of Saturday, February 9, Paramount Famous Lasky Corporation brought Hollywood's glitz and glamor to New York with their presentation of the eighth annual charity Motion Picture Ball at the Hotel Astor.[16] Appropriately, the evening's entertainment highlighted various stars of the silver screen: Ruth Etting, Irene Delroy, Nancy Carroll, and Richard Dix. Emcee was Paul Ash.[17] Roger, and his band (renamed 'Society Serenaders' for the occasion), provided the musical accompaniment. Having Roger perform at such an event was tremendously good PR for the bandleader and the Kahn family, especially as Roger was now airing strong desires for developing a career as a film composer.

Throughout February, New York's weather was relentlessly cold. During the second week of the month, broken boilers, failed electrics, and a coal shortage lowered temperatures further. On Monday, February 11, Roger and his orchestra breezed into the Palace Theatre in Times Square for a week's engagement sharing top billing with husband-and-wife team Frank Fay and Barbara Stanwyck. It was his third appearance at the famed venue in as many years. Its impact on the Kahn band and its maestro was resoundingly uplifting. Roger's popularity was still immense. Evening shows sold out regularly. It was heartening for him to behold, especially on home turf.

Roger's setlist at the Palace contained rhythmic dance numbers aimed more at night-clubbers than at a sit-down vaudeville audience. *Variety* wondered why this should be, as Kahn could well have put across a more 'suitable' performance tailored specifically for a vaudeville show. Nonetheless, Roger was insistent his musicians play as if they were performing at a club. 'The musical excellence and Kahn's direction were there,' assured the critic, but he still questioned why Roger was so adamant at delivering such a fast tempo set.[18] The big surprise, revealed the critic, was 'to see the cute and shifty Williams girls flop.' Such is life! The Williams Sisters had an attack of nerves. It was, after all, their first appearance at the hallowed Palace. *Variety* summed up the Kahn production with the recommendation that Roger finds an additional supporting act apart from the Williams Sisters and ditches the syncopated rhythms in the larger venues. What the reviewer failed to take on board was the fact that Roger was maturing. He was now aged twenty-one and, as such, was playing music that appealed to him, tailored for a more musically sophisticated audience.

On Tuesday, WEAF radio hooked up with RKO to present an hour-long live broadcast from the Palace stage. The program aired from 11 p.m. to midnight and gave listeners a flavor of what to expect if they came to see the show.[19] Roger and his band were allotted the longest airtime of all the acts appearing (twelve minutes, divided into three sections) and kicked off with a current favorite, '*She's Funny That Way.*'[20] Roger remained true to form and delivered up-tempo renditions of all his numbers. The Williams Sisters reprieved themselves admirably after their hiccup the previous evening by offering a splendid a cappella version of '*I Can't Give You Anything but Love, Baby,*' swiped from *Blackbirds* score. Two musicians from Kahn's band played an original composition of their own titled '*Wild-Cat.*' Before the hour reached twelve, Roger and his orchestra committed a cracking rendition of '*Crazy Rhythm*' to get the radio listeners dancing in their pajamas.[21]

Stutz-Bellanca Airplane Corporation

When the announcement came in mid-February that Harry C. Stutz (former president and general manager of the Stutz Motor Car Company) and Ralph Bellanca (designer and aeronautical engineer) were to form the Stutz-Bellanca Airplane Corporation, few people could have imagined the growth and impact aviation would have over the coming decades. The new company would manufacture private and airbus aircraft designed by Bellanca, powered by Stutz air-cooled airplane engines built at Bridgeport, Connecticut, and Orlando, Florida.[22]

The news was of particular interest and importance to Roger, for he was one of the principal shareholders of Bellanca Aircraft Corporation, based in Newcastle, Delaware. It was at this plant that

Ralph Bellanca had been the in-house production and experimental engineer. That company would now fold. The new company would operate from Bridgeport at the Commercial Aircraft Corporation of America plant, where Bellanca would take on the position of vice president, and Harry C. Stutz would become president. Production of the new Stutz-Bellanca planes would start immediately.

Setting The Record Straight

'Becoming a successful jazz leader was no cinch,' insisted Roger in a full-page interview in the *Brooklyn Daily Eagle*.[23] The article was part of a series the newspaper was running, focusing on young men who had gone against their families' wishes and made good. 'People seem to think that because my father is rich and influential, my career was just one rose-strewn path and that all I had to do was to announce my intention to organize an orchestra, and in a jiffy, everything was arranged. Such people believe that it is absolutely impossible for a rich man's son to have any difficulties whatever. Speaking from experience, I can assure them they are all wrong.'

Roger may have upset the family tradition by not going into the banking profession, but by following his instincts and becoming a successful bandleader, he put to rest all the naysayers that from the offset derided his decision. Undoubtedly, his father's money and influence had been a safety net with regards to financial institutions loaning him money, but Roger made sure he settled every cent of such loans. The debts he and his father had jointly sustained more recently were the result of failed ventures.

In some respects, his father's initial disparaging of jazz had spurred him on, as if to prove his father was wrong.

Ever since President Coolidge invited Roger and his orchestra to play at the Inaugural Ball four years ago in Washington, D.C., Otto's opinion of jazz and his son's career had changed considerably. Otto now readily encouraged Roger in his chosen profession. By giving this interview to the *Brooklyn Daily Eagle*, Roger intended to set the record straight. 'He could not see my point,' claims Roger. 'I was only [sixteen] at the time, and I guess a little impetuous.' Happily, for Roger, he admits the day he finished paying back the loan to his dad was a real turning point in his life. 'I felt then that the fight I had made to support my convictions was at last justified.'

Concerning his future goals in music, Roger had this to say. 'I expect some time in the future to concentrate my attention on composing, because I feel that the only way jazz can permanently establish itself is by being furnished with the proper sort of music through which to express those qualities, which are peculiarly its own life, vitality and rhythm.'

Just as the interview was about to wind up, Roger added earnestly, 'Jazz has a future, and I intend to tie up my future to it.'

Dangerous Days For The Dollar

During the 1920s, Otto was estimated to be worth around $160 million at his financial peak. Over at the Stock Exchange in Wall Street, something was stirring. The market had recently shown indications of the jitters, sudden drops, only to regain losses the following day. It was difficult to ascertain who was taking note of these little signals because most dealers were still merrily going about their business, showing little concern. Shares were booming. The Dow Jones was singing. For some, however, the stock market was getting a bit too greedy. Tensions were beginning to rise that something on the horizon might be amiss.

Moreover, the boom had come off the back of borrowed money. Without margin to maneuver, the market would collapse. These were dangerous days for the dollar.

Who was listening? Who was taking note?

On Friday, March 22, the stock market had a severe case of nerves. Suddenly, all eyes turned to the Federal Reserve Board in Washington, D.C., for reassurance. They had the power to curb borrowing. Unbeknown to the public, the Board had tacitly been monitoring the market day after day, carefully observing, but, for some unexplained reason, had issued no official statements or warnings. Thankfully the weekend arrived, giving the market time to rest and settle down again.

On the contrary, the respite gave shareholders time to reassess their investments. Many got cold feet.

Come Monday 25th, a significant number of investors took heed of their intuition and began to sell. Blue-chip shares fell considerably below the 10 percent down payment margin required to purchase stock, which in theory meant they lost their down payment. Any investor wanting to hold onto stock had to make an additional down payment. By Tuesday, millions of investors found themselves sinking fast. Dealers felt compelled to sell stock to keep afloat. If an investor could not secure an extra loan, they lost their investment. The more stock dealers sold, the lower the price fell. With so many borrowers requiring hard cash, interest rates rose to 20 percent, leaving those hit hardest in the impossible situation of putting themselves further in debt. The market had only one end in sight, collapse.

Suddenly, like a knight in nickel-plated armor, Charlie Mitchell, Governor of the National City Bank, announced his bank would provide $25 million of credit to help soothe the market. However, attached to his offer, he added the fateful words 'whatever the Federal Reserve Board thinks.'[24] The Fed did not take kindly to Mitchell's intrusion and took it as a direct slap across the face, leaving many to believe the Board should have acted quicker.

Mitchell's intervention did the trick; within 24 hours, the market rallied. Interest rates on short-term loans (call money) fell from 20 to 8 percent, halting the panic. Mitchell may have singlehandedly averted a crash, but the warning signs remained. For the time being, the stock market got back to its day-to-day business of buying and selling stock, but the undercurrents of things not being quite right in the American economy persisted.

A Libel Writ

On Friday, March 29, Otto slipped quietly out of New York Harbor on board the *Île de France* bound for Europe with two security guards positioned outside his stateroom.[25] He declined to give any statement to the waiting press at the quayside, nor did he pose for any photographs on deck. Instead, Kahn went straight to his quarters, where he remained until the ship had left Upper Bay and entered open water.

A week later, on the exact day that Otto arrived at Claridge's Hotel in London, American-born coloratura soprano Rosalinda Morini boldly announced to the press that she had commenced a libel action against Otto Kahn claiming $250,000 damages.

The issue came about after Morini placed an advertisement in the *Musical Courier* (in the hope of attracting future concert bookings). She claimed Otto had described her voice as 'one of the most beautiful voices I have ever heard.'[26] Kahn's quote was said to have originated after he and Gatti-Casazza heard the singer audition at Carnegie Hall the previous year. However, Otto could not remember whether she had been given a hearing and denied ever making any comment. Morini ignored Otto's denial and subsequently billed herself as 'one of the greatest singers of all time,'[27] using Kahn's alleged 'quote' to boost her reputation.

The press latched on to the story and printed Kahn's denial. As a result of Kahn's rebuttal, Morini claimed her career had significantly suffered through her subsequent loss of work. She was now facing bankruptcy.[28] The plaintiff had sought an order for Kahn's arrest. In anticipation of such an event taking place aboard the liner on which Otto was traveling, a deputy sheriff had boarded carrying bail bonds should they be required. Although Morini's lawyer had filed sealed papers in the Supreme Court, no warrant of civil arrest arrived. Otto sailed without being detained.[29]

It came as no surprise to Otto or his family when news of the writ appeared splashed across the newspapers.[30] Otto had received a discreet tip-off and, as such, had acted accordingly to help minimize the damage to his and his family's good name. Hence, he timed his departure from the U.S. to coincide with the release of the news.

Otto emphatically hated it when companies or individuals (without his consent) used his name to further their own goals. Everyone acquainted with Otto and his family knew this. Morini's persistence in doing so provoked Kahn's response. He issued a retraction printed in the *Musical Courier* in which he protested against the use of his name in advertisements endorsing Miss Morini's voice. His letter dated February 1 read:

'My attention has been called to an advertisement of Rosalinda Morini, which says, 'One of the most beautiful voices I have ever heard - Otto H. Kahn, Metropolitan Grand Opera Company.' I wish to say that the statement attributed to me, that Miss Morini had one of the most beautiful voices I have ever heard, was never made by me. In fact, to the best of my recollection, I made no comment on Miss Morini's vocal qualifications on the one and only occasion when I heard her sing. I certainly never authorized her or anyone else to quote me as having expressed an opinion concerning her.'[31]

Kahn also protested against her use of the Met's name after his own. This usage, he purported, was 'evidently intended to exploit for Miss Morini's benefit the name of the Metropolitan Grand Opera Company, with which Miss Morini has no connection whatever.'

It was this letter Morini was using as the basis of her defamation case against Kahn.[32]

Unfortunately for Otto, even though he was out of the country, the matter did not disappear. Misleading advertisements and fake criticisms were the basis of the libel writ. Who said what, and was what was said expressed with honesty or pity? The 26-year-old singer was stepping on dangerous ground, especially with the legal team Kahn had behind him. Nathan Burkan, attorney for Kahn, had only one thing to say publicly: 'There is no basis for this suit.'[33]

After Otto's letter of retraction was published, Morini claimed that doubt seeped into the public's mind, and engagements were not forthcoming, hence her 'malicious libel' suit. Neither side would back down, and over the next couple of years, the case dragged on unremittingly before it reached any conclusion, and in the process, added more stress to Kahn's already pressured life. Morini milked the case and the subsequent press coverage for every dollar's worth of publicity she could get. Proving just how highly regarded Kahn's opinion was and how careers were built and destroyed upon it.

'The frown of the man who is [the] overlord of the Metropolitan has reduced me to a position where I find it difficult to obtain even mediocre engagements,' declared Morini, who claimed her startling testimony would 'shock the musical world.'[34]

The summons had yet to be served upon Otto; hence the two security guards now shadowing his every move. For the time being, Otto intended to keep it that way. 'Mr. Kahn, who left a week ago for Europe, naturally could not be asked for his version of the case. London dispatches say he has gone into seclusion there!'[35] When Kahn did consent to speak to one reporter about the writ, the only rejoinder he uttered was, 'I have nothing to say.'[36]

The only statement forthcoming on Kahn's behalf came from a Kuhn, Loeb representative at their New York office. He confirmed Kahn was on a tour of Europe seeking new talent for the Metropolitan Opera Company.[37]

On May 11, Justice Peters in the Supreme Court reversed a decision on a motion of counsel made by Kahn's defense to dismiss the complaint.

A few days before Morini announced her libel writ, and just as concerning for Otto, was a report in the papers that opera singer Lydia Lindgren had brought about a $250,000 slander suit against Metropolitan Opera singer Mme. Julia Claussen. Lindgren's counsel, Robert E. Dempsey, confirmed his client would attest in her evidence the names of several wealthy and prominent men whom she allegedly states had improper close 'relationships' with her.[38] Claussen had purportedly instigated a whispering campaign against Lindgren over a six-year period that had resulted in Lindgren being driven into early retirement, suffering an inferiority complex, and bringing about her attempted suicide by drinking poison. Such scandal was not the kind of publicity the Metropolitan Opera Company coveted, nor was it good news personally for Otto.

To add to Otto and Addie's worries, on April 12, gossip columnist Walter Winchell of the *New York Evening Graphic* noted in his editorial that 'Otto Kahn's boy Roger has told intimates he intends eloping with Hannah Williams.' That Roger should even contemplate having a romantic interest with a showgirl, let alone a coal miner's daughter, was the last thing his parents wanted to hear.

Thankfully for the elder Kahns, the Williams Sisters were presently out of town playing vaudeville dates in Cambridge, Massachusetts, followed by an engagement in Des Moines, Iowa, and would not be returning to New York City any time soon.

From Nightclubs to Flying Clubs

Now that Roger's vaudeville tour had ended, he had more time to devote to his aviation activities. Several Broadway musicians and bandleaders (all flight enthusiasts) had formed a private aviation club, the Albatross Flying Club, with a clubhouse and hangars based at Roosevelt Field.[39] Roger was the club president.[40] The number of pilots among Broadway bandsmen had increased considerably over the past few years. The club brought like-minded musicians and flight aficionados together. Such was its popularity that membership had already reached over one hundred and fifty.

Roger's final recordings for Victor arrived in April. *'Shady Lady'* and *'You're the Only One For Me'* were the songs, the former plucked from the Pathé Exchange gangster movie *Shady Lady*. Interestingly, neither offering received the thumbs up from *Variety*.[41] In truth, Roger was glad to see the end of his association with Victor.

In May, brighter news arrived for Roger; he signed a one-year record deal with Brunswick on a guarantee and royalty basis.[42] The terms of the contract were more lucrative than had been with Victor. Roger hoped the new agreement would help achieve higher sales and generate sizable royalties. His debut recordings for the label came soon after: *'Heigh-Ho, Everybody, Heigh-Ho,'* and *'Pretty Little Thing'* with vocals by Frank Munn.[43] Munn was a new choice of vocalist for Kahn, a tenor with a distinctively smooth, resonant tone. He had recently garnered recognition as a regular vocalist on *The Palmolive Hour*, broadcast weekly on NBC Radio. Since 1923, the number of American families with radios had grown from 300,000 to 10 million. Munn was now a household name and would later attain significant success as the 'Golden Voice of the Radio.' Encouragingly for Roger, both of his new tracks achieved far stronger sales than his previous two offerings on Victor.

In New York on April 26, a new company, The Mogmar Art Foundation Inc., listed at 52 William Street, New York, was registered at the Department of State. Otto and Addie set up the private corporation to manage and protect their extensive and valuable art collection. The acronym **Mogmar** derives from the initials of the Kahn family's Christian names: **M**aud, **O**tto, **G**ilbert, **M**argaret, **A**ddie, and **R**oger.*

Over the past couple of years, Gilbert had industriously and diligently built up his reputation in banking. Working at Kuhn, Loeb, in such close contact with his father, had also given him a privileged insight into how his father handled and promoted his dealings within the realms of show business. As a result, Gilbert now felt confident enough to try his hand in the entertainment industry. He became a partner in Bela Blau Inc. production company, formed to produce stage plays of worth by attracting exceptionally gifted new playwrights, actors, and directors.[44]

The initial aim of its founder Bela Blau (a Hungarian film producer) was to launch a subscription theater company. Blau had already attracted several influential associates, including publisher and writer George Palmer Putnam. In addition, $105,000 had presently been deposited with the Equitable Trust Company to finance the operation.[45] The company hoped to stage its first production during the forthcoming autumn season.

Otto's European Escape

'Shout KAHN to a representative group of U.S. citizens and most will think of Otto, a few of Genghis, and a sprinkling of Kublai.'[46]

Otto's European escape took on the guise of an art hunt, property clear out, and all-inclusive vacation. In truth, his swift departure from the U.S. was anything other than what it claimed to be. It was arranged as a necessary deterrent to keep the press off his back. Otto remained in ready contact with his attorney in New York throughout his absence, lest any further worrying developments arose.

In London, Otto put his Regent's Park property, St Dunstan's Lodge, up for auction.[47] *The Times* carried a notice on May 13, informing any prospective purchaser that Curtis and Henson of Mount Street were handling the sale. The estate of twelve acres came with a forty-five-year unexpired Crown lease with a yearly ground rent of £540. The property was eventually sold the following year to the newspaper proprietor Lord Rothermere.

Otto's next stop was Paris, where comedian Harpo Marx of the Marx Brothers was in town.[48] Paramount Pictures had signed the brothers to a five-film deal. Their first offering, *The Cocoanuts,* had just hit the big screen. Harpo was in Europe helping promote it. The comedian once spent a weekend as a guest at the Kahns' Cold Spring Harbor estate, creating havoc in his wake. Ever since his visit, Addie had felt it undignified of her husband to befriend such brash personalities.

From Paris, Otto journeyed north to Berlin and then on to Hamburg, where he boarded the handsome steam-yacht *Albion.*[49] Otto had chartered the splendid vessel for approximately three weeks to sail around Scandinavian waters and the Norwegian fjords. Among the mixed party of eleven guests invited to join him were a wing commander and his wife, two married ladies minus their partners, two unattached bachelors, a beautiful young German girl (who Otto had met a couple of nights earlier), devoted friend Rudolf Kommer, and the 22-year-old aspiring writer Daphne du Maurier. Du Maurier, at times, found the whole experience rather daunting.[50] The yacht docked at various picturesque ports on the way: Copenhagen, Visby on Gotland, and Stockholm.

Daphne wrote an account of the trip in her diary. 'We sailed through the Kiel Canal to Gothenburg, and thence to Denmark, Sweden, Norway, and the fjords ... Otto Kahn was the most wonderful host and a great conversationalist, but he was also an indefatigable sightseer. When onshore, we tramped around museums, castles, and churches at his bidding; and his guests were weary long before he ever was ... a truly remarkable man.' She also noted the uninvited romantic advances she dodged from Otto, a man almost three times her age. When Kahn offered to buy Daphne a fur coat to keep her warm, she refused such a personal gift and instead asked for a dagger, which she thought would be more useful. Kahn obliged.

During the cruise, Otto received the gladdening news from his attorney in New York that Supreme Court Justice Peters had dismissed the $250,000 libel suit brought against him by the singer Rosalinda Morini.[51]

While Otto was swanning around Scandinavian waters, Addie had sailed over to the UK on the *Aquitania* and installed herself at Claridge's Hotel in London from where she was courting the auction

houses, sending prices rocketing.[52] When the private collection of
Baron Vladimir de Grüneisen came up for sale at Sotheby's, Addie felt
compelled to attend. One hopeful bidder observed, 'Grüneisen's sale
here was a disappointment, (a) because there were few good things
and a lot of fakes, and (b) because Mrs. Otto Kahn was in London and
ran everything up to fancy prices.'[53] On the day Addie arrived in
Southampton she also received good news from New York; her
daughter-in-law Anne had given birth to daughter Claire Anne Kahn.*
Mother and baby and Gilbert were all doing fine.

For a while, Roger had been toying with the idea of lending his hand
to writing film scores. Reports of the rich pickings to be made in
Hollywood were a constant inspiration; even bandleader Paul
Whiteman had scuttled west to top up his bank balance. Whiteman
was currently based in a specially built lodge on the backlot at
Universal, discussing storylines for his first movie, *King of Jazz.*
Newspaper reports claimed the bandleader's fee for the film was
$100,000 on account, with an equal sum upon completion.

Fifteen million picturegoers weekly visited a Publix theater in the
U.S., in addition to the countless millions across the globe who
enjoyed movies in their respective countries.[54] When Universal
Pictures purchased the film rights to *Here's Howe!*, Roger's attention
went up a notch.[55] The call from Hollywood now seemed real and too
strong for him to resist. Hollywood producers viewed young Kahn as
a modernistic composer, and interest from MGM was said to be
especially keen.[56] Universal intended to adapt *Here's Howe!* for the
big screen and launch it as their first all-talking and singing musical
feature. If all went to plan, such exposure would be immensely
beneficial for the young composer.

In some respects, Los Angeles was the perfect antidote to
Manhattan; wide, open avenues, clean air, and an altogether slower
pace of life, and continuous sunshine. What was not to like about it?

In June, Roger purchased another Bellanca biplane to add to his
growing collection of aircraft. This plane he intended to use solely for
long-distance cross-country flights.[57] Roger now owned five planes, a
small fleet, one for every day of the week (excluding weekends),
inferred the press upon hearing of his latest acquisition.[58] Young
Kahn's hangar at Roosevelt Field was getting so crowded with
aircraft he now had to employ extra mechanics to service and
maintain them.

Roosevelt Field, along with its member's facilities, was becoming so
popular with out-of-town flyers that airport officials and regular

users decided to form a 'volunteer vigilance committee' to monitor the 'comings and goings' of aircraft to help reduce the volume of dangerous and hazardous flying incidents that were occurring.[59] Of particular concern were pilots not heeding foul weather warnings. Accordingly, the committee (on which Roger sat), were asked to keep a check on any pilot or any plane attempting to take off under 'unsafe' conditions and report such incidents to the general manager of the field. In turn, he had the authority to deny the pilot any future use of the airfield. By adopting such a practice, the committee hoped, within time, the procedure might become routine.

Otto returned to the UK immediately after his Scandinavian cruise came to an end. In London, he was reunited with his wife. On Monday, July 22, from his suite at Claridge's Hotel, Kahn dictated a letter to his secretary inscribed to the politician and former Chancellor of the Exchequer (and MP for Epping) Winston Spencer Churchill. In the letter, he suggests holding a private meeting with American finance and industry leaders during Churchill's forthcoming three-month trip to North America. Kahn proposed an informal dinner to take place at his home 'without the presence of reporters' and asked Churchill to choose a convenient date.* Churchill's tour of Canada would last throughout August. 'I will travel across Canada via Montreal, Toronto, Winnipeg, Calgary, and the Peace River district arriving on the Pacific at Vancouver not later than September 1,' confirmed Churchill in a private letter to American financier Bernard M. Baruch.* From California, Churchill would take the eastward transcontinental route across the U.S., arriving in New York on October 6. Churchill was making the trip as a private individual while Parliament was in recess.

Otto departed from Britain aboard RMS *Majestic* on Thursday, July 25.[60] His private secretary Elizabeth Mutke and valet Frederick Cooper accompanied him.[61] Addie sailed home several weeks later.

Although Otto and Addie returned to the U.S. on separate liners on different dates, it was a clear indication the Kahns believed 'things' had calmed down somewhat in New York since they were last there. Otto even managed to find time to chat with the ship reporters at New York Harbor. When asked how well he found the economy in Europe, he joked: 'I am better posted on European affairs by reading the newspapers in America than by going to Europe.'[62] Otto also had a new grandchild Claire Anne Kahn to be introduced to and a christening to attend when his wife returned.

Churchill accepted Otto's dinner invitation and proposed Thursday,

October 17, as the date for the meal. On September 13, Otto cabled Churchill to confirm their dinner arrangement and asked if anyone else from Churchill's party would be attending other than Winston's brother Jack.* In Churchill's reply, also delivered by telegram, he added two other names to the guest list, Lord Feversham and Horace Cecil Vickers, founding partner of Vickers da Costa (the London brokerage house).*

On Tuesday, October 8, Otto was elected as chairman of the Suffolk County Republican Campaign Committee.[63] Otto had previously spoken in passing conversations about his willingness to assist his local Long Island branch of the Republican Party. The committee took his word at face value. Kahn feigned surprise by his nomination but promptly accepted the post in a telegram sent the following day to the Suffolk County Republican Committee chairman W. Kingsland Macy.[64] In the cable, Kahn confessed to his lack of qualifications for such a position but thanked the executive committee for the unexpected honor and said he hoped what little he might be able to do would be helpful towards serving the Republican organization of Suffolk County.[65]

One almost senses a hint of unease in Otto's acceptance of the post. In a sly dig at Kahn's expense, the *Brooklyn Daily Eagle* assured the regional constituents, 'Suffolk County farmers, we are sure, will contribute more freely to the Republican campaign fund now that Otto H. Kahn, the trusted aid of Woodrow Wilson, has consented to be chairman of the campaign committee. Confidence is everything in such contributing.'[66]

Sixth Plane for Roger

The size of Roger's air fleet increased yet further when he purchased an Ireland amphibian for $29,000 from the Curtiss Flying Service (who operated flights from Boston).[67] With his latest addition, newspapers reckoned young Kahn's six planes had cost him over $100,000.[68] Otto took more than a passing interest in Roger's newfound obsession and made it his business to keep a close eye on his youngest sons flying activities and would on occasions visit Roosevelt Field to monitor his goings-on.[69] Although Roger had yet to entice his father into the cockpit of his machines, his mother was warming to the idea.

Meanwhile, reports filtered through to Otto from South Dakota that troubled opera singer Rosalinda Morini was to perform a recital at Huron College for their pow wow night scheduled for the last week of October. The local *Daily Plainsman* carried a short piece about the soprano to publicize the concert claiming (incorrectly) she was a star of the Metropolitan Opera House and had been lauded, by no less an authority than Otto Kahn, as the possessor of a 'truly remarkable voice.' Allegedly, Kahn had articulated, 'your lyric voice is the most beautiful I have ever heard.'[70] The article also declared the singer had performed in front of the late Caruso, who immediately wrote to his teacher in Naples, exclaiming that he had never heard such material in all his life. The fact that Morini's concert was to take place in the Midwest over 1,500 miles away may have had some bearing on Kahn's action. He remained silent, presumably in the hope of preventing any further adverse publicity or lawsuits?

Dark Days Ahead

In October, a series of unsettling incidents occurred, of which Otto had no, or little, control over. On Thursday, October 10, Kahn's former secretary William J. Wilson committed suicide. Wilson, who lived in Kearny, New Jersey, was reported missing three days earlier.[71] Cops discovered Wilson's body on Thursday morning in his garage. He died from carbon monoxide poisoning. When the cops found him, the automobile's engine was still running. Local reports suggested Wilson had lost heavily on the stock market. In a sense, his death was a precursor of what lay ahead.

Throughout the '20s, New York's stock market had risen sixfold, underpinning support in the strength of the U.S. economy. Industry and emerging technologies were thriving. Although the disparity between rich and poor was widening, overall prosperity was noticeably increasing. The feel-good factor was evident all around, continually reinforced by the entertainment industry and cheap goods.

Otto's prearranged dinner party at which Winston Churchill attended, went ahead at Kahn's Fifth Avenue mansion on October 17. I can find no record of any topics they discussed during the evening or whether Addie or other Kahn family members attended. Following dinner, Churchill caught an overnight train to Washington, D.C., where he arrived at 6:05 a.m. in preparation for a meeting with President Hoover at the White House later that morning.[72] *

On Monday, October 21 - the 50th anniversary of Thomas A. Edison's creation of the incandescent light bulb - Otto was in Dearborn, Michigan, as a guest of car manufacturer Henry Ford at the dedication of Ford's new Thomas Edison Institute (later renamed Henry Ford Museum). Inside the museum was a reconstruction of Edison's original research laboratory from Menlo Park.[73] Other distinguished guests invited to the gathering were President and Mrs. Herbert Hoover, John D. Rockefeller Jr., steel magnate Charles M. Schwab, Walter P. Chrysler (founder of Chrysler Corporation), physicist Marie Curie, and actor Will Rogers. The timely guest of honor was the aged inventor Thomas A. Edison himself. At the press call, Ford and Edison sat jointly at a table in the middle of a vast field watched by a posse of reporters and photographers. There was no cornerstone to lay, just an announcement to relay. The scene could not have been more surreal.

After the golden jubilee dedication, lunch followed in a replica of Philadelphia's Independence Hall (built especially for the occasion). After the meal, Otto returned to New York City by train. That evening's newspapers carried concerning reports of unprecedented volatility on the day's dealings at New York's Stock Exchange.

The following day, Winston Churchill received the sad news from England that his aunt, Lady Sarah Wilson, had passed away. On Wall Street, some recovery from the previous day's stock market falls came as welcome news.

On Wednesday, October 23, in the final hours of trading, when share prices plummeted dramatically, driven down 20 points, the dip came unexpectedly to many, although not a total surprise to everyone.[74] Analysts at the Federal Reserve (U.S. central banking system) who had been monitoring the New York stock market over the past year had quietly suspected a dramatic U-turn was on the horizon. Predicting exactly when it would happen had demonstrated to be the tricky part. The following morning many American newspaper headlines ran the story, 'Wall St. in Panic As Stocks Crash.'[75] The fuse was lit and slowly burning.

Thursday would prove to be a particularly stressful day. October 24 started much like every other day on Wall Street. Otto had his business meetings to attend and, as usual, arrived promptly at his William Street office at 9:45 a.m. A certain buzz was circulating the Stock Exchange that Winston Churchill was to visit that morning. The rumor was correct.

Churchill and his party were back in New York on the final leg of their three-month North American tour residing at the Savoy Plaza

Hotel on Fifth Avenue and 59th Street. The start of the day for the ex-Chancellor had been ominously eventful. At approximately 8:30 a.m., Dr. Otto Matthies, a Berlin chemist occupying a room on the 16th floor of the Savoy Plaza, opened his window and fell to his death.[76] The doctor landed on the roof of a four-story extension directly beneath Churchill's window. Churchill's attention was drawn to the tragic incident when he overheard a disturbance coming from the street outside. 'Under my very window a gentleman cast himself down fifteen storeys and was dashed to pieces, causing a wild commotion and the arrival of the fire brigade,' he later wrote in his diary.[77]

Churchill's visit to the Stock Exchange that day turned out to be a grueling experience for him. That morning, stocks sustained another terrific drop. By one-thirty that afternoon, stockholders had dumped over 10 million shares regardless of cost or value. Many traders watched in silence, unable to comprehend, as the share prices tumbled.

After lunch, an emergency summit took place at J.P. Morgan's, where heads of various banks were present. At the close of the meeting, Thomas W. Lamont Jr., acting head of Morgan's, announced to the media: 'We are not going to give out a statement. There seems to be some disturbed selling on the Stock Exchange, so far as we can see, and we had a meeting of the heads of several institutions to discuss the situation. We considered the situation, which arose on the floor late Wednesday afternoon and today, more in the nature of a technical situation rather than a fundamental one.'[78] Lamont Jr. hoped such reassuring words would do the trick and bring some stability back into the arena.

Soon afterward, share prices began to rally, and the market took an upward swing.[79]

Unlike many of his associates, Otto did not visit the Stock Exchange that day to witness the unfolding mayhem on the trading floor, preferring to remain in the calm surroundings of his office, where he conducted business in his usual collected manner. Only one employee of Kuhn, Loeb, laboring in a back office, kept note of the twists and turns of the stock market's gyrations. Kahn made no public statement to the press about the turmoil the financial markets were suffering. Otto was renowned for inspiring confidence; at no point could he be seen to waver.

That evening Otto attended a dinner in Manhattan at the University Club, hosted by Jeremiah Milbank for the industrialist Claudius H. Huston (the new chairman of the Republican National Committee).[80]

Also attending was Vice President Charles Curtis, Secretary of Commerce Robert P. Lamont, and Undersecretary of the Treasury Ogden L. Mills. During the meal, Senator George H. Moses (chairman of the Republican Senatorial Campaign Committee) spontaneously announced to the other guests that he had decided to select Otto Kahn as the new treasurer of the Republican Senatorial Campaign Committee, urging him to accept.[81] Jeremiah Milbank had previously held the post. Moses named Kahn on the spot without consulting him beforehand or calling a committee meeting to discuss the matter. Whether out of a sense of duty or in embarrassed haste, Kahn accepted the position.

Friday brought a day of respite for the stock market. A more orderly trading session followed as the market held firm despite the forced sales of stock due to weak speculators having to sell. Billions of dollars of paper losses got converted into cash losses.[82] It became evident to many that banks were actively supporting stocks in certain instances.

By way of some light relief, the *Brooklyn Daily Eagle* printed the outcome of a poll conducted by the Kiwanis Club of the best-dressed men in America, in which Otto was amid the top five.* The order of the list was as follows: 1. Mayor Jimmy Walker, 2. Oscar O. McIntyre (columnist), 3. Archibald Klufph (Cleveland Banker), 4. Otto H. Kahn, 5. Condé Nast (publisher).[83]

Investors hoped Saturday morning's trading would bring further orderliness and that Monday would be the start of a new week of optimism. President Hoover's statement to the nation on business conditions added to the general reassurance and did much to inspire confidence. He affirmed: 'The country's fundamental business, that is, the production and distribution of commodities is on a sound and prosperous basis.'[84]

At four o'clock on Saturday afternoon, Otto entertained 250 members of the local Republican Suffolk County Committee at his Cold Spring Harbor estate.[85] The constituents were first escorted around the gardens and then gathered inside the mansion's ballroom for a formal meeting. Here they were addressed by various local Party officials. Otto thanked the Suffolk County leader W. Kingsland Macy for selecting him as their Republican Party Campaign Committee chairman. In doing so, he expressed his hopes of a rousing Republican victory in Suffolk this fall. 'I can talk well of finance, economic affairs, and art, but this is my first venture as a political speaker,' said Kahn.[86] To be accurate, the last part of his sentence was not wholly accurate. Otto had delivered political addresses in the past, in the U.S. and England.

When the New York Stock Exchange reopened on Monday at ten o'clock, the rush to sell stock resumed. Throughout the morning, the market suffered another manic trading session, with leading issues down 30 points or more, bringing record lows for the year. After another emergency meeting of bankers at J.P. Morgan's, a rallying point followed in the early afternoon. Once again, the House of Morgan gave no official statement after the consultation as 'the situation did not call for it.'[87] They assessed the break was the result of forced selling of stock.

To aggravate Otto's situation, this was the week Lydia Lindgren's litigation against Julia Claussen went to court.[88] Since Lindgren's arrival in the U.S. as a protégée of Kahn's, her life had been a pyrotechnic panorama of melodrama. She now claimed her career ambitions in the world of opera were over, wrecked by malicious gossip.

That evening, Otto and Addie dressed in their finery to attend the Met's opening night of the new opera season. The Kahns watched the performance from their parterre box No. 14. On stage, while Puccini's opera *Manon Lescaut*, conducted by Tullio Serafin, played out all the melodramatic convolutions written into the plot by French author Abbé Prévost, another, more worrying drama was converging in the wings of the Stock Exchange. As the 'Golden Horseshoe' glittered from the abundance of expensive jewels bedecking the slender necks of the social elite, a lone photographer from the *Daily News* captured a single picture of diminutive Dowager Mrs. Cornelius Vanderbilt (she was scarcely five feet in stature) and her guests seated in their box, all blissfully unaware of the financial devastation that for many of them lay but a few hours away.*

The gray, austere buildings of Wall Street could neither conceal nor yet reveal the catastrophic chain of events that were about to unravel. The following day the stock market crash came with lightning speed.

No signals could halt it.

No matter how much track was laid down ahead of it, the train rattled on, regardless, to its destination, obliteration.

'What happened?'

'The stock market crashed.'

'Anybody get hurt?' came back the reply.*

Black Tuesday!

It was dubbed the 'worst' crash in history. Stock prices fell to what some traders claimed was the lowest ever. Banks offered financial support to save the market. How much would depend upon how badly wounded the economy was. Things, surely, could not get any worse! News agencies continuously blocked Otto's phone line, pleading for a ninety-second segment they could relay. None was forthcoming.

Wednesday forenoon brought a glimmer of confidence to the day's dealings.[89] The previous day had seen over twenty-six million shares dealt in a record transaction frenzy. Today's session was crucial in trying to bring back some stability for investors.

The market held out through Wednesday as if waiting for a miracle to happen. That evening's papers were more optimistic, 'Wall St. Business Better.'[90] 'Strong Buying Support Stops Selling Panic.' Projections of a long-term rally were forecast. The hysteria may have momentarily paused for a deep breath, but the underlining cause of the tumble remained. President Hoover sought to assert calm and alleviate further worries by claiming the drop in the stock market was not, as yet, hurting the country's industrial structure. In truth, it was way too early to express such an opinion. The Stock Exchange announced it would not open the following day until noon and would close all day Friday and Saturday. This action was to allow brokers time to catch up with their work. Everyone hoped the devastating selling of stock over the past week had waned.[91]

The fact that Winston Churchill chose to visit New York's Stock Exchange on October 24 has since invoked speculation that maybe he and other authority figures knew more about the crash than they publicly professed. Some reports claim the British were the cause of the panic selling and that the City of London had conspired to catalyze the crash. A Federal Reserve memo dated February 7, 1929, notes that the Bank of England demanded American interest rates, 'be raised, at some specific time by a full 1 percent with a view to breaking the spirit of speculation, and then subsequently if necessary by another 1 percent, to provoke liquidation, and then after a fall in the stock market, similar rate action at the first sign of the next revival. By thus prostrating the stock market ... we should be cutting at the root of the current situation.'

When Churchill wrote about his visit to the Stock Exchange, he documented it as occurring 'quite by chance.' But was it?

Josiah Hirst, the editor of the London *Economist*, who by a curious coincidence was also present at the Stock Exchange on that fateful day, explained in a letter he wrote: 'The rise of the London Bank (of

England) rate to 6.5 percent on 26 September precipitated the Stock Exchange crisis and slump of October.'[92]

Nonetheless, the fact remains, Churchill also lost a tidy sum in the crash. On the evening of October 29, Churchill was guest of honor at a curious 'celebration' attended by over forty bankers and master plungers (speculators) held at the magnificent Fifth Avenue mansion of financier and stock investor Bernard M. Baruch.* The following day, Churchill left America aboard the *Berengaria* en route to the UK.

News of Otto's appointment as treasurer of the Senatorial Campaign Committee came as a surprise to everyone in the Republican Party, including President Hoover. So much so, friends of the president in Washington, D.C., were reported as saying the president had adopted a hands-off policy (not to interfere) on the matter of Kahn's selection. Otto had earlier that month been elected chairman of the Suffolk County Republican Campaign Committee. Perhaps Kahn's sudden admittance within the Party was difficult for some Republican officials to digest. The president's lukewarm response certainly got tongues wagging. 'Otto H. Kahn is coolly viewed as a Republican chairman. Because of his cool millions, do you suppose?' asked the *Brooklyn Daily Eagle* on its front page on Tuesday, October 29.[93] 'The debut in Republican politics of Otto H. Kahn ... has been a splendid 'frost.' To date, there are just two persons who think that a partner in Kuhn, Loeb & Co. and the president of the Metropolitan Opera would make a good treasurer of the Republican committee in charge of the Senate elections of 1930.'[94] Members of the committee threatened to resign unless Kahn withdrew from the post immediately.

The matter quickly became an embarrassment for Kahn and the Republican Party and reflected poorly on Kuhn, Loeb & Co., and the Metropolitan Opera Company. On Wednesday, October 30, Otto announced in a letter to Senator Moses that owing to the 'divided reception with which the report of the appointment of a separate treasurer for your committee, and my designation as such treasurer has met,' he had decided to 'abstain from occupying it.'[95] Moses accepted Kahn's withdrawal.[96]

It was a humiliating slight on Kahn's name and character and one dispensed by such a prominent figure in such a public manner. Maybe it was Kahn's comeuppance for openly disapproving and criticizing President Hoover's antiquated stance on Prohibition. Loyal friends rallied round in Otto's defense: 'He would have made an excellent treasurer.'[97] The *Brooklyn Daily Eagle* noted: 'His declination of the honor of being [the] chief fundraiser for the

Republican Senatorial Campaign Committee is perfectly understood by all his friends and admirers.'[98]

Otto photographed on October 30 (given
the press treatment), putting on a brave
face 24 hours after the Wall Street Crash.
The strain clearly shows in his eyes.

At the beginning of 1929, Kuhn, Loeb's assets were worth over $120 million. That figure dropped considerably after the Wall Street Crash.[99]

If ever there was a reason for acting so harshly against one's principles, now was that time. The Kahn fortune was just as vulnerable as all the others. Otto never did divulge how much of his wealth evaporated on that fateful day; that fact, he kept a closely guarded secret, even from Addie, preferring to soldier on as if nothing problematic had occurred. He was determined to remain a pillar of strength upon whom those less fortunate than him could lean. That said, there was one trusted person Otto did divulge everything to; that fellow was his brother Felix.

~

Wall Street Booze Party Bust

Why a dinner party in Washington, D.C., on December 1, 1926, should grab the headlines and hog newspaper coverage during November 1929 seemed inconceivable, given the economy's dire state and all the other newsworthy items that were circulating at the time. But the 'Wall Street Booze Party' did just that.

Senator Smith Wildman Brookhart, a Republican representing Iowa in the U.S. Senate, had an axe to grind and was the adversary that brought the disclosure to light. Brookhart was due to go before the District of Columbia Grand Jury on November 6 to relay to the chamber precisely what went on almost three years prior at a celebratory dinner hosted by New York broker Walter J. Fahy at the Willard Hotel in Washington, D.C.

Brookhart was known to be a 'fervent dry' and champion of the temperance movement. In his efforts to help push forward his belief that finance to ensure the enforcement of Prohibition should be increased by a whopping $240 million, he had already lobbied various congressmen and prominent 'wets' in support of the repeal of Prohibition. What irked Brookhart more than anything was the fact that he had attended Fahy's dinner and, as such, witnessed at close hand the consumption of illicit alcohol at the dining table at which he was a guest.

On November 5, one day before Brookhart's appearance in front of the Grand Jury, he spoke at the Senate. Brookhart stood in his usual place on the rear row as he relayed to the presiding officer and his fellow Senators the facts as he remembered them. The chamber was packed. By now, everyone was hankering to know who was on Fahy's guest list at the infamous dinner.

'Soon after I was elected in 1926,' began Brookhart in his high-pitched voice, 'I received an invitation at my home in Iowa to attend a dinner in Washington. I threw it into the wastebasket. When I returned to Washington, I met the distinguished president pro tempore of the Senate, George H. Moses of New Hampshire, who said to me, 'You haven't answered Fahy's invitation.' I said, 'I don't know, Fahy.' Senator Moses said, 'Oh, he is an old friend of Norris (Senator George W. Norris) and La Follette (Senator Robert M. La Follette Jr.)' I said, 'All right. That's good enough for me. I'll go.'[100]

Brookhart proceeded slowly with his eyewitness account, making sure to express every morsel of information he could summon up: 'I went down to the Willard Hotel. The first fellow I met was Otto Kahn. I didn't recognize him as a particular friend of Norris and La Follette.

I looked around that bunch, and it seemed to me there was something doing.'

The Senate fell silent in anticipation of what Brookhart might reveal next; 'Somebody lifted a curtain from in front of a bookcase or over a table, and there were a lot of silver hip flasks filled with Scotch. I did not take one. Neither did Senator Gooding and neither did Senator Smoot.'

'On my right when we went into dinner sat Otto Kahn and on my left Edward E. Loomis of J.P. Morgan & Co. Right off, Mr. Kahn began discussing my attitude on railroad valuation in relation to a proposition I had made to the Interstate Commerce Commission. After demolishing all my theories about economic matters,' the Iowan continued, 'Kahn proceeded to eulogize the New York Stock Exchange and said what a wonderful benefit it was to the people of my State!' When he finished, Mr. Loomis took up the subject. After a while, Mr. Loomis took out a hip flask and poured himself a drink of Scotch. It was so strong he had to put some water in it.'

Senators around the room roared with laughter.

Brookhart continued earnestly with his tale; 'Similar operations were proceeding around the table. Just as I was leaving, Senator Edge of New Jersey called me back and said, 'Do you realize where you were sitting? You had Kuhn, Loeb & Co. on your right and J.P. Morgan & Co. on your left. Don't you think you got a little contaminated?'

Brookhart fell silent for a moment to accentuate his response.

'If I did, I never got contaminated again, because I was never invited to another Fahy dinner.' Again, Senators howled raucously.

The guests Brookhart recalled being present at the dinner were host Walter J. Fahy, Otto Kahn, Edward Eugene Loomis (president of Lehigh Valley Railroad), and Senators Reed Smoot of Utah, George Moses of New Hampshire, Walter E. Edge of New Jersey, the late Frank R. Gooding of Idaho, and Senator-elect from Pennsylvania William H. Vare.[101]

As Brookhart mentioned Mr. Edge's name, the latter sat bolt upright and grew very red in the face, while Senator David A. Reed of Pennsylvania, seated directly beside Edge, burst into laughter. Worryingly for some, Brookhart had yet to disclose the names of the other guests that attended. When Senator Thomas of Idaho sneakily reached over to Brookhart's desk to grab his notes, Brookhart halted his speech to declare: 'Get away from there.' Both he and Thomas laughed.

Three reporters from the *Washington Times* had recently been sent to jail for contempt of court for refusing to reveal their sources of information on liquor violations.¹⁰² Only last week, an alleged bootlegger, upon entering the Senate Office Building, was arrested after a bottle of liquor was found stashed in his pocket. The intruder referred to covertly as the 'Man with the Green Hat,' was overtly charged under his real name of George L. Cassidey.

Brookhart contended that Fahy, Kahn, Loomis, and other figures present at Fahy's dinner should be summoned before the jury and made to testify concerning their actions at the party. 'No man can invite me,' said Brookhart, 'to dinner where crime is in evidence, and shut my mouth thereafter on the plea that it was in confidence. It's my duty to tell.' And tell, Brookhart certainly did.

The case and subsequent media coverage it received could not have come at a more inopportune time for Otto. For those Republicans that saw fit to denounce Kahn, it was just the sort of ammunition they sought to back up their beliefs of Kahn's unsuitability for any role of importance within the Republican Party.

Brookhart then recited a letter he had received that had swayed his decision to spill the beans regarding Fahy's dinner party.¹⁰³

> *Quincy House*
> *Boston, Mass.*
> *November 2, 1929*

Hon. Smith W. Brookhart, U.S. Senate

Dear Sir

If the enclosed represents your idea of the ethics of a guest invited to a private dinner to broadcast tales about his host, the suspicion that you are a charter member of the great American Polecat club seems amply confirmed.*

The East may be effete, but it is not yellow, and I notice that all this kind of cheap snooping comes from the comical states of Kansas and Iowa. You might take a lesson in the code of honor among gentlemen from those common reporters of Washington who preferred jail to information obtained in confidence. Pretty sickening disclosure of the standard of honor of a Senator of the United States.

Yours truly

Roger W. Mintone

After Brookhart finished reciting the letter, members of the chamber rose to their feet and howled with laughter. Senator Moses rapped his gavel loudly, calling for order. He then bellowed up to the balcony, 'The Chair must admonish the occupants of the galleries that they are present by courtesy of the Senate, and the rules of the

Senate forbid any demonstration whatever in the galleries.' Moses was known to be sharp-tongued and adept in his manner.

The room quietened down.

'I am against alcohol in all forms,' Brookhart began his summing up, 'either as a beverage or medicine. I wish to congratulate President Hoover for his stand, and I want to commend Sir Esmé Howard, the British Ambassador, for drying up his Embassy. If the other ambassadors do not follow suit, I am ready to make them by law.' He ended his thunderous denunciation by calling for the resignation of the Secretary of the Treasury, Andrew W. Mellon; the man he believed was responsible for failing to enforce Prohibition.[104]

For the reporters attending, Brookhart's exposés and his theatrical way of delivering them were the stuff of dreams, and headline upon headline appeared in the dailies. In New York City, when the Associated Press approached Otto for a statement over Brookhart's revelations, he refused to comment. Likewise, at the home of Walter J. Fahy, where a spokesperson for the broker said curtly, 'Mr. Fahy has no comment to make.'

The following day Brookhart dutifully went before the District of Columbia Grand Jury and recounted the whole story again.[105] In doing so, he lay the blame for the slackness of Prohibition enforcement agencies in implementing the law, directly at the doorstep of the White House.

Brookhart's allegation that Fahy had made available a silver hip flask filled with Scotch for each of his dinner guests might well have been correct. The fact that the liquor was drunk during the meal now presented the Grand Jury with the awkward task of determining whether or not, from Brookhart's declaration, they could find grounds for an indictment.

The majority of public opinion was that an indictment of Fahy would be nigh impossible because the dinner guests consumed the evidence.

On the morning of Saturday, November 8, more worrying news arrived for Otto. The dailies announced that the manager Frank S. Hight of the Willard Hotel in Washington, D.C. (where the 'Wall Street booze party' had taken place), and railroad president Edward E. Loomis (who attended the dinner), had been requested by District Attorney Leo A. Rover (a stern Prohibition advocate, and the person that jailed the three *Washington News* reporters), to appear on Monday before the Grand Jury to testify.[106] When reporters sought a comment from Loomis at his Manhattan office, his secretary stated, 'Mr. Loomis has no comment to make on the suggestion that he appear before the Washington Grand Jury on this so-called booze party story. The whole thing is too absurd to be discussed.'[107] At the Senate, a joker placed a bottle of mineral water on Senator Brookhart's desk.[108]

That Sunday, in the grounds at Otto's Cold Spring Harbor estate, Special Officer Paul Schreiner of the Huntington Division apprehended and arrested a lone gunman.[109] The marksman, Mr. A. Ambrosino of 26 Conselyea Street, Brooklyn, was found trespassing on Otto's property while carrying a rifle. The following Wednesday, Ambrosino appeared in court at Huntington and was fined $10. He alleged he was hunting game and charged with violation of the Sunday shooting law. The incident, nonetheless, clearly highlighted the vulnerability of Otto and his family.

Details of the 'Wall Street booze party' may have wet the gossipmonger's appetite, caused a minor public uproar, and brought rapped knuckles to those associated with it, but the Grand Jury, after further consideration, decided not to take the case any further. If nothing else, it brought some light relief amid the gloomy newspaper headlines of late.

Though times were considerably more challenging of late, the House of Kahn continued to function much the same as it had always done. On November 25, Addie hosted a *lecture-musicale* in the ballroom at 1100 Fifth Avenue, at which the Russian violinist Nathan Milstein gave his New York debut.[110] The ticketed recital was held to benefit the Schola Cantorum.

Thanksgiving

Thanksgiving Day fell on Thursday, November 28, although it seemed to Otto and everyone around him in the banking profession the 'thanks' and 'giving' had become disengaged this particular year.

On Thanksgiving Eve - the night when old friends meet up - Roger and His Famous Orchestra performed in the town of Merrick on Long Island at the Police Officers and Patrolmen's Association of Nassau County Annual Masque Ball.[111] It was a significant event in the police calendar, with several thousand guests attending. The ball was held in the vast new Hampstead Armory. Kahn's orchestra played on a stage at one end of the hall, and Harry Reser and His Clicquot Club Eskimos played on another platform at the opposite end.

Among the guests were many high-ranking Nassau police officials and detectives, some of whom Roger was on first-name terms with from his days spent carrying out detective work.

A personal appearance by a big-name bandleader still drew the biggest crowds at parties. Their frequency of personal appearances measured their worth; Roger could add $500 to $1,000 to his orchestra's fee when he appeared in person.[112] Though Roger seldom performed these days, his agency still handled several orchestras that worked under the Kahn name. If a lucrative offer came in, Roger would front one of these bands for the engagement. Flying was now his weakness. Music had become the currency to fund his passion.

Also, in November, Brunswick released a new offering from the Kahn stable, 'Through! (How Can You Say We're Through),' which really took off with the public.[113]

Variety had recently introduced a monthly sales table of sheet music and phonograph records, a forerunner to what would eventually evolve into the 'Charts' or 'Hit Parade.'[114] The report came from the accounts of sales taken by leading music jobbers and disk distributors across the U.S. in the three significant sales territories: New York, Chicago (Midwest), and Los Angeles (West Coast). In November's graph, Roger's rendition of '*Through! (How Can You Say We're Through)* charted at number 3 in Brunswick's best-seller category. *Variety* noted that among the most popular songs in the Midwest (Chicago) '*Through!*' 'showed the most strength' being third on Brunswick's sales list played by Roger Wolfe Kahn, 'a stranger to Chicago disk collectors.' It was an encouraging sign for Brunswick and Roger, and one he took heed of by contemplating a possible spring tour or a string of concerts in the region to cash in on his popularity there.

By December, Roger had over 2,000 flying hours to his credit.[115] He now owned the largest private fleet of airplanes in America, if not the world, six aircraft to date.[116] All were housed in his personal hangar No. 55 at Roosevelt Field, which he named Roweka. The building overlooked Field 2 and had the name Roweka Hangar painted in white capitals across the roof. He employed two full-time mechanics to maintain and keep the craft operational 24 hours a day, should he require to fly any one of them at a moment's notice. His favorite plane was the fastest he owned, a $22,000 Vought O2U Corsair with a speed of around 150 mph. Neither did he fit the role of fashion plate aviator, preferring to ditch the latest flying togs for the more conventional three-quarter-length leather flying coat, which he wore over an ordinary business suit with the addition of a helmet and his goggles.

Roger thought nothing of flying to Washington, D.C., or another city for a business appointment and returning a few hours later. He would often drop in at his parent's Long Island estate just to say 'Hi' to his folks. Then, when Roger had finished flying for the day, he would drive himself home (still in his flying gear) behind the wheel of his plush Lincoln Sedan, with his chauffeur riding passenger on the back seat. To everyone who knew Roger, it seemed he spent more time in the clouds these days than he did on land.

What he intended to do next in aviation, he had yet to disclose.

On December 7, the Paramount movie *Glorifying the American Girl* opened simultaneously in New York and across the States. The musical comedy depicting the rise of a showgirl was the first movie produced by Florenz Ziegfeld Jr. and was one of the earliest films shot in Technicolor. The score featured songs by Irving Berlin and Rudolf Friml. '*A pretty girl is just like a pretty tune,*' sings actress Mary Eaton in her role as Gloria in the opening sequence that perfectly sets the frothy tone of the production.

The movie was of particular interest to the Kahn family, for making a cameo appearance in it was Otto, playing himself. Shot at Paramount's Long Island studios, Otto did not have far to travel to shoot his part.

Otto's scene occurs in the mock-up foyer of a Broadway theater at the fictional premiere of the musical, *Glorifying the American Girl*. During the segment, a procession of first-nighters pass through the lobby: Irving Berlin, actor Noah Beery, producer Charles Dillingham, Queen of the nightclubs Texas Guinan, writer and columnist Ring Lardner, and Mayor Jimmy Walker, all of them making cameos playing themselves.

'*Oh, here comes—here comes a big shot,*' broadcasts the Columbia radio announcer Norman Brokenshire enthusiastically. '*Here comes a big shot—the banker, philanthropist, art patron, I want you to see—Otto Kahn!*'

The camera pans directly to Otto as he walks briskly through the lobby while beaming directly at the camera. Following closely behind him enters Texas Guinan.

Though *Glorifying the American Girl* was hardly 'high art,' the movie was a pleasant enough diversion for the festive season.

Brunswick were eager to capitalize on Roger's current popularity and dropped two more tracks, 'Here Am I' and 'Why Was I Born?' just in time for the busy Christmas market. Both songs were plucked from the hit Broadway musical Sweet Adeline and came with a vocal chorus by 'Scrappy' Lambert. 'Agreeable dance stuff,' wrote Variety's music reviewer.[117]

As if the year hadn't already dealt Otto enough blows, on December 16, the Appellate Division of the Supreme Court held that Justice Sherman was in error in tossing opera singer Rosalinda Morini's $250,000 libel suit against Kahn out of court.[118] Morini's charge that Kahn's letter to a music publication in which he denies ever praising the quality of her voice had subsequently ruined her career was back to haunt him. The court ruled that parts of Kahn's letter were libelous. Otto now had twenty days in which to file affidavits and briefs and prepare for trial.

The Roar of the Twenties

A few months before the stock market crashed, signs of the impending recession had been evident, disproving later theories that the collapse triggered the subsequent depression. Inflation was one of the causes of the slump of 1929.[119] The effects of the crash and the subsequent economic decline would continue and steadily worsen through to midsummer 1933 when the stock market struck its nadir, where five-sixths of its September 1929 pre-crash value had merely evaporated into the ether.

Predictably, throughout this whole bleak period, the House of Kuhn, Loeb remained mute and composed, releasing no statements to the press.

'In 1929, our guide was greed,' said Otto when questioned about the crash a couple of years later. 'At the end of 1929, our guide was fear. I think they are the two worse guides in the world, fear and greed.'

That life can change so dramatically from one day to the next was never more apparent than in the Roaring Twenties' last days. The bellow that epitomized the decade had become all but a distant echo.

The glory days of big spending were over. As December rolled thunderously to a close, no one in the Kahn family could have predicted where the family's future lay. Things were about to change beyond recognition.

On New Year's Eve, in an extraordinary act of wanton destruction, the celebrated and sumptuously upholstered Puncheon speakeasy at 42 West 49th Street was unceremoniously destroyed by machine-gun fire, wrecking ball, cleavers, sledgehammers, and brute force. As if to erase any memory of what the 1920s had represented, the owners of the establishment, cousins and business partners Jack Kreindler and Charlie Berns, organized the 'demolition party' and invited all their wealthy friends to join in the act. Gilbert and Roger Kahn took great pleasure in helping smash the place to smithereens. When the central wooden staircase was chopped in half, Roger and his friend Robert Benchley found themselves temporarily stranded on the upper floors of the building. As an emblem of a gilded age, the once chic speakeasy ended up being obliterated.

The roar of the Twenties came to a sudden, abrupt halt.

PART III

KAHNIVOROUS FOR MORE

1930–1933

*1930, and America was on the brink
of the Great Depression*

*'Otto H. Kahn's greatest gift to the musical arts was
that of his talented son Roger Wolfe Kahn.'*
William Jerome (songwriter)

13

HERE'S THAT BAND AGAIN

'Roger Wolfe Kahn spends hours operating miniature railroad at father's home.'[1]

1930

So this is where we came into the story at the beginning of the book in Chapter 1, with the revelation that Roger locks himself away from the world inside his private suite of rooms at his father's sprawling Long Island estate. Hardly a disclosure of mammoth proportions, but one the media felt inclined to report, such was the public's appetite for gossip relating to the Kahn family.

When life got too insufferable for the young musician, he would shut himself away and play with his miniature electric railroad, knowing full well no one could disturb him. His retreat was his way of escaping the pressures of everyday life that had now become so invasive and intolerable it had left him with only one option, his impulsive decision to temporarily 'quit' the stage to concentrate on being a composer.

The Thirties arrived without the welcoming fanfare and manic revelries usually bestowed upon the birth of a new decade. Instead, any public celebrations that did go ahead were noticeably muted and toned down. The difference was markedly apparent, especially among the rich, smart set, who now preferred to stay at home rather than openly flaunt their wealth. This fresh approach brought with it an unexpected new direction for almost everyone. For some, it had been forced upon them by the troubling events of the past few weeks. For others, such as Roger, it had evolved more organically. Over the coming months, his life would alter further, in ways even he had not anticipated.

The Ivy League Look

Appearing in character is an integral part of any actor or stage performer's job. This line of thought can also relate to any job a person undertakes in their daily life. However, when the actor or stage performer is a 'star' or 'celebrity,' it puts that person in a more compromising position. Consequently, the person is under an abiding amount of pressure to appear during everyday rituals as glamorous as the public perceives them to be. Such activities might involve shopping, walking the dog, or just hanging out relaxing. Ordinary humans in whatever job or role they undertake do not receive such intense scrutiny.

Nevertheless, we expect to see a nurse dressed as a nurse, a policeman is required to wear his uniform, and a banker must also put across a smart, suited appearance. Otto's 'stage' presence had the unfailing task of convincing the world everything he did, meant something important. Otherwise, he would not be doing it.[2] Roger, too, had adopted various guises throughout his career, changing his style to suit the occasion; the child prodigy, the wayward teenager, the suave bandleader, and, more recently, the intrepid aviator.

Once more, Roger's image acquired a makeover.

Over the past couple of years, Roger had taken his outward appearance more seriously. For his latest guise, he adopted the Ivy League look made fashionable on university campuses. He visited the American tailor, Bill Feinstein; '*The best tailor I have ever had,*' wrote Roger on an inscribed photograph he gifted to his new tailor.[3] Roger was constantly in the public eye and, as the press often intimated, one of America's most eligible young bachelors. Alongside his famous bandleader tag, he now got dubbed a flyboy (a glamorous term for an aviator), having joined the ranks of that small clique of elite young American pilots.

Jewish tailor Bill Feinstein was known for his preppy style worn widely on campuses at Princeton, Harvard, and Yale in New Haven. Oversized custom-made tweed suits and classic trench coats cut in shiny leather had become a quintessentially American style, a look Roger now wholeheartedly embraced.

Having veered away from the gigging circuit, Roger now fraternized more with his buddies at Roosevelt airfield than with his friends on the Manhattan club scene. Through the help of his Uncle Felix, Roger was contracted on to the staff of Paramount Pictures as a resident in-house composer at their Long Island studio,[4] with the added possibility he might also record musical numbers for them.[5] It was a lucky break into the movie industry for the young composer and one he had every intention of extending and developing.

Yet again, Otto got thrust into the world of celluloid. He became the subject matter of an amusing new song composed by Billy Rose. Titled *'Is There Something The Matter With Otto Kahn?'* the comedienne Fanny Brice sang it in the musical comedy movie *Be Yourself!*[6] Otto had already heard the song and given United Artists full approval to go ahead and use it.

> *'Is something the matter with Otto Kahn*
> *Or is something the matter with me?*
> *I wrote a note and told him what a star I would make*
> *He sent it back and marked it 'opened by mistake.'*
> *I'd even get fatter for Otto Kahn, as all prima donnas must be:*
> *I studied with Scotti if you know what I mean*
> *He said I had the finest diaphragm he had seen!*
> *And if my high C don't hand Otto a thrill*
> *I think my tra-la-la will.'* [7]

For most of Otto's working life, he had championed enterprising new projects. However, since the stock market crash last October, his financial predicament had changed dramatically.

When the prospective publisher Alex Hillman approached Otto with a business plan to fund a new magazine publishing company, Otto recoiled nervously. Otto was in no mood for haphazardly throwing his cash around at any entrepreneur that approached him with an ill-judged idea. $25,000 was the sum Hillman hoped Otto would invest to kick-start his business.[8] Otto discreetly pulled Hillman aside and uttered in his ear that his fortune too had been hit. Presently his money was all tied up.

Hillman did not take kindly to being fobbed off and assured Otto that all he required to obtain a bank loan was a note of good character signed by a responsible person. 'If you could sign that note,' urged Hillman, I'm sure the bank would 'let me have the money.'

Otto was not so sure.

'If you'd bring me a note signed by someone like me,' Kahn replied flippantly, 'I'd give you the money myself.'

Hillman stuck to his guns and did not let Otto's dissuasion discourage him. Instead, he went ahead and secured the money from an alternative source. In the grip of the deepening Depression, he founded Hillman Publications, which he built into a prosperous company.

Roger had been entertaining vague hopes of a cinematic career in Hollywood for some time. Not as a screen performer but as a background artist composing and performing the soundtracks accompanying movies. Now that he was on the payroll at Paramount's Long Island studio, his route to California seemed but a few frames from his reach. He'd recently spent more time at the studio studying and mastering the methods and techniques required for producing film soundtracks.[9]

The art of cinema is undoubtedly the art of motion; movies were first termed 'motion pictures' and celebrated all the possibilities of movement. In jazz music, the motion of movement encompassed its whole ethos and existence. So the notion of placing jazz into motion pictures seemed as fitting as sliding a hand into a glove. It seemed only a matter of time before more bandleaders headed west to Los Angeles.

Roger got the call to head out west sooner than he anticipated.[10] On January 7, the papers announced young Kahn's arrival in Hollywood was imminent within the next few weeks. He planned to take up a post at Paramount Pictures and devote the first couple of months there becoming acquainted with the business and mastering the technique of movie scoring. After this, the serious task of composing and directing screen musicals would begin. The move would also see Roger relocating to the City of Angels. It was a bold career change for the young musician but a move he felt ready to take on.

The announcement came as a surprise to his friends but not his family, who could see firsthand the stress and limitations his success in the music industry had placed upon him.

Margaret and Maud had spent Christmas and New Year back home with their parents in New York. Gilbert had also remained in town. It was the first time in a while the whole family had been together in the same place.

Roger's Uncle Felix had played a significant role in helping Roger to realign his career. It was a positive way to start a new decade. In the meantime, Roger would continue to operate his booking agency on Fifth Avenue, leaving George Lottman in charge. He would also keep writing songs and numbers for stage musicals.

In January, Roger recorded two cracking tunes for Brunswick, 'When A Woman Loves A Man' and 'Cooking Breakfast For The One I Love,' both borrowed from the forthcoming United Artists movie Be Yourself! This time Roger took the singer and stage actress Libby Holman into the studio with him. It was the first time Roger had recorded a female vocal with his orchestra. While the outcome was euphonious to the ear, overall, it gave a mellower dynamic to the Kahn sound.

The *Nine Fifteen Revue*, directed by Broadway novice Ruth Selwyn, was already in rehearsal. Roger had a featured composition in the production.[11] George Gershwin, Rodgers and Hart, and Cole Porter also contributed numbers. A short out-of-town tryout tour opened on January 21 at the Shubert Theatre in New Haven, where it played for one week. The following week the show anchored at the Wilbur Theatre in Boston.[12] First reports were promising, with the papers giving it the thumbs up. Everyone involved crossed their fingers for a healthy Broadway transfer.

The show was aimed more at a sophisticated after-dinner crowd than a traditional theater audience, with its title *Nine Fifteen Revue* referring to the exact time the curtain rose. As with most revues, it included musical numbers, skits, and comedy sketches. There was even a series of half-a-minute dramas written by the likes of Noël Coward and Eddie Cantor. The song Roger placed, '*I Actually Am,*' had lyrics by his former *Here's Howe*! cohort, Irving Caesar. Thelma Temple and James Howkins performed the number as a duet. The couple had recently appeared in the phenomenally successful Broadway revue *Rain or Shine* that clocked up 356 performances. The financial backers were hoping some of their stage magic would rub off on this production.

In New York City, the Kahn sisters were having such good fun hanging out together that they decided to stick around for a while longer and prearranged their upcoming itinerary to join their parents later in the month in Palm Beach. Maud's 8-year-old son John Marriott was packed off back to England with his nanny aboard RMS *Olympic* to return to school,[13] giving Maud more leisure time on her hands. The sisters' friend, Princess Jean-Louis de Faucigny-Lucinge, who was currently staying as a houseguest at the Kahns' Fifth Avenue mansion, would also join them in Florida.

As with all best-laid plans, things can go awry. Roger came down with chickenpox. His physician instructed him to take several weeks off recuperating before heading west to take up his new post in Hollywood.[14] His illness could not have come at a worse time. On top of the inconvenience of having contracted an acutely contagious disease, his physician also ordered total isolation. A chauffeured limousine promptly whisked Roger off to his father's Long Island

uginoutatinellaitatelpeusegicodictahtumine

estate. In the meantime, Roger put everything to do with his career on hold while he took time out to convalesce.

An extraordinary 'inaccurate biography' of Otto created by Claude Binyon appeared in *Variety* during the fourth week of January.[15] The satire reads as follows:

Inaccurate Biographies
Otto H. Kahn by Claude Binyon

"Otto H. (Harp) Kahn, banker, was born on a little farm near Xzylych, which was later taken over by the Russians and converted into a Turkish bath. Kahn was later reported [to be] one of the angels behind the project, but when they looked, he was gone. He is one of the few angels known to have disappeared from behind a project without losing at least a shirt.

Coming to America with a load of steers, Otto followed his nose and landed a livery stable job in New York. Within three weeks, he was aired for investing his salary in a new-fangled horseless carriage gag. Otto's defense delivered at arm's length in a crowded courtroom was later condensed and transformed into a vulgar slogan by a well-known five-cent cigar company.

In no time at all, thanks to his genius and a couple of well-to-do relatives, Otto had enough money saved to buy the Woolworth building. Inasmuch that Woolworth hadn't built it yet, Otto decided not to wait and slapped the dough into a couple of investments. If the investments flopped, so would all of Otto's cousins, and Otto knew his cousins better than that.

Otto eventually became the offstage voice in an act called Kuhn, Loeb & Co. This act makes Clayton, Jackson, and Durante look like what they really are. Time progressed, and so did Otto. He started bankrolling things, such as operas and little theaters, and a boy named Roger Wolfe Kahn. Roger, being pretty good at a saxophone, took about $1,000,000 worth of lessons and then decided it was an airplane he had been thinking of all the time.

As chairman of the board of directors of the Metropolitan Opera House, Otto has the perfect right to wear tailcoats. As President of the United States of America, Calvin Coolidge had a perfect right to wear cowboy suits. So there you are." (Binyon, Claude., 1930, p. 45)

Did Otto demand an immediate apology or issue a civil lawsuit against the newspaper for defamation of character, or did he take it in jest and laugh it off as an amusing distraction? As it turned out, he chose the latter option. No doubt, he was already starting to nurture a great dislike of courtrooms.

Interestingly, on a different matter, but during the same week, Kahn did assert his legal right regarding an issue to do with his Palm Beach residence Oheka Cottage. On January 21, Otto sought to reclassify the zone of his beachfront property on Sunset Avenue. The town council had approved the reclassification of the adjoining estate owned by the banker Simon William Straus from solely residential to business designation [Residence C], thereby giving Straus unrestricted access to the ocean.[16] Kahn's attorney Joel W. Massie, in a statement issued at a meeting of the Palm Beach town council, asked for the Kahn property to be classified in the same zone.[17] The letter, headed by the declaration that 'the change be sought in the strongest possible terms,' contended 'as his [Mr. Kahn's] property joins the [Straus] property on the south, he [Mr. Kahn] seeks to have his ocean property placed in Residence C; that in justice to Mr. Kahn, it was thought he was entitled to this courtesy.'

New York banker and real-estate developer Simon William Straus had purchased the beachfront villa for $500,000 the previous year from the industrialist Jacob Leonard Replogle and, through his counsel, filed an application in March that year applying for planning permission to establish a beach casino and to furnish the grounds with bathing equipment.[18] The request was granted in spring.

During the summer, the property had undergone refurbishments costing over $100,000, constructing bathhouses and beach cabanas to accommodate 100 bathers Also installed were tennis courts, a swimming pool, and other leisure facilities. Straus already owned the Ambassador Hotels in New York, Atlantic City, and Los Angeles. His Palm Beach property would adopt the same name. On January 15, the Palm Beach Ambassador Hotel opened to the public, with the Ambassador Beach Club opening the following day.[19]

The Kahns were livid over the prospect of losing their tranquility and were in no mood for pussyfooting around with the dithering council. Due to the unsatisfactory position the Kahns now found themselves in, Otto and Addie devised a plan of their own to build a new, more secluded beach home further along the coastline.

At Palm Beach, where the sea was unbelievably blue, and life ordinarily took on a restful setting, things suddenly took an unwelcome turn. Scores of holidaymakers descended upon the Ambassador Hotel and Beach Club.

Undeterred by the intrusion on their privacy, the Kahn family put on a united front. Their arrival at the resort for their annual vacation went ahead as planned. The family was determined life would continue as usual.

The Palm Beach Post noted Otto was out and about leisurely strolling along the Breakers Casino boardwalk, chatting amiably to passersby.[20] Otto even had luck shooting quail near West Palm Beach, no doubt in an attempt to perfect his shot should it be needed elsewhere. Margaret and Maud went ahead with their regular morning and afternoon tennis matches on the Hotel Royal Poinciana courts. Their houseguests, Princess Jean-Louis de Faucigny-Lucinge and tobacco heiress Nancy Yuille, joined them. The group perfected their strokes under the expert tuition of tennis guru George Agutter.

On January 28, Otto hosted an evening dinner party for Mrs. William Bateman Leeds Jr. (Princess Xenia) at the fashionable Patio Lamaze restaurant.[21] Princess Xenia was also a houseguest of the Kahns. Many prominent guests attended the party, including Captain and Mrs. R. A. McOtts Wilson, Countess Carlo di Frasso, Mrs. Joshua A. Cosden, Mrs. Mortimer L. Schiff (Adele), the Marquis de Saline, Sir Hugh Zeeley, architect Addison Mizner, Nancy Yuille, and Otto's dear traveling companion Rudolf Kommer.

Roger may have missed out on all the fun in Palm Beach, but his recovery from chickenpox was quicker than he had anticipated. By the beginning of February, he was back in his Manhattan bachelor apartment at 100 Central Park South.[22]

On Friday, February 7, the New York Aviation Commission hosted a celebratory dinner in the Crystal Room of the Hotel Manger.[23] A Kahn Orchestra was hired for the event, an event Roger had every intention of personally attending. Dinner commenced promptly at 7 p.m. At 7:15, State Senator J. Griswold Webb - chairman of the New York State Aviation Commission - introduced F. Trubee Davison, Assistant United States Secretary of War in charge of aeronautics. Davison gave a short speech that was relayed live on radios WEAF and NBC. Following dinner, guests proceeded to the Grand Central Palace exhibition hall for the formal opening of the 1930 Aviation Show, where over forty planes were on display.[24] Several guests flew in, especially for the occasion, including the Mayor of Albany, John Boyd Thacher II, and his wife.[25]

The organizers contracted a Kahn Orchestra from Roger's agency to perform each day during the nine-day event. Roger made guest appearances with the unit as and when he could fit in with his other commitments. WLTH radio transmitted a live broadcast from the hall featuring Roger and the Kahn Orchestra on Sunday afternoon.[26] Hundreds of thousands of flying enthusiasts visited the event, with some of the wealthier visitors even purchasing aircraft.[27] Practically every American pilot and aviator of note attended.

Nine Fifteen Revue

Having just played two weeks in Boston with weekly grosses hitting the $20,000 mark,[28] and with some splendid reviews to boot,[29] the *Nine Fifteen Revue* opened on February 11 at Broadway's George M. Cohan Theatre with a spring in its step.[30] The production boasted several novelties: Frances Gershwin, two choruses (one Black, one white), movie star Marion Davies' niece Pepi Lederer, and the aging Black vocalist J. Rosamond Johnson coaxed out of retirement. The dancer Arline Judge (an ex-girlfriend of Roger's)[31] had also secured a role in the chorus. The biggest draw of the show was the star, Ruth Etting. Her rendition of '*Get Happy*' penned by Harold Arlen and Ted Koehler was a guaranteed showstopper. When George Gershwin saw Etting perform it, he described her delivery as 'the most exciting finale he had ever heard in a theater.' *Variety* hollered, 'much improved out of town.'[32] Such positive feedback was hugely encouraging for everyone associated with the show.

So what went wrong! The show crashed out after only seven performances. It seemed the New York public was not ready for a mid-evening revue and could not fit it into their evening schedule. The financial loss incurred by its backers amounted to $140,000. Among the audience on the first night were Otto Kahn, film mogul Adolph Zukor, and the actress Hope Hampton. The final curtain fell at midnight, prompting many that attended to moan it was way too late for a midweek performance. The consensus among reviewers was that it was just 'so-so.'[33] And so, it went.

Villa Oheka, Palm Beach

Otto had recently snapped up a stretch of realty further along the Palm Beach coast at 691 North County Road overlooking the beachfront for $110,000. He'd also bought five-and-a-half acres of additional surrounding land stretching as far back as Lake Worth Lagoon.[34] The Kahns' dream of constructing a new, more secluded villa hastily evolved. They commissioned New York architects Maurice Fatio and William A. Treanor to design a Florentine-inspired 40-room villa with Art Deco interior decor.

Construction of the property began later in the year. The grounds would boast a 70-foot infinity pool directly facing the ocean. It was the third villa the Kahn's had built in Palm Beach, and they intended to get it as near perfect for their needs as possible. They would christen the house Villa Oheka.

Otto's health had, again, shown niggling signs of concern for Addie. Although nothing specific that she could lay her finger on, she had noticed her husband had lost some of his usual vitality. She was also aware that Otto was just as vulnerable as any other overworked, stressed individual. He may have looked the picture of health as he strolled along the Breakers boardwalk enjoying the warm breeze, but that did not stop her from keeping a watchful eye upon him lest any further health issues should develop.

After Roger's recent appearances at the Aviation Show, some folk may have assumed he was back on the bandwagon. Although this was not strictly the case, he had warmed to the idea. His name (though not his person) was still attached to several orchestras, including the Roger Wolfe Kahn Serenaders that broadcast weekly on WMCA Radio.[35] Furthermore, he was still contracted to Brunswick records. At the end of February, the label released four new tracks from the young maestro: 'Don't Ever Leave Me' and ''Twas Not So Long Ago' both from the current Broadway success Sweet Adeline, and 'Without A Song' and 'Great Day' from the flop musical of the latter song title. Kahn's orchestrations for the numbers held some effective, well-thought-out treatments,[36] steering the songs away from the show tune genre.

Healthy sales encouraged Roger to return to the studio to lay down four additional tracks. The session took place on March 5 and captured 'Exactly Like You' and 'Montana Call,' as well as the optimistic 'On The Sunny Side of The Street' and the mellower 'The Moon is Low.'[37] The sizably talented 'Scrappy' Lambert sang on the first song, and new boy Dick Robertson handled song No. 3. Both numbers came from Lew Leslie's International Revue. Vocalist Dick Robertson also officiated on 'Montana Call' (snatched from the soundtrack of MGM's western Montana Moon before its official release on March 20). Tenor and radio star Frank Munn got lassoed for 'The Moon is Low.' All four tracks hit the stores in the following weeks. 'A melody of real appeal,' noted Variety in their review of 'The Moon is Low.'[38]

In New York City, the stark silhouette of winter hung on, where nothing familiar seemed welcoming. Society was either ship-bound for Europe or planning their next trip on the horizon. Following the exodus came a natural lull. In March, Otto and Addie sailed to Europe for their annual three-month trip to visit family and friends and indulge their passion for the arts. As the *Majestic* gracefully glided into Southampton docks on March 21, thoughts of the turmoil in America's economy temporarily lifted from Otto's shoulders. Even the stock markets briefly rallied.* In London, the Kahns checked into Claridge's, their home from home. From the capital, they traveled across to the continent where they planned to spend time leisurely exploring coastal resorts along the French and Italian Rivieras.[39]

Roger experienced a scary incident in late March when his plane got caught up in a snowstorm.[40] He ended up having to circle his aircraft for half an hour as he blindly tried to locate the field at Rochester Airport after the weather turned pretty nasty. Only his cool-headedness saw him averting a crash-landing.

On April 8, a front-page report confirmed Roger and his orchestra had agreed to appear at this year's Junior Prom at Villanova College in Philadelphia.[41] The concert would take place in a few weeks. There was, however, no mention of exactly which orchestra Roger would be fronting. He presently did not have one. That information was announced three weeks later. The line-up came as a surprise; Roger would be fronting the Serenaders outfit.[42]

'With the signing of Roger Wolfe Kahn and His Serenaders, the Junior Prom Committee has completed what it fondly hopes and has good reason to believe, will be the most lavish and most entertaining program ever presented at any Villanova function.' The committee had also rented the largest ballroom in the city for the evening - the Penn Athletic Club. The Serenaders had to date (without their namesake at the helm) played at many university 'Hops' ranging from Princeton, Yale, Cornell, and Dartmouth, besides appearing at the *Café des Ambassadeurs* in Paris, France.

The confirmation that Roger would be fronting the unit had tongues wagging and hopes high that he might sometime soon announce a full return to the stage. However, that announcement, if at all, was not forthcoming.

Before his engagement in Pennsylvania, Roger agreed to test fly a new aircraft.[43] The all-metal new Burnelli monoplane, designed by Vincent J. Burnelli, was similar, yet smaller in design, to the Burnelli transport plane. Roger collected the aircraft on April 30 from Aeromarine Airfield at Keyport, New Jersey, from where he flew to

Roosevelt Field. There followed a complete check of the plane, collecting data from every aspect of its performance. It was the first test flight Roger had piloted. Pleasingly for all involved, the mission was a success.

The following day, Roger took one of his planes out for a spin. Having every reason to feel good about his preceding days' work, this trip was for enjoyment. As the weather that day was particularly good, Roger flew his Ireland amphibian. During the flight, the plane developed engine trouble.[44] Not wanting to bail out, he undertook a forced landing. Fortunately, he was close to Port Washington on Long Island. He aimed the plane directly for Manhasset Bay and managed to glide it down onto the water without damaging the craft or injuring himself. The lumbering seaplane was later towed ashore, with Kahn still on board. Had it not been for Roger's quick thinking, the outcome could have so easily been different.

On May 8, Otto arrived back in New York on RMS *Majestic* earlier than expected from his European vacation. He looked rested; the physical change of routine and surroundings had done him good. As was customary, reporters had gathered at the quayside to welcome him home. Otto made no statement to the press that day, preferring to sidestep any fuss or questions. He appeared to have other things on his mind. Addie had remained in Europe, choosing not to return to America until mid-June.

The following week on Friday, May 14, Roger and his orchestra broadcast three separate radio programs on WLTH: the first aired from 3 to 3:15 p.m., the second at 3:30 until 3:45 p.m., and the final at 9 to 9:15 p.m.[45] Had Roger's on-off relationship with performing been rekindled?

On Sunday that weekend, Roger test piloted another aircraft for the Burnelli Corporation. The biplane was the oddest-looking design he'd come across. It looked like a pilot's nightmare, yet it did fly. The large prototype had many queer gadgets, namely, 'ailerons,' created to make the plane easier to control and give additional lift.

Early that morning, Roger flew from Roosevelt Field to Newark Metropolitan Airport, New Jersey, where a large posse of press and hundreds of spectators had turned up to witness the strange beast in operation. It was at Newark airfield that Roger carried out the various tests.

'Freak planes are nothing new,' noted *Modern Mechanix* magazine, 'but a ship of unconventional design that really flies is a distinct novelty. This new type of Burnelli plane, recently flown at Newark

Airport by Roger Wolfe Kahn, not only flies but also seems to be nearly foolproof.'[46]

Roger in the Remington-Burnelli RB-2GX-3 preparing for takeoff.

The aforementioned 'ailerons' (little wings) were attached on the upper and lower sides of the central wing and helped control the aircraft's flight dynamics. Additional drop-shaped, concave anti-spin plates, fixed to the wingtips, also gave added direction. The undercarriage had six small, covered wheels, three on either side of the central cockpit, and two propellers. It certainly was a peculiar-looking craft, straight out of a science fiction novel, and created much attention from the public and press alike.

Newark airfield was still undergoing construction. The runway was shorter than it looked if a little too short for comfort. It took a skilled pilot to lift off and land on such a modest airstrip. The aircraft was parked in front of a hangar in preparation for its tests.

Roger talked briefly with executives from the Burnelli Corporation before climbing into the cockpit to prepare for takeoff. His mechanics ushered back any spectators too close to the runway. A conical windsock waved casually in the wind on a mast in the distance - fine weather for flying. An airport mechanic motioned the 'all clear.' Roger started the propellers to ignite the engines. He then pulled his aviator goggles down over his eyes, took hold of the navigation wheel, and rechecked the field ahead was clear. From now on, Roger was flying solo.

As the cumbersome craft taxied slowly forward, spectators stepped further back as it approached. Within seconds she had gathered speed and, with a gentle tilt, lifted gracefully into the air.

Roger flies the RB-2GX-3 over the hangars.

Roger flew the plane for almost an hour, checking and rechecking all the apparatus was up to spec. Several times he delighted the gawping crowds by flying low overhead. The trial was an undeniable success for its designer and pilot, and the reporters came away with some excellent shots of the plane.

The following day, Roger hauled a bunch of session musicians into the studio to record 'Into My Heart' coupled with 'Dark Night.'[47] Both numbers were lifted from the MGM movie Gay Madrid and came with the smooth vocals of 'Scrappy' Lambert, now a regular contributor to the Kahn camp. These would be Roger's last recordings for Brunswick. The two ballads were targeted at a mainstream audience, no doubt in the hope of achieving higher record sales.

Rene Racover, who had previously been Roger's business partner several seasons ago at Le Perroquet de Paris, had arrived back in New York City and was slumming it at the Ritz Towers.[48] He now had a new occupation as manager of the French pilot Dieudonné Costes. Though Roger and Rene had parted company under less than amicable circumstances, it seems Roger's influence and enthusiasm for flight had remained with the Frenchman. During the previous September, Costes had set the world distance record flying from

Paris to Qiqihar in China. He now had his sights on attempting the first non-stop transatlantic Paris to New York flight via the more challenging westbound direction. Racover was looking for sponsorship. Costes had his eye on the $25,000 prize offered by Colonel William E. Easterwood Jr. of Dallas to achieve the first flight from Paris to New York, finishing in Dallas, Texas.

With co-pilot Maurice Bellonte, Costes accomplished the transatlantic flight later in the year, arriving at Curtiss Field on September 2, having taken 37 hours and 18 minutes to cover 4,100 miles. Upon their arrival in New York City, the Mayor gave them a ticker-tape parade along Broadway. Early in the morning on September 4, Costes and Bellonte flew to Dallas to claim the $25,000 prize from Colonel Easterwood Jr.[49] Rene Racover followed in a plane behind them.[50]

The fact that large amounts of prize money were up for grabs for completing maiden flights had also caught Roger's attention. He, too, had his sights set on attempting one later in the year. However, unlike some pilots, Roger was not an advocate of endurance flying and openly criticized it, believing it was an unsafe practice.

When an inventor and pilot hailing from Boston named Godfrey Lowell Cabot approached Roger with a proposal to trial a new device he'd designed for picking up mail sacks during flight, Roger agreed to help out.[51] The gadget was christened the Cabot Aerial Pickup Device. On Friday, May 23, Roger made four successful preliminary flights at Roosevelt Field, testing the device.[52] Cabot was now keen to showcase his invention to the Post Office Department. Their assessment and criteria for accepting such apparatus would be more rigorous and involve operating the pickup effectively in at least 75 out of 100 attempts.

Cabot had previously been president of the National Aeronautic Association. The preliminary trials were a test to see whether the device was worth considering as a means to transport mail. Roger had proved the idea was viable. Cabot now had to convince the U.S. Post Office Department it was worthy of an official trial.

Roosevelt Field had recently begun operating early evening Airplane Stunt Exhibitions in which Roger and several other pilots participated. Members of the public paid an entrance fee to watch the pilots in action. These events were well attended and became a lucrative money earner for all involved. Spectators were thrilled to observe at close hand the aerobatics such pilots could perform. Reporters were usually in attendance to catch sight of any celebrity that might turn up or to witness any mishaps that might occur. The press frequently singled out Roger for his daredevil antics, guaranteed to delight the crowds. 'The pilot who thrilled spectators in the air circus at Roosevelt Field last week (May 29) was Otto Kahn's li'l boy Roger Wolfe.'[53] Such capers would have had his mother on her sickbed had she heard about them, let alone witnessed them.

At the end of May, Gilbert and Anne and their young daughter, Claire, took off to the continent for their summer outing. The family arrived in Southampton on June 4 aboard SS *Europa* and headed straight for Claridge's Hotel in London, where, conveniently, Addie was still resident. From here, Gilbert and his family journeyed to France and other European country's visiting relatives and friends.

On June 14, Addie departed from Southampton aboard RMS *Berengaria* on her return journey to New York. Perhaps, had she known of the dramas that were to unfold later in the year, she might have delayed her return home yet further.

On the same day Addie left the UK, Roger was test-flying a new Junkers all-metal low wing freighter at Roosevelt Field, designed chiefly for carrying freight.[54] The $30,000 aircraft had recently been imported from Germany and was a sister ship of the Bremen. The freighter was heavier than her relative and had a more powerful engine: a 425 horsepower Pratt & Whitney radial air-cooled motor capable of flying up to 135 mph. Roger flew the machine for more than an hour, under the watchful eye of Junkers representative who had shipped her to the U.S.*

The following Saturday, Roger was back flying one of his planes over Long Island when around 5 p.m., the weather took a sudden and nasty turn for the worse.[55] The sky grew gray and low, and drizzle began swirling around. The rain soon turned to hailstones, large hailstones, bigger than usual, with the consistency of marble, and a mighty wind took hold. Roger and an estimated ten other aircraft were high in the sky above the island when the weather turned foul. It was the third time Long Island had encountered a ferocious storm in the past four days, except this one was fiercer. The torrential downpour and thunder and lightning sent sightseers and visitors at Roosevelt and Mitchel Fields running for shelter. After realizing there was little else he could do, Roger nosed his plane towards land and headed straight for Roosevelt Field, flying directly through the storm. Miraculously he landed safely without incident. Several minutes later, the foul weather eased, and the sun burst through the rain clouds decorating the sky with a colorful rainbow. Roger's quick-thinking actions in the face of danger were a testament to his skills as a pilot. Unluckily, twelve yachts out at sea participating in the weekly races organized by Cold Spring Harbor Beach Club were not so fortunate. They capsized and sank, leaving their occupants bobbing in the water, yelling for help.[56] Motorboats sped to the scene to rescue them.

Regular updates of Roger's flying activities kept the press busy. It was these reports that Addie vexed over. 'Roger Wolfe Kahn keeps up his aeronautical [displays] despite several ugly scares he has had on flights. The other day he was in an airplane accident that, for a minute or so, looked pretty bad, but he pulled out.'[57]

The press calculated that since Roger had stepped away from his lucrative live appearances, his salary had decreased substantially. He was now purportedly living on little more than $60,000 a year (the equivalent to just under $1 million in 2021) and was struggling to make ends meet.[58]

Through early July, New York was bubbling under a blanket of heat. Although the fine weather with clear visibility and light winds were ideal flying conditions, the forecast did mention the possibility of thunderstorms breaking the city heatwave. Under such pleasant circumstances, Roger did what any young man with disposable time and a seaplane might do and took his Ireland amphibian up for a spin, taking three of his chums with him. Not satisfied with the cool breezes wafting through the plane, Roger flew back down and parked on the water's surface on Long Island Sound around a mile offshore from Port Washington. Here Roger dropped anchor so he and his buddies could go fishing.[59] In two hours, they caught more than fifty fish. When asked by a curious reporter back at Roosevelt Field where he got the fish from, Roger quipped, he and his friends had sat on the wings of his ship with their fishing tackle and 'reeled 'em in.'[60]

By the summer of 1930, the spontaneous, indulgent parties Otto hosted at Cold Spring Harbor had all but faded. Otto, too, had made visible cutbacks on his many extravagances. The stopover parties were one such casualty. The carefree jovialities came to an end.

His health was also playing up again, slowly and noticeably deteriorating, as it would continue to do over the next couple of years. If the financial markets appeared in permanent turmoil, then 1930 proliferated the fact. As a Wall Street titan of finance, Otto would personally take on board a lot of the angst and frustrations vented by the public, which accumulatively added to the slow decline of his health.

When things could not get any worse for Otto, they did. His prized yacht *Oheka II* caught fire.[61] The incident happened while the boat was moored off Pilot Street on City Island at Robert Jacob Shipyard, where the ship was undergoing an overhaul. During a routine trial by Captain William T. Young, the exhaust of one of the 300 horsepower engines backfired, igniting woodwork in the engine room. By chance, only three deckhands were on board at the time. Firefighters swiftly arrived and managed to contain the fire, preventing it from spreading to further sections of the vessel. In all, the mishap caused $10,000 worth of damage, most being caused by water.

Cabot Aerial Pickup Trials at Mitchel Field

The Post Office showed great interest in Cabot's Aerial Pickup Device and agreed to attend a test trial. The airfield chosen for Roger to carry out the test flights was Mitchel Field on Long Island, as the field was smaller with less air traffic than Roosevelt or Curtiss. Friday, August 8, was the agreed date.

The expansion of Air Mail was an ongoing consideration for the postal service, and Godfrey Cabot hoped to corner the market with his innovative device. The pickup apparatus was positioned on top of a trailer. The driver parked the vehicle in the center of the field.

Roger, Godfrey Cabot, A. W. Card (builder of the device), and Francis E. Smith (a U.S. Post Office representative) met up at the field early that morning and familiarized themselves with the day's procedure and discussed how the results would be determined.

Roger would make 100 flights. Each flight would be meticulously logged and timed for efficiency and accuracy of the mailbag pickups. Finally, after 100 attempts, the experiment would finish.

A movie camera fitted atop a truck was there to film the action. Also on hand was a photographer to capture stills. Those present to witness the display included Lieutenant Colonel Gerald C. Brant of the Army Air Services, Commander J. Ross of the Navy, and a couple of rival airmail contractors. Cabot had a lot riding on the trials, as did Roger.

'The device consists chiefly of a catapult actuated by a series of ½-inch special shock cords. The catapult propels a carrier along a twelve-foot runway, and it is during this action the plane picks up the mail sack.'[62] The pouch was then drawn up into the aircraft through a trap door using an automatic winch.[63]

The weather was ideal with few clouds and no rain forecast. The Post Office required at least 75 of the 100 pickups delivered correctly before committing to use the device. Roger had his work cut out; concentration and precision were the two key factors that would govern his performance. Roger flew his Bellanca, equipped with a Wright J-5 engine. Under Post Office guidelines, he would have to fly at speeds no less than 85 mph.

Cabot Air Trials, August 8, 1930, (left to right): Roger, A. W. Card, Godfrey Lowell Cabot, and Francis E. Smith. 'Roger Wolfe Kahn piloted the plane; A. W. Card built the device; Francis E. Smith watched the test on behalf of the Post Office Dept. It enables Air Mail planes to pick up without stopping.'

It would be a long day; the first flight lifted off at 11:12 a.m.

The trials continued throughout the day in five-block sections of twenty maneuvers that took until 5:55 p.m. to complete. Two one-hour and two ½-hour breaks separated the five blocks. One hundred and two flights were accomplished, with a total success rate of 101 percent. Only one pickup missed the target due to the hook not being in the correct position.

The loads Roger lifted ranged from 5 to 40 pounds in weight. The day-long experiment was deemed a resounding success and gave Cabot the result he had hoped. The U.S. Post Office was interested in taking the tests further. They arranged to have six devices installed in Norfolk, Virginia, to carry out a six-month trial using the system on one of their legitimate airmail routes.

Roger picks up a mailbag during the Cabot Air Trials, August 8, 1930.

Five days later, at 11 a.m., Roger set off from Roosevelt Field, piloting his Bellanca cabin monoplane to Virginia, accompanied by A. W. Card and his wife as passengers. The purpose of the trip was to organize the construction of the six airmail pickup devices in Norfolk for use in the city.[64]

In mid-August, a delegation of foreign pilots arrived in New York in transit to attend the National Air Races in Chicago. Not wanting to miss the opportunity of meeting them, Roger headed over to Long Island, where the group was checking out Curtiss and Roosevelt Airfields. The visitors were guests of Lt. Alford Joseph Williams Jr., a former Naval pilot and good pal of Roger's.[65] Among their ranks were the French racing pilot Marcel Doret, English RAF pilot Richard L. Atcherley, Schneider cup winner Friedrich Lohse of Germany, and Italian Marshal Pietro Columbo. Roger joined them on several demonstration flights. They first flew from Curtiss Field in two Curtiss Kingbirds circling New York City. There followed a second flight over Manhattan in a 22-passenger twin-motored Burnelli monoplane. Roger, Marcel Doret, and over-water flying record holder Roger Q. Williams alternated at the wheel. It was the largest plane young Kahn had handled.

On Thursday, August 20, Roger drove to the Hamptons on Long Island to front 'his orchestra' at an evening charity presentation of *Quogue Quips*, an annual musical revue held at the Quogue Field Club.[66] *Quogue Quips* was regarded as the blue-ribbon event of the Hamptons' social calendar and attracted capacity audiences from all sections of eastern Long Island. Roger's appearance was in keeping with his custom to support local events on the island whenever possible. It also highlights how Roger had now happily taken to guest appearances fronting orchestras that were not his.

A couple of weeks later, in keeping with Roger's wacky sense of humor, he turned up at Roosevelt Field, driving a kid's automobile, built to his design and specifications.[67] The car was no larger than a rideable showroom model made to carry one person. It came fitted with a Harley-Davidson JDH motorcycle engine that could reach a speed of 90 mph. Perhaps, this was an early birthday gift to himself. The vehicle became a fixture at the airfield, where Roger would regularly drive himself around in it.

In keeping with Otto's aim to raise additional capital, he sold his land on West 57th Street previously allotted for the new Metropolitan Opera House.[68] The plot was now earmarked for an apartment block. For the present, the Met would remain where it was, as would its numerous inconveniences: draughty corridors, endless flights of stairs, obstinate pillars, and such.

On a more harmonious note, the luxury Pierre Hotel at 2 East 61st Street, which Otto helped finance, opened for business on October 1. The new hotel was created and jointly owned by Charles Pierre Casalasco and various financiers. Through its gilded revolving doors, the Pierre welcomed the crème de la crème of New York society.[69] Casalasco was said to have specified that the last rivet hammered into the copper-clad mansard be one of solid gold. The $15 million French château-style hotel, 'a majestic monument to simplicity, beauty, and refinement,' arrived with a hefty price tag. After opening, the Pierre attracted healthy business. But, with the ailing economy, how long that would continue was anyone's guess.*

A New Assignment

In the seven years since Roger established his first professional jazz orchestra, he'd spent a considerable amount of time doing things that were unexpected of him. Now, at the worldlier age of twenty-three, he veered off course yet again, this time into the world of journalism. He accepted the temporary position of aviation columnist for the *Newark Free Press*. In some respects, it was the most routine task he'd undertaken, being bound to a desk, although he would write his pieces from home, not at the newspaper's head office.

Whether the term 'nepotism' crept into the newsroom is not documented; what is known is that Roger's brother-in-law John Barry Ryan Jr. co-founded the *Newark Free Press*.[70] Roger's first article appeared on Monday, November 3. He conveys his opinions on aviation and gives his readers up-to-date news and developments from the airfield. Two more pieces followed, published on the two consecutive Mondays. In one article titled 'Aero Plain Talk,' Roger lays into 'endurance flyers' labeling them 'pseudo-d'Artagnan's of the air.'[71] Whether this rant was directed at his former business partner Rene Racover over his allegiance with the endurance flyer Dieudonné Costes, Roger does not articulate. His damnatory views of such aviators were no secret and had previously been documented.

Night-flying

Night-flying took one giant leap forward on November 7, with the inauguration of a night lighting system at Curtiss Field.[72] Boundary lights, beacon lights, obstruction lights, ceiling beam lights, and wind direction indicator lights had all been newly installed, along with giant floodlights, the brightest of which lit up the far corner of the landing field. The system was the largest at any airport. The light projected was the equivalent of 4 million candlepower and illuminated the airport at night as if it was daytime. Despite the cold weather, the evening unveiling ceremony attracted thousands of sightseers and flight enthusiasts. Roger was also there to witness and participate in the occasion.

New York Commissioner of Public Works, John J. Halleran, threw the switch just as a Curtiss Condor biplane carrying eighteen passengers flew into the airport and landed smoothly directly in front of the terminal building, timed perfectly for the event. A roar of boisterous applause from the spectators greeted its arrival. A demonstration of aerial acrobatics followed, the more daring of which was performed by Roger in his Bellanca biplane as he attempted, and succeeded, to dodge searchlight beams aimed at him. The evening's entertainment came to a thrilling end when George Pynchon Jr., amateur aviator, and son of Wall Street broker George M.

Pynchon, took up a plane equipped with calcium flares and lit up the skies with a pyrotechnics display.

The *'Cheerful Little Earful'*

All of a sudden, Roger looked happy again as if he'd just received some heartening news. He had. Hannah Williams was back in town and had decided to get in touch with him. To everyone in their circle, it seemed they had become an item again.

Hannah was currently appearing on Broadway as a solo act in the smash musical revue *Sweet and Low*, in which she had a featured song, the aptly named *'Cheerful Little Earful.'* The tune had become a hit and a Broadway favorite with audiences. Suddenly Hannah was hot property.

By coincidence, the cast of *Sweet and Low* had appeared on the bill of a benefit show organized by the *Evening Graphic* at the Broadhurst Theatre on December 14, the same show Roger had performed at with one of his orchestras. Had Roger gotten wind that Hannah was performing at the benefit and thus accepted the gig? Did Roger and Hannah run into one another backstage?

News travels fast, but not always for the right reasons. The gossip among stage door Johnnies was that Roger and Hannah had become secretly engaged. The rumor trickled back to Otto and Addie. That's when the real fireworks began.

Candlelit meals for two in well-regarded restaurants had become a regular occurrence for the couple. Of course, tongues were wagging; they were young, impetuous, and so obviously smitten with one another. Before long, the press hit on them. After all, Roger was one of the most eligible young bachelors in America and Hannah, a mere showgirl. Reporters were soon stalking their trail. Roger had grown up under the glare of the public spotlight; it seemed only natural that the same public should scrutinize and take an interest in whom he was dating. Hannah, in comparison, was new to such press shenanigans. For her, such intrusive behavior was difficult for her to navigate.

Hannah had only recently gone solo, trying her luck on stage without her sister Dorothy alongside her. She had been lucky and secured her most prominent role to date. *Sweet and Low* starred Fanny Brice and George Jessel, two of the biggest names on Broadway. Jessel also had an eye for the pretty lassies and would later recall in his biography titled *So Help Me*, 'Little Hannah and I had a tiny crush, but she was keeping company with Roger Wolfe Kahn, the son of the famous banker. She was told by Fanny Brice that I was the last guy in the world she should fall in love with.' Hannah took Fanny's advice.

The festive season came all too soon. At the Kahn residence, the usual sackful of social invitations arrived. The only headache for Otto and Addie was choosing which invites to accept and which ones to decline. On Sunday ahead of Xmas day, *The Bohemian Club* (a musicians' club) held a celebratory dinner at the Hotel Commodore. This year's event honored the Austrian-born conductor Artur Bodanzky, a regular presence at the Metropolitan Opera House. Otto sat at Bodanzky's table along with soprano Gertrude Kappel, Giulio Gatti-Casazza and his wife Frances, and Gatti's assistant Edward Ziegler. Around five hundred guests attended. For some unexplained reason, Addie was absent from her husband's side at the guest of honors table; she sat elsewhere in the ballroom accompanied by Bohemian Club member Siegfried H. Kahn.

The evening before Christmas Eve saw Otto out enjoying a visit to the Astor Theatre as the guest of soprano Grace Moore* to see the premiere of *New Moon*, a movie operetta she was starring in alongside baritone Lawrence Tibbett. Both were leading stars of the Metropolitan Opera. It was their first appearance on screen together. The following day's reviews were less than enthusiastic about the coupling, with the *Brooklyn Daily Eagle* declaring harshly, '*New Moon* is less than a first-rate talking picture.'[73]

New Year's Eve took on an air of expectancy. After the celebrations had passed, the very next day, Otto returned to his office at Kuhn, Loeb. Big changes were on the horizon. In a statement to the press, Otto confirmed that Kuhn, Loeb had promoted three company employees to general partners.[74] All three were the sons of present senior members of the firm; Johnny Schiff, offspring of Mortimer L. Schiff, Felix M. Warburg's firstborn son Frederick, and Otto's eldest son Gilbert. Gilbert had worked his way up the company ladder in just over three years since joining Kuhn, Loeb in September 1927.

Back at the Kahn household, things were not as cordial as they might seem. Something was brewing.

14

THE SECRET'S OUT!

'Having a millionaire father has been a terrible nuisance.'[1]
Roger W. Kahn

1931

On Tuesday, January 20, Addie attended a charity ball at the Ritz-Carlton Hotel, accompanied by her daughter-in-law Anne. The annual benefit aided New York's Nursery and Child's Hospital.[2] It was an event Addie felt particularly close to and one she had associated herself with for many years. To the guests, nothing seemed in the least bit out of the ordinary regarding Addie's demeanor. On the contrary, Addie had an enjoyable evening socializing with her friends without reason to arouse any suspicion that something might be awry. There was no mention of the prevailing gossip circulating among society about her son Roger and the Broadway actress Hannah Williams. Why should she be alarmed, or indeed, act out of character when the rumors were, after all, unsubstantiated! Addie and Anne remained tight-lipped about the subject, side-stepping any mention of Roger's private affairs. Even reporters in their reviews of the ball omitted any reference to the Kahns' youngest son. Perhaps they knew otherwise and were reasonably sure this was the calm, albeit a tempered lull before the proverbial storm broke. It was a game of cat and mouse, an activity the press and the Kahns were adept at playing.

Reporters were already on the scent and stationed tactically outside the Kahns mansion on Fifth Avenue and at the stage door of the Broadway theater[3] where Hannah was appearing in *Sweet and Low*.[4] It was most uncharacteristic of the Kahn family not to be vacationing in Palm Beach at this time of the year, as they generally did each January. The official explanation handed out by Otto's publicist mentioned his ailing health. But surely, Florida would have been more conducive for his physical well-being?

That weekend a great deal of activity took place at the Kahns' Cold Spring Harbor estate, as staff prepared the house for visitors. Otto, however, was still nowhere to be seen.

Early on Monday morning, a small fleet of limousines departed from the Kahns' Fifth Avenue mansion and headed southeast in the direction of Long Island and Jericho Turnpike. Around an hour later, the vehicles pulled up outside the entrance to the Kahn estate and drove through the open gates and continued along the graveled driveway towards the mansion. The gatekeeper hurriedly shut the wrought iron gates after the last vehicle had cleared the gatehouse. Roger, Addie, Gilbert, and his wife Anne, were spotted inside the cars, along with several unidentified passengers. What followed was a bizarre series of comings and goings and unexplained behavior sworn to secrecy.

That evening Hannah Williams appeared on Broadway as billed in *Sweet and Low.* As she arrived at the backstage door, she looked particularly radiant but spoke to no one as she brushed aside the waiting reporters and entered the theater. She then walked briskly to her dressing room to ready herself for her performance.

Over the succeeding two weeks, the rumors and gossip hit fever pitch. Something had taken place at the Kahns' country estate, and the press were itching for the story.

ROGER WOLFE KAHN,
ORCHESTRA LEADER, OWNS
HIS OWN PLANE AND HAS A
TRANSPORT PILOT'S LICENSE.

Roger was now the proud owner
of a transport pilot's license.

On Thursday, January 29, Roger sat his transport pilot's license exam at Roosevelt Field.[5] As expected, reporters were on hand to capture the occasion. Roger knew the airfield well; it was where he housed his aircraft. Part of the assessment included a series of practical maneuvers, which he carried out in one of his own planes. Oren P. Harwood of the Department of Commerce was there to assess his handling of the controls. For the final part of the exam, Roger sat a written paper. He passed all sections with flying colors. His transport pilot's license (No. 104) was the highest issued by the Department of Commerce. As a fully qualified pilot, Roger could now fly paying passengers, which suddenly opened up a whole new flight path for him to consider.[6]

In Friday's late edition newspapers, reports surfaced of a young lady accompanying Roger to the airfield that morning, during which he took up a single-seat biplane. At the time, the identity of the female remained a mystery.[7] Later updates confirmed the young lady was Hannah Williams.

On Monday, February 2, Addie journeyed to Palm Beach to prepare Oheka Cottage for occupancy.[8] Otto, who showed definite signs of improvement from his recent health concerns, did not join his wife and remained in New York City to catch up with business matters.*

On the afternoon of Saturday, February 7, producer Billy Rose issued a press statement announcing that Dorothy Williams, Hannah's sister, would be taking over Hannah's role in *Sweet and Low* taking effect from Monday, February 9. Rose declined to explain why Hannah was leaving the show.

Finally, on Sunday morning, February 8, Otto issued an official statement to the press from his family home on Fifth Avenue; Roger and Hannah Williams had wed.

A Showgirl!

No matter what Roger said, Addie and Otto were never going to approve of Hannah. She was a miner's daughter from a working-class family, with one failed marriage behind her, and was a showgirl.[9] On no account did Hannah Williams tick any of the right boxes as a suitable wife for their youngest son.

Otto forbade the marriage. Addie agreed with her husband. Roger remained intransigent and took no notice of his parents. After all, he was a grown man, aged over twenty-one, and could make his own decisions. Hannah stayed put. Otto was adamant he would not be provoked into saying or doing something he might later regret.

Father and son both remained taciturn on the matter. Neither would back down. As Roger intended, the marriage went ahead.

Unfortunately, the bride was a little less convenient with her dialog. Word soon ricocheted along Broadway's theater district, from backstage door to backstage door, of the prince and the showgirl's alliance, bringing reporters crawling from their offices sniffing for an exclusive. In the media's eyes, it was a true-life Cinderella story.[10] Kahn marries his 'cheerful little earful' echoed many of the dailies. They also noted that Roger's preference for jazz and aviation over the banking profession was second in drama to the rise of his bride's fame on the stage and her triumph at securing the hand and heart of a scion of one of the wealthiest families in America. 'From small beginnings, by her own faith in herself, she has risen to an envied place.'[11]

So here is the story as and when it happened:

On Monday, January 26, Roger and Hannah secretly wed on Long Island at the Kahns' country estate.[12] It was not the big society wedding everyone would have expected, especially considering their three other offspring's marriages had been such colorful occasions with invitations mailed to hundreds of guests apiece. Furthermore, there was no prior announcement of the wedding in the society columns, not even a whisper of an engagement. Instead, the simple, quiet ceremony took place in a manner that was totally out of character with the family's usual tradition. Neither did Otto, or Roger's sisters, or the parents of the bride attend the ceremony. No member of Hannah's family was present, not even her close sister, Dorothy. The two witnesses at the marriage were Roger's mother and his brother Gilbert. Even the Justice of the Peace who performed the ceremony, John Deans, was local, from the parish of Huntington on Long Island.[13]

Later that evening, the newlywed couple toasted their union with an intimate reception at the Kahn home on Fifth Avenue,[14] after Hannah had delivered her performance in Sweet and Low.

When Otto released the statement confirming the marriage had taken place, it was thirteen days after the event. In doing so, maybe Otto had hoped the item might be regarded as old news and assigned to the back pages. If so, his hopes fell flat. The next day the story hit the front pages of many of the national newspapers.[15]

'Miss Williams has retired from the stage, and the couple has left for an extended wedding trip.'

The unusual circumstances surrounding the announcement aroused the media's suspicions. It also became apparent that not all members of the Kahn family were in favor of the bond. Indeed, reports claimed, 'Otto gave his approval to the union, it was understood, only on the condition that she [Hannah] forsake her stage career.'[16] Hannah did forgo her stage career, not willingly, but under pressure, and on the insistence from Billy Rose, who handled Hannah's business affairs, that she serve two weeks' notice as per her contract. Otto's failure to be present at his youngest son's wedding, and his late endorsement of the union, merely provided further fuel for speculation. Did Otto purposely exclude himself from his son's wedding? Otto claimed illness (influenza) prevented him from being present. Was he really too ill to attend? Somehow, his excuse for being absent did not ring true. Otto had been adamant he would not approve the alliance until Hannah had officially quit her stage career. The day after Hannah gave her last performance in *Sweet and Low*, Otto acknowledged the marriage by releasing the press statement.

When a reporter questioned minister John Deans about the marriage, he readily revealed what took place when Roger and Hannah exchanged their vows. On the morning of January 26, Deans received a phone call from the Kahn home asking if he could officiate at a marriage ceremony later that day.[17] It was an unusual request, insofar as it sounded so rushed. That aside, he agreed and arranged for the interested parties to drop by Huntington Hall at 10 a.m. to collect the license. When Roger, Hannah, and Addie arrived, Hannah told the Town Clerk, William B. Trainer, that she had previously been married and had the marriage annulled. Annoyingly for everyone, she did not have the official documentation with her to confirm the fact, and the clerk could not issue the license without first seeing it. The party immediately left to secure the annulment decree, which was back in Manhattan. Later that day, they produced the document, and the marriage license was issued. Roger and Hannah exchanged vows at half-past four that afternoon in the music room at the Cold Spring Harbor mansion. Justice Deans admitted the groom had asked him to withhold any mention of the union for the time being, to which he complied. However, since the news was now in the public domain, Deans felt comfortable talking about it.

The press portrayed Hannah as a fresh-faced *ingénue*, a young showgirl with little experience in life who had only recently achieved minor recognition on Broadway in a musical comedy. That Hannah had abandoned her stage career at the insistence of her father-in-law to devote all her time to her husband did not sit well in the minds of friends close to the bride. Nevertheless, in the public's eyes, it would seem the lovers were all set to live a life of marital bliss in relative luxury. From that moment onward, the media became insufferable, following the couple's every move.

Happily ever after, it was never going to be.

Tonight You Belong To Me

Roger and Hannah may have forgone a lavish wedding, but Otto did fork out for their extended honeymoon, whether as a belated gift or as an order from Addie is unclear. The couple's itinerary would take nine months to complete.

Early on Monday morning, the press gang hurried down to Roosevelt Field to snap pictures of the newlyweds as they prepared for their departure. When the reporters arrived, a hive of activity was taking place. Roger's Bellanca cabin monoplane had been wheeled out of the hangar and put through the usual checks by an engineer. Such tests, as occur before a long-haul flight: compass, fuel, instruments, etc.[18] Roger and Hannah, on the other hand, were nowhere to be seen. The newsmen hung around all day, but to no avail, the honeymooners never turned up. The couple's first stop was to have been a brief visit to Hannah's mother in Scranton, Pennsylvania, to inform her of the marriage. But that trip got canceled at the last minute due to Mattie being unwell and her reluctance to entertain visitors.

Instead, Roger and Hannah rearranged their plans and decided to fly to Florida the following day to stay at Oheka Cottage in Palm Beach. Early that morning, back at Roosevelt Field, those same reporters from the previous day dashed back to the airfield and did this time manage to capture pictures of the couple just as they were about to depart.

Before Roger and Hannah visited Palm Beach, they checked into the smart Roney Plaza Hotel on Miami Beach, where they spent the first few days of their honeymoon relaxing around the pool.[19] In doing so, they hoped to get the media off their backs. Despite their ploy, the newshounds quickly sniffed out their whereabouts. Pretty soon, pictures of them looking smitten began appearing in the dailies. Also staying at the same hotel were Vincent J. Burnelli (the airplane designer) and his wife, the former model Hazel Goodwin.* The recently married couple were friends of Roger's. During their visit, the two couples hung out together.[20]

Roger, looking extremely pleased with himself, holding
Hannah's hand at the Roney Plaza Hotel, Miami Beach.

A few days later, Roger and Hannah journeyed south. Due to bad
weather, they abandoned plans for an all-flying honeymoon and left
by automobile. There was still some light left in the day when they
arrived in Palm Beach, so Roger drove straight to Oheka Cottage to
join his parents and their guests for supper.[21]

Roger was feeling dangerously happy; he'd married the girl of his
dreams, followed the musical path of his passion, and proved many a
cynic wrong. He and Hannah had every intention of enjoying their
honeymoon irrespective of the tensions within their family circle.

Oheka Cottage was fully occupied with family and houseguests
when Roger and Hannah arrived, with further visitors due in the
coming days. Consequently, Roger and Hannah remained only one
night, preferring to drive back to Miami. They planned to return to
Palm Beach in early March when the villa would be empty. Maud had
also turned up to spend time with her parents and acquaint herself
with her new sister-in-law. Having Maud around for the evening took
the heat off Roger and Hannah. One of the couples staying at Oheka
was the Earl and Countess of Moray. The Earl planned on spending
most of his visit playing golf.[22] Winston Churchill's son Randolph and

his mother Clementine were also enjoying a few days break in Palm Beach courtesy of the Kahns' hospitality, as was Sir William George Eden Wiseman and the tobacco heiress Nancy Yuille.[23]

Back in Miami, the press continued to hound Roger and Hannah.[24] Newsreel reports of the marriage and footage of the elusive couple relaxing in Miami flashed across movie theater screens. Pictures of Hannah's sister Dorothy, hugging up to Fanny Brice - the star of *Sweet and Low* - also appeared in the dailies, giving the now ailing Broadway show some much-needed publicity. It also, unnervingly, reminded Hannah of what she had forfeited for the sake of her marriage. Strangely, it seemed Otto and Addie had finally gotten their way, albeit in a roundabout manner.

The Palm Beach season had begun to wind down when Roger and Hannah returned to take up residence at Oheka Cottage in early March.[25] New York society had traveled back whence they came, giving the newlyweds some peace and the chance of privacy. It also allowed Roger to visit Palm Beach County Airport to check out the new up-to-date facilities and amenities the local council had installed to attract more flight paths to the area.[26]

On Saturday, March 7, Roger hired a Sikorsky five-passenger amphibious plane at the airport and spent the day flying with his wife.[27] Hannah was becoming quite addicted to the thrill of being airborne. Roger even offered to give her private flying tuition in exchange for her giving him one-to-one dance lessons. Roger may have been a brilliant bandleader, but he had two left feet when he danced.[28] With no pressing schedules, Roger and Hannah lingered on in Palm Beach for several weeks, unwinding, planning their future, and piecing together the itinerary for the European leg of their honeymoon to begin in late April.[29]

Roger and Hannah Return to New York

When Roger and Hannah arrived back in New York City, they took up temporary residence at the Kahns' Fifth Avenue mansion. Although Roger stressed the arrangement was short-term, until the couple found a suitable property of their own, Hannah viewed the prospect of living with her in-laws wholly unsatisfactory and put up stiff opposition to the plan from the offset. Roger stubbornly refused to be swayed on the matter. Moneywise, it seemed the sensible option given his present precarious financial circumstances. It also meant he could work from the music studio he'd built on the top floor. Given their stay would be transitory, Hannah bit her lip and busied herself catching up with friends, shopping, and generally keeping herself occupied away from the house.

On April 9, Roger flew Hannah to Detroit in his Bellanca monoplane.[30] The trip coincided with the National Aircraft Show. It was the first time the show had been held at Detroit City Airport.[31] The event officially opened on Saturday, April 11, and ran for ten days.

It was advertised as one of the biggest airshows ever staged and turned out to be one of the finest to date. What made the exhibition so unique was how the exhibits were presented in the hangars and on the airport's apron, encouraging the public and prospective buyers to view the machines close up.[32]

Although Roger was coaching Hannah to fly, tensions between the couple came to light at the event when a reporter approached Roger and sneakily inquired how his wife was taking to flying? Caught in an off-guarded moment, Roger let slip his opinion that women had no business being aviators.[33]

Aviation History and Roger's First U.S. Flight Cover

Roger had one further impending appointment inked in his diary before he and Hannah could head off to Europe on the second leg of their honeymoon. He'd promised Godfrey L. Cabot he would test-fly his Aerial Pickup Device in Norfolk, Virginia, on April 21. The trials would be the first-ever mail pickup attempt from a building situated in a city center. A lot was riding on this demonstration, and Roger had no intention of letting Cabot or the U.S. Postal Department down.

Roger and Hannah flew from Roosevelt Field in his Bellanca CH-400 Skyrocket monoplane early that morning directly to Norfolk, Virginia, for the trial. When they arrived, Cabot's device was in position atop a tall warehouse in the heart of the city close to Union Station. Also, on top of the flat-roofed building to view the display were officials from the U.S. Postal Department, Godfrey Cabot, engineer A. W. Card, officials from the U.S. Army and Navy, and news crews, photographers, and a Universal film unit. Roger knew the drill inside out. After dropping Hannah off so she could watch from the roof, Roger flew straight off to begin the trials.

The first two attempts were unsuccessful due to stiff crosswinds. On the third, Roger, flying at 80 mph, made a daring low altitude dip (swooping to within a few yards of the pickup point), swung the steel hook into the catapulting machine, and darted away with two mail pouches weighing 25 pounds apiece.

Roger maneuvering his plane on April 21 during a pick up from the Aerial Pickup Device positioned on the roof of a building in Norfolk, Virginia.

It was the first time in aviation history an object had been snatched from the roof of a building by an aircraft.[34]

Cheers and howls of delight spilled out over the rooftop. Hannah waved her hat in the air, thrilled at her husband's achievement and his nerve. Her jubilation was the result of a mixture of giddy emotions, for each time she had watched her husband swoop towards the building, she had ducked and looked away, burying her head in her arms until the plane had flown by, fearing he might come a cropper and crash.[35]

The U.S. Postal Department was so impressed with the trial and Roger's demonstration that the following day they issued an official postmarked envelope to commemorate his accomplishment.

Footage of the pickup was captured for posterity by Universal Pictures and broadcast in one of their newsreel features released under the heading: 'Speeding airplane successful in first mail rooftop pick up. Bandleader aviator Roger Wolfe Kahn makes daring low altitude pickup of mail in Norfolk, Virginia.' The newsreel played in picture houses across America.

An original Roger Wolfe Kahn official U.S. Postal Flight Cover Envelope to commemorate the first mail pick up from the roof of a building in the heart of a city. The flight took place in Norfolk, VA., on April 21, 1931.

The Kahns Are Back In Europe

Otto had already made the voyage across the Atlantic in mid-April, accompanied by his valet Frederick Cooper. He was now in London comfortably installed in Claridge's Hotel, awaiting his wife's arrival at the end of the month.* Otto's unstable health was the prime reason for this year's lengthier than usual summer vacation.

Almost immediately after Roger's historic flight in Norfolk, he and Hannah returned to New York to prepare for their imminent departure to Europe. Addie had prearranged for her and the newlyweds to sail first-class aboard the North German Lloyd liner SS *Bremen*.

In London, Roger and Hannah checked into the Savoy Hotel. Addie joined her husband at Claridge's.[36] A few days later, Otto and Addie journeyed across to the continent, where they planned to remain until early July.

Hôtel Ritz, Paris, April 29, 1931

On a beautiful Paris afternoon, Otto met up with the poet and literary impresario Ezra Pound in the splendid surrounds of the Hôtel Ritz, where they shared a table in the restaurant. The date was April 29.

Pound had initiated the meeting to convey his thoughts to Kahn on 'American civilization.'

Otto was ever willing to lend an ear on matters regarding America and the arts. However, just how far he would bend it, was called into question, as, at times, their discussion became quite fiery over various conflicting opinions. Pound was obsessively troubled with economics and the role of Jewish financiers within it. He appealed to Otto to invest more of his own money into Jewish culture and literature, especially in advancing the merit of poets such as Louis Zukofsky and George Oppen, two of the chief exponents of the Objectivism poetry movement founded earlier that year.

Pound's argument did not convince Otto, and the two became at loggerheads over the matter. Kahn's refusal to play along to Pound's tune caused Pound to later denounce the banker as a symbolic figure of economic injustice that would eventually lead to ethnic degeneration. Pound failed to grasp the real effect of the stock market crash globally, both in commercial and personal terms. Otto was in no position to invest capital in anything that would not prove financially profitable.

In the French capital, the Kahns met up with Adele Schiff, Mortimer L Schiff's wife. Mortimer was a senior partner at Kuhn, Loeb. Adele was killing time waiting for her husband to join her from New York for their summer vacation together.

From Paris, the Kahns journeyed by car to Germany, where in Berlin, they stayed at the plush Hotel Adlon on Unter den Linden boulevard overlooking the imposing Brandenburg Gate. Here, they met up with their son Gilbert, his wife Anne, and their grandchild Claire who were visiting relatives in the city.

On June 4, Otto received the shattering news that his Kuhn, Loeb colleague Mortimer L. Schiff had died from heart disease. Schiff passed away aged fifty-three, just one day short of his 54th birthday. Mortimer's wife, Adele, had remained in Paris anticipating her husband's arrival when she received the news of his passing. Adele and Addie had recently spent much time together in Paris.

The news came as a profound shock to Otto, not least because they were such close work colleagues, having both handled important railroad accounts, but because Schiff's death now placed Otto at the helm of Kuhn, Loeb & Co. The failing health of Kuhn Loeb's other senior partner Felix M. Warburg had recently caused him to lessen his workload. The tides of change were slowly passing over the old regime and, in its wake, heralding the new.

Gilbert, Anne, and Herr Kahn outside the Hotel Adlon, Berlin, May 1931.

(Photograph by Georg Pahl © German Federal Archive (Deutsches Bundesarchiv). The original negative was incorrectly accredited as being Roger, Hannah, and Otto.

The Russian Connection

A short mention appeared in *The Sentinel* saying Addie Kahn had visited Russia in June;[37] Otto had remained in Berlin. A couple of weeks later, Otto journeyed to Paris and then to Le Touquet on the northern coast of France, where Addie joined him there. From Le Touquet, the couple crossed to the UK and returned to London.

In April the following year, the French newspaper *Le Figaro* ran a series of damning articles, five in total, drawing attention to Addie's visit to Russia.* Two of the reports were splashed across the front page. The pieces, written by François Coty (founder of Coty cosmetic company and owner of *Le Figaro*), claimed Kuhn, Loeb & Co. had helped finance the Russian Revolution,[38] and that in June 1931 Addie had traveled to Russia as a guest of Joseph Stalin.[39]

Coty was known to hold deep-seated anti-Semite and anti-Communist views and had over the years adopted an extreme right-wing political stance believing Jewish bankers and financiers were at the root of the worldwide economic depression.

Coty alleged Mrs. Kahn had enjoyed a month-long trip to the USSR, 'where she was officially received there by the Soviet government, which gave in her honor a grand diplomatic dinner and several brilliant receptions. The ceremonial displayed exceeded in pomp and solemnity that of the journey of Amanullah (Khan) when King of Afghanistan. The Red Army lined the roads exhibiting their weapons . . . It was the least that the head of the 'Proletarian Dictatorship' could do in order to honor the wife of one of their sovereigns.'[40]

Prior to these articles, no account of Addie's visit to Russia had ever emerged, indicating there was either a pre-arranged news blackout on the matter or that the trip was conducted in secrecy outside of the Russian Federation.

Seven years earlier, on December 30, 1924, in a speech to the radical left-wing League for Industrial Democracy, Otto offered the socialist revolutionaries a friendly hand and shared goals. 'What you radicals and we who hold opposing views differ about, is not so much the end as the means, not so much what should be brought about as how it should, and can, be brought about . . .'[41]

Talk of Kuhn, Loeb & Co. professedly having financed the Bolshevik uprising in 1917, fitted in neatly with Coty's exposé of Addie's alleged Russian tea party. Indeed, Rev. Denis Fahey, in his 1938 pamphlet *The Rulers of Russia*, wherein he sets out his view that Bolshevism was really 'an instrument in the hands of the Jews for the establishment of their future Messianic kingdom,' questions the supposed political love affair between capitalist Otto Kahn and the anti-capitalist Soviet government, and reveals that during Stalin's reign, long after the 1917 revolution, Kahn enjoyed a special relationship with the Soviet Empire, which should have raised questions back home in the U.S. as to where his true loyalties lay.[42]

Whether Addie made the trip to Leningrad as an official guest of the Soviet government or visited on her own account is uncertain. Her itinerary indicated she could easily have sailed from Hamburg via the Baltic Sea to the USSR as she was geographically close enough at the time to do so. Addie spoke six languages and often traveled unaccompanied by her husband.[43] It was hearsay in certain circles that Ivy Lee handled public relations for the Soviet government in the U.S., a claim Lee was at pains to deny.[44] Lee had also made several trips to Russia.* If the Soviet government had been clients of Lee's, he could easily have arranged such a trip for Addie through his contacts. Addie never publicly responded to the allegations printed in *Le Figaro*. Indeed, no member of the Kahn family ever spoke openly about the revelations, a matter that, to this day, remains a mystery.

Boy Jazz King Retires (again)

A five-month tour of Europe was an extravagance Hannah had never experienced before. In England, Roger accompanied his wife to the usual round of tourist sites, mainly for Hannah's benefit, as it was her first trip to the UK. The couple also made time to drop by and see Maud and John and their growing son John Jr. at the Marriotts country home in Ascot. During a visit to Hendon Aerodrome at Colindale, Roger met up with the pilot Captain Walter Lawrence Hope to look over a de Havilland Puss Moth high-wing monoplane that Hope was selling.* After putting it to the test and giving the engine a thorough inspection, Roger bought the aircraft and arranged to have it shipped over to the States.[45]

On July 16, Hannah celebrated her 21st birthday, and where better to celebrate it than on her honeymoon. Roger's surprise gift to his wife was probably the largest present she had ever received in her entire life; an open two-seater Hornet Swallow car straight out of the showroom window.[46] Hannah was thrilled with her gift and took to driving it at every opportunity that presented itself.

In another unexpected shift, the press reported Hannah had not altogether given up her dream of conquering the stage and was in her leisure time studying opera singing, hoping to impress her father-in-law and secure a career at the Met.[47]

During the couple's stay at the Savoy Hotel, Roger gave an interview to a *Daily Mail* columnist. He talked frankly about the dilemma he currently faced regarding his music career, having achieved most of what he set out to do since entering the profession at the age of sixteen. Now, at the seasoned age of twenty-three, he found himself in a quandary, deliberating what to do next.

Though Roger sensed his father admired him for his tenacity, he still suspected he would probably have preferred it if he quit the music industry entirely. 'Maybe this trip is his thank-offering because I have given up jazz, but I may take up flying as a career, and father is not too keen about that either.' He paused briefly for a moment before adding, 'Oh, dear, another shock for father.' Roger concluded the interview by stressing a point that was still niggling him: 'The world seems to accept as gospel truth a story that my father settled $600,000 on me when I came of age. There is not a word of truth in that report. My father is not that kind of man, and he has not settled five cents on me. Having a millionaire father has been a terrible nuisance.' The article appeared beneath the banner 'Boy Jazz King Retires.' One can forgive the reader for thinking this would probably not be the last word they'd be hearing from Roger Wolfe Kahn.[48]

A few days later, the honeymooners were spotted in Juan-les-Pins on the Côte d'Azur dining at the ultra-expensive *Joseph* restaurant, a former favorite of Queen Victoria when she stayed at the French resort.[49]

Otto set sail from Southampton for New York on July 19 onboard SS *Bremen*.[50] Addie did not return to the U.S. until September.

No sooner had Otto settled back into his office routine at Kuhn, Loeb than he set to work compiling an ambitious report to bring an end to the economic slump. Otto issued a press statement outlining his new report during a brief trip to Chicago the following month to attend the outdoor Ravinia music festival.[51] In it, he prescribed a series of sweeping suggestions for improving the economy, urging the Government to repeal the Volstead Act and bring in changes to Trust Laws. Kahn also advocated help for the railroads and favored the introduction of higher interest rates. In addition, he warned of tax evils and strongly recommended more care and assistance for those most in distress. It was a bold move on Otto's part and one he firmly stood by, especially after experiencing firsthand the impact the recession was now having on the economy at home and abroad.

The Little Matter of Sachem's Neck

W. Kingsland Macy had been chairman of the Suffolk County Republican Committee since 1926. Suffolk County on Long Island was a stronghold for the Republicans. Within his circle, many viewed Macy as dictatorial and unreasoning. Nevertheless, he promoted himself to the public as a man of high ideals and character and as crusader for unflinching honesty in politics. Contrary to this, in September 1931, it came to light that Macy and his Republican machine had earlier in the year on March 30 secretly introduced a proposal in favor of a $5 million bond issue for public improvements. $3 million was allocated to build a three-span suspension bridge connecting Shelter Island to the mainland (at the eastern end of Long Island).[52] Such a scheme would have personally benefitted Macy and Otto Kahn, who owned, or had a substantial interest in, large tracts of land on Shelter Island.[53] By approving the resolution, the Suffolk County Board of Supervisors denied taxpayers the right to vote on the issue. Despite their speed in passing the motion, the bridge's construction could not proceed without federal permission. Documentation appertaining to the proposal was leaked, purportedly in a bid to influence voters in the run-up to next year's presidential election.

Senator John J. Dunnigan (the Democratic minority leader in the State Senate) brought corruption charges before the District Attorney of Suffolk County. He claimed 'influence' was placed upon the County Board of Supervisors to adopt the bond issue for public improvements by a political leader [W. Kingsland Macy] and a property owner [Otto H. Kahn].

The hearing took place on September 9. After weighing up the testimony, the grand jury found no evidence of criminal misconduct.[54] The jury invited Dunnigan to appear in person before the tribunal on September 28 to explain his allegations of wrongdoing. In his testimony, Dunnigan detailed two donations made the previous year to the Suffolk County Republican Campaign Committee fund, one by Kahn for $2,000, the other for $500 by Suffolk Consolidated Press, in which Macy held an interest.[55] Both payments were said to violate a section of the penal code. Dunnigan intimated Kahn's contribution might well have influenced the Board of Supervisors to approve the $5 million bond issue. His claim did not convince the grand jury. They dismissed the charges, and the investigation was closed.

Many years later, documents surfaced naming former newspaper editor C. S. Thompson as the possible whistleblower. Macy's attempt to slide through the bond issue failed. The bridge never got the go-ahead. For the present, Otto's 500 acres of undeveloped land at Sachem's Neck remained just that, untouched by a bulldozer.

The Lydia Lindgren Case Resurfaces

On the morning of September 29, a $500,000 breach of contract lawsuit brought against Otto by former opera singer Lydia Lindgren got underway before the Supreme Court and Jury at Long Island City Courthouse. Neither the defendant nor the plaintiff was in court for the proceedings.[56] Noting Kahn's absence, the singer's attorney, Emil Baar, made a motion to Justice Charles J. Druhan to compel the defendant's presence during the trial. Kahn's counsel George W. Whiteside successfully opposed the request. Whiteside then asked for permission to hold a private conference with opposing attorneys, which Justice Druhan granted. After thirty minutes, the lawyers returned, and the case proceeded.

The issue was whether or not a verbal agreement was made between Kahn and Lindgren back in 1930. Lindgren claimed the defendant had purportedly arranged to pay the singer $160,000 if she discontinued a slander suit against the opera singer Julia Claussen. The plaintiff's counsel affirmed that their client accepted Kahn's arrangement and subsequently dropped her case against Claussen, but she has only received $13,000 from Kahn since doing so.

Since the contract between Kahn and Lindgren was purportedly oral and with little evidence and no written documentation to present to the jury, the case was thrown out of court two days later.[57] The court also declared the slander action in the lawsuit fraudulent. The outcome brought a huge sigh of relief in the Kahn camp, not least from Otto. Predictably, Lindgren was furious with the result and vowed to appeal against the decision.

Roger and Hannah Return to New York

On October 7, Roger and Hannah, and Hannah's new Hornet Swallow, arrived in New York Harbor onboard SS *Bremen*.[58] Hannah was now becoming quite accustomed to all the attention they received from the media. True to form, as they made their way off the ship, the reporters were waiting to greet them. 'Harmony still reigns' and 'Smiling in Kahn-cert' were just a couple of the headlines that greeted them in the following day's newspapers, along with pictures of the duo smiling affably on the deck of the liner.[59]

Roger and Hannah onboard SS *Bremen*, returning from their honeymoon.

From the harborside, the couple headed straight to 1100 Fifth Avenue, which, for the foreseeable future, they would be calling home. Their return to America signaled the end of their honeymoon, and with it brought a new set of rules, challenges, and headaches.

Aviation had experienced the most staggering period of progress and growth during the past few years. The aircraft industry represented a total public investment of half a billion dollars and employed an estimated 100,000 people, and growing. If any sector was worth getting a foot in the doorway, it was the aviation business.[60] All trends in the market were pointing in the same direction, upwards.

Roger was now in two minds whether to continue with his original plan to compose music for the movies, resume his stage career as a bandleader, or take the giant leap into the aviation industry professionally. He'd been flirting with the idea of a full-time job as a pilot for some time. The coming months would see him toying to and fro, from one decision to another. His indecisiveness stemmed from his financial predicament. He had grown accustomed to earning and spending his own money; the thought of not having that financial safety net did not appeal to him. Furthermore, he now had a wife to support and, as such, incurred extra expenses. The fact that his daily monetary outgoings were increasing was a major concern to him.

Roger's immediate response was to streamline his operations. He ended his seven-year work collaboration with George Lottman and hired George Effenbach as his personal and agency manager. He continued operating his booking agency at 1607 Broadway that presently handled around half a dozen bands.[61] He did not, however, renew the lease on his Manhattan bachelor apartment. For the present, the newlyweds would carry on residing at the Kahns' Fifth Avenue mansion.

The idea of living out of a trunk under the same roof as her in-laws did not sit happily with Hannah. From the offset, she had aired her reservations about the proposal. Since the arrangement had taken effect, she had begun to feel confined, like a caged bird, with eyes watching every move she made. Her only ally in the house was Roger, and when he was not around, a deep sense of loneliness descended upon her. Roger had initially impressed upon her that they would either rent or purchase their own home. That option now appeared less likely as the weeks progressed.

After carrying out adjustments to his finances, Roger realized he still needed to make more changes. The obvious and quickest option available was to resume his stage career. The offers were already there, with contracts waiting for him to sign. Roger called George Effenbach and gave him the go-ahead to set the wheels in motion.

Meanwhile, Hannah, too, was facing a dilemma of her own. Since her marriage and her in-laws' insistence that she could no longer pursue her theatrical career, she had acquired an excessive amount of free time, which she was at odds to fill. Furthermore, the notion of having children was currently not a priority due to their domestic arrangements. Neither was she keen on filling in time by attending formal afternoon tea soirees or knitting circles.

Goodbye Mr. President

Otto's delicate health was of continual concern to his physician and those closest to him, although, to the outside world, it appeared he had the unlimited strength of Apollo. With his finances now compromised beyond immediate repair, he, too, was forced to confront some significant vicissitudes in his life. Knowing he could no longer bail out the Met at the drop of a baton, he made a momentous decision; on Monday, October 26, Otto resigned as president and chairman of the board of the Metropolitan Opera Company.[62] The official explanation he offered for his retirement was the increase of duties he now had to undertake at Kuhn, Loeb, since the death of his associate, the late Mortimer L. Schiff.[63] Exactly one week later, the Met's 1931-32 season opened with a performance of *La Traviata* with Rosa Ponselle in the lead role of Violetta.

Did he jump, or was he coerced? It was a question many were thinking. Undoubtedly, the recession had cut away a deep slice of the Met's sponsorship and donations. Ticket sales were also down. Maybe Otto knew more about the state of the Met's finances than he was letting on and, as such, wanted only to be associated with the good times. The full extent of the Met's debts would not become apparent until a year later, under the chairmanship of Kahn's successor Paul D. Cravath.

Otto had, for some years, been the cornerstone of the Metropolitan Opera Company. Each year when the board of directors assembled to dissect the current deficit report, all retinas fell on Otto to utter the decisive words 'charge it to me.'[64] From now on, that courtesy had gone. The Met would have to stand on its own foundations.

One report reckoned it cost Otto a cool quarter of a million dollars a year to make up the Met's losses.[65] Otto later admitted he'd spent over two million dollars on the company during his tenure in office.[66] Otto no longer had that sort of capital to lavish upon pet projects. He may have had a highly seasoned taste for music and all things grand, but he no longer had a bottomless purse. With Otto's resignation, his forays into grand opera came to a sudden and abrupt end, as did the sorties on his bank account.

Also, on October 26, Otto resigned as vice president and director of the New York Philharmonic Symphony Orchestra Society.[67] *

On November 9, the American playwright Samuel Nathaniel Behrman had his new play, a three-act comedy titled *Brief Moment*, produced on Broadway at the Belasco Theatre. The reviews were positive, and the show ran profitably for 129 performances. What made the work of great interest to everyone in the Kahn household was the suggestion that Behrman had based the plot around the dramas involving Roger and Hannah's relationship and their subsequent marriage.[68] Certainly, the resemblance between the newlyweds and the two lead characters in the play was uncanny; Robert Douglas, a rich, young male heir, falls deeply in love with Francine Larrimore, a working-class showgirl trying her luck on Broadway. Yet more tantalizingly, Behrman never actually denied if he had based the two lead characters on Roger and Hannah. That scintillating piece of tittle-tattle was left up to the audience to decide. Indeed, theater critic Brook Atkinson who worked for the *New York Times* was convinced of the roman à clef similarity.

The Bottom Line

As for Roger's music career, he had taken his eyes off the prize. Roger was presently a bandleader without an orchestra to lead. Some of his peers, such as Paul Whiteman, Vincent Lopez, Duke Ellington, et al., were reaping healthy rewards for their diligence. Also, Roger had been without a record deal for almost a year. If he were to make a fully-fledged comeback, he would have to form a new orchestra, sign a recording contract and jump back into the studio to lay down some hits. Annoyingly for Roger, he had to start from the beginning again; that was the bottom line.

Roger, being a Kahn, never did things by halves and formed not one but two new orchestras: one white, the other Black. He picked some of the hottest players on the New York club scene for the Black ensemble, rehearsed them, and had Chicago bandleader Lucky Millinder front it.[69] The outfit was booked on an RKO tour and played a long line of engagements, including dates in Harlem at the Lafayette, Opera House, Lincoln, Alhambra, and Apollo theatres. After Millinder left the band to join a rival outfit, Donald Heywood took over as leader.[70] The unit also secured a gig at a fashionable Broadway nightclub performing as the nucleus of an all-Black musical comedy.[71]

Included in his white orchestra, Roger secured the services of new boy, clarinetist Artie Shaw, who had previously been working as a session musician backing Bing Crosby on Crosby's CBS radio show.[72] With his new orchestra rehearsed and new connections to investigate, Roger began broadcasting on the radio again. His manager also had some good news in the pipeline, which he hoped to announce to the press in a couple of weeks at the start of the New Year, once Roger had approved and signed the contract.

On the evening of Wednesday, November 25, during the intermission of a performance of *La Bohème* at the Metropolitan Opera House, Otto walked out onto the stage to address the audience. He made a fervent appeal on behalf of the Emergency Relief Committee to help aid the jobless. It was a selfless act delivered by the former president. It also assured people that he might have resigned from his posts as chairman and president at the Met, but he was still a director and intended to retain a visible presence.

Otto at the Senate Finance Committee in Washington, D.C., December 21.

Christmas week began ominously for Otto, with him sitting before the Senate Finance Committee in Washington, D.C., as part of the Pecora Investigation. The U.S. Senate had established the Pecora Commission to study the causes of the 1929 Wall Street Crash. In front of the committee, Kahn appeared relaxed, and during the questioning, he expressed his confidence that the repayment of foreign loans would proceed as arranged.

Early on Christmas day morning, Roger left the Kahn mansion at Fifth Avenue and drove to Roosevelt Field, where, at 10:05 a.m., he and a fellow pilot D. E. Whittler flew off in Kahn's de Havilland Puss Moth plane en route to Glenn H. Curtiss Airport. A report of his departure appeared in the *Brooklyn Daily Eagle* the following day.[73] Why Roger should be away from his home and family on the first Christmas he and his wife should have been sharing was not explained.

By marrying Roger, Hannah had become a member of the upper echelons of New York society and was now expected by her husband and in-laws to act as such whether she liked it or not. Those demands were beginning to gnaw away at her. Hannah was headstrong and stubborn. She found her lack of freedom stifling and slowly began to rebel. Her change in attitude did not sit well with Roger, Addie or Otto, or any other member of the Kahn household. A noticeable rift developed between her and the Kahn family that put her marriage under tremendous strain. Roger's loyalty was slowly evaporating. He, too, held the same views as his parents, that Hannah should make more effort to settle down and turn change into a positive. For Hannah, trying to be a housewife without her own home was not an easy role to play. Hannah was pining for her former life. Driving around in Roger's world was not the life she had envisaged. She missed Broadway's glamor, the bright lights, the roar of the crowd, and the adulation that Broadway bestows upon its favorite stars.[74] Most of all, she missed her freedom.

Roger now found himself facing another quandary, one that required delicate handling. Somewhere along the line, someone had to back down. The way forward would not be easy for either Roger or Hannah.

15

A CHANGE IS IN THE AIR

When you're facing a blank page,
you have to look elsewhere for inspiration.

1932

A huge ray of optimism arrived at the beginning of January when Columbia Records offered Roger a lucrative recording deal.[1] His reinvention had commenced. Roger signed an exclusive contract with Columbia for one year. Over the coming twelve months, he would make a dozen recordings for the label. His manager penciled in the first studio session for early May. Meanwhile, Roger continued rehearsing and refashioning his orchestra, adding budding instrumentalists to take with him on the next chapter of his career.

Regrettably, the year did not start so optimistically for Otto, who, on January 4, was summoned back to Washington, D.C., to testify again before the Senate Finance Committee. Kuhn, Loeb & Co. had sold more than a billion dollars' worth of foreign securities in the past ten years. Questions arose asking whether Kuhn, Loeb's tactics in selling these bonds had been too bullish. The Committee requested Otto to clarify whether the current low prices of bonds materialized because the public had purchased them at higher rates than they warranted. In his reply, Kahn assured the Committee that bond prices were not determined by bankers but by the law of supply and demand. That the market had fallen was indicative of their current low value.

Since that fateful day on Wall Street back in 1929, Kuhn, Loeb & Co.'s assets had plummeted from a staggering $120,402,103 to $66,974,845 in 1931.[2] The fall in value emphasized what was happening in the global economy. It also gave some indication as to how severely Otto's fortune must have taken a battering. Kahn's worrying concerns about cutting back and changing course were genuine and became increasingly evident in his daily activities, most noticeably by his less extravagant lifestyle. Although his continuing health issues were also a determining factor in his quieter, calmer approach to life, he was adamant there was still life in the old German Shepherd. His vacations may have lasted longer, but that did not stop his workload from piling up no matter how much attention he gave to the details.

From Washington, D.C., Otto and Addie journeyed south to Palm Beach, where on January 6, they joined family members and friends for their winter break at Oheka Cottage.[3] The following day, Otto and Addie were guests at a small private party given by architect Maurice Fatio and his wife Eleanor at their family villa.[4]

Otto's days spent golfing at Palm Beach Country Club proved just the tonic he needed. He even made time to attend the first night of a new production at the local Playhouse Theatre to catch Rachel Crowthers' comedy Let Us Be Gay.

Once again, Oheka Cottage played host to a cluster of cosmopolitan houseguests. Family members included Margaret and John and their young son John Barry Ryan III and Maud and her husband, John.[5] Other guests were the exiled Grand Duke Dmitri Pavlovich of Russia (said conspirator in the death of Grigori Rasputin) and his attractive wife, Princess Anna Romanovsky-Ilyinsky. On Friday, January 8, Roger and Hannah flew into Palm Beach to join the party. Roger rented a private villa, Bellamar, so he and Hannah could spend some quality time on their own. Here Hannah could escape the meddling of her disapproving in-laws. A local reporter captured a picture of the couple out bicycling together.[6]

For the elder Kahns, their stay turned out not to be the quiet, relaxed, recuperative sojourn they had hoped. Back in the winter of 1928-29, when their former neighbor Jacob Leonard Replogle sold Sunrise Villa to Simon William Straus, they never suspected Straus would convert the villa into a hotel and bathing complex. He did. Straus had since died. Over the past few months, the hotel had undergone a refurbishment. On January 15, the exclusive hotel and beach resort reopened for business. Rebranded the Sun & Surf Beach Club, the grounds now boasted new tennis courts, extra bathing facilities, and more than $800,000s of improvements. The prospect of intense activity and persistent noise from an influx of vacationers socializing at all times of the day and night was a reality the Kahns now had to face.

The thought of having their idyll compromised had, in 1930, prompted Otto and Addie to purchase a more secluded tract in an enclave further along the seafront in North End. The Council approved an architectural plan drawn up by Treanor & Fatio, and work had commenced clearing the land and laying the foundations of the new property.

As construction work proceeded throughout 1931, albeit at a snail's pace, various problems arose. The contractor's use of dynamite - to reform a rock ledge reef - led to windows shattering and surface damage to nearby Villa Artemis, causing its owner Frederick Guest to file a civil suit and the Town Council to issue a halt to the works. Encouragingly, matters were eventually resolved in Otto's favor enabling the building works to resume.

The continual pressure from keeping one step ahead of everything going on around him, plus the additional stress that generally accompanied such actions, had taken its toll on Otto's health. With each delay, the prospect of inhabiting their luxurious new villa grew farther and farther away. With the amount of construction taking place in Palm Beach, life in the resort was fast becoming just as hectic as New York City. 'I have found while at Palm Beach, I literally some days have had scarcely enough time to sit down for a quiet meal during which there are not some interruptions,' Otto later moaned in a letter to his daughter Margaret.

Cut to 1932: Work on the villa had now significantly progressed. To help hurry the matter along, Addie had instructed her London decorator Curtis Moffat to design the interiors for the new house in the latest modern Art Deco style. When details of his designs arrived, Otto and Addie could not have been happier. Moffat chose chrome fixtures, indirect lighting, and soft neutral-toned leather furniture in yellow, beige, and white. The effect was stunning yet purposefully restful on the eye.

In contrast, for the dining room floor, Moffat chose stylish black-and-white terrazzo tiles. Again, the trick worked; Otto and Addie's spirits were if only temporarily, lifted. They returned to New York, feeling more sanguine about the project.

A paparazzi snapshot of Otto captured during his visit to Germany the previous year surfaced in the Hamburg-American Line and North German Lloyd January edition of *The Seven Seas Magazine*. Otto's image sat alongside various famous stars of the day: Douglas Fairbanks, Gloria Swanson and her husband Michael Farmer, and the Russian composer Sergei Rachmaninoff. It was a measure of the level to which Otto's fame as a world celebrity had now risen.[7]

On February 17, Otto resumed his spree of resignations and dispatched a letter to the *Société Cercles des Annales* at 36 East 58th

Street, New York. In it, he informed the secretary that 'Pursuant to a general rule, which I have adopted, to withdraw from membership in organizations in which I am not taking an active personal interest, I hereby resign as a member of *Cercles des Annales*.'[8]

Similar notifications arrived in the in-trays of many other organizations over the following months. It was as if Otto was clearing out his desk drawers, decluttering, discarding what he no longer deemed necessary, scaling back, making way for a simpler lifestyle. On February 21, Otto quietly celebrated his 65th birthday at home.

On March 4, the Kahns hosted a luncheon at 1100 Fifth Avenue in honor of the German playwright, poet, and novelist Gerhart Hauptmann.[9] The writer was visiting the States for a four-week lecture tour accompanied by his wife Margarete and son Benvenuto. In the evening, Otto made his box available at the Met for the Hauptmanns to see the Rimsky-Korsakov opera '*Sadko*.'

At New York's Capitol Theatre during March, footage of Roger and Hannah, incorporated within columnist *Louis Sobol's Newsreel Scoops*, was relayed daily on the big screen.[10] The reel supplemented the main feature film and the accompanying live stage show. Audiences at the Capitol always found Sobol's newsreels hugely entertaining and would regularly applaud them at the final fade-out.

Whether Hannah crept into the Capitol to view herself on screen is not documented. One can only assume such broadcasts in Broadway theaters would have intensified the feelings of alienation she already felt.[11] It was an impasse Hannah had yet to overcome. Roger's announcement that he was to make a stage comeback and return to live performances came as a further thorn for her to bear.

On most weekdays, Roger was out at work, rehearsing, auditioning new band members, composing, or writing song arrangements. He also spent a fair amount of time flying or socializing at the Long Island Aviation Country Club at Hicksville.[12] Hannah's streamlined role in their marriage was beginning to appear almost incidental. Although Roger was well aware of the sizable cultural and social divide between him and his wife, he showed little effort to lessen it. So when Roger suggested they go away together and spend a couple of weeks in Florida, Hannah jumped at the idea, which is where the couple headed at the beginning of April.

On the evening of April 12, in New York City, Otto and his son Gilbert attended the private screening of the wildly anticipated MGM movie

Grand Hotel. The film starred Greta Garbo, John and Lionel Barrymore, Wallace Beery, and Joan Crawford.[13] The sidewalk outside the Astor Theatre where the showing took place was crammed to the curb with excited onlookers as limousine after limousine pulled up, depositing their occupants onto the red carpet. Otto, too, received the red carpet treatment; he was, after all, quite the celebrity. The screening, held to judge people's reactions, came long before the film went on general release. If tonight's reception was anything to go by, MGM was onto a winner. The outing also gave father and son time to reconnect and catch up on personal matters, away from the business environment of Kuhn, Loeb's office. It seemed Gilbert was having marital problems, too, although how serious they had become had yet to be made public.

Roger and Hannah returned to New York in mid-April, feeling closer than when they departed.[14] The break had done them good. Roger's theatrical comeback timetable now shifted up a gear. He was aiming to stage his first performance in around five weeks. Further auditions took place to replace players in the band that Roger felt weren't up to the grade. As an influx of unemployed musicians had arrived in the city from out of town, Roger could afford to be selective and had no difficulty hiring some of the hottest instrumentalists available.

At 1100 Fifth Avenue, on April 28, Addie welcomed the Italian conductor Arturo Toscanini to a large dinner party she hosted for the Walter Damrosch Symphony Committee.[15] As was customary, Addie had the house decorated with flowers, and the best silver and china adorned the dinner table. It was at times like these that the cold, unhomely mansion came alive with the warm glow of flickering candlelight, mellifluous music, special reserve wine, and riveting conversation. As Roger and Hannah currently occupied Roger's fourth-floor suite in the house, the elder Kahns would have expected them to attend such functions if they were in residence.

For Hannah, attending such dinner party's was never easy for her, being surrounded by people she had little in common with, who showed little interest in her. Such gatherings only served to heighten her feelings of loneliness, isolation, and inadequacy.

This summer, Otto and Addie chose not to open their Cold Spring Harbor estate to the public. They even went as far as canceling a Girl Scout pilgrimage scheduled to take place in the grounds on June 4.[16] The last thing they wanted was herds of inquisitive outsiders snooping all over the place. Besides, there were far too many family goings-on that the Kahns wanted to shield from the public eye.

To publicize his return to music, Roger gave an interview in *Variety*. In it, he whines about the predicament he now finds himself courting regarding his career.[17] He bemoans the fact that he now earns a mere pittance compared with what he was making in his late teens. He also threatens that if the dry period he was presently experiencing continues, he might just pack up his belongings and head over to Europe to live. He reckons it's far cheaper to loaf around on the continent than it is in the U.S. He believes the dilemma he is now facing is all down to relativity; 'One guy hasn't enough to eat, another hasn't enough to get that sixth plane. Or maybe it's a yacht. Not that that bothers me, but if it isn't money, it's something else.'

Yet, Roger concedes that he never wanted to follow his father's footsteps into the banking profession and praises his father's prudence for allowing his son to forge his own template in life and experience his own mistakes and triumphs. He intimates his future ambition was to compose a hit musical or become a big radio star as the maestro of an ultra-hot aggregation. He then acknowledges he is still studying harmony and orchestration and that the chances of any producer in this economic climate gambling on any musical he writes were pretty slim. 'Who's gonna gamble on Broadway shows these days? I don't blame the two, or three, producers who have nerve enough to produce these days, for going after Gershwin and Jerry Kern, why bother with anything I might write?'

He then denounces the fact that he has to pay rent for an office suite he rarely uses; 'I wish I could give it up. I want to get off Broadway and sit at home and write, but who am I to have such ambitions and enjoy something which only a Kern or Gershwin can do?' It was eight years ago when Roger first entered the entertainment business. Times had since changed. 'It's all a new business today,' observed Roger. 'Everything is radio. Four years ago, when I wanted a hotel job, I'd negotiate with the hotel management. Now they immediately refer me to a radio station. The hotels that is; the choicer spots state it's now out of their control.'

Most of the quality hotels had leased out their broadcasting privileges to a radio station, much as they might lease out the cloakroom concession or employ caterers for an event from which they would receive a cut. Such stations as NBC or CBS paid the hotels thousands of dollars annually for the broadcasting rights. It was the radio station that now installed the orchestras in the hotels. If Roger wanted to make a successful comeback, he would have to affiliate his name and band to a radio station.

Although Roger had spent the last two years away from the public stage, he was still very much in the spotlight. Roger's comeback tour would see him playing at the larger theaters across New York, timed to coincide with his first record releases on Columbia. Finally, on May 4, Roger took his newly kitted band into the recording studio to cut his first disks for Columbia. He had lined up an impressive cadre of musicians: Ruby Weinstein and Frank Zullo blew trumpets, Artie Shaw and Elmer Feldkamp were on clarinet. Ward Lay was on string bass. Russ Carlson tinkered the ivories, Leo Arnaud-Vauchant commandeered French trombone, and Chauncey Morehouse hammered the drums.

The studio engineer captured four songs, 'Lazy Day,' 'There I Go Dreaming Again,' 'My Silent Love,' and 'Tell Me Why You Smile, Mona Lisa.' Columbia earmarked the tracks for a June release.

Just a few days after the recording session, everything in Roger's life changed drastically.

On The Rocks

Reports of Hannah's unhappiness in her marriage were beginning to filter through to the media. On May 7, the front page of Saturday's morning edition of the *Pittsburgh Post-Gazette* carried the leader, 'Eager For Stage,' beneath which was a picture of Hannah smiling happily. Yet confusingly, the accompanying report filed from New York on May 6 asserted her marriage was all but on the rocks. Hannah claimed the rift arose because of her wish to return to the stage, whereas her husband wanted nothing more than for her to 'do her singing at home.'[18]

Love and happily ever after were not to be.

The press boys were digging for dirt, and soon enough, were handed a clod in a bold and uncompromising statement directly from Hannah. Without fear of recrimination and with little restraint, the former entertainer confessed all. The juicy facts commanded full-page articles in countless newspapers; such was the public's interest in the Kahn family.

It was official. Hannah had walked out on her husband. The marriage was over. The actress now wanted a divorce.

Talk of Hannah's unrest within the Kahn household had flourished among Broadway and society gossip for some time. From the start of her marriage, Hannah had never been happy in her role as a 'live at home' housewife. Perhaps that arrangement was at the core of the problem; the 'live at home' housewife did not have a home she could call her own. What she did have at her disposal was some of the finest property in America. The couple even had an apartment in the Kahn mansion on Fifth Avenue. However, the fact that she did not have her own front door to open and close as she desired was a continuing gripe for her. Roger's refusal to relocate was purely a financial decision. He had no necessity to pay rent at the family home, and with his business debts mounting weekly, every dollar he could save was crucial for his bank balance.

In a short space of time, their marriage had manifested into little more than a charade. The arrangement was not the deal Hannah had pledged her love and devotion to when she wed. The level of bickering and bruised egos they inflicted upon one another escalated out of control. There were four in this marriage, Roger, Hannah, and the in-laws. No sooner was their divorce announced than the elder Kahns sought legal representation for Roger and appointed Max Steuer of the law firm Chadbourne, Stanchfield & Levy.[19]

Dancing with the Wolffs

The idea of sitting on social committees and attending afternoon tea gatherings horrified Hannah. She didn't know about art or which books to read or commend, and, as for politics, she had no interest in current world affairs whatsoever. Hannah, though, had a fire in her belly. She was first and foremost a stage performer and yearned to get back out there in the glare of the footlights, singing her heart out, baring her soul, and tapping out her dance routines for the love of the audience's roar. Performing to the public was all she knew and all she had ever known since the age of seven. As the tension in her marriage mounted, just as Otto and Addie had feared, it became more apparent to everyone in the Kahn household that nothing was going to extinguish the fire inside Hannah.

It wasn't Hannah's fault she was ill-prepared for entering such an alliance. Circumstances had manipulated her hand.

Addie doted on Roger. Otto was much sterner in his affections towards his sons. In a private letter, he admitted he was closer to Margaret than any of his other children. Addie and Otto made no bones about the fact they had never approved of Hannah. Yes, they had initially laid down certain conditions for the marriage to go ahead, but the deep rift that had developed between them and their son, ever since Roger first met Hannah, had not healed. In her way,

Hannah had tried to assimilate within the family, to the point of even rejecting her own family and background, but it had all been to no avail. No matter how far she moved the goalposts, she would never fit in with the Kahn family or be the gentile stay-at-home wife they all desired. The marriage was doomed from the start.

Addie could not stand by and watch as her son's life was ripped apart. So, of course, she intervened, as many a mother would.

It took several weeks before the unabridged version of the altercation hit the newspapers, and when it emerged, it caused a sensation. Otto and Addie dodged the full impact of the revelations, having slipped out of the country[20] over to Europe.[21]

The Pros and Kahns

The story behind the big bust-up happened something along the lines as follows: The troubles first began when the couple returned from their European honeymoon and moved into the Kahn residence on Fifth Avenue to live.[22] As Roger and Hannah were residents of the house, Otto and Addie expected the couple to join them at mealtimes as and when they were all present. Hannah never found meal times were the relaxed, amiable family affairs they were supposed to be. Instead, she felt left out of the conversations and, at times, was even shunned by the elder Kahns. If Hannah complained to Roger, her protests would fall on deaf ears. Soon after Hannah had moved into the house, she politely asked her mother-in-law how she preferred to be addressed, whether as 'mother' or 'Mrs. Kahn.' 'Well,' came back the chilling reply, 'I suppose you might as well call me Mrs. Kahn.'[23] Hannah realized there and then that her mother-in-law had no spark of affection or feelings of warmth towards her whatsoever and was, no doubt, probably viewed in the same light as any member of the household staff. Nor did any of the Kahn family except Roger ever express any inclination to meet Hannah's relatives. Neither was Hannah's mother nor any of Hannah's friends ever invited to the Kahn home. Even Hannah's sister Dorothy had only managed to spend half an hour with her since her marriage to Roger.

Inside the Kahn mansion, Hannah could do no right. 'Mrs. Kahn [even] objected when I put a bit of makeup on in the daytime,' recalled Hannah.[24] Roger was rarely around during the daytime to back up his wife, and when he was, he would always side with his mother. Roger quickly grew weary of Hannah's argumentative attitude and regularly sought guidance from his mother on what he should do.

Hannah was bored with being a stay-at-home housewife without a home of her own. She pleaded with Roger to allow her to return to the stage. To compromise, she even offered to ditch her married name and use her maiden name instead.[25] Still, Roger would not agree.

Naturally, there was more to the hostilities between the couple than was initially revealed. It took columnist Walter Winchell to get the low down on the real nitty-gritty.[26] Through Hannah's good friend Kim Moran, he discovered one specific incident that lit the fuse. Hannah was given a diamond bracelet as a gift from a friend, purportedly Kim Moran. When Hannah arrived home wearing the bracelet, Roger let rip and marched his wife to a jeweler's to have the wristlet valued. The jeweler placed a $10,000 price tag on it. Roger insisted there and then that Hannah hand the gift back to the person who had given it to her, and as a replacement, he offered to buy her a $2,000 bracelet. Hannah categorically refused to do as Roger requested and stormed out of the store. From that moment onwards, the fight was on.

'My last quarrel with Roger,' Hannah revealed to the press, 'started when he wanted to go up to one of those places in Harlem, and I told him I'd rather go to a place where my friends went.'[27] There followed another argument, which ended with the couple going nowhere. Of course, Roger immediately relayed the whole caboodle back to his mother in the library. Addie lost control of her senses and marched out of the library, straight up the stone stairs to Roger's suite on the fourth floor, where she confronted her daughter-in-law, who was lying on the bed.[28]

Addie unleashed her anger. Hannah greeted her mother-in-law's sharp tongue with disdain. 'When Mrs. Otto Kahn came upstairs,' Hannah articulated to the journalist, 'and said the awfullest things to me, and then shook me, I decided I had stood enough of Roger running to his mama every time we had a spat.'[29] Hannah retaliated. The words tumbled from her lips, nouns, and adjectives, she later probably wished she had never uttered, yet she did. She'd had enough. 'So, I just walked out.'

Her departure did not happen overnight. She could not have left that sudden if she had wanted to because the mansion's front door was securely bolted each night and a liveried night porter was on guard duty. So she had to wait until the early morning when the house began to come alive again after the servants and house staff arrived. As soon as she heard the staff pottering about, she left her bed, dressed hurriedly, put on her hat, grabbed her handbag, and exited the building by the front door. She left with nothing except the clothes she was standing up in, the keys to the car Roger had given her on her birthday, and one dollar in her purse. Once outside, Hannah drove away as fast as she could into the morning rush of traffic heading downtown.

Her abrupt departure was no surprise to anyone in the Kahn household, not least Addie and Otto, who liberally welcomed it. As to Roger's inner feelings about the matter, they were airbrushed out of the equation. In print, it became a war of words. Hannah moved into a suite of rooms at the fashionable Hotel Delmonico on Park Avenue, where her friend Kim Moran was staying.[30] Roger threw himself headfirst into his career. The couple never met face to face again.

Initially, Hannah wanted a divorce. A few days later, after reevaluating her situation, she had second thoughts.[31] 'I've changed my mind about a divorce, and I'm not going to sue for separation, either,' she informed a journalist lurking persistently outside the Hotel Delmonico. 'I'm just going to keep right on being Mrs. Roger Wolfe Kahn. I earned my own living long before I met Roger, and I can do it again.'[32]

Hannah had cottoned onto the fact that being associated with the Kahn name carried a certain cachet. However, after taking legal advice, she quickly changed her mind and announced she intended to sever all ties with her husband. The final indignity for Hannah came after Roger's attorney advised him to insert a prominent notice in the Public Notices column of a well-known New York newspaper advising all retailers that he would not be liable for any debts incurred by his wife. The notification read thus:

'Notice is hereby given that Mrs. Roger W. Kahn or Hannah W. Kahn
is not authorized to contract any obligation of any kind in my name
or on my behalf on my credit or responsibility.'
Signed, Roger W. Kahn.[33]

Roger took such action after receiving the bill for a shopping spree his wife had been on to Hattie Carnegie's famous millinery store at 42 East 49th Street. Here she purchased 24 costly gowns and charged them to her husband's account, running up a bill for several thousand dollars.[34]

When two forces collide, there will always be fallout.

Hannah had in one calculated swoop, by conveying her exposé of life spent living under the Kahns' roof, blown wide open the myth of a harmonious, caring, loving family. Of course, the Kahns were furious.

With one vengeful swipe, Hannah had wiped away years of careful PR work. From that moment onwards, the Kahns agreed the sooner they got shot of her, the better.

Over in Europe, Otto and Addie remained in the loop with developments. Any further breath of scandal had to be stamped on at all costs. Through his attorney, Otto offered Hannah a sum of money to keep her mouth shut and leave peacefully. But would she? Hannah retaliated by announcing she did not want a single cent from the Kahn family and would instead forge ahead with her stage career.[35] The Kahns thought Hannah ungrateful for all the things they had done for her. Hannah never saw that side of the family; all she experienced was how they suppressed her liberty and freedom.

The enormous volume of publicity generated by the split brought Broadway agents and radio producers flocking to the reception desk at the Delmonico, asking for Hannah. She may well have been estranged from her husband and his wallet, but fortunately for her, the lucrative offers of work came pouring in.[36]

While Roger and his orchestra were rehearsing for their highly anticipated return to the stage,[37] Hannah accepted an engagement as a late-night lounge singer at the swanky Central Park Casino,[38] receiving a guarantee of $750 a week.[39] Should any friends of the Kahns happen to drop by, Hannah would dance with a frisson of extra abandon in her step.

She also signed a lucrative contract with RKO to perform several legit theater engagements, including a solo performance at the mighty Palace. Her agent commanded a whopping $4,000 fee for her appearance. Ironically, Roger and Hannah were now in direct competition with one another on Broadway.

At the last minute, the Palace booker got cold feet and pulled Hannah from the bill. He cited her exorbitant fee as being the reason why.[40] Was someone in the background deviously trying to derail her comeback?

No sooner had the press announced Hannah's withdrawal than they reported, Roger and his orchestra would be headlining at the Palace in July. Hannah soldiered on irrespective of any double-dealing that may or may not have been going on behind her back. She secured more dates, this time for Marcus Loew's theater chain.

Notice is Hereby Given [II]

On June 9, one month after Roger placed a notice in a New York newspaper informing the world he was no longer responsible for his wife's debts, another appeared. This time from Roger's brother.[41]

'Notice is hereby given that Mrs. Gilbert W. Kahn or Anne W. Kahn
is not authorized to contract any obligation of any kind in my name
or on my behalf on my credit or responsibility.'
                                              Signed, Gilbert W. Kahn.[42]

It was official; the marriage had failed. Gilbert and his wife, Anne, had separated. The couple had been married for almost eight years before their domestic troubles came to the fore.[43] The problems, however, had been manifesting over several years.

At the time of their estrangement, Gilbert was five weeks short of his 29th birthday. Custody of their 3-year-old daughter Claire was granted to Anne. Though Gilbert and Anne were heirs individually to fortunes, the only unconventional aspect to their marriage was the 'modest' five-story townhouse they resided in at 8 East 80th Street, bought so as not to live financially beyond their means. The first public indication of trouble within their marriage arrived when Gilbert inserted the notice of responsibility in the paper. Anne had been suffering from postnatal depression since the birth of their child. Her mood swings, anxiety attacks, and general listlessness had recently become more concerning. She took medication to help relieve the symptoms and employed a full-time nurse.

A *New York City News* reporter with an eye for a story contacted Gilbert at Kuhn, Loeb asking him for a statement. Gilbert confirmed he and his wife had separated but stressed, 'no legal steps have been taken as yet. Everything is still up in the air. I am leaving the entire matter to Max Steuer.'[44]

After the separation, Anne and their daughter Claire moved out of the family home and into an apartment on Park Avenue.

Across the pond in London, Otto and Addie went about their business in their customary unruffled, dignified manner. At no point did they issue any statement regarding their two sons' marital problems. The press were under the impression that Otto had arrived in Europe on a 'secret mission,' although what that assignment was, and for whom, they were unable to discover. Otto, the maleficent spy, somehow did not fit his cuddly image. Away from matters of 'espionage,' Otto managed to grab a round of golf and to visit the theater.

Otto on his 'secret mission' to Europe photographed in London, June 1932.

Over in New York, Roger continued to relieve his frustrations in the manner he knew best by taking to the air. On Sunday, June 5, a New York air cop spotted a plane flying erratically and dangerously low over Long Island and gave chase before finally driving the aircraft to the ground.[45] Both planes landed at Roosevelt Field, where the policeman, Jack Friedman, was surprised to discover the pilot he'd been chasing cat and mouse with was Roger Wolfe Kahn. He then reprimanded Kahn for low flying. Earlier that morning, Roger had taken off from Glenn H. Curtiss Airport and flown over water and bushland before the air cop caught sight of him and followed in pursuit. The officer stated Roger had dipped lower than 500 feet, the altitude advocated by the Department of Commerce not to pass below. Roger said he was under the impression it was okay to do so if the land beneath was uninhabited.[46]

Air rage was a new phenomenon that some cartoonists had great fun depicting, drawing cops directing traffic from captive balloons. Roger got a real buzz flying his plane as low as he could get away with, especially over New York City, weaving overhead across the avenues and circling the skyscrapers.

Three weekends later, on Sunday, June 26, Roger had a close call during a regular flight. Roger had offered to fly his friend Ramon del Castillo Palop (from the dancing team Ramon and Rosita) to the Lido Beach Country Club on Long Island. The Bellanca set off from Roosevelt Field in near-perfect weather conditions, and the flight proceeded with no hiccups. As the plane came down to land on a sandy strip of beach belonging to the Lido Flying Field, it crashed.[47] A tire blew as it touched down and toppled the plane, sending it nose first, bending the propeller, and bringing the craft to a sudden, jolting halt, parked with its tail sticking perpendicular at an angle.[48]

Roger managed to crawl from the cockpit unscathed. Unfortunately, his passenger was not so lucky. Ramon sustained multiple lacerations to his legs and was stretchered to the hospital.[49] The dancer was due to appear at the Lido's seasonal opening on the following Friday. Irrespective of his injuries, he vowed to honor the engagement.

The new airfield currently had no runway constructed; the lack of which Roger blamed for the accident. Luckily the plane's propeller sustained most of the impact and damage. That afternoon Roger had his mechanics drive over from Roosevelt Field to repair the aircraft in preparation for him to fly it back home later that evening.

The sad news that Adele Schiff (wife of the late Mortimer L. Schiff) had passed away at her country home on Long Island reached Otto and Addie while they were in Europe. Adele never recovered from the shock of her husband's death the previous year.

Yet further unsettling news reached the elder Kahns after the Appellate Division in Manhattan reversed the dismissal of Lydia Lindgren's former $500,000 lawsuit against Otto. Lindgren had been granted the right to sue Otto again.[50] The retrial date was set for November.

~

Roger's return to the stage saw the youthful-looking bandleader transformed into a dashing young heartthrob. Though still fresh-faced and doe-eyed, the new-look Roger Wolfe Kahn had the suave look of a matinée idol about him.

When bandleaders looked like movie stars, Roger Wolfe Kahn, ca. 1932.
(Picture by Murray Korman courtesy of Leslie Greaves, grandniece of Murray Korman.)

New York's music scene had changed significantly during Roger's absence. Bandleaders and musicians were now more anxious to showcase their talents on the radio than appearing in nightclubs or vaudeville. Throughout the long, sweltering summer months of 1932, the city became awash with jobbing musicians, all looking for the best-paid gigs. The marketplace became insanely overcrowded; many hired themselves out for ridiculously low rates just to remain employed. On the plus side, cut-price musicians did have one positive effect, if not for the musicians themselves, then for roadhouse and nightclub proprietors. Bookers were now hiring bands for reduced rates of 50 percent or less. If Kahn's primary objective had been to top up the coffers in his bank account, his planned comeback would need handling carefully.

Roger's first disks for Columbia arrived in record stores in June; 'Tell Me Why You Smile, Mona Lisa' came with a smooth vocal by Elmer Feldkamp, with 'There I Go Dreaming Again' offering the flawless tones of tenor Dick Robertson. The latter came via the spicy Mexican-flavored musical Hot-Cha!, which had arrived on Broadway earlier in the year. 'Mona Lisa' was snatched from the 1931 German movie Der Raub der Mona Lisa. Variety's brief appraisal of the recordings noted: 'Kahn has assembled a good dance combination again and they produce brisk 'dansapation'* with this couplet.'[51] To capitalize on the public's interest in the bandleader, Columbia fast-tracked the band's follow-up, 'Lazy Day' coupled with 'My Silent Love.'

Reports surfaced that Roger might be hooking up with Alex Aarons again (of Aarons and Freedley Stage Productions) over a potential joint venture.[52] Variety finally confirmed the rumor. The Broadway musical was Ballyhoo, set to open in summer. Kahn's orchestra would perform from the pit.

In the interim, Roger and his sixteen-piece orchestra played nightly at the Waldorf-Astoria. He also agreed to undertake a short RKO tour in and around New York. Three days at the RKO Fordham were already confirmed from July 20-22, followed by a week's headlining run at the Palace in Times Square. Kahn's fee for the Palace gig was $2,250.[53] He would also receive a percentage of the gross takings, a regular practice for most headliners at the Palace.

Just when Roger thought his days courting picturegoers had passed him by, Sam Sax, head of the Brooklyn Vitaphone Studios, contracted Roger to star in a movie short. The film was part of their Vitaphone 'Melody Masters' series, which featured nationally known bandleaders and orchestras.[54] A tailor-made script crafted around Kahn's background and lifestyle was presently being prepared by Herman Ruby and his staff writers.[55]

In a striking turnabout, Hannah's questionable past caught up with her when an article appeared in a newspaper announcing the marriage of writer and columnist Damon Runyon to Patrice Amati del Grande.[56] The bride's professional name was Patrice Gridler. She had been one of the original members of Texas Guinan's scantily-clad dance troupe at the infamous 300 Club at 151 West 54th Street. The article confirmed Patrice was the last of the 'give the little girl a great big hand' troupe to bag a husband. The journalist then named the other members of the troupe who had since married, Hannah and her sister Dorothy being two of those girls. The revelation cannot have come as a surprise to the Kahn household and would only have added ink to their list of objections for wishing to get rid of her.

Hannah's agent had been decidedly productive in securing some stellar stage bookings for her. Not wishing to be overshadowed by her husband's top of the bill appearance at the Palace, and no doubt in a calculated effort to capitalize from all the publicity he was generating, Hannah, billed under her maiden name of Williams while retaining 'Mrs. Roger Wolfe Kahn' attached to her advertising, clinched a featured spot at Loew's Capitol in New York. Also on the bill were the Abe Lyman Orchestra, the Boswell Sisters, Phil Baker, and Lou Holtz. The management was shelling out over $19,000 for salaries in producing what they claimed to be the most expensive stage show ever placed in a picture house. Their confidence paid dividends; the show was held over for the following week due to robust advance sales.

On opening night, disaster struck. Hannah was rushed to the hospital to have an emergency operation on her tonsils.[57] Although she missed that week's performances, she danced on stage to thunderous applause the following week. Hannah had that uncanny knack of being able to wow an audience exactly when she needed to, which came from her many years of treading the boards from such an early age.[58] She opened her act with '*Let's Have Another Cup of Coffee*' taken from the musical comedy *Face the Music* and tailed it with a fiery rendition of '*Goin' to the Promised Land*,' during which she put across a hot cha-cha dance routine. She encored with '*Cheerful Little Earful*,' the buoyant number many knew her for. *Variety* warmly reported Hannah was still a draw with the audience. 'Miss Williams is one of the brightest spots of the show. While she hasn't a voice that would win ribbons, she's got personality and selling ability.'[59]

Back at The Palace

Even the mighty Palace Theatre in the heart of Times Square had bowed to public opinion and succumbed to the lure of the moving image. RKO had installed a massive film screen above the revered wooden stage upon which the latest blockbusters flickered. Their change of heart took effect during the third week of July 1932 when they announced their weekly program would feature a 'first run' movie besides a regular vaudeville show. Their first week had been a resounding success at the box office. For their second week, the feature film was the blood-and-thunder pirate adventure melodrama *The Roar of the Dragon*, starring the rugged hero, Richard Dix.

In a surprise announcement, Roger and his eponymous orchestra headlined the vaudeville line-up on the second week of the Palace changeover.[60] After his two-year absence from a Broadway stage, it was an impressive coup for Roger and RKO. Snuggling alongside him on the bill was another Broadway and Harlem favorite, songstress Adelaide Hall.

On the first night, Roger and his sixteen-piece orchestra blew the audience sideways; such was their impact and stage presence. Their set lasted twenty-three minutes and was unashamedly dance-orientated, goading the audience to tap their feet, nod their heads, or stand up and dance in the aisles. Joining Roger on stage was the male harmony trio, the Kahn-a-Sirs (a pun on the word 'connoisseurs'), the loose-limbed dancer Melissa Mason, and the popular torch singer Gertrude Niesen.[61]

Variety was under no doubt, 'Kahn's selection of numbers and the arrangement make the straight music interesting enough for stage purposes. It sounds extremely danceable, and that should re-establish Kahn among the standard dance bandleaders of the town.'[62]

Roger's initial releases on Columbia were selling encouragingly well. '*There I Go Dreaming Again*' and '*Tell Me Why You Smile, Mona Lisa*' were placed jointly at No. 3 in Columbia's New York chart, with '*My Silent Love*' positioned at No. 3 in Los Angeles.[63]

Young Kahn was enjoying his return to the limelight so much that he decided to resign from the upcoming Broadway production *Ballyhoo*, citing his decision to extend his RKO vaudeville dates would clash with rehearsals for the new show.[64] In truth, he was making more bucks from appearing on stage than he would have earned as a pit orchestra. RKO hastily arranged future dates for the unit securing Cleveland, Chicago, Boston, and the E. F. Albee Theatre in Brooklyn. Overnight, Kahn's office and the RKO agency became locked in negotiations over Kahn's hefty fee. New York ticket prices were not attainable in lesser cities. Roger's unit carried 22 people plus an electrician. Negotiations were battled out right up to the last minute until finally, Kahn pulled out of the RKO extension. He had no intention of operating the unit at a reduced capacity.[65]

In the meantime, Kahn's office continued discussions with a major radio station, hoping to secure Roger a regular slot on the air. After all the work Roger had devoted to reforming his orchestra, he had no intention of disbanding the ensemble any time soon. CBS took the bait and contracted the unit to record a radio commercial.[66] Shortly afterward, Roger took the band back into the recording studio to lay down four more tracks for Columbia. The session took place on August 5. This time Roger had a helping hand from the harmony trio, the Kahn-a-Sirs, who clinched the leads on 'You've Got Me In The Palm of Your Hand' and 'Sheltered by The Stars.' Del Porter of the Kahn-a-Sirs also sang solo on 'I Can't Believe It's True' and 'Another Night Alone.' Each track received Roger's arranging skills. A month later, upon their release, *Variety* critic Abel Green was mightily impressed with the offerings, 'All four foxtrots are purveyed in big league manner, intricately orchestrated and excellently interpreted.'[67]

On the same day that Roger took his band into the recording studio, his wife re-emerged in the newspaper headlines; 'Broadway Shows For Paramount, Hannah Williams is Here Today.'[68]

Hannah was starring at the Brooklyn Paramount in their new production *Bringing Broadway to Brooklyn.* The show featured an impressive array of talent: comedian Jack Haley, the youthful Mitzi Mayfair (dancing sensation of the recent *Ziegfeld Follies*) and smiling Eddie Lowry presiding as the emcee.

At last, this was Hannah's chance to make it big on her terms. In a bold move, Hannah's agent had recently snubbed Paramount's offer to stage her with Paul Whiteman's band, insisting on more dough than singer Mildred Bailey, who'd been occupying the slot.

The Yacht Party

In mid-August, Roger filmed *The Yacht Party,* his new short for Warner Bros. Pictures.[69]

Shorts had become a competitive business. A good one featuring a top-notch name could draw in as many customers as a full-length feature. Warner's new summer advertising campaign was aimed directly at the picture house managers, enticing them to feature their latest series of Vitaphone shorts instead of rival products by RKO Radio Pictures.

'Before you buy any Short product, ask yourself whether it will look good on your marquee as well as your screen!'[70] The ace attractions in the RKO pack were Charlie Chaplin, the ever-popular Tom and

Jerry animated cartoon series, and their informative Pathé newsreels. RKO had recently reissued six of Chaplin's most famous silent shorts adding music soundtracks.

The competition was fierce, but Warner's were confident of attracting profitable business after signing some of the most popular bandleaders, comedians, and singing stars to their roster. Names such as Paul Whiteman, Rudy Vallée, Ruth Etting, Roscoe 'Fatty' Arbuckle, the Boswell Sisters, Ben Bernie, Abe Lyman, Jack Denny, Fred Waring, and Roger Wolfe Kahn. Indeed, many a picture house manager went as far as to advertise the stars featured in the shorts upon their outdoor marquees, leading some disgruntled customers to believe that the actual stars featured in the shorts would be appearing live at the theater.

Roger and his orchestra arrived on the sound stage at the Brooklyn Vitaphone film studio to discover a massive set resembling the deck of a superyacht. The studio had built it for the band to perform on. In-house director Roy Mack was there to greet them as they arrived. He discussed the shots he required before any filming took place. Although *The Yacht Party* runs for just under ten minutes and has no actual plot, the short is a musical film, with a specially written script and characters, and song and dance numbers. After the opening credits, the initial scene shows a luxury yacht anchored offshore; the coastline depicted is probably the Gold Coast on Long Island. The name of the two-mast single funnel yacht is not mentioned in the credits, though I believe it to be J. P. Morgan Jr.'s 343-foot *Corsair IV* anchored offshore at Glen Cove, on the North Shore of Long Island.

The cast comprised Roger and his sixteen-piece orchestra (with two pianists), vocal harmony group the Foursome, the mimic and vocalist Gertrude Niesen, eccentric dancer Melissa Mason, a couple of uncredited one-line actors, and tables of seated extras. Most of the name performers had appeared at Roger's headlining gig at the Palace Theatre a couple of weeks earlier.

The majority of the action takes place at a private party on board the luxury yacht, during which the guests enjoy various forms of entertainment. Roger and his orchestra, attired identically in sailor's uniforms with white caps, set the scene with their first number, '*Way Down Yonder in New Orleans,*' in which clarinetist Artie Shaw gives a splendid solo. The number segues seamlessly into a smooth interpretation of '*Gosh Darn!*' sung by three clean-cut sailors (all members of the Foursome quartet).

Gertrude Niesen appears next singing '*Sweet and Hot,*' and spends her entire performance imitating the singer and actress Lyda Roberti (a current Broadway favorite). So good is Niesen at portraying Roberti that if the announcer had not introduced her, the viewer might easily have believed it was Roberti on the screen.

Roger and his orchestra follow Niesen with a frantic rendition of 'Crazy Rhythm.' 'Crazy' becomes the theme throughout the film; both in the song titles - 'You're Driving Me Crazy (What Did I Do?),' 'Crazy Rhythm,' and 'Crazy People' - and within the quirky turns that take place. The zaniness comes to the fore with the extraordinary loose-limbed dancing of Melissa Mason, a tall, lithe lady with long pencil-straight legs that she somehow manages to throw around as if they are attached to a ragdoll. Mason is mercilessly comical to watch and would invariably have the audience roaring with laughter wherever she performed.

Roger holds the whole shebang together in his relaxed, inimitable style, seemingly unfazed by any of the whacky antics taking place around him. The band delivers a cracking rendition of the evocatively titled 'Lullaby of the Leaves' for the finale.

The following day's shoot took place away from the studio, possibly on Long Island at Roosevelt Field, where the director captures footage of Roger flying his 1929 Vought Corsair biplane. Whether to kiss the whole madcap affair farewell or show off his aerobatic skills, the end sequence has Roger ingeniously conducting his orchestra (still playing onboard the yacht) from the open cockpit of his plane. Rather impressively, he then steers the aircraft through a series of loop-the-loop stunts across the sky before the fade.

In August, Otto and Addie motored down to the South of France, where in Cannes, they were guests at the Palais Miramar.[71] Otto returned to New York aboard SS Europa during the third week of August. Accompanying him was his valet Frederick Cooper and secretary Elizabeth Mutke.[72] Addie did her customary routine of returning to the U.S. later than her husband and arrived back aboard SS Bremen the following week.

Upon his arrival home, Otto must have been hugely relieved to receive news from his attorney that a further lawsuit brought against him had reached a satisfactory outcome. William Reswick, a former press correspondent in Moscow, effectuated the claim for $300,000. His lawyer settled the case out of court for less than $5,000.[73] The action grew out of Otto's failure to bring the All-Russian Ballet Company to the USA, as he had agreed.[74]

On August 19, Hannah glided into Loew's Paradise Theatre in the

Bronx, collecting a plump fee of $1,150 for a weeklong engagement.[75] The production had a whopping budget of $15,000 thrown at it, a record high for a New York neighborhood theater. Regardless of all the expensive staging, Hannah still had her work cut out; audiences in the Bronx were tougher to win over than on Broadway. *Variety* noted in their review, 'Williams didn't have them coming her way in full accord until she uncorked a number associated with her from way back.'[76]

Now that Hannah and Roger appeared more accustomed to their separation, their calmer attitude became apparent in their daily lives. Hannah was happily rebuilding her career, as too was Roger. Any vitriol and backstabbing had temporarily been put aside. This momentary truce came as a timely relief for Otto and Addie, whose thoughts were now focused on Gilbert's estrangement, especially as their grandchild Claire was caught up in the split.

Though Otto's fluctuating health had been causing concern over the past couple of years, the Kahn family were unprepared for his physician's latest diagnosis - a previously undetected lesion in Otto's left lung, which was most probably tubercular. Treatment for the condition would last at least six months.

In mid-September, Roger conceded to do something he had vowed on many occasions not to do; he accepted an RKO booking in the provinces. His turnabout was a direct consequence of keeping the wolf from the door, and his band happily fed. Roger and his orchestra journeyed separately to the gig; Roger flew in his Bellanca with a couple of band members while the remaining musicians and their instruments traveled by rail. Their destination was Boston, Massachusetts, where they appeared at the Keith Theatre for a week commencing on September 17.[77]

No sooner had Roger arrived in Boston than he undertook the usual round of interviews to help publicize his shows. 'He is a little fellow, very boyish-looking with straight black [sic] hair and dark eyes, little of the showman about him, very keen in his appraisal of his own abilities,' observed a correspondent from the *Boston Evening Globe*.[78]

When quizzed why audiences did not see him playing on stage these days, his quick reply came as a bit of a jolt to the journalist. 'I don't like to play standing up,' he revealed pragmatically. 'That's alright for Ted Lewis or someone like that, but I wouldn't look right blowing a horn out front there.' He then explained that when he played dance engagements at clubs or hotels, he occasionally sat with his boys and picked up an instrument. He also mentioned that he had filled in on many occasions playing various instruments when sickness had caused gaps in the line-up.

The stage show came with the now-familiar movie presentation. This week's feature was *The Most Dangerous Game*, an adventure, horror mystery starring Joel McCrea, Fay Wray, and Leslie Banks. Whether the film was a stinker, or the weather was just way too hot for sitting indoors, the week's takings took a nosedive on the previous seven days, causing concern for RKO and Roger. Was his popularity waning? It was hard to ascertain, especially as this was his first provincial date in almost five years. The theater grossed just shy of $17,000 for the week.[79] From Boston, the band returned to New York City in preparation for a four-week residency at the ever-popular Hotel Pennsylvania, starting the first week in October.

On September 29, Roger's latest movie short, *The Yacht Party*, premiered in New York at the Strand Theatre. 'An entertaining short, with the best that Kahn offers boiled down to a nice compact whole,' affirmed *Variety* in their trim appraisal.[80]

When the editor of *Our Westchester* magazine commissioned Roger to write a brief article covering the current music scene, he jumped at the opportunity. The outcome titled 'The American Style in Music is Here' appeared in their October issue.[81] It provided Roger a means to air his impressions of modern-day American bands compared to their foreign counterparts. He believed American groups played unlike bands abroad and were easy to recognize by their 'tempo, attack and breeziness.'

'I have been asked if I am not of the opinion that someday we will have an American style in music - a distinctive one. I think we have a definite American style right now.' He follows on by explaining how American composers of popular music had already set a standard of individuality, which is neither matched nor approached in distinctiveness by any other nation, and picks George Gershwin as the best example of an American stylist composer. Kahn also suggests that his readers catch one of Paul Whiteman's Sunday evening concerts at the Hotel Biltmore if they wish to hear a demonstration of American-style music. 'He plays semi-classical and popular music written by Americans and makes [it] a practice [to give] new composers a chance. A Whiteman concert will demonstrate my contention that there already exists an American style in music.'

As to the notion of there being a 'great American composer,' Roger hastened to add, 'he may be alive now, but, if so, he'll never gain the title until long after he is dead. When he passes on, his works will remain, and will become classics in their own right.' Who Roger was thinking of, he never let on.

Up in Canada, Hannah Williams starred in the fifth edition of the *Chez Maurice Revue* in Montreal. Featured alongside her was the singer and emcee Joey Ray, formerly of Earl Carroll *Vanities*.[82] Hannah's contract ran until October 15, after which she was due to return to New York City to commence rehearsals for her lead role in Billy Rose's new Broadway revue.

Otto Kahn Is Too Ill To Appear In Court

Rosalinda Morini vs. Otto H. Kahn

The $250,000 Rosalinda Morini lawsuit that had plagued Otto for the previous three years came back to haunt him. Morini had managed to secure a retrial. The case took place in the Supreme Court during the first half of October. At the hearing, the singer claimed that Kahn's persistent denial of ever praising her voice as 'one of the most beautiful' he had 'ever heard' had irreparably damaged her professional reputation. Frustratingly for Morini, Otto was not in court to defend himself. When the judge asked where Mr. Kahn was, Dr. Charles G. Taylor explained that Otto was so ill that moving him from his Fifth Avenue home 'might prove fatal.' The news came as a shock to everyone present.[83] Taylor had been Kahn's physician for the past twelve years. Otto's counsel then put forward an application requesting that Mr. Kahn be questioned by deposition due to his current circumstances. Before granting the request, Justice Phillip J. McCook assigned an independent physician, Dr. Robert Hurtin Halsey, to go to Kahn's house to examine the defendant in the presence of Kahn's physician and a third medical practitioner Dr. Harold Thomas Hyman. The following day in court, Dr. Halsey's report affirmed what Kahn's physician had informed them. 'I find him to have high blood pressure and angina pectoris, with complicating pulmonitis (pneumonitis), and his condition to be such that an appearance in court would place his life in jeopardy.'

The Chief Justice granted the proposal for a deposition.

It was also a testing time for Addie, having to witness the tremendous stress her husband had to endure. The following week, in a surprise shift, Morini's counsel accepted an out-of-court settlement offered by Kahn's attorney.[84] First indications claimed the sum Morini agreed was a mere $7,500 plus a letter of apology for publication, with her attorney taking a $5,000 cut.[85] Morini swiftly denied such a paltry figure and issued her official statement wherein she verified Kahn had paid her $100,000 in settlement of her abandoned lawsuit.[86] Her lawyer was in for a quarter share of the payment.[87]

Roger's anticipated return engagement at the Hotel Pennsylvania got delayed by two weeks. When the premiere finally took place on October 17, the grillroom was jam-packed. New York's elite, headed by Mayor Joseph V. McKee, turned up in their hundreds.[88] The turnout far exceeded the hotel management's expectations.[89] Roger and his orchestra were contracted for a four-week residency with a nationwide radio hook-up on NBC as part of the deal.[90] NBC would also air the programs on various satellite links with WEAF and WFBR.[91]

Roger was thrilled to be back at the Pennsylvania among old friends fronting his band. He even entered into negotiations with vocalist Mildred Bailey to sing with the unit during their tenure.[92] The only obstacle delaying the deal was a clause in Bailey's former contract with Paul Whiteman stipulating she could not sing with any other organization for six months after being released from her contract with him. That timescale had not yet elapsed. Cautious to avert any legal action, Roger instead featured the singer James A. Lilliard who had appeared in the Broadway productions of *Show Boat* and *Brown Buddies*.[93]

Hannah returned to the Big Apple fired with enthusiasm and threw herself straight into rehearsals for *Billy Rose's Revue*. What's more, Radio WABC featured her on their *Sunday Matinee of The Air* variety show.[94] For this broadcast, the Victor Arden Orchestra accompanied her. Billy Rose's most recent Broadway show *Crazy Quilt* had been a great success and only recently closed. He had a lot riding on his new production, as did Hannah.[95] Early reports were optimistic. Hannah must have quietly been hoping this was the show that would finally put her name back up in lights on Broadway.

'Warm Intimacy'–The Lydia Lindgren Lawsuit

Lydia Lindgren vs. Otto H. Kahn

It was now Lydia Lindgren's turn to sue the ailing Otto Kahn. The soprano had waited almost fourteen months to bring her breach of contract lawsuit back to the Queens Supreme Court at Long Island City. The retrial commenced on November 10. Lindgren's $500,000 claim arose because of Kahn's alleged promise to support her financially if she came to America from her homeland of Sweden.[96] The opera singer had followed Kahn's advice but alleged his funding had not been forthcoming. As such, she claimed her music career had suffered considerably through Kahn's withdrawal of patronage. The hearing could not have come at a better time for the plaintiff; the compromise of Morini's case fell straight into Lindgren's lap.

Lindgren had three grievances she wanted to settle. She insisted Otto had agreed to replenish a $150,000 trust he set up for her in 1926, the promise of $30,000 in an annuity, and his help in securing her professional engagements. Otto agreed to the terms on the understanding Lindgren dropped her $250,000 slander suit against Met soprano Julia Clauseen in which she implied Otto was named. Lindgren withdrew the lawsuit but claimed Kahn had only paid her $13,000.

In court, Kahn's attorney Max Steuer did not hold back with his opening statement. He informed the judge that Lindgren had forced his client to pay through the nose. He told how Kahn had already spent more than $200,000 to purchase Lindgren's silence after a 'warm intimacy' had existed between the pair since 1913 when the Swedish singer first arrived in the USA. Steuer then charged Lydia, with forcibly extracting thousands after thousands of dollars from Kahn by threats of suit. Her behavior, he told the judge, was the real story behind the lawsuit against Kahn.[97] Otto was not in court to hear his counsel's bitter denunciation of the singer due to his ailing health, but Lydia Lindgren was.

'It's not true, it's not true,' she protested loudly from the stand, throwing her arms about wildly, causing Justice Adel to immediately order her to move outside the metal railing surrounding his dais.

In their respective addresses to the court, Kahn's attorney and the plaintiff's counsel conveniently skirted around the exact definition of the phrase 'warm intimacy' that had allegedly existed between Kahn and the singer.

'The only person who ever advertised her as the mistress of Kahn, was herself,' said Steuer, adamantly. 'Whatever their relations were, I want you to remember that she knew Mr. Kahn was a married man, and she certainly was no infant.' Steuer directed his words straight towards the judge. 'During all these years, he has been buying his peace. He has been bled through the nose. She made demand after demand and signed releases, promising never to write him or telephone him. But she never kept these promises.'

The following day, Lindgren's testimony created more fireworks. She affirmed that after her first meeting with Kahn at the Metropolitan Opera House, she entertained him at her home.[98]

'Mr. Kahn said I had a most beautiful voice,' regaled Lindgren, 'that I made a stunning appearance, and that I had a beautiful figure.' Then as an afterthought, she added, 'I hate to say all these compliments about myself.' The court was not taken in by any of it. The case descended into a travesty. Lindgren's behavior was shambolic; she sobbed during parts of her testimony, openly fought with the defense counsel, and repeatedly interrupted discussions between the court and counsel. Even worse, she criticized the judge. It left Judge Adel with no other option but to warn Lindgren that he would not tolerate such behavior in court. Despite all her histrionics and glycerine tears, Lindgren conceded she would be willing to accept $160,000 to settle the case there and then.

After the summing up, a four-hour deliberation followed, during which both parties reached an agreement. Unluckily for the plaintiff, her melodramatic performance in court and tale of woe did not convince anyone. The press later revealed Lindgren received the meager sum of $20,000 from Kahn subject to her signing a document releasing him from all claims, past, present, or future.[99] Mr. Kahn was unavailable for comment.

Predictably, the scandal made front-page news across America, adding yet more stress to Otto's already stressful life.

On the day before the Lindgren vs. Kahn case resurfaced in court, Roger headed back into the studio with his orchestra to record four tracks for Columbia. These would be his last offerings for the label before his contract expired at the end of the year. Perhaps, in light of this, all the songs he delivered were secondhand. He chose not to consign any new material of his own. Under his baton came 'Fit As A Fiddle,' 'It Don't Mean a Thing (If It Ain't Got That Swing)' written by Duke Ellington and Irving Mills, 'A Shine On Your Shoes' from the energetic Broadway revue Flying Colors, and 'Just A Little Home For The Old Folks (A Token From Me).' Each number came garnished with a vocal arrangement handled by the Kahn-a-Sirs, or by an individual member of the vocal trio. Roger's song choice for his last recording leads one to wonder if he committed it to shellac as a dedication to his parents in light of their current predicament at home.

To encourage higher sales, Columbia released a special limited edition of 'It Don't Mean a Thing (If It Ain't Got That Swing)' coupled with 'A Shine On Your Shoes' in exquisite blue shellac, bluer than a Kashmir sapphire.

During Roger's residency at the Hotel Pennsylvania, he landed a prime-time slot on the hugely popular *Lucky Strike Magic Carpet Show* broadcast on the NBC Red radio network.[100] As the title suggests, the program was sponsored by the manufacturers of Lucky Strike cigarettes. The hour-long show aired at 10 p.m. on Tuesday, Thursday, and Saturday and regularly attracted millions of listeners. It introduced the slogan 'Reach for a Lucky instead of a sweet.' The live show came from two locations, the host site being NBC's New York City radio station. A magic carpet piloted by the multi-talented personality Walter O'Keefe was the 'imaginary' mode of transport listeners would travel on between locales. The correspondent Walter Winchell of the New York *Daily Mirror* had a guest spot on Thursday's show. He would narrate up-to-the-minute news reports and lively chat, most of which he harvested from his newspaper column 'On-Broadway.' Winchell's straightforward delivery grabbed you by the collar, keeping the listener's ears transfixed to the speakers. If there was any hot gossip worth relaying, he knew about it. Winchell and Roger were good buddies. Roger and Hannah appeared together on the program back in December 1931 under Winchell's scrutiny.[101] When Roger and his orchestra were on the show, the magic carpet only had to fly the short hop between the Pennsylvania Grill and the NBC New York studio.[102] It was a good gig for Kahn; he commanded a fee of $2,250 for each broadcast.[103]

Roger's stint at the Pennsylvania was extended for an additional week and ended in the final week of November.[104] To keep his band functioning full-time, Roger had to secure regular employment for them. Luckily, their next gig arrived via Roger's previous work associate, stage producer Alex Aarons, and Roger's former music tutor, composer George Gershwin.

Pardon My English

George Gershwin had just completed a score for the musical comedy *Pardon My English,* on which George's brother Ira collaborated.

Plans to stage the musical on Broadway got underway in autumn. Aarons and Freedley were brought on board to produce it. The Gershwin brothers had an association with Aarons and Freedley that stretched back over eight years when, in 1924, they staged the duo's first collaborative Broadway hit, *Lady, Be Good!* Since then, they had produced several Gershwin musicals that had been hugely successful. It was a proven and tested formula that worked well for both parties. The staging of *Pardon My English* progressed with enthusiasm. The talk was of another winner. The news that Roger and his orchestra were to play in the pit came in late November.[105] Rehearsals spilled over into a two-week tryout in Philadelphia, where on December 2, the musical premiered. Frustratingly, the show's failure to attract positive reviews put its Broadway debut in doubt. This scenario was not what the backers had wanted to hear.

Part of the problem was the lack of big names in the cast. Presently, the main star was English music hall entertainer Jack Buchanan, who had only a limited appeal in the U.S. The only other established actors the show could boast were vaudevillian Jack Pearl and actress Lyda Roberti.

The show's mediocre reception in Philly persuaded the producers to postpone its Broadway premiere until January 20, 1933. In the interim, they set about adding new characters.

Pardon My English was 'a headache from start to finish,' Ira Gershwin later reminiscenced[106] and ultimately led to the production team Aarons and Freedley breaking up.

The reworked and newly expanded production was sent on another trial run, this time gracing the Majestic Theatre in Brooklyn, where it opened on Boxing Day for a one-week engagement. With a cast of 125 and costs spiraling out of control, the producers were keen to cash in on the lucrative festive season. To accommodate Jack Pearl, who was contracted to appear in his weekly slot on the *Lucky Strike* radio show, the producers canceled Thursday evening's performance. In its place, they added an extra matinee on Wednesday.[107]

However, the rescheduled performance overlooked the fact that the radio station had Roger and his orchestra booked to perform as guests on the same radio show on Tuesday, December 27. Without Roger and his musicians, the musical could not operate.

Reviewer Arthur Pollock in the *Brooklyn Daily Eagle* found little good to say about the production. 'Yes, it all sounds like something important. It isn't, however, quite so first-rate as it sounds.'[108] He then explains why: 'In the first place *Pardon My English* takes too long to get to the end. It even takes a little too long to get funny.' Pollock then laments that Buchanan has very few amusing lines to deliver, and when he does get one, 'Mr. Buchanan shines only dimly.' Pollock acknowledges it's an ambitious show to have produced in the first place but heeds it will have to smooth itself out if it wants the public to take it seriously.

From Brooklyn, the production traveled a short distance across the Hudson River to Newark, New Jersey. Here it opened on January 2. Sadly, audience attendance figures were worryingly low. Buchanan was thought not to have enough pulling power. To cut further losses, the financial backers bought Buchanan out of his contract and replaced him with the comedian George Givot.

When the show limped into Broadway's Majestic Theatre in January, Roger and his orchestra had also left the cast. His $2,250 fee was way too high for the production company to sustain. The show got panned by the critics and lasted all of 43 performances before the final curtain fell. It was the first significant flop the Gershwin brothers had experienced.

Disappointingly for Hannah, *Billy Rose's Revue* had a similar fate and even shorter shelf life. The show disappeared without a trace before it ever reached Broadway. With Christmas on the doorstep, Hannah secured an engagement at the tropically themed Cocoanut Grove atop of Mid-Manhattan's Park Central Hotel on Seventh Avenue. Also appearing in the floorshow was the crooner Russ Columbo and his band.[109] The restaurant had a spectacular view of New York's skyline and adopted the motto 'It is always June in the Cocoanut Grove' - even in mid-winter. During this engagement, Hannah had a brief, passionate fling with her fellow artiste, handsome, tall, dark-eyed Russ Columbo.*

For Roger, the stark reality of maintaining an orchestra was staring him straight in the eye. He may have been endowed with a 'million-dollar name,' but his failure to reconnect with the public at large was becoming all too evident.[110] After an initial rush at the Pennsylvania Grill, business cooled. His radio appearances were now sporadic, and his contract with Columbia Records was about to end. His comeback was not quite the success he had envisaged. The curiosity factor of a rich kid rebelling against his folks had worn thin with the public. There was no denying his abilities as a jazz maestro, and his new band was a cracking unit, but the music scene and entertainment world had moved on. Things were changing at a rapid speed. Several of his musicians sought alternative employment. Clarinetist Artie Shaw temporarily returned to freelance radio work, something he detested.[111] To add to Roger's setbacks, George Effenbach, who had been acting as Roger's manager, quit just before the Christmas holiday.[112]

What was once second nature was now unfamiliar. Popular music was evolving. Swing was breaking into the mainstream. New bandleaders were grabbing the limelight, musicians such as Benny Goodman and Bennie Moten. And man, could they swing!

Roger now faced a new dichotomy; performing on stage was growing less and less fulfilling for him. Show business was losing its glamor. The notion of being stuck in an office had also never appealed to him. Although Roger was still undecided where his future lay, a career in aviation now seemed more of an obvious route for him to take.

Over the past few weeks, Gilbert Kahn had gradually transferred his attention towards an attractive young dancer who was appearing in a musical comedy, appropriately titled *Take A Chance*. The young lady was Sara Jane Heliker. News of his fondness for the actress had not escaped the newspapers.[113] Gilbert had recently traveled to Newark to catch her performance in the show. During his visit, he aired his disapproval over the flimsiness of one of Miss Heliker's stage costumes, which saw her wearing lingerie. He thought it far too revealing under the powerful stage lighting. Sara had since taken the matter up with the show's producers, Larry Schwab and Buddy DeSylva, but they were adamant her costume remained just as it was. As a consequence of her concerns, Sara was taken out of the production and replaced by another actress.[114] In light of Gilbert's intervention in her career, he and Sara had become an item.

Strange Days

Otto's continuing ill health was still causing concern.

In an extraordinary move, Otto and Addie quietly agreed their beloved mansion at Fifth Avenue had become a financial and oversized burden that, at some point soon, had to be sold. Although Roger presently still occupied his fourth-floor suite, the two elder Kahns and their live-in servants were the property's primary residents. The remainder of the Kahn children had long since flown the nest and had their own family homes. With this in mind, Otto and Addie tentatively sought a new owner for their noble Fifth Avenue palazzo. Preliminary discussions took place with interested parties, but nothing concrete was agreed upon or settled.[115] It would take a while longer before Otto and Addie could fully come to terms with such a significant upheaval. For the present, Otto and Addie bided their time.

Further household staff members were dismissed over the coming months to help reduce the elder Kahns' everyday expenses. One such employee was Addie's faithful chauffeur Robert McCulloch whom she had employed for seven and a half years.[116]

Earlier in summer, before Otto became ill, he permitted the German photographer Erich Salomon to shadow him during a regular day at the office. A selection of Salomon's photographs appeared in the September issue of *Fortune* magazine.[117] The pictures give a rare and fascinating glimpse into the working-day practices of Kuhn, Loeb's headquarters at 52 William Street.

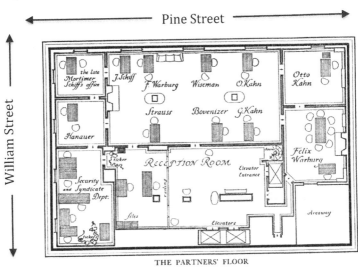

THE PARTNERS' FLOOR

The second-floor offices of Kuhn, Loeb & Co. at 52 William Street.

Around one hundred people worked across the four floors that Kuhn, Loeb occupied, from runners to cashiers, security clerks, stenographers, bookkeepers, secretaries, filing clerks, statisticians, elevator and door attendants, and twelve agents in the foreign department.

The white Georgian second-floor partner's room was known as the heartbeat of Kuhn, Loeb. It overlooked Pine Street and housed seven individual partners' desks. Otto had two desks, one in the partners' room, where he preferred to sit, the other in his mahogany-paneled private office tucked into the far corner of the second floor alongside Felix Warburg's office and adjoining the partners' room. The jumble of books piled on Otto's desks were mostly unread first-editions presented by their grateful authors. Partners' meetings took place around the boardroom table in Felix Warburg's private office. Under Otto's direction, the office environment was very informal; clients and friends would 'roll in' for a chat and then 'roll out' again.

In summer, when the office got uncomfortably muggy, Otto took to swatting flies. He kept a flyswatter by his desk and made great use of it. However, it appears his aim was not very skillful, as he had yet to kill a fly. According to his co-workers, there were no flies in the office; 'Otto just has a fly mania.'

Kuhn, Loeb currently had ten partners.* Otto's office colleagues referred to him as 'the Boss,' a nickname he purportedly liked; everyone regarded him as the 'star' salesman of the firm. Jerome Jonas Hanauer, a conscientious, fastidious worker known to be a 'mathematical genius,' had been a partner since 1912 and was a member of Otto's office team. It had been routine over the years that neither Kahn nor Hanauer took a vacation simultaneously. One always had to cover in the office.

In November, Hanauer announced he was to retire at the end of the year. Although Otto was currently not well enough to occupy his desk at Kuhn, Loeb, the news came as another unsettling shift in Otto's accustomed daily practices.

As if to see out the old and welcome in the new, Roger appeared as the cover boy on the December issue of *Family Circle* magazine, kitted out in his flying gear as he peered down from the open cockpit of his sleek Vought Corsair biplane. Maybe deep in his heart, he already knew what future changes lay ahead for him.

These truly were strange days for the Kahns.

ROGER WOLFE KAHN
. . . born into one of the
richest homes in the world,
gave it all up for the satisfaction of doing what
he liked best. So today he
is one of America's out-
standing orchestra lead-
ers and flyers. (Story on
Page 14.)

RWK

Roger, the cover boy, on *Family Circle*, December 1932. Note his
monogram on the side of the plane.

16

WHAT A SONG AND DANCE!

1933

The elder Kahns annual January vacation to Palm Beach took on a less hectic schedule this year than was usual. Otto's health, which was slowly on the mend, remained the stabilizing factor in their decision; ample rest, with few distractions, was in all probability just what his physician ordered.

Under the watchful eyes of architects Treanor & Fatio, the Kahns' new villa at 690 North County Road was nearing completion. Everyone hoped the property would be ready to occupy soon. As plans moved forward for the family to relocate to their new property, Otto arranged for the title deeds of Oheka Cottage to be transferred. The pink villa sold for $122,000 to Florida Mogar Realty of Jacksonville.*

The Kahns returned to New York, rested and reinvigorated in the last week of January. On the evening of January 27, Otto and Addie attended a benefit concert at Carnegie Hall presented by the Philharmonic Symphony Orchestra to aid the Orchestra Pension Fund.[1] Addie had contributed financially to stage the fundraiser. That evening the Kahns could not have looked happier or more relaxed and appeared totally at peace with the world. There certainly was no hint of the impending storm hovering ominously on the horizon. Few people could have predicted the catalog of crises that unfolded so publicly and so awkwardly in the media's glare over the coming months.

During Addie and Otto's recent vacation in Florida, news of their elder son Gilbert's marriage had hit the front pages of the papers yet again. On January 11, at a private court hearing in Reno, Nevada, Anne was granted a divorce on the grounds of 'extreme cruelty.'[2] Their eight-year marriage was officially over. Custody of Gilbert and Anne's child Claire was handed to the mother. In social circles, news of the annulment had not been unexpected, though what came next was.

Gilbert and Sara Jane Heliker tied the knot on February 1, 1933.

Three weeks after their divorce, on the afternoon of Wednesday, February 1, Gilbert tied the knot to 22-year-old Sara Jane Heliker. The marriage took place in the oak-paneled library at the Kahn residence on Fifth Avenue. Roger and half a dozen close family friends attended the ceremony conducted by Justice Edgar J. Lauer.[3] A small reception followed. Otto and Addie were not present at the wedding, as they had quietly slipped away to Europe.[4] Neither did the bride's parents Mr. and Mrs. Albert J. Heliker, attend the happy occasion.

Sara hailed from Jacksonville, Florida, and had appeared on stage in various Broadway productions, usually in minor ensemble roles performing as a singer and dancer.* Sadly, the starring roles had eluded her. In 1926 she won the 'Miss Miami' beauty contest, and the following year she was crowned 'Miss West Palm Beach' representing the local Miami Lions Club. Minor roles in short comedies at Fox Studios were added to her CV. She also appeared in the original 1926 Broadway run of the Gershwin brothers musical comedy *Oh, Kay*! One of her more notable parts had been in the 1931 edition of *The Third Little Show*. It was during her time in *The Third Little Show* that Gilbert first met Sara.

'We never announced it,' said Gilbert readily to the press, 'but we were engaged for quite some time.'

The marriage announcement came via an official news agency statement issued by Gilbert from Kuhn, Loeb's office.[5] Photographs of the couple with the pretty bride cuddling up to her husband appeared on the front pages of many newspapers the following day.[6] The new Mrs. Gilbert Kahn announced she had retired from a career on the stage to concentrate on her new role as a wife. Unfortunately, due to his father's absence, Gilbert was unable to take leave from his responsibilities at Kuhn, Loeb, and, as such, the couple had temporarily put their honeymoon on hold. Gilbert promised his wife they would take a trip overseas later in the year, probably in spring, to make up for the delay.

News of the marriage reached Otto and Addie in the mid-Atlantic on board the ship they were sailing to the continent on. Unusually for Otto, he issued no statement about his son's divorce or current union. A few days after the elder Kahns arrived in the UK, they received the timely announcement they were grandparents once more with the birth on February 9, in Newport, New Jersey, of Margaret and John's daughter Virginia Fortune Ryan.

In the same month, Roger's rocky marriage to Hannah also hit the papers again with the news he had coughed up $625 to settle one of his estranged wife's dress bills.[7] No doubt, he took the rational approach upon advice from his wise attorney and paid the invoice just days before Hannah's divorce suit was set to go to court.

Roger had been vigorously angling to spot his band into the recently opened classy Manhattan nightclub *El Patio*. The dance partners Ramon and Rosita owned the establishment. Roger and Ramon were pals. The trouble was, a new kid had arrived on the block, who was keen to make his mark. That kid was Walter P. Chrysler Jr., who, with his band of college students, had set his sights on the same gig.[8] 23-year-old Walter Jr. was the son and heir of automotive tycoon Walter P. Chrysler and had as much clout socially along Park Avenue as young Kahn had. Although Walter Jr.'s band was untested, the novelty factor attached to it and thus the press interest would be huge. It was an extraordinary turn up for the books for Roger, the here and now mimicking history. Roger and Ramon may have been good pals, but Ramon was just as astute as Roger when it came to business. Ramon chose Walter's band over Roger's, which must have come as a real kick in the jaw for young Kahn. Perhaps it was further proof, if proof were needed, that times were changing fast, and the next generation of bright, aspiring musicians were eager to grab the limelight.

Otto celebrated his 66th birthday in Europe. There was no lavish party with an extensive guest list for society columnists to pick over. Instead, he spent a leisurely day enjoying the company of friends.

On January 30, Adolf Hitler was appointed Chancellor of Germany. Four weeks later, on February 27, the Reichstag fire in Berlin acted as the catalyst for Hitler to bring in sweeping changes to the German constitution. While in Europe, Otto had toyed with the suggestion to visit a medical specialist in Berlin. However, in a letter written to George Sylvester Viereck on February 20 (the day before Otto's birthday), he admits that such a visit would lay heavy on his conscience. 'I cannot avail myself of his professional skill as I do not feel compatible with my self-respect as a Jew to visit Germany now, much as I always like to be there.' Viereck, a German-born writer, now living in America, was a supporter of National Socialism. Otto had witnessed Germany's shifting wave of opinion towards Jews when he last visited Berlin. One senses his unceasing curiosity would have drawn him towards the country because of the momentous changes taking effect and his desire to see them first-hand.

In Italy, Otto relaxed at a health spa before journeying to the French Riviera with Addie. Here they spent several agreeable weeks on the coast with their daughter Maud and her family. In the last week of March, Otto and Addie caught the Italian liner SS *Rex* for their return voyage to the U.S.[9] Had Otto not come down with a nasty bout of flu on board, he might have felt happier about his homecoming.[10] The vast, rushing metropolis of New York was probably the last place he should have been if he was to recuperate fully. Still, his trip to Europe had rejuvenated his health enough for him to throw himself back into a busy work schedule. Otto's re-emergence at the office meant his son Gilbert could now take time off to whisk his wife Sara away on honeymoon.

Before the honeymooners departed, Otto and Addie met with Gilbert to discuss their collective unsecured holdings in Paramount Publix Corporation bonds, valued at $200,000.[11] On January 26, Paramount Publix had toppled into receivership. A new bank committee was set up to rescue the company, of which Otto was elected to lead.[12] The reorganization of Paramount would keep Otto busy. Surprisingly, Adolph Zukor retained his position as head of the film company under the bank committee's exacting watch.

Shadows on a Dance Floor

At the beginning of March, Hannah Williams journeyed east to Reno, Nevada, where she was now enjoying the local hospitality.[13] Her visit was not merely to savor the lively surroundings; she had gone to commence divorce proceedings. While Hannah was awaiting her legal papers to come through, she hooked up with her former lover, the popular orchestra leader, and radio crooner Russ Columbo who just happened to be in the city. To be accurate, the handsome American heartthrob had canceled a ten-week theater tour and flown out especially to be with Hannah. Reporters spotted the couple out together regularly. Newspapers began speculating whether they were an item?[14] Hannah denied such claims, as did Columbo. Hannah was simply killing time while waiting for her decree absolute.

On April 2, an article about the Kahn brothers and their respective wives surfaced in the *Milwaukee Sentinel*. In it, Hannah spoke openly about her marriage to Roger and laid bare her inner feelings.

'I simply couldn't stand it anymore,' she professed to the journalist. 'Things were so bad that finally, I just had to get up and walk out.' She ends her recount by venting how she feels about the way she's been treated. 'I never want to see Roger or any of his family again, and I don't want any of their money. All I am asking is to be let alone.'[15]

Two days later, on April 4, Hannah got her wish. At Reno Courthouse, the judge granted her a divorce.[16] Hannah testified that her husband was 'impossible to live with anymore.' The decree was awarded on the grounds of cruelty.[17] On the steps outside the building, Hannah posed for the photographers, flashing her best smile.[18] Roger was not there for the proceedings; he was flying one of his airplanes over Long Island. After all the happy and exciting times the couple had shared so intimately, their relationship now represented nothing more than shadows on a dance floor.

That Hannah and Roger never spoke to one another again bears testament to how wretched their attachment had become. Their marriage had lasted all of sixteen months. The pretty, slender, auburn-haired showgirl of five years ago had taken on more than she could handle, and in doing so, became entangled in a web of her own undoing. In some ways, Roger had wanted Hannah to be a copy of his mother. Not a replacement. It begs the question, what else could she have done except walk out and leave? Addie was not the forgiving kind, and Otto was opposed to the union from the beginning.

Hannah was now a free woman again.

In the cold light of day, it all seemed quite surreal: 'I'm a little fool,' she spluttered to one reporter as she wiped away a tear with her silk handkerchief. 'This [indicating her tears] doesn't mean a thing.'[19] Newspapers claimed Hannah received a $50,000 settlement from Otto. Some papers stated it was as much as $150,000.[20] Hannah said the elder Kahn was a 'prince.'[21]

From the courthouse, Hannah went directly to her hotel to change her outfit. She put on a riding habit and then rode off to a dude ranch with Russ Columbo. News reporters reckoned the couple's romance was back on, and they could soon be heading for the altar.[22] As before, Hannah denied such claims, and so did Columbo. The papers also figured NBC's San Francisco office had submitted a script titled *True Romance* to Standard Oil for sponsorship, based on the Williams-Columbo pairing.[23]

Just as the newspapers were getting overheated with gossip about the couple, a new character arrived in the ring, former World Heavyweight boxing champion Jack Dempsey. Throughout the '20s, only baseball ace Babe Ruth rivaled Dempsey's popularity as a sportsman. Dempsey arrived in Reno at precisely the same time as Columbo. When Dempsey was in town, everyone wanted to meet the champ. However, it seemed Dempsey had his eye on meeting someone too, Hannah Williams. Dempsey had divorced his wife, Hollywood actress Estelle Taylor, in 1931. Having retired as a boxer, he was now building a new career as a sports promoter.

Jack first met Hannah in 1924 when she was 'just a little girl' appearing on Broadway in *George White's Scandals*. A few years later, Jack and Hannah met again, this time at New York's Paradise Restaurant on 49th and 8th.[24] The year was 1932. Hannah had just made her widely publicized exit from the Kahns' Fifth Avenue mansion. Dempsey was out having drinks with friends. One of those buddies was Nils Thor Granlund, formerly Loews theaters' press agent. Bandleader Abe Lyman was performing at the restaurant that evening. Hannah turned up to meet Lyman. She was early. Lyman was still on stage. Hannah knew Granlund, so she joined the Dempsey table. As soon as Dempsey's eyes fell on Hannah, he was hooked. It was now one year later. Once again, Dempsey and Hannah met up by chance. This time in Reno.

Suddenly, so much was going on in Hannah's life. It was as if she was about to combust with happiness. Hannah and Dempsey's lascivious desire for each other was instantaneous. Initially, they denied any attraction existed between them when questioned by the media. What else could they say?

Dempsey did hint that maybe such a 'development' might be on the cards in the future. For the present, though, the ex-boxer had an important assignment to attend to, which just happened to be in the same city Hannah Williams was heading for, New York.

One Out, One In

At 11 a.m., three days after his divorce from Hannah, Roger walked briskly into the Town Clerk's Office in Hempstead, Long Island, with 22-year-old Edith May Nelson on his arm and married her.[25] Edith, who went by the name of Daisy, also came from a theatrical background, having been a dancer since she was twenty.[26]

This time, Otto and Addie never interceded. From one showgirl to another, the dye seemed firmly cast in the Kahn brother's genes. Following the ceremony, the couple left in Roger's Bellanca airplane flying south for a brief honeymoon, where Roger had a gig at the Club Forest in downtown New Orleans. Accompanying them was Roger's hangar manager Dell Whitten. Upon their return to New York, the newlyweds took up temporary residence in an apartment at 46 East 91st Street while looking for a home of their own.

Daisy was the daughter of the former Congressman and lawyer John E. Nelson and his wife, who hailed from Augusta, Maine. Roger and Daisy first met when she secured a role in the chorus of the Gershwin brothers musical *Pardon My English*, in which Roger and his orchestra were performing. Although the bride's proud parents were not present at the service, they announced the marriage via a press statement issued by the Kahns.

Roger and Daisy at the Air Races, ca. 1933.

Daisy had studied at Cony High School in Augusta and graduated in 1929. She then went to the Rayson School in New York and later attended the innovative Sonia Serova School of Dancing. She had since appeared in several Broadway musical comedies. There was no mention of whether Daisy would continue her theatrical career, although she was expected not to.[27] Roger planned to drop by with his bride and meet his new in-laws sometime in late spring, just as soon as his schedule would allow.[28]

Gilbert and his wife Sara had now taken up residence in a modern apartment at 912 Fifth Avenue that came with stunning views directly overlooking Central Park. On April 14, the couple departed from New York Harbor on their long-overdue honeymoon aboard the cruise liner SS *Santa Lucia* bound for the Caribbean Sea and Panama before cruising north along the California coastline. It appeared the Kahn brothers were slipping into the cruise-set, multi-marriage lifestyle with incredible ease.

Roger was still operating his Broadway booking agency and presently represented around half a dozen bands. Ever since his former manager quit at the tail end of the previous year, Roger had been handled by heavyweight Irving Mills. Mills had Duke Ellington on his roster, along with many other established artists.[29] Perhaps by having Mills guide his career, Roger hoped more opportunities to work in the movies might arise.

Roger also signed the lease on a large penthouse at 7 Gracie Square on East 84th Street, the building known for its Art Deco 'elephant' entrance doors, said by some to be the most beautiful doors in New York City. The triplex apartment overlooking Carl Schurz Park and the East River contained a pipe organ installed by its previous tenant. The residence remained Roger and Daisy's Manhattan abode for many years.

On the evening of Saturday, April 22, Roger and his orchestra performed at a benefit for the Parkway Policemen's Benevolent Association. Fifty percent of the ticket price went to the Emergency Work Bureau.[30] With breadlines growing longer by the day and soup kitchens a vital necessity, such charity concerts greatly assisted in helping raise cash to feed the unemployed.

When the budding author Esther Eberstadt Brooke approached Otto to write an introduction for her debut book, *The Girl and her Job; A Handbook for Beginners*, Otto could not have foreseen the hostility her view on women's employment opportunities - or lack of them - would have upon the business sector in the coming years. Within her capacity as a vocational counselor, she openly challenged the general perception taught widely at colleges that women should prepare themselves to enter the workplace, generally as a man's lapdog. In the rapidly changing economy of the period, such outspoken rhetoric, as championed by Esther - demanding better rights and higher pay for women in their workplace - was surveyed with suspicion and annoyance by many of her male counterparts.

Otto gladly wrote the introduction for her book, which arrived in bookstores on May Day 1933.[31]* Her philosophy that women applying for a job should 'look your best; talk your best; act your best; bring your best' certainly stood Esther in good stead for her burgeoning career. Championing new writers was something Otto had keenly advocated over the years, and his endorsement of Esther's book added extra weight to her argument. Interestingly, in Otto's preamble, he does not mention his Eberstadt family connection; Esther, and her two brothers, Ferdinand A. Eberstadt (a New York lawyer and investment banker), and industrialist Rudolph Eberstadt, and her sister Zalie Eberstadt, were Otto's first cousins. Their father, Edward Frederick Eberstadt, was Otto's uncle.

On May 1, the Senate Finance Committee announced they would call some of America's most prominent bankers to testify at the ongoing Pecora Inquiry into private banking to determine what effect their company's dealings had on the 1929 Wall Street Crash.[32] The hearing was scheduled to reconvene on May 23 and would last for several weeks. John Pierpont Morgan Jr. was subpoenaed, along with fellow members from J.P. Morgan & Co., as was Otto of Kuhn, Loeb, and Clarence Dillon of Dillon, Read & Co. Not since the Pujo banking investigation of 1912-13 had the head of the House of Morgan testified before a congressional committee investigating banking.

Otto arrived in Washington, D.C., on Sunday, June 25, two days before his appearance before the committee, arranged for the afternoon of the 27th. His arrival in the capital brought the government press corps out in force. Otto was always ready to seize a photo opportunity. He gave reporters a front-page picture when he randomly purchased $25 worth of baseball tickets from a Washington police officer for that week's Firemen vs. Policemen game. As soon as Otto handed over the money, he requested the tickets be given to inmates of the Walter Reed Hospital in Bethesda, Maryland, knowing full well he would be unable to attend the match. Otto's testimony at the inquiry took longer than he had anticipated and covered four days of intense cross-questioning.

A few weeks earlier, Morgan Jr.'s grilling had resulted in him receiving a severe reprimand by Ferdinand Pecora after the banker acknowledged he had not paid income tax in 1931 and 1932. The revelation left Morgan's reputation tarnished. Otto came well prepared for battle.

The inquiry resumed on Tuesday afternoon in the marbled Caucas Room of the Senate Office Building on Capitol Hill. After being sworn in, Otto was the first witness to testify. He explained to the committee the business methods of Kuhn, Loeb and spoke frankly about the 'unloading' of foreign bonds on the American public during the boom.

Several Kuhn, Loeb representatives, notably Benjamin J. Buttenwieser, Sir William Wiseman, and Percy M. Stewart, were present throughout the four-day inquiry. Also attending was the firm's attorneys Carl A. de Gersdorff, Mr. M. T. Moore, and Robert Swaine. Otto learned early on in his career never to stray too far from an attorney when it involved complicated financial matters.

The following day, Otto sat through the morning and afternoon sessions with little to do. Instead, Benjamin J. Buttenwieser testified. He disclosed that Kuhn, Loeb's $90 million loan to Chile, which had since defaulted, was given the Commerce Department's approval in 1925.

On Thursday, June 29, the proceedings were particularly fiery. Kahn was again the first witness to testify and received intense questioning from the Senate Subcommittee. He told how U.S. bankers 'bid foolishly and recklessly' for foreign securities in 1926 and 1928 in a quest to unload stocks on the American investing public. He also revealed that Kuhn, Loeb held a 'preferred list' of select clients. The buyers got opportunities in advance to invest in new issues, including those for the Pennroad Corporation's floatation. To date, the public had lost $106 million from Pennroad stock alone (based on the current price). Kuhn, Loeb made a $10,540,000 profit on the original transaction. 'No one was more surprised than we were,' said Kahn, commenting on the gain. 'The profits came solely through the action of the market. People were buying securities at wholly unreasonable prices.'[33] Otto revealed Kuhn, Loeb made $18 million profit from securities sold between 1927 and 1931. Since the 1929 stock market collapse, the firm's assets had lost 50 percent in value during 1932 and shrunk to a fourth of their 1929 figure.

Otto freely admitted that many bankers acted like 'sinners' during the 1929 bubble and sincerely hoped that Wall Street had learned its lesson since the crash. However, he vehemently denied that Kuhn, Loeb's profits were excessive, considering the risk factor of launching Pennroad. He then pointed out flaws in the U.S. tax law, which he confidently believed were a factor in the 1929 crash, claiming America had been 'the biggest stock market gambler through the 'capital losses and gains' phrase of the income tax law.'[34] Through these provisions in the act, he maintained the government acted as a speculator in the markets, which contributed to inflation and subsequently helped cause the slump. He did, nonetheless, offer his support for government measures to kick-start the economy. He showed a willingness to give the 'New Deal' - a series of plans and strategies and financial reforms established by President Franklin D. Roosevelt to restore prosperity to American citizens - a chance.*

When Otto was quizzed over his income tax payments, he divulged he had not paid any during 1930, 1931, or 1932.[35] The revelation took many in the room by surprise, not least Ferdinand Pecora. When pressed, he revealed he had suffered such heavy losses he had no income to declare. Kahn then had to explain a sale of stock he made directly (not through any exchange) to his daughter Maud (Marriott) on December 30, 1930, that generated a loss of $117,000, which qualified him to avoid paying income tax that year.[36] The sale was implemented to create a new trust fund for Maud. She had executed a transfer of the stocks in March 1931 at full market value. For purposes connected with the trust fund, the assignment was backdated to December 31, 1930. In April 1932, a treasury department official challenged the transaction, but the bureau of internal revenue held it to be lawful. Under further pressure from Pecora, Kahn admitted he had also sold stocks at the end of other tax years to family members.

On the final day of Otto's testimony, the emphasis shifted from his income tax arrangements to a preferred list of prominent persons and corporations that shared in Kuhn, Loeb securities (at no personal financial cost) in return for their advice. Pecora then delved into the ongoing battle for railroad dominance between Kuhn, Loeb, and J.P. Morgan & Co. that centered around the creation of two railroad holding companies. In 1929, Morgan & Co. had backed the Van Sweringen brothers (Mantis and Oris) of Cleveland in forming the Allegheny Corporation for the purchase of rail property in a manner beyond the control of the regulatory Interstate Commerce Commission. Two months later, Kuhn, Loeb floated the Pennroad Corporation for the Pennsylvania Railroad, from which they made a hefty profit. The battle was over oil. Otto concluded by telling the committee optimistically 'a new economic era' was unfolding. At day's end, Pecora adjourned the inquiry for a summer recess until October 3, when more witnesses would testify.

The *Brooklyn Daily Eagle*, in their summing up of Kahn's grilling, claimed it was a stale rehashing of the Morgan Inquiry, staged because the Morgans had private reassurance they would not be the only ones to feel the heat.[37] As such, at least one of Morgan's competitors would get publicly fried, Kuhn, Loeb being the obvious choice. They also felt the investigators did not bear down too hard on Kahn, and thus the general opinion on the inside was that Kahn would not be prosecuted over his income tax sales.

'No suaver, more fluent, and more diplomatic advocate could be conceived.' Otto and Benjamin J. Buttenwieser at the Senate Committee on Capitol Hill.

Otto's charming and personable disposition shone throughout his four days of testimony. Never once did he falter, nor did he show any incongruity in his statements. It was an admirable performance and one that successfully helped defuse public antagonism towards the banking community. The Senate's lead counsel Ferdinand Pecora wrote of Kahn in his 1939 memoir, 'No suaver, more fluent, and more diplomatic advocate could be conceived. If anyone could succeed in presenting the customs and functions of the private bankers in a favorable and prepossessing light, it was he.'[38]

Hannah and the 'Manassa Mauler'

'Naw, I'm not going to marry Hannah Williams,' said a chirpy Jack Dempsey when a reporter cornered him unexpectedly. 'We're a coupla' good friends, but we're not even engaged. I'm too busy to think of marrying.'[39] The trouble was, no one believed him, least of all, Hannah. The pair were smitten with one another and had been since they met in Reno while Hannah was awaiting her divorce papers. Rumors of a romance had persisted ever since.

In the boxing ring, Manassa-born Dempsey had the prowl of a tiger. His moniker, the 'Manassa Mauler,' did his slugs justice. That there should be a softer side to him, that craved and idealized family life stood at odds with the image he portrayed in the 'squared circle.' He longed for a wife to start a family. In Hannah, he felt confident he'd met the woman he could settle down with and raise that family.[40] Currently, though, he had far too much on his scorecard to concentrate on marriage plans. He was promoting the 60,000-seat Max Baer vs. Max Schmeling fight at the Yankee Stadium in the Bronx. Recently, Dempsey and Hannah had regularly been spotted in one another's company. Speculation of a romantic attachment between the pair originally emanated via Broadway circles. Although both parties had hotly denied any romance, the Broadway-wise were smiling, knowingly, and preparing to say, 'I told you so.'[41]

Like many speculators investing in stocks, Dempsey had lost a fortune in the crash. As such, he had a lot riding on his new venture as a boxing promoter, especially the Baer vs. Schmeling match on June 8. The fight sold out. In the searing heat, part-Jewish Baer defeated the German heavyweight and former world champion Max Schmeling in the 10th round after the referee ended the fight. Soaking up the atmosphere at the stadium that night was Hannah Williams.

This Is America

Addie quietly celebrated her 58th birthday on Saturday, June 10, with friends in New York City. On the same evening, in the auditorium of the National Press Club in Washington, D.C., a distinguished audience gathered to view a screening of the new movie *This Is America*, produced by Frederick Ullman Jr. and edited by Gilbert Seldes.[42] The film was a compilation of news stories and events that had shaped America after WWI, set to an orchestral score composed by Hugo Riesenfeld. It was the first full-length documentary feature movie of its kind ever made. Not one seat was empty in the auditorium that evening, with journalists, film reviewers, and special guests occupying most of them. They were all curious to witness how the producer had condensed the shape of America's persona into seventy minutes. It was a brave move on Ullman's part to bring such an ambitious project to the screen, considering not all the significant incidents defining the past fifteen years of American history had been captured on celluloid. To circumnavigate that dilemma, Ullman ingeniously shot scenes to imply those events not recorded through a lens. A *Variety* reviewer at the preview was mightily impressed with what he saw: 'Ullman and Seldes have done rather a fine job in assembling these scenes' and conceded 'the picture stands as the super-newsreel.' When the film was released nationally in mid-July, the American public flocked en masse to see it and unanimously gave it the thumbs up, ensuring it remained a box-office hit for well over a year.

One scene in the movie that must have caught Otto and Addie's, and every other member of the Kahn family's, attention, was the footage of Roger.[43]

The film stood as a social document of the unprecedented changes that had taken place during the previous two decades.[44] The producer deemed Roger had contributed to that transformation.

With the Baer/Schmeling fight out of the way, Dempsey could now focus his mind on matters closer to home. On June 29, Dempsey and Hannah were photographed sitting together at the Jack Sharkey vs. Primo Carnera fight at Madison Square Garden Bowl in Long Island City.[45] Carnera knocked Sharkey out in the sixth round to win the World Heavyweight Championship. Stories of a possible marriage linking Hannah and Dempsey continued to circulate.

Otto and Addie penciled a further three months out of their diaries to travel to the continent, the second time they'd visited this year. On July 5, the couple substituted the sweltering heat of New York City for a calm, relaxing, six-day voyage across the Atlantic to the UK. Otto's health was the primary reason for this additional trip. In Europe, they planned to stay at various health spas before returning to the tranquil coastline of the French Riviera. A prescription of indolence and languorous afternoons beckoned.

The Audition

By now, it was common knowledge Hannah and Jack were dating. Pictures of the couple had graced the dailies for nigh on three months, ever since Hannah's divorce in Reno. It did not take a genius to figure out they'd become more than just good friends.

On July 8, Warner Bros. released a nine-minute one-reel short titled *The Audition* starring Hannah.[16] The film, directed by Roy Mack, was shot at Vitaphone Studios in Brooklyn the previous October. A reviewer could easily have summarized the flimsy plot in one sentence: a booking agent advises bandleader Phil Emerton to liven up his act with a novelty; hence an audition is held to find such a performer. Hannah auditions for the part and sings *'Get Happy'* accompanied by Emerton and his band. She also delivers several lines of dialog, capably, in her light, breezy manner. As the title implies, it's a vehicle for Hannah to showcase her talents.* Various acts audition for the part, but it's fair to acknowledge Hannah's performance is by far the best and stands out for all the right reasons. Whether she'd done enough to forge a full-time career in the movies was a different matter.

From New York, Hannah and Dempsey traveled to Kansas City, Missouri. Jack had some work to attend to.[47] Pictures of the couple hanging out together, looking very much at ease with one another, continued to appear in the newspapers.[48] Jack even went as far as admitting to reporters 'there may be some truth' in the hearsay Hannah was now his fiancée, and then joked, 'but I don't think I'll get married right away.'[49] On the evening of July 12, Hannah caught the night train alone from Kansas City and journeyed to Los Angeles, where she had a bit part in a low-budget picture. Dempsey remained in Kansas City.

During the night of July 17, under cover of darkness, a car sped westwards along the highway from Salt Lake City, Utah, across the Nevada desert. Early the following morning, the same vehicle pulled up outside a local hotel in Elko, where its passengers Mike Costello and Jane Gray alighted and registered at the hotel.[50] The couple immediately retired to their room.

That afternoon Costello and Miss Gray exchanged vows in the County Courthouse at Elko. Justice of the Peace Alvin McFarlane omitted the word 'obey' from the ceremony.[51] When the bride and groom made their exit by the front of the building, they had no idea of the reception or commotion that awaited them. News of the marriage had spread across the city much like a dry sandstorm might blow in from the Great Basin Desert. In the street outside the Courthouse waited hundreds of locals keen to catch a glimpse of their champ and his sweetheart. Their whirlwind romance had paid dividends. It was the biggest scoop Elko had seen in years.

Pandemonium erupted. Reporters jostled for a closer position while waving notepads aloft. Flashbulbs exploded into the afternoon sunlight. Cheers rang out for the happy couple as they appeared on the stone steps of the Courthouse, looking somewhat overwhelmed by the impromptu reception.[52]

Hannah was happier now than she had felt for a long time. Jack shook as many hands of the fans who had waited excitedly to see him as was humanly possible. Hannah blushed and waved bashfully to the crowds. When a cameraman bellowed for more photographs, Hannah objected, saying, 'I look like such a mess after traveling all night.' Jack just smiled, then put his arm reassuringly around her shoulder before uttering, 'you're a liar.' They both folded up laughing. 'Well, if you must take our picture, go ahead,' Hannah succumbed. 'Sure darling, give the newspapermen a break,' Jack pleaded. The newlyweds affectionately snuggled arm in arm under the warm summer sunshine as they posed for the cameras. Though they spoke little about how they'd secretly arranged their marriage, they did express surprise at the turnout of so many well-wishers.

This union was Hannah's third marriage in under six years. It was also Jack's third attempt, having wed Maxine Gates in 1916 for three years, and then in 1925 tying the knot with Hollywood actress Estelle Taylor. Third time lucky, they were both hoping.

The day after the marriage, Hannah received a whopping big theatrical offer paying $5,000 a week, which, after giving serious consideration, she turned down. 'We want to have a home of our own,' she explained to the press. 'From now on, my whole life will be devoted to making Jack a good wife.'[53] The couple returned to Reno for their honeymoon, where their relationship first blossomed and where Dempsey had established a home and base since his divorce from Estelle Taylor.

Hannah and Jack were not the only pair heading off on honeymoon: at the beginning of August, Roger and his new wife Daisy sailed from New York for the French Riviera.[54] In Europe, they planned to cover ground by plane and, towards the end of their stay, had arranged to meet up with Otto and Addie in the South of France. Beforehand, Roger stopped off in the UK. On September 12, he drove from London to Croydon Aerodrome, where he met his friend and fellow pilot Captain Walter Lawrence Hope. From him, he purchased a Comper CLA-7 Swift plane for £250. The SS *American Merchant* promptly shipped the aircraft to America. The small, British-made single-seat monoplane, fitted with a de Havilland Gipsy engine, was one of only three of the forty-one Swift's ever built to have such a motor. The Prince of Wales owned a similar one.

When the plane arrived in New York Harbor, it was transported directly to Roosevelt Field to await Roger's return. The Swift was a natural for air racing; it had a top speed of 190 mph. Roger intended to fly the plane in various American flying competitions. One such event, the Roosevelt Field Air Races, was in December. He also had his sights set on entering the Cleveland Air Races the following year.

Anne's Extraordinary Fall

During the elder Kahns' summer exodus from New York, something extraordinary and unexpected happened on Park Avenue that would have a far-reaching effect on the family.

Gilbert and Sara had arrived back from their Panama honeymoon in early September and were now settling into married domesticity at their apartment at 912 Fifth Avenue. His former wife Anne and their daughter Claire had taken up residence in a modern third-floor 10-room apartment at 764 Park Avenue. Over the past few months, Anne had been under the care of her physician and was receiving treatment for a 'nervous condition' for which she was taking prescribed medication.[55] To help with the day-to-day running of her home, Anne had employed a full-time, live-in housekeeper.

Anne and Claire, accompanied by Anne's friend Agnes Dyer (a trained nurse), had recently paid a brief visit to Canada. From Canada, they returned to Anne's Manhattan apartment on the morning of Sunday, September 10. Before her arrival home, Anne had felt unsteady and complained to her friend Agnes of dizziness. Agnes phoned Anne's physician when they arrived back at the apartment and asked if he might call around to see Anne. The physician agreed and arranged to be there shortly.

The 'official' log of what happened next is as follows:

Anne retired to her bedroom in preparation for when the doctor arrived. Agnes assisted her. As Anne reached over to open a window to let in fresh air, she allegedly leaned too far, lost her balance, and fell forward. Agnes instinctively reached out to grab Anne to help pull her back but caught her flimsy blouse instead. The garment ripped in her hand, and Anne hurtled out of the window.[56]

Anne plunged three floors and hit the sidewalk below on East Seventy-fourth Street, where she lay injured, unable to move but still conscious.[57] Passersby rushed to her assistance. A crowd soon gathered. Anne became agitated and shouted vigorously, urging bystanders to clear off. 'I certainly don't want to be stared at,' she scowled as they looked on.

Anne's physician was already on his way to visit her when she took the fall. He arrived at the apartment block minutes later, where he, along with the porter and elevator attendant, gently carried her into the entrance lobby to await an ambulance.[58]

The ambulance arrived soon after and rushed Anne to Harbor Sanitarium at 667 Madison Avenue, where the initial report stated she was fighting for her life. By Monday, Anne showed slight signs of improvement, although the extent of her internal injuries were still unclear. She had also sustained a hip fracture and was suffering from nervous exhaustion. Nevertheless, surgeons at the hospital were hopeful Anne would, in time, make a full recovery.

When the incident occurred, Anne's parents had been holidaying at their summer residence in Allenhurst, Orange, New Jersey. After being notified of their daughter's accident, they immediately abandoned their vacation and motored to the hospital to be at their daughter's bedside. There was also the question of Anne's 4-year-old daughter Claire and who would now take care of her?

Agnes Dyer gave a statement to the police authorities at the hospital. In her interpretation of the accident, she stressed she was at Anne's apartment, not in her capacity as a nurse, but as a friend.[59] The police informed Gilbert what had happened. For the present, Gilbert was granted custody of his daughter, Claire.

On Thursday, September 28, Roger and Daisy arrived back in New York aboard the SS *Conti di Savoia*.[60] Also on the passenger list were Otto and Addie and their friend, soprano Rosa Ponselle. Miss Ponselle was returning to the U.S. after making her Italian debut at the Maggio Musicale Fiorentino arts festival in Florence.[61] Onshore, when a reporter pressed Otto to comment on the Jewish situation in Germany, he appeared almost lost for words. 'As a German Jew, what can I say?' and shrugged his shoulders as if to apologize.

No sooner had Roger set foot in the city than he rushed over to Temple Emanu-El on the corner of Fifth Avenue and 65th Street to attend the funeral service of Sime Silverman, founder of *Variety*.[62] Three thousand six hundred friends, including many stars and celebrities, packed the congregation. Broadway actor George Jessel gave a heartfelt eulogy for his old buddy, with tears welling up in his eyes. Over 600 floral wreaths decorated the Sanctuary. It was some production.

Silverman passed away in Los Angeles on September 23, having traveled there to aid his health. It was a particularly poignant occasion for Roger, for Sime had shown him great willingness in offering support and advice at the start of his fledgling theatrical career, such help that was not forthcoming from Roger's parents.

Otto was now dividing his time between work and vacation, spending only a few months at Kuhn, Loeb, followed by long spells absent on holiday. In doing so, he hoped his health would show signs of improvement or, at least, remain stable. Plans to restructure Paramount Publix were going ahead smoothly,[63] and Gilbert had taken on a more senior role within Kuhn, Loeb.

On a more pressing note, Otto received news from his 43-year-old cousin Marianne Mathy (Otto's Uncle Emil's son Richard's daughter), who, along with her husband Francis Friedenstein, had been placed under house arrest in Berlin. Marianne was an opera singer and singing teacher; her Jewish husband was a respected architect. Otto immediately sent her an affidavit permitting her to emigrate to the United States. Alarmingly, the German authorities informed Marianne there was a two-year waiting list for processing emigration documents. For the moment, she and her husband were trapped.*

Over the past couple of years, Roger had gradually tuned his interests away from music and more towards aviation. This trend continued over the remainder of 1933. On October 7, Roger and Daisy were among the mass of aeronautical figures and guests attending the opening day events of the two-day Charity Benefit National Air Pageant at Roosevelt Field. A crowd of over 30,000 spectators watched New York's most spectacular aerial show since 1925. On the field, Roger exhibited his latest purchase, his Comper CLA-7 Swift.[64] *

Anne Elizabeth Whelan Kahn

Anne Elizabeth Whelan Kahn died on Sunday, November 19, at the Harbor Sanitarium. For ten weeks, she had bravely fought to recover from the injuries she sustained after plunging from her bedroom window in her third-story apartment on Park Avenue.[65] The 30-year-old's courageous spirit had not been enough to save her. Her father, Charles A. Whelan, and grieving sister Clara Whelan Gray were among family members by her bedside when she passed away. Although hospital attendants initially gave her cause of death as bronchial pneumonia, her physician Dr. John J. Moorhead, in his report to the Medical Examiner, attributed her demise to the injuries she suffered in her fall.[66] Dr. Moorhead had helped save Gilbert's life back in 1921 after Gilbert sustained severe injuries in a motorcycle accident. Anne's passing came as a tremendous shock to everyone who knew her, not least her family and friends and her young daughter Claire.

The following week, a hearse carried Anne's body to Allenhurst, Orange, New Jersey, where she had grown up. Here she was buried in the Whelan family vault at Holy Sepulchre Cemetery.

No member of the Whelan or Kahn families made any public statement regarding Anne's death. However, the newspapers picked up on the extraordinary coincidence that Anne died on the ninth anniversary of her former marriage to Gilbert.[67] They also spoke of how unwell she had been since her divorce to Gilbert was granted in Reno the previous January.

An additional, more delving report in *The Chicago Daily Tribune* hinted that perhaps her tumble had not been accidental and that certain aggravating factors may have contributed to its cause.[68] The paper also contradicted initial accounts of the lead-up to the fatal event. Allegedly, Gilbert Kahn had paid a 'brief and somewhat mysterious call' at his first wife's apartment at 764 Park Avenue two weeks before her fall from the third-floor window. Ever since Gilbert's visit, Anne had been much agitated. Some friends mentioned how she had become 'moody and uncommunicative.' The article informed readers that on Sunday, September 10, at 11 a.m., the heiress had walked towards an 'open third-floor window' where she had 'tottered a moment and pitched through it.' Anne's friend, Agnes Dyer, who was staying at the apartment, leaned forward to grab 'Mrs. Kahn's chemise but the silk garment ripped in two, and the young woman plunged to the sidewalk three stories below.'[69]

Did Anne deliberately lunge forward through the open window in the act of suicide? *The Chicago Daily Tribune* account was dissimilar to any previously published and certainly gave an alternative interpretation of events.

Anne left no will. Although an heiress in her own right to her father's tobacco fortune (now much depleted due to the stock market crash), her estate at the time of her death amounted to 'not more than $50,000' in personal assets and no realty.[70] This news came to light when Judge James A. Foley granted letters of administration to Gilbert. Because Anne and Gilbert had divorced, her entire estate would pass directly to their young daughter Claire Anne Kahn.

Guardianship of Claire reverted to Gilbert. For the present, the young child resided with her grandparents Otto and Addie at the Kahn family home at 1100 Fifth Avenue.[71]

On November 22, 51-year-old Albert Comos of 222 East 39th Street, Brooklyn, was arrested at his home on a disorderly conduct charge for sending bothersome letters to Otto Kahn.[72] Neither the police nor Otto ever disclosed the nature of the content or the intention behind the correspondence, apart from a specific demand by Comos for $100,000.[73] The police were now seeking a mental health assessment of the suspect.[74]

Over the past few months, Roger had taken time to reflect upon his career. After being away from his band for several months, most of which was spent in Europe honeymooning, Roger was yearning to give music another try.[75] His decision coincided with the repeal of Prohibition on December 5. Perhaps he was hoping that dance halls and hotel ballrooms would now become busier, and as such, more work would be available.

'Here's to Prohibition; hippy days!'[76]

The night Prohibition ended was one heck of a party, with everyone invited. Although for some - the racketeers and those that profiteered from the illicit booze trade - the Eighteenth Amendment's repeal was the last thing they wanted. For them, the fun and games finally came to an end.

In another telling move, the week after the Twenty-First Amendment came into effect, Roger applied for a job at an oil and petroleum company, reportedly Tydol, affiliated with Tide Water Oil Company.[77]

Xmas this year brought more fun and merriment than usual into the Kahn household on account that Otto and Addie had their young granddaughter Claire to consider.

On Boxing Day, the Met opened their 1933-34 season with *Peter Ibbetson*, the Deems Taylor opera, followed by the Met Opera Ball. The fundraiser dominated New York's social festive celebrations, and anyone of note, who was in town, attended. Although Otto no longer wielded any real power at the Met, he still turned up for such occasions.

This year's spectacle adopted a Louis XV theme, with the Met's stage taking on the enchanted appearance of the Forest of Fontainebleau. The orchestra pit was boarded over, and upon it, Joe

Moss and His Orchestra played dance numbers. Guests were requested to dress the part, appropriately reflecting the chosen theme. Most attendees obliged, none more so than Mrs. S. Stanwood Menken, who at past events was famed for having turned up in outrageous outfits adorned with ostrich plumes, pearls, turkey wings, birds' nests, and taffeta.

Fundraisers were vitally important for the Met's survival, and this year's ball was no exception. Now that Otto was no longer the old dame's financial guardian angel, new liberal benefactors were sought to feed the ravenous, aging institution.

Trends in the music industry come and go quickly. The development of jazz was continually evolving. On the horizon, the big band sound of swing was now making an impression. Roger and his symphonic syncopated dance music had begun to sound dated alongside the music the new kids were playing.

History had made it impossible for the public to see Roger as anything other than Otto Kahn's rich renegade son and not the serious musician he had worked so hard to be. In the open, father and son may have had their differences, but in private, Roger still referred to his dad as 'the Governor.'[78]

It now seemed only a matter of time before Roger threw in the towel and pursued a more gratifying career. That option would present itself sooner than he could have imagined.

PART IV
THIS IS AMERICA
1934–After

*The world was changing
quicker than a racing heartbeat*

17

THE FALL OF THE HOUSE OF KAHN

'Success is not a free gift. Like everything else really worth having in life, it has to be paid for.'[1] Otto H. Kahn

1934

With the Christmas holidays out of the way, the Palm Beach season in Florida officially commenced in the first week of January. Addie and Otto were due to stay at their new beachfront villa at the end of the month.[2] Perhaps Roger and his wife Daisy, and Gilbert and his wife Sara might join them for a couple of weeks. Otto and Addie hoped so.

In New York City on the afternoon of Sunday, January 14, the American humanitarian James G. McDonald and his wife Ruth were scheduled to arrive at 1100 Fifth Avenue for an informal meeting with Otto and Addie. The visit would take place over tea.

As certain hopeful beneficiaries in the past had discovered, the doorway of generosity was not always open at the Kahn household.

During the previous year, McDonald had been appointed as an autonomous High Commissioner by the League of Nations to help aid and assimilate the growing influx of German refugees crossing into adjoining European countries. However, his office had to appropriate all funds privately to appease German objections to the League of Nations.

McDonald arranged his meeting with the Kahns to discuss the worrying increase of Jewish and non-Jewish refugees in Europe. He hoped they might lend a sympathetic ear towards the cause and offer a financial donation to help subsidize his work.

McDonald was passionate in his belief that European states had only a limited power to absorb refugees and that the escalating crisis had to be tackled at its source to avoid a disaster. He believed that the efforts of the private organizations and the League organizations for refugees could realistically only mitigate the problem 'of growing gravity and complexity,'[3] not eradicate it.

James and Ruth arrived at the Kahn mansion late for their appointment. A liveried footman promptly escorted them to the opulent French salon on the second floor, where Otto and Addie were. Otto especially did not like being kept waiting. In McDonald's absence, he had arranged another meeting for five o'clock with Louis Lipsky - former president of the Zionist Organization of America - that he now could not postpone.[4] Consequently, his discussion with McDonald would have to be brief. Unfortunately for McDonald, the meeting did not go satisfactorily, and no donation was forthcoming. Although the Kahns were genuinely interested in his cause, they were anxious not to associate themselves financially due to their detachment from Jewish cultural and religious affairs.

McDonald had visited Addie in October the previous year, after which he noted in his diary that Addie was active in the Foreign Policy Association, a non-profit organization founded to help spread awareness and understanding of foreign policy issues.[5] Otto was not present at the meeting. Neither did Addie offer McDonald any financial support during their discussion.

It would later become apparent to McDonald that his department's separation from the League of Nations made his role untenable. The division diminished his power and, ultimately, his success as a fundraiser. This dichotomy led to his resignation from the post in December the following year.[6] The outcome of McDonald's meeting with the Kahns was a clear example of the Kahns' religious ambivalence, which caught up with them on many occasions.

After a lifetime of fabricated allegations appearing in the press that Otto was either Episcopalian or Catholic, he recently informed one reporter: 'My parents were not practicing Jews and did not bring me up to be a practicing Jew. But I have never left Judaism and have no idea of doing so.'[7] Nonetheless, the Kahn family had been members of the fashionable congregation of St Bartholomew's Episcopal Church on Park Avenue for many years.

Otto could read a person like a passport. He had no intention of getting caught up in foreign affairs, in which he held no sway. Otto was known not to be an advocate of the League of Nations. 'Nothing that we fought for makes it incumbent upon us to act henceforth as policemen for Europe and Asia,' he wrote in 1919 in a letter to Senator Miles Poindexter of the U.S. Senate regarding the formation of the League.* 'I have been at pains to read the Peace Treaty, including the Covenant, from beginning to end. I laid it away sore at heart and sickened,' Kahn informed Poindexter. 'I am convinced ... the more we are left free to do things in our own way, the more willingly, generously and effectively we shall do them.'[8] Otto still held the same opinion. Interestingly, the U.S. never did join the League of Nations.

'Feeling for art, has nothing to do with a man's pocketbook.'[9]
Otto H. Kahn

New York's Museum of Modern Art at 11 West 53rd Street drew on all of its pulling power as a dominating force in modern art when it opened its doors on Monday, January 15, to preview the International Exhibition of Theater Art.

During the evening, a host of celebrities turned up, bringing West 53rd Street to a halt. Among those attending were the actresses Mary Pickford and Dolores Del Rio and the lesser-known visiting Soviet Ambassador Alexander Antonovich Troyanovsky.[10] Otto, too, was there to check out the collection of artworks by 120 global artists and designers. Exhibited on one wall were curtain paintings by Picasso. Other displays contained sketches by Norman Bel Geddes of costumes and stage sets for *The Miracle* and drafts by Oliver Messel of scenery for Offenbach's opera *La belle Hélène.*

Almost 4,000 invitees shuffled into the museum that evening, past a score of eager photographers and flickering movie cameras. Inside, guests moved slowly up and down the stairs, mingling, in and out of the rooms, with most spending more time chatting and sipping champagne than viewing the actual artworks.

Two days later, Otto attended a benefit concert in the Fifth Avenue home of his friend, investment banker Adolph Lewisohn, at which the scientist Albert Einstein had agreed to play the violin.[11] Proceeds from the event were to aid Dr. Einstein's scientific colleagues in Berlin. Other participating musicians were Russian violinist Toscha Seidel, violin-cellist soloist Ossip Giskin, British pianist Harriet Cohen, and viola player Léon Barzin.[12] Due to the nature of the concert - it was Einstein's American debut playing the violin at a recital - and the curiosity factor, the three hundred $25 tickets sold out. Upon arrival, each ticket holder received a polite word of etiquette before taking their seat in the ballroom: Einstein had barred all criticism of his playing.[13] Thus, as per the scientist's wishes, no negative critique of his performance was written up. To help lessen the impact of his playing on the audience, Einstein practiced on his fiddle that afternoon for three hours before the concert.

In March, the previous year, Einstein had handed in his German passport and renounced his German citizenship at the German consulate in Brussels. He was now an exile in America, his new home. 'Because of Hitler, I don't dare step on German soil,' he wrote to a friend in Berlin. Einstein's open denunciation of the Nazi Party now meant he had a price on his head.

Otto was back in the public eye, attending functions and looking healthier than he had done for some time. It was encouraging for Addie and his family to see. Their fears and worries for the great man had, of late, been of genuine concern.

Addie journeyed to Palm Beach ahead of her husband to oversee any last-minute arrangements at their new villa in preparation for her family's arrival.

Roger, too, had been busy since the start of the New Year rehearsing a new band.[14] He had hopes of securing a prestigious New York club residency with a radio hook-up.[15] He was presently awaiting confirmation. Although Roger's musical aspirations had waned recently, with his interest in aviation occupying more of his time, music still paid his bills.

Sand, Sea, and Sun in Palm Beach

New York was endlessly cold. At the turn of January, Otto traveled south to join his wife in Palm Beach. At last, their handsome new beach house was ready for occupancy.

Villa Oheka, with its red-tiled roof and beige painted walls, directly faced the Atlantic Ocean and gave the impression of a Spanish hacienda.* Only the manicured lawn and evenly placed palm trees separated the shoreline from the house. For the first time in many a year, the elder Kahns got to enjoy the peace they had so earnestly sought. Margaret and Maud had already arrived at the villa with their spouses, and Gilbert, Sara, and Gilbert's daughter Claire were due presently.[16] Roger and Daisy were hoping to fly down, making use of Palm Beach's Belvedere Airport.[17]

It had been a routine practice over the past twenty-five years for Otto and Addie to spend part of winter together in Palm Beach, where more recently, the warm breezes and temperate weather had brought some relief to Otto's persistent health problems. Although they arrived slightly later this year than was usual, their plans would be no different from any other visit. On most days, Otto would take in the fresh Atlantic air as he leisurely strolled along the seafront promenade dressed casually in plus fours and a blazer, wearing his trusty linen hat to protect his head from the sun's beating rays. This break was Otto's quality time when he could mull over his many thoughts without fear of any unwanted distractions. He planned to remain in situ for around four weeks.

A picture of Otto captured during an afternoon stroll to Breakers Casino was published in a local newspaper on February 4. He appeared relaxed and welcomed the attention of the photojournalist.

Villa Oheka, Palm Beach, with Atlantic waves crashing on the shoreline.
(Picture courtesy of the Historical Society of Palm Beach County)

It was customary for the Kahns to invite friends to stay with them for short visits. In early February, they welcomed socialite and bon vivant Captain Alistair Mackintosh and his wife Lela down from New York.[18] The couple spent several days as houseguests at Villa Oheka. Otto's friend and fellow Kuhn, Loeb partner Sir William Wiseman also dropped by, and together, they spent a leisurely afternoon at Hialeah Park racetrack having a flutter on the horses.[19] On February 14, Gilbert and Sara showed up at a Valentine party held at the Palm Beach Patio accompanied by their friends, the coal and iron magnate Benjamin Throop II and his beautiful wife, movie actress Rubye De Remer.

Addie briefly returned to New York in the third week of February to undertake a social function.[20] Otto remained in Palm Beach with his daughters and son Gilbert and his boisterous young grandchildren to keep him occupied. He even found the time to be a judge at an impromptu beauty contest on the beach. Addie returned to Palm Beach in time to celebrate her husband's 67th birthday on February 21. Otto spent the day modestly, enjoying the things he loved most: playing golf in the warm Florida sun and relaxing with his family and close friends around him.

On the day following Otto's birthday, the Pecora investigation reared its ugly head yet again. A newspaper report intimated Otto might be recalled to Washington, D.C., to face further questioning before the Senate Committee.[21]

Mason Day (a former associate of the oil baron Harry F. Sinclair) - both of whom had previously served jail terms for contempt of court as a result of President Warren G. Harding's 'Teapot Dome' oil scandal - had revealed to the Pecora Commission his knowledge of a pool set up last June by Kuhn, Loeb & Co. The pool involved the car manufacturer Walter P. Chrysler and Harry F. Sinclair (among others) and made a handsome profit of $395,238. While being questioned by Ferdinand Pecora, Day stated the pool allegedly intended 'to distribute at a profit' 145,000 Libbey-Owens-Ford glass company shares. Pecora was keen to hear what Otto had to say about the matter. At the hearing the previous year, Otto had pointed out that: 'the watchfulness of the Stock Exchange ought to be most carefully concentrated against any attempt to take advantage of the one function for which it exists, namely, to offer a fair and free market for securities.' Accordingly, Kahn felt anything that artificially interfered with that market ought to be punished not merely by the Stock Exchange but otherwise.

No date had yet been set for the rehearing, as Pecora was still ascertaining whether or not there was the need for additional circumstantial evidence to back up Day's claim.

The implication that Otto might have to face the committee again was not the news he had hoped for, especially after having given such robust and effective testimony during his previous appearance last June. For the moment, the matter remained filed under 'pending.'

At sixty-seven, Otto cut a restrained figure compared with the former erect, dashing silhouette of his past. His once proud, dark, finely clipped mustache was now white and coiled with balm. His dress, though still as immaculate as it had always been, now looked dated. Fashions had changed, yet Otto's sense of style remained constant. Though he left Germany forty-five years ago, he habitually used his hands in a European manner to express his words and describe his emotions. On rare occasions, when he let his guard down, you could still hear a faint flavoring of a German accent. Yet, behind his manicured façade, the most visible change in him was his acceptance of mortality, that, and a distant gaze of sorrow in his eyes.

Otto celebrated his 67th birthday at Palm Beach. Captured by a single journalist, this is one of the last informal photographs of Otto.

After extending his vacation in Palm Beach to last almost six weeks, Otto handed the villa keys over to his daughters and returned to New York with Addie in mid-March.[22] Their retreat from the hustle and bustle of city life may have lasted longer than they anticipated, but the change of pace appeared to have hugely benefitted Otto's health. Back in the metropolis, Otto resumed his duties at Kuhn, Loeb.

Roger and Daisy had now settled into their new modern apartment overlooking East River.[23] Their relocation was all part of Roger's plan to reorganize his life. He had also recently sold two of his aircraft. Since Roger first got the flying bug, he'd clocked up over 3,000 hours in the air, more than any other private transport pilot in the U.S. except for Colonel Charles Lindbergh. His experience and qualifications as a pilot were starting to pay dividends. Airplane manufacturers were lining up to employ his skills as a test pilot.

Roger had not given up all hope of reigniting his music career; it just seemed, the older he became, there were fewer opportunities. Moreover, the ones that did arise were not as well-paid as he might have hoped. Nevertheless, his orchestra was presently under consideration for a new production penned by Irving Caesar and Samuel Pokrass destined for Broadway's Paradise Restaurant.[24] He was also auditioning for radio shows.[25] If the right booking came along, Roger was open for business. In the meantime, his work as a test pilot kept him busy.

Just as it seemed things were on the up, everything changed.

At the beginning of the year, Roger had been full of anticipation, planning his return to the stage. Whether in a fit of anger or during a momentary meltdown, in mid-March, Roger's office issued a press statement confirming he was ready to retire from the entertainment industry for good: 'Roger Wolfe Kahn quits Broadway to become a test pilot.'[26] The news came as no surprise to his family or those closest to him. His patience had finally worn thin. 'What new nightlife scion will crop up to perpetuate the doings of Roger Wolfe Kahn?'[27] wondered one Ohio newspaper.

That said, as past events had clearly shown, Roger could just as quickly change his mind again.

Almost As If to Say Goodbye

At the beginning of the last week in March, Otto occupied his box in the 'Golden Horseshoe' for a performance at the Metropolitan Opera House.[28] * Throughout the evening, he was in a relaxed mood.

Wednesday, March 28

On the evening of Wednesday, March 28, Otto was a guest at a dinner given in honor of the English economist Sir George Paish. During the meal, Otto contributed to the lively conversation with great interest. He was notably in good spirits.[29] His health had improved as of late, and he appeared his former magnetic and cheerful self. Otto returned home to the Kahn mansion on Fifth Avenue at his usual time, just before midnight.

Maundy Thursday, March 29

The following morning, Otto rose early, as was his custom. He dressed, took breakfast with Addie, bade her farewell, and departed for the office. His chauffeur drove him the usual route, along the familiar avenues and streets Otto traveled most days when he was resident in New York City. He had a hectic day ahead of him, and the thought of spending Easter weekend at his beloved Long Island estate had a pleasing ring to it. During the car ride, Otto checked his appointment diary, familiarizing himself with the day's meetings. Fifteen minutes later, his limousine pulled up outside Kuhn, Loeb's main entrance in William Street, at 9:45 a.m.

Death at No. 52

The grand coda arrived unexpectedly. Roger was at 1100 Fifth Avenue with his mother when the call from Kuhn, Loeb came through. Otto had been taken ill and could Mr. Kahn's chauffeured limousine be sent immediately to the office to collect him.[30] The driver and vehicle promptly set off as requested. Ten minutes later, a second call came into the Kahn household from the Kuhn, Loeb office, notifying the family that Otto had passed away. It was Roger that attended to his mother directly after Kuhn, Loeb delivered the tragic news. Before the two phone calls, things were much the same as usual, with nothing out of the ordinary to report. Of all the days for such heartbreak to unfold, today had been nothing special. In the space of ten minutes, all that changed.

Otto died just after 1:45 p.m.* The lead up to the event and what happened after was reported as follows:

Otto arrived at the office that morning in an upbeat mood.[31] He went about his business in his usual manner and displayed no outward signs of pain or discomfort. Shortly after one o'clock, he took lunch with two junior partners in the firm's private dining room on the fourth floor.[32] One of those partners was Benjamin J. Buttenwieser, whom Otto had become particularly fond of from their work together on the Pecora Inquiry. It was some way into the luncheon when Otto suddenly became ill. He replaced his coffee cup onto the saucer and directly slouched forward in his chair before slumping to the floor, where he remained lifeless. Otto had suffered an apoplectic stroke.[33]

Buttenwieser rushed to Otto's aid and tried to resuscitate him but could get no response.[34] Gilbert, who was nearby in the building, was immediately summoned. A call was placed to the Kahn house at Fifth Avenue to inform the family of the situation and ask for Otto's chauffeured limousine. Otto's physician, Dr. Harold Thomas Hyman, was then contacted. A few minutes later, an emergency call went to Beekman Street Hospital in Lower Manhattan requesting an ambulance. The ambulance turned up within minutes, accompanied by Dr. Stanley Sigorski.[35] Shortly afterward, Otto's physician Dr. Hyman arrived. Both physicians attended to Otto, and both confirmed they could not resuscitate the patient. A second call went to the Kahn family at 1100 Fifth Avenue.

All partners of Kuhn, Loeb who were in the building were summoned to an emergency meeting. Those present agreed it would be tactful to impose a temporary media blackout. Everyone who worked for the company was placed under strict gagging orders and informed not to talk to reporters.

Addie was in the library when Roger broke the news to her. A moment of quiet pervaded, after which she fell backward and collapsed into the depths of a large couch.

Otto was dead!

The mighty whirlwind of energy that was Otto Hermann Kahn was gone. As the reality washed through the Kahn household, it was as if the world momentarily stopped turning on its axis and stood still. Life for the Kahn family and everyone around them would never be the same again.

Roger took charge of the situation at the Kahn mansion, ensuring his mother was promptly attended to by a physician. Maud and Margaret were contacted and told of their father's death. Gilbert remained at Kuhn, Loeb, to help deal with the unfolding drama.

Otto Kahn Just Died!

Unsurprisingly, given the enormity of the news, rumors of Otto's passing soon leaked out into the financial district. 'Otto Kahn just died!' The word spread on a gust of wind, down Broad and Wall Streets, ripping through the Stock Exchange and into innumerable banking and brokerage houses. Before long, the media picked up the scent and rushed down to William Street. A crowd began to gather outside the Kuhn, Loeb building. Most people were in shock, bewildered, their faces etched with disbelief, with many just wanting to pay their respects.

After hearing the news, John Pierpont Morgan Jr. slipped out of his office building at 23 Wall Street, accompanied by two senior Morgan partners, Thomas W. Lamont Jr., and Russell C. Leffingwell. The three walked hurriedly around the corner into William Street and entered the Kuhn, Loeb building, where they were escorted directly into Otto's private office on the second floor. They stayed for five minutes. As they departed, Morgan remained silent. He looked visibly moved. When pushed by a reporter asking for a comment, Morgan cut him down curtly, 'Comment? No, I have nothing to say.'[36] Lamont added, 'Mr. Morgan never makes a public statement.' Kuhn, Loeb requested security at the front of the building to be tightened. The doorman drew shut the sliding metal grilles across the entrance. No one was permitted to enter the building unless they had prior approval.

Hanover 9200: Kuhn, Loeb's office phone rang incessantly. Still, Kuhn, Loeb issued no statement, and no press calls got through. Outside in the street, the crowd of onlookers grew. Soon, people spilled out onto the road. Police officers arrived and began moving bystanders back onto the sidewalk in an attempt to keep order. All regular traffic into the street got redirected.

When Otto's chauffeured limousine turned into William Street, the crowd surged forward and toppled back onto the roadway. Police officers attempted to cut a path through so the automobile could park close to the Kuhn, Loeb building. As it braked, reporters hastened forward to capture pictures.

Just before three o'clock, Dr. Hyman phoned the Chief Medical Examiner's office and informed them that Otto Kahn had died. Yet, still, Kuhn, Loeb released no formal statement to the media. Hence, the mystery of exactly what had happened to Otto Kahn continued to baffle everyone outside of Kuhn, Loeb's inner circle.

Newsrooms across America were alerted. Teleprinters spewed out updates as and when events unfolded.

Breaking News. Unconfirmed reports are coming through that the Wall Street financier Otto H. Kahn has passed away. Hold the front page. Await further reports.

The word that Otto had died spread rapidly across Manhattan, but still, the banking firm issued no statement.[37] As usual, the Stock Exchange ended trading for the day at 3 p.m. precisely. By then, the crowds in William Street had grown considerably. A window directly above the main portal of the Kuhn, Loeb building opened, and a uniformed concierge appeared. All eyes in the street settled upon him. The concierge leaned forward towards the white flagpole and slowly lowered the Stars and Stripes flag to half-staff. Onlookers in the street fell silent as they watched.

The metal grille barring entrance to the building was wrenched open. Benjamin J. Buttenwieser stepped forward from behind the grille onto the front steps. In his hand was a sheet of paper from which he read out a brief statement on behalf of Kuhn, Loeb & Co.; 'Otto H. Kahn died suddenly today of a heart attack while at lunch in his office. I hope...' he paused for a moment to straighten his composure, 'I never have to give out such sad news again.'[38] He then announced Kuhn, Loeb would remain closed for four days.

The bulletin was not released earlier to prevent stocks on the markets from falling.[39]

'Mr. Kahn had had general arteriosclerosis for some years,' said Dr. Hyman to the waiting reporters. 'With that, he had high blood pressure and had suffered attacks of angina pectoris. He was suddenly seized today with what was probably an acute occlusion of the coronary artery and died instantly.'[40]

Still, the crowds in William Street grew. Hundreds of inquisitive members of the public milling around, stunned, caught up in the suddenness of the financier's death. Among the first callers at Kuhn, Loeb's office offering their sympathy were senior figures in the banking world. Afterward, a steady flow of visitors followed.

By the time the black hearse turned into William Street, the crowd now stretched the entire length of the block. Police officers struggled to contain order as people surged forward to grasp a closer look. Following directly behind the hearse was a black sedan. The vehicles slowly edged towards the Kuhn, Loeb building, where they came to a halt. Four smartly suited pallbearers stepped out of the sedan. The four attendants removed a wooden casket from the hearse and carried it inside the building.

The Medical Examiner, Dr. Charles Norris, was informed of Otto's death during a lecture he was giving at the Police Academy. He interrupted his lesson and rushed over to the Kuhn, Loeb building to provide an autopsy. Soon after, the doctor gave his permission for the undertakers to remove the body.[41] At 4:30 p.m., the coffin, draped in black, bearing Otto's corpse, was carefully carried down the front steps of the Kuhn, Loeb building and loaded into the hearse. Many of the bystanders lining the sidewalk doffed their hats as a mark of respect. The vehicle then slowly drove away and proceeded north towards Fifth Avenue and the Kahn family home.

A small but persistent bunch of reporters were waiting outside the Kahn mansion when the black hearse carrying Otto's casket turned right from Fifth Avenue into East 91st Street. The driver slowed the vehicle to a crawl as he maneuvered the sweep of the *porte cochère* at the front of the Kahn house. Most of the press corps remained respectful of the family's wishes by not invading their private property. Instead, they remained on the sidewalk to scribble notes and take pictures. Nevertheless, one overly eager photographer did break rank and ran into the carriage entrance to capture an image as the pallbearers removed the casket from the vehicle. A butler pounced on the intruder pushing him aside.

The pallbearers carried the black-draped coffin through the vestibule into the stone reception hall, after which the heavy double front doors of the Kahn mansion shut hurriedly behind them. Otto's body was then taken to an adjoining room and laid out. Throughout the evening, a steady flow of automobiles drew up to the house, depositing their occupants. Many were friends of the family or business associates calling to pay their respects.

A sky full of kindness rained upon the Kahn family. Tributes from world leaders, royalty, and politicians, as well as from countless members of show business, the art world, and the music fraternity, flooded into the Kahn household in an overwhelming display of reverence and heartfelt sadness. Each condolence expressed a personal sense of numbness and grief.

'Extra! Read All About It'

'Extra! Read all about it ... Otto Kahn dead!' hollered the newsie on William Street corner.*

Reports of Otto's death hit some late editions that evening. The following day, it seemed every paper in the U.S. led with the story. In death, Otto's dominating influence was as apparent as it had been during his lifetime. The ramifications and knock-on effect of his passing would be enormous.

The *New York Times* leader read: 'Otto Kahn, 67, Dies of Heart Attack in Bank's Offices - Wall Street is Shocked.' The *Pittsburgh Press* went one further and announced: 'Entire World Mourns Death of Otto Kahn.'[42] The news went global.

'I am shocked and saddened by Mr. Kahn's death,' expressed Thomas W. Lamont Jr. in the *New York Times*.[43] 'He had a long and honorable career in banking and in railway development. His mind and methods were always constructive. His activities were extraordinarily varied, and his influence most helpful in music and the arts. His death is a heavy loss to the community.'

Governor of New York, Herbert H. Lehman, conveyed his sincere regret upon hearing the news. 'He was not only a great business leader but also his interest in art, music and the sciences were very earnest, and to each he brought a breadth of vision and unusual devotion.'

Veteran Broadway producer George C. Tyler spoke of Kahn's, 'willingness to invest money regardless of self-glorification or a possible financial profit. This, he did for the benefit of the better theater.'

Winthrop W. Aldrich, chairman of the Chase National Bank, affirmed he would long remember Kahn as one of the ablest and most influential bankers of his time. 'For more than a quarter of a century, he has occupied an important place in the field of international and domestic finance. He was a man of genuine personal charm and an outstanding patron of music and art.'

In a handwritten letter to Addie signed by Helen Todd on behalf of the Artists and Writers House residents in Soho (which Otto had established seven years earlier), the tenants expressed their deepest sympathy upon hearing the 'unutterably sad news. What Mr. Kahn's goodness and kindness has meant to this group of struggling, young people through the past dark years I have no words to express.'[44]

Otto's death happened at the tail end of the current Metropolitan Opera season, with only seven more New York stage performances scheduled. It seemed highly likely and fitting that a mention of his passing would take place at one of them. On Friday, March 30, at the matinee performance of *Parsifal*, the Mayor of New York City, Fiorello La Guardia, walked on stage during the second intermission and delivered a short eulogy in honor of the Met's former president; 'May we pause just one moment to pay a silent tribute to the memory of a great New Yorker whose name is linked with this institution and who has done so much to make grand opera in New York possible - a tribute to the memory of Otto H. Kahn.'[45]

As the Mayor paused, the entire audience, filling every floor of the opera house, rose to their feet and stood with bowed heads for a moment's silence. After the silent tribute, the Mayor resumed his address, urging operagoers to continue the generous efforts made by Mr. Kahn for so many years.

Curiously, an alternative account of Otto's death appeared in at least one newspaper. *The Montana Standard* specified Otto died slumped at his desk alone in his office.[46] He was discovered later by his private secretary. Her initial reaction was to sit down in a chair in Otto's office and sob hysterically. In the interim, his doctor was phoned and arrived soon after.

Meanwhile, Kuhn, Loeb staff were told to continue business as usual, which they did, for at least half an hour before the veracity of the situation sank in. When it did, confusion ensued throughout the office. The report claimed Otto's demise occurred at 2:45 p.m. However, it has a couple of inaccuracies, namely, the mention of Mrs. Kahn's death a few years earlier.

Whether this is an accurate version of events and the statement Kuhn, Loeb issued to the press was falsified, I can only speculate. It could, however, account for Kuhn, Loeb's decision to temporarily hold back news of Otto's death and the confusion that followed. Did Kuhn, Loeb, use poetic license to stage-manage Otto's finale? Alas, the answer is probably something we will never know.

Otto's Funeral

That weekend the funeral arrangements were released to the press.[47] The service would be private and held at the family's Long Island estate on Easter Monday. The interment would take place nearby among woodland in the Memorial Cemetery of St John's Church.

As morning dawned on Monday, April 2, it seemed the whole of Manhattan was in mourning for the former Wizard of Wall Street; such was the city's somber mood.

At the Kahn mansion at Fifth Avenue, the servants awoke early to prepare for the day's mammoth event, as did their counterparts at the family's Long Island estate.

Addie and her family took breakfast together at the house. At 10:45, the funeral vehicles arrived in East 91st Street outside the Kahn mansion. The hearse drove directly into the *porte cochère*, followed by a limousine for the widow and immediate family members. For the next fifteen minutes, the heavy outer doors remained shut to obscure any view from the street. Soon after 11 a.m., the hearse and limousine departed from East 91st Street, trailed by a short motorcade.[48] Close friends and Otto's work associates independently made their way to Long Island. Addie had arranged for a blanket of lilies to cover the casket.

The drive to Long Island and the Northern State Parkway took just over an hour. As the cortège reached sight of the Kahn estate, police officers from the Syosset Precinct came into view. The motorcade entered the grounds via the gatehouse on Jericho Turnpike. Motorcycle police officers remained stationed at all entrances to the estate and around its western boundary throughout the afternoon.[49]

The warm midday sun cast rays upon the cobblestones as the hearse drew into the courtyard, where it came to a halt. Otto had returned to his beloved château one last time.

The service commenced promptly at three o'clock in the music room. Rev. Dr. Samuel H. Goldenson, rabbi of Temple Emanu-El, officiated. During the sacrament, Addie remained composed, comforted by the close presence of her two sons and two daughters. Other family members and friends were present. Several of Otto's work colleagues from Kuhn, Loeb also attended. Representing Wall Street aristocracy were Felix M. Warburg, Col. Theodore Roosevelt Jr., and John Pierpont Morgan Jr. Around 100 guests were at the gathering. Edward T. Stotesbury, a senior partner of the Philadelphia banking house Drexel & Co., acted as a pallbearer.

The ceremony was simple, with no instrumental music or singing, in observance of Otto's wishes. A garden of flowers decorated the interior of the music room. Many of the blooms came from the greenhouses of neighboring estates.

Though Otto had held himself aloof from everything Jewish throughout his life, Rev. Goldenson conducted the service, pushing all doubt of Otto's Jewishness to one side.[50]

After the formalities, the casket, still draped in lilies, was returned to the hearse in the courtyard. Mourners followed solemnly behind. Each offered their condolences to the family before climbing into their respective automobiles. A short while later, the cortège with a police escort began its twenty-minute drive to St John's Memorial Cemetery. Roger had arrived at the cemetery thirty minutes ahead of the motorcade to guide two large florists' trucks carrying over 100 floral tributes to the burial plot. Among the displays were flowers from the staff at the Metropolitan Opera House and many of its singers and conductors.

The wooded hillsides along the route looked sparse and gray; the spring leaves had yet to awaken. The stately remains of winter melted into the landscape. A crowd of onlookers had gathered by the roadside and at the entrance to the graveyard. Many were just curious bystanders; some were reporters; all were there to pay their respects. Police officers were stationed at various points around the perimeter of the burial ground to keep the press and the public at bay. The cortège wound its way past the crowds and entered the open gateway from where it disappeared from view.

The burial plot lay at the foot of a wooded knoll beside a narrow winding valley road, at a point where the surrounding laurel and rhododendron shrubbery partly blocked it from view. Otto had chosen this plot specifically because of its closeness to the one occupied by his dear friends, Mortimer L. Schiff, and his wife, Adele. Overhead circled a lone airplane. Onboard was a *Daily News* photographer snapping pictures for the following day's paper.

Rev. Goldenson presided over the committal service at the graveside. Otto was then laid to rest.

After the burial, and after everyone had said their final tearful farewells, and after the freshly dug soil had been shoveled back into the grave, the florists arranged an elaborate floral display that obscured any sight of the grave. After the sexton had carried out everything to the family's wishes, only then did police officers allow members of the public to enter the cemetery to view the plot and pay their last respects to Otto Hermann Kahn.[51] Over two hundred converged upon the grave. The public's curiosity was never-ending.

His Place in The Order of Things Will Be Hard to Fill

The library at 1100 Fifth Avenue was tidily arranged, as it always was. Everything in its place, even down to the late-afternoon edition of the *New York Evening News*, folded neatly on the silver tray upon the rosewood side table. Once again, Otto's name hogged the headlines. Addie's marriage had lasted 38 years, two months, and 21 days. The patriarch of the family was now gone. As one correspondent rightly noted, 'His place in the order of things will be hard to fill.'[52]

Otto's death left the Kahn family emotionally adrift. The suddenness of having lost such a powerful head instantly brought the family's hierarchical structure into question. Who would now guide and steer the family into the belly of the 20th century?

The granting of probate immediately went ahead. Otto's last will was dated June 26, 1933.[53] Roger and Addie, along with Benjamin J. Buttenwieser and George Wallace Bovenizer (both junior partners at Kuhn, Loeb), were appointed executors and, along with the attorneys, were left with the immensely complicated task of putting Otto's affairs in order.* At the time of his death, Otto owned 14 percent of Kuhn, Loeb & Co. stock[54] valued at $2.5 million. His estate - taking into consideration the effects of the depressed economy - was liberally estimated to be valued at around $19 million.

Otto's will was made public on Monday, April 16.[55] In a surprising twist, his entire estate went to his four children, Maud, Margaret, Gilbert, and Roger. Addie was not a beneficiary. A single paragraph in the document certified the reason behind Otto's decision: his wife was 'otherwise adequately provided for.' The four children would receive equal shares in their father's estate. Otto also explained why he had not left a single cent to charity: 'Having given largely during my life to the various altruistic activities in which I interested myself, I refrain from making charitable bequests.' Otto left the matter of minor provisions and legacies to his household and office employees for his children to settle.

Winding up Otto's legal affairs took longer than imagined. It took two and a half years before the true value of his estate was publicly revealed.[56]

During Otto's lifetime, he amassed a fortune, spent a fortune, and in his will, he left a fortune, although the money he bequeathed to his children was not the sizable pile most people might have expected. His entire financial settlement was less than $4 million. It seemed a meager amount compared with the sum his estate was previously valued, which prompts the question, where did all the money go?

Considering what he had once been worth, Otto died practically a pauper. After paying all his debts, the net value of his estate was a mere $3,970,869.[57] At his peak in the mid-1920s, his wealth had soared to over $100 million.[58] In comparison to some American family fortunes, the relatively modest size of Otto's estate led some in high society to utter, 'he was broke.'[59]

Otto once offered a revealing insight into his philosophy of life: 'I measure my words when I say that not the most profitable transaction of my business career has brought me results comparable in value and in lasting yield to those which I derived from the 'investment' of hearing, in my early youth, Beethoven's *Fifth Symphony*, or of seeing Botticelli's *Primavera* or of reading the classics of various nations.'[60]

Irrespective of the substantial amounts of money Otto accumulated and spent so copiously and enjoyably in his lifetime, he also believed, 'no life is quite complete, however worthy if it does not include a responsiveness to the call and beauty of art.'[61]

As a result of his spectacular generosity, it is fair to say Otto Hermann Kahn richly deserves his distinction as being one of America's most significant patrons of the arts there has ever been.

Two months before Otto's death, just before his last visit to Palm Beach, he made an extraordinary move in reassessing his Judaism. He gave a public address on January 28 at Temple Emanu-El on the corner of Fifth Avenue and 65th Street at the opening rally of the Federation for the Support of Jewish Philanthropic Societies of New York. No other member of the Kahn family attended the gathering. In his talk, he pleaded to the audience 'to reaffirm their loyalty to Jewry in the face of a bitter and ruthless persecution.' It was the only time throughout his life that Otto made a speech at a Jewish campaign.

It's believed no other member of the Kahn family had any affiliation with Jewish organizations, activities, or causes. However, Otto did, on occasions, give financial donations to Jewish philanthropy. Despite Otto's secularist lifestyle, could his discourse at the rally have led to his religious homecoming to Judaism had he lived longer? Perhaps witnessing the rise of Nazism and the growing persecution of Jews in Germany compelled him to stand up alongside his fellow Jews. It is a thought we can now only feel curious about and deliberate.

1100 Fifth Avenue

Addie must have found it hugely challenging to continue living at 1100 Fifth Avenue after her husband's death. The house was way too large for one person to reside in. Without Otto and his numerous distractions, the place seemed even larger. It was now more like a museum than a home. So much in her life had changed during the last few days, yet everything in each room she entered remained precisely the same as if time had stopped. Otto's pipe was still in the rack where he had left it on his writing desk, the smell of his Virginia tobacco still hung in the air. Each painting on the wall, the rare tapestries, all the precious artifacts scattered about the rooms retained a memory, a date, a touch, and an image evoking her husband. Every room in the house bore Otto's DNA. His passing was a splintering loss for Addie. It would take her many years to come to terms with it fully. There is no cure for grief but time.

During the weeks that followed, Addie found herself sitting at her desk for long periods. The longer she thought things over, the easier she made decisions. Important decisions. The family home had to be sold. It was far too costly for a widow to maintain. A purchaser must be found. That buyer was closer to the Kahn residence than Addie realized.

Otto's limited attention span, which had been most noticeable in his transactions over property, had also affected his judgment when dealing with theatrical and artistic projects. It is quite probable had he lived longer, he would have tired of his Long Island estate as well as his mansion on Fifth Avenue. Before his passing, Otto had tentatively started making plans for his and Addie's future regarding their homes. A prospective purchaser for their Fifth Avenue property had been in discussions with Otto, but nothing yet was agreed upon.

None of the Kahn family wore their private grief on their public sleeves. As a unit, they had strength, much more than as individuals. However, collectively that strength did not amount to anything that replicated the authority that Otto's name commanded. The future of the Kahn dynastic fortune now weighed heavily upon Gilbert and Roger's shoulders.

18

THE ECCENTRIC MR. KAHN

1934 (April–December)

Ever Restlessly Forward

Otto initially came to the U.S. with the premise that if you work hard, you can achieve anything. Sadly, the dreams that had built America were dissipating fast into the clouds of dust blown in by the recession. 'The land of unlimited possibilities' was struggling to live up to the vision. The Kahn family were resilient when Otto was around; now he had gone, the cracks slowly began to show.

The fallout from Otto's death would take months, if not years, to unravel. Meanwhile, life and business had to carry on, and with it came an entirely new set of challenges for the Kahn family. For now, the days of monochromatic memories remained neatly affixed inside family scrapbooks. A new chapter commenced. Moreover, each Kahn offspring now had a partner to consider. It was Addie who, for obvious reasons, would take Otto's death the hardest.

Over the coming months, life slowly regained some manner of normality, though what was thought standard in the Kahn household would be regarded as unorthodox to most other people.

It had been ten years since the onset of Roger's music career. He would reassess his life's vocation for one last time. Since his earlier attempt to quit show business to concentrate on his flying activities, he had led a less social lifestyle, becoming increasingly more solitary and withdrawn in his ways. The boy had finally grown into an astute, level-headed young man.

Radio had initially played a key role in helping establish Roger's career in the entertainment industry, and it was through this medium Roger now sensed his future livelihood might lie. A change in circumstances brought that goal ever closer.

'My future plans will in no way be affected by the death of my father,' declared Roger in a newspaper report published on Monday, April 9.[1] 'I propose to continue my musical activities and devote as much time to aeronautical pursuits as my music will permit.' The $150,000 interim payment Otto's will stipulated to help individually tide over his two sons during probate may have influenced his decision. The money would undoubtedly give Roger the leeway to allow him to plan his future.[2] His absence from the stage had not dulled his appetite for performing. He put out feelers across New York for his former musical sparring buddies. Many of them returned the call. A short residency followed. The Roger Wolfe Kahn Orchestra was back in business.

Otto spent thirty-seven years occupying a desk at Kuhn, Loeb & Co. He rose through the ranks from in-law to leader. During the immediate days following his death, the highly polished desk in his Kuhn, Loeb office remained just as clean as it had always been, the Oriental rug that once lay beneath his feet spotlessly hoovered. Rumors persisted that in Kuhn, Loeb's basement was a great vault in which rows of gold ingots were stored. Indeed, press reports in the past stated Kuhn, Loeb had purchased gold from South Africa.[3]

A few days after Otto's funeral, a removal firm unceremoniously emptied his former Kuhn, Loeb office. The mahogany bookshelves containing a small library of first edition, leather-bound hardbacks were cleared and packed to make way for the next senior partner's possessions. The neatly loaded wooden crates were delivered to the Kahn residence at Fifth Avenue.

For the time being, Gilbert and Addie remained on the board of directors of Paramount Publix Corporation, as did Otto's brother Felix.[4]

Although it was hardly business as usual at Kuhn, Loeb, staff at the company rallied round and put on a united front. Gilbert remained with the company in his present position as a general partner. It was a new era, and exactly which direction the company was heading was not yet mapped.

Perfecting the delicate balance between self-support and self-care was now Addie's main priority.

With a fleet of black motorcars idling in the Kahn garage at 422 East 89th Street and a small battalion of chauffeurs, servants, maids, and gardeners on the Kahn payroll draining the family finances, things in the Kahn household were about to change drastically and immediately.

In New York on May 24, Gilbert Kahn attended a meeting at financier Henry Ittleson's office with around twenty other prominent Jewish businessmen.[5] Seated at the table were Felix M. Warburg and his sons Paul and Frederick, banker James J. Speyer, and lawyer James N. Rosenberg. Humanitarian James G. McDonald was also in attendance. One of the matters discussed was the increasingly worrying anti-Semitic zeal expanding throughout Germany and its effect on the Jewish communities living there. The outcome of the meeting saw Ittleson launch an appeal to help Jews and non-Jews displaced by the Nazis, the result of which raised $230,000.[6]

The Claremont on the Knoll

'At 7:00 we gave our appetizer order. At 7:30 the medium-priced crab meat came, and with it Roger Wolfe Kahn, a tiny leader in tails, winking wisely at his players, waving a tiny baton, thin as a reed.'[7]

At the end of May, the Kahn Orchestra docked at the newly opened and fully refurbished Claremont Inn nestling in New York's picturesque Riverside Park. The licensed restaurant - accessed via Riverside Drive at 124th Street alongside the Hudson River - had an enviable open-air dance terrace and landscaped gardens ideal for summer rendezvous. The Berman-Schleifer family, headed by Arnold Schleifer, who already owned numerous restaurants and concessions in New York, had just taken over the Claremont management after it had lain dark for a period.[8] Because the restaurant was in a public park, it came under the jurisdiction of the Parks Commission headed by Commissioner Robert Moses and, as such, had to abide by the new ruling to serve a low-priced table d'hôtel menu that would appeal to the general public. Roger's band was the first to be featured at the establishment.[9] By 7 p.m. on opening night, the restaurant had taken over 500 reservations for that evening alone.[10]

The venue was not the usual high-end, pricey concern associated with the Kahn orchestra. With the country in the throes of a recession, bookings for large bands were not as lucrative as they had been throughout the '20s. A Kahn orchestra had previously played at the Claremont Inn during one of its many incarnations, but this was the first time Roger had personally fronted a band at the place.[11] On the bill were the vocalists Evelyn Poe, Joan Blane, Vincent Calendo, and The Three Marshalls.[12] Somewhat ominously, on opening night, the heavens opened.

'Up Riverside Drive on a fog-muffled night, past the ghostly outlines of Grant's Tomb, to the historic Claremont Inn, where Roger Wolfe Kahn and his orchestra are bowing in. Rain has forced the guests to take shelter within the Inn, ruining the elaborate ceremonies deftly planned for the Terrace,' observed the *Brooklyn Daily Eagle*'s roving reporter Art Arthur.[13]

'Nearly 500 guests out there eating chicken salad,' wailed Roger as he ran indoors for cover. The weather certainly played havoc with the evening schedule. But, despite the unwelcoming showers, it did not deter the guests, celebrities, and officials from enjoying the food and music on offer. Even Gilbert Kahn turned up to support his little brother.

During Roger's tenure at the Claremont, his eponymous orchestra returned to the airwaves playing late-evening sessions on WGY[14] and WEAF-NBC Radio.[15]

In May, Roger took a leaf out of his mother's notebook and had a sort-out. He sold his deluxe Duesenberg car.

Even though his father was dead, Roger still had to contend with the tag of being a rich man's son. Newspapers continued to assess his worth falsely. The *Jewish Post* in Indianapolis erroneously claimed he had inherited $8 million upon his father's death.[16] Such reports only served to add further untruths to Roger's public persona. Since his recent return to show business, several musicians from his band had tried to take a swipe at his wallet. Most were unsuccessful. Such behavior happened at the Claremont. At the start of the engagement, Roger's attorney insisted on a clause in Roger's contract that specified the usual employees' concession for a 40 percent cut on food checks applicable during his stint. The management verbally agreed but never actually put it in writing. At the end of the residency, Roger discovered his musicians had lumbered him with an additional check totaling $150 for food and drinks ordered on full-priced restaurant tabs without his authority.[17]

Roger and Daisy had settled comfortably into their Upper East Side neighborhood and were now hoping to start a family of their own. In the interim, they had the interior of their Gracie Square penthouse refurbished and hired the modernist designer Paul T. Frankl to undertake the commission. In the refit, Frankl adopted a similar vision and palette of materials to the ones he used in his most recent exhibition at the Frankl Gallery in Midtown Manhattan, using cork, nubby fabrics, grass matting, and oversized mirror, with walls covered in grasscloth.[18]

Upon completion, the apartment 'belonging to the eccentric Mr. Kahn' had no sharp edges. The graceful curve had taken the place of the rigid rectangle. Even the master bedroom was furnished with a specially designed circular bed draped in satin bedding.[19] *House and Garden* magazine featured the innovatively styled interior in their June edition with photographs by Alfredo Valente. The editor claimed it exemplified the new tenets of Modernism by abandoning 'grotesque angles.'[20] The contemporary decor owed a nod to Art Deco and German Modernism. The one piece of furniture that remained in situ unaltered was Roger's black Steinway grand piano.

Jazz and modern art went hand in hand. Jazz-loving artist Piet Mondrian was known to paint in his studio while listening to jazz recordings, including ones by Louis Armstrong, Ethel Waters, and Roger Wolfe Kahn. The music inspired him. It seemed only fitting that Roger should become just as fascinated with the modernist art movement and embrace it as he had embraced jazz. Mondrian claimed jazz had an important influence on his work and that he would quite literally 'jazz' paintings up with garish colors and more intense rhythmic lines.

Death Day Movie

Before *Death Day* opened in U.S. theaters on June 27, little was known about the movie or who was involved in making it. The Mexican Film Trust produced the seventeen-minute short from clips culled from unused footage of the 1932 movie *Que viva México!* - a patchwork portrayal of Mexican culture and politics, with Russian dialog and English subtitles. The Soviet *émigré* Sergei Eisenstein directed it. It had initially been Eisenstein's vision to edit the remaining footage into six shorts. However, a lack of funding prevented him. Several producers are credited on *Death Day*, including Kenneth Outwater - said to be a pseudonym for a New York banker, a name long suspected of being connected to Otto Kahn. Otto was also rumored to have invested $10,000 in *Que viva México!* which also coincidently accredits Outwater as a producer.* Who Outwater was, or where he materialized from, has never been explained.

Kenneth Outwater's signature appears on several stock certificates that came to light soon after Otto's death. They were discovered in a safe in Otto's private office at Kuhn, Loeb & Co. Whether Kenneth Outwater was a fictitious name has since remained a mystery. No one has been able to produce decisive evidence to support the story. However, after carrying out research, I believe I have solved the puzzle. I explain my theory and present my evidence at the end of this book under the subheading, 'It's Not Beyond the Realms of Possibility.' From the data I have uncovered, I believe I have unraveled the secret of who Kenneth Outwater was.

In some respects, the film *Death Day* could be viewed as an illustrative epitaph to Otto and the many artistic endeavors he became passionately involved with during his lifetime.*

Tea with Mrs. Otto Kahn

That summer, Addie sold her Fifth Avenue palazzo,[21] not to the highest bidder but to house the Convent of the Sacred Heart, a Roman Catholic all-girls school.[22] It was an institute close to Addie's heart. The sale included several items of expensive, bulky furniture individually handmade to adorn various rooms in the house. Valuable paintings and historical artifacts from the Kahns' private collection, registered under the Mogmar Art Foundation, were removed from their Fifth Avenue and Long Island mansions and placed in storage with Duveen Brothers in New York.

Addie downsized and purchased an apartment at 25 Sutton Place alongside the East River. To add a more contemporary feel to her new home, she employed British-born furniture designer Terrence H. Robsjohn-Gibbings.

After her husband's death, Addie did not become the 'bookish' spinster. On the contrary, she continued to be the constant tourist, traversing the ebb and flow of the Atlantic to Europe and back as and when she desired. As Otto's frequent travels across the Atlantic had kept him abreast of things culturally and businesswise, Addie intended to continue the practice, especially as her daughter Maud and grandchild John were permanently resident in the UK. Addie also succeeded her husband as a director of the Metropolitan Opera Association and, with time, became a capable sculptor.

As if to honor her husband's memory, Addie's impending summer trip to the continent went ahead. At the end of June, she bade New York adieu from the first-class deck aboard RMS *Aquitania*. Before her departure, she had a benevolent change of mind regarding the humanitarian matter James G. McDonald had pressed her and Otto about at the beginning of the year. Although at the time, McDonald was seen off the Kahns' Fifth Avenue premises without a cent for his begging bowl, it seems Addie had since had second thoughts. She made a donation to the JDC (American Jewish Joint Distribution Committee), although not directly to McDonald. She extended her contribution through her best friend Frieda (Mrs. Felix M. Warburg).[23]

On American Independence Day, the *Aquitania* sailed into Southampton's Ocean Dock, after which Addie traveled directly to London and checked into Claridge's, her unofficial home from home.

At the start of July, Roger packed his eighteen-piece band off to Long Beach, on the South Shore of Long Island, for a summer season at the exclusive Sun & Surf Club.[24] It gave him and his musicians a welcome respite from the encroaching heat of the city. During afternoons, the band (positioned on wooden decking) played to bathers on the club's private beach. At one of these open-air sessions, Fox Movietone News captured Roger and his orchestra in full swing.[25] Filmed on July 7, sixteen attractive Broadway babes dressed in skimpy bathing costumes joined Roger on the beach, strutting their routines to his music. In slacks and open polo shirt, Roger looks relaxed and much happier than he had looked for a long time.

'Broadway goes to the beach, and will you look what happens,' utters the announcer over the film footage, just as dance instructor Bobby Sandford arrives to mix up the proceedings. Sandford, dressed in slacks and a t-shirt, issues the girls with his verdict: 'That was lousy. You've gotta do it all over again,' at which point the girls chase after Sandford and pile on top of him.

The summer seemed endless, but as with all things enjoyable, the Long Beach engagement drew to a close. Roger and his orchestra returned to the smoke with an uncertain future.

A Weekend at the Air Races

During the last weekend in August, Roger flew his Comper CLA-7 Swift plane to the National Air Races in Ohio. Daisy joined him for the four-day event held at Cleveland's Municipal Airport. Although Roger never won a prize in any of the races he entered, the press noted he 'performed well.' Fox Movietone News and its competitors Universal News were on hand to record the highlights. On Labor Day, Monday, September 3, air formations, stunts, parachutists, and daredevil pilots thrilled the crowds estimated at 100,000. Such occasions gave Roger a temporary hiatus away from the trials of the orchestra business, a business he was growing ever more distant from.

In a curious twist of fate, on September 21, Robert Fulton Cutting died of a heart attack. As president of the Metropolitan Opera and Real Estate Company, he had played a keen part in successfully denying Otto his dream of building a modern new Opera House in New York.[26] That vision would not now be realized for a further 32 years when the present Metropolitan Opera House opened in 1966 at Lincoln Center.

At the end of September, Addie arrived back in New York on board the *Aquitania*.[27]

By October, Roger had clocked up 4,000 hours in the air.[28] He was now one of the ablest and capable pilots in the U.S. To some folks, it seemed he was spending as much time in the air as he was on the ground. And, to those same folks, he was viewed very much as a lone cloud in the vast open sky.

Somewhat closer to earth, Roger's fixation with radio continued. At his chic New York penthouse, he had three radio sets. Every car he owned had a radio in it. As did his planes and yet another in his speedboat.[29] Roger was so hooked; he purposely made sure he was always within earshot of a radio speaker lest he should miss something of importance. He now had his eyes set on television, and in his spare time, began experimenting at creating TV programs.[30]

Otto's loyal friend, publicist Ivy Ledbetter Lee, passed away aged fifty-seven from a brain tumor on November 9, in New York City.[31] When times were difficult, Ivy stood firmly by Otto's side, offering solid, practical advice and representation.* Lee had been a director of the Metropolitan Opera Company since 1929. It seemed particularly poignant that Otto and Ivy's demise should follow within a few months of one another.

Passing Ships

Back in late 1933, Otto had invited Louis J. Horowitz (president of the construction firm Thompson-Starrett Co.) to have luncheon with him at his Kuhn, Loeb office.[32] The invitation came unexpectedly and puzzled Horowitz why he should receive it. Thompson-Starrett had built Otto's Fifth Avenue palazzo and the Kuhn, Loeb office block on William Street. It was regarding the Kahn mansion that Otto wished to talk to Horowitz. During lunch, Otto asked his guest his opinion on the future of 1100 Fifth Avenue.

At first, Horowitz was hesitant to answer, especially as his company had been responsible for its construction. 'It's a noble house,' he said courteously before inquiring, 'What is the matter with it?'

Otto stopped eating his Persian melon before giving his reply. 'Mrs. Kahn and I rattle around ... it is so big.' He then explained how the house no longer met either of their needs, especially as their days of entertaining with extravagant dinner parties were long gone. Besides, they had an even roomier mansion on Long Island to entertain guests in, should the need arise.

1100 Fifth Avenue had been appraised modestly at $2 million in the 1930 U.S. Census. 'Shall I get rid of it, even though it would entail a considerable financial loss on my behalf?' Otto quizzed Horowitz.

Horowitz noted a touch of unease in his host's voice. His reply was simple. If the house had no value anymore to him or Mrs. Kahn, and his children had no interest in it, and the dwelling no longer fulfilled its initial purpose, the time had come to let it go. 'Get rid of it,' Horowitz assured him.

Horowitz's response calmed Otto. His guest had given him the reassurance he had sought.

After a moment of silence, Otto turned to Horowitz and, in an almost melancholic tone, explained what was troubling him. 'What Mrs. Kahn and I would like is a little apartment overlooking the East River. We want one with a window placed so that we can sit together and watch the ships go by and see the lights come on in the evening.'[33] He then went on to tell Horowitz how a Catholic Society had approached him to buy the property so that they could turn it into something useful, like a girl's school. In exchange for the mansion, their offer entailed a plot of land on Madison Avenue at 53rd Street, said to be worth $1 million, plus an additional sum of cash.

Horowitz cautiously contradicted Otto by stating the tract was probably not worth a million dollars, but that its worth should not worry him and think of the deal as a trade-off, lot for lot. 'Tell yourself you are paying to be relieved of a burden. Make the trade.'

Several weeks before Otto's death, he and Addie authorized in principle the sale of the building to go ahead to the Society of the Sacred Heart.[34] The deal was conditional on any restrictions imposed upon the property being removed beforehand. One of the chief difficulties the Kahns had encountered in bringing the sale forward was the constraint imposed on buildings in the neighborhood to remain as family dwellings. Subsequently, the Kahns filed an affidavit in the Supreme Court via their attorney Robert D. Steefel of Stroock &

Stroock. It explained that since the time, many years ago, when the council imposed the restrictions, 'great radical and permanent changes have occurred, and the character of the neighborhood has radically and permanently changed.' The Society of the Sacred Heart firmly assured the court that they would continue to maintain the required high standards of the area upon taking ownership.

In mid-May 1934, the court reached an agreement. They removed all obstacles preventing the sale, thereby allowing the exchange of contracts to proceed.*

Otto died before he saw his dream of watching ships at dusk on the East River fulfilled. Addie kept their dream alive. No sooner did she sign the papers to release 1100 Fifth Avenue into the cupped hands of the Convent of the Sacred Heart than she moved into her apartment at 25 Sutton Place, from where in the evenings, through the large picture window in her sitting room, the lights from the passing ships on the East River could clearly be seen.

A few months later, in the fall, Addie went to see Horowitz at his office to seek advice over another matter. It was the first time he had seen Mrs. Kahn since her husband's passing. He was gratified to hear his talks with Otto in his final months had, in some small way, been helpful to her and her husband during moments of uncertainty. Addie assured Horowitz she and Otto had followed his advice.

Addie was a strong independent woman, who found it difficult to display her true emotions to people outside her inner circle. I believe her visit to see Horowitz was her way of letting him know everything was okay and that she had now moved forward with her life.*

FOR REASONS LOST IN TIME

1935 (onwards)

Addie Wolff Kahn

After the storm had passed, after the dust had settled, after the crates and boxes had all been emptied, after the lingering trail of Otto's cologne had long faded, there came a period of quiet regret, followed by an endless peace. Addie slowly rebuilt her life according to her own rules and needs. Slipping graciously into old age was not an option Addie invited. Her husband had altruistically changed the landscape of American culture. After his passing, Addie had every intention of continuing to color the picture. Every summer, she opened her Long Island country estate for her children, grandchildren, and guests to enjoy. Addie rarely spent time there herself; she found the house summoned too many memories.

In 1939 Addie visited her daughter Maud in Cairo and enjoyed the expat lifestyle so much she remained for two and a half years. She returned to New York in January 1942 and moved back into her apartment at 25 Sutton Place to pick up where she had left off.

Travel still played a significant part in her itinerary. There was talk that she might relocate to Europe, but, like Otto, her roots were intangibly tangled in American soil. Her grandchildren took pride of place in her heart, and she kept busy with her charitable and benevolent work. She keenly continued her pursuit of exquisite art and expanded her collection. It was rumored she became particularly close to her art advisor Bernard Berenson whose summer retreat (Casa al Dono in Vallombrosa in the Tuscan Apennines) she visited, although how intimate their relationship was is debatable. A knowledgeable traveling companion in matters of art was how she likened him. When in London, she preferred to reside at her beloved Claridge's Hotel, usually in the same suite. In her final years, Addie lived contentedly as the wealthy dowager Mrs. Otto H. Kahn, the last of a dying breed.

It was at Claridge's that Addie passed away on May 15, 1949. She had been due to travel to Paris the following day.[1] Her body was returned to America and reunited in burial with her husband.

Lady Maud Emily Wolff Marriott (née Kahn)

Maud and John's marriage lasted the course, although, at times, they appeared to have had an open relationship with indistinct, blurred boundaries. The Marriotts had only one child, John Oakes Marriott.*

Like her father, Maud had a restless spirit and adored nothing better than to travel to exotic places and party elaborately with the artistic set. During WWII, her husband was stationed in Cairo. Here the Marriotts ran an open house for expats and foreign visitors. Maud quickly became Cairo's leading hostess, with a penchant for sleeping until noon and reading in the bathtub before dinner. Her vivacity and long red fingernails belied her intellect and strength of character. She made it her business to know all the 'right' people and entertained generously in the process. When Randolph Churchill (Sir Winston's son) arrived in the capital in the summer of 1941 to take up the post of Intelligence Officer at the British Army's Middle East headquarters, Maud and Randolph became inseparable. They purportedly had an affair.[2] She dubbed Randolph 'the problem child,' presumably for his seemingly reckless behavior bordering on foolhardiness and his fondness for enjoying the company of an ever-changing harem of stylish Levantine women.[3] After the war, Maud continued to travel extensively. Newspaper society columns often noted her visits. John retired from military service in 1950. Maud passed away in New York on October 24, 1960. Her husband lived for almost eighteen years more.*

Roger Wolfe Kahn–Flying Solo

'He was a composer at 13, an orchestra leader at 15, a writer of hit musical shows before he was 20, and just turned 26, he gave up the bright lights and billings in theaters, nightclubs and swanky hotel dining rooms to brood over his future. In between times, he did a dangerous stretch as a test pilot.'[4]

Roger was a man of enormous virtues and enormous faults; the latter were inbred; the former can be attributed to talent and single-mindedness.

How things stood, and what they could have been, were the two spectrums of Roger's life after his father died. Popular music was going through a significant transition. The swing era would dominate the music scene for the next twelve years, from 1935 to 1947. Roger's music was beginning to sound dated. He had two choices; change with the flow or quit. He decided to take more of a backseat role and accept freelance work, which he could do from home.

Roger and Daisy were blessed with two children: Virginia 'Dacia' W. Kahn (b. May 10, 1935)[5] and Peter W. Kahn (b. September 7, 1938).[6] The family resided at 7 Gracie Square until the early 1940s, where they employed seven servants to look after them. In 1937, Vitaphone released a new one-reel short of Roger and his orchestra.[7] His band was comprised mainly of session musicians.

The Kahn orchestra gave a one-off reunion concert on October 15, 1938, believed to be one of the last public performances by the orchestra. The show was staged at Roosevelt Field Airport to honor the unveiling of the enormous *Golden Age of Aviation* mural painted by the artist and licensed pilot Aline Rhonie Hofheimer. The 126-foot-long fresco spanned the northern brick wall of Hangar F at Roosevelt Field. It commemorated the enormous advancements made in aviation history from 1908 to 1927, ending with a depiction of Charles Lindbergh's record-breaking trans-Atlantic flight. Whether Aline used her pilot network to coax Roger out of retirement to reform his orchestra or if he offered on his own accord is unclear. Over five hundred guests attended the all-night party, which ran from 10 p.m. until the break of dawn.[8]

Roger's obsession with aviation was no secret. He had maintained his flying headquarters at Roosevelt Field since 1927. The following year he joined the Advisory Board for the American Society for the Promotion of Aviation and the Advisory Board of the Manhattan Aero Club.[9] Four years later, he was appointed lieutenant in the aviation division of the Nassau County Police Department.[10] In 1933, he became a test pilot for Grumman Aircraft Engineering Corporation on Long Island. Roger and aviation had grown up together. The two were too tightly knit for him ever to consider giving it up.

Roger quit music for good in 1940 and went to work full-time for Grumman. The motion of flight replaced the rhythm of jazz. He moved his family to Long Island, where he lived in a detached house on Muttontown Road, Syosset - a five-minute drive from Woodbury. It was here he and Daisy watched their two children grow up. The residence was probably chosen not because it was close to the Cold Spring Harbor estate but because it was near his work. Roger also purchased a farm in the White Mountains of New Hampshire, where the family spent many vacations.

During World War II, Roger test piloted Wildcat and Hellcat fighter planes for Grumman's. Both aircraft were credited with playing an essential role in the Pacific. His highly prized twin-engine monoplane was requisitioned by the U.S. Army to aid the war effort. The plane was removed from its hangar at Roosevelt Field on July 10, 1941, and used for transporting military officials across America.[11] Where formerly a fleet of planes had been housed, now only Roger's Fairchild monoplane remained. In January 1942, Roger became a member of the planning staff at the Civil Air Patrol headquarters.

Roger continued to assist the Police as and when they called upon him to do so. In 1937, the Air Service Division of the Nassau County Police Department conferred upon him the rank of Lieutenant. One widely publicized case in which Roger offered his assistance arose in May 1941 during an air search for a missing Beechcraft biplane, presumed to have crashed into West Mountain near Bellefonte, en route to Warren Airport, Ohio. The plane was carrying New York broker Benjamin Brewster and his 31-year-old wife, Leonie DeBary Lyon.[12] Leonie was heiress to the DeBary real estate. Benjamin and Leonie both died in the accident.

After the war, Roger served as director of Grumman's Worldwide Service Department,* and was a former vice president and Member of the Council of the Institute of Aeronautical Sciences. In his role at Grumman's, Roger visited Naval Air Stations across the U.S. and would usually fly himself there in a commercial G-38 (F8F-2) Bearcat: a classy way to arrive at any airport.[13] Roger was a member of various aviation and test pilot associations and served as a vice president of the Wings Club. He was also affiliated with the Quiet Birdman and the National Aeronautical Association.

Roger died at Columbia Presbyterian Medical Center, New York City, on July 12, 1962, from a fatal heart attack, three months short of his 55th birthday.[14] He is buried two plots away from his parents at Laurel Hollow in St John's Memorial Cemetery. Daisy Kahn died in September 1994.*

In quitting jazz, some might say the boy finally grew up.

Gilbert Sherburne Wolff Kahn

Gilbert never quite followed in his father's footsteps, though it was doubtful anyone could. He remained employed at Kuhn, Loeb for his entire working life. By 1940, Gilbert and his family were residing in an apartment at 834 Fifth Avenue. During WWII, Gilbert served with the U.S. Navy as a lieutenant commander in the South Pacific and was awarded the French *Légion d'Honneur* for distinguished service. His family was understandably immensely proud of him. In 1960, at the age of 57, Gilbert became a limited partner of Kuhn, Loeb & Co.

For a short period, Gilbert and his family lived in the *Médoc* region of France, where he held financial interests in several vineyards. Gilbert carried on his father's legacy in America by becoming a patron of the Met and other art and music organizations. He fathered two children: Claire Anne to his first wife Anne Elizabeth Whelan and a son, Gilbert S. Kahn, to his second wife, Sara Jane Heliker. In 1948 he married his third wife, Polly Stover. The marriage lasted for the rest of his life.* Gilbert died at New York Hospital on December 15, 1975, at the age of 72 and is buried at Laurel Hollow in St John's Memorial Cemetery.[15]

Margaret Dorothy Wolff Ryan (née Kahn)

If parents are allowed favorites among their children, Margaret was Otto's. Margaret certainly took after her father. She inherited his love of opera and, like her father, became a generous patron of the Metropolitan Opera Association. Margaret's effervescent personality was contagious and made her popular and fun to be around. Her marriage to John Barry Ryan Jr. was suitably paired and relatively harmonious, albeit they had different tastes in music and the arts.

John and Margaret accumulated an impressive art collection containing several Impressionist paintings, including a Monet. In addition, they owned various properties: a London home, two elegant Manhattan apartments in the Campanile building at 450 East 52nd Street, and a fifty-acre country estate Moorland Farm (renamed Moorland Lodge) in Newport, Rhode Island. The latter was a summer retreat that Margaret used her design skills to renovate.

The Ryans had two children: John Barry Ryan III and a daughter Virginia Fortune Ryan. John Barry Ryan Jr. died in 1966.

Like her parents, Margaret was a tireless traveler throughout her life and would, on occasions, happily circumnavigate the globe on her own, feeling no need for a traveling companion. Margaret died at her apartment in New York City on January 26, 1995, having lived to the grand age of 93.[16] Her daughter Virginia married the Scottish peer David George Coke Patrick Ogilvy on October 23, 1952, at St Margaret's Church, Westminster, London. When Virginia's husband became the 8th (or 13th) Earl of Airlie in 1968, she acquired the title Countess of Airlie. Since 1973, Virginia Ogilvy, Countess of Airlie, has been a Lady of the Bedchamber to HM Queen Elizabeth II. Their son,

David John Ogilvy, Lord Ogilvy, has inherited the Kahn creative gene and is a professional musician.[17]

Otto and Addie's Marriage

Otto's infidelity was never in question; it was his indiscretions that were. It may have appeared to the wider world that Addie bit her lip and wore her dignity with an elegance that befits the matriarch of a wealthy dynasty, but her motives were rarely selfish. On the contrary, her loyalty to her family was infinite and became ever more apparent following the death of her husband.

After Otto's funeral and burial, and after all the reporters had left from outside the Kahn Fifth Avenue mansion, and after her emotions had settled, Addie and her daughter Margaret dutifully sifted through boxloads of Otto's private papers and diaries, meticulously selecting which to keep and those to dispose of. Letters got burnt, diaries torn to shreds, evidence of his affairs and extramarital activities erased. Addie was adamant the Kahn name and brand should live on untarnished. She had no choice. It was what she was good at, sustaining the dream and protecting her family's honor, and upholding her respectability.

Otto laid the foundations of an empire. Unfortunately, the 1929 stock market crash put pay to his ambitions of expanding it.* When Otto died, he left a net taxable estate valued at just short of $4 million. His attorneys attributed the shrinkage of his fortune to 'severe depression losses,' especially in real estate. Nevertheless, Otto was once regarded as one of America's wealthiest men.[18] In death, it was his cultural legacy that was estimated to be priceless.

Otto and Addie were patrons individually to dozens of charitable organizations, committees, and councils throughout their lives. A couple of the more unusual associations they loaned their names to were; Addie, a patroness of the Bide-A-Wee Home for Friendless Animals;[19] and Otto, a patron of the National Association for the Improvement of American Speech.[20]

Otto always was going to be an impossible act to follow.

Hannah Williams

Hannah gave birth to her first child by Jack Dempsey, a daughter Joan Hannah in August 1934. Around fifteen months later, when Hannah was pregnant with her second baby, Dempsey received several worrying late-night phone calls from an underworld tipster warning the couple their young child was in danger of being kidnapped and held for ransom.[21] The 1932 Charles A. Lindbergh Jr. kidnapping and murder of the one-year-old infant, and subsequent 1935 murder trial, was still headline news at the time and very much in everyone's mind. Dempsey and Hannah took the caveat seriously. The family immediately went into hiding. After laying low in Atlantic City under house guard for several weeks, the scare passed, and life for the Dempseys resumed a semblance of normality. For a while, family life seemed rosy for Hannah. Her second newborn, Barbara Judith, arrived in August 1936.

The family was comfortably off financially. The ex-champ was a publicist's dream, charismatic, handsome in a rugged, down-to-earth style, and made a healthy living from exhibition tournaments and product endorsements. Jack was also a successful businessman in his own right, having opened a restaurant in New York named Jack Dempsey's on the corner of Eighth Avenue and 50th and was co-owner of the chic Dempsey-Vanderbilt Hotel on Miami Beach.*

In 1937, Hannah got lucky and secured a featured role in the new E. Y. Harburg and Harold Arlen musical comedy *Hooray for What!*, starring Ed Wynn. Arlen and Harburg wrote the song '*Buds Won't Bud*' specifically for Hannah, which turned out to be one of their most memorable collaborations.[22] On October 30, the show opened at the Colonial Theatre in Boston, where it ran for two weeks before transferring to Philadelphia and then on to Broadway's Winter Garden Theatre.[23] Unfortunately for Hannah, during its rigorous tryout in Boston, she was fired from the production, as were two of her fellow cast members, including the female lead Kay Thompson.* The press blamed her departure on her husband Jack Dempsey after he verbally threatened the show's producer Harry Kaufman.[24]

Hannah briefly separated from Dempsey in 1940, stating she agreed to disagree with her husband and wished to resume her nightclub career, something Dempsey was vehemently against her doing. Hannah's attorney Moses Polakoff affirmed to the press on her behalf, 'I guess incompatibility would cover it.'[25] Soon afterward, the couple kissed and made up, although their truce was short-lived. In January 1943, in an extraordinary move, Dempsey sued Hannah for divorce, citing her unfaithfulness.[26] She had allegedly been intimate with former Lightweight Champion Lew Jenkins and on a separate occasion with Jenkins' onetime trainer Benny Woodall. Hannah countersued. Dempsey and Hannah's sixteen-year age difference had finally taken its toll on their marriage. Their divorce hit national headlines and wound up in the State Supreme Court in White Plains.

After the decree absolute was granted, Hannah reclaimed her maiden name and attempted to resuscitate her stage career, albeit with only the occasional vaudeville, nightclub, or restaurant engagement.[27] She opened in vaudeville at Loew's State Theatre, Broadway, on October 14, 1943, followed by a club residency at The Riobamba in Manhattan commencing on October 21, where she sang her signature tune *'Cheerful Little Earful,'* the song that brought her fame. Unfortunately, her dreams of becoming a big Broadway star were well and truly over; she now had to make do with whatever booking her agent could offer her.[28] She married again, this time in 1950, to 38-year-old Hollywood comedian Tommy J. Monaghan.[29] The marriage ceremony in Los Angeles was conducted twice due to the late arrival of Hannah's daughter Barbara. The ill-chosen union ended in divorce the following year. Sadly, things did not pan out the way she might have hoped, and on March 24, 1953, Hannah hit the headlines yet again, but for all the wrong reasons. Pictures of her looking disheveled and badly shaken appeared in the newspapers showing her being led away from a Los Angeles hotel by two police officers towards a waiting ambulance after being rescued from a fire in her hotel bedroom.[30] Early reports said the fire started from a lighted cigarette that ignited her bedsheets. At the hospital, she was treated for burns on her hands, face, and arms. Reports in the tabloids later mentioned her arrest for suspected arson.

Hannah died in Los Angeles on January 11, 1973, and is buried at Forest Lawn Memorial Park in Hollywood Hills, Los Angeles County.

George D. Lottman

Roger and his valued friend and former business manager George D. Lottman remained close buddies throughout their lives. George even took flying lessons from Roger and became a competent pilot.[31]

As a press agent, George handled stars such as Eddie Cantor, Dorothy Lamour, Paul Whiteman, Texas Guinan, Russ Columbo, Rudy Vallée, and Tommy Dorsey. Early in his career, he was hired as the first radio press agent and represented practically every club and hotel of note in New York during the 1920s and '30s. He was known to be the only press agent that employed a chauffeur.[32] George died at his home in New York City on September 25, 1942, aged 43, after a year-long illness.[33]

Il Palazzo Kahn, 1100 Fifth Avenue

The Kahn palazzo at 1100 Fifth Avenue was designated 'the finest Italian Renaissance mansion In New York' by the Landmarks Preservation Commission, and in 1974 was classified as a New York City landmark. Many of the elaborate mansions of the Upper East Side no longer remain. The Vanderbilt, Astor, Schwab, Webb, McK. Twombly and other such iconic homes all fell under the developers wrecking ball. Through the diligence of the New York City Landmarks Preservation Commission and the institutions that look after such buildings, the Kahn, Carnegie, and Warburg palaces have survived.

The Cold Spring Harbor Estate

In 1939, reports that the Kahn family were considering demolishing their grand 127-room château at Cold Spring Harbor filtered into the newspapers. The estate still employed 25 permanent members of staff, although the Kahn family were rarely in residence. Taxes for the property that year amounted to over half a million dollars. It had become an oversized burden for the family. The heartbeat of the house had gone. Addie finally laid the ghost to rest and let her husband's mistress go.

There was talk it might become the President's Summer White House.[34] Alas; it was not to be. Instead, the magnificent estate was swept up for the ridiculously low price of $100,000 on June 19 by the New York City Department of Sanitation Welfare Organization, who turned it into an all-year holiday camp for its 15,000 employees.[35] The street cleaners and dustmen were overjoyed at the news.

'I'd be heartbroken to sell this place at such a price to any individual,' Addie was quoted as saying immediately after the sale. 'But you can see I'm happy, can't you?'[36]

The Sanitation Department christened it Sanita Lodge, and the street cleaners swept into the place. 'That's making a long stride in one sweep.'[37] On opening day, upwards of 20,000 people invaded the property, causing havoc and tailbacks for miles on the surrounding highways.[38] 'I still can't believe what I am seeing here today!' quipped Roger after handing over the keys.[39]

The Kahns former Long Island neighbors held their breath in horror. The plush lawns, where once the carefree sound of laughter resonated, were now trodden underfoot by sandal-wearing, hamburger-munching sanitation workers and their vacationing families.

Gilbert (2nd left) and Roger (far right) handed over the keys to Otto's beloved Cold Spring Harbor estate to the New York City Department of Sanitation on July 9, 1939. 'I can't believe what I'm seeing here,' Roger kept repeating as thousands of day-trippers invaded the grounds.

New York City Department of Sanitation only briefly occupied the estate. They relinquished it in early 1940 because of local opposition and controversy over a tax assessment by the town council. The property immediately went back on the market.

In March 1940, reports surfaced that the Greek Orthodox Church had considered buying the estate as a home for orphans and the aged.[40] Archbishop Athenagoras of the Greek Orthodox Church in North and South America disclosed he had visited Huntington on March 16 to view the property. The church had been interested in it even before the New York City Department of Sanitation acquired it. Residents of the nearby town expressed concern over the latest developments and pointed out that the estate would be tax-exempt if sold to the church.

Soon afterward, the château had a bit-part in director Orson Welles' classic 1941 mystery drama *Citizen Kane*.

Over the following years, the Cold Spring Harbor estate changed hands several times. Eventually, the building was stripped of its elegant fixtures and decor and abandoned. By the 1980s, the rotting and crumbling shell had become a charmless relic of 1920s decadence. It was as if the house had fallen into a coma and was on its last journey, close to death. Otto must have been turning in his grave.

Although written reports after Otto's death claim he attached $1,000 bills around Easter eggs and hid them in the garden at Cold Spring Harbor for children to find during egg hunts, I could unearth no evidence to support this engaging anecdote. Some say the estate was Otto's monument to 1920s excess and extravagance. Others imply it was a folly to cater for a whim - close enough to Manhattan to commute to, yet far enough away to contain any gossip of the wild parties and shenanigans that purportedly took place there.

In 1984, in the capable hands of property developer Gary Melius, the venerable mansion rose once again. It remains the second-largest private residence in the U.S. Now renamed Oheka Castle, the house stands as an everlasting monument of the artistic and cultural influence Otto Hermann Kahn brought to America and will forever be remembered as his wonderfully beautiful, nonchalant mistress.

Oheka Cottage, Sunrise Villa and Villa Oheka, Palm Beach

Oheka Cottage and Sunrise Villa in Palm Beach were demolished to make room for the Sun & Surf condominium complex. The Kahns' Villa Oheka on North County Road was sold in 1941 and converted into the Graham-Eckes preparatory boarding school for boys. The Otto Hermann Kahn Estate retained additional land stretching from North County Road to Lake Worth Lagoon. In 1974, the school became a day school but closed in 1989 after facing financial difficulties. The villa has since been renovated and fully reinstated to a residential property.

Kuhn, Loeb & Co., 52 William Street, NY

Kuhn, Loeb & Co. remained working in the Kuhn, Loeb building at 52 William Street until long after Otto's death. In 1955, the company moved its head office to 30 Wall Street. The original Kuhn, Loeb building in William Street is today occupied by a Radisson Hotel.

Le Perroquet de Paris

Nothing remains of *Le Perroquet de Paris* nightclub. For many years the Little Carnegie Playhouse[41] - with modernistic decor by Viennese interior designer Wolfgang Hoffmann - occupied part of the club's premises.[42] The building was torn down in the 1980s. The 68-story postmodern style Metropolitan Tower now stands in its place.

The Metropolitan Opera Company

At the end of the 1934-35 opera season, Giulio Gatti-Casazza retired from the Met and returned to Italy, where he died on September 2, 1940. The Metropolitan Opera Association now governs the Met. The present Metropolitan Opera House is located on Broadway at Lincoln Square on the Upper West Side of Manhattan.

Roosevelt Field, Long Island

Roosevelt Field, the once proud and busy airfield where so many aviation triumphs and achievements took place, has since become a distant memory imprisoned in old Movietone newsreels. The airport closed on May 31, 1951. Today part of the former airfield is covered by a 125-acre shopping mall.[43] Some might say the evocative lyrics of songwriter Joni Mitchell's 1970 hit song *'Big Yellow Taxi'* may so easily have summed up the fate of the late airfield, now a soulless concrete jungle and a dull parking lot.

Roger and his flying instructor Charles T. Homer at the air races, ca. 1939.

Elisabeth 'Lili' Kahn

On October 17, 1893, Elisabeth 'Lili' Kahn, Otto's sister, married Felix Deutsch (co-founder of AEG). The family was well-to-do and lived in Berlin W10 at Rauchstr, 16, where 'Lili' held a salon frequented by leading lights such as composer Richard Strauss, German Foreign Minister Walther Rathenau, and influential journalist Maximilian Harden. Felix died in 1928. In 1939, 'Lili,' with her daughter Gertrud and Gertrud's husband, Gustav Brecher, fled Nazi Germany and escaped to Belgium, intending to travel to the UK to stay with Lili's son Georg. Their valuable possessions were transported ahead via Luxembourg to Ostend. Addie Kahn financially supported the family during this challenging period. At their Ostend hotel, Lili and the Brechers waited for their belongings to arrive; alas, they never did. The last correspondence from 'Lili' was a postcard mailed from Ostend dated April 27, 1940. On May 10, German forces invaded Belgium, after which Lili and the Brechers went missing, presumed killed.[44]

The Man Hanging in the Woods

The mysterious death that came to light at the Kahns Cold Spring Harbor estate on Wednesday, December 8, 1937, was discovered by the patrolman Alexander Warga of the Nassau Division while hunting small game on the estate. The fleshless skeleton of a man was hanging from the branch of a tree.[45] In his statement Warga disclosed that a sash cord noose slung over a tree limb held the suspended body. The fully clothed, partly decomposed corpse was thought to be aged 40 or over and believed to have been dead for at least two or three years. The said tree was in a densely wooded section of the Kahn grounds.

The man hanging in the woods was dressed in a gray suit and a gray felt hat and wore spectacles. He had four gold teeth in his upper jaw. Inside his suit pocket were a gold Waltham watch and a keyring holding seven keys. Another pocket held a fountain pen. Discarded nearby in the undergrowth were a half-empty bottle of whiskey and a wooden cane.*

Did he commit suicide, or was he murdered?

---

* (p. 585) At the completion of this book, I have still not been able to ascertain whether the corpse was ever formally identified.

It's Not Beyond the Realms of Possibility

The Otto H. Kahn and Kenneth Outwater connection.

Kenneth Outwater is credited as being one of the producers of three Mexican documentaries released in the 1930s. Outwater is also named on stock certificates registered during the 1910s, '20s, and '30s. However, no one has been able to verify who Kenneth Outwater was. As a result, some historians believe Outwater to be a fictive character.

Kenneth Outwater's name first surfaced in the public domain in 1933 on the production credits of the documentary *Thunder Over Mexico*. He resurfaced the following year just after Otto Kahn's death when stock certificates issued to and signed by Kenneth Outwater were found in Kahn's safe at his Kuhn, Loeb & Co. office in New York. Ever since their discovery, Kenneth Outwater has been linked to Otto Kahn. But, did Outwater exist, or was he an extension of Otto Kahn's furtive imagination? What makes the Outwater certificates in Kahn's safe so intriguing is that they were signed in blank[1] without being transferred to another person. Furthermore, no one ever stepped forward to claim them after Otto Kahn's death.

It doesn't need a handwriting expert to point out the similarities in Kahn's and Outwater's signatures, particularly the letters o, n, and a.

signature of Outwater[2]

signature of Kahn

---

[1] Signed in blank (assigned in blank) definition: A certificate of stock or a registered bond signed on the back and witnessed, where the space for the name of the new owner is left blank.
[2] Picture courtesy of HWPH Auction House, Zorneding, Germany.

It's not beyond the realms of possibility that Otto Kahn and Kenneth Outwater were one and the same person. Eighty-seven years on, and the story still intrigues people that stumble upon it, including me. Did Otto Kahn purchase stocks covertly?

The earliest stock certificate I've located issued to Kenneth Outwater dates from WWI; 11,500 shares in the Electric Boat Co.[3] The company designed and built submarines, motorboats, and electric machinery intended for use in submarines during WWI. Other certificates, no.'s 12 and 14 for Guild Hall, Inc., registered to Kenneth Outwater in 1925, came up for sale in a 'historical securities' auction on November 7, 2011.[4] Further shares issued to Outwater have also come to auction: no.'s 52 and 53 for Little Picture House, Inc. (1928);[5] no.'s 37193 and 7652 for Kreuger & Toll Company (1929); no. 666 for Kolster Radio Corporation (1930); no. 589 for Murray Hill Allied Corporation (1930); no.'s C10 and P9 for Brockperton Productions Corporation (1931); and no.'s 85232 and 57590 for Grigsby-Grunow Company (1932).

A suggestion that Kahn and Outwater might be the same person came to light after Kahn's death in a series of letters penned in 1930/31 by the novelist Upton Sinclair, who worked as a producer on the Mexican documentary *Que Viva México!* Sergei Eisenstein directed the film. With pressing worries over a shortfall in funding, the production team decided to try and sell the enterprise to someone that could afford to complete it.

Sinclair approached Otto by letter on December 26, 1930, asking if he would like to invest in the movie. This Otto did to the tune of $10k. However, Otto stipulated he did not wish his name to be disclosed as an investor. Thus, from Sinclair's correspondence, it can be determined Kahn's investment was listed under a pseudonym.

On June 15, 1931, Sinclair recontacted Otto by letter to ask if he would be interested in taking over the entire production, possibly through his connection with Paramount Pictures. In the postscript, Sinclair assures Otto, 'Of course if the picture is sold, you will get back your $10,000 and your proportionate share of whatever profit may be made. If you are the purchaser, you will deduct this amount from what you pay us.' Otto turned down the offer.

---

[3] 11,500 shares in the Electric Boat Co. registered to Kenneth Outwater, care of Kuhn, Loeb & Co., 52 William Street, New York, NY.
[4] HWPH Auction House, Zorneding, Germany.
[5] The Little Picture House at 151 E. 50th Street, New York, opened on December 25, 1929. It was reportedly America's first cooperative movie theatre.

In a letter to E. I. Monosson - head of the New York film distributor Amkino - dated October 15, 1931, Sinclair lists the four benefactors that had invested in the film so far: Mary Craig Sinclair $20k (Sinclair's wife), Kate Crane Gartz $5k, S. Hillkowitz $15k, and Kenneth Outwater $10k. In the same letter, Sinclair reveals, 'a New York banker ... has his investment standing in the name of Kenneth Outwater.' Further in the letter, Sinclair confirms, 'The shares of Kenneth Outwater have been made out to him and deposited in the bank to his account.'

Finding subsequent investment difficult to drum up, Upton penned another letter to Monosson a couple of weeks later, on October 25, in which he explains his predicament. 'I am not worried about it, as I feel quite certain at this stage the banker in New York will put up another $10,000 if I ask him to.' Sinclair did contact Otto to invite him to invest a further $10k, but Otto declined.

Although Sinclair teasingly hints Kahn and Outwater were one and the same person, no further evidence substantiating the claim has ever been unearthed. As such, speculation has been rife for many years.

When I realized Kenneth Outwater's initials were Otto Kahn's initials in reverse, I started to wonder if Kenneth Outwater could be a code or acronym, or perhaps an anagram. Otto invented acronyms to name companies and property he owned: Mogmar, Mogar, Oheka, etc. Moving along this line of investigation, I tried to figure out if the names Kenneth and Outwater were acronyms. After two days of trying, I was still nowhere close to an answer. I then looked at the possibility of an anagram and began rearranging the letters; still, I had little luck. I then wondered if Otto had used a foreign language to create an anagram. I tried German as it was Otto's native tongue; that's when things started to get interesting. Using every individual character from Kenneth Outwater, I came up with the German declaration, 'wette unter O Kahn.' The phrase translates to English as: 'bet [or wager] under O Kahn.' Eighty-seven years after Otto's death, I believe the mystery of who Kenneth Outwater was, has finally been solved.

Certainly, Otto did purchase shares under his real name. However, my evidence appears to indicate he also bought them under the alias Kenneth Outwater.

A Note from Baby Peggy

Below is a transcript of an email I received in 2017 from the Hollywood silent movie actress Diana Serra Cary aka Baby Peggy. In it, she gives a short firsthand account of the challenges that arose from being a major child star in the 1920s.* Diana Serra Cary died on February 24, 2020, aged 101.

June 14, 2017

Dear friend

To this day, I vividly remember the week ... I was starred at the Hippodrome [New York] for perhaps a week in an elaborate full stage 'Personal Appearance' presentation with a chorus of adult dancers dressed as children, and all 100 Singer's Midgets [troupe] costumed as toy soldiers and fairy story characters, dancing to a symphony orchestra playing variations of the classic *March of the Toy Soldiers.* At the end, I stepped out of a gigantic golden egg to deliver a tightly memorized speech thanking the audience for coming to see Baby Peggy. This spectacular hoopla was designed to promote Sol Lesser's production of Baby Peggy's [latest] feature film.

A major movie stars appearance 'in the flesh' at that time consisted mainly of 'being seen - shaking hands with fans, giving them an autograph and allowing them to take a snapshot of the two of you together' - preferably in any place outside of Hollywood. Especially for children, this Stone Age celebrity routine was a much bigger thrill than going to the zoo and feeding an elephant or a mile-high giraffe.

The clever imposter Peggy Eames, a one-time 'Our Gang' extra, for several years in the Twenties toured in advance of my vaudeville bookings, cheekily pretending to be the real Baby Peggy and being amazingly successful at earning a sizable income with her convincing deceptions. Because we were both on the road, I was never able to locate or sue her in time to make a successful Out of State arrest. Besides, at that time, and to this day, it is still against the law for a child to hire a lawyer until one is seventeen years old.

I hope Roger Kahn managed to have a career of his own after disobeying his father.

Sincerely

Diana Serra Cary (Baby Peggy)

---

* (p. 589) Baby Peggy made her vaudeville stage debut at the age of six at New York's colossal Hippodrome during the last week of January 1925. Roger Wolfe Kahn made his vaudeville debut aged seventeen on the same bill.

Roger's Legacy

Roger Wolfe Kahn, ca. late 1930s.

Roger's musical legacy in the history of jazz is rich with pointers and road signs. Many early jazz musicians who became noted in their particular fields played in Roger's bands: Artie Shaw, Charlie Teagarden, and Morton Downey are three worth mentioning. Throughout Roger's music career, a continuum was his determination and keenness to help develop popular music, especially American symphonic syncopation.

Testimonials from contemporary musicians who knew or worked with Roger refer kindly to him with the utmost respect. Bandleader Benny Goodman in his 1939 autobiography, claimed: 'Folks who didn't know much about music used to laugh at Kahn in those days (because his father was rich and interested in things like opera, while his son was going in for jazz), but he knew who the good musicians were, and had one of the best bands of the time.'[1]

Probably, having 'one of the best bands of the time' is how Roger would have liked his musical legacy to be remembered, although that was not his only accomplishment; as a musician, composer, and pilot, there was so much more to his talents.

Charting Hits [U.S.]*

Year – Song title – Highest chart position

1926 (Feb.) – I'm Sitting on Top of the World – No. 9
1926 (Mar.) – A Little Bungalow – No. 4
1926 (Sept.) – Mountain Greenery – No. 4
1926 (Oct.) – Cross Your Heart – No. 8
1927 (Feb.) – Tonight You Belong To Me – No. 11
1927 (Feb.) – Clap Yo' Hands – No. 9
1927 (June) – Russian Lullaby – No. 1 [for 15 weeks]
1929 (Nov.) – Through! (How Can You Say We're Through) – No. 3
1932 (Nov.) – My Silent Love – No. 3
1932 (Nov.) – There I Go Dreaming Again – No. 3
1932 (Nov.) – Tell Me Why You Smile, Mona Lisa – No. 3

Minutiae

It was Roger who suggested to musician and bandleader Saul Feldman that he change his name to Shep Fields, thereby christening Shep Fields and His Rippling Rhythm Orchestra.[2]

Roger was posthumously accorded the rank, Honorary Flight Leader of the U.S. Navy Blue Angels by the elite Blue Angels flight demonstration squadron.[3]

Discography

Song title (alphabetical order) – **Year recorded** – **Show/film** – **Vocalist**

A Cup of Coffee, a Sandwich and You - 1925 (*Charlot's Revue*)
A Little Birdie Told Me So - 1927 (*Peggy-Ann*) (v. Johnny Marvin)
A Little Bungalow - 1925 (*Cocoanuts*)
A Room With A View - 1928 (*This Year of Grace*) (v. Franklyn Baur)
A Shine On Your Shoes - 1932 (*Flying Colors*) (Introducing: Louisiana Hayride) (v. Kahn-a-Sirs)
Adorable - 1926 (Earl Carroll *Vanities*) (v. Gladys Rice and Carl Mathieu)
All By My Ownsome - 1927 (v. Franklyn Baur)
Among My Souvenirs - 1927 (v. Harold 'Scrappy' Lambert)
An Old Guitar and an Old Refrain - 1927 (*A Song of Spain*) (v. Franklyn Baur)
Another Night Alone - 1932 (*Rhythm-Mania*) (v. Del Porter)
Anything You Say - 1928 (v. Frank Munn)
At Peace With The World - 1926 (v. Henry Burr)
Baby - 1926 (*Castles In The Air*) (v. Billy Jones)
Bam Bam Bamy Shore - 1925
Birdie - 1926 (whistling by Sybil Sanderson Fagan)
Bluin' the Black Keys - 1926 (Victor reject)
Calling - 1927 (v. Franklyn Baur)
Cheer Up Good Times Are Comin' - 1930 (v. Harold 'Scrappy' Lambert)
Clap Yo' Hands - 1926 (*Oh, Kay!*)
Cooking Breakfast For The One I Love - 1930 (*Be Yourself*) (v. Libby Holman)
Crazy Rhythm - 1928 (*Here's Howe!*) (v. Franklyn Baur)
Cross Your Heart - 1926 (*Queen High*) (v. Henry Burr)
Dance, Little Lady - 1928 (*This Year of Grace*) (v. Franklyn Baur)
Dark Night - 1930 (*In Gay Madrid*) (v. Harold 'Scrappy' Lambert)
Delilah - 1927
Delirium - 1926 (Victor rejected)
Do What You Do! - 1929 (*Show Girl*)
Don't Ever Leave Me - 1929 (*Great Day*)
Down And Out Blues - 1925
Dreaming of Tomorrow - 1925 (recorded as The Deauville Dozen)
El Tango del Perroquet - 1927 (Victor reject)
Exactly Like You - 1930 (Lew Leslie's *International Revue*) (v. Harold 'Scrappy' Lambert)
Fit As A Fiddle - 1932 (v. Kahn-a-Sirs)
Following You Around - 1927
Give Me The Sunshine - 1928 (*Keep Shufflin'*) (v. Franklyn Baur)
Great Day - 1929 (*Great Day*) (v. William C. Elkins Jubilee Singers)
Heigh-Ho, Everybody, Heigh-Ho - 1929 (v. Frank Munn)
Here Am I - 1929 (*Sweet Adeline*) (v. Harold 'Scrappy' Lambert)
Hot-Hot-Hottentot - 1925

I Can't Believe It's True - 1932 (v. Del Porter & Kahn-a-Sirs)
I Can't Believe That You're In Love With Me - 1927
I Love You Sincerely - 1926 (Victor reject)
I Never Knew! - 1925
I'd Climb the Highest Mountain (If I Knew I'd Find You) - 1926
I'm Sitting on Top of the World - 1925
If You're In Love, You'll Waltz - 1927 (*Rio Rita*) (v. Henry Burr)
Imagination - 1928 (*Here's Howe!*) (v. Franklyn Baur)
In A Bamboo Garden - 1928 (v. Frank Munn)
Into My Heart - 1930 (*In Gay Madrid*) (v. Harold 'Scrappy' Lambert)
It Don't Mean A Thing (If It Ain't Got That Swing) - 1932 (v. Kahn-a-Sirs)
Jersey Walk - 1926 (*Honeymoon Lane*)
Just A Little Home For The Old Folks - 1932 (v. Del Porter)
Just The Same - 1927
Lantern of Love - 1926 (*Castles In The Air*)
Lazy Day - 1932 (v. Dick Robertson)
Let A Smile Be Your Umbrella (On A Rainy Day) - 1928 (v. Franklyn Baur)
Liza (All The Clouds 'll Roll Away) - 1929 (*Show Girl*)
Lonely Little Bluebird - 1928 (*Our Dancing Daughters*) (v. Franklyn Baur)
Look Who's Here! - 1925
Looking For A Boy - 1926 (*Tip-Toes*)
Lucky Boy - 1925 (*Cocoanuts*)
Montana Call - 1930 (*Montana Moon*) (v. Dick Robertson)
Mountain Greenery - 1926 (*The Garrick Gaieties 1926*)
My Silent Love - 1932 (*Chamberlain Brown's Scrap Book*) (v. Elmer
    Feldkamp)
Never Without You - 1927 (v. Franklyn Baur) (Victor reject)
On The Road To Mandalay - 1927
On The Sunny Side Of The Street - 1930 (Lew Leslie's *International
    Revue*) (v. Dick Robertson)
One Summer Night - 1927 (v. Henri Garden)
Pep - 1925 (recorded as The Deauville Dozen)
Pretty Little Thing - 1929 (v. Frank Munn)
Raquel Meller Medley - 1926 - 'My Toreador', 'Poor Scentless Flow'r',
    'Your Wonderful Lips' and 'Who'll Buy My Violets?'
Rhythm of the Day - 1925 (Earl Carroll *Vanities*)
Russian Lullaby - 1927 (v. Henri Garden)
Say It With A Red, Red Rose - 1927 (v. J.M.) (Victor reject)
Say 'Yes' Today - 1928
Shady Lady - 1928 (v. Harold 'Scrappy' Lambert renamed Burt Lorin)
Sheltered by The Stars, Cradled by The Moon - 1932 (v. Kahn-a-Sirs, with
    Artie Shaw on clarinet)
She's a Great, Great Girl - 1928
Somebody's Lonely - 1926 (v. Henry Burr)
Sometimes I'm Happy - 1927 (*Hit The Deck*) (v. Franklyn Baur)
Song of The Flame - 1926 (*Song of the Flame*)
South Wind - 1927 (v. Henry Garden) (Victor reject)

South Wind - 1927

Tell Me Tonight - 1926

Tell Me Why You Smile, Mona Lisa - 1932 (*Der Raub der Mona Lisa*) (v. Elmer Feldkamp)

Tenderly Think of Me - 1926 (v. Frank Bessinger)

That's A Good Girl - 1926

The Hours I Spent With You - 1927 (v. Franklyn Baur)

The Moon Is Low - 1930 (*Montana Moon*) (v. Frank Munn)

The Tap-Tap - 1927

Then You've Never Been Blue - 1929 (v. Harold 'Scrappy' Lambert)

There I Go Dreaming Again - 1932 (*Hot-Cha*) (v. Dick Robertson)

Through! (How Can You Say We're Through?) - 1929 (v. Harold 'Scrappy' Lambert)

Ting-a-Ling, The Bells 'll Ring - 1926 (*Cocoanuts*)

Tonight You Belong To Me - 1926 (v. Franklyn Baur)

'Twas Not So Long Ago - 1929 (*Sweet Adeline*)

We'll Have A Kingdom - 1926 (*The Wild Rose*) (v. Johnny Marvin)

When A Woman Loves A Man - 1930 (*Be Yourself*) (v. Libby Holman)

Where The Wild, Wild Flowers Grow - 1927

Whistle Away Your Blues - 1926 (whistling by Sybil Sanderson Fagan) (Victor reject)

Why Was I Born? - 1929 (*Sweet Adeline*) (v. Harold 'Scrappy' Lambert)

Without A Song - 1929 (*Great Day*) (v. William C. Elkins Jubilee Singers)

Wouldn't You? - 1926 (v. Franklyn Baur)

Yankee Rose - 1927

Yearning (Just For You) - 1925 (v. Elliott Shaw)

You Told Me To Go - 1925 (v. Franklyn Baur)

You're A Real Sweetheart - 1928 (v. Frankie Marvin)

You're The Only One For Me - 1929 (*The Flying Fleet*)

You've Got Me In The Palm of Your Hand - 1932 (v. Kahn-a-Sirs)

Other songs composed by Roger Wolfe Kahn *

Cal, Cal, Cal, Cal Coolidge - 1924, m. & w. Roger Wolfe Kahn

Why! - 1925, m. Roger Wolfe Kahn

Nobody Loves Me (And I Wonder Why) - 16 June 1925, m. Roger Wolfe Kahn & Paul Van Loan, w. Lew Brown

Let Me Be The One For You - 1925, m. Roger Wolfe Kahn, w. George D. Lottman

You Should Know - 1926, m. Roger Wolfe Kahn

Gentlemen Prefer Blues - 1927, m. Roger Wolfe Kahn (piano solo)

Solito Estoy - 1928, m. Roger Wolfe Kahn - recorded by Marimba Centro-Americana (Spanish band) and released on Victor

Life as a Twosome - 1928 (*Here's Howe!*) m. Roger Wolfe Kahn & Joseph Meyer, w. Irving Caesar

(On My Mind) A New Love - 1928 (*Here's Howe!*) m. Roger Wolfe Kahn & Joseph Meyer, w. Irving Caesar

Young Black Joe - 1928 (*Americana*) m. Roger Wolfe Kahn, w. Irving
Caesar
No Place Like Home - 1928 (*Americana*) m. Roger Wolfe Kahn, w. Irving
Caesar
The Ameri-Can-Can - 1928 (*Americana*) m. Roger Wolfe Kahn, w. Irving
Caesar
He's Mine - 1928 (*Americana*) m. Roger Wolfe Kahn, w. Irving Caesar
Wild Oat Joe - 1928 (*New Americana*) m. Roger Wolfe Kahn, w. Irving
Caesar
Good Time Charlie - m. Roger Wolfe Kahn

Filmography

Roger Wolfe Kahn Musical Number (1924) B&W (U.S.), short film, directed by
J. Searle Dawley. DeForest Phonofilm Inc. 35mm, sound-on-film sound
system. Survival status unknown.

Roger Wolfe Kahn Musical Number (1925) B&W (U.S.), short film, directed by
J. Searle Dawley. DeForest Phonofilm Inc. 35mm, sound-on-film sound
system. Survival status unknown. IMDb listed.

Night Club (1927) Vitaphone Short B&W No. 468. The Roger Wolfe Kahn
Orchestra assisted by the Mound City Blue Blowers. Roger and his musicians
perform four numbers: '*El Tango del Perroquet*,' '*Following You Around*,'
'*Telling The Birds*' (v. MCBB), and '*Blue Skies*.'

Night Club (1927) Vitaphone Short B&W No. 469. The Roger Wolfe Kahn
Orchestra assisted by Henri Garden (tenor) and the Williams Sisters. Roger
and his musicians perform four numbers: '*Indian Butterfly*,' '*My Heart Is
Calling You*' (v. Henri Garden), '*Thinking Of You*' (v. Williams Sisters), and
'*Yankee Rose*.'

Schrödy The Wolf (1928) (cartoon) - '*Following You Around*' by Roger Wolfe
Kahn and His Orchestra is included in the soundtrack. A twenty-second clip
exists: https://youtu.be/71IabMQp3BU

Yesterday's Newsreels: Otto H. Kahn, financial wizard of yesterday. Filmed
on board a liner, 1920s. Duration: 06:53-07:08, 16 sec.
https://youtu.be/qI-oFaoAcC4

New Airmail Pickup Surprises Officials In Successful Tests. Mitchel Field,
New York (August 1930). Newsreel: Highlights of 1930 (UE30065). 'Roger
Wolfe Kahn demonstrates new Cabot device for Postal officials who required
75 out of 100 perfect pickups.' Duration: 59 sec.
https://www.criticalpast.com/video/65675059953_Cabot-device_aircraft-
in-flight_Roger-Wolfe-Kahn_testing-a-device

Bandleader Aviator Roger Wolfe Kahn makes daring low altitude pickup of mail in Norfolk, Virginia (April 1931). Duration: 1 min. 3 sec. Universal Newspaper Newsreel. Historic footage of Roger in flight. https://www.criticalpast.com/video/65675026605_rooftop-mail_Roger-Wolf-Kahn_ties-mail-to-plane_dropped-in-field

The Yacht Party (1932) Vitaphone Short. Roger Wolfe Kahn and His Orchestra perform six numbers: *'Way Down Yonder in New Orleans,' 'Sweet and Hot'* (v. Gertrude Niesen), *'Crazy Rhythm,' 'You're Driving Me Crazy (What Did I Do?),' 'Crazy People'* (v. The Foursome), and *'Dinah'* accompanied with a novelty dance routine by Melissa Mason.

This Is America (1933) documentary feature (U.S.)
Director: Gilbert Seldes and Frederic Ullman Jr. Narrator: Alois Havrilla
Roger Wolfe Kahn makes an appearance as himself.

Roger Wolfe Kahn and His Jazz Band (1935) (U.S.) Montage Collection: Archive Films: Editorial. Archive: Getty Images, location: United Kingdom Clip No. mr_00027192, created: 1 January 1935, clip length: 00:00:24:08 https://www.gettyimages.co.uk/detail/video/news-footage/mr_00027192

The Bobby Sandford Show outtakes: housed at the Moving Image Research Collection, University of South Carolina. Fox Movietone News, 7 July 1934. Sixteen showgirls dance on the beach at the Sun & Surf Club to the music of Roger Wolfe Kahn and His Orchestra. Kahn leads his band. Bobby Sanford directs the dancers before the dancers pile on top of Sanford. Several outtakes exist. https://mirc.sc.edu/islandora/object/usc:20960

Yesterday's Newsreel (1937). Roger Wolfe Kahn and His Orchestra performing on stage at the Biltmore. Duration: 24 sec. *'Rich man's son drops money for music. Son of banker Otto Kahn, Roger Wolfe Kahn, leads his own orchestra. It's the early 1930s, and this young disciple of George Gershwin is big with a baton. 'This beats banking, and Roger not only made music, music made Roger $30,000 a year.'* https://youtu.be/LTifJFiiKcU

Roger Wolfe Kahn and His Orchestra (1937) Vitaphone, B&W (U.S.) No. 1547. Director: Roy Mack. Starring: Roger W. Kahn, Evelyne Poe, Charles Carlisle, James & Evelyn Vernon. Ten-minute Vitaphone short created: May 1936.* Vitaphone Production Reel No. 2006

Sylvester Ahola Home Movies: In addition to being a brilliant musician, jazz trumpeter Sylvester Ahola was also a keen amateur filmmaker. During the 1920s, he captured various friends and fellow musicians on his home cine camera, including, in one short segment, a teenage, tousle-haired Roger Wolfe Kahn. Some of Ahola's early film footage can be viewed on YouTube, including the ten-second clip of Roger sitting in what appears to be the backseat of a car, although it could easily be an airplane's cockpit. Sitting beside Roger is his friend and flying instructor, Charles T. Homer. Following Roger's scene, a road sign comes into shot, giving directions to ROOSEVELT FIELD AMERICA. I believe this is the earliest known film footage of Roger in existence.*

Rhapsody in Blue (1945) - German-born actor Ernest Golm portrays Otto Kahn in the Warner Bros. feature biopic of George Gershwin.

So This Is Love 'The Grace Moore Story' (1953) - Roy Gordon portrays Otto Kahn (chairman of the Metropolitan Opera Company).

Bibliography

Birmingham, Stephen. *Our Crowd: The Great Jewish Families of New York*, Harper & Row, 1967.

Dempsey, Jack. and Considine, Bob. and Slocum, Bill. *Dempsey: By the Man Himself*, Simon and Schuster, NY, 1960.

Forbes, Bertie Charles. *Men Who Are Making America*, B.C. Forbes Publishing Co. NY, 1917, pp. 214-23 & 331.

Gatti-Casazza, Giulio. *Memories of the Opera*, Charles Scribner's Sons Inc. USA, 1941.

Greenspan, Charlotte. *Pick Yourself Up: Dorothy Fields and the American Musical*, Oxford University Press, 2010.

Holman, Valleri J. *Russian Culture and Theatrical Performance in America, 1891-1933*, Palgrave Macmillan U.S. 2011.

Homans, James E. *Biography of America*, 1918 - Otto H. Kahn.

Horowitz, Louis J. and Sparkes, Boyden. *The Towers of New York The Memoirs of a Master Builder*, Simon and Schuster, NY, 1937.

Kahn, Otto H. *Of Many Things*, Boni & Liveright, 1926.

Kahn, Otto H. *American Stage; Reflections of an Amateur*, (self publ.) 52 William St., NY, 1925.

Kahn, Otto H. *Frenzied Liberty: The Myth of 'A Rich Man's War'* – Extracts from address given by Otto H. Kahn at the University of Wisconsin on 14 January 1918 (self publ.) 1918.

Kahn, Otto H. *Capital and Labor - A Fair Deal* - Extracts taken from an address given by Otto H. Kahn at the Carnegie Institute, Pittsburgh, PA, on 24 April 1919 (self publ.) 1919.

Kahn, Otto H. *The American Stage: Reflections of an Amateur* – An address given by Otto H. Kahn during the Conference on the Drama in American Universities and Little Theatres held at the Carnegie Institute of Technology, Pittsburgh, PA, 27 November 1925 (self publ.) 1925.

Klein, Henry H. *Dynastic America and Those Who Own It*, H. H. Klein, NY, 1921.

Le Moyne, Louis Valcoulon. *Country Residences in Europe and America*, Doubleday, Page and Co., NY, 1908, chapter IV – American places, Cedar Court, pp. 443-49.

Liebman, Roy. *Vitaphone Films: A Catalogue of the Features and Shorts,* McFarland & Co, 2010, pp. 85-86 - Roger Wolfe Kahn's Yacht Party (aka *The Yacht Party*).

Murrells, Joseph. *Million Selling Records: From the 1900s to 1980s,* B. T. Batsford, London, 1984.

Nichols, Beverley. *All I Could Never Be,* Jonathan Cape, London, 1949, chapter VIII Book One, 'Study in Blonde' pp. 111-123.

Phillips-Matz, Mary Jane. *The Many Lives of Otto Kahn,* Macmillan Co. 1963.

Pollack, Howard. *George Gershwin: His Life and Work,* University of California Press, 2006.

Roman, Zoltan. *Gustav Mahler's American Years, 1907-1911: A Documentary History,* Pendragon Press, Stuyvesant NY, 1989.

Rust, Brian. *The American Dance Band Discography 1917-1942:* Vol. I – *Irving Aaronson to Arthur Lange,* Arlington House Publishers, NY, 1975.

Skuria, George M. and Gregory, William H. *Inside the Iron Works: How Grumman's Glory Days Faded,* Naval Institute Press, 2004.

Stravinsky, Igor, and Craft, Robert. *Conversations with Igor Stravinsky* -Doubleday Company Inc., NY, 1959.

Surdam, Charles E. and Osgoodby, William Gardner. *Beautiful Homes of Morris County and Northern New Jersey,* Pierson & Surdam, Morristown, N.J. 1900, Cedar Court, pp. 16-18 (photo).

U.S. Senate Committee on Banking and Currency. *The Pecora Investigation,* Cosimo Inc. Reports, NY, 2010.

Glossary of Abbreviations:
acct. – account
advt. – advertisement
art. – article
capt. – caption
col. – column
n. p. – no page number
obit. – obituary
pict. – picture(s)
publ. – publisher(ed)
rept. – report
rev. – review
suppl. – supplement
Vol. – volume

Roger Wolfe Kahn–Aviation

'Once Kahn was aloft alone, however, the country came by one of its most gifted airmen, and in the recent years his efforts in research and test flying and other phases of aviation have constituted a unique one-man contribution to the advancement of the industry.'[1]

Associations:
- A member of the OX5 Club of America: http://ox5.org
- A director of the National Aeronautic Association: https://naa.aero
- A member of the Advisory Committee of the Quiet Birdmen.
- Vice president and member of the Council of the Institute of Aerospace Sciences: https://www.aiaa.org/about
- Vice president of the National Aeronautic Association and chairman of the NAA Contest Board.[2]
- A member of the Society of Experimental Test Pilots: https://www.setp.org
- A member of the *Ligue Internationale des Aviateurs* (International League of Aviators).
- Vice president and member of the Wings Club: https://www.wingsclub.org
- A member of the Professional Race Pilots Association: http://www.biplaneracing.org/#welcome2
- A member of Long Island Early Fliers Club: http://www.liefc.org
- A member of The Laura Taber Barbour Air Safety Award Board (1962).
- A member of the Aviation Country Club [ACC] of Long Island.

Awards:
- Recipient of The Paul Tissandier Diploma, awarded by the *Federation Aeronautique Internationale.*[3]
- Recipient of the American Legion Air Service Post 501 Medal of Merit for outstanding piloting of new aircraft (1955),[4] and for his contribution to the development of aviation in America.
- Recipient of The William J. McGough Memorial Award: 'for special contribution to, or in, aviation.'[5]

Achievements:
- Burnelli entrant in the Guggenheim safe-aircraft competition.
- At the time of Roger's death, he had over 7,000 flying hours under his belt.

Archives and Special Collections

The Otto H. Kahn Papers at Princeton University Library. A large bulk of the correspondence relates to Otto's business dealings in finance and the arts. The collection was gifted to the Library in 1951 by Gilbert W. Kahn.

The Roger Wolfe Kahn Collection is held at The Institute of Jazz Studies, Rutgers University Libraries Archival Collections: music scores and arrangements, papers, photographs, scrapbooks, broadcasting charts, radio transcripts, and sound recordings. The bulk of the collection dates from 1926 to 1940.

A series of photographs of the Kahns' Morristown estate Cedar Court dating from 1900 to 1920 are housed at the Morristown and Morris Township Public Library, North Jersey History & Genealogy Center.

Otto and Addie built a stunning art collection that contained works by Giovanni Bellini, Benedetto Bonfigli, Botticelli, Boucher, Canaletto, Canova, Clouet, Corot, Lorenzo di Credi, Gerard David, Gaddi, Francesco Lazzaro Guardi, Franz Hals, Lorenzo Lotto, Carpaccio, Lucas Cranach, Mantegna, Matisse, Nattier, Andrea Pisano, Rembrandt, Romney, Jacopo Sansovino, and Martin Schongauer.* After Otto's death the collection was, over time, split up and sold.

The Morgan Library & Museum, Frick Collection, New York, have various items relating to the Kahn family; a portrait of Otto Kahn by Rudolf Herrmann; a letter from Otto Kahn to Isadora Duncan, dated February 27, 1915, New York (ref. MA 5133.8); and Otto Kahn's autograph album presented to him in 1921 by French Prime Minister Aristide Briand, bound by René Kieffer.

The Northrop Grumman History Centre, Bethpage, New York, holds information relating to Roger's employment with Grumman.

Das Bundesarchiv (German Federal Archives) in Koblenz, have four photographs of Otto H. Kahn taken at the Hotel Adlon by the photographer Georg Pahl.

Sources and Notes

* (p. ix) Birmingham, Stephen. *Our Crowd: The Great Jewish Families of New* York, Harper & Row, 1967, p 353, 'Immer rastlos voran' Kahn family motto

PART I. LOOKING FOR THE BOY   1867–1924

Chapter 1. The Rise of the House of Kahn

1. The *Reading Eagle*, 21 January 1930, p. 11 - Flashes of Life (col.).
2. The *Binghamton Press*, 21 January 1930, p. 4 - Roger Wolfe Kahn Spends Hours Operating Miniature Railroad at Father's House.
3. *Robert Kahn and Brahms* (art.) by Burkhard Laugwitz, *Das Orchester*, Hamburg, Vol. 34, No. 65, June 1986, pp. 640-48.
4. *The Sentinel*, 5 April 1934, p. 23 - Otto H. Kahn (obit.).
5. *The National Cyclopædia of American Biography*, 1944 - Otto H. Kahn.
6. *Captains of Industry* - The Story of Otto Hermann Kahn - KEHE Radio Broadcast, Los Angeles, episode No. 42, aired 7 November 1937.
7. *New York Times*, 30 March 1934, p. 18 - Life as a Boy Made Kahn Arts Patron (art.).
8. The *Big Spring, Texas, Daily Herald*, 10 January 1930, p. 4 - Once Upon a Time - Otto H. Kahn, caricature and capt.
9. Forbes, B.C. *Men Who Are Making America*, B.C. Forbes Publishing Co. New York, 1917 - Otto H. Kahn biography pp. 214-223.
10. The *Record-Herald*, Waynesboro, PA., 20 December 1924, p. 8 - *Smart Kid* (rept.) 'Mr. Otto H. Kahn says he won his first promotion as a lad through his rapidity in licking postage stamps. The firm sent out thousands of letters a week...'
11. *The Sentinel*, 5 April 1934, p. 23 - Otto H. Kahn (obit.).
12. *The National Cyclopædia of American Biography*, 1944 - Otto H. Kahn.
13. 1891 England Census, Otto Kahn, 19 Sheffield Terrace, Kensington, London. Tim Read, of Kensington and Chelsea Local Studies and Archives, explains: 'I have pieced together relevant details of the complex building and street naming/numbering history of Sheffield Terrace. From this, it appears that the now 19 was not yet built in 1891. This southeastern end of the street seems to have been developed in the mid-1890s; what is now No. 42 was No. 19 in 1891. Pinning down the date of this building has proved a little troublesome, but it clearly looks second half of the 19th century.' (21/07/2016).
14. Phillips-Matz, Mary Jane. *The Many Lives of Otto Kahn*, Macmillan Co. 1963, p. 255.
15. *The Evening Standard*, 1 May 2009 - Fire Sale at the Savoy (art.).
16. August 1, 1893, Otto H. Kahn, Essex Villa, Datchet, Bucks - UK Naturalization Certificates and Declarations form, number 7604.
17. Ibid.
18. *The Sentinel*, 5 April 1934, p. 23 - Otto H. Kahn (obit.).
19. The *Richmond Times-Dispatch*, 16 February 1920, p. 6 - Otto Kahn bio.
20. Passenger List: 25 April 1894, Otto Kahn arrives in Liverpool, England.
21. Passenger List: 16 Nov. 1895, Otto Kahn arrives in Liverpool, England.
22. *The Journal* (New York, NY), Thursday 9 January 1896, p. 11 - In a Grove of Palms (marriage).
23. Passenger List: 7 Feb. 1896, Otto and Addie Kahn arrive in Liverpool.
24. Marriage certificate - Abraham Wolff and Lydia Cohen, Manhattan,

602   The KAHNS

New York, 1874, marriage ID: 2220816971, certificate number: 2968. Source: Marriage Registers, extracts from Manhattan (1869-1880) and Brooklyn (1895-1897).

25. 1880 and 1900 U.S. Federal Census - Borough of Manhattan, Electoral District 9, NY, Ward 29, New York - Clara Dorothy Wolff (b. Dec. 1876). The 1880 U.S. Federal Census records Lydia's age as 26, born 1854. Clara was 20 when she married Abraham Wolff in 1874.

26. The New York Daily Tribune, 30 January 1896, p. 7, Marriage announcement: Clara D. Wolff and Henri P. Wertheim.

27. Henri Hendrik Pieter Wertheim van Heukelom, b. 2 October 1872, Amsterdam, North Holland, The Netherlands.

28. The New York Tribune, 2 February 1896, p. 7 - The Week in Society (col.) - The marriage of Miss Clara Dorothy Wolff to Henri P. Wertheim - 'The marriage of Miss Clara Dorothy Wolff to Henri P. Wertheim, of Amsterdam, Holland, took place on Wednesday afternoon at the home of the bride's father, Abraham Wolff, at 33 West 57th Street. Dr. Felix Adler performed the marriage ceremony. It was followed by an elaborate seated breakfast. The bride's gown was of white peau de soie, trimmed with white point lace, and her veil was of tulle. Miss Dorothy Wolff, a cousin, was her only attendant.'

29. 1900 U.S. Federal Census - Borough of Manhattan, Election District 9 New York City Ward 29, New York County, New York - Abraham Wolff (b. August 1939), Clara W. Wertheim (b. December 1876) and her husband Henri P. Wertheim (b. October 1872) are all registered as living at 33 West 57th Street. Nine employees (servants) also reside at the property. Clara has already given birth to two children, both of whom are deceased. The 1900 U.S. Federal Census was compiled in June, a few weeks before Abraham Wolff died in August that year.

30. Passenger List: 7 Feb. 1896, Otto and Addie Kahn arrive in Liverpool.

31. The Brooklyn Daily Eagle, 29 December 1930, p. 29 - Firm Changes Announced by Several Houses (rept.).

32. Ibid.

33. Birmingham, Stephen. The Jews in America Trilogy: 'Our Crowd,' 'The Grandees,' and 'The Rest of Us,' Open Road Media, 2016, chapter 25 - Marriage, Schiff Style. German-born Felix M. Warburg (1871-1937) arrived in the U.S. in 1894.

34. Rae, John W. Morristown: A Military Headquarters of the American Revolution, Arcadia Publishing, 2002, pp. 88-90, 138.

35. Upper East Side Historic District Designation Report - East 68th Street, South Side, History, p. 362 - Ref: New York City, Department of Buildings, Manhattan, Plans. Permits and Dockets.

36. The New York Tribune, 3 October 1900, p. 7 - Abraham Wolff death.

37. New York Times, 3 October 1900, p. 7 - Abraham Wolff (obit.).

38. The West Australian Sunday Times, 3 February 1901, p. 4 - A Multimillionaire - Abraham Wolff's Will (rept.). According to the Bureau of Labor Statistics, $20,000,000 in 1900 is equivalent in purchasing power to $610,450,000.00 in May 2020.

39. Kaiser, Harvey H. Great Camps of the Adirondacks, David R. Godine Publisher Inc. 1996, pp. 144-146 - acct. and pict. of Otto Kahn's.

40. The address of the Kahns' Adirondack property was, Bull Point Camp, 525 Bull Point Road, Upper Saranac Lake.

41. Life, 23 December 1946, p. 87 - One Hundred Years of Town and Country - Houses, The Mansions Were Huge and Eccentric (art. and

pict.) - Otto Kahn Camp, Upper Saranac Lake.

42. *New York Times,* 16 August 1903, p. 7 - Mrs. Henri Wertheim dead. (The announcement misreports Clara's year of birth as 1868).

43. The Kahn Papers, Harvard University - Box 111, f. 4 Wolff, Abraham: Trust in favor of his daughter Addie, [1895].

44. Franz Michael Kahn died in Strasbourg on 6 December 1904, aged 43. He worked as a jurist. The French province of Strasbourg became part of the German Empire in 1871 after the Franco-Prussian War.

45. *Democrat and Chronicle,* Rochester, 4 February 1905, p. 8 - Kahn Summer Home at Morristown Destroyed (rept.). *The American Florist,* 11 February 1905, p, 117 - Cedar Court fire (rept.).

46. The *Cornell Daily Sun,* 4 February 1905, p. 2 - News of the Morning (col.) Part of Otto Kahn's Moorish palace near Morristown, N. J. and art objects valued at nearly $500,000, were destroyed by fire.

47. Bernhard Kahn died on 8 March 1905 aged 77, geni.com.

48. *The American Florist,* 11 February 1905, p. 118 - James Fraser tenders the gardens at Cedar Court.

49. *The American Florist,* 15 April 1905 - Cedar Court (rept.).

50. A photograph exists of Otto and Addie Kahn taken in their library at 1100 Fifth Avenue by the photographer Erich Salomon, ca. 1930.

51. Big Old Houses - The King of New York, Otto Kahn (art.) by John Foreman - newyorksocialdiary.com, 6 March 2012.

52. *Prominent and Progressive Americans: An Encyclopaedia of Contemporaneous Biography,* Vol. I, N. Y. Tribune, 1902 - Otto H. Kahn biography.

53. Although a 1910 atlas map of Morris Township (copyright A. H. Mueller) states, Cedar Court occupied 260 acres, when the estate was advertised for sale in 1920 the sales booklet lists: 'In all two hundred and fifty acres, sixty of which are not cleared.'

54. Cedar Court, loc. Columbia Road and Park Avenue, Morris Township.

55. *Prominent and Progressive Americans: An Encyclopaedia of Contemporaneous Biography,* Vol. I, N. Y. Tribune, 1902 - Otto H. Kahn biography.

56. *New York Times,* 9 October 1904 - Morristown Horse Show; Field Club's Seventh Annual Exhibition Closed with a Big Attendance - Morristown, N.J., 8 October 1904 (rept.).

57. The *Richmond Times-Dispatch,* 16 February 1920, p. 6 - Otto Hermann Kahn (short biography).

58. *New Jersey, A Guide to its Present and Past* - The American Guide Series, Viking Press, New York, June 1939, p. 286.

59. *New York Times,* 18 April 1906, p. 1 - Otto Kahn's Deer Killed.

60. Emma S. Kahn, Heidelberg, Germany, died on 25 June 1906, aged 65.

61. Kahn, Otto H. *Our Economic and Other Problems; a Financier's Point of View,* George H. Doran Co. New York, 1920, p. 13.

62. *The National Cyclopædia of American Biography,* 1944 - Otto H. Kahn.

Notes
* (p. 13) Paul M. Warburg joined Kuhn, Loeb & Co. in 1902.

Chapter 2. The New Wizard of Wall Street
1. Quote by a long-standing governess of the Kahn family.

2. The *Boston Evening Transcript,* 12 March 1907, p. 12 - Sailings (col.).

3. *The Greencastle Herald,* Greencastle, Putnam County, 24 April 1907, p. 3 - New Wizard of Finance (art.).

4. Ibid.

5.   The testimony of Edward Harriman before the Interstate Commerce Commission took place in New York on 25, 26 & 27 February 1907.

6.   The *Greencastle Herald*, Greencastle, Putnam County, 24 April 1907, p. 3 - New Wizard of Finance (art.).

7.   Ibid.

8.   The *New York Clipper*, 28 February 1903, p. 7 - Heinrich Conried and the Conried Metropolitan Opera House (rept.).

9.   The Metropolitan Opera House opened in 1883. After a fire in 1892 gutted the stage and auditorium, the 92/93 season was canceled. Reconstruction followed, and the theatre reopened for the 93/94 season. Where previously there had been seventy parterre boxes (referred to collectively as the 'Golden Horseshoe,') the number had been reduced to fifty-four - thirty-five in the Parterre and nineteen in the Grand Tier above. In later years, some journalists labeled the 'Golden Horseshoe' the 'Diamond Horseshoe,' to reflect the glittering diamonds worn by the wealthy occupants. In 1940, the Grand Tier boxes were removed, and rows of seating were installed in their place. Ref: Kolodin, Irving. *The Metropolitan Opera 1883 - 1935*, Oxford University Press, 1936.

10.   *The Opera Season, The Lotus Magazine,* Vol. 4, No. 2, Nov. 1912, pp. 72-74 - The Opera Season (1912-13) Box Holders (list).

11.   The *Greencastle Herald*, Greencastle, Putnam County, 24 April 1907, p. 3 - New Wizard of Finance (art.).

12.   *Le Figaro*, 7 May 1907, p. 4 - Gala of *Salome,* Théâtre du Châtelet, Paris.

13.   *Salome* performed at the Metropolitan Opera House, 22 January 1907.

14.   Excerpt from a review by W. J. Henderson, New York *Sun*, January 1907, of *Salome* at the Conried Metropolitan Opera House.

15.   *New York Times*, 4 August 1907.

16.   *New York Times*, 27 Sept. 1907, p. 6 - *Morristown Horse Show.*

17.   *New York Times*, 29 Sept. 1907, p. 54, Section Four, Sporting News.

18.   Passenger List: 28 July 1908, RMS *Mauretania* arrives in Liverpool from New York. Traveling in first-class were the Kahn family.

19.   *New York Times*, 11 July 1909: London, 10 July - A number of London hotel managers, headed by Mr. Pruger of the Savoy, have undertaken a campaign looking to an extension of the London season.

20.   Passenger List: 12 September 1908, RMS *Mauretania* departs Liverpool bound for New York via Queenstown, Ireland. Traveling in first-class were the Kahn family.

21.   James Gerard elected as a Justice of the New York Supreme Court.

22.   *New York Times,* 15 November 1908, p. 49 - Part 6, Dramatic and Fashion Section (col.).

23.   The *Spokane Press*, 12 July 1909, p. 3 - Gets $660,000 For Five Years Warbling (art.).

24.   *New York Times*, 11 July 1909: London, 10 July - Otto H. Kahn going to Austria to visit E. H. Harriman.

25.   Edward Henry Harriman died on 9 September 1909, aged 61, at his 40,000-acre estate 'Arden' in Ramapo Highlands.

26.   *New York Times*, 10 Sept. 1909 - Harriman Dead; News Delayed.

27.   Passenger List: 23 Oct. 1909, RMS *Mauretania* departs Liverpool, UK, bound for New York. Traveling in first-class were the Kahn family.

28.   *New York Times*, 19 March 1910.

29.   The *Sacramento Union*, 2 April 1910, p. 6 - Big Sums Paid for Paintings (art. reprinted from the *New York Tribune*).

30. Phillips-Matz, Mary Jane. *The Many Lives of Otto Kahn,* Macmillan Co., 1963, p. 65.

31. *New York Times,* 7 August 1910, n. p. - Otto Kahn: A Man of Steel and Velvet.

32. *Variety,* November 1910, p. 23 - From The Boston Opera House Comes A Corrected List of the Board of Directors as it Now Stands.

33. The *New York Sunday American,* 11 Dec. 1910 - Society Flock to Greatest Opera Opening City Ever Saw.

34. The *New York Sunday American,* 11 Dec. 1910 - Incidents of the Night.

35. The *Evening World,* 15 March 1911 - Otto H. Kahn Takes Family to Coronation - Party occupies $11,000 worth of the *Mauretania* and $2,000 of the Caronia (rept.) - The Kahn family sailed on 15 March.

36. Ibid.

37. The *Hawaiian Star,* 1 April 1911, second edition, second section, p. 11 - Pays $11,000 to Cross Atlantic (rept.).

38. The *Charlotte News,* 23 April, p. 4 - Caruso Sailed (to Europe) Tuesday.

39. *New York Daily Tribune,* 31 March 1911, p. 7 - Cassiobury, Watford, historic estate leased by Otto H. Kahn.

40. England & Wales 1911 Census: The Kahn family (minus Otto) are residing at Cassiobury House with twenty-four live-in servants.

41. Letter from Martha Freeman Esmond (Chicago, 23 June 1911) to her friend Julia Boyd in New York, reprinted in the *Chicago Tribune,* 21 June 1959, part 7, p. 4 - When Chicago was Young by Herma Clark.

42. The *Washington Post,* 23 June 1911, p. 3 - report of the coronation from *The Washington Post* correspondent in London.

43. *New York Times,* 23 June 1911, p. 4 - F. T. Martin's Impressions: King George Seemed Crushed Beneath His Burden of Responsibility.

44. *New York Times,* 8 August 1911, p. 9 - 'Our Opera Best, Says Otto Kahn (rept.) Otto H. Kahn, who returned to New York yesterday on the Hamburg-American Liner *Amerika...*'

45. *New York Times,* 1911 - An interview with Otto H. Kahn on operatic and dramatic art in America and other art topics.

46. Ibid.

47. Phillips-Matz, Mary Jane. *The Many Lives of Otto Kahn,* Macmillan Co., 1963, chapter 13, p. 155.

48. *New York Times,* 11 January 1912 - 'Oscar Hammerstein sailed back to London yesterday on the *Lusitania* ... Otto Kahn, one of the directors of the Metropolitan Opera House, sailed on the same ship.'

49. *Variety,* 4 January 1912, front page - Grand Opera Combination Against Covent Garden (art.).

50. *New York Times,* 26 September 1912, p. 1 - Otto Kahn Buys A House in London. More evidence that Otto H. Kahn intends to pass a good deal of his time in the future on this side of the Atlantic ... when he purchased 2 Carlton House Terrace from Mrs. Maldwin Drummond.

51. *New York Times,* 23 November 1912, p. 4 - Kahn Completes Purchase. Now owns famous London mansion, but will not live in it.

52. *New York Times,* 14 February 1912 - Due Here This Morning - Mr. Kahn is on the *Olympic* - His New York career and activities (rept.).

53. Passenger List: 28 August 1912, RMS *Lusitania* - 'Mrs. Kahn sailed with no less than two maids and special stewardesses, her daughter Maud and her governess, her daughter Margaret and her maid, her son Gilbert and his nurse and her son Roger.'

54. The *Times,* 17 September 1912, p. 7 - Court Circular and Social (col.) -

55. Otto H. Kahn arrived in the UK yesterday (16 Sept.) on the *Mauretania*. *New York Times*, 26 September 1912, p. 1 - Otto Kahn Buys A House In London.

56. *New York Times*, 8 October 1912, p. 4 - Another House for Otto Kahn - After buying a mansion in Carlton House Terrace, London, he decides to sell it - Rents a famous villa.

57. The *Courier-Journal*, Kentucky, 10 August 1913, p. 28 - Kahn and His Hobby (art.).

58. *New York Times*, 8 October 1912, p. 4 - Another House for Otto Kahn (art.).

59. Passenger List: 5 February 1913, SS *Kaiser Wilhelm* II departs Southampton bound for New York. Traveling on board is Otto Kahn.

60. Passenger List: 12 April 1913, RMS *Mauretania* departs UK bound for New York. Traveling in first-class, Addie Kahn and her four children.

61. Phillips-Matz, Mary Jane. *The Many Lives of Otto Kahn*, Macmillan Co., 1963, p. 163.

62. The *Courier-Journal*, Kentucky, 10 August 1913, p. 28 - Kahn and His Hobby (art.).

63. *New York Times*, 18 September 1913, p. 11 - Big Prices for Horse Show Boxes at Morristown, N.J., 17 September 1913.

64. The *Sun*, New York, 14 September 1913, sixth section front page - New and Finer Fifth Avenue on Carnegie Hill (art.).

65. The *New York Clipper*, 20 December 1913, p. 15 - More Celebrities Filmed for *'Mutual Girl'* Series (rept.) Belmont and Kahn, Millionaire Bankers, Seen on the Screen with *'Our Mutual Girl'* (rept.).

66. The *New York Clipper*, 4 April 1914, p. 16 - Film Fancies (col.) by HEX.

67. Horowitz, Louis J. and Sparkes, Boyden. *The Towers of New York: The Memoirs of a Master Builder*, Simon & Schuster, NY, 1937, p. 260.

68. Andrew Carnegie's Fifth Avenue mansion, with 56,368 square feet, was New York City's largest single-family home.

69. *Dundee Courier*, 17 June 1914, p. 5 - Britain's largest liner *Aquitania* Completes Memorable Maiden Voyage; Record Number of Passengers.

70. The *New York Clipper*, 17 May 1913, front page - Opera At Popular Prices Assured - Century Opera Company Incorporated (art.).

71. The *New York Tribune*, 21 June 1914, p. 10 - London to Hear Aborn's Opera Co.: Kahn negotiating two-month tenancy of Covent Garden.

72. The *Rock Island Argus*, 22 August 1914, p. 9 - Will There be Opera? - Number of Stars Booked for This Country Are Stranded in Europe.

73. The *Sun*, New York, 10 July 1914, p. 3 - Otto H. Kahn on SS *Imperator*.

74. Ibid.

75. Text taken from Addie Kahn's cable to Otto Kahn dated, 18 July 1914. Otto Kahn papers, box 34, Princeton University.

76. Garafola, Lynn. *The Ballets Russes in America*, Columbia University Academic Commons, 1988, pp. 122 & 125.

77. The *New York Tribune*, 21 June 1914, p. 10 - London Hotels Crowded - Wealthy Men Accept Servants' Quarters Rather than Seek Elsewhere.

78. The *Sun*, New York, 4 August 1914, pp. 1 & 4 - Americans in London Unite for Protection - Plans of the Stranded Americans (rept.).

79. Ibid.

80. Passenger List: 29 Aug. 1914, RMS *Mauretania* departs Liverpool for New York. Traveling in first-class, Addie Kahn and her four children.

81. The *Boston Evening Transcript*, 31 May 1915, p. 11 - War and Italian Singers (art.).

82.   The *New York Tribune*, 15 September 1914, p. 7 - $5,000 For Relief at Opera Benefit (rept.).
83.   The *New York Clipper*, 31 Oct. 1914, p. 4 - Opera Stars Sail.
84.   The *Arizona Republican*, 8 November 1914, p. 4 - News of the Theaters, Music (col.) Helps Young Singers.
85.   The *New York Clipper*, 12 December 1914, p. 19 - Ask Cut In Salaries.
86.   *New York Times*, 21 December 1914, front page - Otto H. Kahn Quits Century Opera Co. (rept.).
87.   The *Daily Book*, 28 Dec. 1914, p. 4 - How Society Leans on Grand Op'ry.
88.   The *New York Clipper*, 2 January 1915, p. 3 - Century Opera Company to Close (rept.).
89.   The *Brooklyn Daily Eagle*, 13 November 1933, p. 15 - Milton Aborn Dies; Noted for Revival of Old Operettas (obit.).

Notes

* (p. 31) Otto arrived at the Met in 1903, the same year as impresario Heinrich Conried and operatic tenor Enrico Caruso; Conried agreed to become the managing director on February 15; Otto was elected a director on February 16; Caruso's debut at the Met took place in *Rigoletto* on November 23. Conried's five-year contract ran from June 1, 1903, until May 31, 1908.

* (p. 33a) Rue Nitot has since been renamed Rue de l'Amiral-d'Estaing.

* (p. 33b) Edgar Speyer was created a Baronet in 1906.

* (p. 37) The Mrs. O. H. Kahn chrysanthemum[1] became a popular seller across America throughout the next decade, winning many floral exhibitions.
    1.   *The American Florist*, 7 November 1908, p, 715 - *The Weekly Florists' Review*, 5 November 1908, p.8 - rept. and pict. of the Mrs. O. H. Kahn chrysanthemum. *The American Florist*, 27 September 1919, p. 527 - 'They are cutting a fine lot of Mrs. O. H. Kahn ...' (rept.).

* (p. 40) Upon Otto's return to New York, he explained to the press how the lack of a strong labor force along the Pacific Coast was holding back the expansion of business there and how a further increase in railroads could benefit the region.[1]
    1.   *New York Times*, 10 November 1910, p. 7 - Lack of Laborers Hold West Back; Otto H. Kahn, Returning from a Tour, Is Much Impressed with Pacific Coast Prospects.

* (p. 58) Passengers sailing aboard the SS *Canopic* included: Arturo Toscanini (conductor), Giorgio Polacco (conductor), Giulio Setti (chorus master), Francesco Romei (assistant conductor), Geraldine Farrar (soprano), Emmy Destinn (soprano), Lucrezia Bori (soprano), Frieda Hempel (soprano), Elisabeth Schumann (soprano), Enrico Caruso (tenor), Jacques Urius (tenor), Luca Botta (Tenor) and Adamo Didur (bass). Passengers to follow included: Hermann Weil (baritone), Otto Goritz (baritone), Carl Braun (basso), Margarete Ober (mezzo-soprano), Albert Reiss (tenor) and Léon Rothier (basso). At the time of the sailing, Dinh Gilly (baritone) was a prisoner of war.

Chapter 3. A Change of Direction
    1.   Kahn, Otto Hermann. *Art And The People*, The New York City Shakespeare Tercentenary Celebration Committee, NY, 1916, p. 6
    2.   *Indianapolis News*, 6 April 1916, p. 11 - Soldier Blinded in War, Studies

Occupations (art.).

3. *The British Journal of Nursing*, 1 May 1915, p. 37 - St Dunstan's Lodge, Regent's Park, London - The Blinded Soldiers' and Sailors Hostel.

4. Rae, John W. *Morristown: A Military Headquarters of the American Revolution*, Arcadia Publishing, 2002, p. 138.

5. The Otto H. Kahn Papers, Dept. of Rare Books and Special Collections, Firestone Library, Seeley G. Mudd Manuscript Library, Princeton, NJ.

6. Phillips-Matz, Mary Jane. *The Many Lives of Otto Kahn,* Macmillan Co. 1963, p. 22.

7. *Duluth Evening Herald*, March 1915 - Maud E. Kahn (pict. & art.).

8. The *New York Tribune*, 28 February 1915, part 3, front page - Many Affairs Held for The Lenten Days (rept.).

9. *New York Times,* 21 March 1915.

10. The *Broad Ax*, 12 June 1915, p. 3 - For The Children - Master Gilbert W. Kahn as an English Officer (pict., capt., & rept.).

11. The *South Bend News-Times*, Vol. 32, No. 181, St. Joseph County, 30 June 1915, p. 13 - Market Factors are all Bearish (rept.).

12. The *Sun*, New York, 14 November 1915, Fourth Section Pictorial Magazine (pict. & capt. of Maud Kahn).

13. The *Daily Telegraph*, 6 January 1916, front page - Prominent Men of Financial and Industrial World visit U.S. in 1916 (pict. & capt.).

14. Schanke, Robert A. *Angels in the American Theater: Patrons, Patronage, and Philanthropy*, Southern Illinois University Press, 2007, p. 56.

15. Birmingham, Stephen. *The Jews in America Trilogy: 'Our Crowd,' 'The Grandees,' and 'The Rest of Us,'* Open Road Media, 2016, chapter 24, - Addie held her debutante ball at Sherry's, New York, at the beginning of 1894.

16. The *New York Herald*, 9 Jan. 1916, Third Section, p. 5 - Society's 'Big Season' Crowded with Events. Sergei Diaghilev and the Ballets Russes troupe land at New York Harbor on 11 Jan. 1916. The Company made its U.S. debut at the Century Theatre on 17 January. Eisenstadt, Peter R., Moss, Laura-Eve., Huxley, Carole F. *The Encyclopedia of New York State*, Syracuse University Press 2005, p. 146.

17. The *New York Press*, 8 January 1916, p. 5 - Miss Kahn's Debut Brilliant Affair - Notables of Social World Attend Presentation in Sherry's - Dinners Precede Ball - Caruso, Pavlova and Yvette Guilbert on List of Entertainers (rept. & pict. of Maud E. Kahn).

18. Lee, Betty. *Marie Dressler: The Unlikeliest Star*, The University Press of Kentucky, 1997, pp. 118-119, mentions '*Melinda and her Sisters'* show.

19. 'Be militant each in your own way ... I incite this meeting to rebellion!' Quote from a speech by Emmeline Pankhurst at the Royal Albert Hall, London, on 17 October 1912. *The Suffragette*, 25 October 1912 (art.).

20. Garafola, Lynn. *The Ballets Russes in America*, Columbia University Academic Commons, 1988, p. 129.

21. The original contract between Nijinsky and the Metropolitan Opera Company is held in the Metropolitan Opera Archives.

22. *New York Times*, 8 February 1916 - Otto H. Kahn Sells Oyster Bay Estate (rept.).

23. Otto and Addie individually purchased their own Rolls-Royce Landaulet Limousine from Brewster & Co. showroom in New York.

24. *New York Times*, 5 November 1916 - Latest Dealings in the Realty Field (rept.). Otto H. Kahn Buys Residence In East 68th Street Adjoining His Present Home.

25.   *New York Times*, 16 May 1916 - Otto H. Kahn in Paris (rept.).

26.   The *New York Tribune*, 3 December 1916, p. 2 - Franco-American association for Musical Art (rept.).

27.   The *Detroit Free Press*, Michigan, 2 August 1916, p. 9 - Women of Today (col.) - pict. & capt. of Maud E. Kahn - 'Maud E. Kahn, of New York, is now on her way to Paris.'

28.   The Great War & New Jersey, holdings of Rutgers University Libraries' Special Collections & University Archives, manuscript collections, Ac. 1551 - Marianne Goodhue McKeever Papers - Marianne Goodhue McKeever correspondence, papers, etc., from 1916 -1919.

29.   The *Sun*, New York, 5 August 1917, section 4, pictorial magazine - pict. & capt. of Maud E. Kahn in her Red Cross uniform.

30.   The *Palm Beach Post*, 19 February 1920, p. 8 - Romance of Pretty Society Girl Had Its Inception at Her Father's Residence (art.).

31.   The *New York Clipper*, 6 December 1916, p. 6 - Kahn Acquires Control of Rialto (rept.).

32.   The *New York Clipper*, June 1914, n. p. - Mutual Film Corporation Holds Annual Meeting - Officers and Directors are Unanimously Re-elected.

33.   Millard, Andre. *America on Record: A History of Recorded Sound*, Cambridge University Press, 1995, Part One: chapter 3, p. 73.

34.   The *World News*, Vol. 28, No. 147, 19 December 1916, p. 10 - Daughter of America's Foremost Banker Succors Needy in France (pict. & capt. of Maud E. Kahn in her Red Cross uniform).

35.   The *Sun*, 25 February 1917, p. 2 - 'Mr. and Mrs. Kahn gave the one dance of note on Monday night at Sherry's for their daughter, Miss Maud Kahn, who returned about a fortnight ago from Paris.'

36.   The *New York Tribune*, 18 Nov. 1917, p. 2 - Maud E. Kahn (pict. & capt.)

37.   Copeau, Jacques., Dasté, Marie-Hélène., Maistre, Susan Saint-Denis. *Appels*, Gallimard, 1974.

38.   The *Indianapolis News*, 5 May 1917, p. 16 - News and Views (col.) 'The eminent French producer will bring his entire Théâtre du Vieux Colombier to the Garrick Theatre, New York, next fall.'

39.   *Jacques Copeau in New York* by Douglas Crowder, *The South Central Bulletin*, Vol. 29, No. 4, Winter 1969, pp. 125-128.

40.   The *Telegram*, 18 February 1917 - The Gridiron Club (rev.).

41.   The *Indianapolis News*, Indianapolis, 19 February 1917, p. 9 - Patriotism and Pranks at the Gridiron Dinner (rept.).

42.   The *New York Herald*, 11 January 1917, p. 4 - The Silent Sentinels at White House for Suffrage Cause are Actually Silent (pict. & rept.).

43.   'Camping Tonight' - Lyrics: writer unknown - Music: composer unknown - Genre: Camp song - Country: USA - Year: February 1917.

44.   The *Los Angeles Herald*, 31 January 1917, front page - Leak Quiz Nears White House - Deny 'Tip' By Wilson Relative (rept.).

45.   *The American Historical Review*, Vol. 54, No. 3, April 1949, pp. 548-552 - The 'Leak' Investigation of 1917 by John M. Blum (art.).

46.   The *Boston Globe*, 10 January 1917, p. 4 - Promise to Give Names by Lawson - Sabin Tells of Peace Statement (rept.).

47.   The *Herald Democrat*, 16 January 1917, front page - Tom Lawson Rips Off Lid In Peace Note Leak Inquiry (rept.).

48.   *New York Times*, 23 February 1917, p. 1 - Committee Blames Leak on Reporters: No Government Official Involved, Report Will Say, and Lawson's Charges Unfounded. Mr. Bolling Exonerated. President's Brother-in-law Gave No Tip on Peace Note (rept.).

49.   *New York Times*, 29 March 1917, front page - Otto H. Kahn Now American Citizen (rept.).

50.   *St. Louis Post-Dispatch*, 27 October 1931, p. 13A - Associated Press NY 27 Oct.: Otto H. Kahn Resigns As Metropolitan Opera Head ... He assumed the additional post of president in 1918 (rept.).

51.   *The Lotus Magazine*, (ed. by Gustav Kobbé) Vol. 9, No. 3, Dec. 1917, p. 140 - List of Box Holders - Parterre Boxes - Otto H. Kahn Box 14 - Box 14 had previously been leased by Mrs. H. H. Jenkins (even Wednesdays), Mrs. J. A. Logan Jr. (odd Wednesdays), Mr. George H. Warren (odd Mondays and odd Matinees), Mrs. W. K. Vanderbilt Jr. (Opening Night), Mr. G. B. Post Jr. (odd Fridays and even Matinees).

52.   The *Reading Times*, Reading, PA, 10 January 1917, p. 8 - Voice of the Press in Short Measure Today (art.)

53.   Ibid.

54.   *The Grand Opera Singers of Today* - The Music Lovers Series, The Page Company, Boston, 1912, p. 355 - The Metropolitan Opera House.

55.   The *New York Clipper*, 7 November 1917, p. 4 - New Opera Company Will Present German Airs (rept.).

56.   *The Étude*, November 1911 - The World of Music - At Home (rept.).

57.   *New York Times*, 9 November 1917, front page - Otto H. Kahn Talks Finance With Wilson (rept.).

58.   The dimensions of the lap pool are 75' long x 11' 6" wide.

59.   *New York Times*, 21 June 1917, p. 10 - Patriotic Rally at Civic Concert, 3,000 Sing National Anthem, 'Fight for art,' says Kahn.

60.   *The Seven Arts*, Vol. 2, No. 4, August 1917 - Music and Recruiting (art.) by Paul Rosenfeld.

61.   *New York Times*, 9 July 1916, p. 3, Civic Orchestral Music; First Concert in Madison Sq. Garden Tuesday Night; Spalding Soloist. *NYT*, 10 July 1916, p. 9 (advt.). The *Sun*, 9 July 1916, p. 6, Summer Concerts.

62.   Toff, Nancy. *Monarch of the Flute: The Life of Georges Barrere*, Oxford University Press, 2005, chapter 11, p. 153.

63.   Ibid., 154.

64.   The *Sun*, 15 August 1917, p. 5 - Notes of the Social World.

65.   Telegram, 12 September 1917, from Arthur Pearson (somewhere in England) to Otto Kahn in New York, acknowledging the imminent arrival of Maud Kahn to 'help with blinded soldiers at St Dunstan's.'

66.   1 June 1917, Otto gave an address titled '*Americans of German Origin and the War*' before the Merchants Association of New York at its Liberty Loan Meeting. The 2nd war bond was launched on 1 Oct. 1917.

67.   The *Indianapolis News*, 26 Sept. 1917, p. 6 - Appeal to Hyphenates.

68.   The *Harrisburg Telegraph*, eve, 27 Sept. 1917, front page: Otto H. Kahn Delighted with Harrisburg and its Beautiful Environment - F. A. Vanderlip is Commended for his Decision by Chamber of Commerce.

69.   The *Indianapolis News*, Indianapolis, Marion County, 27 Sept. 1917, p. 8 - Theater for Each Camp (rept.).

70.   The War Department Commission on Training Camp Activities, Washington, D.C. - Official Report., publ. October 1917, pp. 3-6.

71.   Ibid., 11.

72.   The *Indianapolis Star*, 28 July 1907, p. 56 - the $100,000,000 Theatrical Syndicate (art.).

73.   *New York Times*, 6 May 1909 - Belasco Settles his Syndicate Suit.

74.   Camp Music Division of the War Department, Commission on Training Camp Activities, June 30, 1919, compiled by Frances F. Brundage, publ.

Washington Government Printing Office, pp. 9-13, Music in the Camps.

75. The *Pittsburgh Post-Gazette*, 21 October 1917, p. 17: High Morale in Infantry's Army May Be Built Up by Singing and Music, 'A singing army is a fighting army,' Maj. Gen. J. Franklin Bell, Plattsburg, April 1917.

76. Camp Music Division of the War Department, Commission on Training Camp Activities, Music in the Camps, 18 April 1917 - 30 June 1919, compiled by Frances F. Brundage, publ. Washington Government Printing Office, pp. 7-8, The Singing Doughboy.

77. Hoffmann, Frank B., Cooper, Lee., Gracyk, Tim. *Popular American Recording Pioneers: 1895-1925*, Taylor & Francis, 2012, p. 254.

78. The *New York Clipper,* 13 May 1916, front page - Century Theatre for Dillingham & Ziegfeld (rept.) Secure house after months of rumors.

79. The *New York Clipper,* 17 January 1917, front page - Grove Opens Tomorrow (18 January).

80. *New York Times,* 20 Jan. 1917 - The Century Roof Opens Its Doors; The Cocoanut Grove is a Good-Looking Copy of the Ziegfeld Frolic.

81. Golden, Eve. *Vernon and Irene Castle's Ragtime Revolution*, The University Press of Kentucky, 2007, chapter 31, p. 190.

82. The *New York Clipper,* 4 May 1919, sect. IV, p. 6 - Reisenweber's advt.

83. The *New York Herald*, 25 January 1917, p. 6 - Reisenweber's advt.

84. The *New York Herald*, 25 January 1917, p. 6 - On January 24, Marguerite Wagnière-Horton gave a recital at the home of Henry Louis Reginald de Koven and his wife at 1025 Park Avenue. Three hundred guests attended, including Otto and Addie Kahn.

85. Brunn, H. O. *The Story of the Original Dixieland Jazz Band*, Louisiana State University Press, 1960, chapter 5, New York and the Jass Revolution, p. 57.

86. *The Sentinel*, November 30, 1917, front page - Otto Kahn (pict. & rept.).

87. *The Sentinel*, November 23, 1917, p. 4 - Otto Kahn turns over income.

88. The *South Bend News-Times*, Vol. 35, St. Joseph County, 13 January 1918, pp. 1-2 - Coldest Weather Since 1893 Sweeps Across Nation.

89. The *Jacksonville Daily Journal,* Illinois, 13 Jan. 1918, p. 12 - news.

90. Polk, R. L. *Trow New York Copartnership and Corporation Directory*, R. L. Polk & Co.'s, 1919, p. 1176 - Union Pacific directors.

91. *New York Times,* 14 Jan. 1918 - Blizzard Abates; Blockade Broken - Hundreds of Thousands of Volunteers Dig Paths through Snow.

92. The *South Bend News-Times*, Vol. 35, No. 13, South Bend, St. Joseph County, 13 January 1918, front page - News Bulletin.

93. Extract from Otto Kahn address, University of Wisconsin, 14 Jan. 1918 - Frenzied Liberty - The Myth of a Rich Man's War by Otto H. Kahn.

94. The *Mohave County Miner*, 4 May 1918, p. 3 - Otto H. Kahn quote: 'We seek no 'place in the sun' except the sun of Liberty.'

95. Kahn, Otto H. *Right Above Race*, publ. The Century Co., New York, April 1918, preface by Theodore Roosevelt, forward by Haldane Macfall. 'We will not permit the blood in our veins to drown the conscience in our breast. We will heed the call of honor beyond the call of race.'

96. Dietrich, Kris. *Taboo Genocide: Holodomor 1933 & the Extermination of Ukraine*, Xlibris, 2015 - Ivy Lee (info.).

97. *New York Times,* 27 February 1918, p. 11 - Otto Kahn at Palm Beach; Entertains E. T. Stotesbury at his home (rept.).

98. The *Evening World*, 10 April 1918, final edition p. 9 - League Formed to link France with America (rept.) A meeting was held at the home of Otto Kahn at 1100 Fifth Avenue on 9 April for the purposes of forming

the French League in America.

99.   1918 Passport Application No. 1257 - Otto Kahn states he will depart from New York on board RMS *Adriatic* on 1 May 1918.

100. The *San Antonio Light*, 28 Jan. 1940, p. 8 - Gen. Bundy's Revolt Told.

101. The *Oregon Daily Journal*, Portland, 29 May 1918, p. 5 - Paris: Otto H. Kahn. Banker has arrived here via London on an important mission.

102. *New York Times*, 25 July 1918, p. 16 - Otto Kahn Returns (rept.).

103. The *Indianapolis News*, 1 June 1918, p. 7 - French Orchestra to Give Fifty Concerts (rept.).

104. The *Washington Post*, 17 June 1918, p. 5 - Otto Kahn in Madrid to see King (rept.).

105. The Bodleian Library, University of Oxford, Correspondence: MS. Eng. c. 6595 above, 1953-4 - Shelf mark: MS. Eng. c. 6596 - fol. 298 and fols. 299-308 - the folders hold the Wiseman letter dated 17 September 1918 and a transcript of the Alfonso and Kahn conversation.

106. Birmingham, Stephen. *The Jews in America Trilogy: 'Our Crowd', 'The Grandees,' and 'The Rest of Us,'* Open Road Media, 2016, chapter 40.

107. *The American Jewish Yearbook*, Vol. 22 (Sept. 13, 1920 - Oct. 2, 1921, 5681), publ. American Jewish Committee, p. 153 - Appointment, Honor and Elections.

108. *The American Jewish Yearbook*, Vol. 21 (Sept. 25, 1919 - Sept. 12, 1920), publ. American Jewish Committee, p. 201 - Appointment, Honor and Elections: 'Otto H. Kahn appointed Chevalier of the Legion of Honor, September 1918.'

109. The *Sun*, New York, 11 August 1918, section 4 pictorial magazine - Otto Kahn (pict. & capt.): 'France has just paid an unusual honor to Otto H. Kahn in making him a Chevalier of the Legion of Honor...'

110. *New York Times*, 20 March 1918 - Kahn to House French Actors (art.).

111. Copeau, Jacques., Dasté, Marie-Hélène., Saint-Denis, Susan Maistre. *Appels*, Gallimard, 1974.

112. The *Washington Times*, 10 July 1918, final edition, p. 10 - Happenings in Society (col.) Kahn's Lease Camp.

113. The *New York Tribune*, 7 July 1918, p. 5 - Society (col.) Mrs. Otto H. Kahn and her children are coming to Sagamore Lodge.

114. *New York Times*, 25 July 1918, p. 16 - Otto Kahn Returns (rept.).

115. St. Bernard's School Archive: Nowadays, St. Bernard's School no longer holds Chauffeur races or Sister races. Addie Kahn presented a winning cup for a Sports Day sack race in 1919.

116. *TIME* magazine, 19 September 1927, pp. 18 & 20 - Roger Wolfe Kahn.

117. *American Radio History, Radio Personalities - a Pictorial and Biographical Annual*, 1935 - Roger Wolfe Kahn biography, p. 35.

118. The *Brooklyn Daily Eagle*, 8 November 1927, p. 3 - Kahn Abandons Jazz Band To Become Composer; Tells Of His Struggles As A Leader (art.).

119. *TIME* magazine, 19 September 1927, pp. 18 & 20 - Roger Wolfe Kahn.

120. Ibid.

121. The *Outlook*, 5 May 1926, p. 34-36 - Roger Wolfe Kahn; From Riches to Rags by Ernest W. Mandeville (interview & pict.).

122. The *Brooklyn Daily Eagle*, 8 November 1927, p. 3 - Kahn Abandons Jazz Band To Become Composer; Tells Of His Struggles As A Leader (art.).

123. The *World News*, Vol. 32, No. 95, 18 October 1918, p. 12 - Otto Kahn Assails Present Kaiserism (rept.).

124. The *South Bend News-Times*, Vol. 35, No. 286, South Bend, St. Joseph County, 13 October 1918, p. 11 - Notes of the Financial World.

125.   Extract from an address by Otto H. Kahn at the United War Work Campaign Meeting of the Boston Athletic Association in Boston, Massachusetts, 12 November 1918.

126.   The *Indianapolis News*, 21 December 1918, p. 9 - Statement by Kahn.

Notes

* (p. 74) Allegedly, certain individuals had obtained leaked information that suggested the German Government had instructed the president to approach the Allies on the subject of peace. Such negotiations would affect the price of shares.

* (p. 75) Otto filed his application to become a U.S. citizen at Morristown County Court in January 1917. Kahn was determined to change his allegiance before the War but postponed his application for undisclosed reasons. Finally, he became naturalized before the Common Pleas Court in Morristown on March 28, 1917.

* (p. 77) Otto Kahn became a director of American International Corporation. The (AIC) was founded in 1915 by John D. Rockefeller, Andrew Mellon, Andrew Carnegie, and others, 'to develop domestic and foreign enterprises, extend American activities abroad, and promote the interests of American and foreign bankers, business and engineering.'

* (p. 80) A picture of the Cold Spring Harbor mansion (believed to be one of the first impressions of the building to emerge in the press) appeared in the *Brooklyn Daily Eagle* on February 21, 1917.[1] The main house, though still in the throes of completion, was constructed, with its tiled roof and windows in place.

1.   The *Brooklyn Daily Eagle,* 21 February 1917, p. 8 - Residence of Otto H. Kahn on Jericho Turnpike, Woodbury, now in course of construction.

* (p. 88) The birth of jazz evolved over a longer-than-usual pregnancy. The first variant, dubbed 'jass,' arrived around 1914-15 (possibly earlier) in Black clubs and bars in New Orleans and San Francisco. Jazz progressed from 'jass,' which (for abridged purposes) is referenced to one particular recording session in New York City on February 26, 1917. This date was when the Original Dixieland Jass Band laid down *'Dixie Jass Band One-Step'* and *'Livery Stable* Blues' for the Victor record label. Whether these are the first jazz recordings ever made is still a matter open for debate.

* (p. 92) The Pasco County land title deeds were held in a trust in Otto's name.

* (p. 93) Although Otto did not appear in B. C. Forbes' first-ever American Top 30 Rich List published in *Forbes* magazine on March 2, 1918, his ascendency as a high earner, 'enjoying [a] very large income' from banking, was noted.

Chapter 4. The KAHNS of Fifth Avenue

1.   Kahn, Otto H. *Capital and Labor - A Fair Deal* (self publ.) 1919, p.9 - Quote: 'New wealth has been created at the expense of no one.'

2.   1920 U.S. Federal Census, New York, Manhattan - 1100 Fifth Avenue.

3.   *The DeKalb Daily Chronicle*, 23 June 1926, p. 3 - What To See in New York (col.). Also, Genealogy through houses: housebistree.com

4.   The *New York Tribune*, 1 January 1919, p. 11 - Society to Celebrate New Year with Dancing (rept.).

5.   The *South Bend News-Times,* Vol. 36, No. 35, South Bend, St. Joseph County, 4 Feb. 1919, p. 3 - Receives Order of Crown (rept.).

6.   Confirmed by Douglas Brown, archivist at Groton School, 1 April 2017:

Gilbert Kahn, aged 14, entered Groton School (8th grade) in the fall of 1917, and remained until December 1921 (12th grade). He left aged 18, to be tutored at home prior to entering Princeton University.

7.   *The Sun*, 16 February 1919, p. 4 - Florida Resorts Having Best Season in Their History (rept.).

8.   *The Sun*, 9 March 1919, section 3 pictorial review - Pict. of Otto Kahn and friends on Palm Beach.

9.   The *New York Tribune*, 26 March 1919, p. 5 - Brilliant Reception and Dance in Honor of 27th Division (rept.).

10.   Holman Valleri J. *Russian Culture and Theatrical Performance in America, 1891-1933*, Palgrave Macmillan U.S. 2011, p. 43 - Kahn and Carnegie financially sponsored the first Russian theater company (St Petersburg Dramatic Company) to visit the U.S. The company toured in 1905-06 and performed at New York's Herald Square Theatre.

11.   *The Carnegie Alumnus*, May 1926, Vol. 12 No. 4 & 5, p. 6 - Carnegie Corporation of New York, Board of Trustees, Carnegie Institute of Technology Committee: Otto H. Kahn was a trustee on the board of the Carnegie Institute of Technology Committee - one of six 'outside members' who were not on the Carnegie Institute Board of Trustees.

12.   *New York Times*, 25 April 1919 - Golden Rule is Key to Labor.

13.   *The Washington Times*, 24 April 1919, p. 4 - Golden Rule for Workers.

14.   Kahn, Otto H. *Capital and Labor - A Fair Deal* (extracts from an address) (self publ.) 1919, pp. 4-7.

15.   *The Wall Street Journal*, New York, 9 April 1919, p. 9 - Men of Affairs See Good Times Ahead (rept.).

16.   The *Evening Public Ledger*, Philadelphia, 21 May 1919 - News of the Day at a Glance (pict. & capt. of Maud E. Kahn).

17.   The *Great Falls Daily Tribune*, 28 May 1919, p. 12 - Daughter of Famous New York Banker is Home (pict. & capt. of Maud).

18.   The *South Bend News-Times*, Vol. 36, No. 214, South Bend, St. Joseph County, 2 August 1919, p. 5 - Goes Abroad (Society column).

19.   *The Sun*, New York, 16 July 1919, p. 11 - Notes of the Social World.

20.   Biltmore House in North Carolina built by George Washington Vanderbilt II is the largest private residence in the United States.

21.   *The Brooklyn Eagle*, 20 June 1939, p. 2 - Sanitation Men Buy Long Island Estate of Otto Kahn (rept.).

22.   *Town & Country* magazine, 10 October 1920 issue - Cold Spring Harbor - Otto H. Kahn's estate - feature (pict. & art.).

23.   *New York Times*, 12 August 1919 - Carnegie started as a Bobbin Boy (obit.).

24.   *New York Times*, 12 August 1919 - Gifts and Grants by Andrew Carnegie and the Carnegie Corporation of New York up to 1 June 1918.

25.   Ibid.

26.   *Lawrence Daily Journal-World*, Kansas, 2 October 1919, p. 8 - King Albert is First Reigning Monarch to Visit United States (rept.).

27.   *The Sun*, New York, 26 October 1919, p. 10 - Mrs. C. Vanderbilt Hostess to Queen - Reception with music in Fifth Avenue Home (rept.).

28.   *The Sun*, 26 October 1919, p. 10 - King Flies to West Point to Review Cadets; Prince sees Football Game and Queen Visits her Jeweler.

29.   *The Sun*, 24 October 1919, p. 7 - Albert and Queen to Attend Opera.

30.   *New York Times*, 26 October 1919, p. 18 - Albert Sees West Point - Gets Degree at Columbia (rept.).

31.   The *New York Tribune*, 26 October 1919, p. 12 - Huge Crowd in

Metropolitan Welcomes King and Queen (rept.).

32. *New York Times*, 18 November 1919, front page - King Albert Honors Otto H. Kahn (rept.).

33. The Great War & New Jersey, Holdings of Rutgers University Libraries' Special Collections & University Archives, Ac. 1551 - Marianne Goodhue McKeever Papers (Maud E. Kahn awarded the Medal of French Gratitude in 1919).

34. *The Sun*, New York, 19 November 1919, p. 6 - Wales Cheered by Audience at Opera - 4,000 Stand to Welcome Prince (rept.).

35. The *New York Tribune*, 23 November 1919, p. 12 - The Prince's Farewell letter (rept. & pict.).

36. The *New York Tribune*, 23 November 1919, p. 12 - The Prince's Farewell (rept. & pict.).

37. The *New York Tribune*, 7 December 1919, p. 4 - Society Has Many Plans to Assist Charity Work (rept.).

38. The *New York Tribune*, 28 December 1919, p. 10 - *L'oiseau bleu* Premiere at Metropolitan (rev.) by H. E. Krehbiel.

39. *The Sun and New York Herald*, 15 February 1920, section 3, front page - New York's Greatest Social Season at its Close (rept.).

40. The *New York Tribune*, 26 October 1919, p. 37 - Brilliant Season Ready for Society Debutantes; More than 100 girls to be introduced formally.

41. *The New York Herald*, 2 January 1920, part two, p. 6 - Mr. O. H. Kahn's Daughter Makes Debut at Dance (rev.).

42. *The Sun*, 2 January 1920, p. 9 - Mother Gives Dance For Margaret Kahn.

43. The *New York Tribune*, 4 January 1920, p. 45 - Events of the week in the Society World (col.).

44. *The Sun*, 27 January 1920, p. 7 - *What Next!* Opens for a Charity Run.

45. The *New York Clipper*, 21 January 1920 - Beatrice Byrne will be *première danseuse* (rept.).

46. *The World*, 1 February 1920 - *What Next!* (rev.).

47. *The Sun and New York Herald*, 1 February 1920, section 3, front page - *What Next!* picture of the All Night Rollics Girls (L to R) Vouletti T. Proctor, Marianne 'Billy' McKeever, Dolly Kimball, Sheila Byrne, Suzanne Pierson, and Margaret Kahn.

48. *The Washington Herald*, 17 May 1920, p. 9 - Miss Kahn Felicitated at Palm Beach (rept.).

49. *The Sun And New York Herald*, 16 February 1920, p. 9 - Miss Maud Kahn Engaged To Youngest British Major (pict. of Maud).

50. *The Daily Times*, New Philadelphia, 28 February 1920, front page - Engagement of Banker's Daughter and British Officer Reveals War Romance (pict. of Maud and John & rept.).

51. *The Palm Beach Post*, Florida, 19 February 1920, p. 8 - Romance of Pretty Society Girl Had its Inception at her Father's Residence (art.).

52. The moniker 'Gotham' was first given to New York City by the American writer Washington Irving in his 11 November 1807 periodical *Salmagundi*.

53. *The Sun and the New York Herald*, 20 February 1920, p. 9 - Costume Dance at Palm Beach (rept.).

54. *Los Angeles Herald*, 9 March 1920, front page - New War Romance Bared in Pasadena (rept.).

55. The *New York Tribune*, 15 April 1920, p. 15 - Aeros Float Above Merry Spectacle at Aviators' Ball (rept.).

56. The *Brooklyn Daily Eagle*, 4 July 1920, p. 13 - Otto H. Kahn Suggests

57.   New Taxation System to Help Big Business in U.S. (art. & pict. of Otto). The *Indianapolis News*, 14 June 1920, p. 29 - England's Position (rept. & pict. of Otto).

58.   The *Springfield Missouri Republican*, Missouri, 12 June 1920, p. 2 - Settle War Problems (rept.).

59.   The *Indianapolis News*, 14 June 1920, p. 29 - England's Position (rept.).

60.   *Impressions from a Journey in Europe* by Otto H. Kahn, NY, July 1920.

61.   The *New York Tribune*, 16 May 1920, section IV front p. 15 - Miss Maud E. Kahn Selects June 12 as Her Wedding Date (rept.).

62.   The *Washington Herald*, 19 May 1920, p. 9 - Society (col.).

63.   The *New York Tribune*, 18 May 1920, p. 15 - Kahn-Marriott Wedding is set For June 15 (rept.).

64.   The *Sun and New York Herald*, 23 May 1920, section 3, front page - Bride to be at International Marriage (rept. & pict.).

65.   Ibid.

66.   The *Gazette Times*, 13 June 1920, fourth section, front page - Smart Set Chats From New York (col.) by Polly Stuyvesant.

67.   *New York Times*, 8 June 1920, p. 11 - Maud Kahn's Bridal on June 15.

68.   The *Evening Telegram*, New York, 11 June 1920, p. 10 - Announcements of interest to Society (col.) - Mr. Otto H. Kahn will arrive today on the *Celtic* from England.

69.   *New York Times*, 8 June 1920, p. 11 - Maud Kahn's Bridal on June 15.

70.   The *Washington Herald*, 20 June 1920, p. 2 - Wedding of Maud Kahn Picturesque and Brilliant (rept.).

71.   The *Sunday Star*, Washington, 13 June 1920, part 2, p. 4 - Society (col.).

72.   The *Sun and New York Herald*, 16 June 1920, p. 7 - Miss Maud E. Kahn Married to Major John C.O. Marriott (rept. & pict.).

73.   *New York Times*, 8 June 1920, p. 11 - Maud Kahn's Bridal on June 15.

74.   The *Sun and New York Herald*, 8 June 1920, p. 11 - Miss Maud Kahn to be Married in Country Church (rept.).

75.   The *Sun and New York Herald*, 20 June 1920, section 3, front page - Major John C. O. Marriott and his Bride, Who Was Miss Maud E. Kahn, Now on Their Way to Their New Home in England (rept. & picts.).

76.   The *Washington Herald*, 20 June 1920, p. 2 - Wedding of Maud Kahn Picturesque and Brilliant (acct.).

77.   The *Brooklyn Daily Eagle*, 16 June 1920, p. 5 - Brooklyn Society (col.), Miss Kahn's Wedding.

78.   The *Sun and New York Herald*, 16 June 1920, p. 7 - Miss Maud E. Kahn Married to Major John C.O. Marriott (rept. & pict.).

79.   The *Sun and New York Herald*, 23 June 1920 - Ziegfeld *Follies of 1920* a blaze of color and beauty (rev.).

80.   *Impressions from a Journey in Europe* by Otto H. Kahn, publ. New York, July 1920.

81.   The *Rotarian*, October issue 1920, Vol. XVII, No, 4, p. 207 - *The American War Credits* by Otto H. Kahn (art.).

82.   *New York Times*, 7 July 1920, front page - Kahn Sells Cedar Court.

83.   The *Brooklyn Daily Eagle*, 7 July 1920 - The Realty Market (col.) - Otto Kahn Sells Cedar Court (rept.).

84.   The *Jewish Week - American Examiner*, 11 Dec. 1977, p. 40 - Lehman-Kuhn, Loeb union recalls golden era of Jewish leadership (art.).

85.   The *Indianapolis News*, 23 Sept. 1920, p. 7 - Tax System Censored by New York Banker - Otto H. Kahn says methods are too complex (rept.).

86.   The *Pittsburgh Post-Gazette*, 23 October 1920, p. 14 - Kahn Says All

87.   Want Profits Tax Repealed (rept.).
    New York Times, 6 Nov. 1920 - Otto Kahn Upholds His Naturalization; Statement by Cravath Asserts Congress Nullified Technicality (rept.).

88.   The *Brooklyn Daily Eagle*, 6 November 1920, p. 20 - Woman Attacks Citizenship of Otto Kahn, Rich Banker (rept.).

89.   The *New York Herald*, 6 November 1920, p. 9 - Says Otto H. Kahn is not U.S. Citizen (rept.).

90.   *New York Times*, 6 Nov. 1920 - Otto Kahn upholds his Naturalization; Statement by Cravath Asserts Congress Nullified Technicality (rept.).

91.   Ibid.

92.   The *New York Herald*, 6 November 1920, p. 9 - Says Otto H. Kahn is not U.S. Citizen (rept.).

93.   The *Washington Herald*, 7 November 1920, p. 2 - Woman Seeks Data on Kahn Citizenship (rept.).

94.   The *Washington Herald*, 23 November 1920, front page - Otto H. Kahn, New York financier, was legally admitted to citizenship - District Attorney Leroy Ross announced today following investigation (rept.).

95.   The *Courier-News*, Bridgewater, 24 November 1920, p. 9 - Kahn Citizenship Question Settled (rept.).

96.   The *New York Herald*, 23 Nov. 1920, p. 22 - Ross Clears Kahn's Title to Citizenship - Finds Congressional Enabling Act Verifying Rights (rept.).

97.   *New York Times*, 17 November 1920 - Mrs. de Poy duped, he says; Woman Who Attacked Otto Kahn Makes Statement to Prosecutor.

98.   The *Evening World*, 4 December 1920, final edition, p. 6 - Society page.

99.   The *New York Tribune*, 26 December 1920, part IV, front page - Notes of the Social World (col.).

100.   The *World News*, 22 December 1920, p. 2 - Growing Trend in Favor of Some Sort of a Tax on Sales (rept.).

Notes

* (p. 103a) The salon's French Louis XVI neoclassical interior of gilded paneling and arched mirrors initially lined the walls of the receiving room in the Paris mansion of Jean Bretagne Godefroy de la Trémoille on Rue Saint-Dominique. Otto purchased the interior in Paris from a dealer. It was then shipped to New York and installed in the Kahns' palazzo.

* (p. 103b) The interior panels of the elevator still exist and are decorated with a hand-painted floral and bird mural.

* (p. 103c) Each offspring's fourth-floor suite had a shared sitting room, dressing room, bedroom, bathroom, and a walk-in closet.

* (p. 107) Simon Guggenheim superseded his brother Daniel to the position in January 1919.

* (p. 108) On Grievance Day (Tuesday, July 19, 1921), Otto, through his agent, David C. Bennett Jr., complained to the Board of Assessors at Long Island's County Assessor's Office that they had valued his Cold Spring Harbor property too high at $1,094,000, presumably in an attempt to lower his property tax bill.[1]

    1.   The *Long-Islander*, 22 July 1921, p. 5 - Grievance Day (rept.).

* (p. 119) A bureau of information for the Blue Bird Campaign was established inside the Carry On Tea Room at 587 Fifth Avenue.[1]

1.   *New York Tribune*, 21 December 1919, p. 34 - Society Will Be Out In Force at Brilliant Affair Friday Night at the Waldorf-Astoria (rept.).

* (p. 120) This 1919 photograph of the composer Albert Wolff and set designer Boris Anisfeld was taken at the Metropolitan Opera House's stage door during rehearsals of *L'oiseau bleu*. Captured to the left peering through a glass panel in the stage door is the mischievous-looking, 12-year-old Roger W. Kahn. The photograph is housed in the U.S. Library of Congress Prints and Photographs Division, Bain Collection, ID ggbain.29946.

* (p. 121) On August 26, 1920, the 19th Amendment to the U.S. Constitution, granting all American women the right to vote, was officially enacted.

Chapter 5. Gilbert Takes a Hit

1.   The *Chicago Daily Tribune*, Illinois, 15 March 1921, front page - Young Kahn Hit by Auto - He and Girl Near Death (rept.).

2.   The *New York Tribune*, 4 February 1921, p. 11 - Society News - Outbound on the *Aquitania*.

3.   Passenger List: 9 February 1921, RMS *Aquitania* - traveling in first-class, Addie and Roger Kahn.

4.   The *Palm Beach Post*, 14 February 1921, p. 3 - Local Swimming Fans Attend Miami Races (rept.).

5.   The *Philadelphia Inquirer*, 20 March 1921, p. 27 - Palm Beach Homes.

6.   The *New York Herald*, 4 March 1921, p.8 - Shipping News - Steamers Due in New York on 5 March.

7.   *New York Times*, 8 March 1921, p. 16 - England Will Pay, Says Selfridge (rept.) SS *Imperator* Docks.

8.   *The Evening World*, 14 March 1921, p. 5 - Young Kahn Hurt, also Olive Crowe, in Auto Crash (rept.).

9.   The *Brooklyn Daily Eagle*, 14 March 1921, front page - Banker Kahn's Son and Girl Critically Hurt in Collision (Olive Crowe pict. & rept.).

10.   The *Chicago Daily Tribune*, Illinois, 15 March 1921, front page - Young Kahn Hit by Auto - He and Girl Near Death (rept.).

11.   *Turner's Public Spirit*, Ayer, Massachusetts, 19 March 1921, p. 4 - Groton Schoolboy Hurt (rept.) Groton news items (col.).

12.   The *San Francisco Chronicle*, California, 15 March 1921, p. 2 - New York Bankers Son is Hurt (rept.).

13.   *New York Times*, 15 March 1921, p. 7 - Young Kahn Improves (rept.).

14.   The *Brooklyn Daily Eagle*, 14 March 1921, front page - Banker Kahn's Son and Girl Critically Hurt in Collision (Olive Crowe pict. & rept.).

15.   The *Brooklyn Daily Eagle*, 25 March 1921, p. 9 - Kahn Boy Near Father.

16.   The *New York Evening Post*, 15 July 1925, p. 21 - Younger Men of Wall Street (art.).

17.   The *New York Herald*, 5 April 1921, p. 11 - Personal Intelligence (col.) Major and Mrs. John C. O. Marriott of London (rept.).

18.   The *Washington Times*, 3 May 1921, p. 17 - Society (col.) by Jean Eliot - 'Mrs. Kahn, who is with her daughter, Mrs. Marriott.'

19.   New York City Department of Buildings, Manhattan, Plans, Permits and Dockets.

20.   *New York Times*, 26 April 1921, p. 35 - Otto H. Kahn sells his 'new five-story English basement residence' at 8 East 68th Street ... one of three houses built by Mr. Kahn on the site of his former residence (rept.).

21.   *New York Times*, 19 May 1921 - Mr. and Mrs. Otto H. Kahn Form Corporation to Administer $2,000,000 Country Home (rept.).

22. The *South Bend News-Times*, St. Joseph County, 20 April 1921 - Society Now On its Toes (art.) by Helen Hoffman.
23. The *Washington Times*, 3 May 1921, p. 17 - Society (col.) by Jean Eliot - 'Otto Kahn will sail today for Europe on the *Aquitania*, accompanied by his daughter and son, Miss Margaret D. Kahn and Gilbert W. Kahn.'
24. *The Evening Star*, New York, 18 June 1921, front page - Otto H. Kahn Decorated. *Norwich Bulletin*, 20 June 1921, front page - Brief Telegrams (col.). Premier Briand personally decorated Otto H. Kahn.
25. The original book gifted to Otto in Paris in June 1921 by the French Prime Minister Aristide Briand is housed at the Frick Museum, NY.
26. The *South Bend News-Times*, Vol. 38, No. 215, South Bend, St. Joseph County, 3 August 1921, p. 2 - Caruso's Wish Fulfilled as World Mourns.
27. The *New York Tribune*, 10 August 1921, p. 9 - Kahn Delays Sailing.
28. The *New York Herald*, 11 September 1921, p.4 - Noted Portrait Painters in Colony at Deauville (rept.). Orpen, British Artist, Working on Pictures of Mr. Otto H. Kahn and His Daughter.
29. *Maclean's*, 1 November 1921, p. 29 - Where Fools and Money Part by Lord Beaverbrook.
30. Passenger List: 24 August 1921, RMS *Olympic* departs Southampton bound for New York.
31. The *Washington Times*, 25 August 1921, p. 8 - Society (col.).
32. The *New York Tribune*, 12 February 1922, section IV p. 5 - Caruso Memorial Concert Will Be Given Next Sunday (rept.).
33. *New York Times*, 30 September 1921, p. 17 - Otto H. Kahn Sued for Motor Accident (rept.).
34. The *County Review*, Riverhead, Suffolk, 4 November 1921, p. 5 - Cases Tried in The Supreme Court This Week - Otto H. Kahn (rept.).
35. *New York Times*, 2 November 1921, p. 23 - Verdicts Against Kahn - Jury Awards $2,000 to Two Thrown From Carriage (rept.).
36. The *Washington Times*, 4 October 1921, p. 10 - Society (col.).
37. The *Cumberland Evening Times*, 21 December 1920, front page - Tax Law Revision Necessary if Healthy Growth of Business is to Continue.
38. The *New York Tribune*, 15 November 1921, p. 9 - An Audience of Pre-War Brilliancy Hears Galli-Curci in Opening Opera (rev.).
39. *The New York American*, November 1921 - *La traviata* (rev.).
40. The *New York Evening Post*, 15 July 1925, p. 21 - Younger Men Of Wall Street (art.). Gilbert W. Kahn at 22 starts to learn banking preparatory to follow in footsteps of his father.
41. Information provided by Douglas Brown, archivist at Groton School, 1 April 2017.
42. *New York Times*, 11 December 1921, sec. R, p. 142 - Otto H. Kahn as a Boy Felt Like a Plutocrat; Tells School Art League of First Visit to Opera When Rich Host Fell Asleep (rept.).
43. Kahn, Otto H. *Of Many Things*, Boni & Liveright, 1926.
44. The *Evening Star*, 17 February 1922, p. 5 - Epidemic of Flapperitis - Mothers Now Fear for Sons, Girls' - Protective League Told (rept.).
45. The *Ogden Standard Examiner*, Utah, 17 February 1922, p. 2 - Flapperitis has mother's fearing for their sons' (rept.).
46. The *Brooklyn Daily Eagle*, 17 February 1922, p.20 - Do Flappers Vamp Boys? It's 50/50, says Mrs. Payne (rept.).
47. Kivisto, Peter. *Illuminating Social Life*, Sage Publ., 2012, pp. 145-146.
48. The *New York Tribune*, 13 October 1922, p. 13 - Women Indorse Direct Primary and Dry Rule (rept.).

49. At the age of fourteen, the boys at St. Bernard's School graduated from knickerbockers into long trousers. Roger left St. Bernard's School at the age of fourteen and was allowed to wear long pants at home.

50. The *Brooklyn Daily Eagle*, 8 November 1927, p. 3 - Kahn Abandons Jazz Band To Become Composer; Tells Of His Struggles As A Leader (art.).

51. *TIME* magazine, 19 Sept. 1927, pp. 18 & 20 - Roger Wolfe Kahn (art.).

52. *Variety*, 24 March 1922, p. 6 - Palace's Midnight Show (rept.).

53. *American Art News*, Vol. 20, No. 25, 1 April 1922 (rept.).

54. The *New York Tribune*, 5 April 1922, p. 13 - Music Lovers Favor Idea of City Memorial. Mayor Announces he will Approve Bill, After it is Endorsed by Otto H. Kahn and Other Citizens (rept.).

55. *The Leader*, Guthrie, Oklahoma, 16 May 1922, p. 8 - Local News (col.).

56. *American Art News*, 20 May 1922 - Kahn Loans Museum a Carpaccio.

57. *New York Times*, 14 May 1922 - Morgan and Kahn Sail on *Olympic*.

58. The *Hawera & Normandy Star*, 22 May 1922, p. 5 - (rept.).

59. Stravinsky, Igor, and Craft, Robert. *Conversations with Igor Stravinsky* - Doubleday Company Inc., NY, 1959.

60. *Variety*, 16 June 1922, p. 2 - Cables *(Variety*, London office) col. - New Metropolitan Singer (rept.).

61. *New York Times*, 10 June 1922, p. 18 - Strauss to conduct *Salome* for Otto Kahn (rept.).

62. The *Hammond Times*, Vol. 11, No. 22, Lake County, 17 June 1922, p. 8 - New York Letter by Lucy Jeanne Price. Richard Strauss has gone to Vienna to conduct *Salome* in the presence of the Metropolitan powers.

63. Lojkó, Miklós. *Meddling in Middle Europe: Britain and the 'Lands Between, 1919-1925*, Central European University Press, 2005, p. 137, note 35 - Sir William Athelstane Meredith Goode was president of the Austrian Section of the Reparation Commission, 1920-21, and semi-official adviser of the Hungarian Government, 1922-41.

64. The *South Bend News-Times*, Vol. 39, No. 164, South Bend, St. Joseph County, 13 June 1922, p. 5 - Austria Facing Economic Crisis (acct.).

65. *New York Times*, 16 July 1922, p. 3 - Kahn Expects Good Results From Hague (rept.) - (15 July) Banker Looks for Approach to Unity in British, French and American Policies.

66. The *Wisconsin Jewish Chronicle*, Milwaukee, 14 July 1922, p. 8 - Otto Kahn and Max Warburg Expected in The Hague (rept.).

67. *New York Times*, 16 July 1922, p. 3 - Kahn expects good results from Hague (rept.).

68. *The Times*, 17 July 1922, p. 9 - Mr. Kahn On Europe (art.) - Mr. Kahn arrived in London on July 16 from The Hague.

69. Passenger List: 5 August 1922, RMS *Mauretania* departs Southampton bound for New York. Traveling in first-class, Otto Kahn, address Taplow Court, Taplow, Buckinghamshire, accompanied by valet Frederick Cooper and secretary James Dartt.

70. Passenger List: 4 Sept. 1922, RMS *Aquitania* departs Southampton bound for New York. Traveling in first-class: Addie Kahn, Roger Kahn, Margaret Kahn, Gilbert Kahn, Miss Cooper (maid) and Lorraine Doty (teacher). UK address: Taplow Court, Taplow, Buckinghamshire.

71. The *New York Tribune*, 3 September 1922, p. 8 - Justice Brandeis among 12 picked as Leading Jews. Eleven Others Honored When Jewish Tribune Ballots are counted; 174 men and Women Listed.

72. The *New York Tribune*, 8 October 1922, part IV, front page - Shepherd Dog Club Show to be held October 17-18 (rept.).

73.   The *New York Tribune*, 18 October 1922, p. 12 - Police Dogs Have Big Day on Bench in Armory Show (rept.).

74.   The *New York Tribune*, 18 October 1922, p. 8 - Record is set by 205 Dogs in Shepherd Show - German Expert is Judge (rept.).

75.   The *Biddeford Daily Journal*, Front Page, 18 Nov. 1922, America Greets Tiger of France. Clemenceau Coming to Win States to His Nation.

76.   The *Manning Times*, South Carolina, 22 Nov. 1922, p. 7 - 'Clemenceau Visits Home of Roosevelt.' Clemenceau visited Kahn's Long Island estate on Nov. 21, en route to Oyster Bay to pay his respects at Theodore Roosevelt's grave.

77.   *New Castle News*, 22 Nov. 1922, front page & p. 2 - New World War Brewing French 'Tiger' (Clemenceau's nickname) Declares (rept.).

Chapter 6. Ballroom Syncopation

1.   The *Wireless Age*, May 1923 p. 39 - An Interview With Roger Kahn by Sam Loomis (interview).

2.   A photograph exists of Fred and Adele Astaire sitting at a grand piano, with the inscription to 'Gil - Adele and Fred.' The picture was taken in London by James Abbe and presented to Gilbert Kahn by the Astaires.

3.   Levine, p. xii, The Rostovtzeff lectures were published as *The Animal Style in South Russia and China* - Princeton Monographs in Art and Archaeology, 14, Princeton: Princeton University Press, 1929.

4.   *The 1945 Radio Annual - Radio Daily*, p. 37 - Twenty-Five Years of Radio by Frank Burke (art. by the editor of *Radio Daily*) - Dr. Frank Conrad broadcast the returns of the Harding-Cox presidential election from KDKA in Pittsburgh, on 2 November 1920. Historically, 2 November 1920 is considered the birthdate of radio.

5.   The *Wireless Age*, May 1923, p. 39 - An Interview With Roger Kahn by Sam Loomis (interview).

6.   Ibid.

7.   The *Outlook*, 5 May 1926, pp. 34-36 - Roger Wolfe Kahn, From Riches to Rags by Ernest W. Mandeville (interview and pict.).

8.   The *Brooklyn Daily Eagle*, 25 April 1924, p. 24 - One Word After Another (art.).

9.   Photograph of Roger W. Kahn in his laboratory, 30 October 1924, Kadel & Herbert News Photos No. H18194.

10.   *The 1945 Radio Annual - Radio Daily*, p. 37 - Twenty-Five Years of Radio by Frank Burke (art. by the editor of *Radio Daily*).

11.   Margaret Kahn portrait photograph by Arnold Genthe, 20 March 1923, from Genthe's records.

12.   The *New York Clipper*, 9 May 1923, p. 5 - Otto Kahn to Buy Hippodrome, Gest to Stage *The Miracle* (rept.).

13.   The *New York Clipper*, 4 July 1923, p. 6 - No Chance For *The Miracle*.

14.   Roger Wolff Kahn U.S. Passport Application,16 May 1923.

15.   The *Bulletin*, Augusta, 10 November 1923, front page - Priest-Chancellor of Austria Highly Praised by American Financier (rept.).

16.   The *Republic*, Columbus, Indiana, 31 October 1923, p. 2 - A Trio of Financial Powers (pict. & capt.).

17.   *Jewish Post*, Indianapolis, Marion County, 1 Oct. 1943, p. 10 - '20 Years Ago This Week' (col.) Budapest - 'Anep.' organ of the fascist *Awakening Magyars.'* Otto Kahn told the Hungarian authorities his banking firms would not join in any loan to the Hungarian government unless it took steps to stop the discrimination against Jews.

18.   31 October 1923, RMS *Olympic* departs from the UK.

19.   The *New York Clipper*, 9 November 1923, p. 24 - Arthur Lange and Orchestra (twelve-piece) Cinderella Dancing, New York.

20.   *Zanesville Times Signal* (Ohio), 8 June 1924, p. 30 - And the Daddy of Opera Raised a Jazz Baby Boy! (art. and pict.).

21.   *The New Amberola Graphic*, Autumn 1986, No. 58, pp. 6-7 - Life in the Orthophonic Age: Roger Wolfe Kahn (part 1) Prodigy and Pioneer.

22.   *Personalities* Newsreel, 1930s - The narrator labels Roger '*a former disciple of George Gershwin.*' *See* 'Filmography' section in this book.

23.   *American Magazine*, June 1924 - Paul Whiteman Made Jazz Contagious (art.) by Susie Sexton.

24.   *Sheet Music Review*, Feb. 1924 - Popular Music Recital - 'Mr. Whiteman has, for years, been a leader in advancing the cause of popular music and in the introduction of symphonic effect in his orchestra' (rept.).

25.   The *New York Clipper*, 14 December 1923, p. 24 - First American Jazz Concert Will Be Paul Whiteman's (rept.).

26.   *Sheet Music Review*, Feb. 1924 - Popular Music Recital - 'Three or four years ago I was requested by a number of my admirers to give a concert of popular music...' (rept.).

27.   The *New York Clipper*, 14 December 1923, p. 24 - First American Jazz Concert Will Be Paul Whiteman's (rept.).

28.   *Variety*, 7 February 1924, pp. 1 & 15 - 'Otto Kahn incidentally is one of the patrons of the Whiteman concert' - Mina Schall's 'Rich Catch.'

29.   *Literary Digest*, 30 January 1926 - Roger Wolfe Kahn (art.).

30.   The *New York Clipper*, 11 January 1924, p. 23 - Dance Orchestras Favor Films, Preferable to Vaudeville (rept.).

31.   The *New York Clipper*, 14 December 1923, p. 24 - First American Jazz Concert Will Be Paul Whiteman's (rept.).

Notes

* (p. 161) The legal requirement for drivers in New York to possess a license had not yet been passed and would not become law until 1924.

* (p. 165) In 1928, Otto commissioned Arnold Genthe to take a series of photographs capturing the grounds of Kahn's estate at Long Island.

* (p. 173) In 1923, Paul Whiteman and his orchestra made their first tour of England, lasting from March through to August. Accompanying the bandleader was his wife, Mildred. Before returning to the U.S. on the SS *Leviathan*, the couple caught a ferry across the English Channel to France and traveled to Paris, where Whiteman met up with Otto Kahn. During an afternoon meeting (most probably at the Hôtel Ritz), Whiteman broached Otto with a proposal to stage a concert in New York featuring jazz. Whiteman and his wife arrived back in New York on board SS *Leviathan* on August 13, 1923.

* (p. 174) The Arthur Lange Band continued their residency at Cinderella Dancing until the third week in January 1924.[1] After that, they played nightly at the Lomax in the Romax Building, New York.[2] The band remained at the Lomax until the third week in February 1924.

1.   The *New York Clipper*, 18 January 1924, Listings Page - the Arthur Lange Band are listed as appearing at Cinderella Dancing on 18 January 1924.

2.   The *New York Clipper*, 25 January 1924, Listings Page - the Arthur Lange Band are listed as appearing at the Lomax for the week of 28 January 1924.

Chapter 7. A Song With No Key Signature

1. The *New York Evening Post*, 28 March 1924, p. 3 - Otto H. Kahn Hears Son's Jazz Players.

2. *Étude*, XLI, 10 January 1924, pp. 6-8 - What's the Matter with Jazz?

3. *Cine-Journal*, 26 October 1923 - Musical Adaptation of the Guitar and the Jazz Band (art.).

4. Jordan, Matthew F. *Le Jazz: Jazz and French Cultural Identity*, University of Illinois Press, 2010, chapter 3, pp. 87-88 - Contains part of Nivoixs' article.

5. *Brooklyn Life*, 25 October 1924, p. 18 - *The Miracle* (rept.).

6. The *Southern Cross*, 26 April 1924, p. 9 - *The Miracle* Denounced by Anti-Catholics (art.).

7. *Variety*, 12 March 1930, p. 56 - Gest's Bankruptcy Caused by Illness.

8. The *Brooklyn Daily Eagle*, 9 Nov. 1924, p. 68 - *The Miracle* Moves.

9. *New York Times*, 21 January 1924 - Roland Hayes Sings in Otto H. Kahn's Home (rept.).

10. *Variety*, 7 February 1924, pp. 1 & 15 - Mina Schall's 'Rich Catch' (art.) - Otto Kahn's Son, Roger, In Vaudeville With Jazz Band.

11. The *Milwaukee Journal*, 25 April 1939, pp. 1-2 - Famous Son, Famous Bandleader, Famous Flier (art.).

12. *Variety*, 30 September 1925, p. 46 - Otto told him (Roger) to eschew all mention of the family name in his professional career' (rev.).

13. The *New York Clipper*, 8 February 1924, p. 17 - Otto H. Kahn's Two Sons Broadway Jazz Musicians. *The New York Clipper*, 29 February 1924, p. 17 - More Kahn Publicity When Cabaret Opens (rept.).

14. The *New York Post*, 11 January 1924, p. 9 - Society of Artists' Dinner.

15. The *New York Clipper*, 15 February 1924, pp. 13, 15 & 17 - Whiteman's Jazz Recital - An Experiment in Modern Music (art.) by Abel Green.

16. *Variety*, 7 April 1926, p. 3 - London As It Looks (col.) by Hannen Swaffer - Gershwin Remembers - Cigarette case given as present.

17. The *New York Clipper*, 15 Feb. 1924, pp. 13, 15 & 17 - Whiteman's Jazz Recital - An Experiment in Modern Music - 'Paul Whiteman's jazz recital at Aeolian Hall, New York, the afternoon of February 12, was a complete success as an experiment in modem music' (art.).

18. The *New York Clipper*, 15 February 1924, pp. 1 & 31 - Otto H. Kahn Not Displeased With Son (rept.).

19. The *Journal News*, Ohio, 13 Feb. 1931, p. 6 - Young Roger Kahn, Son of Banker, has Already Earned $40,000 Chose his Own Career in Music, Now Marries his Principal Dancer. *New York Herald Tribune*, 9 February 1931, front page & p. 2 - Secretly Married (pict. and rept.).

20. *Zanesville Times Signal*, Ohio, 8 June 1924, p. 30 - And The Daddy of Opera Raised a Jazz Baby Boy (art.) by Mildred Hardenbergh.

21. Sammarco, Anthony Mitchell. *Milton: A Compendium*, The History Press, 2010, pp. 137-138.

22. *Popular Science,* January 1928 issue, p. 136 - Invention - Hobby of Great men (art.).

23. *Zanesville Times Signal*, Ohio, 8 June 1924, p. 30 - 'And The Daddy of Opera Raised a Jazz Baby Boy' (art.) by Mildred Hardenbergh.

24. The *New York Clipper*, 25 January 1924 - (Listings) - The Arthur Lange Band is listed as appearing at the Lomax in the Romax Building, New York, week commencing 28 January 1924.

25. *The Outlook*, 5 May 1926, pp. 34-36 - Roger Wolfe Kahn, From Riches to Rags by Ernest W. Mandeville (interview and pict.).

26. The *New York Clipper*, 15 Feb. 1924 - (Listings) - The Arthur Lange Band at the Lomax, Romax Building, New York, week 28 January 1924.

27. The *Sun and the Globe*, 26 February 1924 - Knickerbocker Grill (advt.).

28. The *Evening Independent*, Ohio, 20 March 1934, p. 7 - The former Knickerbocker Hotel was called the 'Crossroads of the World.'

29. *New York Times*, 27 February 1924 - Otto H. Kahn's Son Fails To Play Jazz; Respects His Father's Opposition to His Appearance as a Saxophonist at a Cabaret (rept.).

30. The *Sun And The Globe*, 8 March 1924, p. 5 - 'The Roger Wolfe (Kahn) Orchestra, of which Arthur Lange is director, is winning increasing favor at the Knickerbocker Grill ... playing an extended engagement.'

31. The *Sun*, 19 March 1924, p. 19 - R. W. Kahn's Orchestra to Stage 'London Night' (rept.) Kahn gets his musicians union card.

32. The *Reading Eagle*, 28 February 1924, front page - Banker's Son Joins Union (rept.).

33. Ibid.

34. The *New York Clipper*, 29 February 1924, p. 17 - More Kahn Publicity When Cabaret Opens (rept.).

35. The *Outlook*, 5 May 1926, pp. 34-36 - Roger Wolfe Kahn; From Riches to Rags by Ernest W. Mandeville (interview & pict.).

36. *Variety*, 30 December 1925, p. 23 - An Example For Boys - Some Inside Stuff On Roger Wolfe Kahn (rept.).

37. The *New York Clipper*, 29 February 1924, p. 7 - More Kahn Publicity When Cabaret Opens (rept.) - Otto Kahn's Other Son Runs Counter to Father, While Strumming Banjo.

38. The *Brooklyn Daily Eagle*, 10 March 1929, p. 3 (suppl.) - Upsetting Family Tradition by Louis Fribourg (art.).

39. The *New York Clipper*, 29 February 1924, p. 17 - Here and There (col.).

40. *Zanesville Times Signal*, Ohio, 8 June 1924, p. 30 - And The Daddy of Opera Raised a Jazz Baby Boy (art.) by Mildred Hardenbergh.

41. The *Brooklyn Daily Eagle*, 8 November 1927, p. 3 - Kahn Abandons Jazz Band To Become Composer; Tells Of His Struggles As A Leader (art.).

42. *Brooklyn Life*, 15 March 1924 p. 23 - Those Who Can't Resist (col.).

43. The *Sun*, 19 March 1924, p. 19 - R. W. Kahn's Orchestra to Stage 'London Night' (rept.).

44. The *Sun and The Globe*, 26 February 1924, p. 19 - Dance Wave Sweeps London (rept.).

45. *New York Evening Post*, Tuesday, 11 March 1924, p. 2 - Blocked Otto Kahn's Car.

46. The *New York Clipper*, 13 March 1924, p. 13 - Unusual Radio Features Tuesday in Music, Remarks and People - Kahn's Band Broadcast.

47. Ibid.

48. *Radio Digest*, Illustrated, 22 March 1924, p. 16 - Radio Listings - Wednesday 19 March - WJY Radio, New York - 10:30, Roger Wolfe's Hotel Knickerbocker Grill Orchestra live transmission.

49. The *Brooklyn Daily Eagle*, 12 March 1924, p. 11 - Gatti-Casazza Renews Contract (rept.).

50. The *Brooklyn Daily Eagle*, 8 June 1924, p. 2 - Opera Plans for 1924-25 Announced by Gatti-Casazza (rept.).

51. The *New York Clipper*, 6 March 1924, p. 13 - Band Leaders, Efficiency Men - Rule now is Business on Business Line - Good Management.

52. The *Evening News*, Harrisburg, PA, 20 March 1924, p. 10 - Knickerbocker Fires Kahn Orchestra (rept.).

53. The *Evening News*, Harrisburg, PA, 20 March 1924, p. 10 - Knickerbocker Fires Kahn Orchestra (rept.) - 'The orchestra will do a little radio broadcast tonight, through Station BO.' Station BO could, possibly, have been WABO in Rochester, NY.

54. The *New York Evening Post*, 21 March 1924, p. 11 - Many Activities Planned For Post Lenten season - Social Activities (rept.).

55. *The Sun*, 22 March 1924, p. 9 - Peoples Chorus Gives Afternoon of Songs Today (rept.).

56. *The Jewish Transcript*, Seattle, Washington, 25 March 1924, front page - Otto Kahn of New York (rept.).

57. Lundberg, Ferdinand. *America's 60 Families*, The Vanguard Press, 1937.

58. *New York Times*, 1 to 15 September 1925 - tax figures taken from various reports in the *New York Times*.

59. The *Brooklyn Daily Eagle*, 30 March 1924, (Sunday Eagle Magazine suppl.) page two - Gilbert Kahn - Banker's Son, Jazz Leader (art.).

60. Ibid.

61. *Zanesville Times Signal*, Ohio, 8 June 1924, p. 30 - And The Daddy of Opera Raised a Jazz Baby Boy (art.).

62. The *Brooklyn Daily Eagle*, 27 March 1924, p. A8 - On The Screen (rept.) by Martin B. Dickstein - *The Dawn of a Tomorrow* at the Rivoli Theatre.

63. The *New York Evening Post*, 28 March 1924, p. 3 - Otto H. Kahn Hears Son's Jazz Players (rept.).

64. The *New York Clipper*, 10 April 1924, p. 17 - Roger Wolfe's Orchestra With Arthur Lange Conducting, Rivoli, New York (rev.).

65. The *New York Sun*, 23 April 1924 - report by Albert Haim.

66. Riggio, Thomas P. *Theodore Dreiser Letters to Women: New Letters, Vol. 2*, University of Illinois Press, 2009, p. 177.

67. *Brooklyn Life*, 5 April 1924, p. 23 - Society (col.) - Those who sailed last Wednesday [2 April] on the RMS *Berengaria* included Master John Marriott, grandson of Mr. and Mrs. Otto H. Kahn, and his nurse.

68. The *Brooklyn Daily Eagle*, 4 May 1924, p. 2B - News and Views on Current Art - Portrait of Miss Margaret Kahn by Zuloaga (pict.).

69. The *Brooklyn Daily Eagle*, 27 April 1924, p. 2B - Carnegie Salon Opens Doors to Modern Art (rev.). *The American Magazine of Art*, Vol. 15, No. 7, July 1924 pp. 337-344 - Contemporary Painting (art. incl. pict.). Portrait of Miss Margaret Kahn by Ignacio Zuloaga shown in the 23rd International Exhibition Carnegie Institute, Pittsburgh.

70. The *Brooklyn Daily Eagle*, 19 April 1924, p. 7 - Roger Kahn Becomes Popular Song Writer; His Effort Named *'Why!'*

71. *New York Times*, 19 April 1924 - Roger W. Kahn Sells a Foxtrot.

72. The *Music Trade Review*, 3 May 1924, p. 53 - Roger Wolfe Kahn Song.

73. The *Brooklyn Daily Eagle*, 25 April 1924, p. 24 - One Word After Another (art.) by Nunnally Johnson.

74. The *New York Clipper*, 4 July 1923, p. 14 - Nat'l., Music Week Next Spring (rept.).

75. www.nfmc-music.org - National Music Week (page). How did National Music Week begin? (history).

76. Tremaine, C. M. *History of National Music Week*, National Bureau for the Advancement of Music, NY, 1925, chapter 1, The Underlying Philosophy.

77. Tremaine, C. M. *History of National Music Week*, National Bureau for the Advancement of Music, NY, 1925, Foreword, Otto Kahn quotation.

78. The *Brooklyn Daily Eagle*, 4 May 1924, p. 4E - Roger Kahn and his Band in Phonofilms (rept.).
79. *Zanesville Times Signal*, Ohio, 8 June 1924, p. 30 - And The Daddy of Opera Raised a Jazz Baby Boy (art.).
80. The *New York Clipper*, 8 May 1924, p. 32 - Kahn's Band Replaces Rapp.
81. The *Music Trade Review*, 17 May 1924, p. 39 - Roger Wolfe Kahn At The Palais Royal (rept.).
82. The *Music Trade Review*, 17 May 1924, p. 50 - W. Kahn Features '*Why!*'
83. *San Antonio Express*, 8 May 1924, p. 5 - Millionaire's Heir Makes His Debut as Jazz Band Banjoist (rept.) Associated Press, New York.
84. The *Brooklyn Daily Eagle*, 24 May 1924, p. 4 - City to Hold 'May Day on Green' This Afternoon (rept.).
85. *Brooklyn Life*, 31 May 1924, p. 17 - *Lido Venice* Society's Own (rept.).
86. *Variety*, 23 July 1924, p. 38 - Palais Royal is to Reopen - Under New Name - Court Order Granted, with Restrictions (rept.).
87. *Variety*, 25 June 1924, pp. 9 & 47 - Inside Stuff on Vaudeville (col.).
88. The *Brooklyn Daily Eagle*, 07 June 1924, p. 14A - Saxophone Sales Pile Up to $20,000,000 During Year - Make Big Record (rept.).
89. *Variety*, 3 September 1924 - Band and Orchestra Reviews.
90. The *New Yorker*, 24 October 1925 - John McEntee Bowman personally hires the Roger Wolfe Kahn Orchestra (rept.).
91. *The Outlook*, 5 May 1926, pp. 34-36 - Roger Wolfe Kahn; From Riches to Rags by Ernest W. Mandeville (interview & pict.).
92. *Variety*, 11 June 1924, p. 7 - Kahn Band at Biltmore (rept.).
93. *Variety*, 4 June 1924, p. 3 - Kahn's Band To Sail - June 15 (rept.).
94. The *Brooklyn Daily Eagle*, 6 June 1924, p. 11 - Many At Opening.
95. *New York Evening Post*, 6 June 1924, p. 11 - About People You Know.
96. The *Outlook*, 5 May 1926, pp. 34-36 - Roger Wolfe Kahn; From Riches to Rags by Ernest W. Mandeville (interview & pict.).
97. The *Pittsburgh Post-Gazette*, PA, 21 June 1924, front page - Down With Parents, Tyranny, Crusade Cry (rept.).
98. *Nottingham Evening Post*, 1 July 1924, p. 4 - Jazz King's Outfit - Mr. Roger Wolfe Kahn, son of Otto Kahn, is expected in London tomorrow with the largest collection of musical instruments ever brought to England by any one individual for his own amusement (rept.).
99. Passenger List: 2 July 1924, RMS *Berengaria* arrives at Southampton from New York. Traveling in first-class, Addie and Roger Kahn, accompanied by Jacques Kasner (violinist).
100. Passenger List: 13 June 1924, RMS *Olympic* arrives at Southampton. Traveling in first-class, Otto Kahn - address, Claridge's, London.
101. Jane Compton blog - Gershwin in New York (WordPress).
102. *New York Evening Post*, 3 October 1924, p. 2 - Hoot Mon! Roger Kahn Home To Give Jazz A Little Scotch (rept.).
103. The *New York Clipper*, 28 June 1924, p. 37 - Band And Orchestra Reviews - Roger Wolfe Kahn's Orchestra (rev.).
104. The *New York Clipper*, 14 June 1924, p. 2 - Kahn Band Sticks (rept.).
105. *Variety*, 30 December 1925, p. 23 - An Example For Boys - Some Inside Stuff On Roger Wolfe Kahn (rept.).
106. *Variety*, 9 July 1924, p. 11 - Roger Kahn May Become Legit Producer.
107. Ibid., 35 - Cabarets (col.).
108. The *Brooklyn Daily Eagle*, 5 July 1924, p. 11 - Features of Next Week's Radio - Tuesday (listings).
109. The *Brooklyn Daily Eagle*, 12 July 1924, p. 4 - WJZ Radio station - Radio

110. *Variety*, 23 July 1924, p. 38 - Abel's Comment by Abel Green - Unknown leading Band in Vaudeville (col.).
111. *Variety*, 20 August 1924, p. 2 - Americans In Europe (col.) report from Paris, 4 August 1924.
112. *Brooklyn Life*, New York, 5 July 1924, p. 10 - Mrs. Otto Kahn and her son Roger sail on the RMS *Berengaria* (rept.).
113. *New York Times*, 13 August 1924 - Jazz Music Upheld by Otto H. Kahn - Among the passengers who arrived yesterday from Southampton and Cherbourg on the White Star liner *Majestic* was Otto H. Kahn (rept.).
114. Passenger List: 8 August 1924, RMS *Olympic* arrives at Southampton from New York. Traveling in first-class, Gilbert Kahn, aged 21. UK address: Whittingehame, Prestonkirk, Scotland.
115. The *Brooklyn Daily Eagle*, 8 August 1924, p. 14 - Roger Kahn Writes Jazz Campaign Song for Coolidge (rept.).
116. The *New York Evening Post*, 12 August 1924, p. 11: Society In The Suburbs, Long Island. Kahn writes jazz campaign song for Coolidge.
117. The *Detroit Free Press*, 8 August 1924, p. 4 - Coolidge Puts O.K. on Campaign Song by Boy, 16 (rept.).
118. *Variety*, 8 February 1939, p. 47 - 15 years Ago (from *Variety*) column.
119. *Variety*, 27 August 1924, p. 38 - Abel's Comment (col.) by Abel Green.
120. *Variety*, 10 Sept. 1924, p. 40 - Abel's Comment (col.) by Abel Green.
121. *Variety*, 27 August 1924, p. 15 - Hippodrome (rev.).
122. Ibid., & *Variety*, 3 September 1924, p. 40 - Roger Wolfe Orchestra (12) Hippodrome (rev.).
123. *Variety*, 30 September 1925, p. 46 - Inside Stuff on Music (col.) - What The Queen Thinks of Jazz - An off the cuff remark by Col. Mackenzie-Rogan, trainer of the Guards' bands of the British Army, made during his visit to Toronto to take part in the 1925 Canadian Exhibition.
124. *Variety*, 10 September 1924, p. 40 - Abel's Comment (col.) by Abel Green - The Prince, Mr. Mackay, and Bands.
125. *Brooklyn Life*, 16 May 1925, p.11 - Society: The Prince of Wales' 1924 visit to Long Island where he stayed at the Burdens Syosset estate.
126. Passenger List: 30 September 1924, RMS *Aquitania* departs Southampton. Traveling in first-class, Addie Kahn, Roger Kahn, and Jacques Kasner - address, Claridge's, London.
127. *Variety*, 24 September 1924, p. 26B - Lange Quits Kahn Band.
128. *Variety*, 5 November 1924, p. 38 - Arthur Lange and Orchestra (fourteen-piece) Fay Follies Club, New York (rev.).
129. *The New Yorker*, 24 October 1925, p. 3 - Roger Wolfe (rept.).
130. *Rome Daily Sentinel*, New York, 9 October 1924, front page - Anne Elizabeth Whelan to Wed Gilbert W. Kahn (rept.).
131. The *Brooklyn Daily Eagle*, 10 November 1924, p. 22 - Gilbert Kahn Gets License To Marry Anne Whelan (rept.).
132. *New York Times*, 27 October 1924, p. 18 - Favors Otto H. Kahn For Mayor.
133. The *Brooklyn Daily Eagle*, 20 November 1924, p. 7 - Society (col.) - Miss Whelan Bride of Gilbert W. Kahn.
134. The *New York World*, 20 November 1924 - Miss Anne Elizabeth Whelan Marries Gilbert W. Kahn (rept.).
135. *Variety*, 3 September 1924, p. 18 - Opera and Concert by John H. Raftery (art.).
136. The *Brooklyn Daily Eagle*, 12 November 1924, p. 5 - Brooklyn Little

Theatre Movement Gains Momentum as Otto H. Kahn and Others Praise Project at Meeting of Workers (rept.).

137. The *Musical Observer*, May 1924 edition - Vincent Lopez Comments on his Unique Experiment (art.).

138. *Collier's Magazine*, 13 March 1925 - Vincent Lopez (art.).

139. *Springfield Missouri Republican*, 14 December 1924, p. 28 - Symphonic Jazz Concert by Vincent Lopez and his Augmented Orchestra of Forty Selected Soloists, Metropolitan Opera House, Sunday, 23 Nov. 1924.

140. *Music Courier*, 20 November 1924 - Kahn On Jazz.

141. The *Music Trade News*, 28 November 1924 - Musical News (col.) - Kahn Wants A Jazz Opera to Produce On Metropolitan Stage.

142. *Springfield Missouri Republican*, 14 December 1924, p. 28 - Symphonic Jazz Concert by Vincent Lopez and his Augmented Orchestra of Forty Selected Soloists, Metropolitan Opera House, Sunday, 23 Nov. 1924.

143. The *New York Evening Post*, 9 December 1924, p. 11 - Jazz By Radio For Europe - Supper Crowds in Capitals to Dance to Music Broadcast by Wanamaker's (rept.).

144. The *Evening Independent*, St Petersburg, 23 December 1924, p. 21 - Financier's Son Starts as Clerk (rept.).

145. *Radio Digest*, 20 December 1924, p. 16 - Radio listings.

146. The *Brooklyn Daily Eagle*, 24 December 1924, p. 8A - Radio Programs.

Notes

* (p. 176) An alternative interpretation of Otto's original 1924 quotation, *'Jazz is America's contribution to music. It is the artistic expression of American exuberance,'* appeared in print many years later accredited to saxophonist and educator Ahmad Alaadeen. Alaadeen's citation, *'Jazz does not belong to one race or culture but is a gift that America has given the world,'* has since been used to explain how jazz originated. Alaadeen was born in 1934, ten years after Otto first made his citation. Otto's quote was widely documented in newspapers of the day.

* (p. 179) Otto had initially hoped to stage *The Miracle* in New York City at Madison Square Garden in 1914. *New York Times*, 14 May 1914, n. p. - *The Miracle* for Madison Square Garden (rept.).

* (p. 180) Victor ledger - matrix (trial 1924-02-04-05), *'What Do You Do Sunday, Mary?'* Roger Wolfe and Orchestra. Victor ledger - matrix (trial 1924-02-04-06) *'You'*, Roger Wolfe and Orchestra. *'What Do You Do Sunday, Mary?'* was from the Broadway stage musical *Poppy*.

* (p. 185) News reports stated Igor Stravinsky attended the concert. However, after I contacted the Fondation Igor Stravinsky to verify this, they informed me that it was incorrect, as Stravinsky was on a European concert tour through January-March 1924.

* (p. 186) On February 14, Otto's name was mentioned before the Senate committee in Washington, D.C., regarding an investigation into an oil scandal and a mysterious 'million-dollar slush fund.' The fund had allegedly been put on deposit in Washington 'for distribution among men in high places' and set up by oilmen interested in providing leases for government officials'.[1] Otto sent a telegram the following day from Palm Beach to Chairman Lenroot of the Senate committee categorically denying any knowledge of the fund.[2]

1. *The Daily Banner*, Greencastle, 14 February 1924, p. 1 - Slush Fund Raised by The Oil Interests (rept.).

2. *New York Times*, 17 February 1924, p. 2 - Kahn Awaits Subpoena; New York Banker Again Disclaims Dealing With Oil Men (rept.).

* (p. 187) Mabel Hunt was born in 1865 to parents William Morris Hunt (artist) and Louisa Dumeresq Hunt. In 1924, Mabel was aged 59. She died in 1942.

* (p. 198) *The Suffolk County News*, 28 March 1924, p. 6 - Island News Notes.

* (p. 201) Songwriter Herbert P. Stothart, in later years, went on to write the score for the movie *The Wizard of Oz*, for which he received an Academy Award.

* (p. 208) Roger also conducted the orchestra that evening for the actor and dancer Clifton Webb and his dance partner Bonnie Glass, who performed for the audience. *New York Times*, 7 May 1924, n. p. - Roger Wolfe Kahn (rept.).

* (p. 218) When Roger returned to New York in early October 1924, he brought with him a set of bagpipes,[1] and announced to the press he was contemplating forming a bagpipe jazz band with all the musicians clad in kilts.[2]

1. The *Journal News*, Ohio, 13 February 1931, p. 6 - Young Roger Kahn Has Already Earned $40,000. Chose His Own Career In Music (rept.) - Mr. Kahn went to Europe in 1924 for 'serious study' and surprised his father when he returned with a bagpipe.
2. The *Sunday Post*, Scotland, 14 September 1924, p. 11 - Bagpipe Jazz Band - 'Roger Wolfe Kahn, chief of the famous Wolfe Dance Band of New York, has been experimenting with jazz selections on bagpipes while holidaying in Scotland.'

* (p. 221) Italian-born Domenico Savino had migrated to the States early in the 20th century to further his music career. It was Savino who brought to America actor Rudolph Valentino. Hugo Frey and Domenico Savino both became powerhouse arrangers, conductors, and composers and were in huge demand by many large orchestras in classical and popular music.

PART II. SITTING ON TOP OF THE WORLD   1925–1929

Chapter 8. Howling Wolfe

1. The *Brooklyn Daily Eagle*, 30 March 1924, p. 2 - Gilbert Kahn - Bankers Son - Jazz Leader (art.).
2. Letter from Otto H. Kahn to James B. Pond dated 2 January 1925.
3. *Literary Digest*, 30 January 1926 - King Jazz and the Jazz Kings.
4. The *Palm Beach Post*, 27 February 1925, p. 12 - Kentucky Serenaders at The Belleview, Belleair, Palm Beach (advt.).
5. *Variety*, 28 January 1925, p. 50 - Actor's Fund Benefit (rev.).
6. *Variety*, 28 January 1925, p. 9 - Vaudeville Reviews - The Hippodrome.
7. *New York Times*, 15 February 1925 - Otto H. Kahn Sails - Banker to Visit Most of the Capitals of Europe (rept.).
8. The *New York Evening Post*, 7 March 1925, p. 4 - Of Interest in Washington Society (col. 2).
9. Ibid.
10. The *New York Evening Post*, 9 March 1925, p. 9 - The Oranges (rept.).
11. A letter of Reference signed by Addie Kahn for Robert McCulloch, bearing the address, Eleven Hundred Fifth Avenue, dated October 20, 1932, exists. The letter regards the employment of Robert McCulloch as Addie's chauffeur for seven and a half years.

12.   Source: *Encyclopedic Dictionary of Victor Recordings.*
13.   *Variety,* 8 April 1925, p. 48 - 2 New Victor Bands (rept.).
14.   The *Brooklyn Daily Eagle,* 23 April 1925, p. 9 - Victor Records (advt.).
15.   The *Brooklyn Daily Eagle,* 24 March 1925, p. 8 - 100 Fight Grass Fire.
16.   *The Outlook,* 5 May 1926, pp. 34-36 - Roger Wolfe Kahn; From Riches to Rags by Ernest W. Mandeville (interview & pict.).
17.   *Variety,* 15 April 1925, p. 39 - Inside Stuff on Music (col.).
18.   *Variety,* 8 April 1925, p. 47 - Here and There (col.).
19.   *Variety,* 22 April 1925, p. 37 - Inside Stuff on Music (col.).
20.   The *Brooklyn Daily Eagle,* 14 April 1925, p. 11 - In Brooklyn Theaters, Theatrical Notes (rept.).
21.   Goodman, Benny, and Kolodin, Irving. *The Kingdom of Swing,* Stackpole Sons, NY, 1939, p. 84 - June 1925: Joe Venuti was offered an engagement in New York in a band directed by Roger Wolfe Kahn.
22.   *New York Times,* 17 May 1925 - French Fete Otto H. Kahn (rept.).
23.   The *Cincinnati Enquirer,* 10 June 1925, p. 3 - Kahn Misquoted: In European Speeches, He Says Debt Criticism Denied (rept.).
24.   The *London Evening News,* 5 June 1925 - Interview with Otto Kahn.
25.   The *Cincinnati Enquirer,* 10 June 1925, p. 3 - Otto Kahn, prominent New York banker, returning on the *Majestic* today (rept.).
26.   The *New York Evening Post,* 12 June 1925, p. 12 - After Theater Entertainment (col.) Roger Wolfe Kahn Orchestra opens at Cascades.
27.   *Variety,* 1 July 1925, p. 18 - '*I'm For You*' Is Kahn's Title - Bankers Son Likes Show Business (rept.).
28.   *Variety,* 20 May 1925, p. 24 - Young Kahn As Composer (rept.).
29.   *Variety,* 10 June 1925, p. 24 - Royce Gets Kahn Show; Boys Father May Help (rept.).
30.   The *New Yorker,* 20 June 1925, p. 19 - A rumor is circulated that Roger wants to become a detective! (rept.).
31.   The *Springfield Leader,* Missouri, 26 July 1925, p. 27 - Hist! 'Tis Roger the Boy Detective of the '400' (art.) Son of Otto Kahn Has Set Himself the Task of Snaring 'Society Crooks' (pict.).
32.   The *Chicago Daily Tribune,* 11 November 1930, p. 22 - Receivers are appointed for Cosden Oil Co. (rept.).
33.   The *Springfield Leader,* Missouri, 26 July 1925, p. 27 - Hist! 'Tis Roger the Boy Detective of the '400' (art.) Son of Otto Kahn Has Set Himself the Task of Snaring 'Society Crooks' (pict.).
34.   The *Brooklyn Daily Eagle,* 13 June 1925, p. 6 - Seven Years of Progress.
35.   *New York Times,* 3 October 1925, p. 17 - Donahue Gem Theft Seen as Inside Job. *Life,* 12 March 1956, Vol. 40 No. 11, pp. 121-136 - Confessions of Master Jewel Thief by Robert Wallace (art.). Arthur Barry, great second-story man, looks back on a $10m life in crime.
36.   Passenger List: 16 July 1925, RMS *Olympic,* arrives Southampton from New York. Traveling in first-class, Addie Kahn, her maid (Madelein Garcin, French citizen), and Felix Kahn - address, Claridge's, London.
37.   *Brooklyn Life* and Activities of Long Island Society, 16 May 1925, p. 11 - On 4 June the gardens of Mrs. Otto H. Kahn at Woodbury will be opened to the public (rept.).
38.   Passenger List: 14 July 1925, RMS *Berengaria* arrives Southampton from New York. Traveling in first-class, Gilbert Kahn and his wife Anne, and lady's maid Marie Metzner - address, Claridge's, London.
39.   The *New York Evening Post,* 15 July 1925, p. 21 - Younger Men of Wall Street (art.) by Frank J. Williams.

40.   *New York Times*, 21 June 1925, p. 5 - Weekend Trip to Halifax.
41.   *Brooklyn Life*, 22 August 1925, p. 13 - Huntington (col.).
42.   Joe Venuti biography on the Eddie Lang website eddielang.com.
43.   *Presto* magazine, Sept. 1925 issue, p. 20 - Uses Conn Instruments,
44.   *Variety*, 26 August 1925, p. 30 - Roger Kahn's Jazz School (rept.).
45.   *Variety*, 16 September 1925, p. 44 - Kahn's Score and School (rept.).
46.   The *New York Evening Post*, 2 September 1925, p. 6 - Kahn Jr., Plans
      Jazz School (rept.).
47.   The *Music Trade Review*, 21 November 1925, p. 54 - The Roger Wolfe
      Kahn School of Dance Music opened on Wednesday of this week.
48.   *Variety*, 26 August 1925, p. 30 - Roger Kahn's Jazz School (rept.).
49.   *Variety*, 30 December 1925, p. 23 - An Example For Boys - Some Inside
      Stuff On Roger Wolfe Kahn (rept.).
50.   Passenger List: 2 Sept. 1925, RMS *Majestic*, departs Southampton for
      New York. Traveling in first-class, Gilbert Kahn and Anne Kahn, and
      their French maid Margaret Metzner.
51.   1925 State Census (1 June 1925) - Residing at 1100 Fifth Avenue: Otto,
      Addie, Margaret, and Roger. Roger's work is listed as a musical
      director. The English housekeeper is Mary Hogsett (aged 59). 14
      servants and the Scottish cook Jessie Macrea are also resident.
52.   *The New Yorker*, 17 April 1926 - The Talk of The Town (col.) Success.
53.   *Variety*, 9 September 1925, p. 51 - half-page advt.
54.   *Variety*, 30 September 1925, p. 60 - Roger Wolfe Kahn Orchestra
      Vaudeville Tour (advt.).
55.   The *New York Evening Post*, 18 September 1925, p. 12 - Roger Wolfe
      Kahn and his Orchestra at the Palace Theatre (rept.).
56.   *Brooklyn Life,* 3 October 1925, p. 16 - Plays and Players (section).
57.   The *Brooklyn Daily Eagle*, 4 October 1925, p. 2E - Vaudeville Theaters,
      Nora Bayes and Roger Wolfe Kahn and His Orchestra (rev.).
58.   The *Brooklyn Daily Eagle*, 4 October 1925, p. 3E - Kahn and Jazz.
59.   *Variety*, 30 September 1925, p. 46 - Vaudeville Reviews - Riverside.
60.   *Variety*, 7 October 1925, p. 15 - Vaudeville Reviews - Albee Theatre,
      Brooklyn.
61.   *Variety*, 30 September 1925, p. 5 - Kahn's Quick Return (rept.).
62.   *Variety*, 14 October 1925, p. 45 - Inside Stuff on Music (col.) Young
      Kahn and his Music.
63.   *Variety*, 14 October 1925, p. 14 - New Acts This Week Reviews: The
      Palace, New York: Roger Wolfe Kahn (rev.).
64.   *Variety*, 14 October 1925, p. 15 - Vaudeville Reviews: The Palace, New
      York (rev.).
65.   *Variety*, 14 October 1925, p. 14 - New Acts This Week Reviews: The
      Palace, New York: Roger Wolfe Kahn (rev.).
66.   *Variety*, 28 October 1925, p. 39 - Kahn's Concert Tour (rept.) Kahn's
      birthday gift from band.
67.   *Variety*, 30 September 1925, p. 46 - Band and Orchestra Reviews:
      Roger Wolfe Kahn and His Hotel Biltmore Orchestra at the Cascades.
68.   Ibid.
69.   *Variety*, 30 December 1925, p. 23 - An Example For Boys - Some Inside
      Stuff On Roger Wolfe Kahn (rept.).
70.   The *Music Trade Review*, 5 Sept. 1925, p. 61 - Kahn Writing Comedy.
71.   *Variety*, 2 September 1925, p. 39 - Inside Stuff On Music (col.) - Young
      Kahn's Versatility.
72.   *Variety*, 30 September 1925, p. 45 - Band-men Authoring (rept.).

73.   The *Music Trade Review*, 24 October 1925, p. 42 - Conn Line Featured by Kahn Orchestra Tour (rept.).

74.   *'Bam Bam Bamy Shore'* and *'Look Who's Here'* recorded October 1925.

75.   *Presto*, 24 October 1925, p. 23 - Masterly Piano Rolls (col.) The New Victor Electrical Recording Process.

76.   *Variety*, 30 September 1925, p. 46 - Band and Orchestra Reviews: Roger Wolfe Kahn and His Hotel Biltmore Orchestra.

77.   *Variety*, 14 October 1925, p. 45 - Inside Stuff on Music (col.) Young Kahn and his Music.

78.   Ibid., 44 - Roger Kahn's Bookings (rept.).

79.   *Variety*, 7 October 1925, p. 2 - Real and Personal Property (rept.).

80.   The *Suffolk Times*, 9 October 1925 - Otto Kahn has purchased a large tract of land from the Avalon Corporation consisting of about 500 acres in Sachem's Neck on Shelter Island, Long Island (rept.).

81.   Byron, Basil Gordon & Coudert, Frederic Reni. *America Speaks: A Library of the Best Spoken Thought in Business and the Professions*, Cosimo Classics, 2005 - Advertising, p. 493 - Otto H. Kahn quote.

82.   *Variety*, 21 October 1925, p. 17 - Right off the Desk (col.).

83.   *TIME* magazine, 2 November 1925 - Mr. Kahn & Mr. Gatti (art.).

84.   *Variety*, December 9, p. 20 - News From The Dailies (col.).

85.   Kahn, Otto H. *American Stage; Reflections of an Amateur*, (self publ.) 52 William St., NY, 1925. A transcript of an address by Otto H. Kahn at the Carnegie Institute of Technology, Pittsburgh, PA., 27 November 1925.

86.   The *Music Trade Review*, 28 November 1925, p. 48 - Kahn Booking Office (rept.).

87.   The *Music Trade Review*, 12 December 1925, p. 136 - Kahn Writing Symphony (rept.).

88.   *Variety*, 25 November 1925, p. 42 - Inside Stuff on Music (col.).

89.   *'Rhythm of the Day'* - Victor Ledger, Victor matrix BVE-34147, Roger Wolfe Kahn and His Hotel Biltmore Orchestra. Recorded 15 December 1925. Takes 1,2 & 4 destroyed. Take 3 held.

90.   *Variety*, 25 November 1925, p. 43 - Here And There (col.).

91.   *Variety*, 16 December 1925, p. 47 - Inside Stuff on Music (col.) - Sandwich Bearer off Sandwich (rept.).

92.   *Variety*, 2 February 1927, p. 35 - On The Square (col.) - Wrong Meat Sandwiches.

93.   *Marshall Evening Chronicle*, Michigan, 24 December 1925, front page - Today (col.) and 'Funeral of F. A. Munsey' (rept.).

94.   The *Cherokee Times*, 24 December 1925, front page - Death Closes Great Career of Publisher (rept.).

95.   *The New Yorker*, 26 Dec. 1925, p. 35 - Biltmore Hotel (listing): 'Room to dance, good air to breathe, and the Roger Wolfe Kahn Orchestra.'

96.   *Variety*, 9 December 1925, p. 45 - Inside Stuff on Music (col.) - Roger Wolfe Kahn augments his Hotel Biltmore band.

97.   *The New Yorker*, 24 October 1925 - Deems Taylor has finished jazz symphony *Circus Day* for Paul Whiteman. First public performance will be night of December 29th, in Metropolitan Opera House (rept.).

98.   The *Brooklyn Daily Eagle*, 13 March 1927, p. 80 - Deems Taylor's New Opera (art.).

99.   *Variety*, 30 December 1925, p. 23 - An Example For Boys - Some Inside Stuff On Roger Wolfe Kahn (rept.).

Notes

* (p. 235) United News Pictures, 461 Eighth Avenue, New York City, NY.

* (p. 236) A limited-edition souvenir program was published for the event. The thirty-six-page booklet features portraits and biographies of President Coolidge and Vice President Charles Dawes, a brief history of past inaugural balls, and details of that evening's entertainment. There were performances by the United States Navy Band Orchestra, the Vincent Lopez Orchestra, and the Roger Wolfe Kahn Orchestra. The program also contains several advertisements from high-end businesses and a long list of patrons and dignitaries. Each number Roger and Vincent Lopez played is listed. Roger's band performed 28 tunes, including 'Tea for Two' and 'Indian Love Call.' The Lopez unit played 24 pieces, with most identified as foxtrots. Due to the popularity of certain numbers, Lopez repeated several tunes the Kahn orchestra performed, including the two aforementioned.

* (p. 246) Roger was presented with a Gold Badge after he helped a detective catch a burglar in the Bronx.[1]
   1.   New York Sunday Graphic, Magazine Section, Sunday 12 July 1925, pp. 1 & 11 - 'I Won My Detective Star Helping Catch A Thief' by Roger Wolfe Kahn (art.).

* (p. 254) On October 21, Texas Guinan threw a belated 18th birthday bash for Roger at the Del-Fey Club, 107 West 45th Street, at which Roger was her guest of honor. Roger's guest was Arthur Hand, leader of the California Ramblers. At the party, Guinan presented her revue Fascinations of 1925.[1]
   1.   A Texas Guinan invitation card dated October 21 is housed in the Roger Wolfe Kahn Collection at the Institute of Jazz Studies, Rutgers University Libraries Archival Collections.

* (p. 256a) After 'The Girl I Love' was dropped from Lady, Be Good! the song reappeared in 1930 in the musical Strike Up the Band with the alternative lyrics of 'The Man I Love.'

* (p. 256b) The musicians that performed on 'Dreaming of Tomorrow' and 'Pep' are, Tommy Gott & Leo McConville on trumpets, 'Miff' Mole on trombone, Arnold Brilhart & Alfred Evans on alto saxophone, Harold Sturr on tenor saxophone, Joe Venuti & Joe Raymond on violin, Arthur Schutt on piano, Tony Colucci on banjo, Mr. Crawford on tuba, and Vic Berton on drums.

* (p. 257) Roger signed a six-month extension to his Biltmore contract from January to June 1926. Variety incorrectly reported it was for one year.

* (p. 259) Cocoanuts opened at the Lyric Theatre, 213 West 42nd Street, on December 8, 1925, and had a score by Irving Berlin.

Chapter 9. The Dream Palace
   1.   Variety, 21 September, p. 47 - Young Kahn's 3rd Plane: Driving Without Compass (rept.) Kahn's first plane was a Sikorsky monoplane.
   2.   Variety, 20 January 1926, p. 43 - Kahn Band Name Changes (rept.).
   3.   Variety, 6 January 1926, p. 44 - Disk Reviews by Abel Green.
   4.   Levinson, Peter J. Tommy Dorsey: Livin' in a Great Big Way, a Biography, Da Capo Press, 2005, chapter 2, pp. 24-25. 'Bites of the Apple' - During most of the winter of 1926, Tommy Dorsey played alongside Eddie Lang and Joe Venuti in Kahn's dance orchestra.
   5.   The Musical Observer, May 1924 - Vincent Lopez Comments on his Unique Experiment (art.).
   6.   The Brooklyn Standard Union, 12 January 1926, p. 7 - Vaudeville Stars

For Newspaper Club's Show (rept.).

7. *Variety*, 13 January 1926, p. 45 - Inside Stuff on Music (col.).

8. *New York Times*, 24 January 1926, p. 16 - Lamont and Kahn Defend Mussolini at the Hotel Astor Yesterday Afternoon (rept.).

9. At a Hearing in New York City before a Subcommittee of the Committee on Immigration in February 1942, Luigi Criscuolo mentioned that Otto Kahn, in his address before the Foreign Policy Association on January 23, 1926, 'came across as being quite an objective speaker.' - United States Senate, Seventy-Seventh Congress, Second Session, held to amend the Nationality Act of 1940.

10. *The Times*, 14 January 1926, p. 11 - The Metropolitan Opera House - Proposed Rebuilding on New Site (rept.).

11. The *Outlook*, 27 January 1926, pp. 128-129 - The 'Golden Horseshoe.'

12. *The Times*, 23 January 1926, p. 11 - New Opera House For New York.

13. *Variety*, 27 January 1926, p. 16 - New Acts This Week - Jean Goldkette Orchestra (twelve-piece) Roseland Ballroom, New York (rev.).

14. *Variety*, 27 January 1926, p. 45 - Goldkette's NY Plans (rept.).

15. *Variety*, 13 January 1926, p. 45 - Here and There (col.).

16. *Literary Digest*, 30 January 1926 - King Jazz and the Jazz King (art.) Roger Wolfe Kahn (interview).

17. *The Music Trade Review*, 1926, p. 12 - Musical Merchandise Section.

18. *Variety*, 13 January 1926, p. 45 - Here and There (col.).

19. Ibid., 46 - Kahn Delays Doubling (rept.).

20. Ibid., 45 - Inside Stuff on Music (col.).

21. *Literary Digest*, 30 January 1926 - King Jazz and the Jazz King (art.), Roger Wolfe Kahn (interview).

22. *Variety*, 16 December 1925, p. 46 - Bands For Florida (rept.).

23. The *Ram Newspaper*, 18 December 1925, pp. 1-3 - Junior Prom Will Be Held at Hotel Biltmore February 5.

24. *Fordham University, New York,* magazine, 5 February 1926, Vol. 7, p. 16: 26th Anniversary of Junior Prom at Hotel Biltmore this Friday.

25. The *Fordham Ram*, 15 January 1926, front page - Several Arrangements for Coming Jr. Prom Made During Holidays (rept.).

26. Cooper, Diana. *The Light of Common* Day, Houghton Mifflin Co. Boston The Riverside Press Cambridge, 1959, chapter 2, pp. 49-50 - Rudolf Kätchen Kommer visits Kahn.

27. The *New York Sun*, 20 February 1926, p. 11 - Ballet Producers Guests in Parterre at Opera - at the Metropolitan Opera House last evening [19 February] Mr. and Mrs. Kahn in box 14 with their guests Mr. and Mrs. Benjamin S. Guinness and the Misses Guinness.

28. *New York Times*, 19 February 1926, p. 3 - Foils Palm Beach Robbers; Watchman Prevents Thieves From Breaking Into Otto Kahn's Home.

29. The *Evening News*, Harrisburg, PA, 19 February 1926, page 18 - Attempt Made to Rob Kahn's Winter Home in Palm Beach (rept.).

30. *Variety*, 24 February 1926, p. 16 - News From The Dailies (col.) Robbers at Kahn's Palm Beach Villa.

31. *Variety*, 3 February 1926, p. 34 - Literati (col.).

32. *Liberty*, 9 January 1926, pp. 25, 28-29 - Jazz! America is leading the world in a wild financial Charleston. Here is 18-year-old Roger Wolf Kahn, son of Otto Kahn, who makes $2,500 a week out of it. (art.)

33. *Variety*, 24 Feb. 1926, p. 40 - Literati (col.) Young Kahn As Author.

34. *Variety*, 17 Feb. 1926, p. 49 - Disk Reviews by Abel Green.

35. Ibid., 49 - How A Famous Band 'Killed' An Auto Show (rept. & pict.).

36.   *Variety*, 3 March 1926, p. 39 - Kahn's Band Added at $5 Cover Cabaret - 5th Avenue Club (rept.).

37.   *Variety*, 17 March 1926, p. 43 - Music page - Kahn Leaves Club (rept.).

38.   *Variety*, 24 March 1926, p. 41 - Friday Nights Radio Program Should Make Theaters Worry (rev.).

39.   The *Music Trade Review*, 20 March 1926, p. 24 - Popular Victor Concerts Presented Over The Radio (rev.).

40.   The *Brooklyn Daily Eagle*, 20 March 1926, p. 7 - On The Radio Last Night (rept.).

41.   *Variety*, 24 March 1926, p. 21 - Young Singer Feels Regret For Otto Kahn (rept.).

42.   *The Goblin* magazine, Toronto, Canada, Vol. VI, No. 9, April 1926, p. 21 - Beautiful Thought (rept.).

43.   *Variety*, 17 February 1926, p. 46 - Here and There (col.).

44.   *South Bend Tribune*, 14 May 1926 and 15 May 1926 - Jean Goldkette.

45.   The *Pennsylvanian*, 16 April 1926, front page & p. 3 - Annual Ball Tonight Concludes Program of Ivy Week Activities (rept.).

46.   The *Pennsylvanian*, 17 April 1926, front page & pp. 2-3 - Senior Week Terminates With Colorful Ivy Ball (rev.).

47.   The *Music Trade Review*, April, p. 29 - New York Musical Instrument Dealers Promote Elaborate Concert at Aeolian Hall (rept.).

48.   *Variety*, 21 April 1926, p. 44 - Rudy Wiedoft Concert (rev.).

49.   *Variety*, 14 April 1926, p. 40 - Lottman With Kahn (rept.).

50.   *The New Yorker*, 17 April 1926, p. 11 - The Talk of The Town - Success.

51.   The *Brooklyn Daily Eagle*, New York, 2 May 1926, p. 4E - N.V.A. Benefit (advt.), 'Big N.V.A. Benefit Tonight' (rept.).

52.   *Variety*, 26 May 1926, p. 49 - Roger Kahn's Bookings (rept.).

53.   *Variety*, 2 June 1926, p. 43 - Here and There (col.).

54.   *Variety*, 21 April 1926, p. 44 - Girl Band In Pictures (rept.).

55.   The *Music Trade Review*, 8 May 1926, p. 44 - Lottman With Kahn.

56.   *The New Yorker*, 8 May 1926 - More Meller (rept.).

57.   *Variety*, 24 March 1926, p. 19 - $10 For Meller Interesting Experiment.

58.   *The Outlook*, 14 April 1926, p. 582 - By the Way (col.).

59.   The *New York Evening Post*, 22 May 1926, front page - Otto Kahn's Son Sails Abroad To Study Banking Conditions (rept.).

60.   *The Springfield Missouri Republican*, 26 May 1926, p. 2 - Dreamers to Get Home of Dreams building for Writers, Artists and Other Cultural Toilers to Be Dedicated in Greenwich Village Today (rept.).

61.   Ibid., Otto Kahn quote given at the opening ceremony of Twin Peaks.

62.   *The Long Islander*, 6 April 1934, front page - Funeral Services of Otto Kahn Simple - In Music Room (rept.) Helen Todd attends.

63.   *Variety*, 2 June 1926, p. 42 - Forming New Bands (rept.) Kahn closes June 6 (Sunday) at the Hotel Biltmore.

64.   *Variety*, 12 May 1926, p. 22 - Kahn and Pictures (rept.).

65.   *Variety*, 16 June 1926, p. 44 - Roger Kahn Tied Down To 2 Weekly Leadings (rept.).

66.   *Variety*, 2 June 1926, p. 42 - Forming New Bands (rept.) Joe Venuti, violinist of Roger Wolfe Kahn's band, and Eddie Lang of the Mound City Blue Blowers are organizing a new combination of their own. Venuti left Kahn this week. Arthur Schutt (pianist), and Victor Berton (drummer), are also out of the Kahn organization.

67.   *Variety*, 30 June 1926, p. 41 - Here and There (col.).

68.   *Variety*, 6 January 1926 - Irving Berlin yearly income $300,000.

69.   *Variety*, 2 June 1926, p. 43 - Disk Reviews by Abel - Victor Records.

70.   *Variety*, 23 June 1926, p. 44 - Disk Reviews by Abel Green.

71.   Ibid., 34 - News From The Dailies - New York (rept.).

72.   Ibid., 45 - Cabaret Reviews - Castillian Royal, Pelham, New York (rev.) Roger Wolfe Kahn Band.

73.   Ibid., 45

74.   Ibid., 43 - Roger Wolfe Kahn (advt.) Ultimately Ultra Dance Music Universally.

75.   The *Film Daily*, 13 June 1926, p. 9 - Developments In Presentation (col.) Gus Edwards Rehearsing Act (rept.).

76.   *Variety*, 23 June 1926, p. 34 - Big Field Day Sunday At Polo Grounds For Drive (rept.).

77.   The *Brooklyn Daily Eagle*, 20 June 1926, p. 2E - Charity Carnival at Polo Grounds (advt. & rept.).

78.   The *Brooklyn Daily Eagle*, 28 June 1926, p. 9 - Sports Benefit of Jewish Campaign Raises $75,000 (rept.).

79.   The *Brooklyn Daily Eagle*, 18 July 1926, p. 2F - Many Well-Known People in New Hampshire Hills For Season (rept.).

80.   The *Brooklyn Daily Eagle*, 18 July 1926, p. B5 - Musical Program Enjoyed by Guests at the Balsams (rept.).

81.   *Variety*, 21 July 1926, p. 40 - Young Kahn's Score (rept.).

82.   *Variety*, 28 July 1926, p. 46 - Kahn Booking Into Society (rept.).

83.   Ibid., 48 - Kahn Leaving Road House (rept.).

84.   Ibid., 27 - Bands With Loew's (rept.).

85.   *Greenpoint Weekly Star*, 6 August 1926, p. 2 - Jazz King's Boat On Mud in Creek (art.).

86.   *St. Petersburg Times*, 5 August 1926, p. 8 section 2 - Otto Kahn's Son Wants to Compose (rept.).

87.   *Variety*, 4 August 1926 - Kahn Back at Palace (rept.).

88.   The *Brooklyn Daily Eagle*, 8 November 1927, p. 3 - Kahn Abandons Jazz Band To Become Composer; Tells Of His Struggles As A Leader (art.).

89.   *Variety*, 11 August 1926, p. 57 - Kahn's Nightclub at $23,000 Rental.

90.   *Radio Mirror*, Sept. 1934, p. 60 - Harry Richman by Herb Cruikshank.

91.   *The New Yorker*, 25 Sept. 1926, p. 13 - The Talk of the Town (col.) Tour Deluxe.

92.   *Variety*, 11 August 1926, p. 57 - Kahn's Nightclub at $23,000 Rental.

93.   *Variety*, 18 August 1926, p. 66 - Imported Spanish Artiste At Kahn's Nightclub - Kahn Leaves on Motor Trip (rept.).

94.   *The New Yorker*, 25 September 1926, p. 13 - The Talk of the Town (col.) Tour Deluxe - Artist Austin Purves Paints the Kahns' Swimming Pool While They Are On Vacation.

95.   *Variety*, 25 August 1926, p. 51 - Kahn On The Boats (rept.).

96.   Ibid., 52 - Disk Reviews by Abel Green.

97.   *Variety*, 18 August 1926, p. 66 - Imported Spanish Artiste At Kahn's Nightclub (rept.) Kahn off on Motor Trip (rept.).

98.   *Variety*, 29 Sept. 1926 - Kahn opens the New Orpheum Palace, Chicago, (rept.). *Le Perroquet de Paris* scheduled for a November opening.

99.   *El Paso Herald*, Texas, 16 October 1926, p. 14 - Great Opportunity in El Paso, says Kahn, NY Banker (rept.).

100.   *The Princeton Alumni Weekly*, 26 Nov. 1926, Vol. XXVII, No 10, p. 301 - Class Intelligence '22 (col.) 'Len Cushing was a member of Otto Kahn's party, which made a hurried tour of the country in nothing flat' (rept.).

101.   The *Glengarry News*, 17 September 1926, p. 2 - Here and There (col.).

102. The *Oakland Tribune*, California, 25 September 1926, p. 24 - Kahn to Play Golf at Del Monte Lodge (rept.).

103. *San Bernardino County Sun,* California, 1 Oct. 1926, front page - Mirror to Compose Floor of Ballroom Contemplated by Otto Kahn's Son.

104. *El Paso Herald*, Texas, 16 October 1926, p. 14 - Great Opportunity in El Paso, says Kahn, NY Banker (rept.).

105. *The Waco News-Tribune,* Texas, 23 October 1926, p. 9 - Otto Kahn Will See Aggie-S.M.U. Tilt (rept.).

106. The *Music Trade Review*, 9 October 1926, p. 41 - Kahn Orchestra Plays Engagement in Chicago (rept.).

107. The *Vaudeville News and New York Star*, 8 October 1926, p. 5 - The Orpheum's New Palace, Chicago, Opens in Blaze of Glory (rev.).

108. Roger Wolfe Kahn and his Society Orchestra: New Palace Theatre opening night souvenir program, Monday October 4, 1926.

109. *Variety*, 6 October 1926, p. 58 - New Palace, Chicago (rev.).

110. *Swing Music Magazine,* November-December 1935, issue 0005, p. 242-243 - A New Portrait of 'Miff' Mole by B. M. Lytton Edwards.

111. The *Brooklyn Daily Eagle*, 10 October 1926, p. 2E - Events of the Week in the Theaters - Roger Wolfe Kahn and Jean Acker at Albee (rept.).

112. *Orchestra World*, 11 November 1926 - Roger Wolfe Kahn Orchestra at the Palace Theatre, New York, week commencing 18 October 1926.

113. Passenger List: 16 October 1926, *Aquitania*, departs Southampton for New York. Traveling in first-class, Addie, Margaret Kahn, and their maid, Lydia Cooper.

114. *The New Yorker*, 16 October 1926, p. 58 - Roger Wolfe Kahn nightclub opening (rept.).

115. Peretti, Burton W. *Nightclub City: Politics and Amusement in* Manhattan, University of Pennsylvania Press, 2007. p. 13.

116. The *Nassau Daily Review*, 12 October 1926, p. 4 - In New York (col.).

117. *The New Yorker*, 4 December 1926, p. 14 - *Le Perroquet de Paris*; the only mirror floor in New York (rept.).

118. The *Evening Independent*, 6 November 1925 - Dream Palace Opened in NY by Young Kahn (rept.).

119. The *Brooklyn Daily Eagle*, 2 November 1926, p. 2 - Goldfish-Decorated Tables, Mirror Dance Floor Delayed At Young Kahn's Jazz Palace.

120. *Variety*, 27 Oct. 1926, p. 71 - 'Classiest' Nightclub With 50c Invitations.

121. The *Palm Beach Post*, 7 August 1932, p. 10 - Love Troubles of the Kahn Boys (art.) 'Then Roger opened his own nightclub. The opening night is still remembered in society.'

122. Churchill, Allen. *The Year the World Went Mad*, Thomas Y. Crowzz Company, 1960, p. 75, 'Roger Wolfe Kahn's ... club ... was so surpassingly elegant that even Broadway was awed by it.'

123. *Syracuse Herald Journal,* New York, 26 March 1939, p. 23 - The Man On Broadway by Walter Winchell - Jimmy Durante declined Roger Wolfe Kahn's offer to host his nightclub.

124. The *Brooklyn Daily Eagle*, 2 November 1926, p. 2 - Goldfish-Decorated Tables, Mirror Dance Floor Delayed At Young Kahn's Jazz Palace.

125. *Variety*, 13 October 1926, p. 44 - Class Nightclub Wanted Marie Saxon.

126. The *New York Morning Telegraph*, 28 November 1926, n. p. - Roger Wolfe Kahn and Mrs. George D. Lottman (pict. & capt.).

127. *Variety*, 1 December 1926: p. 30 - 'Class' Night Clubs (listings).

128. *Variety*, 10 November 1926, p. 46 - Night Club Reviews - *Le Perroquet de Paris* - New York (Nov. 6).

129.   Ibid.
130.   The *Nassau Daily Review*, 12 October 1926, p. 4 - In New York (col.).
131.   *Brooklyn Life*, 27 November 1926, p. 21 - Merrill Hughes Enjoying Most Successful Season (rept.).
132.   *Variety*, 1 December 1926, p. 30B - Kahn Buys Out Partner: Runs Night Club Alone (rept.).
133.   *The New Yorker*, 5 Jan. 1998, p. 38-55 - The City-Shaper, Robert Moses (art.) by Robert A. Caro. Caro, Robert A. *The Power Broker* (*Robert Moses and the Fall of New York*), Knopf, NY, 1974, ISBN: 0394720245.
134.   The *Pittsburgh Daily Post*, 9 Jan. 1927, p. 74 - Her Life Just One Melodrama After Another. How Prima Donna Lydia Lindgren's Latest Effort to Outdo Grand Opera's Strange Plots Nearly Cost Her Life (art.).
135.   The *News-Herald*, Franklin and Oil City, 6 December 1926, front page - Lydia Lindgren, Opera Star, Swallows Poison (rept.).
136.   The *Pittsburgh Daily Post*, 9 Jan. 1927, p. 74 - Her Life Just One Melodrama After Another. How Prima Donna Lydia Lindgren's Latest Effort to Outdo Grand Opera's Strange Plots Nearly Cost Her Life (art.).
137.   *Variety*, 1 December 1926, p. 30B - *Le Perroquet de Paris*, (listings).
138.   *Variety*, 5 January 1927, p. 26 - Inside Stuff On Vaudeville - *Le Perroquet* Gift Shoppe (rept.).
139.   The *Brooklyn Daily Eagle*, 18 Dec. 1926, p. 5 - On the Radio Last Night.
140.   *Variety*, 5 Jan. 1927, p. 47 - WEAF Moved From NY to Philly New Year's Eve (rev.).

Notes

* (p. 264) Roger's version of *'I'm Sitting on Top of the World'* touched No. 9 in February's sheet music sales chart, with *'A Little Bungalow'* fairing higher at No. 4 in March.

* (p. 267) Otto's admiration for Italy's dictator and fascism would later conflict with his strong condemnation of Germany's National Socialist Party.

* (p. 294) Roger's recording of *'Mountain Greenery'* peaked at No. 4 in September's sheet music sales chart, with *'Cross Your Heart'* reaching No. 8 the following month.

* (p. 296) Otto visited Charlie Chaplin Studios in early fall, 1926. (Getty Images - Charlie Chaplin posing with screen affiliates).

* (p. 297) On October 19 in San Antonio, a plane crashed thirty feet away from a steel tower where Otto and his guests were standing.[1] The incident happened during a mock battle staged by a film company. Hundreds of soldiers were taking part in the scene. As the plane flew overhead, its engine failed, and the aircraft crashed on to the battlefield. The pilot escaped but sustained severe bruising.
    1.   The *Waco News-Tribune*, Texas, 20 October 1926, front page - Plane Crash Endangers Life of Otto Kahn (rept.).

* (p. 306) *Sous le Gui* by *Jean de Parys*: The black glass bottle bearing the gilded inscription *Sous le Gui*, and the trademark *Jean de Parys* had a gilded over-cap embossed with mistletoe, from which dangled a silk tassel. The brand name *Sous le Gui* translates to *Under the Mistletoe*. The bottle was designed by Andre Jollivet and crafted by the renowned French glassmaker René Lalique. Each perfume came packaged in a box that opened like a book. The flacon was as prized as the scent, and every woman entering the establishment aimed to get their hands on one, hence the opening night

$25 admission charge.

* (p. 309) Robert Moses and Addie Kahn were first cousins. Robert's father, Emanuel Moses, married Bella Cohen, who was Addie's aunt and her late mother (Lydia Cohen's) sister.

* (p. 311) Franz Gerhardt Deutsch died tragically in an automobile accident in September 1934 in Ivry-en-Montagne, Burgundy, France.

Chapter 10. The Year New York Went Crazy

1. The *Brooklyn Daily Eagle,* 19 February 1928, p. 15 - The Weekly Book Review (suppl.) - 'What an eyeful he would have had at Roger Wolfe Kahn's jazz palace, where goldfish swam in the very tables and one danced over mirrors.' Quote by George Currie.
2. *Variety*, 26 January 1927, p. 52 - Heavy Snowstorm Uptown Explained Village Bunk (rept.).
3. *Variety*, 23 March, p. 31 - Henry Santrey and his Band (advt.).
4. The *Evening Tribune News*, 7 January 1927, p. 11 - Radio Programs.
5. *Daily Illin*, 7 January 1927, p. 10 - '*Tonight You Belong To Me*' (advt.).
6. *Variety*, 26 January 1927, p. 50 - Kahn-Mills Contract (rept.).
7. *Variety*, 19 January 1927, p. 46 - Here and There (col.).
8. *Billboard*, 9 January 1927 - Kahn has signed 'Miff' Mole, trombonist.
9. Goodman, Benny and Kolodin, Irving. *The Kingdom of Swing*, Stackpole Sons, New York, 1939. - By this time violinist Joe Venuti had returned to play in the Kahn Orchestra.
10. *Vaudeville News and the New York Star*, 29 January 1927, p. 17 - Ramon and Rosita to Sail (rept.).
11. Bogle, Donald. *Bright Boulevards, Bold Dreams: The Story of Black Hollywood*, One World - Ballantine Books, NY, 2005.
12. *Brooklyn Life*, 3 March 1928, p. 22 - Music and Musicians (rept.).
13. *Variety*, 26 January 1927, p. 52 - Music Men Vacationing (rept.).
14. The *Outlook*, 5 May 1926, pp. 34-36 - Roger Wolfe Kahn; From Riches to Rags by Ernest W. Mandeville (interview & pict.).
15. *Variety*, 30 March 1927, p. 53 - Kahn Opening at Penn (rept.).
16. *Variety,* 9 February 1927, p. 47 - (Kahn) Calls Vacation Off (rept.).
17. *The New York Sun*, 9 February 1927, p. 27 - Atlantic City Arrivals.
18. *Variety,* 9 February 1927, p. 46 - Too Much Jazz Forces Rest (rept.).
19. *Variety,* 26 Jan. 1927, p. 50 - Parade of Maestros Welcome Whiteman.
20. *Variety,* 9 February 1927, p. 46 - Paul Whiteman Welcomed Back to New York by Associates of Jazz Organization (rept.).
21. *San Antonio Express*, 10 April 1927 - Vitaphone release *Night Club*.
22. The *Gettysburg Times*, 9 February 1931, p. 2 - Financier's Son Wed to Daughter of Coal Miner (rept.).
23. 1920 U.S. Federal Census, Scranton, PA, Jan. 5 to Feb. 5 - Hannah Williams aged 9, Dorothy Williams aged 11, Leona Williams aged 14.
24. *Utica Herald Dispatch*, 16 August 1918, p. 3 - Vaudeville at the Majestic - The Williams Sisters (rev.) 'The Williams Sisters are a petite and dainty duo of misses, with an act of exceptional vivacity and charm.'
25. The *Film Daily*, 13 March 1927, p. 90 - *Le Perroquet de* Paris (advt.) the Williams Sisters 'a decidedly different offering' are listed as appearing. Note: the sisters are mistakenly advertised as the 'William Sisters.'
26. *Variety*, 31 March 1926, p. 46 - Straight's Brunswick Record's (rept.).
27. *Variety*, 14 April 1926, p. 45 - Chicago: 'Ethel Kendall and Jack Lund's

reconstructed Merry Garden Ballroom opened formally last week.'

28. *Variety*, 12 May 1926, p. 48 - 'K. C. Hotel Booking Big Attractions for Summer' (rept.).

29. *Variety*, 21 July 1926, p. 46 - *Frolics* (rev.).

30. *Variety*, 1 September 1926, p.47 - *Frolics* new edition (rev.).

31. *Variety*, 6 October 1926, p.35 - Chicago's Night Life Draws Same Regulars Nightly Somewhere - *Frolics* new edition (rev.).

32. *EIR*, 9 April 1993, Vol. 20, No. 14, p. 36 - D. W. Griffith's *The Birth of a Nation*, Hollywood, and the KKK by Mark Calney (art.) The article mentions Felix Kahn's involvement with Paramount Pictures Corp.

33. *Variety*, 12 January 1927, p.5 - Williams Sisters banned by B&K.

34. *Variety*, 16 February 1927, p. 50 - 'The Williams Sisters, from Chicago, who opened last week at Roger Wolfe Kahn's *Le Perroquet de Paris*...'

35. Variety, 2 March 1927, p. 48 - Nightclub Reviews - *Le Perroquet De Paris*, February 17 (rev.).

36. *Variety*, 1 September 1926, p. 48 - Cabaret Listings - the Williams Sisters are billed to appear in cabaret at Texas Guinan's nightclub.

37. *Variety,* 9 February 1927, p. 30 - White Signs Team (rept.).

38. *Variety*, 2 February 1927, p. 54 - Williams Sisters First (rept.).

39. ACME News, 25 February 1927 - Otto Kahn Celebrates 60th Birthday by Working (rept.).

40. 'Judging the Stars' (art.) by Mauro Gonzàlez with accompanying caricature by Mauro Gonzàlez, 1927, unidentified newspaper, p. 14.

41. *Variety*, 2 March 1927, p. 2 - Sailings (col.) February 26 Sailings - New York to France (Paris) - Otto Kahn & Max Reinhardt on the *Leviathan*.

42. The *Brooklyn Daily Eagle*, 27 February 1927, p. 18A - Kahn Goes Abroad On Hunt For Art Works And Singers (rept.).

43. *The Times*, 1 April 1927, p. 21 - New Banking Company (rept.).

44. The *Brooklyn Daily Eagle*, 22 March 1927, p. 5 - Giant Buds Bloom in Glory As L. I. Exhibitors Capture Prizes at Flower Show (rept.).

45. *Brooklyn Life*, 19 March 1927, p. 15 - Long Island Society (col.).

46. *Variety*, 2 March 1927, p. 48 - Nightclub Reviews - *Le Perroquet De Paris* - 17 February.

47. *Variety,* 9 February 1927, p. 47 - Kahn Cans Souvenirs, But $5 Cover Stays On (rept.).

48. *Variety*, 9 March 1927, p. 44 - The Waltons at *Le Perroquet de Paris*.

49. The *Brooklyn Daily Eagle*, 21 February 1927, p. A3 - On The Radio Last Night (rev.).

50. The *Times Herald* (Olean), 28 February 1927, p. 1 - 'Otto Kahn's son Roger Wolfe has left his father's Fifth Avenue mansion for an apartment over his jazz parlor on 57th Street' (rept.).

51. The *New York Sun*, 24 February 1927 - Party for Actors Fund To Be Held As Scheduled (rept.).

52. The *New York Sun*, 19 February 1927, p. 13 - British Players Planning Benefit For Actors Fund (rept.).

53. The *Film Daily*, 23 February 1927, p. 6 - A Little From Lots (col.).

54. *Vaudeville News and the New York Star*, 26 February 1927, p. 13 - Along Song Lane by William Jerome (col.).

55. *Variety*, 9 March 1927, p. 19 - Bands on Broadway - Kahn in a new Irving Berlin musical (one-liner).

56. Ibid., 19 - Film House Reviews - Roger Wolfe Kahn and His Orchestra and the Williams Sisters at the Strand Theatre.

57. Ibid., 20 - The Strand, New York, 6 March: Roger Wolfe Kahn and His

Orchestra and The Williams Sisters (rev.).

58. *Variety*, 16 March 1927, p. 9 - Picture House (takings).
59. The *Milwaukee Sentinel*, 21 May 1932, p. 24 - Kahn Mama's Boy His Wife Charges - Roger Ran to Parent With Every Spat: Hannah Leaves.
60. *Variety*, 30 March 1927, p. 2 - Americans Abroad (col.) 20 March: Otto H. Kahn in Paris.
61. The *Milwaukee Sentinel*, 20 March 1927, p. 3, section 1 - Kahn May Buy Jazz Operas (rept.).
62. *New York Times*, 26 March 1927, p. 3 - Kahn Lauds Germany in Speech at Berlin (rept.).
63. *TIME* magazine, 28 March 1927 - People (col.).
64. *Variety*, 23 March 1927, p. 46 - Page's Defense, Publicity (rept.).
65. The *Chicago Sunday Tribune*, 6 March 1927, N section, p. 4 - About Broadway by Mark Helliger (rept.).
66. *Variety*, 9 March 1927, p. 45 - Kahn Lands Pennsylvania, Doubling Into Nightclub (rept.).
67. *Variety*, 2 March 1927, p. 45 - Olsen Supervising All Music For Statler Hotel Chain (rept.).
68. *Variety*, 30 March 1927, p. 53 - Kahn Opening at Penn (rept.).
69. *Variety*, 6 April 1927, p. 55 - Many Broadwayites were on hand to witness the debut of Roger Wolfe Kahn and his band at the Pennsylvania Grill (rept.).
70. *Variety*, 23 March 1927, front page - Kahn To Close Café Costing Him $200,000 (rept.).
71. *Variety*, 23 March 1927, back page - Roger Wolfe Kahn (advt.).
72. The *Film Daily,* 27 March 1927, p. 32 - How Broadway Does It (col.).
73. *New York Times*, 20 March 1927, p. E4 - Editorial General News (rept.).
74. The *New York Evening Post*, 19 March 1927, front page - Roger Kahn In Deal to Sell $2,300,000 In Jazz Statler (rept.).
75. The *Brooklyn Daily Eagle*, 20 March 1927, p. 4A - Jazz Richer Than Bonds, Says Banker Kahn's Son in $2,340,000 Band Deal (rept.).
76. The *Princeton Alumni Weekly*, 25 March 1927, p. 723 - 'Student syncopators at the Prom listened with awe to Ben Bernie and to Roger Wolfe Kahn, that prodigal son who has flown from finance to fiddling.'
77. *Variety*, 23 March 1927, p. 47 - Here And There (col.).
78. Inventory of the Ben Hecht Papers, 1879-1983, box 11, folder 299 - *Hearts and Flowers.*
79. *Buffalo Courier Express*, 20 March 1927, front page - Kahn May Put Orchestra in Statler-Owned Hotels (rept.).
80. *Vaudeville News and the New York Star*, 6 August 1927, p. 3 - As We Go to Press (col.) *Hearts and Flowers* soon to go into rehearsals.
81. *Presto-Times*, 12 February 1927, p. 15 - Appoints Jazz Arbiter (rept.).
82. The *Evening News*, Harrisburg, 5 February 1927, p. 18 - Julian T. Abeles appointed (rept.).
83. The *Music Trade Review*, 16 April 1927, p. 41 - Fred Fischer Threatens To Sue Orchestra Directors (rept.).
84. The *Saratoga Sun*, Saratoga Springs, 6 April 1927, front page - Flashes of Life (col.).
85. *New York Times*, 2 April 1927, p. 20 - Orchestra Leaders Plan Benefit.
86. *Variety*, 20 April 1927, p. 53 - Directors' Ball Against Conditions, Got $5,000 (rev.).
87. Ibid., 53 - Whiteman Calls Off NAOD Membership (rept.).
88. *Variety*, 23 March 1927, p. 35 - Keith-Western (listings): 28 March

1927, Palace Theatre, Chicago - Williams Sisters.

89. *Variety*, 13 April 1927, p. 39 - Orpheum (listings): 11 April 1927, Hennepin, Minneapolis - Williams Sisters.

90. Ibid., 30 - Williams Sisters Prefer dates for Picture House (rept.).

91. *Variety*, 29 June 1927, p. 34 - George White on Stage (rept.).

92. *Variety*, 20 April 1927, p. 53 - Director's Ball Against Conditions Got $5,000 - Ben Bernie was in Chicago on a contract, and Roger Wolfe Kahn, who was also in the city on business, wired from the same place.

93. Laurie Wright's *'Fats in Fact'* - memoir from Ernie Anderson of New York's Liederkranz Hall studio (art.).

94. Roger Wolfe Kahn and His Orchestra recorded *'South Wind,'* and *'One Summer Night'* for Victor at Liederkranz Hall on 28 April 1927.

95. Roger Wolfe Kahn and His Orchestra recorded *'South Wind,'* *'Where the Wild, Wild Flowers Grow,'* and *'Calling,'* for Victor at Liederkranz Hall on 12 May 1927.

96. *Princeton Alumni Weekly*, 2 May 1964, Vol. 84, p. 33 - The Sons of Bix Keep Blowing (art.).

97. *Fiat Lux*, newspaper (Alfred, New York), 10 May 1927, p. 4 - Alfred Varsity Men Hope To Win Mid-Atlantic Challenge (rept.).

98. The *New York Evening Post*, 21 May 1927, p. 10 - 8 Loaded Liners Sail for Europe - Roger Kahn one of 1,550 Passengers on the *Leviathan*.

99. The *Lincoln Star*, Nebraska, 12 June 1927, p. 33 - 'Roger Wolfe Kahn commissioned by Paul Whiteman to write a rhapsody for film' (rept.).

100. The *Music Trade Review*, 28 May 1927, p. 105 - Roger Wolfe Kahn to Write Jazz Number for Whiteman (rept.).

101. *Radio World*, 18 June 1927, p. 12 - Lindbergh's Landing Quickly Announced (rept.).

102. The *Hamilton Daily News*, Ohio, 27 May 1927, front page - Versatile Youngster (pict. & capt.) Roger Wolfe Kahn traveling to Europe.

103. *Variety*, 1 June 1927, p. 36 - Picture Theaters (listings) Marbro, Chicago.

104. *American Bond News*, Vol. 3 No. 3, July 1927, front page - Marbro Theatre Enjoys Tremendous Crowds (rept. and pict.).

105. *Variety*, 8 June 1927, p. 21 - Marbro, Chicago (rev.) *In A Magic Garden*.

106. *Variety*, 1 June 1927, p. 29 - Hannah Williams Knew Chas Kaley Two Weeks (rept.).

107. The *New Amberola Graphic*, Autumn 1986, p. 7 - Life in the Orthophonic Age, Roger Wolfe Kahn (part I) - In May 1927, Roger was the first passenger on the maiden Cherbourg to Paris airline flight.

108. The *Daily Illin*, 3 June 1927, p. 6 - 'Russian Lullaby' (advt.) 'Irving Berlin's latest waltz hit *'Russian Lullaby,'* with balalaika (Russian mandolin) effects woven into the flowing vocal refrain. Weird minor combinations accent the flavor of the frozen steppes.'

109. *TIME* magazine, 19 September 1927, pp. 18 & 20 - Roger Wolfe Kahn.

110. The *Yacht*, 1927, No. 39, pp. 1-3 - *Oheka II*, A test cruise with the fastest American express cruiser (art. & pict.).

111. *New York Times*, 9 June 1927, Section Sports, p. 30 - *Oheka II* Speed Test Halted by Accident (rept.).

112. The *Saratogian*, 9 June 1927, p. 14 - Record Effort on Hudson Ends at West Point (rept.).

113. Sloat, Warren. *1929: America Before the Crash*, MacMillan Publishing Co. Inc., NY, 1979, p. 155.

114. The *Brooklyn Daily Eagle*, 27 February 1927, p. 18A - Kahn Goes

Abroad On Hunt For Art Works And Singers (rept.).

115. *Vaudeville News* and *the New York Star*, 2 April 1927, p. 13 - Along Song Lane (col.) by William Jerome.

116. *Radio World*, 18 June 1927, p. 12 - Lindbergh Day A Radio Event.

117. *Variety*, 8 June 1927, p. 2 - Sailing (col.).

118. *Santa Ana Register* (California), 21 June 1927, p. 4 - New York Banker Helps Golf Club Paris (rept.).

119. *New York Times*, 21 June 1927 - Otto Kahn Due Back Today; Returning on the *Majestic* After Three Months Tour Abroad (rept.).

120. *Long Islander*, 24 June 1927, p. 3 - Kahn's Back From Europe (rept.).

121. *Variety*, 20 July 1927, p. 24 - Hannah Williams Wed; Roger Kahn's Regrets (rept.).

122. The *Indianapolis Star*, Indiana, 14 August 1927, p. 85 - Why A Chicago Jazz King is Now Featuring Hard Hearted Hannah While Otto Kahn's Syncopating Son Smiles (rept. & pict.).

123. *New York Times*, July 4, 1927 - Coney Island (rept.).

124. The *New Yorker*, 9 July 1927, p. 4 - Roger Wolfe Kahn and Orchestra providing excellent music in circus surroundings (rept.).

125. *The New Yorker*, 27 August 1927, p. 4 - Roger Wolfe Kahn and Orchestra still playing at Pennsylvania up to 27 August in a 'good old circus tent' (rept.).

126. *Variety*, 20 July 1927, p. 45 - *Variety's* Broadway Guide (col.) New Kahn Releases.

127. *The New Yorker*, 2 July 1927, p. 9 - Roger (art.).

128. Ibid., 11 - Roger Wolfe Kahn has 8 orchestras working under his name.

129. The *Brooklyn Daily Eagle*, 27 August 1927, p. 3 - On the Radio Last Night (col.).

130. *New York Times*, 8 August 1927, p. 4 - Sir George Lewis, Lawyer, Dead.

131. The *Brooklyn Daily Eagle*, 10 August 1927, front page - Banker Kahn's Son, Caught Speeding, Flashes A Badge (rept.).

132. Ibid.

133. *Variety*, 17 August 1927, p. 40 - News From The Dailies (rept.) 'Roger Wolfe Kahn ... nabbed for eating up the road with his car.'

134. The *Brooklyn Daily Eagle*, 15 August 1927, p. 2 - Roger Wolfe Kahn Fined $25 For Eastern Parkway Speeding (rept.).

135. The *Southeast Missourian*, 18 August 1927, p. 8 - News Flashes (rept.).

136. Crow, Bill. *Jazz Anecdotes: Second Time Around*, Oxford University Press, 1990, p. 319 - Joe Venuti.

137. *Variety*, 27 July 1927, p. 54 - Kahn Claims Salary Is Due (rept.).

138. *Variety*, 30 November 1927, p. 54 - Aaronson Lasted 9 Days At His Own Club (rept.).

139. *Variety*, 3 August 1927, front page - Young Kahn's $200,000 Nite Club Is Cold (rept.).

140. The *Buffalo Courier Express*, 16 January 1929, p. 8 - Manhattan Days and Nights (col.).

141. *Variety*, 21 September, p. 47 - Young Kahn's 3rd Plane: Driving Without Compass (rept.).

142. The *Brooklyn Daily Eagle*, 4 August 1927, p.3 - Roger in New Role (rept. & pict.) Roger Wolfe Kahn Enters Plane Race.

143. *Variety*, 24 August 1927, p. 54 - Inside Stuff On Music (col.).

144. *Variety*, 31 August 1927, front page & p. 2 - Roger Kahn Retiring From Dance Band Field (rept.).

145. *Variety*, 24 August 1927, p. 54 - Kahn To Freelance (rept.).

146. The *Music Trade Review*, August 1928, p. 36 - Still Manages Kahn.
147. *The Hartford Daily Courant*, 1 September 1927, p. 7 - Roger Wolfe Kahn Orchestra At Hotel Bond (rept. & advt.).
148. The *Brooklyn Daily Eagle*, 3 Sept. 1927, front page - Roger Wolfe Kahn to Wed Virginia Franck, Specialty Dancer, latter Announces (rept.).
149. *The Standard Union*, Brooklyn, 3 September 1927, front page - Kahn's Engagement to Stage Dancer Not Denied (pict. & art.).
150. *El Paso Herald*, Texas, 3 September 1927, p. 6 - Young Jazz Artist and Dancer Engaged (rept. & pict.).
151. The *Standard Union*, Brooklyn, 3 September 1927, front page - Kahn's Engagement to Stage Dancer Not Denied (pict. & art.).
152. The *Philadelphia Inquirer*, 4 September 1927, front page - 'To Be Or Not To Be?' (rept.).
153. The *Milwaukee Sentinel*, 4 September 1927, p. 11, Section - Engaged To Roger? (pict. & capt. of Virginia Franck).
154. Ibid., 11 Section - Son of Kahn and Dancer's Names Linked (rept.).
155. The *Nassau Daily Review*, 6 September 1927, front page - Roger Wolfe Kahn Denies Engagement To Lynbrook Girl (rept.).
156. Ibid.
157. *TIME* magazine, 19 September 1927, pp. 18 & 20 - Roger Wolfe Kahn.
158. *Variety*, 7 September 1927, p. 43 - Romance Blows Up (rept.).
159. *Variety*, 16 March 1927, p. 46 - Van With Kahn (rept.).
160. *Variety*, 28 September 1927, p. 56 - Roger Kahn's Farewell (rept.).
161. *Variety*, 21 September 1927, p. 57 - Chance on Broadway (rept.).
162. *Variety*, 14 September 1927, p. 50 - Is Pittsburgh Shot? (Rept.).
163. *Variety*, 21 September 1927, p. 47 - Young Kahn's 3rd Plane: Driving Without Compass (rept.).
164. *TIME* magazine, 19 September 1927, front cover - Roger Wolfe Kahn.
165. The *Brooklyn Daily Eagle*, 29 December 1930, p. 29 - Firm Changes Announced by Several Houses (rept.) & Passenger List: 14 September 1927, RMS *Majestic*, departs Southampton for New York via Cherbourg. Traveling in first-class, Gilbert and Anne Kahn.
166. *The New Yorker*, 8 October 1927, p. 18 - 'Young Roger Wolfe Kahn continues to attract public attention' (rept.).
167. *Variety*, 12 October 1927, p. 42 - Greenwich Village (col.) by Lew Ney.
168. *Variety*, 7 September 1927, p. 49 - Reinhardt's U.S. Visit for 8 Weeks Under Kahn's Guarantee (rept. from Paris, 6 September).
169. *Variety*, 7 December 1927, p. 50 - Kahn and the Irish (rept.).
170. *New York Times*, 11 June 2009 - A Mansion for Me, Another for My Cars (art.) by Christopher Gray.
171. *Jewish Daily Bulletin*, 9 October 1927, p. 2 - Tokyo (7 October): Schiff and Kahn Honored by Japanese Government (rept.).
172. The *Brooklyn Daily Eagle*, 8 November 1927, p. 3 - Kahn Abandons Jazz Band To Become Composer, Tells Of His Struggles As A Leader (art.).
173. The *Auburn Citizen*, 2 November 1927, p. 7 - Flashes of Life (col.).
174. *Miami Daily News-Record*, 12 August 1927, p. 10 - 'Roger Kahn, jazz artist and airmail, and his father, Otto H. Kahn' by Hortense Saunders.
175. *New York Times*, 27 June 1927 - New York Airfields (rept.).
176. The *Harrisburg Telegraph*, PA, 7 October 1927, p 8 - Curtiss Field, Mineola, L.I., (rept.).
177. *The Daily Mirror,* New York City, October 1927, n. p. - Flying Suit Stolen, Kahn Calls Police (rept.).
178. *The New Amberola Graphic*, Autumn 1986, p. 7 - Life in the

179. Orthophonic Age, Roger Wolfe Kahn, part I (art.).

179. Greenspan, Charlotte. *Pick Yourself Up: Dorothy Fields and the American Musical*, Oxford University Press, 2010, p. 62.

180. *Variety*, 1 August 1928, front page - Kahn's Nite Club May Become Sore Seater (rept.).

181. The *Brooklyn Daily Eagle*, 23 Dec. 1927, p. 8A - News Items (col.) 'Mr. Lew Leslie, the theatrical manager, has acquired the premises, and after Drian, the famous French mural maker, has finished decorating the lobby, will open it once again with a company of twenty colored artists. The opening is scheduled for Thursday evening, 29 December.'

182. *Variety*, 28 Dec. 1927, p. 34 - Around The Square: Those Xmas Cards.

183. The *Daily Sentinel*, Rome, NY, 29 December 1927, p. 2 - Spear's Music House (advt.): New Victor records on sale 30 December.

184. *Radio Broadcast*, April issue, 1928, p. 442 - Disk (rev.).

185. Churchill, Allen. *The Year the World Went Mad*, Thomas Y. Crowzz Company, 1960, p. 299.

Notes

* (p. 318a) Toscanini's afternoon performance with the New York Philharmonic Orchestra took place on February 26, 1927, at the Academy (movie theatre) NY.

* (p. 318b) Considerable excitement was caused during the lunch hour when a fire started in the twenty-story building occupied by Kuhn, Loeb & Co.[1,2] Kuhn, Loeb & Co. had celebrated its 60th anniversary earlier that week - Abraham Kuhn and Solomon Loeb formed the company in 1867.[3]

1. *Jewish Daily Bulletin*, 6 Feb. 1927, p. 4 - 'Fire started at noon on Thursday in the building occupied by Kuhn, Loeb & Co., at 52 William Street.'

2. *The Decatur Herald*, Illinois, 9 Feb. 1927, p. 20 - Last-Minute Photos In The News - William Street, NY (Kuhn, Loeb Building Blaze - photo).

3. *TIME* magazine, 14 Feb. 1927, p. 36-37, 40 - Mortimer Schiff (cover) Pine and William Sts. (report)

* (p. 320a) Roger's fee for the movie was $3,500.[1]

1. Liebman, Roy. *Vitaphone Films: A Catalogue of the Features and Shorts*, McFarland & Co., 2010, pp. 18-19 - Release 468 and Release 469: Roger Wolfe Kahn and His Orchestra.

* (p. 320b) This rare movie still is one of the few remaining from the two-reel short, titled *Night Club,* featuring Roger Wolfe Kahn and His Orchestra. It was discovered in a baseball card shop in Allentown, PA, on December 28, 2008, by Michael Edwards of Jamison, PA. Mr. Edwards donated it to the Smithsonian Institution, Washington D.C., where it is housed in the National Museum of American History, Behring Center Archives Center, Box 25, Folder 22.

* (p. 321a) Copies of the Vitaphone sound disks that accompanied *Night Club* (Nos. 468 & 469) exist at the Library of Congress, Washington. Unfortunately, the film elements of both are missing, presumed lost - Library of Congress: Roger Wolfe Kahn and His Orchestra, 1927.

* (p. 321b) In Taylor, Pennsylvania, Hannah Williams' birthdate was registered as July 16, 1910 (file No.: 107439, July 29, 1910). Hannah's age is recorded as nine on the 1920 US Federal Census (January 5, 1920). However, Hannah was later incorrectly documented as being born on July 16, 1911. Hence, her cast memorial plaque at Forest

Lawn Memorial Park, Hollywood Hills, LA, has her date of birth recorded as July 16, 1911.

* (p. 325) The Williams Sisters appeared at the Avalon Club, Nov. 24, 1926.

* (p. 344a) As a teenage recording artist, Roger's success arguably warrants his recognition as the first adolescent music star in recording industry history.

* (p. 344b) The legal age for marriage in Illinois from 1905-1974 for a male was 21 and 18 for a female. With parental consent, 18 for a male and 16 for a female. www.chipublib.org

* (p. 346) In 1924, L. Gordon Hamersley, in his speedboat *Cigarette IV*, set the Albany-N.Y. speed record for cruising boats at 4 hours, 21 minutes, 57 seconds.

* (p. 352) Roger was presented the Gold Badge in 1925 after aiding a detective catch a burglar in the Bronx.[1] The police had also called upon Roger to help detectives find a master jewel thief who'd been the scourge of New York society for some years. That robber, Arthur T. Barry, had recently been arrested after committing a particularly audacious theft on Mr. and Mrs. Jesse Livermore (May 27, 1927). They were sat up in their bed, chatting to the thief as he robbed them. Barry was later found guilty and sentenced to 25 years in Auburn Prison.[2] He was estimated to have stolen more than $10 million worth of jewels during his life of crime.

    1.   *New York Sunday Graphic*, Magazine Section, Sunday 12 July 1925, pp. 1 & 11 - 'I Won My Detective Star Helping Catch A Thief' (art.) by Roger Wolfe Kahn.
    2.   *Life*, 12 March 1956, Vol. 40, No. 11, pp. 121-136 - Confessions of Master Jewel Thief (art.). Arthur Barry, great second-story man, looks back on a $10m life in crime.

* (p. 359) Virginia married a bond clerk named Jack Hedden in January 1929.

* (p. 360a) Thrills! Spills! and Speed! The National Air Races took place from September 21 to 25, 1927, and were held in Spokane at Felts Field. It attracted nearly 100,000 people over the five days. The $10,000 grand prize money went to Charles W. 'Speed' Holman, who finished his flight in 19 hours and 42 minutes.

* (p. 360b) Prince Michael 1 of Romania (Bonny King Michael) was the youngest person to appear on the cover of *TIME* magazine on August 1, 1927, aged 5. Roger Wolfe Kahn became the third youngest to have the privilege.

* (p. 361) Roger passed his pilot's license test on November 1.

Chapter 11. America's New Son

    1.   The *Binghamton Press*, 17 Jan. 1928 - Nephew of Former Binghamton Woman Soon to Wed Daughter of Mr. and Mrs. Otto H. Kahn (rept.).
    2.   The *Brooklyn Daily Eagle*, 17 Jan. 1928, front page - Kahn's daughter to Wed John Ryan Jr., Reporter and Heir to Fortune (pict. & rept.).
    3.   The *Leeds Mercury*, 18 Jan. 1928, p. 5 - Mrs. William B. Leeds - Divorce Decree for former Princess (rept.).
    4.   The *Binghamton Press*, 17 Jan. 1928 - Nephew of Former Binghamton Woman Soon To Wed Daughter of Mr. and Mrs. Otto H. Kahn (rept.).
    5.   The *Pittsburgh Post-Gazette*, 18 Jan. 1928, p. 3 - Never Left Judaism, Otto Kahn Declares (rept.).

6. The *New York Evening Post*, 15 February 1928, p. 12 - Forecasts and Postscripts (col.) by Wilella Waldorf. A new Aarons and Freedley Musical Comedy *Here's Howe!* (rept.).

7. *Record Research 29* (The Magazine of Record Statistics and Information), August 1960, issue 29, publ. Brooklyn.

8. *Variety*, 8 February 1928, p. 30 - Kahn's Reviving Band (rept.).

9. The *Brooklyn Daily Eagle*, 12 February 1928, p. 4E - Roger W. Kahn Featured on New Fox Savoy Bill (rept.).

10. The *Brooklyn Standard Union*, 12 February 1928, p. 10 - advert for Roger's appearance at the Savoy and the report 'Kahn At The Savoy.'

11. *The Daily News*, 10 February 1928, p. 70 - Otto Kahn Daughter Marries Ryan Scion. Nuptials at Financier's 5th Ave. Mansion (rept. & pict.). *New York Times*, 27 January 1995 - Margaret Kahn Ryan (obit).

12. The *World of Aviation*, 12 February 1928, p. 24 - Name New Supervisor For Fliers (rept.).

13. The *Brooklyn Daily Eagle*, 27 January 1928, p. 3 - Young Kahn Gets Hangar Site At Roosevelt Field (rept.).

14. The *Brooklyn Daily Eagle*, 26 February 1928, p. 56 - Roger Wolfe Kahn Becomes Flier - Just To Idle Around In Air Sedan (rept.).

15. *Popular Aviation*, March edition 1928, p. 52 - Manhattan Aero Club - Aero Club News (col.).

16. The *New York Evening Post*, 9 April 1928, p. 3 - Our Own Star Gazer Sees Traffic Jams in the Air (rept.) by Nunnally Johnson.

17. The *Brooklyn Daily Eagle*, 26 February 1928, p. 56 - Roger Wolfe Kahn Becomes Flier - Just To Idle Around In Air Sedan (rept.).

18. *New York Times*, 22 Feb. 1928 - Otto H. Kahn at 61 leaves for Florida.

19. *The Miami News*, 4 March 1928, p. 4 - Otto Kahn and His Party in Miami (pic. & caption). El *Paso Herald*, 16 March 1928, front page - Gotham Banker Lauds El Paso as Art and Commercial Center (rept.).

20. *Brooklyn Life*, 3 March 1928, p. 22 - Music and Musicians page (rept.).

21. The *Chicago Tribune*, 22 Sept. 1934, p. 16 - Fulton Cutting, NY Real Estate Head, Dies at 82 (rept.) 'As president of the Metropolitan Real Estate Co. he successfully blocked the plan of Otto Kahn and other directors to build a new opera house on West 57th St. six years ago.'

22. The *Brooklyn Daily Eagle*, 20 February 1928, p. 5 - Society Wins in Fight to Keep Opera on Old Site (rept.).

23. The *Brooklyn Daily Eagle*, 19 February 1928, p. 47 - Home Buying on Long Island Increasing (rept.).

24. The *New York Evening Post*, 28 January 1928, p. 10 - Supper Clubs - 'Among the instant successes of this season, Lew Leslie's *Ambassadeur's* on W. 57th Street probably has been the most noted.'

25. Jr., *Judge. Here's How*, John Day Co., NY, November 1927.

26. Jr., *Judge. Here's How*, Leslie-Judge Co., NY, 1927.

27. *Variety*, 22 February 1928, p. 46 - Legitimate page: Keeps House Open.

28. The *Brooklyn Daily Eagle*, 10 March 1928, p. 12 - Roger Kahn Takes The Air (rept.).

29. The *New York Evening Post*, 15 February 1928, p. 12 - Forecasts and Postscripts (col.) by Wilella Waldorf. A new Aarons and Freedley Musical Comedy *Here's Howe!* (rept.).

30. *Variety*, 22 February 1928, p. 46 - Legitimate page: Keeps House Open.

31. *Ziegfeld Follies of 1927*, New Amsterdam Theatre, program, p. 45, Franklyn Baur short biography.

32. Sloat, Warren. *1929: America Before the Crash*, MacMillan Publishing

Co. Inc., NY, 1979, p. 174 - Otto Kahn's visit to Hollywood.

33. *El Paso Evening Post*, 16 March 1928, p. 7 - Banker Sees Big E. P. Gain.

34. Ibid., Front page - Gotham Banker Lauds El Paso as Art and Commercial Center (rept.).

35. Nichols, Beverley. *All I Could Never Be*, Jonathan Cape, London, 1949, chapter VIII, Book One, 'Study In Blonde' pp. 111-123.

36. ACME News Pictures, 5 April 1928 - Photograph of Otto H. Kahn planting a tree at the Botanical Gardens, LA.

37. The *Indianapolis Star*, 7 January 1929, p. 6 - 'Carl Van Vechten assures reporters...' (rept.).

38. *Variety*, 11 April 1928, p. 60 - Salt Lake City, Variety News (col.).

39. Passenger List: 28 March 1928, RMS *Aquitania* arrives in Southampton from New York. Traveling in first-class, Addie Kahn - address, Claridge's, London.

40. The *Brooklyn Daily Eagle*, 29 February 1928, p. 12A - Theater Notes.

41. *Variety*, 11 April 1928, p. 52 - Legitimate (theater) - *And Howe!*

42. *Variety*, 11 April 1928, p. 52 - Plays Out of Town: Philadelphia, April 10, *And Howe!* (rev.).

43. Sloat, Warren. *1929: America Before the Crash*, MacMillan Publishing Co. Inc., NY, 1979, p. 174 - Otto Kahn's visit to Hollywood.

44. *Variety*, 11 April 1928, p. 52 - Legitimate (theater) - *And Howe!*

45. *Variety*, 10 October 1928, p. 43 - Chatter In New York (col.).

46. *Variety*, 2 May 1928, p. 56 - Legitimate, Estimates for Last Week (col.).

47. Ibid., 57 - 23 Dark Houses; 40 Open Now As Season Seems Folding Up.

48. The *Brooklyn Daily Eagle*, 2 May 1928, p. 14A - *Here's Howe!* Arrives.

49. *Variety*, 9 May 1928, p. 64 - What's in *Here's Howe?*

50. Ibid., 67 - Aarons and Freedley Markedly Spurn Shubert Interference.

51. Ibid., 69 - *Here's Howe!* (rev.) by Abel Green.

52. Vets - veterans.

53. *Variety*, 6 June 1928, p. 54 - Roger Wolfe Kahn - Disc Reviews.

54. *Variety*, 9 May 1928, p. 69 - *Here's Howe!* (rev.) by Abel Green.

55. The *Music Trade Review*, 11 August 1928, p. 37 - '*Crazy Rhythm*' Takes Hold as Dance Number (rept.).

56. *Variety*, 23 May 1928, p. 53 - On The Square (col.) Mad Now Patch.

57. *Variety*, 16 May 1928, p. 54 - Williams Sisters Move (rept.).

58. The *Exhibitors Herald*, 26 May 1928, p. 75 - Paramount Elects Son of Otto H. Kahn Member of Board of Directors (rept.).

59. George Barr Mallon was one of the 11 founding members of the Dutch Treat Club. He was presently the city editor at *The Sun* (NY) daily.

60. Dutch Treat Club Annual 1905 - 1943 (38th anniversary), Published in New York, 1943, p. 77 - History of the Dutch Treat Club (art.).

61. *New York Evening Post*, 5 June 1928, p. 28 - *Here's Howe!* Luncheon.

62. Passenger List: 23 July 1928, RMS *Majestic* arrives in Southampton from New York. Traveling in first-class Addie Kahn.

63. The *Brooklyn Daily Eagle*, 30 July 1928, p. 10A - Reverting To Type by Rian James, It Ain't So (editorial) Otto H. Kahn denial letter printed.

64. *Variety*, 18 July 1928, front page - A Few Millions for Roger Kahn at 21.

65. *Variety*, 15 August 1928, p. 3 - Roger Kahn Will Not Be Millionaire at 21: Otto H. Kahn denial letter to *Variety*.

66. *Variety*, 25 July 1928, front page - Kahn Is A Liberal Donator But Banker's System 50-50 on Year (rept.).

67. Ibid., 50 - *Legitimate* - *New Americana* with McEvoy and Young Kahn.

68. *Variety*, 15 August 1928, p. 5 - Mindlin's Kahn Deal (rept.).

69. *Variety*, 19 September 1928, p. 43 - Greenwich Village as Iz (col.).

70. Passenger List: 8 August 1928, RMS *Aquitania* arrives Southampton from New York. Traveling in first-class, Otto Kahn - address, Claridge's, London.

71. *Variety*, 29 August 1928, p. 57 - Ballroom With Kahn (rept.) Star, at 110 West 42nd Street.

72. *Variety*, 5 September 1928, p. 59 - This Is Paris (col.) Superman and Everyman.

73. Otto Kahn photographed in his suite at the Hotel Adlon, Berlin, October 1928, during Otto's meeting with Hugo Eckener. Das Bundesarchiv, photograph by Georg Pahl. Ref: Bild 102-06711.

74. The *Thanet Advertiser*, 14 September 1928, front page - Ramsgate Visitors (rept.).

75. The *Leeds Mercury*, 13 September 1928, front page - Millionaire Ship (rept.). RMS *Olympic* set sail from Southampton on 12 September.

76. The *Brooklyn Daily Eagle*, 23 September 1928, p. 7 - Us Busy Executives - You Know (art.) by Jo Ranson.

77. *Variety*, 10 October 1928, p.39 - Women folks (col.) by Molly Gray. Talk and Clothes Vie.

78. The *Brooklyn Daily Eagle*, 23 September 1928, *Sunday Eagle Magazine*, p. 7 - Us Busy Executives - You Know, J. P. McEvoy by Jo Ranson.

79. *Variety*, 10 October 1928, p. 50 - Legitimate (page) Advance for *Americana* OK (rept.).

80. *Variety*, 17 October 1928, p. 51 - Legitimate (page) *Americana* $18,000 Sole Hub Prospect (rept.).

81. Ibid., 72 - Legitimate (page) Plays Out of Town, *Americana* (rev., Boston October 11).

82. The *Reading Times*, Reading, PA, 30 November 1928, p. 22 - Roger Kahn Hunts Fugitive in Plane (rept.).

83. The *Milwaukee Sentinel*, 29 November 1928, p. 4 - Young Kahn Back to Band After Air Hunt (rept.).

84. The *Brooklyn Daily Eagle*, 31 October 1928, p. 12A - More *Americana* (rev.) by Arthur Pollock.

85. *Variety*, 5 September 1928, p. 64 - full-page advt. of the Williams Sisters featured in *Parisian Nights* at the Paramount Theatre.

86. The *Evening Independent*, Florida, 16 November 1928, p. 11A - At The Theaters (col.).

87. *Variety*, 7 November 1928, p. 49 - McEvoy's *Americana* Off; Closed Without Notice (rept.).

88. *Exhibitors Herald World*, 18 January 1930, p. 57 & 62 - The Cinema Art Movement (art.).

89. Klein, Henry H., *Dynastic America and Those Who Own* It, H. H. Klein, NY, 1921, p. 128 - 'Among the chief contributors to the Republican state committee fund were John D. Rockefeller ... Otto H. Kahn ...' etc.

90. The *Harrisburg Telegraph*, 29 October 1928, p.11 (second edition) - Otto Kahn Lends Support to Hoover (rept.).

91. The *Daily Deadwood Pioneer-Times*, South Dakota, 27 October 1928, front page - (rept.).

92. *Variety*, 14 November 1928, p. 51 - Young Kahn Bringing Back *Americana* (rept.).

93. *Variety*, 19 August 1936, p. 61 - News From The Dailies (rept.).

94. The *Biloxi Daily Herald*, 24 November 1928, front page - Thomas F. Ryan - Ryan Leaves Huge Estate (rept.).

95.   *The New Yorker*, 10 September 1955, p. 43 - Rummaging Around With The Ryans (art.) by Geoffrey T. Hellman.
96.   The *Brooklyn Daily Eagle*, 30 November 1928, page 18A - The Theaters - *New Americana* (rev.) by Arthur Pollock.
97.   *Variety*, 7 November 1928, p. 51 - Legitimate: *Americana* (rept.).
98.   Ibid., 45 - McEvoy's *Americana* Off Closed Without Notice (rept.).
99.   *Brooklyn Life*, 8 December 1928, p. 17 - *New Americana* (rev.).
100.   The *Brooklyn Daily Eagle*, 15 Dec. 1928, p. 12, Staccato Stuff (col.).
101.   The *Indianapolis Star*, 18 November 1928, p. 73 - Activities in Music.
102.   *Variety*, 12 December 1928, front page - Kahn $210,000 in Red On *Americana*; And Off (rept.).
103.   *Variety*, 19 December 1928, p. 25 - Vaudeville page - Kahn Prefers New York (rept.).
104.   *Vaudeville News*, 29 December 1928, p. 79 - Vaudeville Routes.

Notes

* (p. 369) 'Among My Souvenirs' originated from the UK. When it arrived in the U.S., Victor record company leaped on it and had five of its top orchestras record a version. Paul Whiteman made a twelve-inch concert adaptation, and Roger and his band produced a dance arrangement. Roger's version was issued some weeks in advance of the others. To publicize its release, Victor featured three of the recordings in a car-card cross-country advertising campaign starting on January 6, 1928.[1] The Philadelphia music store H. A. Weymann & Sons devoted an entire shop window to promote the sheet music; such was the song's popularity. In America, publishing sales alone for the song were unprecedented in the short time since its release.[2]

    1.   *Talking Machine World*, January 1928 (issue).
    2.   *Talking Machine World*, January 1928 (issue), p. 113 - H. A. Weymann & Sons, Philadelphia, Give window to '*Among My Souvenirs*'.

* (p. 370a) Madame Blanche Le Ralec was an impoverished French aristocrat when she immigrated to Canada and then the U.S. to turn her fortunes around. She built a cake business that revolutionized the wedding cake industry. Her celebrated Black Douglas cake graced more society weddings than any other cake in the world, including those of the Rockefeller, Vanderbilt, Carnegie, and Morgans.[1] Every lauded wedding cake since 1911 had originated in the pocket-sized workroom of Madame Blanche's smart New York kitchen in the Upper East Side. Her secret Black Douglas cake recipe was a gift from an Englishwoman, the recipe having originated in the 13th century from Scotland's Black Douglases.

    1.   The *Los Angeles Times*, 4 June 1944, page 97 - Wedding Cake Queen by Clementine Paddleford (art.).

* (p. 370b) On February 17, as the SS *Leviathan* neared Southampton, she ran ashore near Calshot at the head of Southampton Water and became stuck on a sandbank. Four tugs helped move her astern. She reached port 45 minutes behind schedule with no damage reported to the hull.[1]

    1.   The *Brooklyn Daily Eagle*, 17 February, front page - *Leviathan* Ashore at Southampton, Freed by Four Tugs.

* (p. 377) The photo was likely taken at the Texas & Pacific Passenger Train Station in Fort Worth, Texas, after or before a visit with Amon G. Carter at his Shady Oaks Farm.
AR406-6-67-3

* (p. 381) *Crazy Rhythm* lyric p. 387 & p. 391 @ Roger Wolfe Kahn, Joseph Meyer, Irving Caesar (Warner Songs).

* (p. 383) *Blackbirds of 1928* struggled at first to make an impact on Broadway. Mixed reviews and low attendance figures plagued the production for the first few weeks until Leslie added a late-night show that attracted the after-theater crowd. Ticket sales increased, and the show became a hit.

* (p. 384a) The Dutch Treat Club had previously selected Roger as their guest of honor in 1925, a place hitherto filled by Vincent Lopez and Paul Whiteman.[1] At the time, it helped put young Kahn on the map; 'Kahn arrived when, guest of honor, of Dutch Treat Club.'
    1.   *The New Yorker*, 24 October 1925, p. 3 - Talk of the Town (col.): Roger Wolfe.

* (p. 384b) In 1928, Otto invited New York photographer Arnold Genthe to Long Island to capture his Cold Spring Harbor estate. Dull, overcast weather conditions dogged the photographer's visit, and the surviving prints are gray and unimpressive. Genthe's eye for detail appears lost in the vastness of vistas and open space surrounding the château. On July 22, 3.21 inches of rain fell during the day in Syracuse, New York.

* (p. 385) *Here's Howe!* performed a total of 71 performances on Broadway.

* (p. 393) Confusingly, the address of *Le Perroquet de Paris* appeared incorrectly in certain adverts. Most listed 146 West 57th Street, but some printed 145 West 57th Street. The address of *Les Ambassadeur's* was 146 West 57th Street, and the address of The New Little Cinema that later became the Little Carnegie Playhouse was also at 146. The Russian Art Chocolate and Russian Tea Room was at 145 West 57th Street, which later moved to 150 West 57th Street.

* (p. 395a) Roger discovered after his father died that the $30,000 (three $10,000 checks) that J. P. McEvoy had loaned from Otto to produce *Americana* remained unpaid. Roger issued legal proceedings against McEvoy to reclaim the money. 'A separate charitable branch in the Kuhn, Loeb & Co. office takes care of Kahn's endowments, but the banker must be personally sold on the worthiness and merit of the enterprise before he authorizes any monetary succor. The same department also takes care of the out-and-out charity donations to campaign drives, organized federations and whatever meritorious individuals might come to Kahn's attention.'[1]
    1.   *Variety*, 25 July 1928, front page - Kahn Is A Liberal Donator But Banker's System 50-50 on Year.

* (p. 395b) Thomas Fortune Ryan was a dominant figure in finance until he retired from thirty-five of his corporations in 1908. Even in retirement, he was still active in business and was frequently seen working in his office at the Guaranty Trust Company. On Monday, November 19, 1928, during a luncheon at his office, Ryan took ill. Two days later, he was suffering from acute inflammation of the gallbladder. His elderly age prevented an operation. He passed away at his home at 858 Fifth Avenue during the afternoon on November 23 with his children and grandchildren at his bedside.

Chapter 12. Hot Depression Jazz
    1.   *Brooklyn Life*, 5 January 1929, p. 17 - Brooklyn Life (col.).
    2.   *Variety*, 9 January 1929, front page - $500,000 Show loss for Young Kahn and worth it in Broadway Experience (rept.).

3.　Ibid., 65 - Disk Reviews by Abel Green.

4.　The *Pittsburgh Press*, PA, 18 September 1927, p. 61 - Paddles Own Canoe (rept.) 'Roger (Wolfe Kahn) ranks on the lists of the Victor Co., as one of the producers of the first 25 most popular records they supply to the millions of phonograph buyers.'

5.　The *Brooklyn Daily Eagle*, 6 January 1929, page 53 - On The Keith-Albee Circuit (col.).

6.　*Variety*, 23 January 1929, p. 40 - Flu (rept.).

7.　The *Brooklyn Daily Eagle*, 8 January 1929, page 19 - Theater News (col.) E. F. Albee Theatre (rev.).

8.　*The Palm Beach Post*, 20 January 1929, section 2 p. 2 - Palm Beach Society and News Happenings (col.).

9.　The *New York Sun*, 5 January 1929, p. 18 - Otto Kahn Catches Forty-Pound King Fish (rept.).

10.　The *Standard Union*, 12 January 1929, p. 13 - In The Keith Theaters - Roger Wolfe Kahn (rept.).

11.　The *Brooklyn Daily Eagle*, 18 January 1929, p. 12A - Next Week at The Albee (rept.).

12.　Pollack, Howard. *George Gershwin: His Life and Work*, University of California Press, 2006, p. 412.

13.　*New York Times*, 23 January 1929, p. 13 - Otto Kahn is ill at home.

14.　The *Asbury Park Press*, New Jersey, 23 January 1929, p. 4 - (rept.).

15.　*New York Times*, 27 January 1995 - Margaret Kahn Ryan, aged 93, Financier's Daughter Dies (obit.).

16.　The *Exhibitors Herald-World*, 2 February 1929, p. 22 - Full-page advert for The Motion Picture Ball.

17.　The *Exhibitors Herald-World*, 16 February 1929, p. 32 - Big Attendance Features Paramount Pep Club Ball; Ash Puts Over Stage Show (rev.).

18.　*Variety*, 13 February 1929, p. 45 - New Acts (vaudeville) Roger Wolfe Kahn and band (fifteen-piece) with the Williams Sisters (rev.).

19.　Ibid., 34 - Keith's Fourth Radio (rept.).

20.　The *Brooklyn Daily Eagle*, 13 February 1929, p. A - On The Radio Last Night (col.).

21.　The *Daily Sentinel* (Rome, New York), 13 February 1929, p. 9 - Last Night On The Air (col.) by Georgie Flanders.

22.　The *Brooklyn Daily Eagle*, 18 February 1929, p. 24 - Stutz-Bellanca Combine Formed To Build Planes (art.).

23.　The *Brooklyn Daily Eagle*, 10 March 1929, p. 3 - Upsetting Family Tradition (interview).

24.　American Experience - The Crash of 1929 - transcript.

25.　The *Chicago Daily Tribune*, 5 April 1929, p. 3 - Otto H. Kahn Sued For Libel by Girl Singer - Otto H. Kahn sailed for Europe unannounced on the *Ile de France* [29 March] with two guards watching his stateroom.

26.　The *Musical Courier*, 31 January 1928, p. 11 - Advert placed by Rosalinda Morini.

27.　The *Arizona Republican* (Phoenix), 26 October 1930, p. 6 - Songbird Comes to Arizona (rept. & pict.).

28.　The *Morning Call* (Laurel, Mississippi), 7 April 1929, front page - Alleges Kahn Caused Her to Lose All Future (rept.).

29.　The *New York Evening Post*, 5 April 1929, p. 5 - Otto Kahn is Sued For $250,000 Libel (rept.).

30.　The *Waco News-Tribune* (Texas), 2 May 1929, p. 4 - Rosalinda Morini Will Sing in Amarillo (rept.).

31. The *New York Evening Post*, 5 April 1929, p. 5 - Otto Kahn is Sued For $250,000 Libel (rept.).

32. The *Chicago Daily Tribune*, 5 April 1929, p. 3 - Otto H. Kahn Sued For Libel by Girl Singer (rept.).

33. The *Morning Call* (Laurel, Mississippi), 7 April 1929, front page Alleges Kahn Caused Her to Lose All Future (rept.).

34. The *Springfield Leader*, 11 May 1929, front page - Suing Singer To 'Shock Musical World,' Woman Asking $250,000 Confident of Vindication (rept.).

35. The *Morning Call* (Laurel, Mississippi), 7 April 1929, front page - Alleges Kahn Caused Her to Lose All Future Bookings: 'Mr. Kahn, who left a week ago for Europe, naturally could not be asked for his version of the case. London dispatches say he has gone into seclusion there!'

36. The *Morning Call* (Laurel, Mississippi), 6 April 1929, p. 3 - Otto Kahn Sued Girl Singer (rept.).

37. The *Times Herald* (Olean, New York), 5 April 1929, front page - Otto H. Kahn Named Defendant in Libel Brought by Soprano (rept.).

38. The *Pittsburgh Post-Gazette*, PA, 27 March 1929, p. 1 - Singer Asks $250,000 for Slander (rept.).

39. *Variety*, 24 April 1929, p. 55 - Flying Bandsmen (rept.).

40. The *Pittsburgh Press*, 9 June 1929, p. 8 (automobile section) - New Note in Aviation (pict. & capt.).

41. *Variety*, 24 April 1929, page 56 - Disk Reviews by Abel Green.

42. *Variety*, 15 May 1929, page 64 - Edison Lateral Record (short art.).

43. *Variety*, 24 July 1929, p. 73 - Disk Reviews by Abel Green.

44. *Variety*, 15 May 1929, p. 52 - Chatter in New York (col.).

45. *Vaudeville News*, 4 May 1929, p. 9 - As We Go To Press (col.).

46. *TIME* magazine, 20 May 1929, n. p. - Business and Finance: Great Kahn.

47. The *Times*, 14 May 1929, p.11 - The Estate Market, St Dunstan's - Auctions Today (rept.).

48. *Variety*, 19 June 1929, p. 64 - Americans Abroad (col.).

49. *Variety*, 3 July 1929, p. 99 - Kahn in Stockholm (rept.).

50. Forster, Margaret. *Daphne Du Maurier*, Arrow, 1993, chapter 4, p. 65.

51. *Variety*, 3 July 1929, p. 88 - News From the Dailies (rept.).

52. Passenger List: 26 June 1929, RMS *Aquitania* arrives in Southampton from New York - traveling in first-class, Addie Kahn.

53. Letter from American Historian Royall Tyler to American Art Collector Mildred and Philanthropist Barnes Bliss, dated 17 July 1929.

54. *Variety*, 7 August 1929, front page (rept.) & p. 2 (advt.).

55. The *Film Daily*, 7 July 1929, p. 6 - 'U' Buys *Here's Howe*! (rept.).

56. *Variety*, 3 July 1929, p. 96 - Words About Music (col.) by Abel Green.

57. The *Brooklyn Daily Eagle*, 15 June 1929, p. 7 - Aviation News Notes.

58. *Variety*, 17 July 1929, front page - Young Kahn's 5 Planes (rept.).

59. The *Brooklyn Daily Eagle*, 11 July 1929, p. 15 - Vigilance Group Created at Long Island Field to Control Flying of Private Pilots (rept.).

60. The *Times*, 26 July 1929, p. 17 - Court Circular (col.) 'Mr. Otto Kahn has left Claridge's for the U.S.'

61. Passenger List: 25 July 1929, RMS *Majestic* departs Southampton for New York. Onboard is Otto Kahn, Frederick Cooper (valet), and Elizabeth Mutke (secretary).

62. The *Daily Sentinel*, Rome, New York, 31 July 1929, p. 9 - Flashes From Press Wires (col.).

63. *New York Times*, 10 October 1929, p. 20 - Otto H. Kahn to Lead Suffolk

Republicans (rept.). Banker Accepts Chairmanship of Campaign Committee - Surprise to Politicians.

64.   The *Brooklyn Daily Eagle*, 3 p.m. edition 10 October 1929, p. 16 - Otto Kahn to Head Suffolk GOP Drive (rept.).

65.   The *Brooklyn Daily Eagle*, 11 October 1929, p. 25 - Otto Kahn Sees GOP Victory In Acceptance Note (rept.).

66.   The *Brooklyn Daily Eagle*, 14 October 1929, p. 20 - Suffolk County farmers ... (rept.).

67.   The *Brooklyn Daily Eagle*, 28 September 1929, p. 4 - Buys Sixth Plane.

68.   The *Brooklyn Daily Eagle*, 11 October 1929, p. 24 - Roger Wolfe Kahn Tests New Amphibian (rept.).

69.   The *Decatur Herald* (Illinois), 1 October 1929, p. 16 - Last Minute Photos in the News (pict. of Roger and Otto standing in front of a Vought Corsair plane at Roosevelt Field). 'Roger Wolfe Kahn, bandleader and aviation enthusiast, shows his father, Otto H. Kahn, his new Vought Corsair plane at Roosevelt Field, New York. The army model has top speed of 160 mph and landing speed of 60 miles.'

70.   The *Daily Plainsman* (Huron, South Dakota), 16 October 1929, p. 6 - Famous Soprano to be Here Soon - Metropolitan Opera Star Will Appear in First recital of 1929-30 season on 26 October (rept.).

71.   The *Brooklyn Daily Eagle*, 3 p.m. edition, 10 October 1929, front page - Ex-Secretary of Kahn Suicide by Garage Gas (rept.).

72.   Tolppanen, Bradley P. *Churchill in North America, 1929: A Three Month Tour of Canada and the United States*, McFarland & Co. 2014, p. 207.

73.   The *Brooklyn Daily Eagle*, 22 October 1929, front page & p. 43 - Edison Resting At Ford Home After Big Day (rept.).

74.   The *Brooklyn Daily Eagle*, 23 October 1929, 3:30 edition, front page - Stocks Driven Down 20 Points As Bears Force Record Lows (rept.).

75.   The *Brooklyn Daily Eagle*, 24 October 1929, front page - Wall St. In Panic As Stocks Crash (rept.).

76.   Ibid., front page - German Chemist Plunges to Death at Savoy Plaza.

77.   Tolppanen, Bradley P. *Churchill in North America, 1929: A Three Month Tour of Canada and the United States*, McFarland & Co., 2014, p. 224.

78.   The *Brooklyn Daily Eagle*, 3:30 edition, 24 October 1929, front page - Lamont is Optimistic on Wall St. Outlook (rept.). J. P. Morgan Jr. was away on vacation in Europe.

79.   Ibid., front page - Stocks Rally After Worst Crash (rept.).

80.   The *Brooklyn Daily Eagle*, 25 October 1929, p. 22 - Vice President Curtis Attends Huston Dinner (rept.).

81.   The *Brooklyn Daily Eagle*, 29 October 1929, p. 5 - Kahn Feared Too Effete For GOP in Rough West (rept.). Old guard doubts if provinces would shell out campaign cash to opera patron and wearer of foreign medals - Financier wants to withdraw.

82.   The *Brooklyn Daily Eagle*, 3:30 edition, 25 October 1929, p. 43 - Stocks Hold Well Under Heavy Distress Selling; Turn Up After Early Dip.

83.   Ibid., 30 - The Top of The New by Frederick Boyd Stevenson (col.).

84.   The *Brooklyn Daily Eagle*, 26 October 1929, front page & p. 2 - Hoover Declares Business In U.S. Generally Sound (rept.).

85.   The *Brooklyn Daily Eagle*, 22 October 1929, p. 20 - Kahn Will Greet Suffolk Workers (rept.).

86.   The *Brooklyn Daily Eagle*, 27 October 1929, p. 2 - Kahn Entertains GOP of Suffolk (rept.).

87.   The *Brooklyn Daily Eagle*, 3 p.m. edition, 28 October 1929, front page -

Stocks Rally As Bankers Confer (rept.).

88. The *Brooklyn Daily Eagle*, 28 October 1929, p. 19 - Mad, Gay Life in America Stills Nightingale's Song (rept.).

89. *Chicago Daily Tribune*, 30 October 1929, front page - Stock Slump Ends In Rally (rept.).

90. *Green Bay Press-Gazette*, 30 October 1929, front page - Wall St. Business Better (rept.).

91. The *Brooklyn Daily Eagle*, 3 p.m. edition, 30 October 1929, front page - Stocks Gain: Exchange Will Close (rept.).

92. Letter by Josiah Hirst editor of the London *Economist*, Executive Intelligence Review, 6-12 November 1979, p. 33 - Britain Caused the 1929 Crash (art.).

93. The *Brooklyn Daily Eagle*, 29 October 1929, front page - Stocks Sink Despite Banks; Rally (rept.).

94. Ibid., pp. 5 & 14 - Kahn Feared Too Effete For GOP in Rough West.

95. *Chicago Daily Tribune*, 30 October 1929, front page - Otto H. Kahn Refuses GOP Finance Post (rept.).

96. The *Brooklyn Daily Eagle*, 3 p.m. edition, 30 October 1929, p. 28 - Moses Accepts Kahn Refusal of Campaign Post (rept.).

97. Ibid., front page - Today's News (col.).

98. The *Brooklyn Daily Eagle*, 2 November 1929, p. 12 - Otto H. Kahn would have found neither pleasure nor profit in making himself a political punching bag for the Republican insurgents (rept.).

99. Cottrell, Philip L. and Cassis, Youssef. *Private Banking in Europe: Rise, Retreat, and Resurgence*, OUP Oxford, 2015, p. 227.

100. The *Brooklyn Daily Eagle*, 5 November 1929, front page & p. 2 - Kahn and Morgan's Aid Booze Party, Brookhart Swears (rept.).

101. The *Brooklyn Daily Eagle*, closing prices edition, 6 November 1929, p. 2 - Crime Problem In Capital Gets Hoover's Notice (rept.).

102. Ibid.

103. The *San Bernardino Sun*, 6 November 1929, front page - Brookhart Exposes Booze Party (rept.).

104. The *Brooklyn Daily Eagle*, 5 November 1929, front page & p. 2 - Kahn and Morgan's Aid Booze Party, Brookhart Swears (rept.).

105. The *Brooklyn Daily Eagle*, closing prices edition, 6 November 1929, front page - Brookhart Asks Atterbury, Kahn Grill On Liquor (rept.).

106. The *Brooklyn Daily Eagle*, closing prices edition, 8 November 1929, front page - Hotel Manager Called to Quiz on Booze Dinner (rept.).

107. The *Brooklyn Daily Eagle*, closing prices edition, 7 November 1929, front page - Grand Jury Calls Loomis to Tell of 'Booze Party' (rept.).

108. Ibid., front page - Today's News (col.).

109. The *Brooklyn Daily Eagle*, 13 November 1929, p. 16 - Game Wardens Arrest Two; Fined At Huntingdon (rept.).

110. The *Brooklyn Daily Eagle*, 3 November 1929, p. 70 - Schola Cantorum.

111. The *Brooklyn Daily Eagle*, 21 October 1929, p. 13 - Nassau Police Prepare For Ball (rept.).

112. The *Telegraph*, UK, 20 November 1929 - About New York by Richard Massock (rept.).

113. *Brunswick Records: New York sessions, 1927-1931* by Ross Laird, Brunswick-Balke-Collender Co., Brunswick Radio Corporation, p. 726.

114. *Variety*, 11 December 1929, p. 70 - Monthly Music Survey (col.) November 1929.

115. *Variety*, 4 December 1929, p. 46 - New York Chatter (col.).

116.   The *Brooklyn Daily Eagle*, 13 December 1929, front page - Roger W. Kahn at 22 Owns Six Airplanes (art.).

117.   *Variety*, 25 December 1929, p. 55 - Disc reviews by Bob Landry (rev.) Roger Wolfe Kahn *'Here Am I'* and *'Why Was I Born?'*

118.   *St. Louis Post-Dispatch*, 17 December 1929, p. 2 - Appellate Court Rules Kahn Libeled Singer Who Sued Him (rept.).

119.   *Chicago Daily Tribune*, 30 June 1933, front page - Kahn Points Out Flaws in U.S. Tax Law (rept.).

Notes

* (p. 411) Museum of Fine Arts Boston - Artwork: Andiron - accession number: 57.8.1 - The Mogmar Art Foundation was a private corporation that looked after parts of the Kahn art collection after Otto's death. Pieces from the archive were stored with Duveen Brothers in New York from June 1934 onwards.

* (p. 413) Claire Anne Kahn was born on June 26, 1929.

* (p. 414a) A letter from Otto Kahn to Winston Churchill written on Claridge's, London, headed notepaper, dated 22 July 1929. Ref: CHAR 1/206/62 - The Winston Churchill Archive Trust & content copyright 2003 (1 file (99 folios) Personal: Visit to Canada and the United States: Correspondence.)

* (p. 414b) Churchill confirmed his Canadian itinerary in a private letter to Bernard M. Baruch, 10 July 1929, written from 71 St Stephen's House, Westminster, London.

* (p. 415a) A telegram from Otto Kahn to Winston Churchill, dated 13 September 1929, in which Kahn confirms the date of their forthcoming dinner. Ref: CHAR 1/207/73 - The Winston Churchill Archive Trust & content copyright 2003 (1 file (137 folios) Personal: Visit to Canada and the United States: Correspondence.)

* (p. 415b) A telegram from Otto Kahn to Winston Churchill, dated 11 October 1929, in which Kahn confirms Lord Feversham and Horace Cecil Vickers attendance for dinner. Ref: CHAR 1/208/34 - The Winston Churchill Archive Trust & content copyright 2003 (1 file (125 folios) Personal: Visit to Canada and the United States: Correspondence.)

* (p. 416) That afternoon Churchill returned by train to New York City. He attended an evening party thrown in his honor by Millicent Hearst (wife of the media tycoon William Randolph Hearst). After the meal, Churchill caught another night train, this time to Virginia.

* (p. 419) Kiwanis was founded in 1917 in Detroit, Michigan, and is a global organization of volunteers dedicated to improving the world, one child and one community at a time.

* (p. 420a) New York Daily News Photo Archive: Metropolitan Opera, 1929: 'The night before the stock market crash' by Harry Warnecke (*New York Daily News*). The dowager Mrs. Cornelius Vanderbilt (center above the aisle) and guests seated in a 'Golden Horseshoe' box on the opening night of Puccini's *Manon Lescaut* at the Metropolitan Opera House, October 28, 1929.

* (p. 420b) A gag told by the comedy duo Amos 'n' Andy.

* (p. 422) Churchill's friend Bernard M. Baruch contributed financially to the cost of Churchill's New York Savoy Plaza hotel bill.

* (p. 426) The letter's author (Roger W. Mintone) had enclosed a copy of Brookhart's summons before the Grand Jury. However, who Mr. Mintone was and his connection with the case were never entirely ascertained.

PART III. KAHNIVOROUS FOR MORE   1930–1933

Chapter 13. Here's That Band Again

1. The *Binghamton Press*, 21 January 1930, p. 4 - Roger Wolfe Kahn Spends Hours Operating Miniature Railroad at Father's Home.
2. *Variety*, 8 January 1930, p. 74 - National Celebs Always in 'Character' (art.) by Courteney Allison.
3. The inscription, *'To Bill Feinstein the best tailor I have ever had,'* is written on a photograph of Roger Wolfe Kahn inscribed to Bill Feinstein. On the reverse is a department store sticker from Edw. Malley Co., New Haven, where the photograph was framed. The photograph is in the private collection of Iain Cameron Williams.
4. The *Brooklyn Daily Eagle*, 5 January 1930, p. E3 - Studio and Screen.
5. *Motion Picture News*, 4 January 1930, p. 44 - Roger Kahn at L.I. Studio.
6. The *Brooklyn Daily Eagle*, 5 January 1930, p. E3 - Such Popularity Must Be Deserved (section).
7. *Variety*, 1 January 1930, p. 11 - Song of Otto Kahn in Talker (rept.).
8. The *Pittsburgh Post-Gazette*, PA, 26 June 1944, p. 19 - The Lyons Den.
9. *Variety*, 15 January 1930, p. 73 - Young Kahn and Paramount (rept.).
10. The *Buffalo Courier Express*, 7 January 1930, p. 11 - What's News In Hollywood by Florabel Muir.
11. *Variety,* 18 December 1929, p. 51 - Shows In Rehearsal (col.).
12. The *Brooklyn Daily Eagle*, 7 January 1930, p. 14 - Ought To Be Good.
13. The *Hanover Evening Sun*, PA, 10 January 1930, p. 1 - Sailings today.
14. *Variety*, 22 January 1930, p. 35 - Ill And Injured (col.). Roger Wolfe Kahn is confined to his home in Long Island, a case of chickenpox.
15. Ibid., 45 - Inaccurate Biographies: Otto H. Kahn by Claude Binyon.
16. The *New York Sun*, 16 January 1930, p. 29 - Ambassador at Palm Beach Ends Bathing Beach Fight (rept.).
17. The *Palm Beach Post,* 22 January 1930, p. 11 - Kahn Asserts Rights To Protect Residence In Classification Deal (rept.).
18. *New York Times*, 5 March 1929, p. 32 - S.W. Straus to Build Palm Beach Casino (rept.).
19. Ibid., 29 - Hotel Ambassador Opens (rept.).
20. The *New York Evening Post*, 29 January 1930, p. 13 - Otto H. Kahn Host to Mrs. W. B. Leeds at Palm Beach (rept.). *The Republican-Journal*, 28 January 1930, p. 7 - Multi-Millionaire Marksman (pict.).
21. The *Palm Beach News*, Palm Beach, 22 January 1930, p. 2 - Catches In The Social Stream - Breakers Beach (rept.).
22. 1930 Federal Census, New York, Manhattan, 100 Central Park South, Roger Wolfe Kahn (aged 22) head of the household (rent $580 per month) occupation, musician (concert stage).
23. The *Brooklyn Daily Eagle*, 2 February 1930, p. C7 - War Dept. Plans on 1930 Aviation Will Go on Radio (rept.).
24. The *Brooklyn Daily Eagle*, 6 February 1930, p. 11 - Albany Flight To Open Legion Airplane Show (rept.).

25. The *Brooklyn Daily Eagle*, 7 February 1930, p. 12 - Today's Radio Programs (listings).
26. The *Brooklyn Daily Eagle*, 9 February 1930, p. E9 - Today's Radio Programs (section).
27. The *Brooklyn Daily Eagle*, 16 February 1930, p. D11 - Aircraft Sold To Visitors At The NY Aero Show (rept.).
28. *Variety*, 5 February 1930, p. 54 - *9:15* revue, $20,000 (rept.).
29. Ibid., 55 - *Nine Fifteen Revue*, (rev.).
30. Bordman, Gerald Martin. *American Musical Theatre: A Chronicle*, Oxford University Press, 1978, p. 514 - *Nine Fifteen Revue*.
31. *Silver Screen*, June 1931 (issue), p. 37 - *The Lucky Twenty-Eight* by John Auburn (art.) Arline Judge.
32. *Variety*, 12 February 1930, p. 59 - Shows In New York And Comment.
33. The *Brooklyn Daily Eagle*, 13 February 1930, p. 23 - *The 9:15* Ruth Selwyn's Revue Is No More Than So-So (rev.).
34. The *Palm Beach Post*, 30 May 1930, p. 1 - Half-Million Additional Announced As Permits Are Issued (rept.).
35. The *Brooklyn Daily Eagle*, 24 February 1930, p. 13 - Today's Radio Programs (listings) Roger Wolfe Kahn's Serenaders.
36. *Variety*, 5 March 1930, p. 65 - Disk Reviews (col.).
37. Laird, Ross. *Brunswick Records: New York sessions, 1927-1931*, Brunswick-Balke-Collender Co., Brunswick Radio Corporation, p. 756.
38. *Variety*, 7 May 1930, p. 73 - Disk Reviews (col.).
39. *The Times*, 1 April 1930, p. 19 - Court Circular (col.).
40. *New York Times*, 29 March 1930, p. 6 - Storm Halts Roger Kahn.
41. *Villanovan, PA.*, 8 April 1930, Vol. 2, No. 25, p. 1 - Junior Prom Band announced.
42. *Villanovan, PA.*, 29 April 1930, Vol. 2, No. 26, p. 1 - Roger Wolfe Kahn and His Serenaders to Furnish Rhythm for Junior Prom (art. & pict.).
43. The *Brooklyn Daily Eagle*, 1 May 1930, p. 19 - Kahn As Test Pilot.
44. The *Brooklyn Daily Eagle*, 2 May 1930, p. 19 - Kahn in Forced Landing.
45. The *Brooklyn Daily Eagle*, 14 February 1930, p. 25 - Today's Radio Programs - 1400k - WLTH - 214M (listings).
46. *Modern Mechanix*, September 1930 - Many Queer Gadgets Found on Burnelli's New Airplane (art. with a diagram of the airplane).
47. *Variety*, 2 July 1930, p. 66 - Disk Reviews (col.).
48. *Variety*, 21 May 1930, p. 42 - Paris Chatter (col.).
49. The *Morning Herald* (Hagerstown, Maryland), 5 September 1930, front page - Crowds Welcome French Fliers at Dallas (rept.).
50. The *Portsmouth Herald* (New Hampshire), 4 September 1930, front page - Question Mark on Way To Dallas From New York (rept.) New York's Welcome to French Airmen (pict. & capt.).
51. The *Brooklyn Daily Eagle*, 24 May 1930, p. 24 - Kahn Tests Pickup.
52. The *Standard Union*, 24 May 1930, p. 3 - Young Kahn Passes Mail Plane Tests (art.).
53. The *Brooklyn Daily Eagle*, 7 June 1930, p. 9 - Fore And Aft (col.).
54. The *Brooklyn Daily Eagle*, 14 June 1930, p. 24 - Kahn Tests New Plane.
55. The *Brooklyn Daily Eagle*, 22 June 1930, front page - Long Island Hail Storm Drives Planes From Air to Ground Shelter (art.).
56. Ibid.
57. *Variety*, 21 May 1930, p. 48 - Broadway Chatter (col.).
58. *Variety*, 9 July 1930, p. 49 - Editorial - Round The Square (col.).
59. The *Lawrence Daily Journal World*, 9 July 1930, p. 4 - Flashes of Life.

60. The *Brooklyn Daily Eagle*, 9 July 1930, p. 13 - Kahn Fishes From Plane.
61. The *Standard Union*, 1 Aug. 1930, front page - Otto Kahn's Yacht Afire.
62. Report of Official Test, 8 August 1930 (courtesy of *Aviation News*).
63. *Skyways Magazine*, April 2010, p. 11 - Aviation In The Newsreels (art. and pict. of Roger Wolfe Kahn piloting his Bellanca plane).
64. The *Brooklyn Daily Eagle*, 14 Aug. 1930, p. 15 - Kahn Flies to Norfolk.
65. The *Brooklyn Daily Eagle*, 18 August 1930, p. 13 - Daily Aviation Record and News From Fields (rept.).
66. *Brooklyn Life*, 23 August 1930, p. 11 - Quogue (rept.).
67. The *Brooklyn Daily Eagle*, 6 September 1930, p. 22 - Daily Aviation Records And News From The Fields (rept.).
68. The *Outlook*, 24 September 1930, p. 138 - Relic (rept.) 'With old New York landmarks steadily vanishing, it is nice to know that the Metropolitan Opera House will remain where it is.'
69. Stewart, Jules. *Gotham Rising: New York in the 1930s*, I. B. Taurus & Co. Ltd., 2016, chapter 10, p. 166.
70. *TIME* magazine, 8 December 1930, n. p. - Roger Wolfe Kahn Aviation Columnist for the *Newark Free Press* (rept.).
71. *Newark Free Press*, New Jersey, 10 November 1930, n. p. - Aero Plain Talk by Roger Wolfe Kahn (art.).
72. The *Daily Star* (Long Island City), evening, 8 November 1930, p. 2 - Night Flying Inaugurated at Curtiss Airport (rept.).
73. The *Brooklyn Daily Eagle*, 24 December 1930, p. 15 - Movie Operetta, *New Moon*, Opens at the Astor Theatre (rev.).
74. The *Brooklyn Daily Eagle*, 29 December 1930, p. 29 - Firm Changes Announced by Several Houses (rept.).

Notes

* (p. 445) After the stock market rallied in April 1930, it crashed yet again, eventually ending 89 percent down from its 1929 high. The market did not reach its 1929 high for another quarter of a century.

* (p. 450) The freighter was probably a prototype variant of a Junkers W33. Junkers representative at the test flight was the pilot Carl Anderson.

* (p. 455) Hotel Pierre Inc. filed for bankruptcy on March 7, 1932. Charles Pierre Casalasco died in September 1934.

* (p. 458) Otto helped develop Grace Moore's operatic singing career.

Chapter 14. The Secret's Out

1. The *Northern Miner*, 1 September 1931, p. 2 - Boy Jazz King Retires.
2. The *New York Sun*, 5 January 1931, p. 28 - Vice Presidents Are Appointed for Charity Ball (rept.).
3. The *Brooklyn Daily Eagle*, 10 January 1931, p. 9 - *You Said It* Coming (rept.). *You Said It* featuring Lou Holtz will make its New York debut at Chanin's 46th Street Theatre on the same night (19 January) *Sweet and Low* will move to the 44th Street Theatre.
4. Ibid., 9 - Promoted on Merit (rept.). Billy Rose, producer of *Sweet and Low*, has promoted Hannah Williams to the position of featured player in recognition of her unusual talents. She will share honors with Fanny Brice, James Barton, and George Jessel.
5. The *Standard Union*, 30 January 1931, p. 3 - Roger Wolfe Kahn passes

6. Transport Air Pilot Test (rept.).

6. The *Brooklyn Daily Eagle*, 30 Jan. 1931, p. 17 - Kahn Gets Transport License (rept.).

7. The *Brooklyn Daily Eagle*, 9 Feb. 1931, front page - Honeymoon in the Air for Roger Kahn's (rept. & pict.). Plane of Banker's Son, Who Wed Hannah Williams, Actress, Quietly Jan. 26, is tested at Roosevelt Field.

8. The *New York Sun*, 2 February 1931, p. 26 - Palm Beach Dispatch (col.). Mrs. Otto H. Kahn has arrived in Palm Beach to prepare villa Oheka.

9. The *Gettysburg Times*, 9 February 1931, p. 2 - Financier's Son Wed to Daughter of Coal Miner (rept.).

10. The *Binghamton Press*, evening edition, 11 February 1931, p. 5 - Bride of Roger Wolfe Kahn Made Start In Binghamton (rept.).

11. *The Long Islander*, 13 February 1931, front page - Roger Wolfe Kahn Marries Star Actress (rept.).

12. United States Marriage Certificate, 26 Jan. 1931 - Roger Wolff Kahn (23) and Hannah Williams (20). Huntington, Suffolk, New York State. Hannah's parents are Thomas Williams and Martha Hughes.

13. The *Troy Times*, 9 February 1931, front page - Roger Wolfe Kahn, Son of Banker, and Actress are Wed (rept.).

14. The *Journal News* (Ohio), 13 February 1931, p. 6 - Young Roger Kahn, Son of Banker, Has Already Earned $40,000, Chose His Own Career In Music Now Marries His Principal Dancer (rept.).

15. The *Evening News* (New York), 9 February 1931, front page - Roger Wolfe Kahn and Bride on Honeymoon (rept.).

16. *The Portsmouth Times*, 9 February 1931, front page - Roger W. Kahn Weds Actress (rept.).

17. *The Long Islander*, 13 February 1931, front page - Roger Wolfe Kahn Marries Star Actress (rept.).

18. The *Brooklyn Daily Eagle*, 9 Feb. 1931, front page - Honeymoon in the Air for Roger Kahn's (rept. & pict.). Plane of Banker's Son, Who Wed Hannah Williams, Actress, Quietly Jan. 26, is Tested at Roosevelt Field.

19. The *Brooklyn Daily Eagle*, 12 February 1931, p. 2 - Roger Wolfe Kahn and Hannah Williams (pict. & capt.).

20. The *Evening News* (Harrisburg), 18 February 1931, p. 8 - (pict. & capt.) Vincent J. Burnelli and his wife in Miami.

21. *Palm Beach News*, 25 Feb. 1931, p. 2 - Catches In The Social Stream.

22. The *New York Evening Post*, 13 February 1931, p. 9 - Otto Kahn Due At Palm Beach (rept.).

23. *Palm Beach News*, 25 Feb. 1931, p. 2 - Catches In The Social Stream.

24. *Chicago Sunday Tribune*, 1 March 1931, p. 5 - Roger and Hannah relaxing together on a garden bench-swing in Miami (pict. & capt.).

25. The *Palm Beach Post*, 8 March 1931, p. 11 - Honeymooners Arrive In Palm Beach on Friday 6 March (pict. & short art.).

26. The *New York Sun*, 6 January 1934 - Bath And Tennis Club Has Opening Palm Beach Party (rept.).

27. The *Palm Beach Post*, 8 March 1931, p. 11 - Activities In Brief (col.).

28. *Radio Digest/Radio Fan Fare*, October 1933, p. 11 - Not all orchestra leaders were nifty on their feet. Roger Wolfe Kahn remembers Hannah Williams' many attempts to teach him steps.

29. The *Brooklyn Daily Eagle*, 22 March 1931, p. 12 B - Brooklyn and Long Island Guests Linger At Palm Beach (rept.).

30. The *Saratogian*, 9 April 1931, front page - Flashes of Life (col.).

31. *New York Times*, 12 April 1931, p. 3 - National Air Show Displays 83

Planes (rept.).

32.   *Flying Magazine*, June 1931 issue, pp. 32-34 - The Detroit Show: Who was there, and what they had to offer (rev.).

33.   The *Saratogian*, 9 April 1931, front page - Flashes of Life (col.).

34.   *Reading Times* (Reading), 22 April 1931, p. 1   Roger Kahn Tests Air Mail Device Norfolk. Va. (rept.).

35.   The *Lewiston Daily Sun* (Maine), 21 April 1931, n. p. - Kahn in Successful Test of Mail Pickup Device (rept.).

36.   The *New York Evening Post*, 28 April 1931, p. 9 - Social Notes (col.) Mrs. Otto H. Kahn.

37.   *The Sentinel*, June 26, 1931, p. 16 - Society (col.).

38.   *Le Figaro*, 18 April 1932, front page - *Les Financiers Qui Mènent Le Monde* - *Réponse A Quelques Objections par François Coty (Quatrième Article)* - *La dynastie qui s'élève en Israël (Suite)* - The Financiers Who Lead The World - Answer To Some Objections by François Coty (fourth art.) - The dynasty rising in Israel (continued).

39.   *Le Figaro*, 20 April 1932, front page - *Les Financiers Qui Mènent Le Monde* - *Réponse A Quelques Objections by François Coty (Cinquième Article)* - *Le filet qui enserre les nations, la position de 'Angleterre* - The Financiers Who Lead The World - Answer to Some Objections by François Coty (fifth art.) - The net that surrounds the nations, the position of England.

40.   Ibid., French to English translation of the extract taken from François Coty's art. (No. 5) titled '*Les Financiers Qui Mènent Le Monde.*'

41.   Kahn, Otto H. *Of Many Things*, Boni & Liveright, 1926. p. 175.

42.   Fahey, Rev. Denis. *The Rulers of Russia*, Cahill & Co. Ltd. Dublin, Ireland, 1938, pp. 6 & 24.

43.   *The Sentinel*, February 21, 1930, p. 4 - Addie spoke six languages.

44.   The *New York Times*, March 28, 1926, front page - Ivy Lee Moved to Aid Soviet; Sends out 'Confidential' Letters to Men of 'Influence' Urging Recognition. A Cold Reply from Root. Says he is acting on his own, not in this case for Standard Oil.

45.   *Vintage Airplane* (The Magazine of the EAA Antique/Classic Division) February 1991 (issue), pp. 33-34 - Mystery Plane by George Hardie - de Havilland DH-80A Puss Moth belonging to Roger Wolfe Kahn.

46.   *Motion Picture Herald*, 20 August 1932, p. 66 - Stage Attractions: Up and Down the Alley (col.).

47.   The *Daily Illini*, 16 July 1931, p. 4 - A New Yorker at Large (col.).

48.   The *Northern Miner*, 1 September 1931, p. 2 - Boy Jazz King Retires (The original *Daily Mail* art. reprinted in *The Northern Miner*).

49.   *The Bystander*, 12 August 1931, p. 322 - In Juan-les-Pins (rept.).

50.   Passenger List: 19 July 1931 - Otto Kahn and valet Frederick Cooper depart Southampton for New York on board SS *Bremen*.

51.   *New York Times*, 30 August 1931 front page - Otto H. Kahn Gives Plan To Bring End To Economic Slump (rept.).

52.   Jakkula, A.A. *Bulletin: A History of Suspension Bridges in Bibliographical Form*, The Agriculture and Mechanical College of Texas, 1941, p. 432 - Greenport Bridge.

53.   Otto purchased 500 acres in Sachem's Neck (now named Mashomack Preserve) on Shelter Island in October 1925: *see* Chapter 8, source 80.

54.   *The County Review*, 10 September 1931, front page & 2 - Grand Jury Starts Suffolk County Probe (rept.).

55.   *The County Review*, 1 October 1931, front page & 2 - Grand Jury Finds No Grounds For Indictment (rept.).

56.   The *Brooklyn Daily Eagle*, 29 September 1931, p. 12 - Singer's $160,000 Suit Against Kahn On: Both Absent (rept.).

57.   The *Anniston Star* (Alabama), 3 October 1931, p. 5 - A Suit Brought Against Otto H. Kahn (rept.).

58.   *Variety*, 29 September 1931, p. 2 - Sailings (listings).

59.   The *Southeast Missourian*, 12 October 1931, p. 6 - Smiling In Kahn-cert.

60.   Aeronautical Chamber of Commerce of America Inc. *The Aircraft Year Book for 1930*, D. Van Nostrand Co. Inc., NY, 1930, chapter 1, pp. 1-6.

61.   *Variety*, 29 April 1931, p. 87 - Bands and Orchestras (listings).

62.   *St. Louis Post-Dispatch*, 27 October 1931, p. 13A - Otto H. Kahn Resigns As Metropolitan Opera Head (rept.). Kahn remains as a director of the Metropolitan Opera Company.

63.   *Variety*, 3 November 1931, p. 42 - News from The Dailies (col.).

64.   The *Brooklyn Daily Eagle*, 19 Feb. 1926, p. 18 - Night and Day (col.).

65.   The *Orrville Courier*, 19 February 1931, p. 4 - Opera (rept.).

66.   Birmingham, Stephen. *The Jews in America Trilogy: 'Our Crowd,' 'The Grandees,' and 'The Rest of Us,'* Open Road Media, 2016, chapter 39. In 1932, Kahn was asked by a young composer how much he had gifted to the Met. He replied, 'for your personal and confidential information, I may say that my endeavors, in one way or another, to aid the cause of the Metropolitan Opera have cost me over two million dollars.' Add to that figure the $1.2 million he paid Oscar Hammerstein to disband the Manhattan Opera Company in 1910 (who were in direct competition with the Met) to get a more accurate idea of what his involvement with the Met cost him.

67.   The *Palm Beach Post*, 6 November 1931, front page - Otto H. Kahn Resigns as Philharmonic Official (rept.).

68.   Mordden, Ethan. *All That Glittered: The Golden Age of Drama on Broadway 1919-1959*, St. Martin's Press, 2007, chapter 6.

69.   Griffiths, David. *Hot Jazz: From Harlem to Storyville*, Scarecrow Press Inc., 1998, p. 235.

70.   The *New York Age*, 26 Dec. 1931, p. 6 - Theatrical Notes (col.). Roger Wolfe Kahn's colored orchestra appears at the Lafayette Theatre, Harlem, week beginning 2 Jan. 1932. Will also open in the fashionable nightclubs of Broadway.

71.   The *New York Age*, 2 Jan. 1932, page 6 - Advert: Lafayette Theatre, Harlem, new revue *Harlem Bound* featuring Butterbeans and Susie and Donald Heywood's Band presented by Roger Kahn (opens Jan. 2).

72.   Ciment, James & Russell, Thaddeus. *The Home Front Encyclopedia: United States, Britain, and Canada*, Vol. 1, ABC-CLIO Ltd., 2006, p. 715.

73.   The *Brooklyn Daily Eagle*, 26 December 1931, p. 18 - Daily Aviation Record and News from Fields (col.).

74.   The *North Countryman* (New York), 22 February 1933, n. p. - (rept.).

Notes

* (p. 461) Otto planned to arrive in Palm Beach on Friday, February 13.

* (p. 464) Hazel Goodwin won the title of 'America's Sweetest Girl' in a nationwide contest in 1925.

* (p. 469) A photograph exists of Otto Kahn asleep on a deckchair on the SS *Bremen*'s sundeck, dated April 21, 1931 - TT News Agency archive.

* (p. 472) During April 1932, François Coty published five leading articles in *Le Figaro* titled '*Les Financiers Qui Mènent Le Monde*,' all written by Coty. The first appeared on April 12, and, afterward, every second day until April 20.

* (p 473a) In 1931, Ivy Lee head-hunted 25-year-old Welsh-born Gareth Jones - the Foreign Affairs Advisor in London to the former Prime Minister Lloyd George. Lee offered Jones a job in New York at Ivy Lee & Associates, which Jones accepted. Lee hired Jones for his language and writing skills; he spoke Russian and German and, for a short period, had been a journalist on *The Times*. Jones was to assist Lee with the research and preparation for a book about the Soviet Union. Jones arrived in New York in April 1931. In May, Lee presented Jones with the assignment to chaperone Jack Heinz II (heir to the Heinz food manufacturing empire) to Russia on a month-long fact-finding mission. Heinz, aged 23, and Jones departed for Russia in August. Large swaths of Russia were in the grips of a famine brought on by Stalin's Five-Year-Plan, implemented in 1928. Jones had previously visited the USSR for three weeks in 1930 and written a series of carefully worded articles published in *The Times* about his trip. With Lee's close connections with the Kahn family, it would not be alarming to discover he had a hand in organizing Addie's Soviet visit. Moreover, that Addie appears to have seemingly traveled unchaperoned indicates 'someone' made assurances for her safety. Was she also on a secret mission? If so, for whom?

* (p. 473b) Captain W. L. Hope won the King's Cup (a 540-mile air race around Britain that began and ended at Hucknall Aerodrome) in 1927 and 1928.

* (p. 479) On October 26, 1931, Otto sent a simple, one-paragraph letter of resignation to the Philharmonic Symphony Orchestra Society - The New York Philharmonic Archives, Otto H. Kahn letters (June 1, 1923 - April 11, 1934).

Chapter 15. A Change Is In The Air

1. The *News Owl*, 1 January 1932, p. 7 - Famous Gossip Gossips With Famous: Walter Winchell talks to Roger and Hannah (pict. & rept.).
2. *New York Times*, 28 June 1933, front page - $35,000 Was Paid To Davis To Promote Chile Loans, Otto H. Kahn Testifies (rept.).
3. The *New York Evening Post*, 6 January 1932, p. 13 - Otto H. Kahn's Join Family In Party At Palm Beach (rept.).
4. The *New York Sun*, 8 January 1932, p. 28 - Mrs. Maurice Fatio Gives Party in her Palm Beach Villa (rept.).
5. The *Brooklyn Daily Eagle*, 10 January 1932, p. 29 - report from Palm Beach. The *Palm Beach Post*, 6 January 1932, p. 5 - Palm Beach Notes (rept.). The *New York Evening Post*, 6 January 1932, p. 13 - Otto H. Kahn's Join Family In Party At Palm Beach (rept.).
6. Photograph of Roger and Hannah bicycling, Bellamar, Palm Beach, 12 January 1932, TT Nyhetsbyrån Archive, Sweden.
7. *The Seven Seas*, January edition 1932, n. p. - pict. of Otto Kahn.
8. Letter of resignation from Otto H. Kahn to the *Cercles des Annales* Society at 36 East 58th Street, New York, dated 17 February 1932.
9. *TIME* magazine, 28 March 1932, p. 27 - People (pict. and rept.).
10. The *Film Daily*, 13 March 1932, p. 12 - *Louis Sobol's Newsreel Scoops*.
11. *Variety*, 29 March 1932, p. 69 - Roger Kahn May Pick Up His Baton Again (rept.).

12.   The *Spur*, 15 March 1932, n.p. - And Two Who Own Their Own Aircraft.

13.   Photograph of Otto and Gilbert Kahn attending the premiere of *Grand Hotel*, Daily News Pix Archive.

14.   *Variety*, 19 April 1932, p. 59 - Kahn Casting (rept.).

15.   The *Brooklyn Daily Eagle*, 29 April 1932, p. 19 - Mrs. Otto H. Kahn Hostess to Damrosch Symphony Committee (rept.).

16.   The *Brooklyn Daily Eagle*, 1 May 1932, p. 4B - Long Island Society.

17.   *Variety*, 3 May 1932, front page & p. 31 - Roger Kahn Has A Squawk at 24 - He Is Not Earning As Much As When 14 (art.).

18.   The *Pittsburgh Post-Gazette*, 7 May 1932, front page - Eager For Stage.

19.   The *Milwaukee Sentinel*, 7 May 1932, front page - Roger Doesn't Want Her To Go Back On Stage (rept.).

20.   Passengers List: 26 May 1932, SS *Bremen*, sailing from New York, arrives in Southampton. Traveling onboard in first-class were Otto and Addie Kahn.

21.   *The Times*, 28 May 1932, p. 15 - Court Circular (col.). Mr. and Mrs. Otto H. Kahn have arrived at Claridge's from New York.

22.   The *Milwaukee Sentinel*, 2 April 1933, p. 3 - One Song and Dance Daughter-in-Law Walks Out Another Walks In (art.).

23.   *The Milwaukee Sentinel*, 26 June 1932, p. 34 - Hannah Williams, Show Girl, Married the Multi-millionaire's Son and Moved Up From Theatrical Boarding-House Life to the Great Otto Kahn Mansion on Fifth Avenue - and Her Troubles Began (rept.).

24.   The *Milwaukee Sentinel*, 21 May 1932, p. 24 - Kahn Mama's Boy His Wife Charges - Roger Ran to Parent With Every Spat: Hannah Leaves.

25.   *Urbana Daily Courier*, 9 May 1932, p. 4 - Moaning Blues in Kahn House.

26.   The *Reading Times* (Reading), 11 June 1932, p. 4 - Walter Winchell on Broadway (col.).

27.   The *Milwaukee Sentinel*, 21 May 1932, p. 24 - Kahn Mama's Boy His Wife Charges - Roger Ran to Parent With Every Spat: Hannah Leaves.

28.   The *Milwaukee Sentinel*, 26 June 1932, p. 34 - Hannah Williams, Show Girl, Married the Multi-millionaire's Son and Moved Up From Theatrical Boarding-House Life to the Great Otto Kahn Mansion on Fifth Avenue - and Her Troubles Began (rept.).

29.   The *Milwaukee Sentinel*, 21 May 1932, p. 24 - Kahn Mama's Boy His Wife Charges - Roger Ran to Parent With Every Spat: Hannah Leaves.

30.   The *Reading Times* (Reading), 11 June 1932, p. 4 - Walter Winchell on Broadway (col.).

31.   *Variety*, 24 May 1932, p. 60 - News From the Dailies (col.). Hannah Williams Kahn drops divorce action against Roger Wolfe Kahn.

32.   The *Milwaukee Sentinel*, 21 May 1932, p. 24 - Kahn Mama's Boy His Wife Charges - Roger Ran to Parent With Every Spat: Hannah Leaves.

33.   *Variety*, 10 May 1932, pp. 31 & 42 - Kahn's Walkout Bride in Demand for Jobs (rept.). At the same time, Otto Kahn's son published a legal notice disclaiming responsibility for any debts contracted by the wife who had walked out on him.

34.   The *Reading Times* (Reading), 11 June 1932, p. 4 - Walter Winchell on Broadway (col.).

35.   The *Milwaukee Sentinel*, 11 May 1932, front page - New York Daily Letter (col.). Hannah Williams Kahn lets it be known that she doesn't want a cent of the Kahn millions.

36.   *Variety*, 10 May 1932, pp. 31 & 42 - Kahn's Walkout Bride in Demand for Jobs (rept.).

37. The *Brooklyn Daily Eagle*, 25 May 1932, p. 22 - Kahn In *Ballyhoo*.

38. The *Brooklyn Daily Eagle*, 22 May 1932, p. C12 - Roger Wolfe Kahn Back On Broadway (rept.). Hannah Williams will open in the Central Park Casino.

39. *Variety*, 13 December 1932, p. 54 - Inside Stuff - Radio (col.).

40. *Variety*, 7 June 1932, p. 31 - Vaudeville page: Wide Difference Over Hannah Williams' Pay (rept.).

41. The *Palm Beach Post*, 7 August 1932, p. 10 - Love Troubles of the Kahn Boys (art.).

42. The *Milwaukee Sentinel*, 13 June 1932, p. 16 - New Kahn Divorce Plans Announced (rept.).

43. The *St. Louis Post-Dispatch*, 3 August 1932, p. 26 - Marital Troubles of the Kahn Boys (art.). One is a dignified disciple of his wealthy father; the other is a saxophone tooter. But they both failed at marriage.

44. The *New York City News*, 10 June 1932, n. p. - 2D, Kahn Son Admits Parting From Mate (pict. & rept.).

45. The *Chicago Daily Tribune*, 6 June 1932, p. 8 - Wealthy Youth Chased by Cop (rept. & pict.).

46. The *Miami Daily News*, 15 June 1932, p. 4 - Air Cops Needed (rept.).

47. The *New York City Journal*, 27 June 1932, n. p. - Plane Crash Fails To Hurt Kahn (rept.).

48. The *New York City News*, 27 June 1932, n. p. - Roger Kahn's Plane Hits Nose Landing; Ramon Gets Bump (rept.).

49. The *New York City American*, 28 June 1932, n. p. - Ramon In Air Crash But To Dance At Lido (rept.).

50. The *Daily News* (New York), June 15, 1932, p. 2 - Mme. Lydia Lindgren, the Swedish Nightingale (The News in Tabloid, col.).

51. *Variety*, 28 June 1932, p. 53 - Disc Reviews by Abel Green.

52. *Variety*, 28 June 1932, p. 43 - Alex Aarons - Roger Kahn Deny Legit Partnership (Legitimate theater, rept.).

53. *Variety*, 19 July 1932, p. 40 - Kahn at $2,250 (rept.).

54. The *Film Daily*, 19 July 1932, p. 7 - Vita Signs Roger Kahn (rept.).

55. The *Film Daily*, 23 July 1932, p. 4 - Short Shots from Eastern Studios.

56. The *Milwaukee Sentinel*, 8 July 1933, p. 2 - Damon Runyon Gives Guinan Girl Big Ring (rept.).

57. *Variety*, 26 June 1932, p. 29 - Capitol, NY, (rev.).

58. *Motion Picture Herald*, 30 July 1932, p. 67 - Spots and Shots on Broadway (col.).

59. *Variety*, 2 August 1932, p. 34 - Film House Reviews - The Capitol, New York, 29 July.

60. The *Brooklyn Daily Eagle*, 25 July 1932, p. 18 - At The Palace (rept.).

61. *Variety*, 26 July 1932, p. 30 - Vaudeville House Reviews - The Palace, New York, Roger Wolfe Kahn's orchestra (22-piece) and Specialties.

62. Ibid., Roger Wolfe Kahn's Orchestra at the Palace (rev.).

63. *Variety*, 19 July 1932, p. 61 - June Music Survey (rept.).

64. The *Brooklyn Daily Eagle*, 28 July 1932, p. 10 - Kahn Leaves *Ballyhoo*.

65. *Variety*, 2 August 1932, p. 27 - Roger Kahn No Like RKO Dough, So He Blow (rept.).

66. Ibid., 51 - Looks Like Dough But Contract Didn't Say So; Kahn Off *Ballyhoo* (rept.). CBS Radio Commercial.

67. *Variety*, 13 September 1932, p. 84 - Disk Reviews by Abel Green.

68. The *Brooklyn Daily Eagle*, 5 August 1932, p. 7 - Broadway Shows For Paramount (rept.). Hannah Williams is Here Today.

69.   *The Yacht Party*, 1932, Roger Wolfe Kahn and His Orchestra directed by Roy Mack, Vitaphone - Library of Congress, USA.

70.   The *Daily Film*, 17 September 1932, pp. 12-13 - Warner Bros. Vitaphone Shorts (advt.).

71.   *The Sentinel*, August 26, 1932, p. 12 - Society (col.).

72.   Passenger List: 16 August 1932 - Otto Kahn departs from Southampton for New York on board RMS *Europa*.

73.   The *Daily News* (New York), 12 August 1932, p. 179 - O. H. Kahn Settles Suit on Ballet (rept.).

74.   *Variety*, 16 August 1932 p. 32 - News From The Dailies, East - Suit of William Reswick against Otto Kahn dropped (rept.).

75.   *Variety*, 9 August 1932, p. 23 - Nabe's Houses $15,000 Show (rept.). Hannah Williams at $1,150.

76.   Ibid., 30 - Loew's Paradise (rev.).

77.   *Variety*, 13 September 1932, p. 65 - Variety Bill listings.

78.   *Boston Mass Eve Globe*, 19 September 1932, n. p. - Son of Otto Kahn Here Leading Own Jazz Band (art.).

79.   *Variety*, 20 September 1932, p. 8 - 'Okay' $17,000 Blah (rept.).

80.   *Variety*, 18 Oct. 1932, p. 14 - Roger Wolfe Kahn *The Yacht Party* (rev.).

81.   *Our Westchester*, October 1932, page 28 - The American Style in Music is Here by Roger Wolfe Kahn (art.).

82.   The *Montreal Gazette*, 8 October 1932, p. 10 - Hannah Williams Closes at Chez Maurice 15 October (rept.).

83.   The *Brooklyn Daily Eagle*, 8 October 1932, p. 2 - Otto H. Kahn Too Ill to Appear in $250,000 Suit of Singer (art.).

84.   *Variety*, 18 October 1932, p. 36 - News From The Dailies (col.).

85.   The *Daily Mirror*, NY, 18 October 1932, n. p. - Walter Winchell Man About Town Column (Rosalinda Morini - Otto H. Kahn lawsuit).

86.   *Variety*, 25 October 1932, p. 36 - News From The Dailies (col.).

87.   *St. Louis Post-Dispatch*, 22 October 1932, p. 3 - Singer Says Otto Kahn Paid Her $100,000 To Drop Suit (rept.).

88.   *Variety*, 18 Oct. 1932, p. 48 - Radio Chatter (East) Frolic at the Pennsy.

89.   *Variety*, 25 October 1932, p. 53 - More Openings (col.).

90.   *Ithacan*, 12 October 1932, p. 4 - Autumn Leaf by Phil Lang (col.). Roger Wolf Kahn will soon sign with NBC network with his band from the Pennsylvania Grill.

91.   The *Cadet* (Lexington, Virginia), 24 October 1932, p. 2 - Pick of the Programs (Radio Listings). Tuesday 25 October 1932, Roger Wolfe Kahn and His Orchestra from 11 p.m. to 12 a.m. on WEAF and WFBR.

92.   *Variety*, 1 November 1932, p. 51 - No Bailey - Kahn (rept.).

93.   The *Pittsburgh Courier*, 10 December 1932, p. 6 second section - Singer James A. Lilliard (art. & pict.).

94.   *Variety*, 1 November 1932, p. 50 - *Sunday Matinee of The Air* with Harry Rose, Jimmy Lyons, Hannah Williams, and the Victor Arden Orchestra (rev.).

95.   The *Oakland Tribune*, 24 July 1932, p. 15 - Howard Barnes (col.). Later this month Billy Rose will start rehearsals.

96.   *Variety,* 1 November 1932, p. 36 - News From The Dailies (col.).

97.   The *Waco News-Tribune*, 11 November 1932, front page & p. 2 - Otto Kahn 'Taxed' by Singer Friend (rept.).

98.   The *Pittsburgh Press*, 11 Nov. 1932, p. 4 - 'Banker Told Her She 'Had a Beautiful Voice and Figure and Made a Stunning Appearance" (rept.).

99.   *Variety*, 15 November 1932, p. 42 - News From The Dailies (col.).

100. The *Daily Inter Lake* (Kalispell, Montana), 15 Nov. 1932, p. 3 - Lucky Strike Dance Orchestra: Roger Wolfe Kahn Orchestra Tuesday Nov. 15.

101. The *News Owl*, 1 Jan. 1932, p. 7 - Famous Gossip Gossips With Famous (col.). Walter Winchell interviews Roger and Hannah (pict. and brief art.) re: *Lucky Strike Magic Carpet Show*.

102. *The Lucky Strike Dance Hour* scripts (November - December) held by the Old Time Radio Researchers Group (OTRR).

103. *Variety*, 11 October 1932, front page - Salaries of Names (col.). Roger Wolfe Kahn Orchestra $2,250 (radio & musicals).

104. The *Cadet* (Lexington, Virginia), 24 Oct. 1932, p. 3 - Lend Thine Ears (col.). Ted Weems and His Orchestra follow Roger Wolfe Kahn at the Pennsylvania.

105. *Variety*, 6 December 1932, p. 49 - Kahn Cedes Band (rept.).

106. Furia, Philip. *Ira Gershwin: The Art of the Lyricist*, Oxford University Press, 1996, chapter 5.

107. The *Brooklyn Daily Eagle*, 25 December 1932, Section E, front page - New Show at Majestic (rept.).

108. The *Brooklyn Daily Eagle*, 27 December 1932, p. 12 - The Theaters by Arthur Pollock (rev.): *Pardon My English*.

109. *Variety*, 13 Dec. 1932, p. 54 - Inside Stuff, Radio (col.). Russ Columbo, Hannah Williams, 3 Pickens Sisters, & Bob Royce at Park Central hotel.

110. *Variety*, 29 November 1932, front page - 'Million Dollar Name' Not Enough To Click (rept.).

111. Nolan, Tom. *Artie Shaw, King of the Clarinet: His Life and Times*, W. W. Norton & Co. reprint 2011, pp. 42-43.

112. The *Brooklyn Daily Eagle*, 24 December 1932, p. 12 - Radio Dial-Log (col.). George Effenbach, formerly manager for Roger Wolfe Kahn has severed his connection with the band man.

113. The *Urbana Daily Courier*, 20 September 1932, p. 4 - Dancer Attracts Banker's Son - Sara Jane Heliker (pict. & capt.).

114. *Variety*, 6 Dec. 1932, p. 42 - Inside Stuff, Legit: Evangeline Raleigh will replace Sara Jane in *Take A Chance* at the Apollo, New York.

115. *Jewish Daily Bulletin*, 23 May 1934, p. 3 - Otto Kahn Home to Echo Soon to Lessons of Catholic Misses. 'The Academy of the Sacred Heart, one of the oldest teaching orders in the Roman Catholic Church, opened negotiations with Mr. Kahn for the purchase of the building back in 1932.'

116. A Letter of Referral exists typed on the Kahns' distinctive green Eleven Hundred Fifth Avenue notepaper, dated October 20, 1932, signed by Addie Kahn, in which she praises Robert McCulloch's skills as a chauffeur and offers a personal reference to any future employer.

117. *Fortune*, Sept. 1932, pp. 32-36 - Kuhn, Loeb: Citadel of Conservatism.

Notes

* (p. 499) 'Dansapation' - silken renditions of melodies (a style Paul Whiteman and His Orchestra had popularized).

* (p. 513) Hannah performed two shows a night (dinner & supper) with Russ Columbo and His Band. During the engagement, Russ fell impossibly in love with Hannah. He had recently separated from his former girlfriend, actress Dorothy Dell, and, like Hannah, who had recently parted from Roger, felt vulnerable and lonely. Their union was insufferably torrid and short-lived. Dorothy Dell died tragically in an auto accident

in June the following year, just months before Columbo's death from a gun shooting accident in September.

* (p. 516) Kuhn, Loeb & Co. partners in 1932: Otto H. Kahn, Jerome Jonas Hanauer, Lewis Lichtenstein Strauss, John Mortimer Schiff, Felix Moritz Warburg, Benjamin Joseph Buttenwieser (baby of the firm, made a partner in January 1932), Frederick Marcus Warburg, Sir William George Eden Wiseman, Gilbert W. Kahn, George Wallace Bovenizer.

Chapter 16. What A Song And Dance

1. The *New York Sun*, 27 January 1933, p. 94 - Orchestra Pension Fund to be Helped By Concert Tonight (rept.).
2. *Niagara Falls Gazette*, 12 January 1933, front page - Divorced (pict. & capt. of Anne W. Kahn).
3. The *Palm Beach Post*, 2 February 1933, p. 6 - Gilbert Kahn Marries Local Girl, Sara Jane Heliker, in New York (rept.).
4. *New York Times*, 2 February 1933, p. 14 - Otto H. Kahn in Europe.
5. The *Brooklyn Daily Eagle*, 1 February 1933, front page - Otto H. Kahn's Son, Gilbert, Weds Again (rept.).
6. *Shamokin News-Dispatch*, PA, 3 February 1933, front page - Gilbert Kahn and Sara Jane Heliker marriage (pict. and rept.).
7. *Variety*, 7 February 1933, p. 56 - News From the Dailies (col.).
8. *Variety*, 21 February 1933, front page - Young Chrysler's Band (rept.).
9. *New York Times*, 30 March 1933, n. p. - Ship Arrivals: Italy's liner SS *Rex* arrives in New York (rept.). Otto H. Kahn and Mary Pickford among tourists returning from Europe on the *Rex*.
10. *New York Times*, 31 March 1933, p. 17 - Otto Kahn Returns Ill (rept.).
11. *Variety*, 21 March 1933, p. 6 - $450,000 Bondholders (rept.).
12. Bingen, Steven. with Wanamaker, Marc (Bisson Archives). *Paramount: City of Dreams*, Taylor Trade Publishing 2016, chapter 2, pp. 39-40.
13. *Variety*, 7 March 1933, p. 53 - Reno (col.).
14. The *Cortland Standard* (Cortland), 5 April 1933, p. 5 - Snapographs - Denies Romance (Hannah Williams Kahn).
15. The *Milwaukee Sentinel*, 2 April 1933, p. 3 - One Song and Dance Daughter-in-Law Walks Out Another Walks In (rept.).
16. *New York Times*, 4 April 1933, Section Amusements, p. 15 - Wife At Reno Sues Roger Wolfe Kahn; Hannah Williams, in Divorce Action.
17. The *Milwaukee Sentinel*, 5 April 1933, p. 3 - Divorce is granted to Hannah Williams (rept.).
18. The *Brooklyn Daily Eagle*, 7 April 1933, p. 11 - Divorces Kahn (pict.).
19. The *Southeast Missourian*, 6 April 1933, p. 4 - Hannah Kahn Becomes Tearful Over Divorce (rept.).
20. The *Lincoln Star* (Nebraska), 22 July 1934 p. 35 - Hannah got divorced in Reno on April 4, 1933, with a settlement reported to be $150,000.
21. The *Daily News*, 4 April 1933, n. p. & p. 29 - Hannah Sues Kahn But Ma Decrees Nix On Russ (rept. and pict.).
22. *Variety*, 4 April 1933, p. 29 - Kahn's Divorcing, It's Hannah and Columbo (rept.).
23. Ibid.
24. Dempsey, Jack. Considine, Bob. Slocum, Bill. *Dempsey: By the Man Himself*, Simon and Schuster, NY, 1960, chapter 27, pp. 190-194 - Hannah Williams.
25. The *Ottawa Citizen* (Canada), 8 April 1933, p. 5 - Roger Wolfe Kahn and

Edith Nelson Married on April 7 (rept.).

26. *Variety*, 11 April 1933, p. 51 - Marriages (col.).

27. The *Lewiston Daily Sun*, 8 April 1933, p. 3 - Kahn-Nelson Nuptials.

28. The *Lewiston Evening Journal*, 17 April 1933, p. 3 - Mrs. Roger Wolfe Kahn (pict. & brief capt.).

29. The *Film Daily*, 22 May 1933, p. 7 - Along The Rialto (col.) with Phil M. Daly - Irving Mills is now managing Roger Wolfe Kahn.

30. The *Scarsdale Inquirer*, 7 April 1933, p. 11 - Features at Police Benefit for Emergency Work Bureau (rept.).

31. *Catalog of Copyright Entries. New Series: 1933, Part 1*, Library of Congress. Copyright Office, publ. D. Appleton & Co., 1933, p. 635, entry 4307 - Brooke, Esther Eberstadt. *The Girl and her Job; A Handbook for Beginner*, D. Appleton & Co., 1933, p. 9 - Introduction by Otto H. Kahn.

32. *San Bernardino Sun*, 2 May 1933, front page - J.P. Morgan to Face Quizzing (rept.).

33. The *Decatur Daily Review* (Illinois), 30 June 1933, front page - Kuhn, Loeb Losses Enormous Despite Pennroad Profit (rept.).

34. The *Chicago Daily Tribune*, 30 June 1933, front page - Kahn Points Out Flaws in U.S. Tax Law (rept.).

35. *Cape Girardeau Southeast Missourian*, 8 July 1933, p. 4 - So They Say (col.). 'Otto Kahn paid no income tax for 1930, 1931 or 1932.'

36. The *Urbane Daily Courier*, 29 June 1933, front page - Otto Kahn Sold Securities to Daughter (rept.).

37. The *Brooklyn Daily Eagle*, 1 July 1933, p. 9 - News Behind the News by Paul Mallon (rept.).

38. Pecora, Ferdinand. *Wall Street Under Oath: The Story of Our Modern Money Changers*, Simon and Schuster, 1939, p. 293.

39. The *Pittsburg Post-Gazette*, 8 June 1933, p. 7 - Rumors Denied (pict. & capt. of Hannah).

40. *True Experiences*, Monthly, February 1939 - The Amazing Story of Jack Dempsey and Hannah Williams (art. & pict.).

41. The *Daily Iowan* (Iowa City), 15 June 1933, p. 5 - Triple Knockout Credited to Cupid (art.).

42. *Variety*, 13 June 1933, p. 21 - Pictures, Newsreel: *This Is America*.

43. *Variety*, 1 August 1933, p. 14 - *This Is America* (rev.) by Abel Green '… the hectic nightlife (there's a shot of Roger Wolfe Kahn in one of these Broadway clips).'

44. The *Brooklyn Daily Eagle*, 23 July 1933, p. 20 - *This Is America* (rev.): Rivoli Theatre, New York, July 19.

45. The *Fresno Bee and The Republican*, 13 July 1933, p. 7 - Dempsey and Hannah (pict. & capt.).

46. Liebman, Roy. *Vitaphone Films: A Catalogue of the Features and Shorts*, McFarland & Co., 2010, p. 91 - The Audition with Hannah Williams.

47. The *Brooklyn Daily Eagle*, 14 July 1933, p. 24 - There Seems to be a Romance (pict. & capt. of Jack Dempsey and Hannah Williams).

48. The *Chillicothe Constitution Tribune*, 17 July 1933, p. 2 - Dempsey and Hannah (pict. & capt.).

49. The *Daily Illin*, 13 July 1933, p. 4 - Dempsey Admits He May Marry Actress (rept.).

50. The *Daily Illin*, 19 July 1933, p. 4 - Dempsey Marries New York Actress.

51. The *Salt Lake Tribune*, 20 August 1933, p. 75 - Hannah Williams, Fashionable Fifth Avenue Couldn't Hold Her (art.).

52. The *Pittsburg Press*, 18 July 1933, front page - Dempsey, Hannah

53.   Williams Wed in Nevada Desert Town (rept.).
The *Salt Lake Tribune*, 20 August 1933, p. 75 - Hannah Williams, Fashionable Fifth Avenue Couldn't Hold Her (art.).

54.   *Variety*, 8 August 1933, p. 52 - Chatter (col.) Broadway.

55.   The *Daily Banner*, Greencastle, Putnam County, 13 September 1933, front page - Injured In Plunge (rept.).

56.   The *Gettysburg Times*, 12 Sept. 1933, p. 2 - Heiress Falls Three Floors - Nurse Attempts To Stop Plunge But Woman's Clothing Tears (rept.).

57.   *New York Times*, 11 September 1933, p. 19 - Mrs. Anne W. Kahn is Injured in Fall (rept.).

58.   The *Brooklyn Daily Eagle*, 11 September 1933, p. 15 - Mrs. Anne W. Kahn Breaks Hip in Fall (rept.).

59.   *The Gettysburg Times*, 12 Sept. 1933, p. 2 - Heiress Falls Three Floors - Nurse Attempts To Stop Plunge But Woman's Clothing Tears (rept.).

60.   *Variety*, 3 October 1933, p. 59 - Chatter (col.) Broadway. Roger Wolfe Kahn & Mrs. Kahn return to NY on the *Conti di Savoia*, September 28.

61.   The *New York Evening Post,* 28 September 1933, n. p. - Arriving today on the *Conte di Savoia* (pict.). Marconi Arrives, Lauds Radiophone.

62.   The *Pittsburgh Press*, 29 September 1933, p. 29 - Sime Silverman Laid To Rest (rept.). *New York Times*, 29 September 1933, p. 22 - Broadway Mourns Sime Silverman (rept.).

63.   *Variety*, 19 September 1933, p. 4 - Bankers Figure New Company For Paramount Following Discharge From Bankruptcy (rept.).

64.   Volaré Products, Comper Swift; Documentation: Racing in America (art., pict. & video) volaréproducts.com.

65.   The *Pittsburgh Press*, 20 November 1933, p. 21 - Fall Kills Former Wife of Kahn's Son (rept.).

66.   The *Chicago Daily Tribune*, 20 November 1933, page 3 - Anne W. Kahn, Heiress Hurt in Fall, Dies at 30 (rept.).

67.   The *Brooklyn Daily Eagle*, 20 November 1933, p. 13 - Mrs. Anne Kahn Dies in Hospital; Ill Nearly a Year (rept.).

68.   The *Chicago Daily Tribune*, 20 November 1933, page 3 - Anne W. Kahn, Heiress Hurt in Fall, Dies at 30 (rept.).

69.   Ibid.

70.   The *Brooklyn Daily Eagle*, 4 December 1933, p. 3 - Daughter Inherits Mrs. Kahn's Estate (rept.).

71.   Ibid.

72.   *New York Times*, 23 November 1933, p. 4 - Kahn Annoyer Seized.

73.   The *Palm Beach Post* (West Palm Beach, Florida), 23 November 1933, front page - Albert Comos, accused of writing a letter to Otto Kahn asking for $100,000 (rept.).

74.   The *Daily Plainsman* (South Dakota), 23 November 1933, p. 5 - Asked $100,000 (rept.).

75.   *Variety*, 5 December 1933, p. 40 - Air Line News by Nellie Revell (col.). 'Roger W. Kahn, after several months' rest from baton waving, is planning a comeback.'

76.   Jr., *Judge. Here's How*, Leslie-Judge Company, NY, 1927, p. 59 - The Flapper's Delight.

77.   *Variety*, 19 Dec. 1933, page 173 - Air Line News by Nellie Revell (col.).

78.   The *Montgomery Advertiser* (Alabama), 23 June 1929, p. 18 - Roger Wolfe Kahn calls his dad 'Governor' (quote).

Notes

* (p. 518) Florida Mogar Realty could have been another holding company set up by

Otto. The word 'Mogar' is similar to 'Mogmar,' as used for the Mogmar Art Foundation, founded by the Kahns in 1929: Mogmar is an acronym compiled from the initials of the Kahn family's forenames. **Mogar** can also be created from their initials: **M**aud or **M**argaret, **O**tto, **G**ilbert, **A**ddie, **R**oger,

* (p. 519) Sarah was billed as Sarah Jane or Sarah Jane Heliker for her theatrical career.

* (p. 527) Otto's introduction in the book contains his Ten Golden Rules of Success, which he set down many years previously and had abided by ever since.

* (p. 529) In the 1932 U.S. presidential election, Otto voted for the Democrat candidate Franklin D. Roosevelt even though he'd always been a steadfast Republican. Kahn's action may indicate his annoyance at the frostiness he received in October 1929 by President Hoover and his cronies over his short-lived appointment as treasurer of the Republican Senatorial Campaign Committee. Then again, Otto's decision to vote Democrat might purely have been because Roosevelt made the repeal of Prohibition part of his campaign platform, a change Otto fully supported.

* (p. 533) *The Audition* (Vitaphone, 1933), directed by Roy Mack, is thought to be the only known film that features footage of Hannah Williams performing. However, some of her biographical addenda claim she appeared in the 1935 RKO movie *The Last Days of Pompeii* as a Pompeii citizen, although her role is said to have been a non-speaking part and as such is uncredited.

* (p. 537a) Marianne and Francis finally escaped from Germany in 1939, just before the declaration of war. They traveled to the UK, from where they sailed to Australia.

* (p. 537b) Comper Swift - American registration NC27K.

PART IV. THIS IS AMERICA   1934–After

Chapter 17. The Fall Of The House Of Kahn

1. Brooke, Esther Eberstadt. *The Girl and Her Job; A Handbook for Beginners*. D. Appleton & Co., 1933, p. 9 - Introduction by Otto H. Kahn.
2. The *New York Sun*, 6 January 1934 - Bath And Tennis Club Has Opening Palm Beach Party (rept.).
3. Centre of Migration, Policy and Society, University of Oxford Annual Conference 2009 - Asylum-seeking in Europe in the 1930s and 2010s Compared - Irial Glyn.
4. Breitman, Richard., Stewart, Barbara McDonald. and Hochberg, Severin. *Advocate for the Doomed: The Diaries and Papers of James G. McDonald 1932-1935*, Indiana University Press, 2007, p. 257.
5. Ibid., 132.
6. McDonald's Letter of Resignation, December 27, 1935 - League of Nations Archive.
7. The *Wisconsin Jewish Chronicle* (Milwaukee), 6 January 1928, p. 4 - 'Mr. Kahn may not call himself a 'practicing Jew,' but he is doing many practical Jewish things...' 'My parents were not practicing Jews...'
8. America and the League of Nations: A Letter to Senator Poindexter by Otto H. Kahn, Nov. 29, 1919: Reprinted by the Committee of American Businessmen: Dec. 22, 1919. Copy held at Harvard University.
9. The *Capital Times* (Madison, Wisconsin), 12 January 1930, p. 27 -

Quotations: Otto H. Kahn: 'Feeling for art...'

10. *TIME* magazine, 29 January 1934 - Art: Stage Design (col.).

11. *New York Times*, 6 January 1934, p. 12 - Einstein To Play For Charity Here (rept.).

12. *Jewish Telegraph Agency*, 14 January 1934 - Einstein At Fiddle In Benefit Concert (rept.).

13. *New York Times*, 18 January 1934, p. 23 - Einstein In Debut As Violinist Here (rept.).

14. The *Brooklyn Daily Eagle*, 23 Jan. 1934, p. 18 - Radio Dial-Log (col.).

15. *Variety*, 9 January 1935, p. 33 - Air Line News by Nellie Revell (col.).

16. The *Palm Beach Daily News*, 30 March 1934, p. 4 - The Shiny Sheet.

17. The *New York Sun*, 6 January 1934, n. p. - Bath and Tennis Club Has Opening Palm Beach Party (rept.).

18. The *New York Sun*, 8 February 1934, p. 24 - Palm Beach Group.

19. *Logansport Pharos-Tribune* (Indiana), 31 March 1934, p. 6 - Today (col.) by Arthur Brisbane.

20. The *Palm Beach Post*, 16 February 1934, p. 2 - Society, Sports, Fashion, News of Seasonal Activities (col.).

21. The *Jacksonville Daily Journal*, 22 February 1934, front page - Otto H. Kahn Faces Another Summons From Senate Market Investigating Committee (rept.).

22. Birmingham, Stephen. *Our Crowd: The Great Jewish Families* of New York, Harper & Row, 1967, p. 423.

23. The *Tuscaloosa News*, 20 February 1934, p. 4 - The Younger Kahn Decides to Make His Own (editorial).

24. *Variety*, 27 February 1934, p. 46 - Hollywood: Paradise Digging New Show (col.).

25. The *Brooklyn Daily Eagle*, 24 Feb. 1934, p. 11 - Radio Dial-Log (col.).

26. *Variety*, 13 March 1934, p. 62 - News From The Dailies - East (col.) Roger Quits Broadway.

27. The *Evening Independent* (Ohio), 20 March 1934, p. 7 - New Galaxy of Colorful Characters in The Making on Broadway (art.).

28. *Escanaba Daily Press*, 30 March 1934, front page - Otto H. Kahn, Banker, Philanthropist Stricken With Clot On the Heart (rept. & photo.) 'He occupied early this week his box in the Golden Horseshoe of the Metropolitan Opera House.'

29. The *Advertiser*, Adelaide, 31 March 1934, p. 15 - Otto H. Kahn (obit.).

30. *New York Times*, 30 March 1934, front page - Otto Kahn, 67, Dies of Heart Attack in Bank's Offices (rept.).

31. *The Sentinel*, 5 April 1934, p. 23 - Otto H. Kahn (obit.).

32. *Delaware County Daily News* (Chester, PA), 30 March 1934, p. 7 - Otto H. Kahn Aged 67 Dies Suddenly (rept. & last known photo of Otto).

33. The *Advertiser*, Adelaide, 31 March 1934, p. 15 - Otto H. Kahn (obit.).

34. *Nevada State Journal*, 30 March 1934, p. 3 - Otto Kahn. Financier, Dies Of Heart Attack New York (rept.).

35. *Delaware County Daily News* (Chester, PA), 30 March 1934, p. 7 - Otto H. Kahn Aged 67 Dies Suddenly (last known photo of Otto).

36. The *Salt Lake Tribune*, 30 March 1934, p. 4 - Otto H. Kahn, Banker and Arts Patron Dies (rept.).

37. The *Abilene Reporter-News* (Texas), 30 March 1934, front page & p. 3 - Kahn, International Banking Head, Dies From Heart Attack.

38. The *Salt Lake Tribune*, March 30, 1934, p. 4 - Otto H. Kahn, Banker and Arts Patron Dies (rept.).

39. The *Daily News* (NY), 30 March 1934, front page & pp. 2 & 34 - Otto H. Kahn Drops Dead in His Office (rept. & pict.) 'News withheld until stock markets closed for the day.'

40. *Delaware County Daily* Times (Chester, PA), 30 March 1934, p. 7 - Otto H. Kahn, 67, Dies Suddenly (rept. & pict.)

41. *Ballymena Weekly Telegraph*, 12 October 1935, p. 11 - The Queerest Case (art.), Dr. Charles Norris.

42. The *Pittsburgh Press*, 30 March 1934, p. 12 - Entire World Mourns Death of Otto Kahn (rept.).

43. *New York Times*, 30 March 1934, front page - Otto Kahn, 67, Dies of Heart Attack in Bank's Offices (rept.).

44. The *Long Islander*, 6 April 1934, front page - Funeral Services of Otto Kahn Simple; In Music Room (rept.).

45. Ibid.

46. *The Montana Standard* (Butte), Friday Morning, 30 March 1934 - Otto Kahn, Famous Financier, Dies in NY (rept.).

47. *Motion Picture Daily*, 2 April 1934, p. 1 - Otto H. Kahn Funeral Today.

48. The *Long Islander*, 6 April 1934, front page - Otto H. Kahn Funeral.

49. The *Brooklyn Daily Eagle*, 3 April 1934, p. 13 - Police on Guard At Funeral Rites For Otto H. Kahn (rept.).

50. The *Spokesman*, 6 April 1934, front page - Kahn Is Buried by Rabbi Goldenson (rept.).

51. The *Brooklyn Daily Eagle*, 3 April 1934, p. 13 - Police On Guard At Funeral Rites For Otto H. Kahn (rept.).

52. The *Daily Banner* (Greencastle, Putnam County), 30 March 1934, p. 2 - A Hodge-Podge from Here and There (col.).

53. *Jewish Daily Bulletin*, 17 April 1934, p. 8 - Kahn Leaves Entire Estate to Children. (rept.).

54. *Jewish Daily Bulletin*, 30 March 1934, front page - Otto H. Kahn, Banker, Philanthropist, Dead (obit.). 'According to *TIME* magazine his interest in the firm was fourteen percent.'

55. The *Milwaukee Journal*, 17 April 1934, p. 4 - Philanthropist's Estate Is Left To His Children (rept.). Klein, Henry H., *Dynastic America and Those Who Own* It, New York, Henry H. Klein 1921, p. 155 - Estimated Wealth of Richest Families - Kahn, $100,000,000.

56. The *Lewiston Daily Sun*, 1 January 1937, p. 9 - Otto Kahn Estate Left Estate of Less Than $4 Million (rept.).

57. *Jewish Post* (Indianapolis, Marion County), 8 January 1937, p. 2 - Mish-Mash (col.) by Paul A. Peters.

58. The *Jewish Transcript* (Seattle, Washington), 25 March 1924, front page - Otto Kahn of New York (rept.).

59. Lundberg, Ferdinand. *America's 60 Families*, Vanguard Press, 1937.

60. The *Brooklyn Daily Eagle*, 30 March 1934, p. 18 - Otto H. Kahn, Patron of the Arts.

61. The *Brooklyn Daily Eagle*, 30 March 1934, p. 5 - Music and Finance Lose Dominant Figure in Death of Otto Kahn.

Notes

* (p. 544) Otto wrote a 19-page letter dated November 29, 1919, to Hon. Miles Poindexter, United States Senate, Washington, D.C., putting forward his exposition for the case against the acceptance of the League of Nations Covenant.[1]

1. *'America and the League of Nations'* - The Otto H. Kahn letter to Hon. Miles
    Poindexter is held at Harvard University (Ref: 182a - 7025), reprinted by The
    Committee of American Businessmen, New York.

* (p. 546) The completed villa had 23 rooms, as larger rooms were thought to fit more
with Treanor & Fatio's vision.

* (p. 550) At the Metropolitan Opera House, Otto attended either a Charity Gala
Concert on Sunday, March 25, or the Gaetano Donizetti opera *Lucia di Lammermoor* on
Monday 26, conducted by Vincenzo Bellezza.

* (p. 551) The time of Otto's death differed in the following day's newspapers from
1:14 p.m.[1] through to 2:20[2] and 2:45,[3] with the *New York Times* confirming the time as
being 1:45.[4]
    1. *Escanaba Daily Press*, 30 March 1934, front page - Otto H. Kahn Banker,
        Philanthropist Stricken With Clot On the Heart (rept. & photo) 1:14 p.m.
    2. The *Daily News*, 30 March 1934, front page - Otto H. Kahn Drops Dead in his
        Office (rept.) 2:20 p.m.
    3. *Montana Standard*, Butte, Friday Morning, 30 March 1934 - Otto Kahn, Famous
        Financier, Dies in NY (rept.) 2:45 p.m.
    4. *New York Times*, 30 March 1934, front page - Otto Kahn, 67, Dies of Heart Attack
        in Bank's Offices (rept.) 1:45 p.m.

* (p. 555) 'Newsie' - a newspaper boy.

* (p. 560) Hugh Pettitt and Charles Geoffrey Vickers were the appointed attorneys that
handled Otto's will.

Chapter 18. The Eccentric Mr. Kahn
1. The *Brooklyn Daily Eagle*, 9 April 1934, p. 22 - Radio Dial-Log (col.) by
    Jo Ranson.
2. *Jewish Post* (Indianapolis), 13 April 1934, front page - Interesting Facts
    of Interesting Jews (col.): 'Roger Wolfe Kahn is preparing a return to
    radio with a new orchestra soon.'
3. *TIME* magazine, Feb. 14, 1927, p. 36 - Pine and William Sts. (report) -
    Kuhn, Loeb recently purchased $3,000,000 of South African gold.
4. *The Film Daily Year Book 1934*, p. 545 - Lists the members of the board
    of directors of Paramount Publix Corporation.
5. Henry Ittleson was the founder of the Commercial Investment Trust.
6. Breitman, Richard., Stewart, Barbara McDonald., and Hochberg,
    Severin. *Advocate for the Doomed: The Diaries and Papers of James G.
    McDonald 1932-1935*, Indiana University Press, 2007, p. 397.
7. *The New Yorker*, 9 June 1934, p. 14.
8. The *Brooklyn Daily Eagle*, 25 May 1934, p. 10 - Casino Bides Edict
    Claremont Accepts (rept.).
9. The *Brooklyn Daily Eagle*, 27 May 1934, p. E3 - Claremont Opens.
10. The *Brooklyn Daily Eagle*, 29 May 1934, p. 26 - Claremont Opens Under
    Moses Plan (rept.).
11. The *Daily Sentinel*, NY, 19 April 1935, p. 18 - New York Day by Day
    (col.) by Oscar O. McIntyre. McIntyre mentions a Roger Wolfe Kahn
    band had previously played at the Claremont Inn.
12. The *Brooklyn Daily Eagle*, 28 May 1934, p. 11 - Radio Dial-Log.
13. The *Brooklyn Daily Eagle*, 4 June 1934, p. 9 - Reverting To Type by Art
    Arthur (col.). Cuttin' The Corners.

14. 2 June 1934, WGY Radio - 12:30 a.m., RWK Orchestra.

15. 18 June 1934, WEAF-NBC Radio - 11:30, RWK Orchestra.

16. *Jewish Post* (Indianapolis), 8 June 1934, front page - Interesting Facts of Interesting Jews (col.) by Leonard Rothschild.

17. *Variety*, 3 July 1934, p. 54 - Inside Stuff - Music (col.).

18. Long, Christopher. *Paul T. Frankl and Modern American Design* Yale University Press, 2007, chapter 9, pp. 110-111.

19. Walker, Stanley. *Mrs. Astor's Horse*, Frederick A. Stokes Co. 1935, p. 142 - 'One of his [Frankl's] triumphs is a circular bed designed for Mrs. Roger Wolfe Kahn in the summer of 1934.'

20. *House and Garden*, July 1934, pp. 54-55 - The Apartment of Roger Wolfe Kahn by Paul T. Frankl (art. & photos).

21. *The Sentinel*, July 5, 1934, p. 9 - 'More than $500,000 in cash changed hands in the transaction, with the Kahn estate also receiving the $750,000 property on which the Order's school now stands.'

22. *Jewish Daily Bulletin*, 23 May 1934, p. 3 - Otto Kahn Home to Echo Soon to Lessons of Catholic Misses. 'The Academy of the Sacred Heart, one of the oldest teaching orders in the Roman Catholic Church, opened negotiations with Mr. Kahn for the purchase of the building back in 1932.'

23. Breitman, Richard., Stewart, Barbara McDonald., and Hochberg, Severin. *Advocate for the Doomed: The Diaries and Papers of James G. McDonald 1932-1935*, Indiana University Press, 2007, p. 409.

24. The *Nassau Daily Review*, 5 July 1934, p. 4 - Beach Colonists Assail Surf Club (rept.).

25. Fox Movietone News story 22-595, 22-596, 7 July 1934. A copy of the newsreel is housed at the Moving Image Research Collection, Digital Video Repository, University of South Carolina, University Libraries.

26. *Chicago Tribune*, 22 September 1934, p. 16 - Fulton Cutting, NY Real Estate Head, Dies at 82 (rept.).

27. Passenger List: 22 September 1934, Addie Kahn departs from Southampton, England, on board RMS *Aquitania* bound for New York.

28. *Radio Mirror*, October 1934 issue, p. 5 - Behind The Mikes (col.). Roger holds pilot's license No. 104.

29. *Radio Mirror*, August 1934 issue, Vol. 2, No. 4, p. 73 - Hot and Airy (col.). Gossip and news of the air world.

30. *Radio Mirror*, November 1934 issue, p. 58 - Hot and Airy (col.).

31. *The Bradford Era*, 10 November 1934, front page - Ivy L. Lee, Dean of Publicists, Is Taken By Death (rept.).

32. Horowitz, Louis J. and Sparkes, Boyden. *The Towers of New York: The Memoirs of a Master Builder*, Simon and Schuster, NY, 1937, pp. 261-263.

33. Ibid.

34. *Jewish Daily Bulletin*, 23 May 1934, p. 3 - Otto Kahn Home to Echo Soon to Lessons of Catholic Misses (rept.).

Notes

* (p. 567) Kenneth Outwater is also credited as a producer in Eisenstein's 1933 movies *Thunder over Mexico* and *Eisenstein in Mexico*.

* (p. 568) *Death Day* is classed as 'lost,' as no copies of the movie are known to exist. The movie's title is believed to refer to *The Day of the Dead* (*Día de Muertos*), an annual

public holiday and feast celebrated throughout Mexico in remembrance of dead relatives and friends.

* (p. 570) Ivy Lee is now widely considered the father of modern public relations.

* (p. 572a) The interior wall paneling of the Kahns' Louis XVI French salon was not part of the deal. Addie was determined the Convent would not have the 'gold lounge' and sold it to the Duveen Brothers art dealership. Duveen installed it in their gallery at 720 Fifth Avenue. The Salon Doré, as it was later renamed, is now housed in the Legion of Honor museum in San Francisco.

* (p. 572b) Horowitz retired from Thompson-Starrett Co. and the construction industry in 1934 to run the Louis J. and Mary E. Horowitz Foundation.

For Reasons Lost in Time

1. The *Chicago Tribune*, 16 May 1949, p. 55 - Widow of Otto Kahn, New York Art Patron and Banker, is Dead.
2. *Vanity Fair,* October 1996, p. 276. & Smith, Sally Bedell. *Reflected Glory: The Life of Pamela Churchill Harriman*, Simon & Schuster, 1996, Ch. 9.
3. *Al-Ahram* Cairo (weekly), 9-15 December 1999, Issue No. 459 - In The Pashas' Den - The Former Mohamed Ali Club has been revealed in all its splendor, (art.) by Fayza Hassan.
4. *The Milwaukee Journal*, 25 April 1939, pp. 1-2 - Famous son, Famous bandleader, Famous flier (art.).
5. The *Brooklyn Daily Eagle*, 14 May 1935, front page - Mother, Mrs. Roger Wolfe Kahn (pict. & short art.).
6. 1940 U.S. Federal Census - Dacia W. Kahn & Peter W. Kahn.
7. *The Film Daily*, 6 February 1937, p. 4 - Vitaphone Releasing 9 Shorts.
8. *New York Times*, 17 October 1938, n. p. - Aline Rhonie Hofheimer mural unveiled (rept.). 7b. An invitation card to the mural unveiling party exists that reads: 'DANCE! A Roger Wolfe Kahn Orchestra, Hangar F, Sat. October 15 - Enough Said! - Gambling at its Best - Join Public Auction - Monte Carlo Currency - No Tariff - Ten till Dawn at Roosevelt Field - Informal.'
9. *Popular Aviation*, March edition 1928, p. 52 - Manhattan Aero Club - Aero Club News (col.).
10. The *Brooklyn Daily Eagle*, 26 February 1938, p. 11 - Nassau Police Raise Whitney to Captain (rept.).
11. The *Brooklyn Daily Eagle*, 10 July 1941, p. 11 - Kahn Plane Taken Over by U.S. Army (rept.).
12. The *Brooklyn Daily Eagle*, 12 May 1941, pp. 1-2 - 70 Fliers Hunting Brewsters' Plane (rept.).
13. Meyer, Corwin H. *Corky Meyer's Flight Journal: A Test Pilot's Tales* of *Dodging Disasters - Just in Time*, Specialty Press, 2006, chapter 16, p. 149 - Clipping The Bearcat's Wings.
14. *New York Times*, 13 July 1962, p. 23 - Roger Wolfe Kahn Dies at 54; Orchestra Leader and Test Pilot; Son of Otto Kahn Organized Jazz Band When He Was 15 - Composed Song Hits (obit.).
15. *New York Times*, 16 December 1975, p. 42 - Gilbert W. Kahn, Arts Patron and Investment Banker, Dead (obit.).
16. *New York Times*, 27 January 1995 - Margaret Kahn Ryan (obit.) by James Barron.
17. Davidogilvy.co.uk

18. *The Long Islander,* 8 January 1937, front page - A Large Shrinkage in Taxable Estate of Otto H. Kahn (rept.).

19. The *New York Tribune,* 12 December 1920, part IV front page - Notes of the Social World (col.).

20. The *New York Tribune,* 14 November 1920, part IV front page - Notes of the Social World (col.).

21. Dempsey, Jack. and Considine, Bob. and Slocum, Bill. *Dempsey: By the Man Himself,* Simon and Schuster, NY, 1960, chapter 27, pp. 190-210 - Hannah Williams.

22. Jablonski, Edward. *Harold Arlen: Rhythm, Rainbows, and Blues,* Northeastern University Press, 1996, pp. 114, 116-117.

23. The *Brooklyn Daily Eagle,* 29 October 1937, p. 13 - Stage News (col.).

24. Jablonski, Edward. *Harold Arlen: Rhythm, Rainbows, and Blues,* Northeastern University Press, 1996, p. 116.

25. The *Pittsburg Post-Gazette,* 21 May 1940, front page - Jack Dempsey and Wife Parted, Lawyer Reveals - Hannah Williams Likely to Resume Career as Singer (rept.).

26. *TIME* magazine, 18 January 1943 - Milestones (col.).

27. *Variety,* 8 September 1943, front page - Hannah Williams to Make Stage Comeback in Vaudeville (rept.).

28. *Variety,* 7 February 1945, p. 46 - Night Club Reviews: Hannah Williams at the Greenwich Village Inn, NY.

29. *St. Petersburg Times,* 24 March 1950, front page - Married (rept. & pict. of Hannah).

30. *Spokane Daily Chronicle,* 24 March 1953, front page - Hannah Williams Severely Burned (rept.).

31. *Variety,* 4 January 1939, p. 201 - Chatter (col.) Broadway.

32. *Who's Who in Radio,* 1936, p. 114 - George D. Lottman.

33. *Billboard,* 3 October 1942, p. 28 - The Final Curtain (col.). George D. Lottman (obit.).

34. *The Sentinel,* June 8, 1939, p. 9 - Strictly Confidential (col.).

35. The *Brooklyn Eagle,* 20 June 1939, p. 2 - Sanitation Men Buy Long Island Estate of Otto Kahn (rept.).

36. *New York Times,* 27 December 1981 - Otto Kahn's Mansion Set On Condominium Course by James Barron (rept.).

37. *The Evening Independent,* Florida, 14 July 1939, p. 6 - Free Speeches by Bill Wiley (col.).

38. *The Suffolk County News,* NY, 14 July 1939, pp. 1 & 8 - Beer, Hotdogs and Hamburgers Reign as Cleaners Take Over Kahn Estate (rept.).

39. *New York City Sun,* 10 July 1939 - '20,000 Crowd Kahn Château' (rept.).

40. The *Brooklyn Daily Eagle,* 21 March 1940, p. 2 - Church May Buy Kahn Estate, Once Occupied as Sanita Lodge.

41. The Little Carnegie Playhouse, 146 West 57th Street, NY 10019.

42. *Exhibitors Herald World,* 18 January 1930, p. 57 & 62 - The Cinema Art Movement (art.).

43. Area Development Bulletin: Vol. 1-2, January 1955, U.S. Dept. of Commerce. p. 4.

44. Breitman, Richard. *The Berlin Mission: The American Who Resisted Nazi Germany from Within,* Public Affairs, 2019, ISBN-13: 978-1541742161.

45. *Nassau Daily Review Star,* 9 December 1937, front page - Cop Finds Skeleton Hanging From Tree (rept.).

Notes
* (p. 574a) John Oakes Marriott (b. 1921 - d. 2007).

* (p. 574b) Major-General Sir John Charles Oakes Marriott, KCVO, CB, DSO & Bar, MC, died on September 11, 1978.

* (576a) Roger's hopes of rising within Grumman's chain of command were dashed when he was overlooked for the vice president's role. Grumman's decision upset him so much, he allegedly locked himself away in his office for three days, surfacing only to use the bathroom. Roger always suspected that it was because of his Jewish blood that drew him the short straw.

* (p. 576b) Daisy Kahn died in September 1994 at Glenn Cove, Nassau County.

* (p. 577) Polly Kahn (née Stover) died December 1, 2006, at Old Brookville, NY.

* (p. 578) Otto never put in place an endowment to benefit future scholars. Nor did he create a foundation to house his art collection, which may reflect his realization that his fortune had been eroded too severely to fund such projects.

* (p. 579a) The Dempsey-Vanderbilt Art Deco hotel, designed by architect Henry Hohauser, still operates as a hotel and is renamed The Setai Miami Beach Hotel.

* (p. 579b) Hannah's song 'Buds Won't Bud' was also dropped from the show but resurfaced three years later, sung by Judy Garland in the 1940 movie Andy Hardy Meets Debutante.

Roger's Legacy (& Minutiae)
1. Goodman, Benny. and Kolodin, Irving. *The Kingdom of Swing*, Stackpole Sons, New York, 1939.
2. *Radio Mirror*, November 1936, p. 100 - Orchestral Anatomy (rept.).
3. Keillor, Maureen Smith. and Wheeler, Evelyn L. *The Blue* Angels, Arcadia Publishing, 2017, p. 27 - Honorary Flight Leaders.

Notes
* (p. 591) Sheet-music sales and the peak positions in *Billboard*'s Hot 100 Chart using *Billboard*'s best sellers in store, most played by jockeys, most played on jukeboxes, and top 100 Charts pre-1958.

Other Songs Composed by Roger Wolfe Kahn
Notes
* (p. 594) Songs not mentioned in Roger's discography.

Filmography
Notes
* (p. 596) Roy Mack directed the film as part of Vitaphone's 'Melody Master' series. It was shot at Brooklyn Vitaphone studios in May 1936[1] but was not released until February 1937.
1. The *Brooklyn Daily Eagle*, 4 May 1936, p. 12 - Kahn Starts 'Short' (rept.).

* (p. 597) Sylvester Ahola movie: YouTube: ten-second clip 4:17 - 4:26 https://youtu.be/0zmxNw26W0U

Roger Wolfe Kahn–Aviation
1. *US Air Services* (magazine), January 1942, p. 36-38 - Off the Ground Most of the Time.
2. *Air Force Magazine*, April 1959, p. 75 - The National Aeronautic Association.

3. 'Awarded to those who have served the cause of Aviation in general and Sporting Aviation in particular, by their work, initiative, devotion, or in other ways.':
https://www.fai.org/awards
4. Administered by Air Service Post 501 of the American Legion - *The American Legion Monthly*, May 11, 1955.
5. [5]*Significant American and International Awards in Aviation*, publ. 1954, United States, Navy Dept, Bureau of Aeronautics, p. 65 - The William J. McGough Memorial Award.

Archives
Notes
* (p. 600) Art list courtesy of the Frick Collection, New York.

Musicians
* (p. 686) Williams, Aeneas Francon. ***Dreamdrift: by a young lover***, Stockwell, London, 1932 - extract from the poem *Musicians*.

Photo Credits

Individual photographs and works of art appearing herein may be protected by copyright in the U.S. and elsewhere and may thus not be reproduced in any form without the copyright owners' permission. The following list applies to photographs and works of art appearing herein for which copyrights and acknowledgments are known.

P. 1 - The Kahn palazzo, 1100 Fifth Avenue & 1 East 91st Street - The Kahn Collection © I. C. Williams.

Chapter 1
P. 12 - Otto Hermann Kahn - Unknown photographer.
P. 17 - Cedar Court, Morristown - Detail from a postcard.
P. 23 - Morristown Races - The Kahn Collection © I. C. Williams.
P. 24 - Morristown Field Club - Library of Congress, Prints & Photographs Division, George Grantham Bain Collection (LC-DIG-ggbain-14352).
P. 25 - The Kahn villa, Cedar Court - Image ID: MT022-004 © collections of the North Jersey History Center, The Morristown and Morris Township Library.

Chapter 2
P. 39 - Addie Kahn - Library of Congress, Prints & Photographs Division, George Grantham Bain Collection (LC-DIG-ggbain-04831).
P. 43 - Cassiobury House - Photograph permission English Heritage.

Chapter 3
P. 92 - Oheka Cottage, Palm Beach - Courtesy Historical Society of Palm Beach County.

Chapter 4
P. 109 - Cold Spring Harbor Estate (Aiglon Aerial Photos) - The Kahn Collection © I. C. Williams.
P. 120- Roger W. Kahn, Albert Wolff & Boris Anisfeld, Metropolitan Opera House, Library of Congress, Prints & Photographs Division, (LC-DIG-ggbain 29946).
P. 124 - Maud Emily Kahn (detail). Unknown photographer. George Grantham Bain

Collection, Library of Congress Prints and Photographs Division Washington, D.C.

Chapter 6
P. 163 - Roger Wolfe Kahn - The Kahn Collection © I. C. Williams.
P. 169 - Roger Wolfe Kahn - The Kahn Collection © I. C. Williams.

Chapter 8
P. 229 - Roger Wolfe Kahn - the Roger Wolfe Kahn Collection, Institute of Jazz Studies, Rutgers University Libraries Archival Collection. Photograph by G. Maillard Kesslère
P. 231 - Roger Wolfe Kahn - The Kahn Collection © I. C. Williams.
P. 236 - Inaugural Ball Program - The Kahn Collection © I. C. Williams.
P. 237 - Inaugural Ball Program - The Kahn Collection © I. C. Williams.
P. 238 - Inaugural Ball - The Kahn Collection © I. C. Williams.
P. 241 - Roger Wolfe Kahn - Library of Congress, Prints & Photographs Division, George Grantham Bain Collection (LC-DIG-ggbain-30011).

Chapter 9
P. 263 - Fifth Avenue, ca. 1920s - The Kahn Collection © I. C. Williams.
P. 273 - Roger Wolfe Kahn - the Roger Wolfe Kahn Collection, Institute of Jazz Studies, Rutgers University Libraries Archival Collection. Unknown photographer.
P. 296 - Charlie Chaplin group picture, Oct. 29, 1926 - Copyright © Roy Export Company Limited.
P. 305 - *Le Perroquet de Paris* - Photograph by F. M. Demarest - the Roger Wolfe Kahn Collection, Institute of Jazz Studies, Rutgers University Libraries Archival Collection.
P. 307 - Roger Wolfe Kahn and Mrs. George D. Lottman - The *New York Morning Telegraph*, Nov. 28, 1926.

Chapter 10
P. 321 - *Night Club* movie still - Picture © Duncan P. Schiedt Photograph Collection, Archives Center, National Museum of American History, Smithsonian Institution. Box 25, Folder 22.
P. 322 - *Night Club* movie still - Ibid.
P. 346 - *Oheka II* yacht - The Kahn Collection © I. C. Williams.
P. 363 - Roger Wolfe Kahn, Curtiss Field - The Kahn Collection © I. C. Williams.

Chapter 11
P. 377 - Otto Kahn on a train, March 1928 - Fort Worth Star-Telegram collection, University of Texas Arlington, Special Collections Library.
P. 378 - Botanic Garden, Brentwood - The Kahn Collection © I. C. Williams.
P. 386 - *Oheka II* yacht - The Kahn Collection © I. C. Williams.

Chapter 12
P. 399 - Roger Wolfe Kahn portrait - Photograph by G. Maillard Kesslère, the Roger Wolfe Kahn Collection, Institute of Jazz Studies, Rutgers University Libraries Archival Collection.
P. 423 - Otto H. Kahn - The Kahn Collection © I. C. Williams.

Chapter 13
p. 433 - The Kahn palazzo, 1100 Fifth Avenue & 1 East 91st Street - The Kahn Collection © I. C. Williams.
P. 447 - Roger at Newark Metropolitan Airport - The Kahn Collection © I. C. Williams.
P. 448 - Roger flying the Burnelli plane - The Kahn Collection © I. C. Williams.

Acknowledgments

Special thanks go to Eric Koch (descendent of Hermann Kahn), who, unknowingly, helped me piece the Kahn genealogy in order and whose homemade videos recounting his lineage were a joy to watch. My thanks also go to Tim Reid and Dave Walker of Kensington and Chelsea Archives; to Mia Anderson and Janine St. Germain at St. Bernard's School, NY; to Timothy H. Horning, University Archives, University of Pennsylvania; to Bill Stolz, Special Collections and Archives, Wright State University Libraries, Dayton, Ohio; and Douglas Brown, the archivist at Groton School.

To Oheka Castle owner Gary Melius and his daughter Nancy, I offer my appreciation for their warm welcome and hospitality during my brief visit to the estate in 2018. In addition, to Sally Brazil and Susan Chore at the Frick Art Reference Library and the Frick Collection, NY; Adriana Cuervo and Elizabeth Surles at the Institute of Jazz Studies, Rutgers University Libraries; Carolyn Vega at the Morgan Library & Museum, NY; Richard J. Berenson, former president of the Society of Illustrators; Debi Murray and Rose Guerrero at the Historical Society of Palm Beach County; Sara Pezzoni at Special Collections, the University of Texas at Arlington Libraries; and to the Fondation Igor Stravinsky, I offer my deep gratitude for their assistance with my research.

My thanks also reach out to Oxford's Bodleian Library for permitting me copies of Sir William G. E. Wiseman's letter dated September 17, 1918 (Folio 298, shelfmark 6596) and copies of the translation of an interview held in Madrid on June 19, 1918, between Alfonso XIII and Otto H. Kahn (Folios 299-308, shelfmark 6596); to Arnold Lozano at charliechaplin.com for permitting me to include the Charlie Chaplin photograph; to Kay Peterson at the Smithsonian Institution; to Ron Hutchinson at the Vitaphone Project; to Brad Bayley at Santa Barbara Vintage Photography; to Leslie Greaves, grandniece of the photographer Murray Korman for allowing me to include the Korman photograph; to Howard Kroplick, president of the board of trustees of the Roslyn Landmark Society; and Joel Friedman at The Cradle of Aviation Museum and Education Centre.

I extend my appreciation to Virginia Fortune Ogilvy, Countess of Airlie; The Hon. David John Ogilvy, Lord Ogilvy; Christof Eberstadt; and Frederick 'Freddy' Eberstadt for sharing their family recollections. This book will forever be associated with Edinburgh and all the people there who made me feel so welcome. When I arrived in the city in January 2017, I decided what better place to write a book about a family who were great friends of Andrew Carnegie than inside an Andrew Carnegie Library! I thank all the staff at Edinburgh Central Library for their assistance; I'm indebted to you and Andrew Carnegie's generosity. My gratitude also goes to the National Library of Scotland and the New York Public Library. Thank you, Motel One, for giving me a bay of calm in which to shelter and to their staff for looking after me so attentively and, last but not least, I'd like to thank Fiona Graham for her unwavering words of encouragement.

Portrait of Roger Wolfe Kahn

Conclusion

In 1942, a report stated Roger first developed an interest in flying after taking a flight when he was seven. He was visiting Santa Barbara with his family when he persuaded his mother to let him go on a five or ten-dollar seaplane hop. The experience had a profound effect on him, and he instinctively sensed his life would become aligned with aviation and airplanes. Unfortunately, I've been unable to ascertain whether the Kahn family did visit Santa Barbara or California in 1913 or 1914.

Interestingly, during this period, the pioneering aviation engineers Allan and Malcolm Loughead were based in San Francisco, 300 miles further along the West Coast. In 1913, they built a two-passenger seaplane, which they operated from a boat ramp in San Francisco Bay. For the privilege of a 10-minute sea hop, the public paid $10. In early 1916, the brothers moved their flying operation to Santa Barbara Bay, where they flew summer seaplane hops from a beach ramp. Roger would have been aged eight at the time. Could this have been the plane Roger flew in?

In London, in 1924, Roger convinced his parents that the easiest and quickest way to travel to Paris was by plane. Otto and Addie took their son's advice and gave it a shot. The family flew on a charter flight with Imperial Airways direct from Croydon Airport to Paris. It was the first flight the Kahn family flew collectively. Between these two markers, Roger's interest in aviation grew.

After Otto's death, Roger gradually alienated himself from the public arena. It is now apparent he took on too much too soon during his teenage years, which led to his music career imploding. The continual expectations demanded by his parents and the media became stifling and too difficult to handle. Eventually, those demands became a burden that wore Roger down. His escape was aviation.

Roger never did get to study full-time at a European conservatoire as he and his parents had wished. Nor did he get to reopen his beloved Manhattan nightclub *Le Perroquet de Paris*, and nor did he realize his dream of composing and staging that elusive hit Broadway musical. Even more upsetting for him was that he never followed through with his hope of performing his symphony, *Americana*, on stage. His extensive archive housed at the Institute of Jazz Studies at Rutgers University, Newark, contains dozens of boxes of original handwritten music scores and songs composed and arranged by Roger. Some of the compositions may have never been performed or heard in public before. Perhaps, among this rich archive, lies Roger's elusive symphony or his jazz rhapsody, *Birth of the Blues*, just waiting to be discovered.

Roger Wolfe Kahn was a veritable product of the Roaring Twenties, an era he helped define. In many ways, his family were his co-stars. Had Roger's life been different, would he have accomplished everything he longed for? Unfortunately, this question is something we will never know. Hopefully, in the future, history will be kinder to the young musician who, through his musical genius and dogged determination, achieved so much in such a short space of time. During an interview in August 1932, Roger was asked if he had any heroes? In his telling response, Roger admitted he had only one hero, and that person was his father.

Roger turned his hand to jazz one last time; the date was April 30, 1958. With his friend 'Brownie' - Arthur William Brown, illustrator, and honorary president of the Society of Illustrators in New York - the pair teamed up as 'entrepreneurs extraordinaire' to promote the Second Society of Illustrators' Jazz Festival presented at their HQ at 128 East 63rd Street. Nothing suggests that after the one-day festival, Roger had anything to do with jazz ever again.

However, Roger did one final act to ensure his legacy would remain intact for future generations to discover, even though news of it would not seep into the public domain until fifty-six years after his death. In 1959, Roger set up a trust to care for his wife Daisy and their two offspring. After their demise, the residual monies were earmarked to benefit the Institute of the Aeronautical Sciences (one of the American Institute of Aeronautics and Astronautics [AIAA] precursors), of which Roger had been a former vice president. The trust, upon its maturity in 2018, amounted to $7 million. After receiving news of the gift, AIAA announced the money was the largest gift in the Institute's history and a classic example of 'paying it forward,' a topic the Institute feels passionate about. Due to Roger's forward-thinking, his legacy is now to take on an ever more exciting course with the creation of AIAA Roger W. Kahn Scholarships. No matter how history views Roger's accomplishments in life, there's no denying Roger Wolfe Kahn was a pretty cool dude.

At the end of this book, the Kahn family have finally been returned to their palazzo at 1100 Fifth Avenue, where they rightly belong. And, after all the marvelous adventures, inspirational triumphs, and saddening disappointments I've unearthed and shared, there is, still, a little idling thought at the back of my mind, thinking I will forever be looking for the boy.

I. C. Williams, 2022

Musicians
by Aeneas Francon Williams *

There are conductors pale who stand
tiptoe before the band,
and all the instrumentalists are dumb
until the white-hot baton,
and the thumb of the magician
makes cryptic potion.
And with the motion,
there comes the strange effusion
of dreamy cadence
like incense smoke
that winds and sways
all ways.

Index

160-161, 168, 175, (plays banjo with the California Ramblers) 183, 191, (argues with his parents, storms out of 1100 Fifth Avenue) 192-193, (hedonistic lifestyle) 199-200, 215, (travels to Scotland **1924**) 218, 219, 220, (engagement to Anne Whelan, **1924**) 222, (marriage to Anne, **1924**) 222-223, (quits Princeton, secures job at Equitable Trust) 228, 232, 238, (visits London, **1925**) 248-249, 250-151, (travels to Europe to study banking methods, **1926**) 281, 293, 295, 299, 330, 340, 347, (returns from Europe, joins Kuhn, Loeb & Co., **1927**) 360, (elected to the board of Paramount, **1928**) 383, 395, (becomes entrepreneur, **1929**) 411, (birth of Claire, **1929**) 413, 432, 438, (family visit to Europe, **1930**) 450, (becomes general partner at Kuhn, Loeb, **1931**) 458, 460, (witness at his brother's marriage, **1931**) 462, (visits Berlin, **1931**) 470, 471, 486-487, (Anne gets custody of Claire) 495, 505, (meets Sara Jane Heliker) 514, (Gilbert and Anne divorce, **1933**) 518, (Gilbert and Sara wed, **1933**) 519,-520, 522, 526, (Anne's fall) 535-536, (a more senior role at Kuhn, Loeb) 537, (Anne's death, **1933**) 537-539, 543, 546, 547-548, (father's death, **1934**) 552, 560, 562, 564, 566, (**1935** onwards) 576-577, 582, 600

Kahn, Mrs. Gilbert (née Whelan, Anne Elizabeth), 222-223, 228, 238, 248, 250, 281, 330, 347, 360, 413, 450, 459, 460, 470-471, 495, (divorce) 518, (Anne's fall) 535-536, (death) 537-539

Kahn, Mrs. Gilbert (née Heliker, Sara Jane, 514, 519-520, 522, 526, 535, 543, 546, 547, 577

Kahn, Hedwig, 7

Kahn, Hermann, 5-7, 8

Kahn, Leopold, 5, 7

Kahn, Margaret Dorothy W., vii, 4, (birth, **1901**) 19, 41, 62, (dance classes) 63, 70, 78, 103, 104, (invitation to the Vanderbilts mansion) 105, (2nd invitation to

the Vanderbilts mansion) 113, (attends Edward, Prince of Wales' Met Gala, **1919**) 116, (debutante party, **1920**) 121, (appears on Broadway, **1920**) 122-123, 124, (drives across America to California, **1920**) 125-126, 128, (maid of honor at Maud's marriage, **1920**) 129, 135, 137, 138 (Gilbert's motor-cycle accident) 140-141, (ballet classes) 142-143, 146, 150, 152, 154, 155, (photographed by Arnold Genthe) 165, 191, (painted by Ignacio Zuloaga y Zabaleta) 202, 223, 232, 238, 248, 279, (moves into Twin Peaks) 281-282, 292, 293, 299, (attends the opening of Roger's nightclub) 307, 347 (marriage announcement) 367-368, (marriage) 370
see also Ryan, Margaret,

Kahn, Maud Emily W., vii, 4, (birth, **1897**) 17, 19, 23, 34, 41, 62, 63, 64, (debutante ball, **1916**) 65-66, (War Service, French Red Cross, **1916**) 70-71, (British War Service, **1917**) 72, 78, (British volunteer work at St Dunstan's, London, **1917**) 83, 96, 97, 103, 104, 105, 107-108, 113, (Maud receives the *Médaille de la Reconnaissance française*) 115, 116, 120, 121, (*What Next!* show) 122-123, (engagement & marriage) 124-130
see also Marriott, Maud

Kahn, Michael, 5-8

Kahn, Otto Hermann, vii, 3, 4, (ancestry) 4-5, (birth, **1867**) 7, 8, (upbringing) 9, (move to U.K., **1889**) 10-11, (move to USA, **1893**) 11-12, (marriage, **1896**) 12-13, (joins Kuhn, Loeb & Co., **1897**) 13, 14, 15, (birth of 1st child, Maud, **1897**) 17, 18, (birth of Margaret, **1901**) 19, (birth of Gilbert, **1903**) 20, (Cedar Court fire, **1905**) 21-22, (anti-Semitic hostility) 22-24, 25 (deer slaughtered, **1906**) 26, (Edward Harriman association) 27-28, (New Wizard of Wall Street, **1907**) 29-30, (elected chairman of Metropolitan Opera Company) 31-32, (summer in

Private pilot license) 361,
(interview) 361-362, (more time to
fly) 363-364, (Lew Leslie rents
Roger's club) 365, (**1928**) (snap
New York tour) 369-370, (new
Bellanca plane) 371-372, 373-374,
(1st Broadway musical *Here's Howe!*)
374-375, 379, 380-383, (Dutch
Treat Club luncheon) 383-384,
(Broadway) 384, (*Here's Howe!*
closes) 385, (no financial
endowment for Roger's 21st) 387,
(unbeknown to Roger, father
invested in *Here's Howe!*) 387-388,
(new tenant for Roger's club) 388,
(Star Club) 401, (*Americana* stage
show) 389-393, 394, (*New
Americana*) 395-397, (brief
vaudeville tour) 398, ($500,000
loss, **1929**) 399, (more vaudeville
dates) 400, (catches influenza) 401,
402, 403-404, 405-406, (news
report claims Roger to elope with
Hannah Williams) 410, (signs
to Brunswick Records) 410,
(Hollywood) 413, 414, (sixth plane
for Roger) 415, 428-429, (clocks up
2,000 flying hours) 429-430, 431,
432, 434, (**1930**) (reclusive
behavior) 435, (image makeover)
436, (cinematic career) 438, (*Nine
Fifteen Revue*) 439, (ill with chicken
pox) 439-440, 442, (*Nine Fifteen
Revue* opens) 443, 444, (scary
incident) 445, (1st test flight) 445-
446, (2nd test flight) 446-448, (flight
competitions) 448-449, (Cabot's
Pickup Device trial) 449, (stunt
exhibitions & test flights) 449-450,
(financially worse off) 451, (2nd
Cabot's Pickup Device trial) 452-
454, (demonstration flights) 454,
(drives a kid's automobile) 455,
(journalist) 456, (night-flying) 456-
457, (Roger happy again; secret
engagement) 457-458, (media
frenzy, **1931**) 459-460, (transport
pilot license) 460-461, (Roger weds
Hannah) 461, (Otto & Addie
disapprove of the marriage) 461-
463, (Otto not at the wedding) 463,
(honeymoon in Florida) 464-466,
(Roger makes aviation history) 467-

469, (5-month honeymoon in
Europe) 469, 473-474, (return to
NY, but no marital home) 476-477,
(reignites his music career) 477-
478, 479-480, (forms 2 orchestras)
480, (vanishes on Christmas day)
481-482, (signs a new record deal,
1932) 483, 484, 486, 487, (music
dealings, new recordings) 488-489,
(marriage fails, divorce beckons)
489-493, 494, (air rage) 496-497,
(plane crash) 497, (comeback tour)
498-499, (Vitaphone movie) 499,
(back at the Palace) 500-502, (*The
Yacht Party*) 502-504, 505-506,
(return residency at Hotel
Pennsylvania) 508, 510-511, (pit
orchestra for new Gershwin
musical) 512-513, (comeback fails)
513-514, 516, 517, (**1933**) 519,
520, 521, (divorce granted) 522-
523, (marries Edith May Nelson)
524-526, 532, (honeymoon in
Europe) 534-535, (return to NY)
536-537, 539, 540, (**1934**) 543,
(forms new band) 546, (clocks up
3,000 flying hours) 550, (quits
Broadway, again) 550, (father's
death) 551, 552, 559, (inheritance)
560, 562, (attempts another music
comeback) 563-564, 565-567, 569,
(clocks up 4,000 flying hours) 570,
(**1935** onwards) 574-576, 580, 581-
582, 584, 589, (legacy) 590-591,
599, 683, (conclusion) 684-685
Kahn, Siegfried H., 458
Kahn, Sigismund, 5
Kahn, Virginia W. 'Dacia', 575
Kahn & Co., 7
SS *Kaiser Wilhelm II*, 29
Kaley, Charles, 343-344, 350, 359
Kane, Helen, 375
Kappel, Gertrude, 458
Karsavina, Tamara, 55
Kasner, Jacques (music tutor), 99,
167, 168, 170, 171, 193, 204, 215,
218, 220
Kassel, Morris, 139, 141
Kaufman, Harry, 579
Kearns, Allen, 375, 381
Keith-Albee Corporation, 166, 219,
243, 253, 292
Keith Theatre, Boston, 501, 505

Dempsey, an item) 530-531, 532,
(weds Jack Dempsey, **1933**) 532-
534, 578-580
Williams, Martha 'Mattie,' 321-322,
344, 350, 464
Williams, Roger Q., 454
The Williams Sisters, 320-325, 329,
330, 338, 342-343, 344, 359, 383,
392, 395, 396, 398, 399, 400, 404,
410, 595
Williams, Thomas C., 321-322, 350
Wills, Helen, 328
Wilson, Lady Sarah, 417
Wilson, William J., (secretary), 416
Wilson, President Woodrow, 73, 74,
79, 80, 415
Winans, General Edwin B., 297
Winchell, Walter, 374, 380, 396, 410,
492, 511
Winchester College, 45
The Wings Club (aeronautical), 576,
599
Winter, Mrs. Thomas G., 149-150
Winter Garden Theatre London, 215-
216
Winter Garden Theatre, NY, 579
Winthrop (family), 130
Winthrop, Henry Rogers, 91
Julie Wintz Orchestra, 356
Wiseman, Sir William George Eden,
94, 466, 528, 547, 682
'Wizard of Wall Street' (title), 29, 50,
110, 257, 557
WJY Radio, 164, 196
WJZ Radio, 159-160, 164, 217, 221,
275, 333, 348
WLTH Radio, 442, 446
WMCA Radio, 314, 444
WNAC Radio, 164
WNYC Radio, 228
WRC Radio, 348
Wolfe, Elsie de, 184, 299
Wolff, Albert, 119-120
Wolff, Abraham O., 13-15, 16, 17, 18-
19, 20, 21, 25
Wolff, Addie, 13-15
Wolff, Clara, 13-14
Woodall, Benny, 579
Woodlands, Long Island, 220
Woods, Albert Herman, 293
Woods, Mrs. Albert Herman, 293
Woods, Harry, 375

Woolworth, F. W., 247
Wray, Fay, 506
WSB Atlanta Radio, 228
Wynn, Ed, 338, 579

X

Y

The Yacht Party (film, **1932**), 502-
504, 596
Yale University, 4, 271, 436, 445
'Yankee Rose' (song), 320, 334, 595
Yarrow, Rev. Phillip, 149
'Yearning (Just for You),' 239-240,
275
Yellman, Duke, and his Irene Castle
Orchestra, 207
'Young Black Joe' (song), 392
Young, Edward Hilton, 231-232
Young, Captain William T., 345-346,
452
'You Should Know' (instrumental),
299, 312
'You've Got Me in The Palm of Your
Hand' (song), 502
Yuille, Nancy, 442, 466

Z
Zeeley, Sir Hugh, 442
Ziegfeld, Florenz Jr., 87, 123, 131,
201, 271, 375, 391, 430
Ziegfeld Follies of 1920 (show), 131
Ziegler, Edward, 458
Ziegler, William Jr., 51
Zukofsky, Louis, 470
Zukor, Adolph, 443, 522
Zullo, Frank, 489
Zuloaga y Zabaleta, Ignacio, 202

Otto H. & Addie Kahn Ancestry Chart

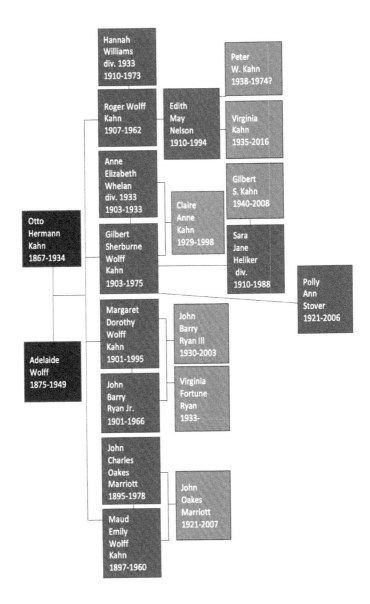

The KAHNS

iwp

Made in the USA
Middletown, DE
01 September 2024

60230692R00404